The Complete CPA Reference

WITHDRAWN

NICK A. DAUBER, MS, CPA

JAE K. SHIM, PhD

JOEL G. SIEGEL, PhD, CPA

WILEY

John Wiley & Sons, Inc.

Published by John Wiley & Sons, Inc., Hoboken, New Jersey.
Fourth edition (*The Vest Pocket CPA*) published in 2008 by John Wiley & Sons, Inc.
Published simultaneously in Canada.

For general information on our other products and services or for technical support, please contact our Customer Care Department within the United States at (800) 762-2974, outside the United States at (317) 572-3993 or fax (317) 572-4002.

Wiley also publishes its books in a variety of electronic formats. Some content that appears in print may not be available in electronic books. For more information about Wiley products, visit our web site at www.wiley.com.

Library of Congress Cataloging-in-Publication Data:

Dauber, Nick A.
  The complete CPA reference / Nick A. Dauber, Jae K. Shim, Joel G. Siegel.
     p. cm.
  Includes bibliographical references and index.
  ISBN 978-1-118-11588-6 (cloth); ISBN 978-1-118-22440-3 (ebk);
  ISBN 978-1-118-23761-8 (ebk); ISBN 978-1-118-26252-8 (ebk)
  1. Accounting–Handbooks, manuals, etc.   I. Shim, Jae K.   II. Siegel, Joel G.   III. Title.
  HF5636.D377 2012
  657–dc23

                                                                            2011041537

Printed in the United States of America

10 9 8 7 6 5 4 3 2 1

To

Karen J. Dauber
Loving wife and dear friend
Katie and Michael Dauber
Precious children
Margie, Marc, and Susan Dauber
Loving and wonderful mother, father, and sister

and

Roberta Siegel
Loving wife and colleague
Philip E. Levine
Dear and precious friend

and

Chung Shim
Dedicated wife

Contents

About the Authors

NICK A. DAUBER, MS, CPA, is an accounting practitioner specializing in auditing and taxation. Prior to starting his practice more than 25 years ago, he was an audit and tax manager at a CPA firm.

Mr. Dauber is also an instructor of auditing and taxation at Queens College of the City University of New York. He was the president of Person-Wolinsky CPA Review Courses and has instructed over 100,000 CPA Exam candidates during the past 31 years. Mr. Dauber was the writer of the review course's auditing and taxation material and served as the editor of the law and financial accounting material.

In 1992, Mr. Dauber was named Professor of the Year at Queens College of the City University of New York and was recipient of the Golden Apple Award bestowed by the Golden Key National Honor Society. He has also served as an award-winning lecturer in auditing and taxation for the Foundation for Accounting Education at the New York State Society of CPAs as well as for the American Institute of Certified Public Accountants.

Mr. Dauber has served as a book reviewer for major book publishers and has published articles in many professional accounting journals, including the *CPA Journal* (New York), *Massachusetts CPA*, *Virginia Accountant Quarterly*, and *National Public Accountant*.

Books by Mr. Dauber include *The Complete Guide to Auditing Standards and Other Professional Standards for Accountants, Corporate Controller's Handbook of Financial Management*, and *Barron's How to Prepare for the CPA Exam*. He has also been a contributor to professional books in accounting and auditing.

JAE K. SHIM, PhD, is one of the most prolific accounting and finance experts in the world. He is a professor of accounting and finance at California State University, Long Beach, and CEO of Delta Consulting Company, a financial consulting and training firm. Dr. Shim received his MBA and PhD degrees from the University of California at Berkeley (Haas School of Business). He has been a consultant to commercial and nonprofit organizations for over 30 years.

Dr. Shim has over 50 college and professional books to his credit, including *Barron's Accounting Handbook, Barron's Dictionary of Accounting Terms, 2012 GAAP: Handbook of Policies and Procedures, Budgeting Basics and Beyond, 2011–2012 Corporate Controller's Handbook of Financial Management, US Master Finance Guide, Uses and Analysis of Financial Statements, Investment Sourcebook, Dictionary of Real Estate, Dictionary of International Investment Terms, Dictionary of Business Terms, The Vest-Pocket CPA, The Vest-Pocket CFO*, and the best-selling *Vest-Pocket MBA*.

Thirty of his publications have been translated into foreign languages such as Chinese, Spanish, Russian, Polish, Croatian, Italian, Japanese, and Korean. Professor Shim's books have been published by Commerce Clearing House, Barron's, John Wiley & Sons, McGraw-Hill, Prentice Hall, Penguin Portfolio, Thomson Reuters, Global Publishing, American Management Association (Amacom), and the American Institute of Certified Public Accountants (AICPA).

Dr. Shim has also published numerous articles in professional and academic journals. He was the recipient of the Financial Management Association International's 1982 Credit Research Foundation Award for his article on cash flow forecasting and financial modeling.

Dr. Shim has been frequently quoted by such media as the *Los Angeles Times*, the *Orange County Register*, *Business Start-Ups*, *Personal Finance*, and *Money Radio*.

JOEL G. SIEGEL, PhD, CPA, is professor of accounting and finance at Queens College of the City University of New York. He is also an accounting practitioner to various clients.

Dr. Siegel was previously a member of the audit staff of Coopers & Lybrand, CPAs, and a faculty resident with Arthur Andersen, CPAs. He has acted as a consultant in accounting issues to many organizations, including International Telephone & Telegraph, United Technologies, Person-Wolinsky CPA Review Courses, and Citicorp.

Dr. Siegel is the author of 67 books and approximately 300 articles on accounting topics. His books have been published by Prentice Hall, McGraw-Hill, John Wiley & Sons, Barron's, Richard Irwin, Probus, Macmillan, HarperCollins, International Publishing, Southwestern, Commerce Clearing House, the American Management Association, and the American Institute of Certified Public Accountants.

His work has been published in numerous accounting and financial journals, including *Massachusetts CPA*, *Ohio CPA*, *Michigan CPA*, *Virginia Accountant Quarterly*, *Delaware CPA*, the *CPA Journal*, *National Public Accountant*, *Financial Executive*, and the *Financial Analysts Journal*.

In 1972, he was the recipient of the Outstanding Educator of America Award. He is listed in *Who's Who Among Writers* and *Who's Who in the World*. He is the former chairperson of the National Oversight Board.

Acknowledgments

Permission to quote from the *Audit and Accounting Manual, Professional Standards, Statements on Auditing Standards, Statements on Standards for Accounting and Review Services, Statements on Standards for Attestation Engagements*, and the May 1983 *Auditing CPA Exam* (Question 5) was received from the American Institute of Certified Public Accountants (AICPA). Copyright by the American Institute of Certified Public Accountants, 1211 Avenue of the Americas, New York, New York 10036.

Permission to reprint Example 1 of Appendix C (pages 44–51) of FASB Statement 95, *Statement of Cash Flows*, and the example on page 32 of FASB Statement 96, *Accounting for Income Taxes*, was received from the Financial Accounting Standards Board. Copyright by the Financial Accounting Standards Board, High Ridge Park, Stamford, CT 06905. Reprinted with permission. Copies of the complete document are available from the Financial Accounting Standards Board.

Introduction

The Complete CPA Reference is a useful reference and problem solver for today's busy certified public accountant (CPA). Organized in a handy question-and-answer format, it will help you quickly pinpoint:

- What to look for
- What to watch out for
- What to do
- How to do it

This valuable book will guide you through the complex, ever-changing world of accounting. You'll find financial measures, ratios, procedures, techniques, and rules of thumb to help you analyze, evaluate, and solve most accounting-related problems as they come up. Throughout, you'll find this book practical, quick, comprehensive, and useful. Carry it with you for constant reference wherever you go—on a business trip, visiting a client's office, meeting corporate executives, and at your office. The content of the book applies to public and private accountants whether employed by large, medium-size, or small firms. The uses for this book are as varied as the topics presented.

This practical reference contains the latest information on proven approaches and techniques for understanding and solving problems of:

- Financial accounting
- Financial statement analysis
- Financial planning
- Managerial accounting
- Quantitative analysis and modeling
- Auditing
- Taxation

Part I takes you through accounting principles, financial reporting requirements, disclosures, and specialized accounting topics, to keep you up to date with generally accepted accounting principles (GAAP). It points out differences between U.S. GAAP and International Financial Reporting Standards (IFRS) where applicable. FASB Accounting Standards Codification is referenced throughout this part.

Part II examines the financial health and operating performance of a business entity. You'll learn about:

- Analytical tools used in appraising a company as a basis for determining the extent of audit testing, financial reliance on testing, and going-concern problems
- The viability of a targeted company for a merger
- Achievement of optimal investment return while controlling risk
- Investment analysis techniques

Part III presents internal accounting applications to help you:

- Evaluate your own company's performance, profitability, effectiveness, efficiency, marketing, and budgeting processes.
- Highlight problem areas with variance analysis.
- Move your company toward greater profits through breakeven analysis.
- Apply quantitative decision modeling.

Guidelines are presented for evaluating proposals, whether they are short-term or long-term, for profit potential and risk-return comparison. Operations research, quantitative, and modeling techniques are clearly presented so that the accountant can use up-to-date approaches in solving business problems.

Part IV relates to audit planning, procedures, and reporting. The chapters address means of gathering audit evidence, evaluating internal control, appraising financial statement items, and preparing audit work papers, and discuss review and compilation services. The practitioner is provided with a handy guide for designing audit plans. There are checklists to assist the auditor in developing work programs for any client environment. Chapter 12 guides the practitioner through the many Statements on Auditing Standards (SASs) and Auditing Standards (ASs) of the Public Company Accounting Oversight Board and exposes him or her to the many types of reports pertinent to various engagements. Given a standard report, the practitioner can prepare modifications with a minimum of effort. The pronouncements relevant to the various reporting situations have been streamlined for easier application. Chapter 13 discusses the major provisions of the Sarbanes-Oxley Act from the practitioner's point of view.

Part V applies to conducting income tax research.

Part VI addresses other professional standards. Specifically, the practitioner is provided guidance in connection with consulting services, quality control, and the AICPA Code of Professional Conduct.

The Complete CPA Reference provides instant answers to any accounting or finance question you may have.

The content of the book is clear, concise, and current. It is a valuable reference tool with guidelines, checklists, illustrations, step-by-step instructions, practical applications, and how-to's for you, the up-to-date, knowledgeable accountant. Keep this book handy for easy reference and daily use.

PART I

Commonly Used Generally Accepted Accounting Principles

CHAPTER 1

Financial Statement Reporting: The Income Statement

The reporting requirements of the income statement, balance sheet, statement of changes in cash flows, and interim reporting guidelines must be carefully examined. Individuals preparing personal financial statements have to follow certain unique reporting requirements, as do those who are accounting for a partnership. Points to note are:

- Income statement preparation involves proper revenue and expense recognition. The income statement format is highlighted in this chapter along with the earnings per share computation.
- Balance sheet reporting covers accounting requirements for the various types of assets, liabilities, and stockholders' equity.
- The statement of cash flows presents cash receipts and cash payments classified according to investing, financing, and operating activities. Disclosure is also provided for certain noncash investment and financial transactions. A reconciliation is provided between reported earnings and cash flow from operations.
- Interim financial reporting allows for some departures from annual reporting, such as the gross profit method to estimate inventory. The tax provision is based on the effective tax rate expected for the year.
- Personal financial statements show the worth of the individual. Assets and liabilities are reflected at current value in the order of maturity.

This chapter deals with the reporting requirements on the income statement. Chapter 2 deals with the balance sheet, and Chapter 3 covers the remaining statements.

IFRS Connection

The elements of financial statements are assets, liabilities, equity, income, and expenses.

Presentation of comparative financial statements is mandatory. Accordingly, the first statements must include at least one year of comparative information.

Personal financial statements are not specifically addressed by the International Financial Reporting Standards (IFRS).

Income Statement Format

With respect to the income statement, the certified public accountant (CPA)'s attention is addressed to:

- Income statement format
- Comprehensive income
- Extraordinary items
- Nonrecurring items
- Discontinued operations
- Revenue recognition methods
- Accounting for research and development costs
- Presentation of earnings per share

How are items on the income statement arranged?

In the preparation of the income statement, continuing operations are presented before discontinued operations.

Starting with income from continuing operations, the format of the income statement is:

> Income from continuing operations before tax
> Less: Taxes
> Income from continuing operations after tax
> Discontinued operations:
> Income from discontinued operations (net of tax)
> Loss or gain on disposal of a division (net of tax)
> Income before extraordinary items
> Extraordinary items (net of tax)
> Net income

Note

Earnings per share is shown on the income statement items as well.

Comprehensive Income

What is comprehensive income?

Comprehensive income is the change in equity occurring from transactions and other events with nonowners. It excludes investment (disinvestment) by owners.

What are the two components of comprehensive income?

Comprehensive income consists of two components: net income and "other comprehensive income." Net income plus "other comprehensive income" equals comprehensive income.

What does "other comprehensive income" include?

Per Accounting Standards Codification (ASC) 220-10-45-3, *Comprehensive Income: Overall* (Statement of Financial Accounting Standards [SFAS] FAS-130, *Reporting Comprehensive Income*), "other comprehensive income" includes:

- Foreign currency translation gain or loss
- Unrealized gain or loss on available-for-sale securities
- Change in market value of a futures contract that is a hedge of an asset reported at present value

How is comprehensive income reported?

ASC 220-10-45-3 has three acceptable options of reporting comprehensive income and its components. We present the best and most often used option, which is an income statement–type format:

Statement of Income and Comprehensive Income		
Net Income		$400,000
Other Comprehensive Income		
Foreign Currency Translation Gain	$20,000	
Unrealized Loss on Available-for-Sale Component	(3,000)	
		17,000
Comprehensive Income		$417,000

The "other comprehensive income" items reported in the income statement are for the current-year amounts only. The total "other comprehensive income" for all the years is presented in the stockholders' equity section of the balance sheet as "accumulated other comprehensive income."

IFRS Connection

The statement of equity must not report the components of comprehensive income.

Extraordinary Items

What are extraordinary items?

Extraordinary items are those that are both unusual in nature and infrequent in occurrence.

- "Unusual in nature" means the event is abnormal and not related to the typical operations of the entity.
- "Infrequent in occurrence" means the transaction is not anticipated to take place in the foreseeable future, taking into account the corporate environment.

- The environment of a company includes consideration of industry characteristics, geographical location of operations, and extent of government regulation.
- Materiality is considered by judging the items individually and not in the aggregate. However, if items arise from a single specific event or plan, they should be aggregated.

Extraordinary items are shown net of tax between income from discontinued operations and net income.

What are some typical extraordinary items?

Extraordinary items include:

- Casualty losses
- Losses on expropriation of property by a foreign government
- Gain on life insurance proceeds
- Gain on troubled debt restructuring
- Loss from prohibition under a newly enacted law or regulation

Exception

Losses on receivables and inventory occur in the normal course of business and therefore are not extraordinary. Losses on receivables and inventory are extraordinary, however, if they relate to a casualty loss (e.g., earthquake) or governmental expropriation (e.g., banning of product because of a health hazard).

IFRS Connection

IFRS does not permit special reporting for extraordinary items.

Nonrecurring Items

What are nonrecurring items?

Nonrecurring items are items that are either unusual in nature or infrequent in occurrence. They are shown as a separate line item before tax in arriving at income from continuing operations. *Example:* The gain or loss on the sale of a fixed asset.

Discontinued Operations

How is a discontinued operation defined?

A discontinued operation is an operation that has been discontinued during the year or will be discontinued shortly after year-end. A discontinued operation may be a business segment that has been sold, abandoned, or spun off.

The two components of discontinued operations are:

1. Income or loss from operations
2. Loss or gain on disposal of division

What disclosure requirements apply to a discontinued activity?

Footnote disclosure regarding the discontinued operation should include:

- An identification of the segment
- Disposal date
- The manner of disposal
- Description of remaining net assets of the segment at year-end

A business segment is a major line of business or customer class. Even though it may be operating, a formal plan to dispose of it exists.

IFRS Connection

Under IFRS, a discontinued operation must be a major line of business or geographic segment. Also, under IFRS, separate disclosure must be made of the cash flows of the discontinued operation.

How do we present discontinued operations?

In an annual report, the income of a component classified as held for sale is presented in discontinued operations in the year(s) in which the income occurs. Phase-out losses are not accrued.

Example 1.1

ABC Company produces and sells consumer products. It has a number of product groups, each with different product lines and brands. For this company, a product group is the lowest level at which the operations and cash flows can be distinguished, operationally and for financial reporting purposes, from the rest of the company. ABC Company has suffered losses related to specific brands in its beauty product group. It has opted to get out of this group.

ABC commits to a plan to sell the beauty product group, and therefore classifies it as held for sale at that date. The operations and cash flows of the group will be eliminated from the ongoing operations of ABC because of the sale transaction, and the company will not have any continuing involvement in

(continued)

(*Continued*)

the activities of the beauty product component. Therefore, ABC should report in discontinued operations, the activities of the group while it is classified as held for sale.

   Assume ABC instead decides to continue in the beauty care business but discontinue the brands with which the losses are associated. Because these brands are part of a larger cash-flow-generating product group and, in the aggregate, do not constitute a group that on its own is a component of ABC, the conditions for reporting in discontinued operations the losses associated with the brands that are discontinued would not be satisfied.

The income of a component of a business that either has been disposed of or is held for sale is reported in discontinued operations only when *both* these criteria have been satisfied:

- The profit and cash flows of the component have been (or will be) eliminated from the ongoing operations of the company due to the disposal decision.
- The company will not have any major ongoing involvement in the activities of the component subsequent to the disposal decision.

In general, gain or loss from operations of the discontinued component should include operating gain or loss incurred and the gain or loss on disposal of a component taking place in the current period. Gains should not be recognized until the year actually realized.

IFRS Connection

IFRS defines revenue to include both revenues and gains. U.S. generally accepted accounting principles (GAAP) provide separate definitions for revenues and gains.

Revenue Recognition

What are the various ways of recording revenue?

Revenue, which is associated with a gross increase in assets or a decrease in liabilities, can be recognized under different methods depending on the circumstances. (Special revenue recognition guidelines exist for franchisors and in sales involving a right of return. A product financing arrangement may also exist.) The basic methods of recognition include:

- Realization
- Completion of production
- During production
- Cash basis

Realization

When is revenue normally realized?

Revenue is realized (recognized) when goods are sold or services are performed. Realization results in an increase in net assets. This method is almost always used. At realization, the earnings process is complete. Further, realization is consistent with the accrual basis of accounting, meaning that revenue is recognized when earned rather than when received. Realization should be used when:

- The selling price is determinable.
- Future costs can be estimated.
- An exchange has taken place that can be objectively measured.

Note

There must be a reasonable basis for determining anticipated bad debts.

Three other methods of revenue recognition are used in exceptional situations, as discussed next.

At the Completion of Production

When can revenue be recognized upon completion of production?

Revenue is recognized prior to sale or exchange.

REQUIREMENTS   There must be:

- A stable selling price
- Absence of material marketing costs to complete the final transfer
- Interchangeability in units

  This approach is used:

- With agricultural products, by-products, and precious metals when the afore-mentioned criteria are met
- In accounting for construction contracts under the completed contract method

During Production

When can I recognize revenue during production?

In the case of long-term production situations, revenue recognition is made when both of the following conditions exist:

- An assured price for the completed item exists by contractual agreement.
- A reliable measure of the degree of completion at various stages of the production process is possible.

Example: The percentage of completion method can be used in accounting for long-term construction contracts.

Which is preferable—the completed contract method or the percentage of completion method?

Under the completed contract method, revenue should not be recognized until completion of a contract. In general, the completed contract method should be used only when the use of the percentage of completion method is inappropriate.

How is revenue matched with costs in the percentage of completion method?

Under the percentage of completion method, revenue is recognized as production activity is occurring. The gradual recognition of revenue, levels out earnings over the years and is more realistic than the completed contract method since revenue is recognized as performance takes place.

Recommendation

The percentage of completion method is preferred over the completed contract method and should be used when reliable estimates of the extent of completion in each period are possible. If not, the completed contract method should be used. Percentage of completion results in a matching of revenue against related expenses in the benefit period.

Using the cost-to-cost method, revenue recognized for the period equals:

$$\frac{\text{Actual costs to date}}{\text{Total estimated costs}} \times \text{Contract price} = \text{Cumulative revenue}$$

Revenue recognized in prior years is deducted from the cumulative revenue to determine the revenue in the current period.

Example 1.2

Given:

- Cumulative revenue (years 1–4)
- Revenue recognized (years 1–3)
- Revenue (year 4–current year)

Revenue less expenses equals profit.

In year 4 of a contract, the actual costs to date are $50,000. Total estimated costs are $200,000. The contract price is $1,000,000. Revenue recognized in the prior years (years 1–3) is $185,000.

$$\frac{\$50,000}{\$200,000} \times \$1,000,000 = \$250,000 \text{ Cumulative revenue}$$

Cumulative Revenue	$250,000
Prior-Year Revenue	$185,000
Current-Year Revenue	$ 65,000

Journal entries under the construction methods using assumed figures follow.

	Percentage of Completion		Completed Contract	
Construction-in-Progress	$100,000		$100,000	
Cash		$100,000		$100,000
Construction Costs				
Progress Billings	80,000			
Receivable			80,000	
Progress Billings on Construction-in-Progress		80,000		80,000
Periodic Billings				
Construction-in-Progress	25,000		No entry	
Profit		25,000		

In the final year when the construction project is completed, the following additional entries are made to record the profit in the final year:

	Percentage of Completion	Completed Contract
Progress Billings on Construction in Progress	Total Billings	Total Billings
Construction in Progress	Cost +	Cost
Profit	Profit Incremental Profit for Last Year	Profit for All the Years

Construction in Progress less Progress Billings is shown net. Usually a debit figure results, which is shown as a current asset. Construction in Progress is an inventory account for a construction company. If a credit balance occurs, the net amount is shown as a current liability.

Note

Regardless of whether the percentage of completion method or the completed contract method is used, conservatism dictates that an obvious loss on a contract should be recognized immediately even before contract completion.

IFRS Connection

IFRS prohibits the use of the completed contract method of accounting for long-term construction contracts. Companies must use the percentage of completion method. If revenues and costs are difficult to estimate, then companies recognize revenue only to the extent of the cost incurred—a zero-profit approach.

Cash Basis

When is cash basis, rather than accrual basis, preferable or required?

In the case of a company selling inventory, the accrual basis is used. However, the cash basis of revenue recognition is used under certain circumstances, namely, when revenue is recognized upon collection of the account. The cash basis instead of the accrual basis must be used when one or more of these situations exist:

- Inability to objectively determine selling price at the time of sale
- Inability to estimate expenses at the time of sale
- Risks as to collection from customer
- Uncertain collection period

How do I compute revenue under the installment method?

Revenue recognition under the installment method equals the cash collected, times the gross profit percent. Any gross profit not collected is deferred on the balance sheet until collection occurs. When collections are received, realized gross profit is recognized by debiting the deferred gross profit account. The balance sheet presentation is:

Accounts Receivable (Cost + Profit)
Less: Deferred Gross Profit
Net Accounts Receivable (Cost)

Note

A service business that does not deal in inventory (e.g., accountant, doctor, lawyer) has the option of using either the accrual basis or the cash basis.

How is revenue recognized if the buyer can return the goods?

When a buyer has a right to return the merchandise bought, the seller can recognize revenue at the time of sale in accordance with ASC 605-15-25-1, *Revenue Recognition: Products* (FAS-48, *Revenue Recognition When Right of Return Exists*), only provided that all of these conditions are satisfied:

- Selling price is known.
- Buyer has to pay for the goods even if the buyer is unable to resell them. *Example:* A sale of goods from a manufacturer to a wholesaler. No provision must exist that the wholesaler has to be able to sell the items to the retailer.
- If the buyer loses the item or it is damaged in some way, the buyer still has to pay for it.
- Purchase by the buyer of the item has economic feasibility.
- Seller does not have to render future performance in order that the buyer will be able to resell the goods.
- Returns may be reasonably estimated.

If any of these criteria are not met, revenue must be deferred along with deferral of related expenses until the criteria have been satisfied or the right of return provision has expired. As an alternative to deferring the revenue, record a memo entry as to the sale.

What factors affect the ability of a company to predict future returns?

These considerations can be used in predicting returns:

- Predictability is hampered when there is technological obsolescence risk of the product, uncertain product demand changes, or other material external factors.
- Predictability is lessened when there is a long time period involved for returns.
- Predictability is enhanced when there exists a large volume of similar transactions.
- The seller's previous experience should be weighed in estimating returns for similar products.
- The nature of the customer relationship and the type of product involved need to be evaluated.

Caution

ASC 605-15-25-1 does not apply to dealer leases, real estate transactions, or service industries.

What is the definition of a financing arrangement?

Per ASC 470-40-25 (FAS-49, *Accounting for Product Financing Arrangements*), the arrangement involving the sale and repurchase of inventory is, in substance, a financing arrangement. It mandates that the product financing arrangement be accounted for as a borrowing instead of a sale. In many cases, the product is stored on the company's (sponsor's) premises. In addition, often the sponsor will guarantee the debt of the other entity.

Typically, the sponsor eventually uses or sells most of the product in the financing arrangement. However, in some cases, the financing entity may sell small amounts of the product to other parties.

The entity that gives financing to the sponsor is usually an existing creditor, nonbusiness entity, or trust. It is also possible that the financer may have been established *only* for the purpose of providing financing for the sponsor.

Note

Footnote disclosure should be made of the particulars of the product financing arrangement.

What are some types of financing arrangements?

Types of product financing arrangements include:

- Company (sponsor) sells a product to another business and agrees to reacquire the product or one basically identical to it. The established price to be paid by the sponsor typically includes financing and holding costs.
- Sponsor has another company buy the product for it and agrees to repurchase the product from the other entity.
- Sponsor controls the distribution of the product that has been bought by another company in accordance with the aforementioned terms.

Note

In all situations, the company (sponsor) either agrees to repurchase the product at given prices over specified time periods or guarantees resale prices to third parties.

How are financing arrangements reported?

- When the sponsor sells the product to the other firm and in a related transaction agrees to repurchase it, the sponsor should record a liability when the proceeds are received to the degree the product applies to the financing arrangement.

Caution

A sale should not be recorded, and the product should be retained as inventory on the sponsor's books.

- In the case where another firm buys the product for the sponsor, inventory is debited and liability is credited at the time of purchase.
- Costs of the product, except for processing costs, in excess of the sponsor's original production cost or acquisition cost or the other company's purchase cost constitute finance and holding costs. The sponsor accounts for these costs according to its typical accounting policies. Interest costs will also be incurred in connection with the financing arrangement. These should be shown separately and can be deferred.

Example 1.3

On 1/1/2X12, a sponsor borrows $100,000 from another company and gives the inventory as collateral for the loan. The entry is:

Cash	$100,000	
Liability		$100,000

Note

A sale is not recorded here, and the inventory remains on the books of the sponsor. In effect, inventory serves as collateral for a loan.

On 12/31/2X12, the sponsor pays back the other company. The collateralized inventory item is returned. The interest rate on the loan was 8 percent. Storage costs were $2,000. The entry is:

Liability	$100,000	
Interest Expense	8,000	
Storage Expense	2,000	
Cash		$110,000

Recognition of Franchise Fee Revenue by the Franchisor

When can franchise fees be recognized?

According to ASC 952-10-25-4, *Franchisors; Revenue Recognition* (FAS-45, *Accounting for Franchise Fee Revenue*), the franchisor can record revenue from the initial sale of the franchise only when all significant services and obligations applicable to the sale have been substantially performed. Substantial performance is indicated when:

- There is absence of intent to give cash refunds or relieve the accounts receivable due from the franchisee.
- Nothing material remains to be done by the franchisor.
- Initial services have been rendered.

The earliest date on which substantial performance can occur is the franchisee's commencement of operations unless special circumstances can be shown to exist.

In the case in which it is probable that the franchisor will ultimately repurchase the franchise, the initial fee must be deferred and treated as a reduction of the repurchase price.

How are deferred franchise fee revenues reported?

If revenue is deferred, the related expenses must be deferred for later matching in the year in which the revenue is recognized. This is illustrated next.

Year of initial fee:
Cash
   Deferred Revenue
Deferred Expenses
   Cash

Year when substantial performance takes place:
Deferred Revenue
   Revenue
Expenses
   Deferred Expenses

What are the requirements for initial franchise fees?

In the case in which the initial fee includes both initial services and property (real or personal), there should be an appropriate allocation based on fair market values.

When part of the initial franchise fee applies to *tangible property* (e.g., equipment, signs, inventory), revenue recognition is based on the fair value of the assets. Revenue recognition may take place prior to or after recognizing the portion of the fee related to initial services. *Example:* Part of the fee for equipment may be recognized at the time title passes with the balance of the fee being recorded as revenue when future services are performed.

How do I handle recurring franchise fees?

Recurring franchise fees are recognized as earned and receivable. Related costs are expensed.

Exception

If the price charged for the continuing services or goods to the franchisee is below the price charged to third parties, this indicates that the initial franchise fee was in essence a partial *prepayment* for the recurring franchise fee. In this situation, part of the initial fee has to be deferred and recognized as an adjustment of the revenue from the sale of goods and services at bargain prices.

Suggestion

The deferred amount should be adequate to meet future costs and generate an adequate profit on the recurring services. This situation may occur if the continuing fees are minimal relative to services provided or if the franchisee has the privilege of making bargain purchases for a particular time period.

When *continuing franchise fees will probably not cover the cost of the continuing services and provide for a reasonable profit* to the franchisor, part of the initial franchise fee should be deferred to satisfy the deficiency and be amortized over the life of the franchise.

What accounting requirements exist?

- *Unearned franchise fees* are recorded at present value. Where a part of the initial fee constitutes a nonrefundable amount for services already performed, revenue should be accordingly recognized.
- *The initial franchise fee is not typically allocated to specific franchisor services* before all services are performed. This practice can be done only if actual transaction prices are available for individual services.
- If the franchisor *sells equipment and inventory* to the franchisee *at no profit*, a receivable and payable are recorded. No revenue or expense recognition is given.
- In the case of a *repossessed franchise*, refunded amounts to the franchisee reduce current revenue. If there is no refund, the franchisor books additional revenue for the consideration retained that was not previously recorded. In either situation, *prospective* accounting treatment is given for the repossession.

Caution

Do not adjust previously recorded revenue for the repossession.

- Indirect costs of an operating and recurring nature are expensed immediately. Future costs to be incurred are accrued no later than the period in which related revenue is recognized. Bad debts applicable to expected uncollectibility of franchise fees should be recorded in the year of revenue recognition.
- Installment or cost recovery accounting may be employed to account for franchisee fee revenue only if a long collection period is involved and future uncollectibility of receivables cannot be accurately predicted.

Requirements

Footnote disclosure is required of:

- Outstanding obligations under agreement
- Segregation of franchise fee revenue between initial and continuing

Other Revenue Considerations

What happens if the vendor gives consideration to a customer?

In general, if the vendor provides the customer something to purchase the vendor's product, such consideration should reduce the vendor's revenue applicable to that sale.

What if the vendor is reimbursed for its out-of-pocket expenses?

The vendor records the recovery of reimbursable expenses (e.g., shipping costs billed to customers, travel costs on service contracts) as revenue.

Note

These costs are not to be netted as a reduction of cost.

How are contributions received recorded?

As per ASC No. 958-605-05 *Not-for-Profit Entities: Revenue Recognition* (FAS-116, *Accounting for Contributions Received and Contributions Made*), contributions received by a donee are recorded at fair market value by debiting the asset account and crediting revenue.

The donor debits contribution expense at fair market value. A gain or loss is recognized if fair market value differs from the book value of the donated asset.

Multiple Deliverables

How are multiple deliverables recognized?

Accounting Standards Update (ASU) No. 2009-13 (October 2009), ASC 605, *Revenue Recognition—Multiple-Deliverable Arrangements*, discusses revenue recognition policy (ASC Topic 205) and provides amendments to ASC Subtopic 605-25, *Revenue Recognition—Multiple-Element Arrangements*, for separating consideration in multiple-deliverable arrangements. A selling price hierarchy is established to determine the selling price of a deliverable. The selling price used for each deliverable is based on vendor-specific objective evidence if available, third-party evidence if vendor-specific objective evidence is not available, or estimated selling price if neither of the two aforementioned types of evidence is available.

Arrangement consideration should be allocated at the inception of the arrangement to all deliverables using the relative selling price method. This method allocates any discount in the arrangement proportionally to each deliverable on the basis of each deliverable's selling price.

A vendor must determine its best estimate of selling price consistent with that used to determine the price to sell the deliverable on a stand-alone basis.

What should be disclosed by multiple deliverables?

The following should be disclosed by similar types of arrangements:

- Timing of revenue recognition for separate units of accounting
- Description of multiple-deliverable arrangements, including nature and terms
- Factors and estimates used to determine vendor-specific objective evidence, third-party evidence, or estimated selling price
- Significant deliverables within its arrangements
- General timing of delivery or performance

Software Revenue Recognition

How are revenue arrangements consisting of tangible products and software accounted for?

Accounting Standards Update (ASU) No. 2009-14 (October 2009), ASC 985, *Software—Certain Revenue Arrangements That Include Software Elements*, relates to the accounting for revenue arrangements consisting of tangible products and software. A vendor must sell a particular element separately to assert vendor-specific objective evidence for that element. If a vendor does not have vendor-specific objective evidence for the undelivered element in an arrangement, the revenues for both the delivered and the undelivered elements are combined into one unit of accounting. Any revenue associated to the delivered products is then deferred and recognized at a later date, which in most instances is when the undelivered elements are delivered by the vendor.

Note

The Accounting Standards Update does not affect software revenue arrangements that do not include tangible products. In addition, the Update changes the accounting model for revenue arrangements that include both tangible products and software elements.

    If software contained on the tangible product is essential to the tangible products' functionality, the software is excluded from the scope of the software revenue guidance. This exclusion includes essential software that is sold with the product and undelivered software elements that relate to the tangible product's essential software.

Research and Development Costs

How are research and development (R&D) costs defined?

Research is the testing done in search of a new product, service, process, or technique. Research can be aimed at deriving a material improvement to an existing product or process. *Development* is the translation of the research into a design for the new product or process. Development may also result in material improvement in an existing product or process.

How are research and development costs accounted for?

Per ASC 730-10-05-1, *Research and Development: Overall* (FAS-2, *Accounting for Research and Development Costs*), research and development (R&D) costs are expensed as incurred.

IFRS Connection

Under IFRS, development costs, which are costs incurred after technological feasibility is established, are capitalized. This matches U.S. GAAP for software development costs, but not for ordinary R&D.

What are R&D costs?

R&D costs include:

- Salaries of personnel involved in R&D activities
- Rational allocation of indirect (general and administrative) costs

Note

R&D costs incurred under contract for others that are reimbursable are charged to a receivables account rather than expensed. Further, materials, equipment, and intangibles purchased from others that have alternative future benefit in R&D activities are capitalized. The depreciation or amortization on such assets is classified as an R&D expense. If no alternative future use exists, the costs should be expensed.

If a group of assets is acquired, allocation should be made to those that relate to R&D efforts. When a business combination is accounted for as a purchase, R&D costs are assigned their fair market value.

Expenditures paid to others to conduct R&D activities are expensed.

Note

ASC 730-10-15-4, *Research and Development: Overall* (FAS-2, *Accounting for Research and Development Costs*) does not apply to regulated industries or to the extractive industries (e.g., mining).

What are typical activities that may or may not be included as R&D?

R&D activities include:

- Formulation and design of product alternatives and testing thereof
- Laboratory research
- Engineering functions until the point the product satisfies operational requirements for manufacture
- Design of tools, molds, and dies involving new technology
- Preproduction prototypes and models
- Pilot plant costs

Examples of activities that are not for R&D include:

- Quality control
- Seasonal design changes
- Legal costs of obtaining a patent
- Market research
- Identification of breakdowns during commercial production
- Engineering of follow-up in the initial stages of commercial production
- Rearrangement and start-up activities, including design and construction engineering
- Recurring and continuous efforts to improve the product
- Commercial use of the product

Note

According to ASC 985-20-25, *Software: Costs of Software to Be Sold, Leased, or Marketed* (FAS-86, *Accounting for the Costs of Computer Software to Be Sold,*

(continued)

(Continued)

Leased, or Otherwise Marketed), costs incurred for computer software to be sold, leased, or otherwise marketed are expensed as R&D costs until technological feasibility exists, as indicated by the development of a detailed program or working model. After technological feasibility exists, software production costs should be deferred and recorded at the lower of unamortized cost or net realizable value. EXAMPLES: Debugging the software, improvements to subroutines, and adaptations for other uses.

Amortization begins when the product is available for customer release. The amortization expense should be based on the higher of:

- The percent of current revenue to total revenue from the product
- The straight-line amortization amount

What are the requirements if another party funds R&D?

Per ASC 730-20-25, *Research and Development: Research and Development Arrangements* (FAS-68, *Research and Development Arrangements*), if a business enters into an arrangement with other parties to fund the R&D efforts, the nature of the obligation must be determined. In the case where the entity has an obligation to repay the funds regardless of the R&D results, a liability has to be recognized with the related R&D expense. The journal entries are:

Cash	
Liability	
Research and Development Expense	
Cash	

A liability does not exist when the transfer of financial risk involved to the other party is substantive and genuine. If the financial risk applicable to R&D is transferred because repayment depends *only* on the R&D possessing future economic benefit, the company accounts for its obligation as a contract to conduct R&D for others. In this case R&D costs are capitalized, and revenue is recognized as earned and becomes billable under the contract.

Requirement

Footnote disclosure is made of the terms of the R&D agreement, the amount of compensation earned, and the costs incurred under the contract.

What if loans or advances are to be repaid depending on R&D results?

When repayment of loans or advances to the company depends *only* on R&D results, such amounts are deemed R&D costs incurred by the company and charged to expense.

How are warrants or other financial vehicles handled?

If warrants or other financial instruments are issued in an R&D arrangement, the company records part of the proceeds to be provided by the other parties as paid-in capital based on the financial instruments' fair market value on the arrangement date.

Advertising Costs

How are advertising costs accounted for?

Advertising must be expensed as incurred or when the advertising program first occurs. The cost of a billboard should be deferred and amortized.

Restructuring Charges

How are restructuring charges treated?

Restructuring charges are expensed as incurred. In general, an expense and a liability should be accrued for employee termination costs. Disclosure should be made of the group and number of employees laid off.

Other Expense Considerations

Start-up costs, including organization costs and moving costs, are expensed as incurred.

Earnings per Share

Who must compute earnings per share?

ASC 260-10-50-1, *Earnings per Share: Overall* (FAS-128, *Earnings per Share*), requires that publicly held companies must compute earnings per share (EPS). This is not required of nonpublic companies. In a simple capital structure, no potentially dilutive securities exist. "Potentially dilutive" means the security will be converted into common stock at a later date, reducing EPS. Thus, only one EPS figure is necessary. In a complex capital structure, dilutive securities exist, requiring dual presentation.

What do basic earnings per share and diluted earnings per share take into account?

Basic EPS takes into account only the actual number of outstanding common shares during the period (and those contingently issuable in certain cases). Diluted EPS includes the effect of common shares actually outstanding and the impact of convertible securities, stock options, stock warrants, and their equivalents if dilutive.

How are basic EPS and diluted EPS calculated?

Basic EPS = Net income available to common stockholders ÷ Weighted-average number of common shares outstanding.

Diluted EPS = Net income available to common stockholders + Net of tax interest and/or dividend savings on convertible securities ÷ Weighted-average number of common shares outstanding + Effect of convertible securities + Net effect of stock options.

How do I calculate the weighted-average common stock outstanding?

Weighted-average common stock shares outstanding takes into account the number of months in which those shares were outstanding.

Example 1.4

On 1/1/2X12, 10,000 shares were issued. On 4/1/2X12, 2,000 of those shares were bought back by the company. The weighted-average common stock outstanding is:

$$\left(10,000 \times \frac{3}{12}\right) + \left(8,000 \times \frac{9}{12}\right) = 8,500 \text{ shares}$$

Note

When shares are issued because of a stock dividend or stock split, the computation of weighted-average common stock shares outstanding mandates retroactive adjustment as if the shares were outstanding at the beginning of the year.

Example 1.5

These events occurred during the year for a common stock:

Shares outstanding—1/1	30,000
2-for-1 stock split—4/1	30,000
Shares issued—8/1	5,000

The number of common shares to be used in the denominator of basic EPS is 62,083 shares, computed:

1/1–3/31: 30,000 × 3/12 × 2	15,000
4/1–8/1: 60,000 × 4/12	20,000
8/1–12/31: 65,000 × 5/12	27,083
Total	62,083

What are the mechanics of the calculation of EPS?

In the numerator of the EPS fraction, net income less preferred dividends represents earnings available to common stockholders. On cumulative preferred stock, preferred dividends for the current year are subtracted out whether paid or not. Further, preferred dividends are subtracted out only for the current year. *Example:* If preferred dividends in arrears were for five years, all of which were paid plus the sixth-year dividend, only the sixth-year dividend (current year) is deducted. Preferred dividends for each of the prior years would have been deducted in those years.

In computing EPS, preferred dividends are subtracted out only on preferred stock that was not included as a common stock equivalent. If the preferred stock is a common stock equivalent, the preferred divided would not be subtracted out since the equivalency of preferred shares into common shares is included in the denominator.

As for the denominator of EPS, if convertible bonds are included, they are considered as equivalent to common shares. Thus, interest expense (net of tax) has to be added back in the numerator.

Example 1.6

This information is presented for a company:

Preferred stock, $10 par value, 6% cumulative, 30,000 shares issued and outstanding	$300,000
Common stock, $5 par value, 100,000 shares issued and outstanding	500,000
Net income	400,000

The company paid a cash dividend on preferred stock. The preferred dividend would therefore equal $18,000 (6% × $300,000). Basic EPS equals $3.82, computed as:

(continued)

(Continued)

Earnings Available to Common Stockholders

Net income	$400,000
Less: Preferred dividends	(18,000)
Earnings available to common stockholders	$382,000

Basic EPS = $382,000/100,000 shares = $3.82

Example 1.7

On January 1, 2X12, Dauber Company had these shares outstanding:

Preferred stock, $100 par value, 6% cumulative	150,000 shares
Common stock, $5 par value	500,000 shares

During the year, these events occurred:

- On April 1, 2X12, the company issued 100,000 shares of common stock.
- On September 1, 2X12, the company declared and issued a 10 percent stock dividend.
- For the year ended December 31, 2X12, the net income was $2,200,000.

Basic EPS for the year 2X12 equals $2.06 ($1,300,000/632,500 shares), calculated as:

Earnings Available to Common Stockholders

Net income	$2,200,000
Less: Preferred dividend (150,000 shares × $6)	900,000
Earnings available to common stockholders	$1,300,000
Weighted-average number of outstanding common shares	
1/1/2X12–3/31/2X12 (500,000 × 3/12 × 110%)	137,500
4/1/2X12–8/31/2X12 (600,000 × 5/12 × 110%)	275,000
9/1/2X12–12/31/2X12 (660,000 × 4/12)	220,000
Weighted-average outstanding common shares	632,500

Diluted Earnings per Share

If potentially dilutive securities exist that are outstanding, such as convertible bonds, convertible preferred stock, stock options, or stock warrants, both basic and diluted earnings per share must be presented.

How does the if-converted method work?

In the case of convertible securities, the *if-converted method* must be used. Under this approach, it is assumed that the dilutive convertible security is converted into common stock at the beginning of the period, or the date of issue if later. If conversion is assumed, the interest expense (net of tax) that would have been incurred on the convertible bonds must be added back to net income in the numerator. Any dividend on convertible preferred stock would also be added back (dividend savings) to net income in the numerator. The add-back of interest expense (net of tax) on convertible bonds and preferred dividends on convertible preferred stock, results in an adjusted net income figure used to determine earnings per share. Correspondingly, the number of common shares the convertible securities are convertible into (or their weighted-average effect if conversion to common stock actually took place during the year) must also be added to the weighted-average outstanding common shares in the denominator.

How does the treasury stock method work?

In the case of dilutive stock options, stock warrants, or their equivalent, the *treasury stock method* is used. Under this method, there is an assumption that the option or warrant was exercised at the beginning of the period, or the date of grant if later. The assumed proceeds received from the exercise of the option or warrant are assumed to be used to buy treasury stock at the average market price for the period. However, exercise is presumed to occur only if the average market price of the underlying shares during the period is greater than the exercise price of the option or warrant. This presumption ensures that the assumed exercise of a stock option or warrant will have a dilutive effect on the earnings per share computation. Correspondingly, the denominator of diluted earnings per share increases by the number of shares assumed issued, owing to the exercise of options or warrants reduced by the assumed treasury shares bought.

Example 1.8

One hundred shares are under a stock option plan at an exercise price of $10. The average market price of the company's stock during the period is $25. The assumed issuance of common shares, because of the assumed exercise of the stock options, is 60 shares, computed as:

Issued shares from option	100 shares × $10 = $1,000
Less: Treasury shares	40 shares* × $25 = $1,000
Additional shares that must be issued to satisfy option holders	60 shares

*It is assumed that 1,000/$25 = 40 shares were acquired.

If options are granted as part of a stock-based compensation arrangement, the assumed proceeds from the exercise of the options under the treasury stock method include deferred compensation and the resulting tax benefit that would be credited to paid-in capital arising from the exercise of the options.

What about the denominator of diluted EPS?

As a result of the if-converted method for convertible dilutive securities and the treasury stock method for stock option plans and warrants, the denominator of the diluted earnings per share computation equals the weighted-average outstanding common shares for the period plus the assumed issue of common shares arising from convertible securities plus the assumed shares issued because of the exercise of stock options or stock warrants, or their equivalent.

Example 1.9

This example assumes the same information about the Dauber Company given in Example 1.7. It is further assumed that potentially dilutive securities outstanding include 5 percent convertible bonds (each $1,000 bond is convertible into 25 shares of common stock) having a face value of $5,000,000. There are options to buy 50,000 shares of common stock at $10 per share. The average market price for common shares is $25 per share for 20X2. The tax rate is 30 percent.

Basic earnings per share = Net income available to common stockholders divided by weighted-average number of common shares outstanding = $1,300,000/632,500 shares = $2.06

Diluted earnings per share equals:

Income for diluted earnings per share:		
Earnings available to common stockholders		$1,300,000
Interest expense on convertible bonds	$250,000	
($5,000,000 × 0.05)		
Less: Tax savings ($250,000 × 0.30)	(75,000)	
Interest expense (net of tax)		175,000
Income for diluted earnings per share		$1,475,000
Shares outstanding for diluted EPS:		
Weighted-average outstanding common shares		$　632,500
Assumed issued common shares for convertible		
bonds (5,000 bonds × 25 shares)		125,000
Assumed issued common shares from exercise		
of option	$　50,000	
Less: Assumed repurchase of treasury shares	(20,000)	30,000
[(50,000 × $10 = $500,000)/$25]		
Shares outstanding for diluted EPS		787,500

Diluted EPS for 2X12 is $1.87 ($1,475,000/787,500 shares). Diluted EPS must be disclosed because the two securities (the 5 percent convertible bond and the stock options) had an aggregately dilutive effect on EPS. That is, EPS decreased from $2.06 to $1.87. The required disclosures are indicated next.

Earnings per Share Disclosure	
Basic earnings per share	$2.06
Diluted earnings per share	$1.87

Antidilutive Securities

Are antidilutive securities included in EPS?

In computing EPS, all antidilutive securities should be ignored. A security is considered to be antidilutive if its inclusion does not cause EPS to go down. In computing EPS, the aggregate of all dilutive securities must be taken into account. However, in order to exclude the ones that should not be used in the computation, it is necessary to determine which securities are individually dilutive and which ones are antidilutive. As was previously noted, a stock option will be antidilutive if the underlying market price of the stock that can be bought is less than the exercise price of the option. A convertible security is antidilutive if the exercise of the convertible bond or preferred stock results in an increase in the EPS computation compared to that derived before the assumed conversion. In this case, the additive effect to the numerator and denominator as a result of the conversion causes EPS to increase. In both cases, the antidilutive securities should be ignored in the calculation.

Example 1.10

A company's net income for the year is $100,000. A 10 percent $2,000,000 convertible bond was outstanding all year that was convertible into 2,000 shares of common stock. The weighted-average number of shares of common stock outstanding all year was 200,000. The income tax rate was 30 percent.

Basic EPS = $100,000/200,000 shares = $0.50
Diluted EPS = $100,000 + $200,000 (1 − 0.30) = $240,000, divided by 200,000 + 2,000 shares = $240,000/202,000 shares = $1.19

Because EPS increased as a result of the inclusion of the convertible bond, the bond is antidilutive and should be excluded from the calculation. Only basic EPS should be disclosed here.

Example 1.11

Davis Company has basic EPS of $14 for 2X12. There were no conversions or exercises of convertible securities during the year. However, possible conversion of convertible bonds would have reduced EPS by $2. The impact of possible exercise of stock options would have increased EPS by $0.38. Diluted EPS for 2X12 equals $12 ($14 − $2).

Note

The dilutive convertible bonds are taken into account in deriving diluted EPS, but the stock options are ignored because they have an antidilutive effect.

What are the reporting requirements for EPS?

Disclosure of EPS should include:

- Information on the capital structure
- Explanation of the computation of EPS
- Identification of common stock equivalents
- Assumptions made
- Number of shares converted

   Rights and privileges of the securities should also be disclosed, including:

- Dividend and participation rights
- Call prices
- Conversion ratios
- Sinking fund requirements

   Another point to remember is:

- A stock conversion may materially affect EPS if it has taken place at the beginning of the year.

Recommendation

Supplementary footnote disclosure should be made reflecting on an "as-if" basis what the effects of these conversions would have been on EPS if they were made at the start of the accounting period.

- If a subsidiary has been acquired under the *purchase accounting method* during the year, the weighted-average shares outstanding for the year are used from the purchase date.

- If common stock or a common stock equivalent is sold during the year and the proceeds are used to buy back debt or retire preferred stock, there should be a presentation of supplemental EPS figures.
- When comparative financial statements are presented, there is a retroactive adjustment for stock splits and stock dividends.
- When a prior-period adjustment occurs that causes a restatement of previous years' earnings, EPS should also be restated.

Example 1.12

Assume that in 2X12 a 10 percent stock dividend occurs. The weighted-average shares used for previous years' computations have to be increased by 10 percent to make EPS data comparable.

CHAPTER 2

Financial Statement Reporting: The Balance Sheet

On the balance sheet, the CPA is concerned with the accounting for and reporting of assets, liabilities, and stockholders' equity.

Assets

What valuation is used for assets?

Assets are recorded at the price paid plus related incidental costs (e.g., insurance, freight). If an asset is acquired for the incurrence of a liability, the asset is recorded at the present value (discounted value) of the payments.

Example 2.1

If a machine was acquired in exchange for making 10, $10,000 payments at an interest rate of 10 percent, the asset would be recorded at:

$$\$10,000 \times 6,145^* = \$61,450$$

---

*Factor using the present value of ordinary annuity table for $n = 10$, $i = 10\%$.

Note

The asset is recorded at the principal amount excluding the interest payments. If an asset is acquired for stock, the asset is recorded at the fair value of the stock issued. If it is impossible to determine the fair market value of the stock (e.g., closely held corporation), the asset will be recorded at its appraised value.

Unearned discounts (except for cost or quantity), finance charges, and interest included in the face of receivables should be deducted from receivables to derive the net receivable.

Some of the major current and noncurrent assets include:

- Accounts receivable
- Inventory
- Fixed assets
- Intangibles

Accounts Receivable

What is the difference between an assignment and factoring?

The assignment of accounts receivable typically requires the incurrence of a financing charge as well as interest expense on the note.

Example 2.2

In an assignment of accounts receivable, the entries are:

Accounts Receivable Assigned	$50,000	
Accounts Receivable		$50,000

to designate specific accounts for assignment and collateralization for the loan;

Cash	$45,000	
Notes Payable		$45,000

to recognize a liability for the advance received from the lending institution;

Allowance for Bad Debts	$XX	
Accounts Receivable Assigned		$XX

to write off an uncollectible assigned accounts receivable.

At a particular date, the transferor's equity in the *assigned* receivables equals the difference between the accounts receivable assigned and the balance of the line ($5,000). When payments on the receivables are received, they are remitted by the company to the lending institution to reduce the liability. Assignment is on a nonnotification basis to customers. It is made with recourse, where the company has to make good for uncollectible customer accounts.

In a *factoring* of accounts receivable, the receivables are in effect sold. Customers typically are notified. Factoring usually is done without recourse, where the risk of uncollectibility of the customer's account rests with the financing institution.

Billing and collection typically are done by the factor. The difference between the factored receivable and the amount received represents a gain or loss, as shown:

Cash
Loss (or Gain)
    Accounts Receivable

Note

Receivables from officers and affiliates require disclosure.

When are transfers of receivables treated as sales?

A sale is recorded for the transfer of receivables with recourse if all of these criteria are satisfied:

- The transferor gives up control of the future economic benefits applicable to the receivables (e.g., repurchase right).
- The liability of the transferor under the recourse provisions is estimable.
- The transferee cannot require the transferor to repurchase the receivables unless there is a recourse provision in the contract.

How are transfer sales disclosed?

When the transfer is treated as a sale, gain or loss is recognized for the difference between the selling price and the net receivables.

- The selling price includes normal servicing fees of the transferor and appropriate probable adjustments (e.g., debtor's failure to pay on time, effects of prepayment, and defects in the transferred receivable).
- Net receivables equals gross receivables plus finance and service charges minus unearned finance and service charges.

In the case in which selling price varies during the term of the receivables owing to a variable interest rate provision, the selling price is estimated with the use of an appropriate going market interest rate at the transfer date.

Note

Later changes in the rate cause a change in estimated selling price, not in interest income or interest expense.

If any one of the listed criteria is not satisfied, a liability is recognized for the proceeds received.

The footnote disclosure includes:

- Amount received by transferor
- Balance of the receivables at the balance sheet date

Inventory

How can inventory be valued?

Inventory can be valued at the lower of cost or market value. Specialized inventory methods may be used, such as:

- Retail
- Retail lower of cost or market
- Retail last in, first out (LIFO)
- Dollar-value LIFO

Losses on purchase commitments should be recognized in the accounts.

If ending inventory is overstated, cost of sales is understated and net income is overstated. If beginning inventory is overstated, cost of sales is overstated and net income is understated.

How does the lower of cost or market value method work?

Inventories are recorded at the lower of cost or market value for conservatism purposes applied on a total, category, or individual basis.

> **Note**
>
> The method used must be consistently applied.

If cost is below market value (replacement cost), cost is taken. If market value is below cost, we start with market value.

- Market value cannot exceed the ceiling, which is net realizable value (selling price less costs to complete and dispose). If it does, the ceiling is chosen.
- Market value cannot be less than the floor, which is net realizable value less a normal profit margin. If market value is less than the floor, the floor value is used.
- Market value is used when it lies between the ceiling and floor. The next diagram may be helpful:

Example 2.3

The lower of cost or market value method is being applied on an item-by-item basis. The bold figure is the appropriate valuation.

Product	Cost	Market	Ceiling	Floor
A	**$ 5**	$ 7	$ 9	$ 6
B	14	12	**11**	7
C	18	**15**	16	12
D	20	12	18	**16**
E	**6**	5	12	7

In case E, a market value of $5 was originally selected. Because the market value of $5 exceeded the floor of $7, the floor value would be used. However, if after applying the lower of cost or market value rule, the valuation derived ($7) exceeds the cost ($6), the cost figure is more conservative and thus is used.

Note

If market (replacement cost) is below the original cost but the selling price has not likewise declined, no loss should be recognized. To do so would create an abnormal profit margin in the future period.

The lower of cost or market value method is not used with LIFO since under LIFO current revenue is matched against current costs.

IFRS Connection

IFRS prohibits the use of the LIFO cost flow assumption and records market value in the lower of cost or market value method *differently*. FIFO and average cost are the only two acceptable cost flow assumptions permitted under IFRS. Both U.S. GAAP and IFRS permit specific identification where appropriate. In the lower of cost or market value test for inventory valuation, IFRS defines market value as *net realizable value*. U.S. GAAP, in contrast, defines market value as replacement cost subject to the constraints of net realizable value (the ceiling) and net realizable value less a normal markup (the floor). In other words, IFRS does not use a ceiling or a floor to determine market value.

When and how should the retail method be applied?

The retail method is used by department stores and other large retail businesses that carry inventory items at retail selling price. The retail method is used to estimate the ending inventory at cost by employing a cost-to-retail (selling price) ratio.

The ending inventory is first determined at selling price and then converted to cost. Markups and markdowns are both considered in arriving at the cost-to-retail ratio, resulting in a higher ending inventory than the retail lower of cost or market value method.

How do I apply the retail lower of cost or market value method?

The *conventional retail* method is a modification of the retail method and is preferable to it. In computing the cost-to-retail ratio, markups but not markdowns are considered. This results in a lower inventory figure.

Example 2.4 illustrates the accounting difference between the retail method and the retail lower of cost or market value method.

Example 2.4

	Cost	Retail	
Inventory—1/1	$16,000	$ 30,000	
Purchases	30,000	60,000	
Purchase returns	(5,000)	(10,000)	
Purchase discount	(2,000)		
Freight in	1,000		
Markups	$25,000		
Markup cancellations	(5,000)		
Net markups		20,000	
Total	$40,000	$100,000	(40%)
Markdowns	$22,000		
Markdown cancellations	(2,000)		
Net markdowns		20,000	
Cost of goods available	$40,000	$ 80,000	(50%)
Deduct:			
Sales	55,000		
−Sales returns	(5,000)	50,000	
Inventory—Retail		$ 30,000	
Retail method: At cost 50% × 30,000		15,000	
Retail lower of cost or market method: 40% × 30,000		12,000	

How does retail LIFO work?

In computing ending inventory, the mechanics of the retail method are basically followed. Beginning inventory is excluded, and both markups and markdowns are included in computing the cost-to-retail ratio. A decrease in inventory during the period is deducted from the most recently added layer and then subtracted from layers in the inverse order of addition. A retail price index is used in restating inventory.

Example 2.5

Retail price indexes follow:

2X10	$100
2X11	104
2X12	110

	Cost	Retail	Notes	Restated
2X11				
Inventory—Jan. 1 (base inv.)	$ 80,000	$130,000		
Purchases	240,000	410,000		
Markups		10,000		
Markdowns		(20,000)		
Total (exclude beg. inv.)	$240,000*	$400,000	*60%	
Total (include beg. inv.)	$320,000	530,000		
Sales		389,600		
2X11 Inventory—End at retail		$140,400		
Cost Basis				
2X11 Inventory in terms of 2X10 prices 140,400 ÷ 1.04		$135,000		
2X10 Base	$ 80,000	130,000	130,000 × 1.04	$135,200
2X11 Layer in 2X10 prices		$ 5,000		
2X11 Layer in 2X11 prices		$ 5,200	5,000 × 1.04	5,200
				$140,400
2X11 LIFO cost 60% × 5,200	3,120			
	$ 83,120	$140,400		

	Cost	Retail		
2X12				
Inventory—Jan. 1	$ 83,120	$140,400		
Purchases	260,400	430,000		
Markups		20,000		
Markdowns		(30,000)		
Total (exclude beg. inv.)	$260,400*	$420,000	*62%	
Total (include beg. inv.)	$343,520	$560,400		
Sales		408,600		
2X12 Inventory—End at retail		$151,800		
Cost Basis				
2X12 Inventory in terms of 2X10 prices 151,800 ÷ 1.10				
2X10 Base	$ 80,000	$138,000		
Excess over Base Year		130,000	130,000 × 1.10	$143,000
2X11 Layer in 2X11 prices	3,120	$ 8,000		
2X12 Layer in 2X10 prices		5,000	5,000 × 1.10	5,500
2X12 Layer in 2X12 prices		$ 3,000		
2X12 Increase in 2X12 prices		$ 3,300	3,000 × 1.10	3,300
2X12 LIFO cost 62% × 3,300	2,046			
	$ 85,166	$151,800		$151,800

What are the steps in dollar-value LIFO?

Dollar-value LIFO is an extension of the historical cost principle. This method aggregates dollars instead of units into homogeneous groupings. The method assumes that an inventory decrease came from the last year.

The four steps under dollar-value LIFO are:

1. Restate ending inventory in the current year into base dollars by applying a price index.
2. Subtract the year 0 inventory in base dollars from the current year's inventory in base dollars.
3. Multiply the incremental inventory in the current year in base dollars by the price index to obtain the incremental inventory in current dollars.
4. Obtain the reportable inventory for the current year by adding to the year 0 inventory in base dollars the incremental inventory for the current year in current dollars.

Example 2.6

At 12/31/2X12, the ending inventory is $130,000, and the price index is 1.30. The base inventory on 1/1/2X12 was $80,000. The 12/31/2X12 inventory is computed next.

12/31/2X12 Inventory in base dollars $130,000/1.30	$100,000
1/1/2X12 Beginning base inventory	80,000
2X12 Increment in base dollars	$ 20,000
2X12 Increment in current-year dollars	× 1.3
	$ 26,000
Inventory in base dollars	$ 80,000
Increment in current-year dollars	26,000
Reportable inventory	$106,000

What are some problems in determining inventory?

Although the basics of inventory cost measurement are easily stated, difficulties arise because of cost allocation problems.

- Idle capacity costs and abnormal spoilage costs may have to be written off immediately in the current year instead of being allocated as an element of inventory valuation.
- General and administrative expenses may be inventoried when they specifically relate to production activity.
- Under ASC 330-10, *Inventory—Overall* (FAS-151, *Inventory Costs*), we must expense as incurred freight and handling.

What if there is a loss on a prospective purchase?

Significant net losses on purchase commitments should be recognized at the end of the reporting period.

Example 2.7

In 2X12, ABC Company committed itself to buy raw materials at $1.20 per pound. At the end of the year, before fulfilling the purchase commitment, the price of the materials dropped to $1.00 per pound. Conservatism dictates that a loss on the purchase commitment of $0.20 per pound be recognized in 2X12. Loss on Purchase Commitment is debited and Allowance for Purchase Commitment Loss is credited.

When can inventory be stated at market value in excess of cost?

Inventories can be stated in excess of cost under unusual circumstances when:

- There is no basis for cost apportionment (e.g., meat packing industry).
- Immediate marketability exists at quoted prices (e.g., certain precious metals or agricultural products).

   Disclosure is necessary when inventory is stated above cost.

What footnote disclosure is required for inventory?

Footnote disclosure for inventory includes the valuation basis method, inventory categorization by major type, unusual losses, and inventory pledged or collateralized.

Fixed Assets

How are fixed assets recorded?

A fixed asset is recorded at its fair market value or the fair market value of the consideration given, whichever is more clearly evident.

- The cost of *buying an asset* includes all costs necessary to put that asset into existing use and location, including freight, insurance, taxes, installation, and breaking-in costs (e.g., instruction).
- *Additions to an existing asset* (e.g., garage attached to a house) are capitalized and depreciated over the shorter of the life of the addition or the life of the house. Rearrangement and reinstallation costs should be capitalized if they have future benefit. If not, they should be expensed.

Recommendation

Obsolete fixed assets should be reclassified from property, plant, and equipment to other assets and shown at salvage value reflecting a loss.

- When *two or more assets are bought for one price*, cost is allocated to the assets based on their relative fair market values. If an old building is demolished to make way for the construction of a new building, the costs of demolishing the old building are charged to the land account.
- Assets that are *self-constructed* are recorded at the incremental costs to build assuming idle capacity. However, they should not be reflected at more than the outside price.
- A fixed asset *donated to the company* should be recorded at fair market value. The entry is to debit fixed assets and credit revenue.

Example 2.8

Incremental costs to self-construct a machine are $15,000. The machine could have been purchased from outside at $10,000. The journal entry is:

Machine	$10,000	
Loss	5,000	
Cash		$15,000

Note

Fixed assets cannot be written up except in the case of a discovery of a natural resource or in a purchase combination. In a discovery of a natural resource (e.g., oil), the land account is charged at appraised value and then depleted by the units of production method.

- *Land improvements* (e.g., sidewalks, driveways, fencing) are capitalized and depreciated over their useful life. Land held for investment purposes or for a future plant site should be classified under investments and not fixed assets.
- *Ordinary repairs* to an asset (e.g., tune-up for a car) are expensed since they have a life of less than one year.
- *Extraordinary repairs* are capitalized since they benefit a period of one year or more (e.g., new motor for a car). Extraordinary repairs add to an asset's life or make the asset more useful. Capital expenditures improve the quality or quantity of services to be derived from the asset.

DEPRECIATION

How do I calculate fractional-year depreciation?

Fractional-year depreciation is computing depreciation when the asset is acquired during the year. A proration is required.

Example 2.9

On 10/1/2X11, a fixed asset costing $10,000 with a salvage value of $1,000 and a life of five years is acquired.

Depreciation expense for 2X12 using the sum-of-the-years'-digits method is:

1/1/2X12–9/30/2X12	
5/15 × $9,000 × 9/12	$2,250
10/1/2X12–12/21/2X12	
4/15 × $9,000 × 3/12	600
	$2,850

Depreciation expense for 2X12 using a double declining balance is:

Year	Computation	Depreciation	Book Value
0			$10,000
10/1/2X11–12/31/2X11	3/12 × $10,000 × 40%	$1,000	9,000
1/1/2X12–12/31/2X12	$9,000 × 40%	**3,600**	5,400

How is depreciation calculated by group and composite methods?

Group and composite depreciation methods involve similar accounting. The group method is used for similar assets, while the composite method is used for dissimilar assets. Both methods are generally accepted. There is one accumulated depreciation account for the entire group.

$$\text{Depreciation rate} = \frac{\text{Depreciation}}{\text{Gross cost}}$$

For a period:

$$\text{Depreciation expense} = \text{Depreciation rate} \times \text{Gross cost}$$

$$\text{Depreciable life} = \frac{\text{Depreciable cost}}{\text{Depreciation}}$$

When an asset is sold in the group, the entry is:

Cash (proceeds received)
Accumulated Depreciation
   Fixed Asset (cost)

Note

Upon sale of a fixed asset in the group, the difference between the proceeds received and the cost of the fixed asset is plugged to accumulated depreciation. No gain or loss is recognized upon the sale. The only time a gain or loss would be recognized is if the entire assets were sold.

Example 2.10

Calculations for composite depreciation follow:

Asset	Cost	Salvage	Depreciable Cost	Life	Depreciation
A	$ 25,000	$ 5,000	$ 20,000	10	$ 2,000
B	40,000	2,000	38,000	5	7,600
C	52,000	4,000	48,000	6	8,000
	$117,000	$11,000	$106,000		$17,600

Composite Rate:

$$\frac{\$\ 17,600}{\$117,000} = 5.04\%$$

Composite Life:

$$\frac{\$106,000}{\$\ 17,600} = 6.02 \text{ years}$$

The entry to record depreciation is:

Depreciation	$17,600	
Accumulated Depreciation		$17,600

The entry to sell asset B for $36,000 is:

Cash	$36,000	
Accumulated Depreciation	4,000	
Fixed Asset		$40,000

Disclosure should be made of the interest capitalized and expensed.

CAPITALIZED INTEREST

When is interest expensed or capitalized?

Disclosure should be made of the interest capitalized and expensed. Interest incurred on borrowed funds is expensed. However, interest on borrowed money is capitalized to the asset account and then amortized in these instances:

- Self-constructed assets for the entity's own use (to justify interest capitalization, a time period must exist for assets to be prepared for use)
- Assets purchased for the company's own use by arrangements mandating a down payment and/or progress payments
- Assets for sale or lease constructed as discrete, individual projects (e.g., real estate development)

Interest is *not* capitalized for:

- Assets produced in large volume or on a repetitive basis
- Assets in use or ready for use
- Assets not in use and not being prepared for use

What interest rate is used?

Interest capitalized is based on the average accumulated expenditures for that asset. The interest rate used is either:

- Weighted-average interest rate of corporate debt *or*
- Interest rate on the specific borrowing

When does the capitalization period begin and end?

The interest capitalization period commences when these situations exist:

- Expenditures have been incurred.
- Work is proceeding to make the asset ready for intended use. These activities are not limited to actual construction but may also include administrative and technical functions prior to the time of construction. Included are costs of unforeseen events taking place during construction. *Examples:* Labor problems and litigation.
- Interest is being incurred.

The capitalization period ceases when the asset is materially complete and usable. When an asset has individual parts (e.g., condominium units), the capitalization period of interest costs applicable to one of the separate units ends when the specific unit is materially finished and usable. Capitalization of interest is not continued when construction ends, except for brief or unexpected delays.

When the total asset must be finished to be useful, interest capitalization continues until the total asset is materially complete. *Example:* A manufacturing plant where sequential production activities must take place.

NONMONETARY TRANSACTIONS

How is an exchange of assets recorded?

Nonmonetary transactions covered under ASC 845-10-05, *Nonmonetary Transactions: Overall* (FAS-153, *Exchanges of Nonmonetary Assets*) deal primarily with exchanges or distributions of fixed assets.

Fair market value in a nonmonetary exchange may be based on:

- Quoted market price
- Appraisal
- Cash transaction for similar items

Per ASC 845-10-05, the asset received in a nonmonetary exchange is recorded at fair market value when the transaction has *commercial substance*. Commercial substance exists when future cash flows change because of the transaction arising from a change in economic positions of the two parties. A gain or loss is recorded for the difference between the book value of the asset given up and the fair market value of the asset received. However, if commercial substance does *not* exist, the exchange is recorded based on book values with no gain or loss recognized.

Example 2.11

Erlach Corporation exchanged automobiles plus cash for land. The autos have a fair market value of $25,000. They cost $32,500 with accumulated depreciation of $12,500, so the book value is $20,000. Cash paid is $8,750. The exchange has commercial substance.

The cost of the land to Erlach Corporation equals:

Fair market value of autos exchanged	$25,000
Cash paid	8,750
Cost of land	$33,750

The journal entry for the exchange transaction is:

Land	$33,750	
Accumulated Depreciation	12,500	
Autos		$32,500
Cash		8,750
Gain		5,000

The gain equals the fair market value of the autos less their book value, as calculated next.

Fair market value of autos	$25,000
Book value of autos ($32,500 − $12,500)	20,000
Gain	$ 5,000

What footnote disclosure is required?

Footnote disclosure should be made of the nature of the exchange transaction, method to account for transferred assets, and gain or loss on the exchange.

IMPAIRMENT OR DISPOSAL OF LONG-LIVED ASSETS

How do we account for the impairment or disposal of long-lived assets?

ASC 205-20-45-3, *Presentation of Financial Statements: Discontinued Operations* (FAS-144, *Accounting for the Impairment or Disposal of Long-Lived Assets*), applies to a company's long-term assets to be retained or to be disposed of.

With respect to long-term assets to be retained and used, an impairment takes place when the fair value of the long-term asset group is below its book (carrying) value. The impairment loss is recorded only when the carrying value of the asset group is not recoverable and exceeds its fair value. A lack of recoverability exists when the book value of the asset group is more than the total undiscounted cash flows expected to arise from the use and eventual disposition of the asset group. The impairment loss equals the carrying value of the asset group less its fair value.

IFRS Connection

Under IFRS, development costs, which are costs incurred after technological feasibility, are capitalized. This matches U.S. GAAP for software development costs, but not for ordinary R&D.

Example 2.12

These data are given for an asset group:

Carrying value	$50,000
Fair value	40,000
Sum of the undiscounted cash flows	47,500

Because the sum of the undiscounted cash flows is less than the carrying value, a nonrecoverability situation exists. The impairment loss to be recognized equals $10,000 ($50,000 − $40,000).

Example 2.13

This information is provided for another asset group:

Carrying value	$50,000
Fair value	53,000
Sum of the undiscounted cash flows	47,000

Because the sum of the undiscounted cash flows is less than the carrying value, a nonrecoverability situation exists. However, an impairment loss is not recognized because the fair value exceeds the carrying value.

Example 2.14

Carrying value	$50,000
Fair value	46,000
Sum of the undiscounted cash flows	52,000

Because the sum of the undiscounted cash flows exceeds the carrying value, a recoverability situation exists. Therefore, no impairment loss has occurred.

IFRS Connection

IFRS also uses a fair value test to measure the impairment loss. However, IFRS does not use the first-stage recoverability test used under U.S. GAAP—that is, comparing the *undiscounted* expected future cash flows to the carrying (book) amount. Thus, the IFRS test is more stringent than U.S. GAAP.

What should be footnoted for an impairment loss?

Footnote disclosure required for an impairment loss includes:

- Description of the impaired asset along with impairment circumstances
- Method used to derive fair value
- Amount of impairment loss and where such loss is included in the income statement
- The business segment associated with the impaired asset

INVOLUNTARY CONVERSION

What is an involuntary conversion?

There may exist an involuntary conversion (transfer) of nonmonetary assets into monetary assets, followed by replacement of the involuntarily converted assets. *Example:* A warehouse is destroyed by a fire, and the insurance proceeds received are used to purchase a similar warehouse.

How is an involuntary conversion recorded?

Per ASC 605-40-05, *Revenue Recognition—Gains and Losses,* (FASB Interpretation No. 30, *Accounting for Involuntary Conversion of Nonmonetary Assets to Monetary Assets*), gain or loss is recognized for the difference between the insurance recovery and the book value of the destroyed asset. *Example:* The new warehouse (replacing the destroyed one) is recorded at its purchase price.

Caution

A contingency results if the old fixed asset is damaged in one period but the insurance recovery is not received until a later period. A contingent gain or loss is reported in the period the old fixed asset was damaged. The gain or loss may be recognized for book and tax purposes in different years, causing a temporary difference requiring interperiod income tax allocation.

ASSET RETIREMENT OBLIGATIONS

How are asset retirement obligations accounted for?

ASC 410-20-05, *Asset Retirement and Environmental Obligations: Asset Retirement Obligations* (FAS-143, *Accounting for Asset Retirement Obligations*) requires companies to record at fair value a liability when a retirement obligation is incurred, provided fair value can be reasonably estimated even though it is years before the asset's planned retirement. The asset retirement obligation must be measured and recorded along with its associated asset retirement cost. Asset retirements may be from sale, recycling, abandonment, or disposal.

When the initial obligation arises, the company books a liability and defers the cost to the long-term asset for the same amount. After the initial recognition, the liability will change over time, so the obligation must be accreted to its present value each year. The long-term asset's capitalized cost is depreciated over its useful life. When the liability is settled, the company either settles the liability for the amount recorded or will have a settlement gain or loss.

Any incremental liability incurred in a later year is an additional layer of the original obligation. Each layer is initially measured at fair value.

DISCLOSURE

What footnote disclosure is given for fixed assets?

Footnote disclosures for fixed assets include:

- Fixed assets by major category
- Contracts to buy new fixed assets
- Description of depreciation method and estimates used
- Fixed assets subject to pledges, liens, or other commitments
- Fixed assets held to be disposed of and any expected losses
- Idle fixed assets
- Fully depreciated assets still in use

Intangibles

What are intangible assets?

Intangible assets are assets that have a life of one year or more and that lack physical substance (e.g., goodwill) or represent a right granted by the government (e.g., patent) or by another company (e.g., franchise fee).

> **Note**
>
> Goodwill does not include identifiable assets.

How are intangible assets accounted for?

ASC 350-20-55, *Intangibles—Goodwill and Other: Goodwill* (FAS-142, *Goodwill and Other Intangible Assets*) covers accounting for intangible assets, whether purchased or internally developed. The costs of intangibles acquired from others should be reported as assets. The cost equals the cash or fair market value of the consideration given.

Individual intangibles that can be separately identified must be costed separately. If not separately identified, the intangibles are assigned a cost equal to the difference between the total purchase price and the cost of identifiable tangible and intangible assets.

According to ASC 350-20-55, intangibles have either a *limited useful life* or an *indefinite useful life*. An intangible asset with a *limited life* is amortized into expense over its useful life. Examples are patents, trademarks, trade names, franchises, licenses, and copyrights. A loss on impairment is recognized on a limited life intangible asset when carrying value exceeds its fair market value. After the impairment is recognized, the reduced carrying amount is the asset's new cost basis. An intangible asset with an *indefinite life* is *not* amortized but rather is subject to a yearly impairment test. An example is goodwill.

The cost of developing and maintaining intangibles should be charged against earnings if the assets are not specifically identifiable, have indeterminate lives, or are inherent in the continuing business (e.g., goodwill).

> **Example**
>
> With respect to internally developed goodwill, the costs incurred in developing a name (e.g., "Burger King") are expensed.

How is useful life determined?

The factors in estimating useful lives for limited life intangibles include:

- Legal, contractual, and regulatory provisions
- Renewal or extension provisions (if a renewal occurs, the life of the intangible may be increased)
- Obsolescence and competitive factors
- Product demand
- Service lives of essential employees within the organization

Note

Footnote disclosure is made of the amortization period for limited life intangibles.

How is goodwill valued?

Goodwill is theoretically equal to the present value of future excess earnings of a company over other companies in the industry.

In buying a new business, a determination often must be made as to the estimated value of the goodwill. Two methods that can be used are:

1. Capitalization of earnings
2. Capitalization of excess earnings

Example 2.15

This information is available for a business that we are contemplating acquiring:

Expected average annual earnings	$10,000
Expected fair value of net assets exclusive of goodwill	$45,000
Normal rate of return	20%

Using the capitalization of earnings approach, goodwill is estimated at:

Total asset value implied ($10,000/20%)	$50,000
Estimated fair value of assets	45,000
Estimated goodwill	$ 5,000

Assuming the same facts except a capitalization rate of excess earnings of 22 percent, and using the capitalization of excess earnings method, goodwill is estimated at:

Expected average annual earnings	$10,000
Return on expected average assets ($45,000 × 20%)	9,000
Excess earnings	$ 1,000
Goodwill ($1,000/0.22)	$ 4,545

Example 2.16

The net worth of ABC Company excluding goodwill is $800,000, and profits for the past four years were $750,000. Included in the latter figure are extraordinary gains of $50,000 and nonrecurring losses of $30,000. It is desired to determine a selling price of the business. A 12 percent return on net worth is deemed typical for the industry. The capitalization of excess earnings is 45 percent in determining goodwill.

Net Income for 4 years	$750,000
Less: Extraordinary gains	50,000
Add: Nonrecurring losses	30,000
Adjusted 4-year earnings	$730,000
Average earnings ($730,000/4)	$182,500
Normal earnings ($800,000 × 0.12)	96,000
Excess annual earnings	$ 86,500
Excess earnings capitalized at 45% ($86,500/0.45)	$192,222

How is goodwill accounted for?

If a firm buys, on a step-by-step basis, an investment using the equity method, the fair value of the acquired assets and the goodwill for each step purchased must be identified separately.

When the purchase of assets results in goodwill, later sale of a separable portion of the equity acquired mandates a proportionate reduction of the goodwill account.

Goodwill is recorded in a business combination accounted for under the purchase method only when the cost to the acquirer exceeds the fair market value of the net assets acquired. Goodwill is then subject to an annual impairment test. If the cost to the acquirer is less than the fair market value of the net assets acquired, a credit arises. This credit represents negative goodwill that is proportionately allocated as a reduction of the acquired assets except for certain deferred assets (e.g., deferred pension and tax assets). If these assets are reduced to zero, the credit balance remaining is recorded as an extraordinary gain.

How should I handle new product costs, organization costs, and leaseholds?

Internally generated costs to derive a patented product (e.g., research and development incurred in developing a new product) are expensed. The patent is recorded at the registration fees to secure and register it, legal fees in successfully defending it in court, and the cost of acquiring competing patents from outsiders. The patent account is amortized over its useful life, not exceeding 20 years.

How are trademarks, trade names, franchises, licenses, and copyrights accounted for?

Trademarks and trade names have legal protection for 10 years and can be renewed an indefinite number of times. Franchises and licenses with a limited life should be amortized over their useful life. Copyrights are granted for the life of the creator plus 70 years. Registration fees and successful legal fees are deferred to the intangible asset.

Note

If an intangible asset is deemed worthless, it should be written off, recognizing an extraordinary or nonrecurring item depending on the circumstances.

Organization costs are the costs incurred to incorporate a business (e.g., legal fees). They are expensed as incurred.

Leaseholds are rents paid in advance and are amortized over the life of the lease.

What footnote disclosures should be made for goodwill and other intangible assets?

The footnote disclosures for goodwill and other intangible assets include:

- Amortization period for limited life intangibles and expected amortization expense for the next five years
- Amount of any significant residual value
- Amount of goodwill included in the gain or loss on disposal of all or part of a reporting unit
- Description of impaired intangible assets and the reasons for such impairment
- Amount of impairment loss
- Method to compute fair value

What should be disclosed about recognized intangible assets?

Companies must disclose information about how recognized intangible assets would aid financial statement users to determine how a company's ability to renew or extend an arrangement impacts the company's anticipated cash flows associated with the asset.

Disclosure should be made of:

- Weighted-average period at acquisition or renewal before the next renewal or extension.
- Accounting policy for costs incurred to renew or extend an intangible asset's term.
- In the event renewal or extension costs are capitalized, the total cost incurred to renew or extend the term of a recognized intangible asset.

Financial Assets

How are transfers of financial assets accounted for?

ASC 860, *Transfers and Servicing* (FAS-166, *Accounting for Transfers of Financial Assets*), requires additional information about transfers of financial assets such as securitization transactions, and where business entities have continuing exposure to the risks associated with transferred financial assets. It eliminates the concept of a "qualifying special-purpose entity." It changes other requirements for derecognizing financial assets, and requires additional disclosures. There is greater transparency about transfers of financial assets and the company's continued involvement in transferred financial assets.

A purpose is to determine if a transferor has surrendered control over transferred financial assets. A participating interest is to establish specific conditions for reporting a transfer of part of a financial asset as a sale. If the transfer does not satisfy those conditions, a transferor should account for the transfer as a sale only if it transfers an entire financial asset or a group of entire financial assets and surrenders control over the entire transferred assets.

A transferor must recognize and initially measure at fair value all assets obtained and liabilities incurred due to a transfer of financial assets accounted for as a sale.

ASC 860 clarifies the principle that the transferor must appraise whether it, its consolidated affiliates, or its agents effectively control the transferred financial assets directly or indirectly.

Note

The pronouncement is effective January 1, 2010, for companies reporting earnings on a calendar-year basis.

Insurance

How is cash surrender value defined?

Cash surrender value of whole-life insurance is the sum payable upon cancellation of the policy by the insured; the insured will, of course, receive less than the premiums paid in.

Note

Cash surrender value is classified under long-term investments.

How is possible reimbursement calculated?

Casualty insurance covers such items as fire loss and water damage. Casualty insurance reimburses the holder for the fair market value of property lost. Insurance companies typically have a coinsurance clause so that the insured bears part of the loss. This insurance reimbursement formula assumes an 80 percent coinsurance clause:

$$\frac{\text{Face of policy}}{0.80 \times \text{Fair market value}} \times \text{Fair market value of loss of insured property}$$
$$= \text{Possible reimbursement}$$

Insurance reimbursement is based on the lower of the face of the policy, fair market value of loss, or possible reimbursement.

Example 2.17

Case	Face of Policy	Fair Market Value of Property	Fair Market Value of Loss
A	$ 4,000	$10,000	$ 6,000
B	6,000	10,000	10,000
C	10,000	10,000	4,000

Insurance reimbursement follows:

Case A:

$$\frac{\$4,000}{0.8 \times \$10,000} \times \$6,000 = \$3,000$$

Case B:

$$\frac{\$6,000}{0.8 \times \$10,000} \times \$10,000 = \$7,500$$

Case C:

$$\frac{\$10,000}{0.8 \times \$10,000} \times \$4,000 = \$5,000$$

What does a blanket policy cover?

A blanket policy covers several items of property. The face of the policy is allocated based on the fair market values of the insured assets.

Example 2.18

A blanket policy of $15,000 applies to equipment I and equipment II. The fair market values of equipment I and II are $30,000 and $15,000, respectively. Equipment II is partially destroyed, resulting in a fire loss of $3,000.

The policy allocation to equipment II is computed next.

	Fair Market Value	Policy
Equipment I	$30,000	$10,000
Equipment II	15,000	5,000
	$45,000	$15,000

The insurance reimbursement is:

$$\frac{\$5,000}{0.8 \times \$15,000} \times \$3,000 = \$1,500$$

How is a fire loss recorded?

When a fire loss occurs, the asset destroyed has to be removed from the accounts, with the resulting fire loss recorded based on book value. The insurance reimbursement reduces the fire loss. The fire loss is an extraordinary item (net of tax).

Example 2.19

This fire loss information applies to ABC Company. Merchandise costing $5,000 is fully destroyed. There is no insurance for it. Furniture costing $10,000 with accumulated depreciation of $1,000 and having a fair market value of $7,000 is entirely destroyed. The policy is for $10,000. A building costing $30,000 with accumulated depreciation of $3,000 and having a fair market value of $20,000 is 50 percent destroyed; the face of the policy is $15,000. The journal entries to record the book loss are:

Fire Loss	$ 5,000	
Inventory		$ 5,000
Fire Loss	9,000	
Accumulated Depreciation	1,000	
Furniture		10,000
Fire Loss	13,500	
Accumulated Depreciation	1,500	
Building		15,000

Insurance reimbursement totals $16,375, computed as follows:

Furniture:

$$\frac{\$10,000}{0.8 \times \$7,000} \times \$7,000 = \$12,500$$

Building:

$$\frac{\$15,000}{0.8 \times \$20,000} \times \$10,000 = \$9,375$$

The journal entry for the insurance reimbursement is:

Cash	$16,375	
Fire Loss		$16,375

The net fire loss is $11,125 ($27,500 − $16,375).

Liabilities

What types of liabilities must I focus on?

In accounting for liabilities, the CPA has numerous reporting and disclosure responsibilities.

- Bonds payable may be issued between interest dates at a discount or premium.
- Bonds may be amortized using the straight-line method or effective interest method.
- Debt may be retired before its maturity date in cases where the company can issue new debt at a lower interest rate.
- Estimated liabilities must be booked when it is *probable* that an asset has been impaired or liability has been incurred by year-end, and the amount of loss is subject to reasonable estimation.
- An accrued liability may also be made for future employee absences (e.g., sick leave or vacation time).
- Special termination benefits, such as early retirement, may also be offered to and accepted by employees.
- Short-term debt may be rolled over to long-term debt, requiring special reporting.
- A callable obligation by the creditor may also exist.
- Long-term purchase obligations must be disclosed.

Bonds Payable

What is the effective cost of a bond?

The cost of a corporate bond is expressed in terms of yield. Two types of yield calculations are:

$$\text{Simple yield} = \frac{\text{Nominal interest}}{\text{Present value of bond}}$$

$$\text{Yield to maturity} = \frac{\text{Nominal interest} + \dfrac{\text{Discount}}{\text{Years}} - \dfrac{\text{Premium}}{\text{Years}}}{\dfrac{\text{Present value} + \text{Maturity value}}{2}}$$

Simple yield is not as accurate as yield to maturity.

Example 2.20

A $100,000, 10 percent, five-year bond is issued at $96,000. The simple yield is:

$$\frac{\text{Nominal interest}}{\text{Present value of bond}} = \frac{\$10,000}{\$96,000} = \underline{10.42\%}$$

The yield to maturity is:

$$\frac{\text{Nominal interest} + \dfrac{\text{Discount}}{\text{Years}} - \dfrac{\text{Premium}}{\text{Years}}}{\dfrac{\text{Present value} + \text{Maturity value}}{2}}$$

$$= \frac{\$10,000 + \dfrac{\$4,000}{5}}{\dfrac{\$96,000 + \$100,000}{2}} = \frac{\$10,800}{\$98,000} = \underline{11.02\%}$$

What is a discount or premium?

- When a bond is issued at a discount, the yield is greater than the nominal interest rate.
- When a bond is issued at a premium, the yield is less than the nominal interest rate.

How is a discount or a premium amortized?

The two methods of amortizing a bond discount or bond premium are:

- *Straight-line method.* This results in a constant dollar amount of amortization but a different effective rate each period.
- *Effective interest method.* This results in a constant rate of interest but different dollar amounts each period.

Recommendation

The effective interest method is preferred over the straight-line method.

The amortization entry is:

Interest Expense (Yield × Carrying Value of Bond at the Beginning of the Year)
Discount
Cash (Nominal Interest × Face Value of Bond)

In the early years, the amortization amount under the effective interest method is lower than under the straight-line method (for either discount or premium).

Example 2.21

On 1/1/2X11, a $100,000 bond is issued at $95,624. The yield rate is 7 percent and the nominal interest rate is 6 percent. This schedule is the basis for the journal entries to be made:

Date	Debit Interest Expense	Credit Cash	Credit Discount	Carrying Value
1/1/2X11				$95,624
12/31/2X11	$6,694	$6,000	$694	96,318
12/31/2X12	6,742	6,000	742	97,060

The entry on 12/31/2X11 is:

Interest Expense	$6,694	
Cash		$6,000
Discount		694

At maturity, the bond will be worth its face value of $100,000.

How is a discount or premium amortized when bonds are issued between interest dates?

The entry is:

Cash
    Bonds Payable
    Premium (or Debit Discount)
    Interest Expense

Example 2.22

A $100,000, 5 percent bond having a life of five years is issued at $110,000 on 4/1/2X07. The bonds are dated 1/1/2X07. Interest is payable on 1/1 and 7/1. Straight-line amortization is used. The journal entries are:

4/1/2X07 Cash ($110,000 + $1,250)	$111,250	
Bonds Payable		$100,000
Premium on Bonds Payable		10,000
Bond Interest Expense ($100,000 × 5% × 3/12)		1,250
7/1/2X07 Bond Interest Expense	2,500	
Cash		2,500
Premium on Bonds Payable ($100,000 × 5% × 6/12)	526.50	
Bond Interest Expense		526.50

4/1/2X07–1/1/2X12, 4 years, 9 months = 57 months

$$\frac{\$10,000}{57} = \$175.50 \text{ per month}$$

$175.50 × 3 months = $526.50

12/31/2X07 Bond Interest		
Expense	2,500	
Interest Payable		2,500
Premium on Bonds Payable	1,053	
Bond Interest Expense		1,053
1/1/2X08 Interest Payable	2,500	
Cash		2,500

How is the bonds payable amount recorded?

Bonds payable is shown on the balance sheet at its present value this way:

Bonds Payable
Add: Premium
Less: Discount
Carrying Value

Bond issue costs are the expenditures incurred in issuing the bonds, such as legal, registration, and printing fees.

Recommendation

Preferably, bond issue costs are deferred and amortized over the life of the bond. They are shown as a deferred charge.

How do I compute the price of a bond?

The price of a bond is determined in this way:

- The face amount is discounted using the present value of $1 table. (Exhibit 8.13)
- The interest payments are discounted using the present value of annuity of $1 table. (Exhibit 8.14)
- The yield rate is used as the discount rate.

Example 2.23

A $50,000, 10-year bond is issued with interest payable semiannually at an 8 percent nominal interest rate. The yield rate is 10 percent. The present value of $1 table factor for $n = 20$, $i = 5\%$ is 0.37689. The present value of annuity of $1 table factor for $n = 20$, $i = 5\%$ is 12.46221. The price of the bond should be:

Present Value of Principal	
$50,000 × 0.37689	$18,844.50
Present Value of Interest Payments	
$20,000 × 12.46221	24,924.42
	$43,768.92

How do I handle a bond conversion?

In converting a bond into stock, three methods can be used:

1. Book value of bond
2. Market value of bond
3. Market value of stock

Book value of bond method. No gain or loss on bond conversion will result, because the book value of the bond is the basis to credit the equity account. This is the preferred method.

Market value methods. Gain or loss will result because the book value of the bond will be different from the market value of the bond or market value of the stock, which is the basis to credit the equity account.

Example 2.24

A $100,000 bond with unamortized premium of $8,420.50 is converted to common stock. There are 100 bonds ($100,000/$1,000). Each bond is converted into 50 shares of stock. Thus, 5,000 shares of common stock are involved. Par value is $15 per share. The market value of the stock is $25 per share. The market

(continued)

(Continued)

value of the bond is $120. When the book value method is used, the entry for the conversion is:

Bonds Payable	$100,000.00	
Premium on Bonds Payable	8,420.50	
Common Stock (5,000 × $15)		$75,000.00
Premium on Common Stock		33,420.50

When the market value of stock method is used, the entry is:

Bonds Payable	$100,000.00	
Premium on Bonds Payable	8,420.50	
Loss on Conversion	16,579.50	
Common Stock		$75,000.00
Premium on Common Stock		50,000.00
5,000 × $25 = $125,000		

When the market value of the bond method is used the entry is:

Bonds Payable	$100,000.00	
Premium on Bonds Payable	8,420.50	
Loss on Conversion	11,579.50	
Common Stock		$75,000.00
Premium on Common Stock		45,000.00
$100,000 × 120% = $120,000		

Extinguishment of Debt

When can debt be retired early?

Long-term debt may be called back early when new debt can be issued at a lower interest rate. It also can be called back early when the company has excess cash and wants to avoid paying interest charges and having the debt on its balance sheet.

How is early extinguishment handled?

The gain or loss on the early extinguishment of debt is an ordinary item that should be shown in the income statement. Ordinary classification occurs whether the extinguishment is early, at scheduled maturity, or later.

Note

Serial bonds do not have characteristics of sinking fund requirements.

Debt may be construed as being extinguished in the case where the debtor is relieved of the principal liability and probably will not have to make future payments.

Example 2.25

A $100,000 bond payable with an unamortized premium of $10,000 is called at $85,000. The entry is:

Bonds Payable	$100,000	
Premium on Bonds Payable	10,000	
Cash (85% × $100,000)		$85,000
Ordinary Gain		25,000

Footnote disclosures regarding extinguishment of debt include a description of extinguishment transaction, including the source of funds used.

How do I record the conversion of debt to equity?

If convertible debt is converted to stock in connection with an *inducement offer* in which the debtor alters conversion privileges, the debtor recognizes an expense. The amount is the fair value of the securities transferred in excess of the fair value of securities issuable according to the original conversion terms. This fair market value is measured at the earlier of the conversion date or the date of the agreement.

An inducement offer can be accomplished by giving debt holders:

- A higher conversion ratio
- Payment of additional consideration
- Other favorable changes in terms

ASC 470-20-30, 27-28 [FSP APB 14-1, *Accounting for Convertible Debt Instruments That May Be Settled in Cash upon Conversion (Including Partial Cash Settlement)*], states that interest costs associated with convertible debt instruments recognized in periods subsequent to their initial recognition should constitute the borrowing rate a company would have incurred had it issued a comparable debt instrument without the embedded conversion option. That objective is achieved by requiring issuers to separately account for the liability and equity components of convertible debt instruments.

What are the steps to be used to initially measure the convertible debt?

The following three steps should be used to initially measure the convertible debt:

1. Determine the carrying value of an instrument's liability component using a fair value measurement of a similar liability (including embedded features, if any, other than the conversion option) that has no related equity component.

2. Determine the carrying value of the instrument's equity component corresponding to the embedded conversion option by subtracting the liability component's fair value from the initial proceeds applicable to the total convertible debt instrument.

3. Appraise the total convertible debt instrument if its embedded features, other than the conversion option, are substantive at the issuance date. If, at issuance, the company concludes that it is probable that a convertible instrument's embedded feature will not be exercised, that embedded feature is considered to be nonsubstantive and would not impact the initial measurement of an instrument's liability component.

Transaction costs incurred with third parties except the investors that directly relate to convertible debt issuance should be allocated to the liability and equity components in the same proportion as the allocation of proceeds and accounted for as costs of issuing debt and equity, respectively.

A temporary tax basis difference associated with the liability component may occur. Additional paid-in capital should be adjusted when deferred taxes are initially recognized for the tax impact of the temporary difference.

The principal amount of the liability component over its initial fair value must be amortized to interest cost using the interest method.

A liability component's anticipated life is not impacted by embedded features determined to be nonsubstantive when the convertible debt was issued.

If a conversion option has to be reclassified from stockholders' equity to a liability measured at fair value, the difference between the amount that has been recognized in equity and the fair value of the conversion option at the date of reclassification should be accounted for as an adjustment to stockholders' equity. On the other hand, when a conversion option accounted for in stockholders' equity is reclassified as a liability, gains or losses recognized to account for that conversion option at fair value while classified as a liability should not be reversed if later the conversion option is reclassified back to stockholders' equity. The reclassification of a conversion option does not impact the accounting for the liability component.

What should be disclosed about conversion?

The following should be disclosed:

- Conversion price and the number of shares used to calculate the total consideration to be delivered on conversion.
- Effective interest rate on the liability component.
- Amount of interest cost applicable to both the contractual interest coupon and the discount amortization on the liability component.
- Carrying value of the equity component.
- Principal amount of the liability component, its amortized discount, and its carrying value.
- Remaining years for which the discount on the liability will be amortized.
- Amount by which the instrument's if-converted value is more than the principal amount, irrespective of whether the instrument is currently convertible.
- Term of derivative transactions, reasons to enter into derivative transactions, and number of shares underlying derivative transactions.

What if a trust is set up for payment of interest and principal?

According to ASC 860-10-05, *Transfers and Servicing: Overall* (FAS-76, *Extinguishment of Debt*), if the debtor puts cash or other assets in an irrevocable trust to be used only for paying interest and principal on debt, disclosure should be made of the particulars, including a description of the transaction and the amount of debt considered to be extinguished.

Estimated Liabilities

How is a probable loss contingency defined?

A loss contingency should be accrued if *both* of these criteria exist:

- At year-end, it is probable (likely to occur) that an asset was impaired or a liability was incurred.
- The amount of loss is subject to reasonable estimation.

What are some typical loss contingencies?

Examples of probable loss contingencies may be:

- Warranties
- Lawsuits
- Claims and assessments
- Expropriation of property by a foreign government
- Casualties and catastrophes (e.g., fire)

How is a probable loss contingency booked?

The loss contingency is booked because of the principle of conservatism. The entry for a probable loss is:

Expense (Loss)
   Estimated Liability

Example 2.26

On 12/31/2X11, warranty expenses are estimated at $20,000. On 3/15/2X12, actual warranty costs paid for were $16,000. The journal entries are:

12/31/2X11	Warranty Expense	$20,000	
	Estimated Liability		$20,000
3/15/2X12	Estimated Liability	16,000	
	Cash		16,000

Notes

A probable loss that cannot be estimated should be footnoted.

If a loss contingency exists at year-end but no asset impairment or liability incurrence exists (e.g., uninsured equipment), footnote disclosure may be made.

A probable loss occurring after year-end but before the audit report date requires only subsequent event disclosure.

If the amount of loss is within a range, the accrual is based on the best estimate within that range. However, if no amount within the range is better than any other amount, the *minimum amount* (not maximum amount) of the range is booked. The exposure to additional losses should be disclosed.

Are there any other requirements on loss contingencies?

- In the case of a *reasonably possible loss* (more than remote but less than likely), no accrual is made but footnote disclosure is required. The disclosure includes the nature of the contingency and the estimate of probable loss or range of loss. If an estimate of loss is not possible, that fact should be stated.
- A *remote contingency* (slight chance of occurring) usually is ignored and no disclosure is made.

Exceptions

Guarantees of indebtedness, standby letters of credit, and agreements to repurchase receivables or properties are disclosed.

- *General (unspecified) contingencies* are not accrued. *Examples:* Self-insurance and possible hurricane losses. Disclosure and/or an appropriation of retained earnings can be made for general contingencies. To be booked as an estimated liability, the future loss must be specific and measurable, such as parcel post and freight losses.
- *Gain contingencies* cannot be booked. This violates conservatism. However, footnote disclosure can be made.

IFRS Connection

Under IFRS, the measurement of a provision related to a contingency is based on the best estimate of the expenditure required to settle the obligation. If a range of estimates is predicted and no amount in the range is more likely than any other amount in the range, the *midpoint* of the range is used to measure the liability. In U.S. GAAP, the *minimum* amount in a range is used.

Accounting for Compensated Absences

What are compensated absences?

Compensated absences include:

- Sick leave
- Holiday
- Vacation time

ASC 710-10-15, *Compensation—General: Overall* (FAS-43, *Accounting for Compensated Absences*) is not applicable to:

- Severance or termination pay
- Deferred compensation
- Post-retirement benefits
- Stock option plans
- Other long-term fringe benefits (e.g., insurance, disability)

When should there be an accrual for compensated absences?

The employer shall accrue a liability for an employee's compensation for future absences when *all* of these criteria are met:

- Employee services have already been performed.
- Employee rights have vested.
- Probable payment exists.
- Amount of estimated liability can be reasonably determined.

Note

If the criteria for a compensated absence are satisfied except that the amount is not determinable, only a footnote can be made, since an accrual is not possible.

Accrual for sick leave is required only when the employer permits employees to take accumulated sick leave days off regardless of actual illness. No accrual is required if employees may take accumulated days off only for actual illness, since losses for these are typically immaterial.

Example 2.27

Estimated compensation for future absences is $30,000. The entry is:

Expense	$30,000	
Estimated Liability		$30,000

(continued)

(Continued)

If at a later date a payment of $28,000 is made, the entry is:

Estimated Liability	$28,000	
Cash		$28,000

Accounting for Special Termination Benefits to Employees

What if employees leave early and take special benefits?

An expense should be accrued when an employer offers special termination benefits to an employee, the employee accepts the offer, and the amount is subject to reasonable estimation. The amount equals the current payment plus the discounted value of future payments.

When it can be objectively measured, the effect of changes on the employer's previously accrued expenses applicable to other employee benefits directly associated with employee termination should be included in measuring termination expense.

Example 2.28

On 1/1/2X12, as an incentive for early retirement, the employee receives a lump-sum payment of $50,000 today, plus payments of $10,000 for each of the next 10 years. The discount rate is 10 percent. The journal entry is:

Expense	$111,450	
Estimated Liability		$111,450
Present value $10,000 × 6.145*	$ 61,450	
Current payment	50,000	
Total	$111,450	

*Present value factor for $n = 10$, $i = 10\%$ is 6.145.

Refinancing of Short-Term Debt to Long-Term Debt

When can a short-term obligation be considered long-term?

A short-term obligation shall be reclassified as a long-term obligation when either of these two conditions applies:

1. After the year-end of the financial statements but before the audit report is issued, the short-term debt is rolled over into a long-term obligation, or an equity security is issued in substitution.
2. Prior to the audit report date, the company enters into a contract for refinancing of the current obligation on a long-term basis and all of these three conditions are met:

1. Agreement does not expire within one year.
2. No violation of the agreement exists.
3. The parties are financially capable of meeting the requirements of the agreement.

How do I show the reclassification of debt from short-term to long-term?

The proper classification of the refinanced item is under long-term debt and *not* stockholders' equity, even if equity securities were issued in substitution of the debt.

Recommendation

When short-term debt is excluded from current liabilities, a footnote should describe the financing agreement and the terms of any new obligation to be incurred.

If the amounts under the agreement for refinancing vary, the amount of short-term debt excluded from current liabilities will be the minimum amount expected to be refinanced based on conservatism.

Caution

The exclusion from current liabilities cannot be greater than the net proceeds of debt or security issuances, or amounts available under the refinancing agreement.

Once cash is paid for the short-term debt, even if long-term debt of a similar amount is issued the next day, the short-term debt shall be shown under current liabilities since cash was disbursed.

Callable Obligations by the Creditor

What if the debtor violates the debt agreement?

If the debtor violates the debt agreement and long-term debt therefore becomes callable, include the debt as a current liability, except if *one* of these two conditions exists:

1. The creditor waives or loses his or her right to require repayment for a period in excess of one year from the balance sheet date.
2. There is a grace period in the terms of the long-term debt issue during which the debtor may cure the violation, and it is probable that the violation will be rectified within such grace period.

Disclosure of Long-Term Purchase Obligations

What are unconditional purchase obligations?

An unconditional purchase obligation is an obligation to provide *funds* for goods or services at a determinable future date. *Example:* A take-or-pay contract obligating the buyer to periodically pay specified amounts for products or services. Even in the case in which the buyer does not take delivery of the goods, periodic payments still must be made.

How are unconditional purchase obligations disclosed?

When unconditional purchase obligations are recorded in the balance sheet, disclosure still is made of:

- Payments made for recorded unconditional purchase obligations
- Maturities and sinking-fund requirements for long-term borrowings

Unconditional purchase obligations that are not reflected in the balance sheet usually should be disclosed if they meet these criteria:

- Noncancellable, except on a remote contingency
- Negotiated to arrange financing to provide contracted goods or services
- A term in excess of one year

The disclosures needed for unconditional purchase obligations when not recorded in the accounts are:

- Nature and term
- Fixed and variable amounts
- Total amount for the current year and for the next five years
- Purchases made under the obligation for each year presented

Disclosure is optional for the amount of imputed interest required to reduce the unconditional purchase obligation to present value.

Exit or Disposal Activities

How do I account for the costs and obligations associated with exit or disposal activities?

ASC 420-10-05-3, *Exit or Disposal Cost Obligations: Overall* (FAS-146, *Accounting for Costs Associated with Exit or Disposal Activities*), applies to costs (e.g., costs to consolidate facilities or relocate workers, one-time termination benefits to current workers, operating lease termination costs) applicable to a restructuring, plant closing, discontinued operation, or other exit or disposal activity. These costs are recognized as incurred (not at the commitment date to an exit plan) based on fair value along with the related liability. The best indication of fair value is the quoted market prices in active markets. If fair value cannot reasonably be estimated, recognizing the liability must be postponed until such time.

The initiation date of an exit or disposal activity is when management obligates itself to a plan to do so or otherwise dispose of a long-lived asset.

What footnote disclosures are made for exit or disposal activities?

These items should be footnoted:

- Description of exit or disposal activity and the anticipated completion date
- For each major type of cost applicable to the exit activity, the total anticipated cost, the amount incurred in the current year and the cumulative amount to date
- If a liability for a cost is not recorded because fair value is not reasonably estimated, a note about that fact along with the reasons why
- Where exit or disposal costs are presented in the income statement

Fair Value Measurements

ASC 820-10-05, *Fair Value Measurements and Disclosures: Overall* (FAS-157, *Fair Value Measurements*), states that a fair value measurement reflects current market participant assumptions about future inflows of the asset and future outflows of the liability. A fair value measurement incorporates the attributes of the particular asset or liability (e.g., location, condition). In formulating fair value, consideration is given to the *exchange price*, which refers to the market price at the measurement date in an *orderly transaction* between the parties to sell the asset or transfer the liability. The focus is on the price that would be received to sell the asset or would be paid to transfer the liability (exit price), *not* the price that would be paid to buy the asset or would be received to assume the liability (entry price).

The asset or liability may be by itself (e.g., financial security, operating asset) or may be a group of assets or liabilities (e.g., asset group, reporting unit).

What about the fair value hierarchy?

A hierarchy list of fair value distinguishes between (1) assumptions based on market data from independent outside sources (observable inputs) and (2) assumptions by the company itself (unobservable inputs). The use of unobservable inputs allows for situations in which there is minimal or no market activity for the asset or liability at the measurement date. Valuation methods used to measure fair value shall maximize the use of observable inputs and minimize the use of unobservable ones.

What about risk and restrictions?

An adjustment for risk should be made in a fair value measurement when market participants would include risk in the pricing of the asset or liability. Nonperformance risk of the obligation and the entity's credit risk should be noted. Further, consideration should be given to the effect of a *restriction* on the sale or use of an asset that impacts its price.

What is the difference between the principal market and the most advantageous market?

In a fair value measurement, we assume that the transaction occurs in the principal (main) market for the asset or liability. This is the market in which the company would sell the asset or transfer the liability with the greatest volume. If a principal market is nonexistent, then the most advantageous market should be used. This is the market in which the business would sell the asset or transfer the liability with the price that maximizes the amount that would be received for the asset or minimizes the amount that would be paid to transfer the liability after taking into account any transaction costs. The fair value measurement should incorporate transportation costs for the asset or liability.

What valuation approaches can be used?

In fair value measurement, valuation techniques based on the market, income, and cost approaches may be used. The *market approach* uses prices for market transactions for identical or comparable assets or liabilities. The *income approach* uses valuation techniques to discount future cash flows to a present value amount. The *cost approach* is based on the current replacement cost, such as the cost to buy or build a substitute comparable asset after adjusting for obsolescence. Input availability and reliability related to the asset or liability may impact the choice of the most suitable valuation method.

A single or multiple valuation technique may be needed, depending on the situation. For example, a single valuation method would be used for an asset having quoted market prices in an active market for identical assets. A multiple valuation method would be used to value a reporting unit.

What are the three levels of the fair value hierarchy?

The fair value hierarchy prioritizes the *inputs* to valuation techniques used to measure fair value into three broad levels. Level 1, the highest priority, assigns quoted prices (unadjusted) in active markets for identical assets or liabilities. Level 3, the lowest priority, is assigned for unobservable inputs for the assets or liabilities.

Level 2 inputs are those except quoted prices included within Level 1 that are observable for the asset or liability, either directly or indirectly. Level 2 inputs include:

- Quoted prices for similar assets or liabilities in active markets
- Quoted prices for similar or identical assets or liabilities in markets that are not active, such as markets with few transactions, noncurrent prices, limited public information, and where price quotations show substantial fluctuation
- Inputs excluding quoted prices that are observable for the asset or liability, such as interest rates observable at often quoted intervals and credit risks
- Inputs obtained primarily from observable market information by correlation or other means

In the case of Level 3, unobservable inputs are used to measure fair value to the degree that observable inputs are not available. Unobservable inputs reflect the reporting company's own assumptions about what market participants consider (e.g., risk) in pricing the asset or liability.

What should be disclosed?

Quantitative disclosures in a tabular format should be used for fair value measurements in addition to qualitative (narrative) disclosures about the valuation methods. Emphasis should be placed on the inputs used to measure fair value, and the effect of fair value measurements on profit or change in net assets. Any change in valuation techniques should be noted.

Fair Value Option for Financial Assets and Financial Liabilities

ASC 825-10-05, 10-10, and 10-15, *Financial Instruments: Overall* (FAS-159, *The Fair Value Option for Financial Assets and Financial Liabilities*), permits business entities to choose to measure most financial instruments and some other items at fair value. The pronouncement is effective as of the beginning of the company's first fiscal year commencing after November 15, 2007. Many provisions of the pronouncement apply only to businesses that select the fair value option. The eligible items for the fair value measurement option are:

- Recognized financial assets and financial liabilities, excluding (1) investment in a subsidiary or variable interest entity that must be consolidated, (2) employers' plan obligations or assets for pension and postretirement benefits, (3) financial assets and financial liabilities recognized under leases, (4) financial instruments classified by the issuer as a component of stockholders' equity (e.g., convertible bond with a noncontingent beneficial conversion feature), and (5) deposit liabilities that can be withdrawn on demand of banks
- Written loan commitments
- Nonfinancial insurance contracts and warranties that can be settled by the insurer by paying a third party for goods or services
- Firm commitments applying to financial instruments, such as a forward purchase contract for a loan not readily convertible to cash
- Host financial instruments arising from separating an embedded nonfinancial derivative instrument from a nonfinancial hybrid instrument

ASC 825-10 allows a business to select to measure eligible items at fair value at specified election dates. Included in earnings at each reporting date are the unrealized (holding) gains and losses on items for which the fair value option has been elected.

The fair value option is irrevocable (except if a new election date occurs) and is applied solely to *entire* instruments (*not* parts of those instruments or specified risks or specific cash flows). The fair value option may be applied in most cases instrument by instrument, including investments otherwise accounted for under the equity method.

FAS-159's amendment to FASB Statement No. 115, *Accounting for Certain Investments in Debt and Equity Securities* (ASC 825-10-15, 4-5), relates to all companies with trading and available-for-sale securities.

Up-front costs and fees associated to items for which the fair value option is chosen are expensed as incurred.

Electing the Fair Value Option

A business entity may select the fair value option for all eligible items only on the date that *one* of these events occurs:

- The company first recognizes the eligible item.
- The company engages in an eligible firm commitment.
- There is a change in the accounting treatment for an investment in another company because the investment becomes subject to the equity method or the investor no longer consolidates a subsidiary because a majority voting interest no longer exists, but the investor still retains some ownership interest.
- Specialized accounting treatment no longer applies for the financial assets that have been reported at fair value, such as under an American Institute of CPAs (AICPA) Audit and Accounting Guide.
- An event occurs that mandates an eligible item to be measured at fair value on the event date but does not require fair value measurement at each later reporting date.

Events

Some events that require remeasurement of eligible items at fair value, initial recognition of eligible items, or both, and thus create an election date for the fair value option, are:

- Business combination
- Consolidation or deconsolidation of a subsidiary or variable interest entity
- Major debt modification

Instrument Application

The fair value option can be chosen for a single eligible item without electing it for other identical items except in these four cases:

1. If the fair value option is selected for an investment under the equity method, it must be applied to all of the investor's financial interests in the same entity that are eligible items.
2. If the fair value option is selected to an eligible insurance contract, it must be applied to all claims and obligations under the contract.
3. If the fair value option is chosen for an insurance contract for which integrated or non-integrated contract features or riders are issued at the same time or subsequently, the fair value option must be applied as well to those features or coverage.

4. If multiple advances are made to one borrower under a single contract, such as a construction loan, and the individual advances lose their identity and become part of the larger loan, the fair value option must be applied to the larger loan balance but *not* to the individual advances.

The fair value option typically does not have to be applied to all financial instruments issued or bought in a single transaction. An investor in stock or bonds, for example, may apply the fair value option to only some of the stock shares or bonds issued or acquired in a single transaction. In this situation, an individual bond is considered the minimum denomination of that debt security. A financial instrument that is a single contract cannot be broken down into parts when using the fair value option. However, a loan syndication may be in multiple loans to the same debtor by different creditors. Each of the loans is a separate instrument, and the fair value option may be selected for some of the loans but not others.

An investor in an equity security can select the fair value option for its entire investment in that security, including any fractional shares.

Balance Sheet

Companies must present assets and liabilities measured at the fair value option in a manner that separates those reported fair values from the book (carrying) values of similar assets and liabilities measured with a different measurement attribute. To accomplish this, a company must either:

- Report the aggregate fair value and nonfinancial fair value amounts in the same line items in the balance sheet and in parentheses disclose the amount measured at fair value included in the aggregate amount *or*
- Report two separate line items to display the fair value and non–fair value carrying amounts.

Statement of Cash Flows

Companies must classify cash receipts and cash payments for items measured at fair value based on their nature and purpose.

Disclosures

Disclosures of fair value are mandated in annual and interim financial statements.

When a balance sheet is presented, these six items must be disclosed:

1. Reasons why the company selected the fair value option for each allowable item or group of similar items must be given.
2. For every line item on the balance sheet that includes an item or items for which the fair value option has been chosen, management must provide information on how each line item relates to major asset and liability categories. Further, management must provide the aggregate carrying amount of items included in each line item that are *not* eligible for the fair value option.

3. When the fair value option is selected for some but not all eligible items within a group of similar items, management must describe those similar items and the reasons for partial election. Further, information must be provided so that financial statement users can understand how the group of similar items applies to individual line items on the balance sheet.

4. Disclosure should be made of investments that would have been reported under the equity method if the company did not elect the fair value option.

5. The difference between the aggregate fair value and the aggregate unpaid principal balance of loans, long-term receivables, and long-term debt instruments with contractual principal amounts for which the fair value option has been chosen must be disclosed.

6. In the case of loans held as assets for which the fair value option has been selected, management should disclose the aggregate fair value of loans past due by 90 days or more. If the company recognizes interest revenue separately from other changes in fair value, disclosure should be made of the aggregate fair value of loans in the nonaccrual status. Disclosure should also be made of the difference between the aggregate fair value and aggregate unpaid principal balance for loans that are 90 days or more past due and/or in nonaccrual status.

When an income statement is presented, four items must be disclosed:

1. How dividends and interest are measured and where they are reported in the income statement

2. Gains and losses from changes in fair value included in profit and where they are shown

3. For loans and other receivables, the estimated amount of gains and losses (including how they were calculated) included in earnings applicable to changes in instrument-specific credit risk

4. For liabilities with fair values that have been significantly impacted by changes in the instrument-specific credit risk, the estimated amount of gains and losses from fair value changes (including how they were calculated) related to changes in such credit risk, and the reasons for those changes

Other disclosures include the methods and assumptions used in fair value estimation. Qualitative information concerning the nature of the event as well as quantitative information, including the impact on earnings of initially electing the fair value option for an item, should also be disclosed.

Eligible Items at Effective Date

A company may elect the fair value option for eligible items at the effective date. The difference between the book (carrying) value and the fair value of eligible items related for the fair value option at the effective date must be removed from the balance sheet and included in the cumulative-effect adjustment. These differences include (1) valuation allowances (e.g., loan loss reserves); (2) unamortized deferred costs, fees, discounts, and premiums; and (3) accrued interest associated with the fair value of the eligible item.

A company that selects the fair value option for items at the effective date must provide in financial statements these five points, including their effective dates:

1. Reasons for choosing the fair value option for each existing eligible item or group of similar items
2. The amount of valuation allowances removed from the balance sheet because they applied to items for which the fair value option was selected
3. The impact on deferred tax assets and liabilities of selecting the fair value option
4. If the fair value option is chosen for some but not all eligible items within a group of similar eligible items, a description of similar items and the reasons for the partial election (further, information to enable financial statement users to understand how the group of similar items applies to individual items on the balance sheet)
5. A schedule presenting by line items in the balance sheet:
   - Before-tax portion of the cumulative-effect adjustment to retained earnings for the items on that line
   - Fair value at the effective date of eligible items for which the fair value option is selected and the book (carrying) amounts of those same items immediately before opting for the fair value option

Available-for-Sale and Held-to-Maturity Securities

Available-for-sale and held-to-maturity securities held at the effective date are eligible for the fair value option at that date. In the event that the fair value option is selected for any of those securities at the effective date, cumulative holding (unrealized) gains and losses must be included in the cumulative-effect adjustment. Separate disclosure must be made of the holding gains and losses reclassified from accumulated other comprehensive income (for available-for-sale securities) and holding gains and losses previously unrecognized (for held-to-maturity securities).

Stockholders' Equity

In accounting for stockholders' equity, consideration is given to:

- Preferred stock characteristics
- Preferred stock conversion to common stock
- Stock retirement
- Appropriation of retained earnings
- Treasury stock
- Quasi-reorganization
- Dividends
- Stock splits
- Stock options
- Stock warrants
- Fractional share warrants

The stockholders' equity section of the balance sheet includes major categories for:

- Capital stock (stock issued and stock to be issued)
- Paid-in capital
- Retained earnings
- Accumulated other comprehensive income
- Treasury stock

Note

Disclosure should be made for required redemptions of capital stock redeemable at given prices on specific dates.

Preferred Stock

What are some characteristics of preferred stock?

Preferred stock can be fully or partially participating. *Participating preferred stock* is entitled to share in dividend distributions in excess of the preferred stock dividend rate on a proportionate basis using the total par value of the preferred stock and common stock.

Cumulative preferred stock means that if no dividends are paid in a given year, the dividends accumulate and must be paid before any dividends can be paid to noncumulative stock.

The *liquidation value of preferred stock* means that in corporate liquidation, preferred stockholders will receive the liquidation value (sometimes stated as par value) before any funds may be distributed to common stockholders.

Note

Disclosure for preferred stock includes liquidation preferences, call prices, and cumulative dividends in arrears.

How is preferred stock accounted for?

When preferred stock is converted to common stock, the preferred stock and paid-in capital account are eliminated, and the common stock and paid-in capital accounts are credited. If a deficit results, retained earnings would be charged.

How distributions to shareholders with components of stock and cash are accounted for?

According to Accounting Standards Update (ASU) No. 2010-01 (January 2010), *Equity* (ASC Topic 505), *Accounting for Distributions to Shareholders with Components of*

Stock and Cash, the stock part of a stockholder distribution that permits stockholders to receive stock or cash with a possible restriction of the cash to be received is deemed an issuance of shares. It is not considered a stock dividend. EPS computation will include these distributions. The effective date for this accounting is December 15, 2009.

Preferred securities redeemable for cash or other assets are to be classified outside of permanent capital if they are redeemable (1) at a fixed or determinable price on a fixed or determinable date, (2) at the holder's option, or (3) upon the occurrence of an event that is not solely within the control of the issuer. There is a major difference between a security with mandatory redemption or whose redemption is outside the control of the issuer and conventional equity capital. The Securities and Exchange Commission (SEC) believes future cash obligations attached to this type of security should be highlighted to distinguish it from permanent capital.

Equity instruments with redemption features that are not solely within the control of the issuer must be classified as "temporary equity."

According to the SEC, the initial carrying amount of a redeemable equity instrument should be its issuance-date fair value.

For a share-based payment arrangement with employees, the amount presented in temporary equity at each balance sheet date should be based on the redemption provisions of the instrument and should take into consideration the proportion of consideration received in the form of employee services.

What should be disclosed for redeemable equity instruments?

Disclosures are required for redeemable equity instruments as follows:

- For a redeemable equity instrument that is not adjusted to its redemption amount, the reason(s) why it is not probable that the instrument will be redeemable
- Description of the accounting method used to adjust the redemption amount of a redeemable equity instrument
- If the registrant decides to accrete changes in the redemption amount of a redeemable equity instrument, the redemption amount of the equity instrument as if it were currently redeemable
- Amount credited to equity of the parent upon the subsidiary's deconsolidation

Stock Retirement

What do I do if stock is retired?

A company may decide to retire its stock. If common stock is retired at par value, the entry is:

Common Stock	} Par value
Cash	

If common stock is retired for less than par value, the entry is:

Common Stock
    Cash
    Paid-in Capital

If common stock is retired for more than par value, the entry is:

Common Stock
Paid-in Capital (original premium per share)
Retained Earnings (excess over original premium per share)
    Cash

> **Note**
>
> In retirement of stock, retained earnings can only be debited, not credited.

Appropriation of Retained Earnings (Reserve)

What is a retained earnings appropriation?

Appropriation of retained earnings means setting aside retained earnings and making them unavailable for dividends. It indicates the need to stockholders to restrict asset disbursements because of expected major uses or contingencies. *Examples:* Appropriations for plant expansion, sinking fund, and contingencies.

How are retained earnings appropriations booked?

The entry to record an appropriation is:

Retained Earnings
    Appropriation of Retained Earnings

When the contingency occurs, this entry is reversed.

Treasury Stock

How is treasury stock accounted for?

Treasury stock is issued shares that have been bought back by the company. There are two methods to account for treasury stock: the cost method and par value method.

COST METHOD Treasury stock is recorded at the purchase cost and is shown as a reduction from total stockholders' equity.

If treasury stock is later *sold above cost*, the entry is:

Cash
    Treasury Stock
    Paid-in Capital

If treasury stock is *sold below cost*, the entry is:

Cash
Paid-in Capital—Treasury Stock (up to amount available)
Retained Earnings (if paid-in capital is unavailable)
    Treasury Stock

If treasury stock is donated, only a memo entry is needed. When the treasury shares are later sold, the entry based on the market price at that time is:

Cash
    Paid-in Capital—Donation

Note

An appropriation of retained earnings equal to the cost of treasury stock on hand is required.

PAR VALUE METHOD Treasury stock is recorded at its par value when bought. An appropriation of retained earnings equal to the cost of the treasury stock on hand is required. Treasury stock is shown as a contra account to the common stock it applies to under the capital stock section of stockholders' equity.

If treasury stock is *purchased at more than par value*, the entry is:

Treasury Stock—Par Value
Paid-in Capital (original premium per share)
Retained Earnings (if necessary)
    Cash

If treasury stock is *purchased at less than par value*, the entry is:

Treasury Stock—Par Value
    Cash
    Paid-in Capital

If treasury stock is *sold above par value*, the entry is:

Cash
   Treasury Stock
   Paid-in Capital

If treasury stock is *sold under par value*, the entry is:

Cash
Paid-in Capital (amount available)
Retained Earnings (if paid-in capital is insufficient)
   Treasury Stock

Quasi-Reorganization

What is a quasi-reorganization?

A quasi-reorganization gives a financially troubled company with a deficit in retained earnings a fresh start. A quasi-reorganization is undertaken to avoid formal bankruptcy. There is a revaluation of assets and an elimination of the deficit by reducing paid-in capital.

How do I handle a quasi-reorganization?

- Stockholders and creditors must agree to the quasi-reorganization.
- Net assets are written down to fair market value. If fair value is not readily available, then conservative estimates of such value may be made.
- Paid-in capital is reduced to eliminate the deficit in retained earnings. If paid-in capital is insufficient, then capital stock is charged.
- Retained earnings become a zero balance. Retained earnings will bear the date of the quasi-reorganization for 10 years subsequent to the reorganization.

The retained earnings account consists of these components:

Retained Earnings—Unappropriated	
Dividends	Net Income
Appropriations	
Prior Period Adjustments	
Quasi-reorganization	

The entry for the quasi-reorganization is:

Paid-In Capital
Capital Stock (if necessary)
   Assets
   Retained Earnings

Caution

If potential losses exist at the readjustment date but the amounts of losses cannot be determined, there should be a provision for the maximum probable loss. If estimates used are subsequently shown to be incorrect, the difference goes to the paid-in capital account.

Note

New or additional common stock or preferred stock may be issued in exchange for existing indebtedness. Thus, the current liability account would be debited for the indebtedness and the capital account credited.

Example 2.29

ABC Company shows these balances before a quasi-reorganization:

Current Assets	$100,000	Capital Stock (80,000 shares, $10 par)	$800,000
Fixed Assets	400,000	Paid-in Capital	200,000
		Retained Earnings	(500,000)
Total Assets	$500,000	Total Liabilities and Capital	$500,000

Current assets are overvalued by $20,000 and fixed assets are overvalued by $100,000.

The entries for the quasi-reorganization are:

Quasi-reorganization	$120,000	
Current Assets		$20,000
Fixed Assets		100,000
Quasi-reorganization	500,000	
Retained Earnings		500,000
Paid-in Capital	200,000	
Quasi-reorganization		200,000
Common Stock	420,000	
Quasi-reorganization		420,000

Quasi-reorganization	
$120,000	$200,000
500,000	420,000
$620,000	$620,000

Dividends

How is a cash dividend recognized?

A cash dividend is based on the outstanding shares (issued shares less treasury shares).

Example 2.30

There are 5,000 issued shares and 1,000 treasury shares, a total of 4,000 outstanding shares. The par value of the stock is $10 per share. If a $0.30 dividend per share is declared, the dividend is:

$$4,000 \times \$0.30 = \$1,200$$

If the dividend rate is 6 percent, the dividend is:

$$4,000 \text{ shares} \times \$10 \text{ par value} = \$40,000$$

$$\$40,000 \times 0.06 = \underline{\underline{\$2,400}}$$

Assuming a cash dividend of $2,400 is declared, the entry is:

Retained Earnings	$2,400	
Cash Dividend Payable		$2,400

No entry is made at the record date.
The entry at the payment date is:

Cash Dividend Payable	$2,400	
Cash		$2,400

Is a property dividend handled like a cash dividend?

Yes, but in the case of a property dividend, the entry at the declaration date at the fair market value of the asset is:

Retained Earnings	
Asset	

Gain or loss arising between the carrying value and fair market value of the asset is recorded at the time of transfer.

How is a stock dividend handled?

A stock dividend is issued in the form of stock. Stock dividend distributable is shown in the capital stock section of stockholders' equity. It is *not* a liability.

- If the stock dividend is *less than 20 to 25 percent* of outstanding shares at the declaration date, the retained earnings account is reduced at the market price of the shares.

- If the stock dividend is *in excess of 20 to 25 percent* of outstanding shares, the retained earnings account is charged at par value. Between 20 and 25 percent is a gray area.

Example 2.31

A stock dividend of 10 percent is declared on 5,000 shares of $10 par value common stock having a market price of $12. The entry at the declaration and issuance dates follows:

Retained Earnings (500 shares × $12)	$6,000	
Stock Dividend Distributable		
(500 shares × $10)		$5,000
Paid-In Capital		1,000
Stock Dividend Distributable	5,000	
Common Stock		5,000

Assume instead that the stock dividend was 30 percent. The entries would be:

Retained Earnings (500 × $10)	$5,000	
Stock Dividend Distributable		$5,000
Stock Dividend Distributable	5,000	
Common Stock		5,000

How is a liability dividend accounted for?

A liability dividend (scrip dividend) is payable in the form of a liability (e.g., notes payable). A liability dividend sometimes occurs when a company has financial problems.

Example 2.32

On 1/1/2X12, a liability dividend of $20,000 is declared in the form of a one-year, 8 percent note. The entry at the declaration date is:

Retained Earnings	$20,000	
Scrip Dividend Payable		$20,000

(continued)

(Continued)

When the scrip dividend is paid, the entry is:

Scrip Dividend Payable	$20,000	
Interest Expense	1,600	
Cash		$21,600

Stock Split

What is a stock split?

In a stock split, the shares are increased and the par value per share is decreased. However, total par value is the same.

How do I handle a stock split?

Only a memo entry is needed.

Example 2.33

Before: 1,000 shares, $10 par value = $10,000 total par value

A 2-for-1 stock split is declared.

After: 2,000 shares, $5 par value = $10,000 total par value

A reverse split would have the opposite effect.

Stock Options

What are noncompensatory and compensatory stock option plans?

Four characteristics of noncompensatory plans are:

1. Employees are offered stock on some basis (e.g., equally or percentage of salary).
2. Full-time employees can participate.
3. A reasonable period of time exists to exercise the options.
4. The price discount on the stock for employees is not better than that afforded to corporate stockholders if there was an additional issuance to the stockholders.

A compensatory plan exists if any one of these four criteria is not met. Consideration received by the firm for the stock equals the cash, assets, or employee services obtained.

What is the purpose of a noncompensatory plan?

The purpose of a noncompensatory plan is to obtain funds and to reduce greater widespread ownership in the company among employees. It is not primarily designed to provide compensation for services rendered. Therefore, no compensation expense is recognized.

How are stock option plans recognized under the fair value method?

ASC 718-10-05, *Compensation—Stock Compensation: Overall* (FAS-123R, *Share-Based Payment*; FASB Statement No. 123, revised 2004, referred to as FASB Statement No. 123R, *Share-Based Payment*), eliminates the intrinsic method to account for stock option plans.

ASC 718-10-05 mandates that the total compensation cost that should be recognized for stock-based compensation plans be equal to the grant-date fair value of all share options that vest with employees. This amount is then allocated over the service years based on the amount of service performance that has been, or will be, performed by workers. At the date of grant, the fair value of the share options *locks* and cannot be changed to later changes in stock prices. Typically, the service period is the vesting period, which is the time from the grant date to the vesting date. The company must estimate the number of share options that will be given to workers based on the services rendered. Compensation cost should be recognized only if performance by the employee is likely to take place. Thus, compensation cost *cannot* be accrued if it is *unlikely* that employee performance will occur. An example is an expected resignation. If at a later date it is ascertained that the initial estimate of the number of share options that are likely to be earned by workers was incorrect, a revision must be made. It is required under ASC 718-10-05 that the cumulative effect on current and previous years of a change in the estimated number of share options for which service is expected to be, or has been, performed, should be recognized as compensation in the year of the change.

The mathematical models used to measure the fair value of share options do so at a single period in time, usually the grant date. The assumptions underlying the fair value measurement are a function of available information at the time the measurement is made. Models used to value share options include the Black-Scholes-Merton option pricing model and the lattice-based models.

Debt Issued with Stock Warrants

How do I distinguish between detachable and undetachable warrants?

If bonds are issued along with *detachable* stock warrants, the portion of the proceeds applicable to the warrants is credited to paid-in capital. The basis for allocation is the relative values of the securities at the time of issuance.

In the event that the warrants are *not detachable*, the bonds are accounted for solely as convertible debt. There is no allocation of the proceeds to the conversion feature.

Example 2.34

A $20,000 convertible bond is issued at $21,000 with $1,000 applicable to stock warrants. If the warrants are not detachable, the entry is:

Cash	$21,000	
Bonds Payable		$20,000
Premium on Bonds		1,000
Payable		

If the warrants are detachable, the entry is:

Cash	$21,000	
Bonds Payable		$20,000
Paid-in Capital—Stock		1,000
Warrants		

If the proceeds of the bond issue were only $20,000 instead of $21,000, and $1,000 could be attributable to the warrants, the entry is:

Cash	$20,000	
Discount	1,000	
Bonds Payable		$20,000
Paid-in Capital—Stock		1,000
Warrants		

IFRS Connection

IFRS requires that the issuer of convertible debt record the liability and equity components separately.

Fractional Share Warrants

What recognition is given to fractional share warrants?

Example 2.35 shows how fractional share warrants are handled.

Example 2.35

There are 1,000 shares of $10 par value common stock. The common stock has a market price of $15. A 20 percent dividend is declared resulting in 200 shares (20% × 1,000). Included in the 200 shares are fractional share warrants. Each warrant equals one-fifth of a share of stock. There are 100 warrants resulting in 20 shares of stock (100/5). Thus, 180 regular shares and 20 fractional shares are involved.

At the declaration date, the journal entries are:

Retained Earnings (200 shares × $15)	$3,000	
Stock Dividends Distributable (180 shares × $10)		$1,800
Fractional Share Warrants (20 shares × $10)		200
Paid-in Capital		1,000

At time of issuance, the journal entries are:

Stock Dividend Distributable	$1,800	
Common Stock		$1,800
Fractional Share Warrants	200	
Common Stock		200

If instead of all the fractional share warrants being turned in, only 80 percent were turned in, the entry is:

Fractional Share Warrants	$200	
Common Stock		$160
Paid-in Capital		40

Disclosure

What footnote disclosures are made for stockholders' equity?

Footnote disclosures for stockholders' equity include:

- Agreements to issue additional shares
- Unusual voting rights
- Participation rights
- Dividend and liquidation preferences
- Dividends in arrears
- Conversion features
- Call features
- Sinking fund provisions

IFRS Connection

Both IFRS and U.S. GAAP consider the statement of stockholders' equity a primary financial statement. However, under IFRS a company has the option of either preparing a statement of stockholders' equity similar to U.S. GAAP or preparing a statement of recognized income and expense (SoRIE). The SoRIE reports the items that were charged directly to equity, such as revaluation surplus, and then adds the net income for the period to arrive at total recognized income and expense. In this situation, additional note disclosure is required to provide reconciliations of other equity items.

CHAPTER 3

Financial Statement Reporting:
Statement of Cash Flows and
Other Disclosures

In addition to the income statement and balance sheet, the CPA must be conversant with:

- Statement of cash flows
- Interim reporting
- Personal financial statements
- Partnerships

Statement of Cash Flows

According to ASC 230-10, *Statement of Cash Flows—Overall* (FAS-95, *Statement of Cash Flows*), a statement of cash flows is required in the annual report. In addition, separate reporting is mandated for certain information applicable to noncash investments and financing transactions.

What is the purpose of the statement of cash flows?

The statement of cash flows:

- Furnishes useful data regarding a company's cash receipts and cash payments for a period
- Reflects a reconciliation between net income and net cash flow from operations
- Shows the net effects of operating transactions on earnings and operating cash flow in different periods
- Explains the change in cash and cash equivalents for the period

What is a cash equivalent?

A cash equivalent is a short-term, very liquid investment satisfying these two criteria:

1. It is easily convertible into cash.
2. It is very near the maturity date so there is hardly any chance of change in market value due to interest rate changes. (Typically, this criterion applies only

to investments with original maturities of three months or less.) *Examples:* Commercial paper, money market funds, U.S. Treasury bills.

How are cash equivalents disclosed?

The company's policy for determining which items represent cash equivalents should be disclosed. A change in such policy is accounted for as a change in accounting principle, which requires the restatement of previous years' financial statements for comparative purposes.

IFRS Connection

In certain situations, bank overdrafts are considered part of cash and cash equivalents under IFRS (which is not the case in U.S. GAAP). Under U.S. GAAP, bank overdrafts are classified as financing activities.

IFRS requires a statement of cash flows. Both IFRS and U.S. GAAP specify that the cash flows must be classified as operating, investing, or financing.

How is the statement of cash flows structured?

The statement of cash flows classifies cash receipts and cash payments as arising from:

- Investing activities
- Financing activities
- Operating activities

The statement of cash flows presents the net source or application of cash by investing, financing, and operating activities. The net effect of these flows on cash and cash equivalents for the period shall be reported so that the beginning and ending balances of cash and cash equivalents may be reconciled.

What are investing activities?

Investing activities include making and collecting loans, buying and selling fixed assets, and purchasing debt and equity securities in other entities.

Cash inflows from investing activities include:

- Collections or sales of loans made by a company and of another firm's debt instruments that were purchased by the company
- Receipts from sales of equity securities of other companies
- Amounts received from disposing of fixed assets

Cash outflows for investing activities include:

- Disbursements for loans made by the company and payments to buy debt securities of other entities

- Disbursements to buy equity securities of other companies
- Payments to buy fixed assets

What are financing activities?

Financing activities include receiving equity funds and furnishing owners with a return on their investment, debt financing and repayment or settlement of debt, and obtaining and paying for other resources derived from creditors on noncurrent credit.
    Cash inflows from financing activities are:

- Funds received from the sale of stock
- Funds obtained from the incurrence of debt

    Cash outflows for financing activities are:

- Dividend payments
- Repurchase of stock
- Paying off debt
- Other principal payments to long-term creditors

What are operating activities?

Operating activities relate to manufacturing and selling goods or the rendering of services, not to investing or financing functions. Cash flow derived from operating activities typically applies to the cash effects of transactions entering into profit computation.
    Cash inflows from operating activities are:

- Cash sales or collections on receivables arising from the initial sale of merchandise or rendering of services
- Cash receipts from returns on loans, debt securities, or equity securities of other entities (including interest and dividends received)
- Receipt of a litigation settlement
- Reimbursement under an insurance policy

    Cash outflows for operating activities are:

- Cash paid for raw material or merchandise for resale
- Principal payments on accounts payable arising from the initial purchase of goods
- Cash payments to suppliers
- Employee payroll expenditures
- Payments to governmental agencies (e.g., taxes, penalties, fees)
- Interest payments to lenders and other creditors
- Lawsuit payments
- Charitable contributions
- Cash refund to customers for defective merchandise

> ## Note
>
> If a cash receipt or cash payment *applies to more than one classification* (investing, financing, operating), classification is made to the activity that is the main source of that cash flow.
>
> *Example:* The purchase and sale of equipment to be used by the company is typically construed as an investing activity.

IFRS Connection

Statement of Cash Flow Items	Classification
Interest and dividends received	U.S. GAAP—operating
	IFRS—operating or investing
Interest payments	U.S. GAAP—operating
	IFRS—operating or financing
Dividends paid	U.S. GAAP—financing
	IFRS—operating or financing
Income taxes paid	U.S. GAAP—operating
	IFRS—operating, investing, or financing

In the case of *foreign currency cash flows*, use the exchange rate at the time of the cash flow in reporting its currency equivalent. The impact of changes in the exchange rate on cash balances held in foreign currencies is shown as a separate element of the reconciliation of the change in cash and cash equivalents for the period.

How are cash flows reconciled in the statement of cash flows?

Reconciliation is achieved by either the direct or the indirect method.

The direct method is preferred, in that companies should report cash flows from operating activities by major classes of gross cash receipts and gross cash payments and the resulting net amount. A company using the direct method should present these types of operating cash receipts and cash payments separately:

- Cash received from customers, licensees, and lessees
- Receipts from dividends and interest
- Other operating cash receipts
- Cash paid to employees and suppliers for goods or services
- Cash paid to advertising agencies and insurance companies
- Payment of interest
- Tax payments
- Other operating cash payments

Additional breakdowns of operating cash receipts and disbursements can be made to enhance financial reporting. Example: A manufacturing company may divide cash paid to suppliers into payments applicable to inventory acquisition and payments for selling expenses.

The indirect reconciliation method can be used, although this is not the preferred practice. Under this method, the company reports net cash flow from operating activities indirectly, by adjusting profit to reconcile it to net cash from operating activities. The adjustment to reported earnings involves effects of:

- Deferrals of past operating cash receipts and cash payments (e.g., changes in inventory and deferred revenue)
- Accumulations of anticipated future operating cash receipts and cash payments (e.g., changes in receivables and payables)
- Items whose cash impact relates to investing or financing cash flows (e.g., depreciation expense, amortization expense, gain and loss on the sale of fixed assets, and gain or loss on the retirement of debt)

Note

Regardless of which method is used, there should be a reconciliation of net income to net cash flow from operating activities. The reconciliation shall identify the principal types of reconciling items.

Example: Major classes of deferrals and accruals affecting cash flows should be reported, including changes in receivables, inventory, and payables that apply to operating activities.

If the indirect method is employed, interest and income taxes paid during the period should be disclosed.

How are operating, financing, and investing activities distinguished on the statement of cash flows?

When the direct method of reporting cash flows from operating activities is used, the reconciliation of profit to cash flow from operations should be disclosed in a separate schedule. When the indirect method is followed, the reconciliation can appear within the body of the statement of cash flows or can be shown in a schedule.

There should be separate presentation within the statement of cash flows of cash inflows and cash outflows from investing and financing activities. *Example:* The purchase of fixed assets is an application of cash, whereas the sale of a fixed asset is a source of cash. Both are shown separately to aid analysis by readers of the financial statements. Debt incurrence would be a source of cash, whereas debt payment would be an application of cash. Thus, cash received of $800,000 from incurred debt would be shown as a source, while the payment of debt of $250,000 would be presented as an application. The net effect is $550,000.

Note

Separate disclosure shall be made of investing and financing activities that affect assets or liabilities but do not affect cash flow. This disclosure may be footnoted

(continued)

(Continued)

or shown in a schedule. Furthermore, a transaction having cash and noncash elements should be discussed, but only the cash aspect will be shown in the statement of cash flows.

Examples: Noncash activities of an investing and financing nature include:

- Bond conversion
- Purchase of a fixed asset by the incurrence of a mortgage payable
- Capital lease
- Nonmonetary exchange of assets

Cash flow per share shall *not* be shown in the financial statements, since it will detract from the importance of the earnings per share (EPS) statistic.

IFRS Connection

IFRS requires that noncash investing and financing activities be excluded from the statement of cash flows. Instead, these noncash activities should be disclosed in the notes to the financial statements instead of in the financial statements. Under U.S. GAAP, companies may present this information at the bottom of the cash flow statement or in a separate note.

Who uses the statement of cash flows, and why?

An analysis of the statement of cash flows helps creditors and investors:

- Evaluate the entity's ability to obtain positive future net cash flows
- Appraise the company's ability to satisfy debt
- Analyze the firm's dividend-paying ability
- Establish an opinion regarding the company's capability to derive outside financing
- Notice a difference between net income and cash flow
- Evaluate the impact on the firm's financial position of cash and noncash investing and financing transactions

What financial information do I need to construct a statement of cash flows?

Example 3.1   Financial Information Necessary to Construct a Statement of Cash Flows

Summarized in the following is financial information for the current year for Company M, which provides the basis for the statements of cash flows.

Company M
Consolidated Statement of Financial Position

	1/1/2X12	12/31/2X12	Change
Assets:			
Cash and cash equivalents	$ 600	$ 1,665	$ 1,065
Accounts receivable (net of allowance			
for losses of $600 and $450)	1,770	1,940	170
Notes receivable	400	150	(250)
Inventory	1,230	1,375	145
Prepaid expenses	110	135	25
Investments	250	275	25
Property, plant, and equipment, at cost	6,460	8,460	2,000
Accumulated depreciation	(2,100)	(2,300)	(200)
Property, plant, and equipment, net	$ 4,360	$ 6,160	$ 1,800
Intangible assets	40	175	135
Total assets	$ 8,760	$11,875	$ 3,115
Liabilities:			
Accounts payable and accrued expenses	$ 1,085	$ 1,090	$ 5
Interest payable	30	45	15
Income taxes payable	50	85	35
Short-term debt	450	750	300
Lease obligation	—	725	725
Long-term debt	2,150	2,425	275
Deferred taxes	375	525	150
Other liabilities	225	275	50
Total liabilities	$ 4,365	$ 5,920	$ 1,555
Stockholders' equity:			
Capital stock	$ 2,000	$ 3,000	$ 1,000
Retained earnings	2,395	2,955	560
Total stockholders' equity	4,395	5,955	1,560
Total liabilities and stockholders' equity	$ 8,760	$11,875	$ 3,115

Source: Statement of Financial Accounting Standards No. 95, Statement of Cash Flows, 1987, Appendix C, Example 1, pp. 44–51. Reprinted with permission of the Financial Accounting Standards Board.

Company M
Consolidated Statement of Income
For the Year Ended December 31, 2X12

Sales	$ 13,965
Cost of sales	(10,290)
Depreciation and amortization	(445)
Selling, general, and administrative expenses	(1,890)
Interest expense	(235)
Equity in earnings of affiliate	45

(continued)

(Continued)

Company M
Consolidated Statement of Income
For the Year Ended December 31, 2X12

Gain on sale of facility	$ 80
Interest income	55
Insurance proceeds	15
Loss from patent infringement lawsuit	(30)
Income before income taxes	1,270
Provision for income taxes	(510)
Net income	$ 760

Company M entered into the following transactions during 2X12, which are reflected in the preceding financial statements:

- Company M wrote off $350 of accounts receivable when a customer filed for bankruptcy. A provision for losses on accounts receivable of $200 was included in Company M's selling, general, and administrative expenses.
- Company M collected the third and final annual installment payment of $100 on a note receivable for the sale of inventory and collected the third of four annual installment payments of $150 each on a note receivable for the sale of a plant. Interest on these notes through December 31 totaling $55 was also collected.
- Company M received a dividend of $20 from an affiliate accounted for under the equity method of accounting.
- Company M sold a facility with a book value of $520 and an original cost of $750 for $600 cash.
- Company M constructed a new facility for its own use and placed it in service. Accumulated expenditures during the year of $1,000 included capitalized interest of $10.
- Company M entered into a capital lease for new equipment with a fair value of $850. Principal payments under the lease obligation totaled $125.
- Company M purchased all of the capital stock of Company S for $950. The acquisition was recorded under the purchase method of accounting. The fair values of Company S's assets and liabilities at the date of acquisition are:

Cash	$ 25
Accounts receivable	155
Inventory	350
Property, plant, and equipment	900
Patents	80
Goodwill	70
Accounts payable and accrued expenses	(255)
Long-term note payable	(375)
Net assets acquired	$ 950

- Company M borrowed and repaid various amounts under a line-of-credit agreement in which borrowings are payable 30 days after demand. The net increase during the year in the amount borrowed against the line of credit totaled $300.
- Company M issued $400 of long-term debt securities.
- Company M's provision for income taxes included a deferred provision of $150.
- Company M's depreciation totaled $430, and amortization of intangible assets totaled $15.
- Company M's selling, general, and administrative expenses included an accrual for incentive compensation of $50 that has been deferred by executives until their retirement. The related obligation was included in other liabilities.
- Company M collected insurance proceeds of $15 from a business interruption claim that resulted when a storm precluded shipment of inventory for one week.
- Company M paid $30 to settle a lawsuit for patent infringement.
- Company M issued $1,000 of additional common stock, of which $500 was issued for cash and $500 was issued upon conversion of long-term debt.
- Company M paid dividends of $200.

Based on the financial data from the preceding example, the next computations illustrate a method of indirectly determining cash received from customers and cash paid to suppliers and employees for use in a statement of cash flows under the direct method:

Cash received from customers during the year:		
Customer sales		$13,965
Collection of installment payment for sale of inventory		100
Gross accounts receivable at beginning of year	$ 2,370	
Accounts receivable acquired in purchase of Company S	155	
Accounts receivable written off	(350)	
Gross accounts receivable at end of year	(2,390)	
Excess of new accounts receivable over collections from customers		(215)
Cash received from customers during the year		$13,850
Cash paid to suppliers and employees during the year:		
Cost of sales		$10,290
General and administrative expenses	$ 1,890	
Expenses not requiring cash outlay (provision for uncollectible accounts receivable)	(200)	
Net expenses requiring cash payments		1,690
Inventory at beginning of year	(1,230)	
Inventory acquired in purchase of Company S	(350)	
Inventory at end of year	1,375	
Net decrease in inventory from Company M's operations		(205)

(continued)

(*Continued*)

Adjustments for changes in related accruals:		
Account balances at beginning of year		
Accounts payable and accrued expenses	$ 1,085	
Other liabilities	225	
Prepaid expenses	(110)	
Total		$1,200
Accounts payable and accrued expenses acquired in purchase of Company S		255
Account balances at end of year		
Accounts payable and accrued expenses	1,090	
Other liabilities	275	
Prepaid expenses	(135)	
Total		(1,230)
Additional cash payments not included in expense		225
Cash paid to suppliers and employees during the year		$12,000

Presented next is a statement of cash flows for the year ended December 31, 2X12, for Company M. This statement of cash flows illustrates the direct method of presenting cash flows from operating activities.

Company M
Consolidated Statement of Cash Flows for the Year Ended December 31, 2X12
Increase (Decrease) in Cash and Cash Equivalents

Cash flows from operating activities:		
Cash received from customers	$ 13,850	
Cash paid to suppliers and employees	(12,000)	
Dividend received from affiliate	20	
Interest received	55	
Interest paid (net of amount capitalized)	(220)	
Income taxes paid	(325)	
Insurance proceeds received	15	
Cash paid to settle lawsuit for patent infringement	(30)	
Net cash provided by operating activities		$ 1,365
Cash flows from investing activities:		
Proceeds from sale of facility	$600	
Payment received on note for sale of plant	150	
Capital expenditures	(1,000)	
Payment for purchase of Company S, net of cash acquired	(925)	
Net cash used in investing activities		(1,175)
Cash flows from financing activities:		
Net borrowing under line-of-credit agreement	$300	
Principal payments under capital lease obligation	(125)	
Proceeds from issuance of long-term debt	400	
Proceeds from issuance of common stock	500	
Dividends paid	(200)	

Company M
Consolidated Statement of Cash Flows for the Year Ended December 31, 2X12
Increase (Decrease) in Cash and Cash Equivalents

New cash provided by financing activities	$ 875
Net increase in cash and cash equivalents	1,065
Cash and cash equivalents at beginning of year	600
Cash and cash equivalents at end of year	$1,665

Reconciliation of Net Income to Net Cash Provided by Operating Activities

Net income		$ 760
Adjustments to reconcile net income to net cash provided by operating activities:		
Depreciation and amortization	$445	
Provision for losses on accounts receivable	200	
Gain on sale of facility	(80)	
Undistributed earnings of affiliate	(25)	
Payment received on installment note receivable for sale of inventory	100	
Change in assets and liabilities net of effects from purchase of Company S:		
Increase in accounts receivable	(215)	
Decrease in inventory	205	
Increase in prepaid expenses	(25)	
Decrease in accounts payable and accrued expenses	(250)	
Increase in interest and income taxes payable	50	
Increase in deferred taxes	150	
Increase in other liabilities	50	
Total adjustments		605
Net cash provided by operating activities		$1,365

Supplemental Schedule of Noncash Investing and Financing Activities

The company purchased all of the capital stock of Company S for $950. In conjunction with the acquisition, these liabilities were assumed:

Fair value of assets acquired	$1,580
Cash paid for the capital stock	(950)
Liabilities assumed	$ 630

A capital lease obligation of $850 was incurred when the company entered into a lease for new equipment.

Additional common stock was issued upon the conversion of $500 of long-term debt.

(continued)

(*Continued*)

Disclosure of Accounting Policy

For purposes of the statement of cash flows, the company considers all highly liquid debt instruments purchased with a maturity of three months or less to be cash equivalents.

Presented next is Company M's statement of cash flows for the year ended December 31, 2X12, prepared using the indirect method.

Company M
Consolidated Statement of Cash Flows for the Year Ended December 31, 2X12
Increase (Decrease) in Cash and Cash Equivalents

Cash flows from operating activities:		
Net income		$ 760
Adjustments to reconcile net income to net cash		
provided by operating activities:		
Depreciation and amortization	$ 445	
Provision for losses on accounts receivable	200	
Gain on sale of facility	(80)	
Undistributed earnings of affiliate	(25)	
Payment received on installment note receivable for		
sale of inventory	100	
Change in assets and liabilities net of effects from		
purchase of Company S:		
Increase in accounts receivable	(215)	
Decrease in inventory	205	
Increase in prepaid expenses	(25)	
Decrease in accounts payable and accrued expenses	(250)	
Increase in interest and income payable	50	
Increase in deferred taxes	150	
Increase in other liabilities	50	
Total adjustments		605
Net cash provided by operating activities		$ 1,365
Cash flows from investing activities:		
Proceeds from sale of facility	$ 600	
Payment received on note for sale of plant	150	
Capital expenditures	(1,000)	
Payment for purchase of Company S, net of cash		
acquired	(925)	
Net cash used in investing activities		(1,175)
Cash flows from financing activities:		
Net borrowings under line-of-credit agreement	$ 300	
Principal payments under capital lease obligation	(125)	
Proceeds from issuance of long-term debt	400	
Proceeds from issuance of common stock	500	
Dividends paid	(200)	
Net cash provided by financing activities		875
Net increase in cash and cash equivalents		1,065
Cash and cash equivalents at beginning of year		600
Cash and cash equivalents at end of year		$ 1,665

Company M
Consolidated Statement of Cash Flows for the Year Ended December 31, 2X12
Increase (Decrease) in Cash and Cash Equivalents

Supplemental Disclosures of Cash Flow Information

Cash paid during the year for:	
Interest (net of amount capitalized)	$220
Income taxes	325

Supplemental Schedule of Noncash Investing and Financing Activities

The company purchased all of the capital stock of Company S for $950. In conjunction with the acquisition, these liabilities were assumed:	
Fair value of assets acquired	$ 1,580
Cash paid for the capital stock	(950)
Liabilities assumed	$ 630

A capital lease obligation of $850 was incurred when Company M entered into a lease for new equipment.

Additional common stock was issued upon the conversion of $500 of long-term debt.

Disclosure of Accounting Policy

For purposes of the statement of cash flows, the company considers all highly liquid debt instruments purchased with a maturity of three months or less to be cash equivalents.

Interim Reporting

How often should interim reports be given?

Interim reports may be issued at appropriate reporting intervals, for example quarterly or monthly. Complete financial statements or summarized data may be given, but interim financial statements do not have to be certified.

What type of report is appropriate for an interim period?

Interim balance sheets and cash flow data should be provided. If these statements are not presented, material changes in liquid assets, cash, long-term debt, and stockholders' equity should be disclosed. Interim reports usually include results of the current interim period and the cumulative year-to-date figures. Typically, comparisons are made to results of comparable interim periods for the prior year.

What are some guidelines in preparing interim reports?

- Interim results should be based on the accounting principles used in the last year's annual report unless a change has been made in the current year.

- A gain or loss cannot be deferred to a later interim period unless such deferral has been permissible for annual reporting.
- Revenue from merchandise sold and services performed should be accounted for as earned in the interim period in the same way as accounted for in annual reporting. If an advance is received in the first quarter and benefits the entire year, it should be allocated ratably to the interim periods affected.
- Costs and expenses should be matched to related revenue in the interim period. If a cost cannot be associated with revenue in a future interim period, it should be expensed in the current period. Yearly expenses, such as administrative salaries, insurance, pension plan expense, and year-end bonuses, should be allocated to the quarters. The allocation basis may be based on such factors as time expired, benefit obtained, and activity.
- The gross profit method can be used to estimate interim inventory and cost of sales. Disclosure should be made of the method, assumptions made, and material adjustments by reconciliations with the annual physical inventory.
- A permanent inventory loss should be reflected in the interim period during which it occurs. A subsequent recovery is treated as a gain in the later interim period. However, if the change in inventory value is temporary, no recognition is given in the accounts.
- When there is a temporary liquidation of the last in, first out (LIFO) base with replacement expected by year-end, cost of sales should be based on replacement cost.
- When a standard cost system is used, variances expected to be reversed by year-end may be deferred to an asset or liability account.

Example 3.2

The historical cost of an inventory item is $10,000 with replacement cost expected at $15,000. The entry is:

Cost of Sales	$15,000	
Inventory		$10,000
Reserve for liquidation of LIFO base		5,000

Note

The reserve for liquidation of LIFO base account is shown as a current liability. When replenishment is made at year-end, the entry is:

Reserve for liquidation of LIFO base	$ 5,000	
Inventory	10,000	
Cash		$15,000

Volume discounts given to customers tied into annual purchases should be apportioned to the interim period based on the ratio of:

$$\frac{\text{Purchases for the interim period}}{\text{Total estimated purchases for the year}}$$

IFRS Connection

LIFO liquidation is not an issue in interim (or annual) periods because LIFO is not a permitted accounting policy under IFRS.

How are taxes reflected in interim reports?

The income tax provision includes current and deferred taxes, both federal and local. The tax provision for an interim period should be cumulative. *Example:* Total tax expense for a nine-month period is shown in the third quarter based on nine-month income.

The tax expense for the three-month period based on three months' income may also be presented. *Example:* Third-quarter tax expense based on only the third quarter.

What tax rate should I use?

In computing tax expense, the estimated annual effective tax rate should be used. The effective tax rate should be based on income from continuing operations. If a reliable estimate is not practical, the actual year-to-date effective tax rate should be used.

Suggestion

At the end of each interim period, a revision to the effective tax rate may be necessary, employing the best current estimates of the annual effective tax rate. The projected tax rate includes adjustment for net deferred credits. Adjustments should be contained in deriving the maximum tax benefit for year-to-date figures.

The estimated effective tax rate should incorporate:

- All available tax credits (e.g., foreign tax credit)
- All available alternative tax methods in determining ordinary earnings

Note

A change in tax legislation is reflected only in the interim period affected.

How are income and losses accounted for in interim reports?

Income statement items after income from continuing operations (e.g., income from discontinued operations, extraordinary items, cumulative effect of a change in accounting principle) should be presented net of the tax effect. The tax effect on these unusual line items should be reflected *only* in the interim period when they actually occur.

Caution

Do not predict items before they occur. Prior-period adjustments in the retained earnings statement are also shown net of tax when they take place.

What should I do about a change in principle?

When a change in principle is made *in the first interim period*, the cumulative effect of a change in principle account should be shown net of tax in the first interim period.

If a change in principle is made *in a quarter other than the first*, we assume the change was made at the beginning of the first quarter showing the cumulative effect in the first quarter. The interim periods (e.g., first, second, and third quarters) will have to be *restated* using the new principle.

When *interim data for previous years* are presented for comparative purposes, data should be restated to conform with newly adopted policies. Alternatively, disclosure can be made of the effect the new practice would have had on prior data if it had been applied to that period.

For a change in principle, disclosure should be made of the nature and justification in the interim period of change. The effect of the change on per-share amounts should be given.

What other factors affect interim results?

- Disclosure should be made of seasonality aspects affecting interim results and contingencies.
- A change in the estimated effective tax rate should be disclosed.
- If a fourth quarter is not presented, any material adjustments to that quarter must be commented on in the footnotes to the annual report.
- If an event is immaterial on an annual basis but material in the interim period, it should be disclosed.

Purchase transactions should be noted.

How do I present prior-period adjustments?

The financial statement presentation for prior-period adjustments:

- Net income for the current period should include the portion of the effect related to current operations.
- Earnings of impacted prior interim periods of the current year should be restated to include the portion related thereto.
- If the prior-period adjustment affects prior years, it should be included in the earnings of the first interim period of the current year.

Criteria to be met for prior-period adjustments in interim periods are:

- Materiality
- Estimable
- Identified to a prior interim period

Examples: Prior-period adjustments for interim reporting include:

- Error corrections
- Settlement of litigation or claims
- Adjustment of income taxes
- Renegotiation proceedings
- Utility revenue under rate-making processes

Notes

Earnings per share are computed for interim purposes the same way as for annual purposes.

Segmental disposal is shown separately in the interim period during which it occurs.

Personal Financial Statements

What are personal financial statements used for?

Personal financial statements may be prepared for an individual or a family to show financial status. The accrual basis is followed. Some uses include:

- Obtaining credit
- Financial planning
- Compliance with disclosure requirements (for public officials)

What information should personal financial statements contain?

Disclosures in personal financial statements include:

- Individuals covered by the statement
- Methods used in determining current values
- Nature of joint ownership in property
- Identification of major investments
- Percentage of ownership in an identified closely held business, including the nature of business activities consummated, as well as summarized financial data for the entity
- Identification of intangibles, including estimated lives
- Amount of life insurance taken out

- Pension rights
- Methods and estimates employed in computing income taxes
- Particulars of receivables and payables (e.g., interest rates, pledged items, and maturities)
- Noncapitalized commitments (e.g., rental agreements)

What are the guidelines for preparing the statement of financial condition?

In the statement of financial condition:

- Assets are reflected at the estimated current value and are listed in the order of liquidity (maturity). Current value can be determined based on recent transactions of similar items, appraisals, present value of future cash flows from the asset, adjusting historical cost for inflation, and so on.
- There is no breakdown between current and noncurrent classifications.
- Material business interests should be shown separately. *Example:* A material interest in a closely held company should be shown separately from the equity investment in other companies.
- If assets are jointly owned, only the individual's beneficial interest should be reported.
- Liabilities should be shown at current amounts by order of maturity.
- The estimated current amount is the lesser of the present value of the debt payments or the amount the liability could be currently paid off for. Usually the liability equals the principal plus accrued interest due.
- Estimated taxes payable are shown as a liability, including provision for unpaid taxes of previous years and the estimated tax for the current year. The estimated tax for the present year should be based on the relationship of year-to-date taxable income to estimated taxable income for the year. The amount is reduced by any withholding and estimated tax payments.
- Net worth is the difference between assets and liabilities.

Example 3.3

An illustrative statement of financial condition follows.

Mr. and Mrs. J. Smith
Statement of Financial Condition
December 31, 2X12

Cash	$ 5,000
Interest and Dividends Receivable	200
Marketable Securities	10,000
Interest in Closely Held Company	6,000
Cash Surrender Value of Life Insurance	1,000
Real Estate	100,000
Personal Property	30,000
Total	$152,200

<table>
<tr><td colspan="2" align="center">Mr. and Mrs. J. Smith
Statement of Financial Condition
December 31, 2X12</td></tr>
</table>

Liabilities	
Credit Cards	$ 6,000
Income Taxes Payable	3,000
Loans Payable	10,000
Mortgage Payable	60,000
	$ 79,000
Estimated Taxes (on the difference between carrying amounts and tax bases of assets and liabilities)	40,000
Net Worth	33,200
Total	$152,200

What role does cost basis play in the statement of financial condition?

The statement of financial condition includes another element for the tax provision based on the difference between the current estimated amounts of assets and liabilities and their respective bases.

Example 3.4

An individual owns ABC stock that was bought five years ago for $8,000. The stock is currently worth $17,000. The individual is in the 38 percent tax bracket. If the individual sold the stock today, there would be a $9,000 gain, which would result in $3,420 in taxes. The $3,420 should be included in the "provision for estimated taxes on the difference between carrying amounts and tax bases of assets and liabilities." Since the $3,420 constitutes an amount of taxes that would be payable upon sale of the stock, it should be presented as a credit in the statement of financial condition, reducing the individual's net worth.

Is there another statement that can be prepared?

As an option, a statement of changes in net worth may be prepared. It is useful in showing the mix of business and personal items in personal financial statements. Increases and decreases in net worth are shown.

Items increasing net worth include:

- Income
- Increases in current values of assets
- Decreases in current amounts of liabilities
- Decreases in estimated taxes on the difference between the estimated current asset values and liability amounts and their tax bases

Items decreasing net worth include:

- Expenses
- Decreases in current values of assets
- Increases in current amounts of liabilities
- Increases in estimated taxes on the difference between the current amount and the tax bases of assets and liabilities

Also optional are comparative financial statements.

Incorporation of a Business

What accounting is needed when forming a corporation?

When an unincorporated entity (e.g., sole proprietorship, partnership) incorporates and issues stock or debt securities in exchange for the assets of the unincorporated business:

- The new corporation does not recognize the gain or loss on the issuance of stock in exchange for the unincorporated entity's assets.
- Assets acquired are recorded at fair market value.
- Current liabilities are recorded at face value.
- Long-term liabilities are recorded at present value.
- Stock issued is recorded at par value.
- The excess of net fair market value of assets acquired over par value is credited to paid-in capital.

The journal entry is:

Cash
Current Assets
Fixed Assets
   Current Liabilities
   Long-Term Liabilities
   Common Stock
   Paid-in Capital

Partnerships

How do I account for a partnership?

When a partnership is formed:

- Assets are debited at fair market value.
- Liabilities are credited for debt assumed, usually at the present value of future payments or fair value.
- Capital is credited for the net difference.

What accounting changes are needed when a new partner is admitted?

A new partner may be admitted to the partnership by:

- *Buying the interest of an existing partner.* When an interest is purchased from an existing partner, it is a private transaction between the two parties not affecting the partnership's financial records. The new partner's capital account is recorded simply by relabeling the old partner's capital account.
- *Contributing assets to the partnership* (e.g., new capital). In this case, the new partner may receive an interest in exchange for the contributed assets and/or goodwill (e.g., client following).

Example 3.5

X and Y form a partnership. X transfers $10,000 cash, and Y provides $30,000 of furniture with a loan thereon of $5,000. The journal entry is:

Cash	$10,000	
Furniture	30,000	
Loans Payable		$ 5,000
X Capital		10,000
Y Capital		25,000

How is the new partner's admission accounted for?

The new partner's admission can be accounted for under either the bonus method or the goodwill method.

Bonus Method

The new partner's capital account is credited for an amount equal to his or her purchased share of the partnership's total capital. The total capital equals the net book value of assets before the new partner's contribution plus the fair value of net assets contributed by the new partner. A bonus arises for the difference between the fair market value of contributed assets and the credit to the new partner's capital account.

- If the fair value of contributed assets exceeds the credit to the new partner's capital account, the excess increases the capital accounts of the old partners based on the profit-and-loss ratio.
- If the fair value of contributed assets is less than the new partner's capital account, the new partner recognizes the bonus. *Result:* The bonus reduces the old partners' capital accounts based on the profit-and-loss ratio.

Goodwill Method

If the new partner's contribution exceeds the ownership interest obtained, the excess assets represent goodwill applicable to the old partners.

When the new partner's asset contribution is less than the ownership interest received, the excess capital allowed to the new partner is construed as goodwill attributable to him or her.

How are profits and losses accounted for in a partnership?

Profits and losses of the partnership are divided equally among the partners unless stated otherwise in the partnership agreement. In dividing profits, the partnership may consider:

- Salary provision and interest on capital balances (interest based on the beginning, ending, or average capital)
- Time spent or capital invested

When interest and salary exceed profit, the resulting loss will be allocated based on the profit-and-loss ratio.

Partner drawing accounts exist to reflect cash withdrawals from the business. The drawing accounts are periodically closed to the capital accounts.

How do I treat partner withdrawals and liquidation of the partnership?

When the amount paid to a withdrawing or retiring partner exceeds that partner's capital balance, the excess is either attributed to goodwill or charged against the remaining partners' capital balances based on the profit-and-loss ratio.

When a partnership is liquidated, gains or losses on sales of assets are divided among the partners based on the profit-and-loss ratio. The initial cash received is used to satisfy the liabilities.

Note

Before the cash can be distributed to a partner, liquidation losses and expenses must have been charged to the capital accounts.

CHAPTER 4

Accounting and Disclosures

Hierarchy of GAAP

Financial Accounting Standards Board (FASB) Statement No. 162, *The Hierarchy of Generally Accepted Accounting Principles*, identifies the sources of accounting principles and the framework to select them in preparing financial statements in conformity with U.S. generally accepted accounting principles (GAAP). The GAAP hierarchy should be directed to the company.

The hierarchy of GAAP applies to the following levels:

Level 1 (highest level): FASB statements and interpretations, Accounting Principles Board (APB) opinions, and American Institute of CPAs (AICPA) accounting research bulletins.

Level 2: FASB technical bulletins and AICPA industry audit and accounting guides and statements of position.

Level 3: AICPA accounting standards executive committee practice bulletins, and consensus positions of the FASB Emerging Issues Task Force (EITF).

Level 4 (lowest level): Implementation guides (questions and answers) published by the FASB staff, and practices widely recognized and prevalent either generally or in the industry.

An accounting entity should follow the accounting treatment specified by the accounting principle from the source in the highest category available. A company should not follow the accounting treatment specified in accounting principles for similar transactions or events in cases in which those accounting principles either prohibit the application of the accounting treatment to the particular transaction or event or indicate that the accounting treatment should not be applied by analogy.

FASB Accounting Standards Codification

On June 3, 2009, the FASB approved the Accounting Standards Codification (ASC) (http://asc.fasb.org/home) and issued FASB Statement No. 168, *The FASB Accounting Standards Codification and the Hierarchy of Generally Accepted Accounting Principles—A Replacement of FASB Statement No. 162* (ASC 105-10).

It is intended to simplify user access to all authoritative U.S. GAAP by providing all the authoritative literature related to a particular topic in one place. The Codification is organized into approximately 90 accounting topics. It is not intended to change existing U.S. GAAP, but rather integrates existing accounting standards by multiple standard setters within the current GAAP hierarchy. The Codification is now the single official source of authoritative, nongovernmental U.S. GAAP, superseding existing FASB, AICPA, EITF, and related literature. Going forward, U.S. GAAP will no longer be issued in the form of an "accounting standard," but rather as an update to the applicable "topic" or "subtopic" within the Codification. As such, accounting guidance will be classified as either "authoritative" or "nonauthoritative" based on its inclusion in or exclusion from the Codification.

The Codification content is arranged within topics, subtopics, sections, and subsections, as follows:

- *Topics*. Topics represent a collection of related guidance and reside in four main areas: (1) presentation (e.g., income statement, balance sheet); (2) financial statement accounts (e.g., assets, liabilities, equity); (3) broad transactions (e.g., business combinations, derivatives); and (4) industries (e.g., airlines, real estate).
- *Subtopics*. Subtopics represent subsets of a topic and are generally distinguished by type or by scope. For example, "Operating Leases" and "Capital Leases" are two subtopics of the "Leases" topic.
- *Sections*. Sections represent the nature of the content in a subtopic (e.g., recognition, measurement, disclosure).
- *Subsections*. Sections are further broken down into subsections, paragraphs, and subparagraphs.

The following is the structure of the classification system: XXX-YY-ZZ-PP, where:

XXX = Topic
YY = Subtopic
ZZ = Section
PP = Paragraph

For example, Statement of Financial Accounting Standards No. 141R (FAS-141R, *Business Combinations*), is now ASC 805-10, *Business Combinations: Overall*.

Accounting Changes

ASC 250-10-05, *Accounting Changes and Error Corrections: Overall* (FAS-154, *Accounting Changes and Error Corrections—A Replacement of APB Opinion No. 20 and FASB Statement No. 3*) provides for accounting changes in principle, estimate, and reporting entity.

Accounting changes include a change in:

- *Principle*, which requires retrospective application to previous years' financial statements

- *Estimate*, which is accounted for prospectively over current and future years
- *Reporting entity*, which mandates the restatement of previous years' financial statements (up to five years' worth) as if both companies were always combined

Corrections of errors adjust the beginning balance of retained earnings. Proper disclosure of accounting changes is necessary.

> ## Note
>
> Significant accounting policies must be disclosed.

Development-stage companies must follow the same generally accepted accounting principles (GAAP) as established companies.

In a troubled debt restructuring, the debtor recognizes an extraordinary gain while the creditor recognizes an ordinary loss.

Segmental disclosures are required when a business segment comprises 10 percent or more of revenue, operating profit, or total assets of the entire company.

In the case of a non-interest-bearing note, interest must be imputed based on the interest rate the borrower would normally pay for a note in an arm's-length transaction.

Accounting for futures contracts and oil and gas accounting problems are also addressed.

Change in Accounting Principle

Can accounting principles be changed?

A change in principle should be made *only when necessary*. Once an accounting principle is adopted, it is presumed that the principle should not be changed for events or transactions of a similar nature. A method used for a transaction that is being terminated or was a single, nonrecurring event in the past should not be changed.

How is a change in accounting principle reflected?

A change in accounting principle is accounted for as an adjustment to the beginning balance of retained earnings.

- The amount equals the difference between retained earnings at the beginning of the year with the old method versus what retained earnings would have been at the beginning of the year if the new method had been used in prior years.
- The new principle is used in the current and future years. Consistency is needed for accurate user comparisons.

> **Note**
>
> Footnote disclosure should be made of the nature of and justification for a change in principle, including an explanation of why the new principle is preferred.

What justifies a change in principle?

A change in principle is justified by:

- A new FASB pronouncement
- A new tax law
- A new AICPA recommended practice
- A change in circumstances
- The need to more readily conform to industry practice

> **Notes**
>
> Specialized accounting practices and principles included in the AICPA Statements of Position (SOPs) and Guides are "preferable accounting principles." Where summaries of financial data for several years are present in financial reports, ASC 250-10-05 applies.
>
> Indirect effects are included in the cumulative effect only if they are to be recorded on the books as a result of a change in accounting principle. The cumulative effect does not include nondiscretionary adjustments based on earnings (e.g., employee bonuses) that would have been recognized if the new principle had been used in prior years.

If an accounting change in principle is deemed immaterial in the current year but is anticipated to be material in later years, disclosure is necessary.

What if I were to change a method, not a principle?

An *accounting principle* is not only an accounting principle or practice, but also includes the methods used to apply such principles and practices.

Example: Changing the composition of the cost elements (e.g., material, labor, and overhead) of inventory qualifies as an accounting change. Changing the composition must be reported and justified as preferable.

The basis of preferability among the different accounting principles is established in terms of whether the new principle improves the financial reporting function. Preferability is not determinable by considering income tax effect alone.

What is required under ASC 250-10-05?

ASC 250-10-05 mandates retroactive application to previous years' financial statements (up to five years' worth) of changes in accounting principle. It is the application of a different accounting method to previous years as if that new method had always been used. If it is impractical to ascertain either the year-specific impact or the cumulative effect of the change, the newly adopted accounting method must be applied to the beginning balances of assets or liabilities of the earliest year for practical retrospective application. Further, a corresponding adjustment must be made to the beginning balance of retained earnings for that year. If the cumulative dollar effect of applying an accounting principle change to previous years is impractical, the new accounting principle must be applied as if it were adopted prospectively from the earliest practical date.

A change in depreciation, depletion, or amortization must be accounted for as a change in estimate effected by a change in principle.

What is presented in the retained earnings statement?

The retained earnings statement after a retroactive change for a change in accounting principle follows.

Retained earnings—1/1, as previously reported
Add: Adjustment for the cumulative effect on prior years of
   applying retrospectively the new accounting method
Retained earnings—1/1, as adjusted

Example 4.1

Akel Construction Company has in prior years used the completed contract method for construction costs. In 2X12, the company changed to the percentage of completion method. The tax rate is 30 percent. These data are presented:

Year	Before-Tax Income from Completed Contract	Percentage of Completion
Before 2X12	$40,000	$60,000
In 2X12	16,000	18,000
Total at end of 2X12	56,000	78,000
Total in 2X12	19,000	20,000

(continued)

(*Continued*)

The basis for the journal entry to record the change in 2X12 is:

	Difference	Tax (30%)	Net of Tax
Before 2X12	$20,000	$6,000	$14,000
In 2X12	2,000	600	1,400
Total at end of 2X12	22,000	6,600	15,400
Total in 2X12	1,000	300	700

The journal entry to record the change in 2X12 is:

Construction-in-Progress	$22,000	
Deferred Tax Liability		$ 6,600
Retained Earnings		15,400

Change in Accounting Estimate

When do I change an accounting estimate?

A change in accounting estimate is caused by new circumstances or events requiring a revision in the estimates, such as a change in salvage value or in the life of an asset.

How is a change in estimate disclosed?

- A change in accounting estimate is accounted for prospectively over current and future years. There is no restatement of prior years.
- A footnote should describe the nature of the change.
- Disclosure is required in the period of the change for the effect on income before extraordinary items, net income, and earnings per share. Disclosure is not required for estimate changes in the ordinary course of business when immaterial. *Example:* Revising estimates of uncollectible accounts or inventory obsolescence.

How is a change in estimate accounted for?

If a change in estimate is coupled with a change in principle and the effects cannot be distinguished, it is accounted for as a change in estimate. *Example:* A change made from deferring and amortizing a cost to expensing it has incurred because of doubtful future benefits. This should be accounted for as a change in estimate.

Example 4.2

Equipment was bought on 1/1/2X06 for $40,000, having an original estimated life of 10 years with a salvage value of $4,000. On 1/1/2X12, the estimated life was revised to eight more years remaining with a new salvage value of $3,200. The journal entry on 12/31/2X12 for depreciation expense is:

Depreciation	$2,800	
Accumulated Depreciation		$ 2,800

Computations follow:

Book value on 1/1/2X12:
Original Cost $40,000
Less: Accumulated Depreciation

$$\frac{\$40,000 - \$4,000}{10} = \$3,600 \times 4$$
   14,400

Book Value $25,600

Depreciation for 2X12:
Book Value $25,600
Less: New Salvage Value   3,200
Depreciable Cost $22,400

$$\frac{\text{Depreciable cost}}{\text{New life}} = \frac{\$22,400}{8} = \$2,800$$

Change in Reporting Entity

How is a change in reporting entity treated?

A change in reporting entity (e.g., two previously separate companies combine) is accounted for by restating prior years' financial statements (up to five years' worth) as if both companies were always combined.

- Restatement for a change in reporting entity is necessary to show proper trends in comparative financial statements and historical summaries.
- The effect of the change on income before extraordinary items, net income, and per-share amounts is reported for all periods presented. The restatement process does not have to go back more than five years.
- Footnote disclosure should be made of the nature of and reason for the change in reporting entity only in the year of change.

Examples include:

- Presenting consolidated statements instead of statements of individual companies
- Change in subsidiaries included in consolidated statements or those included in combined statements

Correction of an Error

What do I do about a mistake?

A correction of an error is accounted for as a prior-period adjustment. The retained earnings account absorbs the difference related to the error for previous years.

Example 4.3

On 1/1/2X10, B Company received $13,000 on account from a customer. It improperly credited revenue. The correcting entry on 12/31/2X12 is:

Retained Earnings	$13,000	
Accounts Receivable		$13,000

Example 4.4

At the end of 2X11, a company failed to accrue telephone expense that was paid at the beginning of 2X12. The correcting entry on 12/31/2X12 is:

Retained Earnings	$16,000	
Telephone Expense		$16,000

Example 4.5

At the beginning of 2X10, a company bought equipment for $300,000, with a salvage value of $20,000 and an expected life of 10 years. Straight-line depreciation is used. In error, salvage value was not deducted in computing depreciation. The correcting journal entries on 12/31/2X12 are:

		2X11 and 2X12
Depreciation Taken ($300,000/10 × 2 years)		$60,000
Depreciation Correctly Stated ($280,000/10 × 2 years)		$56,000
		$ 4,000
Depreciation	$28,000	
Accumulated Depreciation		28,000
Depreciation for Current Year		
Accumulated Depreciation	4,000	
Retained Earnings		4,000
Correct Prior-Year Depreciation Misstatement		

Prior-Period Adjustments

What are prior-period adjustments?

The two types of prior-period adjustments are:

1. Recognition of a tax loss carryforward benefit arising from a purchased subsidiary
2. Correction of an error that was made in a prior year

Errors may be due to mathematical mistakes, errors in applying accounting principles, or misuse of facts existing when the financial statements were prepared. Furthermore, a change in principle from one that is not GAAP to one that is GAAP is an error correction.

Disclosure should be made of the nature of the error and the effect of correction on earnings.

How are prior-period adjustments made?

When a single year is presented, prior-period adjustments adjust the beginning balance of retained earnings. The presentation follows.

Retained Earnings—1/1 Unadjusted
Prior-Period Adjustments (net of tax)
Retained Earnings—1/1 Adjusted
Add: Net Income
Less: Dividends
Retained Earnings—12/31

When comparative statements are prepared, a retroactive adjustment for the error is made insofar as it affects the prior years. The retroactive adjustment is disclosed by showing the effects of the adjustment on previous years' earnings and component items of net income.

Example 4.6

On 1/1/2X10, an advance retainer fee of $50,000 was received covering a five-year period. In error, revenue was credited for the full amount. The error was discovered on 12/31/2X12, before closing the books. The correcting entry is:

12/31/2X12 Retained Earnings	$30,000	
Revenue		$10,000
Deferred Revenue		20,000

Example 4.7

A company bought a machine on January 1, 2X09, for $32,000, with a $2,000 salvage value and a five-year life. The repairs expense was charged in error. The mistake was discovered on December 31, 2X12, before closing the books. The correcting entry is:

Depreciation Expense	$ 6,000	
Machine	32,000	
Accumulated Depreciation		$24,000
Retained Earnings		14,000

Accumulated depreciation of $24,000 is calculated next:

$$\frac{\$32,000 - \$2,000}{5} = \$6,000 \text{ per year} \times 4 \text{ years} = \$24,000$$

The credit to retained earnings reflects the difference between the erroneous repairs expense of $32,000 in 2X09 versus showing depreciation expense of $18,000 for three years (2X09 to 2X11).

IFRS Connection

A prior-period error must be corrected by restatement unless it is impracticable to do so. A change in accounting policy must be made only if it (1) is required by a new standard or interpretation or (2) results in reliable and more relevant information about transactions, financial condition, financial performance, and cash flows.

Disclosure of Accounting Policies

What are accounting policies?

Accounting policies include accounting principles and methods of application in the presentation of financial statements, such as:

- A selection from generally accepted accounting principles
- Practices unique to the given industry
- Unusual applications of generally accepted accounting principles

What should be described regarding accounting policies?

The first footnote or section preceding the notes to the financial statements should be a description of the accounting policies that the company follows.

Examples include:

- The depreciation method used
- Consolidation bases
- Amortization period for a patent
- Construction contract method
- Inventory pricing method

Notes

Financial statement classification methods and qualitative data (e.g., litigation) are not accounting policies.

Nonprofit entities should also disclose the accounting policies followed.

The application of GAAP requires the use of judgment where alternative acceptable principles exist and where varying methods of applying a principle to a given set of facts exist.

Disclosure of these principles and methods is vital to the full presentation of financial position and operations, so that rational economic decisions can be made.

Is disclosure of accounting policies always necessary?

Some types of financial statements do not need a description of the accounting policies followed.

Examples include:

- Quarterly unaudited statements when there has not been a policy change since the last year-end
- Statements solely for internal use

Development-Stage Companies

What are development-stage entities?

A development-stage entity is one that concentrates on establishing a new business, where major operations have not begun or operations have started but no significant revenue has been derived. Some activities of a development-stage enterprise are:

- Establishing sources of supply
- Developing markets
- Obtaining financing
- Financial and production planning
- Research and development
- Buying capital assets
- Recruiting staff

What are the requirements for a development-stage company?

The *same* generally accepted accounting principles for an established company must be followed by a development-stage enterprise. A balance sheet, income statement, and statement of cash flows are prepared.

- The balance sheet shows the accumulated net losses as a deficit.
- The income statement presents cumulative amounts of revenues and expenses since inception of the business.
- Similarly, the statement of cash flows presents the operating, investing, and financing cash receipts and cash payments.
- The stockholders' equity statement shows for each equity security from inception the date and number of shares issued and dollar figures per share applicable to cash and noncash consideration.

The nature and basis for determining amounts of noncash consideration must also be provided.

Notes

Financial statements must be headed "development-stage enterprise."
A footnote should describe the development-stage activities.
In the first year that the entity is no longer in the development stage, it should disclose that in previous years it was in the development stage.

Troubled Debt Restructuring

What is a troubled debt restructuring?

In a troubled debt restructuring, a debtor in financial difficulty receives partial or complete forgiveness of the obligation by the creditor. The concession may be:

- By debtor-creditor agreement
- Imposed by law
- By foreclosure and repossession

Some types of troubled debt restructurings are:

- Debtor transfers to creditor receivables from third parties or other assets in part or full satisfaction of the debt.
- Debtor gives creditor equity securities to satisfy the debt.
- The debt terms are modified, including downwardly adjusting the interest rate, lengthening the maturity date, or reducing the face amount of the obligation.

The debtor recognizes an extraordinary gain (net of tax) on the restructuring, while the creditor recognizes a loss. The loss may be ordinary or extraordinary, depending on whether such arrangement by the creditor is unusual and infrequent. Typically, the loss is ordinary.

Debtor

How is the debtor's gain disclosed?

The gain to the debtor equals the difference between the fair value of assets exchanged and the book value of the debt, including accrued interest. Furthermore, there may be a gain on disposal of assets exchanged in the transaction equal to the difference between the fair market value and the book value of the transferred assets. The latter gain or loss is not a gain or loss on restructuring, but rather an ordinary gain or loss in connection with asset disposal.

Example 4.8

A debtor transferred assets having a fair value of $80 and a book value of $60 in settlement of a payable with a carrying value of $90. The gain on restructuring is $10 ($90 − $80). The ordinary gain is $20 ($80 − $60).

What if the debtor transfers stock to the creditor?

A debtor may transfer an equity interest to the creditor. The debtor enters the equity securities issued on the basis of fair market value rather than the recorded value of the debt satisfied. The excess of the recorded payable satisfied over the fair market value of the securities issued is an extraordinary gain.

What must I do if the original debt agreement is changed?

When a modification in terms of an initial debt agreement exists, it is accounted for *prospectively*. There is a new interest rate computed based on the new terms. This interest rate is then employed to allocate future payments to reduce principal and interest. When the new terms of the agreement cause the sum of all the future payments to be less than the book value of the payable, the payable is reduced and a restructuring gain is recognized for the difference. Future payments are construed as a reduction of principal only. No interest expense is recognized.

Is a transfer of assets the only way to restructure a debt?

A troubled debt restructuring may result in a *combination* of concessions to the debtor. This may occur when assets or an equity interest are transferred for *partial* satisfaction of the debt, and the balance is subject to a modification of terms. Two steps are involved:

Step 1. The payable is reduced by the fair market value of the assets or equity transferred.
Step 2. The remaining part of the debt is accounted for as a modification of terms type of restructuring.

Direct costs (e.g., legal fees) incurred by the debtor in an equity transfer lower the fair value of the equity interest. All other costs reduce the gain on restructuring. If there is no gain involved, they are expensed.

Footnote disclosure by the debtor includes:

- Explaining the particulars of the restructuring agreement
- The aggregate and per-share amounts of the gain on restructuring
- Amounts that are contingently payable, including the contingency terms

Creditor

What is done if the creditor cannot collect?

The creditor's loss is the difference between the fair market value of assets received and the book value of the investment. In a modification of terms situation:

- The creditor recognizes interest income to the extent total future payments exceed the carrying value of the investment. Interest income is recognized using the effective interest method.
- Assets received are recorded at fair market value.
- When the carrying value of the receivable is greater than the aggregate payments, an ordinary loss is booked for the difference.
- All cash received in the future is accounted for as a recovery of the investment.
- Direct costs incurred by the creditor are expensed.

Notes

The creditor does not recognize contingent interest until the contingency is removed and interest has been earned.

Future changes in the interest rate are accounted for as a change in estimate.

Footnote disclosure by the creditor includes:

- Commitments to lend additional funds to financially troubled debtors
- Loans and/or receivables by major class
- Debt agreements where the interest rate has been modified, explaining the particulars
- Description of terms of the restructuring

Example 4.9

The debtor owes the creditor $100,000 and has indicated that because of financial problems, there may be difficulty in meeting future payments. Footnote disclosures by the creditor and debtor are needed surrounding the financial problems.

Example 4.10

The debtor owes the creditor $100,000. The creditor relieves the debtor of $20,000. The balance of the obligation will be paid at a later date. The journal entries are:

Debtor			Creditor		
Accounts Payable	$20,000		Ordinary Loss	$20,000	
Extraordinary Gain		20,000	Accounts Receivable		20,000

Example 4.11

The debtor owes the creditor $50,000. The creditor agrees to accept $45,000 in payment in full satisfaction of the debt. The journal entries are:

Debtor			Creditor		
Accounts Payable	$5,000		Ordinary Loss	$5,000	
Extraordinary Gain		5,000	Accounts Receivable		5,000

Segmental Reporting

What is segmental reporting?

Segmental data occurs when a company prepares a full set of financial statements (balance sheet, income statement, statement of cash flows, and related footnotes) for a business segment. The data are shown for each year presented. Information reported is a disaggregation of consolidated financial information.

Segmental information assists financial statement users in analyzing financial statements by allowing improved assessment of an enterprise's past performance and future prospects.

Financial reporting for business segments is useful in evaluating segmental performance, earning potential, and risk.

Segmental reporting may be by:

- Industry
- Foreign geographical area
- Export sales
- Major customers
- Governmental contracts

An industry segment sells merchandise or renders services to outside customers.

Exception

Segmental information is not required for nonpublic companies.

What does ASC 280-10-05-2, Segment Reporting: Overall *(FAS-131,* Disclosures about Segments of an Enterprise and Related Information*), require?*

ASC 280-10-05-2 requires that the amount reported for each segment item be based on what the *chief operating decision maker* (e.g., chief executive officer, chief operating officer) uses in making a determination as to the amount of resources to assign to a segment and how to evaluate the performance of that segment.

Note

The term *chief operating decision maker* may relate to a function and not necessarily a specific person. This is a management approach instead of an industry approach in identifying segments. The segments are based on the company's organizational structure, income sources, nature of activities, existence of managers, and information presented to the board of directors.

Revenues, gains, expenses, losses, and assets should be allocated to a segment only if the chief operating decision maker considers doing so in measuring a segment's earnings for purposes of making a financial or operating decision.

Note

A start-up operation would qualify as an operating segment even though revenue is not being earned.

Do special principles apply to segmental reporting?

Accounting principles employed in preparing financial statements should be used for segment information, except that numerous intercompany transactions eliminated in consolidation are included in segmental reporting on a gross basis. The financial statement presentation for segments may appear in the body, in the footnotes, or in a separate schedule from the financial statements.

When must a segment be reported?

A segment must be reported if any of these criteria are met:

- Revenue is 10 percent or more of total revenue.
- Operating income or loss is 10 percent or more of the combined operating profit.
- Identifiable assets are 10 percent or more of the total identifiable assets.

How are reportable segments established?

Reportable segments are determined by:

- Identifying specific products and services
- Grouping those products and services into segments by industry line
- Selecting material segments to the company as a whole

A number of approaches are possible in grouping products and services by industry lines. In many cases, management judgment is necessary to determine the industry segment.

A starting point in deriving the industry segment is by profit center. When the profit center crosses industry lines, it should be broken down into smaller groups. A company in an industry not accumulating financial information on a segregated basis must disaggregate its operations by industry line.

Although worldwide industry segmentation is recommended, it may not be practical. If foreign operations cannot be disaggregated, the firm should disaggregate domestic activities. Foreign operations should be disaggregated where possible and the remaining foreign operations be treated as a single segment.

How do I determine whether a segment is significant?

A segment that was significant in the past, even though not meeting the 10 percent test in the current year, should still be reported if it is expected that the segment will be significant in the future.

Segments should constitute a substantial portion (75 percent or more) of the company's total revenue to outside customers. The 75 percent test is applied separately each year.

In order to derive 75 percent, no more than 10 segments should be shown for practical purposes. If more than 10 are identified, similar segments may be combined.

Notes

Even though intersegment transfers are eliminated in the preparation of consolidated financial statements, they are includable for segmental disclosure in determining the 10 percent and 75 percent rules.

Disclosures are not required for 90 percent enterprises (i.e., a company that derives 90 percent or more of its revenue, operating profit, and total assets from one segment). In effect, that segment is the business. The dominant industry segment should be identified.

How is the 10 percent criterion applied?

In applying the 10 percent criterion, the accountant should note:

- *Revenue.* Revenue to unaffiliated customers and revenue to other business segments should be separated. Transfer prices are used for intersegmental transfers. Accounting bases followed should be disclosed.
- *Operating profit or loss.* Operating earnings of a segment exclude:
  - General corporate revenue and expenses that are not allocable
  - Interest expense (unless the segment is a financial type, such as one involved in banking)
  - Domestic and foreign income taxes
  - Income from unconsolidated subsidiaries or investees
  - Income from discontinued operations
  - Extraordinary items
  - Cumulative effect of a change in accounting principles
  - Minority interest

Note

Directly traceable and allocable costs should be charged to segments when applicable.

- *Identifiable assets.* Assets of a segment include those directly in it and general corporate assets that can rationally be allocated to it. Allocation methods should be consistently applied. Identifiable assets include those consisting of a part of the company's investment in the segment (e.g., goodwill). Identifiable assets do not include advances or loans to other segments except for income from them that is used to compute the results of operations (e.g., a segment of a financial nature).

What disclosures do segments have to make?

Disclosures to be made by segments include:

- Measurement or valuation basis, and change therein
- Aggregate depreciation, depletion, and amortization expense
- Capital expenditures
- Company's equity in vertically integrated, unconsolidated subsidiaries and equity method investees (note the geographical location of equity method investees)
- Effect of an accounting principle change on the operating profit of the reportable segment, including its effect on the company
- Material segmental accounting policies not already disclosed in the regular financial statements
- Unusual items included in segmental earnings

- Transfer price used
- Allocation method for costs
- Unusual items affecting segmental profit
- Type of products
- Sales to unaffiliated customers
- Tax effects

How does consolidation affect segmental reporting?

If a segment includes a *purchase method* consolidated subsidiary, the required segmental information is based on the consolidated value of the subsidiary (i.e., fair market value and goodwill recognized), not on the values recorded in the subsidiary's own financial statements. However, transactions between the segment and other segments, which are eliminated in consolidation, are reportable.

Segmental data are not required for *unconsolidated subsidiaries* or other *unconsolidated investees*.

Note

Each subsidiary or investee is subject to the rules requiring that segment information be reported.

Some types of typical consolidation eliminations are *not* eliminated when reporting for segments. *Example:* Revenue of a segment includes intersegmental sales and sales to unrelated customers.

A full set of financial statements for a foreign investee that is *not* a subsidiary does not have to disclose segmental information when presented in the same financial report of a primary reporting entity.

Exception

The foreign investee's separately issued statements already disclose the required segmental data.

Are there other requirements that apply to segmental reporting?

The source of the segmental revenue should be disclosed, along with the percent so derived, when:

- Ten percent or more of revenue or assets is associated with a foreign area. Presentation must be made of revenue, operating profit or loss, and assets for foreign operations in the aggregate or by geographical area. (A foreign geographical area is a foreign country or group of homogeneous countries.

Factors considered are geographical proximity, economic affinity, and similar business environments.)

- Ten percent or more of sales is to one customer. A group of customers under common control is construed as one customer.
- Ten percent or more of revenue is obtained from either domestic or foreign government contracts.

In some instances, *restatement* of prior-period information is required for *comparative* reasons when:

- Financial statements of the company as a whole have been restated.
- A change has occurred in grouping products or services for segment determination.
- A change has taken place in grouping of foreign activities into geographical segments.

The nature and effect of restatement should be disclosed.

Note

Segmental data that are presented in another company's financial report are not required in financial statements if those statements are:

- Combined in a complete set of statements, and both sets are presented in the same report
- Presented for a foreign investee (not a subsidiary of the primary enterprise) unless the financial statements disclose segment information (e.g., foreign investees for which such information is already required by the Securities and Exchange Commission)
- Presented in the report of a nonpublic company

Note

If an investee uses the market value or equity method and is not exempted by one of the preceding provisions, its full set of financial statements presented in another enterprise's report must present segment information if such data are significant to statements of the primary enterprise. Significance is determined by applying the percentage tests (i.e., 10 percent tests) to the financial statements of the primary enterprise without adjustment for the investee's revenue, operating results, or identifiable assets.

Imputing Interest on Notes

What if a non-interest-bearing note exists?

If the face amount of a note does not represent the present value of the consideration given or received in the exchange, imputation of interest is needed to avoid the misstatement of profit. Interest is imputed:

- On non-interest-bearing notes
- On notes that provide for an unrealistically low interest rate
- When the face value of the note is significantly different from the going selling price of the property or market value of the note

---

Notes

If a note is issued only for cash, the note should be recorded at the cash exchanged, regardless of whether the interest rate is reasonable or of the amount of the face value of the note. The note has a present value at issuance equal to the cash transacted.

When a note is exchanged for property, goods, or services, a presumption exists that the interest rate is fair and reasonable. Where the stipulated interest rate is not fair and adequate, the note has to be recorded at the fair value of the merchandise or services or at an amount that approximates fair value. If fair value is not determinable for the goods or services, the discounted present value of the note has to be used.

How do I determine the imputed interest rate?

The imputed interest rate is the one that would have resulted if an independent borrower or lender had negotiated a similar transaction. *Example:* It is the prevailing interest rate the borrower would have paid for financing.

Factors to consider in deriving an appropriate discount rate are:

- Prime interest rate
- Going market rate for similar quality instruments
- Issuer's credit standing
- Collateral
- Restrictive covenants and other terms in the note agreement
- Tax effects of the arrangement

For what kinds of instruments does imputed interest have to be determined?

ASC 835-30-05, *Interest: Imputation of Interest* (APB-21, *Interest on Receivables and Payables*) applies to long-term payables and receivables. Short-term payables and receivables typically are recorded at face value since the extra work of amortizing a discount or premium on a short-term note is not worth the information benefit obtained.

The pronouncement is *not* applicable to:

- Security deposits
- Usual lending activities of banks
- Amounts that do not mandate repayment
- Receivables or payables occurring within the ordinary course of business
- Transactions between parent and subsidiary

How are premiums and discounts determined and handled?

The difference between the face value of the note and the present value of the note represents discount or premium. This must be accounted for as an element of interest over the life of the note. Present value of the payments of the note is based on an imputed interest rate.

The *interest method* is used to amortize the discount or premium on the note. The interest method results in a constant rate of interest.

Amortization = Interest rate × Present value of the liability/
Receivable at the beginning of the year

Interest expense is recorded for the borrower, while interest revenue is recorded for the lender. Issuance costs are treated as a deferred charge.

The note payable and note receivable are presented in the balance sheet this way:

Notes Payable (principal plus interest)
Less: Discount (interest)
Present Value (principal)
Notes Receivable (principal plus interest)
Less: Premium (interest)
Present Value (principal)

Example 4.12

On 1/1/2X11, a machine is bought for $10,000 cash and the incurrence of a $30,000, five-year, non-interest-bearing note payable. The imputed interest rate is 10 percent. The present value factor for $n = 5$, $i = 10\%$ is 0.62. Appropriate journal entries are:

1/1/2X11		
Machine ($10,000 + $18,600)	$28,600	
Discount	11,400	
Notes Payable		$30,000
Cash		10,000

The present value of the note equals $30,000 × 0.62 = $18,600. On 1/1/2X11, the balance sheet shows:

Notes Payable	$30,000
Less: Discount	11,400
Present Value	$18,600
12/31/2X11	
Interest Expense	1,860
Discount 10% × $18,600 = $1,860	$1,860

On 1/1/2X12 the balance sheet shows:

Notes Payable	$30,000
Less: Discount ($11,400 – $1,860)	9,540
Present Value	$20,460
12/31/2X12	
Interest Expense	$ 2,046
Discount 10% × $20,460 = $2,046	$2,046

Accounting for Futures Contracts

What are futures contracts?

A futures contract is a legal arrangement entered into by the purchaser or seller and a regulated futures exchange in the United States or overseas. FASB Statement No. 80, *Accounting for Futures Contracts*, does not apply to foreign currencies futures, which are dealt with in FASB Statement No. 82, *Financial Reporting and Changing Prices: Elimination of Certain Disclosures*. Futures contracts involve:

- A buyer or seller receiving or making a delivery of a commodity or financial instrument (e.g., stocks, bonds, commercial paper, mortgages) at a given date. Cash settlement rather than delivery often exists (e.g., stock index futures).
- A futures contract can be eliminated prior to the delivery date by engaging in an offsetting contract for the particular commodity or financial instrument involved. *Example:* A futures contract to buy 100,000 pounds of a commodity by December 31, 2X12, can be canceled by entering into another contract to sell 100,000 pounds of that same commodity on December 31, 2X12.
- Changes in value of open contracts are settled regularly (e.g., daily). The usual contract provides that when a decrease in the contract value occurs, the contract holder has to make a cash deposit for such decline with the clearinghouse. If the contract increases in value, the holder may withdraw the increased value.

When does a futures position constitute a hedge?

A *hedge* exists when both of these criteria are met:

1. The hedged item places price and interest rate risk on the firm. *Risk* means the sensitivity of corporate earnings to market price changes or rates of return of existing assets, liabilities, commitments, and expected transactions.

Note

This criterion is not met where other assets, liabilities, commitments, and anticipated transactions already offset the risk.

2. The contract lowers risk exposure and is entered into as a hedge. High correlation exists between the change in market value of the contract and the fair value of the hedged item. In effect, the market price change of the contract offsets the price and interest rate changes on the exposed item. For example, a futures contract to sell silver offsets the changes in the price of silver.

How do I handle a change in the market value of the futures contract?

The change in market value of a futures contract involves a gain or loss that should be recognized in earnings.

Exception

For certain contracts, the timing of income statement recognition relates to the accounting for the applicable asset, liability, commitment, or transaction. This accounting exception applies when the contract is designed as a hedge against price and interest rate fluctuation. When these criteria are met, the accounting for the contract relates to the accounting for the hedged item. Thus, a change in market value is recognized in the same accounting period during which the effects of related changes in price or interest rate of the hedged item are reflected in income.

What are the requirements for a "hedge-type" futures contract?

- A change in the market value of a futures contract that meets the hedging criteria of the related asset or liability should adjust the carrying value of the hedged item. *Example:* A company has an investment in a government bond that it anticipates selling at a later date. The company can reduce its susceptibility to changes in fair value of the bonds by engaging in a futures contract. The changes in the market value of the futures contract adjust the book value of the bonds.

- A change in the market value of a futures contract for the purpose of hedging a firm commitment is included in measuring the transaction satisfying the commitment. When the company hedges a firm purchase commitment by using a futures contract and the acquisition takes place, thus satisfying the purchase commitment, the gain or loss on the futures contract is an element of the cost of the acquired item. *Example:* Assume ABC Company has a purchase commitment for 30,000 pounds of a commodity at $2 per pound, totaling $60,000. At the time of the consummation of the transaction, the $60,000 cost is decreased by any gain (e.g., $5,000) arising from the hedged futures contract. The net cost is shown as the carrying value ($55,000).
- The accounting applicable for a hedged futures contract related to an expected asset acquisition or liability incurrence should be consistent with the company's accounting method employed for those assets and liabilities. *Example:* The firm should book a loss for a futures contract that is a hedge of an expected inventory acquisition, if the amount will not be recovered from the sale of inventory.
- If a hedged futures contract is closed prior to the expected transaction, the accumulated value change in the contract should be carried forward to be included in measuring the related transaction. If it is probable that the quantity of an expected transaction will be less than the amount initially hedged, recognize a gain or loss for a pro rata portion of futures results that would have been included in the measurement of the subsequent transaction.

Note

A hedged futures contract requires disclosure of:

- Firm commitments
- Nature of assets and liabilities
- Accounting method used for the contract, including a description of events or transactions resulting in recognizing changes in contract values
- Transactions expected to be hedged with futures contracts

How do I account for an anticipatory hedge contract?

A futures contract may apply to transactions the company expects to conduct in the ordinary course of business but is not obligated to. These expected transactions do not involve *existing* assets or liabilities or transactions applicable to existing firm commitments. *Example:* A company may *anticipate* buying a certain commodity in the future but has not made a formal purchase commitment. The company may minimize risk exposure to price changes by entering into a futures contract. The change in market value of this *anticipatory hedge* contract is included in measuring the subsequent transaction. The change in market value of the futures contract adjusts the cost of the acquired item.

Four criteria must be met for anticipatory hedge accounting:

1 and 2. The first two criteria are the same as the criteria for regular hedge contracts related to *existing* assets, liabilities, or firm commitments.
3. Identification exists of the major terms of the contemplated transaction. Included are the type of commodity or financial instrument, quantity, and expected transaction date. If the financial instrument carries interest, the maturity date should be given.
4. It is probable that the expected transaction will take place. Probability of occurrence depends on:
   - Time period involved
   - Monetary commitment for the activity
   - Financial capability to conduct the transaction
   - Frequency of previous transactions of a similar nature
   - Possibility that other types of transactions may be undertaken to accomplish the desired goal
   - Adverse operational effects of not engaging in the transaction

Oil- and Gas-Producing Companies

What should I know about accounting for oil and gas companies?

Under the successful efforts method used by oil and gas companies, *successful costs* of exploration are deferred and amortized. *Unsuccessful costs* of exploration are immediately expensed.

Capitalization should be made of these expenditures:

- Mineral interests in properties classified as proved or unproved
- Wells and related equipment
- Support equipment and facilities used in oil- and gas-producing activities
- Uncompleted wells, equipment, and facilities

These capitalized costs should be amortized as the oil and gas reserves are produced. Unproved properties should be assessed on a periodic basis and losses recognized. Costs not resulting in the acquisition of an asset should be expensed.

Disclosures include:

- Net quantities of proved reserves and changes during the year
- Capitalized costs
- Property acquisitions
- Exploration and development costs
- Results of operations
- A measure of discounted future net cash flows
- Production (lifting) costs

CHAPTER 5

Key Financial Accounting Areas

Consolidations

What is a consolidation?

Consolidation occurs when the parent owns more than 50 percent of the voting common stock of the subsidiary. The objective of consolidation is to present as one economic unit the financial position and operating results of a parent and subsidiaries. The consolidation shows the group as a single company with one or more branches or divisions rather than as separate companies.

The companies making up the consolidated group keep their individual legal identities. Adjustments and eliminations are for the sole purpose of financial statement reporting.

Note

Consolidation is appropriate even if the subsidiary has a material amount of debt. Disclosure should be made of the firm's consolidation policy in footnotes or by explanatory headings.

When is a consolidation not valid?

A consolidation is negated, even if more than 50 percent of voting common stock is owned by the parent, in these instances:

- Parent is not in actual control of subsidiary. *Example:* Subsidiary is in receivership or in a politically unstable foreign country.
- Parent has sold or contracted to sell subsidiary shortly after year-end. The subsidiary is a temporary investment.
- Minority interest is very large in comparison to the parent's interest; individual financial statements are more appropriate.

How is a consolidation accounted for?

Intercompany eliminations include those for intercompany payables and receivables, advances, and profits. For certain regulated companies, intercompany profit does not have to be eliminated to the extent the profit represents a reasonable return on investment. Subsidiary investment in the parent's shares is not consolidated outstanding stock in the consolidated balance sheet.

Note

Consolidated statements do not reflect capitalized earnings in the form of stock dividends by subsidiaries subsequent to acquisition.

Minority interest in a subsidiary is the stockholders' equity in the partially owned subsidiaries outside of the parent's controlling interest. It should be shown as a separate component of stockholders' equity. When losses applicable to the minority interest in a subsidiary exceed the minority interest's equity capital, the excess and any subsequent losses related to the minority interest are charged to the parent. If profit subsequently occurs, the parent's interest is credited to the degree of prior losses absorbed.

Note

If a parent acquires a subsidiary in more than one block of stock, each purchase is on a step-by-step basis, and consolidation does not occur until control exists.

- *When the subsidiary is acquired within the year*, the subsidiary should be included in consolidation as if it had been bought at the beginning of the year with a subtraction for the preacquisition part of earnings applicable to each block of stock.

Alternative Approach

Include in consolidation the subsidiary's earnings subsequent to the acquisition date.

- *The retained earnings of a subsidiary* at the acquisition date are not included in the consolidated financial statements.
- When *the subsidiary is disposed of during the year*, the parent should present its equity in the subsidiary's earnings prior to the sale date as a separate line item consistent with the equity method.
- A subsidiary whose *major business activity is leasing* to a parent should always be consolidated.

- Consolidation is still permissible without adjustments when the fiscal year-ends of the parent and subsidiary are *three months or less apart*. Footnote disclosure of material events occurring during the intervening period is needed.

What methods of accounting can be used?

The *equity method* of accounting is used for unconsolidated subsidiaries, unless there is a foreign investment or a temporary investment.

When the equity method is not used, the *cost method* is followed. The cost method recognizes the difference between the cost of the subsidiary and the equity in net assets at the acquisition date. Depreciation is adjusted for the difference as if consolidation of the subsidiary was made. There is an elimination of intercompany gain or loss for unconsolidated subsidiaries to the extent the gain or loss exceeds the unrecorded equity in undistributed earnings.

Requirement

Unconsolidated subsidiaries accounted for with the cost method should have adequate disclosure of assets, liabilities, and earnings. Such disclosure may be in footnote or supplementary schedule form.

Aren't combined statements sometimes valid?

Combined financial statements are sometimes more appropriate than consolidated statements. *Example:* A person owns a controlling interest in several related operating companies (brother-sister corporation).

Note

In some cases parent company statements are required in addition to consolidated statements, in order to properly provide information to creditors and preferred stockholders. In this event, *dual columns* are needed—one column for the parent and other columns for subsidiaries.

Accounting Standards Update (ASU) No. 2010-02 (January 2010), *Consolidation* (ASC 810-10) *Accounting and Reporting for Decreases in Ownership of a Subsidiary—a Scope Clarification*, provides the following amendment.

A deconsolidation of a subsidiary by a parent is when the parent no longer has a controlling financial interest. An ensuing gain or loss is recognized by the parent, and a change in a parent's ownership interest is treated as an equity transaction. As a result, gain or loss is not recorded. A parent's ownership changes if it buys, sells, or reacquires shares in the subsidiary.

A deconsolidation should include disclosure of the nature of activities, any related-party transaction, valuation method to determine fair value, fair value inputs, and resulting gain or loss.

Disclosure for a business combination includes the date of purchase, identification and description of acquiree, percentage of ownership bought, way in which control of the targeted company occurred, accounting treatment for the combination, reasons for the combination, transaction description, issuance costs, when a combination occurs in stages, fair value measurements, acquisition costs, valuation method, acquiree's profit after the purchase date, and profit for the combined company for a comparable previous period.

ASC 810, *Consolidation* (FAS-167, *Amendments to FASB Interpretation No. 46(R)*), changes how a company determines when an entity that is inadequately capitalized or is not controlled through voting should be consolidated. The determination is based on factors such as the company's purpose and design and its ability to direct activities that impact its economic performance.

ASC 810 amends Interpretation 46R to replace the quantitative-based risks and rewards calculation to determine which company, if any, has a controlling financial interest in a variable-interest entity with an approach based on identifying which company has the power to direct activities of a variable-interest entity that mostly affects the entity's economic performance and (1) the obligation to absorb the entity's losses or (2) the right to receive benefits from the entity. A qualitative approach will be more effective.

ASC 810 requires a company to provide additional disclosures about its involvement with variable-interest entities and any major changes in risk exposure because of that involvement. Disclosure is made of how the involvement impacts the company's financial statements.

The pronouncement is effective January 1, 2010, for companies reporting earnings on a calendar-year basis.

Noncontrolling Interests in Consolidated Financial Statements

ASC 810-10-65, *Consolidation—Overall—Transition and Open Effective Date Information* (FAS-160, *Noncontrolling Interests in Consolidated Financial Statements*) states that a noncontrolling (minority) interest is the part of equity in a subsidiary not attributable to the parent. ASC 810-10-65 applies to all companies preparing consolidated financial statements and is effective for fiscal years beginning on or after December 15, 2008.

Ownership interests in subsidiaries held by parties other than the parent should be identified and presented in the consolidated balance sheet within equity, but separately from the parent's equity. The consolidated net income attributable to the parent and the noncontrolling interest should be identified and presented in the consolidated income statement. The computation of earnings per share (EPS) amounts, in consolidated financial statements, is based on amounts attributable to the parent.

Changes in a parent's ownership interest in a subsidiary, such as when the parent buys additional equity interest or sells ownership interest, represent an equity transaction if the parent keeps the controlling financial interest in the subsidiary. An equity transaction is also when a subsidiary reacquires or issues additional ownership interests.

If a subsidiary is deconsolidated, any retained noncontrolling equity investment in the former subsidiary should initially be recorded at fair value. The gain or loss on the deconsolidation of the subsidiary is measured based on the fair value of any noncontrolling equity investment instead of the carrying amount of the retained investment. A parent deconsolidates a subsidiary at the date the parent no longer has a controlling financial interest in the subsidiary.

A subsidiary may incur losses with its ensuing negative financial impact on noncontrolling interests. If the noncontrolling interest in the subsidiary's net assets has been reduced to zero due to losses, the noncontrolling interest will continue to be charged for its share of additional losses, even if that causes a deficit balance in the noncontrolling interest account.

Disclosures are made to identify and distinguish between the interests of the parent and the noncontrolling owners of the subsidiary. There should be reconciliation at the beginning and ending balances of the equity associated with the parent and the noncontrolling owners, as well as a schedule that presents the impact of changes in a parent's ownership interest in a subsidiary on the equity related to the parent.

Business Combinations

What are major changes with respect to business combinations and consolidations?

Business combinations in the form of mergers and acquisitions occur when companies choose to combine (rather than grow internally) to take advantage of cost efficiencies or transform their businesses to the next level. The result of a business combination is that the combined company may have additional product offerings, greater geographic presence, and increased market share, as well as control over all sources of production and product distribution (vertical integration). The accountant is frequently called upon to advise management of the impact of proposed combinations, as well as to prepare consolidated financial statements for completed transactions. Knowledge of the emerging accounting rules in this area is critical in supporting both functions.

With the exception of the elimination of pooling of interests for new acquisitions (in 2001) and the required consolidation of variable-interest entities (revised in 2003), the accounting rules for business combinations and consolidations remained largely unchanged for over 50 years until December 2007, when the Financial Accounting Standards Board (FASB), after many years of deliberation, simultaneously issued two new standards, FASB Statement No. 141R (FAS-141R), *Business Combinations* (ASC 805) (a revision of FASB Statement No. 141), and FAS-160, *Noncontrolling Interests in Consolidated Financial Statement—An Amendment of ARB No. 51* (ASC 810-10-65-1). These statements, which require prospective treatment for new business combinations having fiscal years beginning after December 15, 2008, mandate what is referred to as the acquisition method. Moreover, the purchase method of accounting will no longer be permitted for acquisitions closed after the effective date of the new rules. *Note:* FAS-141R completes a joint effort by the FASB and the International Accounting Standards Board (IASB) to standardize the reporting for business combinations as part of the international convergence project. The IASB's IFRS 3,

Business Combinations, was issued in 2007 and for the most part mirrors the rules found in FAS-141R.

A critical distinction is that the new rules abandon the historical cost-based structure of accounting for acquisitions at the price paid and require that consolidation of the acquiree is at *business fair value*. As retroactive adoption of the new standards is not permitted, mergers completed before the effective date must continue to be treated in accordance with the accounting standards that were in effect at the date of the original business combination. Therefore, there will continue to be many mergers that will be grandfathered under the accounting rules in existence at the dates they were completed (i.e., purchase method and pooling of interests method).

Relevant Accounting Pronouncements

Business combinations are accounted for in accordance with FAS-141R, *Business Combinations*, which replaces FAS-141; FAS-142, *Goodwill and Other Intangible Assets* (ASC 350); FAS-160, *Noncontrolling Interests in Consolidated Financial Statements*, which amends Accounting Research Bulletin No. 51, *Consolidated Financial Statements* (ASC 810-10-10); and FASB Interpretation No. 46R, *Consolidation of Variable Interest Entities* (ASC 810-10-30). Applicable Emerging Issues Task Force bulletins issued prior to the effective date of FAS-141R and FAS-160 have been incorporated into the new standards.

How does the acquisition method compare with the purchase and pooling of interests methods?

Prior to the effective dates of FAS-141R and FAS-160, previously completed business combinations were accounted for under the purchase method or the pooling of interests method. Since they are grandfathered under the new rules, those business combinations will continue to be accounted for under the rules that were in place at the time the transaction closed.

A listing of the main points of each method is as follows:

A. Acquisition method (effective for new acquisitions by acquirers having fiscal years beginning after December 15, 2008):
   - Focus is on fair value of the acquired entity.
   - Direct combination costs are expensed.
   - Stock issuance costs are treated as a reduction of additional paid-in capital.
   - Bargain purchase is treated as income to the acquirer.
   - Fair value of contingent consideration at acquisition date is considered part of the fair value of the acquired entity.
   - Subsequent resolution of contingent consideration at a value different from that recorded at acquisition date is run through the income statement.
   - Acquiree in-process research and development costs and other purchased intangibles are recorded at fair value at acquisition date.

- Preacquisition contingencies that are resolved after the acquisition closing date are expensed.
- Acquiree assets and liabilities are reported in the consolidated entity at fair value.

B. Purchase method (effective for acquisitions closed prior to December 15, 2008, that have been accounted for under the purchase method):
- Acquisitions continue to be accounted for under the purchase method.
- Focus is on historical cost of the acquisition (i.e., the price paid to acquire an entity).
- Direct combination costs are capitalized as part of the investment cost.
- Stock issuance costs are treated as a reduction of additional paid-in capital.
- Bargain purchase results in a proportional reduction of noncurrent assets of the acquire, with any excess treated as an extraordinary gain.
- Contingent consideration is not recorded as part of acquisition cost until it is subsequently resolved. (*Note:* If the resolution of the contingency requires an additional payment to be made by the acquirer, that payment will either increase goodwill or lessen the reduction to noncurrent assets in the case of a bargain purchase).
- Acquiree in-process research and development costs are included in acquisition cost only when considered either technologically feasible or subject to alternative future use.
- Assets and liabilities of the acquiree are reported at fair value, subject to any reduction in acquiree noncurrent assets due to a bargain purchase.

C. Pooling of interests method (effective for acquisitions completed prior to June 30, 2001, assuming they met all 12 of the specific criteria in existence at that time):
- Acquisitions will continue to be consolidated under this method until the entities are sold, closed, or otherwise disposed of.
- Assets and liabilities are consolidated at their book values.
- There are no adjustments to either the balance sheet (fair value allocations) or the income statement (amortization of fair value adjustments).
- Income and expense of the acquiree are reported retrospectively; that is, they are retroactively restated for all periods presented.

What are the main differences between the acquisition and purchase methods?

Exhibit 5.1 presents the main differences between the acquisition and purchase methods of accounting.

What does the acquirer disclose for each acquisition?

For each acquisition that occurs during the reporting period or after the reporting period but before financial statements are issued, the acquirer must disclose:

- Name and description of the acquiree.
- Acquisition date.
- Percentage of voting interest acquired.

EXHIBIT 5.1   Acquisition Method versus Purchase Method

	New Rules (Acquisition Method) (ASC 805, FAS-141R); FAS-160	Old Rules (Purchase Method) FAS-141; ARB 51
Focus	Fair value of entity acquired, referred to as "business fair value"	Historical cost (i.e., price paid to acquire the entity)
Direct combination costs	Expensed	Treated as part of cost of acquisition
Bargain purchase	Recognize as income on transaction closing date	Reduce noncurrent assets proportionately; any excess is extraordinary gain
Stock issuance costs	Decrease (debit) to additional paid-in capital	Same
Contingent consideration	Recorded at fair value at transaction closing date; subsequent changes in fair value recorded in income statement	Not recorded as part of acquisition cost until contingency is resolved; this will result in additional goodwill or less reduction to noncurrent assets (bargain purchase)
In-process research and development costs	Capitalized at fair value as intangible assets, subject to impairment testing or amortization	Expensed
Preacquisition contingencies	Contractual contingencies recorded at fair value; noncontractual contingencies recorded at fair value if they meet "more likely than not" criteria for definition of an asset or a liability	Not recorded unless FAS-5 criteria are met (i.e., probable and reasonably estimable)
Valuation of equity issued	Fair value at transaction closing date	Fair value at the date the acquisition is announced
Other intangible assets	Recorded at fair value	Recorded as part of investment cost if meeting contractual criteria (e.g., patents) or separability (e.g., technology)

- Rationale for the business combination and how the acquirer obtained control of the acquiree.
- Qualitative factors supporting any goodwill from the transaction (e.g., expected synergies from combined operations or description of intangible assets not qualifying for separate recognition).
- Fair value of total consideration transferred, as well as fair value of each component.
- Amount and description of any contingent consideration, as well as a discussion of the circumstances in which payment will be made; also included should be a range of possible outcomes or, if a range cannot be estimated, the reasons why.

- Amounts recognized at the acquisition date for each major class of assets acquired and liabilities assumed.
- Nature of recognized and unrecognized contingencies along with a range of possible outcomes.
- Total goodwill expected to be deducted for tax purposes.
- If acquirer is required to disclose segment information, the amount of goodwill by reportable segment (this information will be used in the goodwill impairment test).
- Where acquirer and acquiree have previously had a business relationship, any amounts that are not part of the exchange in the business combination between the acquirer and acquiree should be identified.
- Any acquisition-related costs and where reported in the financial statements (i.e., expense, reduction of paid in capital, or other category).
- For any bargain purchase, the amount of the gain included in the consolidated income statement and the reason why the business combination resulted in a gain.
- Fair value of any noncontrolling interest and valuation techniques used to measure fair value.
- For step acquisitions, the fair value of any equity interest held immediately prior to the acquisition date and the amount of gain or loss recognized as a result of remeasuring to fair value.
- For public companies, the amount of revenue and earnings subsequent to the acquisition date, reported in the consolidated income statement.
- Supplemental pro forma information, showing revenue and earnings for any comparative period for which financial statements are presented, including as of the beginning of the current reporting period.

Accounting Standards Update

Accounting Standards Update (ASU) No. 2010-29 (December 2010), *Business Combinations* (ASC 805), *Disclosures of Supplementary Pro Forma Information for Business Combinations*

When comparative financial statements are presented, disclosure should be made of revenue and profit of the combined business as if the business combination taking place during the current year had occurred as of the start of the comparable previous annual reporting period only. Disclosure should also be made describing the nature and amount of nonrecurring pro forma adjustments applicable to the business combination included in reported pro forma revenue and profit.

What are the advantages and disadvantages of the purchase method?

An advantage is that the fair value is used to recognize the acquired company's assets just as in the case of acquiring a separate asset.

Disadvantages are:

- Difficulty in determining fair value
- Mixing fair value of acquired company's assets and historical cost for the acquiring company's assets

According to Accounting Standards Update (ASU) No. 2010-01 (January 2010), *Equity* (ASC Topic 505), *Accounting for Distributions to Shareholders with Components of Stock and Cash*, the stock part of a stockholder distribution that permits stockholders to receive stock or cash with a possible restriction of the cash to be received is deemed an issuance of shares. It is not considered a stock dividend. EPS computation will include these distributions. The effective date for this accounting is December 15, 2009.

Investments in Securities

Stock Investments

Investments in stock may be accounted for and reported under ASC 320-10-05-1 and 05-2, *Investments—Debt and Equity Securities: Overall* (FAS-115, *Accounting for Certain Investments in Debt and Equity Securities*), or ASC 323-10-15-8, *Investments—Equity Method and Joint Ventures* (APB 18—*The Equity Method of Accounting for Investments in Common Stock*), depending on the percentage of ownership involved in voting common stock.

Market Value Adjusted

Securities are defined as held to maturity, trading, or available for sale.

How are held-to-maturity securities reported?

Held-to-maturity treatment applies just to debt securities because stock does not have a maturity date. Held-to-maturity debt securities are reported at amortized cost, which equals the purchase price adjusted for the amortization of discount or premium. Held-to-maturity categorization applies to debt securities only if the company has the intent and ability to hold the securities to the maturity date.

Note: Under ASC 825-10-35-4, *Financial Instruments: Overall* (FAS-159, *The Fair Value Option for Financial Assets and Financial Liabilities*), a company has the option, if it wishes, to measure held-to-maturity securities at fair market value. If this fair value option is selected, unrealized (holding) gains and losses will be presented separately in the income statement.

How are trading securities reported?

Trading securities can be either debt or equity. The intent is to sell them in a short time period. Trading securities often are bought and sold to earn short-term gain. Trading securities are recorded at market value with the unrealized (holding) loss or gain presented separately in the income statement. Trading securities should be reported as current assets in the balance sheet.

Example 5.1

On 12/31/2X12, the trading securities portfolio had a cost and market value of $500,000 and $520,000, respectively. The journal entry to account for this portfolio at market value is:

Market Adjustment	$20,000	
Unrealized Gain		$20,000

The market adjustment account has a debit balance and is added to the cost of the portfolio in the current assets section of the balance sheet in this way:

Trading Securities (cost)	$500,000
Add: Market Adjustment	20,000
Trading Securities (market value)	$520,000

The unrealized (holding) gain is presented in the income statement under "other income."

How are available-for-sale securities reported?

Available-for-sale securities can be either debt or equity. These securities are not held for trading reasons, nor is the intent to hold them to maturity. They are reported at market value with the accumulated unrealized loss or gain shown as a separate item in the stockholders' equity section of the balance sheet. The portfolio of available-for-sale securities may be presented in the current asset or in the noncurrent asset sections of the balance sheet, depending on how long these securities are intended to be held.

Example 5.2

On 12/31/2X12, the available-for-sale securities portfolio had a cost and market value of $300,000 and $285,000, respectively. The journal entry to recognize the portfolio at market value is:

Unrealized Loss	$15,000	
Market Adjustment		$15,000

The portfolio is presented in the balance sheet at $285,000 net of the market adjustment account of $15,000. The unrealized loss is presented separately in the stockholders' equity section of the balance sheet.

IFRS Connection

Securities are classified as either held to maturity or available for sale under the International Financial Reporting Standards (IFRS).

- A security not at fair value through profit or loss is measured at fair value plus transaction costs. Other securities are measured at fair value.
- Securities are classified upon initial recognition as (1) measured at amortized cost or (2) measured at fair value.

A debt instrument is measured at amortized cost if it meets the business model test (objective: collect the contractual cash flows) and the cash flow test (contract results in specific dates for cash flows that are principal and interest payments only).

How is the sale of securities reported?

When securities are sold, regardless of the type, the realized gain or loss is reported in the income statement. If the decline in market value of either available-for-sale or held-to-maturity securities is deemed permanent, a realized loss is presented in the income statement. When the security is written down, market value at that date becomes the new cost basis.

Example 5.3

On 12/31/2X12, a company presented these accounts before adjustment:

Available-for-Sale Securities	$300,000
Market Adjustment	25,000

It was determined on 12/31/2X12 that the portfolio's market value is $290,000. The journal entry needed to bring the portfolio up to date is:

Market Adjustment	$15,000	
Unrealized Gain		$15,000

What if there is an exchange of stock?

If two or more securities are purchased at one price, the cost is allocated among the securities based on their relative fair market value. In the exchange of one security for another, the new security received in the exchange is valued at its fair market value.

Example 5.4

Preferred stock costing $10,000 is exchanged for 1,000 shares of common stock having a market value of $15,000. The entry is:

Investment in Common Stock	$15,000	
Investment in Preferred Stock		$10,000
Gain		5,000

How is a stock dividend handled?

A stock dividend involves a memo entry reflecting more shares at no additional cost. As a result, the cost per share decreases.

Example 5.5

Fifty shares at $12 per share for a total cost of $600 are owned. A 20 percent stock dividend is declared amounting to 10 shares. This memo entry is made reflecting the additional shares:

Investment

50	$12	$600
10		0
60	**$10**	$600

If 10 shares are later sold at $15 each, the entry is:

Cash	$150	
Long-Term Investment		$100
Gain		50

What effect does a stock split have?

A stock split has the effect of increasing the shares and reducing the cost basis on a proportionate basis. A memo entry is made.

Example 5.6

One hundred shares costing $20 per share are owned. A 2-for-1 stock split would result in 200 shares at a cost per share of $10. Total par value would remain at $2,000.

Equity Method

When is the equity method of accounting used?

The investor company is the owner and the investee company is being owned. The equity method is used if:

- An investor owns between 20 and 50 percent of the voting common stock of an investee.
- The holder owns less than 20 percent of the voting common stock but possesses significant influence (effective control).
- More than 50 percent of the voting common stock is owned but one of the negating factors for consolidation exists.

Note

Investments in joint ventures have to be accounted for under the equity method.

IFRS Connection

The equity method is *not* required if:

- The investment is classified as held for sale.
- The investment is acquired solely to be disposed of within 12 months, or conditions exist similar to those that would exempt an entity from preparing consolidated statements.

How do I account when using the equity method?

The accounting under the equity method as per ASC 323-10-15-8 (APB 18) is illustrated by the T-accounts shown in Exhibit 5.2.

- The cost of the investment includes brokerage fees. The investor recognizes his or her percentage ownership interest in the ordinary profit of the investee by debiting investment in investee and crediting equity in earnings of investee.
- The investor's share in investee's earnings is computed after deducting cumulative preferred dividends, whether declared or not. The investor's share of the investee's profit should be based on the investee's most recent income statement applied on a consistent basis.
- Extraordinary gains or losses as well as prior-period adjustments are also picked up as shown on the investee's books.
- Dividends reduce the carrying value of the investment account.

EXHIBIT 5.2   T-Accounts

Investment in Investee

Cost	Dividends
Ordinary Profit	Depreciation on Excess of Fair Market
Extraordinary Gain	Value less Book Value of Specific
	Assets
	Permanent Decline

Equity in Earnings of Investee

Depreciation	Ordinary Profit

Extraordinary Gain

	Extraordinary Gain

- The excess paid by the investor for the investee's net assets is first assigned to the specific assets and liabilities and is depreciated. The unidentifiable portion of the excess is considered goodwill, which is subject to an annual impairment test. Depreciation on excess value of assets reduces the investment account and is charged to equity in earnings.
- *Temporary decline* in price of the investment in the investee is ignored. *Permanent decline* in value of the investment is reflected by debiting loss and crediting investment in investee.
- When the investor's share of the investee's losses is greater than the balance in the investment account, the equity method should be discontinued at the zero amount.

Exceptions

The investor has guaranteed the investee's obligations or immediate profitability is assured. A return to the equity method is made only after offsetting subsequent profits against losses not recorded.

- When the investee's stock is sold, a realized gain or loss will arise for the difference between the selling price and the cost of the investment account.

Isn't the equity method like a consolidation?

The mechanics of consolidation essentially apply to the equity method. For example, intercompany profits and losses are eliminated. Investee capital transactions impacting the investor's share of equity should be accounted for as in a consolidation. The investee's capital transactions should be accounted for as if the investee was a consolidated subsidiary. *Example:* When the investee issues its common stock to third parties at a price in excess of book value, there will be an increase in the value of the investment and a related increase in the investor's paid-in capital.

What else should I know about the equity method?

Interperiod income tax allocation will occur because the investor shows the investee's *profits* for book reporting but *dividends* for tax reporting. This results in a deferred income tax credit account.

If the ownership goes below 20 percent or if the investor is unable to control the investee, the investor should cease recognizing the investee's earnings. The equity method is discontinued, but the balance in the investment account is maintained. The market value method should then be applied.

If the investor increases ownership in the investee to 20 percent or more, the equity method should be used for current and future years. Furthermore, the effect of using the equity method rather than the market value method on prior years at the old percentage (e.g., 15 percent) should be recognized as an adjustment to retained earnings and other accounts so affected (e.g., investment in investee). The retroactive adjustment on the investment, earnings, and retained earnings should be applied in the same manner as a step-by-step acquisition of a subsidiary.

What disclosures are necessary?

The investor should make disclosures of these items in footnotes, separate schedules, or parenthetically:

- Percent owned
- Name of investee
- Investor's accounting policies
- Material effects of possible conversions and exercises of investee common stock
- Quoted market price (for investees not qualifying as subsidiaries)
- Summarized financial data as to assets, liabilities, and earnings for material investments in unconsolidated subsidiaries
- Material realized and unrealized gains and losses relating to the subsidiary's portfolio occurring between the dates of the financial statements of the subsidiary and parent

Example 5.7

On 1/1/2X11, X Company bought 30,000 shares for a 40 percent interest in the common stock of AB Company at $25 per share. Brokerage commissions were $10,000. During 2X11, AB's net income was $140,000 and dividends received were $30,000. On 1/1/2X12, X Company received 15,000 shares of common stock as a result of a stock split by AB Company. On 1/4/2X12, X Company sold 2,000 shares at $16 per share of AB stock. The journal entries follow.

1/1/2X11 Investment in Investee	$760,000	
Cash		$760,000
12/31/2X11 Investment in Investee	56,000	
Equity in Earnings of Investee		56,000
40% × $140,000 = $56,000		
Cash	30,000	
Investment in Investee		30,000
1/1/2X12 Memo Entry for Stock Split		
1/4/2X12 Cash (2,000 × $16)	32,000	
Loss on Sale of Investment	2,940	
Investment in Investee		
(2,000 × $17.47)		34,940
$786,000/45,000 = $17.47 per share		

Investment in Investee

1/1/2X11	$760,000	12/31/2X11	$30,000
12/31/2X11	56,000		
	816,000		
	$786,000		

Example 5.8

On 1/1/2X12, the investor purchased 100,000 shares of the investee's 400,000 shares outstanding for $3,000,000. The book value of net assets acquired was $2,500,000. The $500,000 excess paid over book value is attributable to undervalued tangible assets. The depreciation period is 20 years. In 2X12, the investee's net income was $800,000, including an extraordinary loss of $200,000. Dividends of $75,000 were paid on June 1, 2X12. These journal entries are necessary for the acquisition of investee by investor accounted for under the equity method.

1/1/2X12 Investment in Investee	$3,000,000	
Cash		$3,000,000
6/1/2X12 Cash	18,750	
Investment in Investee		18,750
25% × $75,000 = $18,750		
12/31/2X12		
Investment in Investee	250,000	
Equity in Earnings of Investee		250,000
$1,000,000 × 25% = $250,000		
Extraordinary Loss from Investment	50,000	
Investment in Investee		50,000
$200,000 × 25% = $50,000		
Equity in Earnings of Investee	25,000	
Investment in Investee		25,000

Note: Under ASC 825-10-35-4, *Financial Instruments: Overall* (FAS-159), a company using the equity method can *elect* to use the fair value option. If that option is selected, the investment in investee account will reflect temporary changes in market value of the investee. The resulting unrealized (holding) loss or gain will be presented as a separate item in the income statement. For example, if the fair market value of the investee decreases, the investor will debit unrealized loss and credit the investment in investee account (or a valuation allowance account) for the decrease in value. If there is an increase in fair market value, the investment in investee account (or valuation allowance account) would be debited and unrealized gain credited for the increase in fair market value.

According to ASC 320, *Investments—Debt and Equity Securities* (FASB Staff Position [FSP] FAS 115-2 and FAS 124-2, *Recognition and Presentation of Other-Than-Temporary Impairments*), an investment is impaired if the fair value is less than the amortized cost. This FSP applies to debt securities classified as available for sale and held to maturity that are subject to other-than-temporary impairment guidance.

If the fair value of a debt security is less than amortized cost at year-end, the company shall assess if impairment is other than temporary. If a company intends to sell the debt security, an other-than-temporary impairment has taken place. If a company is more likely than not to be required to sell the security before there is a recovery in its amortized cost, an other-than-temporary impairment has occurred.

If the company does not anticipate recovering the full amortized cost of the security, the company would be unable to assert that it will recover its amortized cost. In this case, an other-than-temporary impairment has occurred. If the present value of cash flows expected to be collected is less than amortized cost, credit loss still exists, and an other-than-temporary impairment has occurred. To determine whether a credit loss exists, factors such as the time period and degree to which fair value has been less than amortized cost should be considered.

If a company intends to sell the debt security or more likely than not will be required to sell the security before recovery of its amortized cost basis less any current-period credit losses, the other-than-temporary impairment shall be recognized in earnings equal to the difference between the investment's amortized cost basis and its fair value on the balance sheet date. If the entity does not intend to sell the security, the other-than-temporary impairment shall be separated into the (1) credit loss and (2) amount related to other factors. The amount of impairment related to the credit loss is recognized in earnings, while the impairment related to other factors is recognized in other comprehensive income.

Leases

How are leases defined?

Leases are typically long-term, noncancellable commitments. In a lease, the lessee acquires the right to use property owned by the lessor. Even though no legal transfer of title occurs, many leases transfer substantially all the risks and benefits of ownership. Theoretical substance governs over legal form in accounting, resulting in the lessee recording an asset and a liability for a capital lease.

> ## Note
>
> A lease may be between related parties. This occurs when one entity has significant influence over operating and financial policies of another entity.

The *date of inception* of a lease is the time of lease *agreement*, or *commitment*, whichever occurs first.

> ## Requirement
>
> A commitment must be in writing, signed, and provide principal provisions. If any major provisions are to be negotiated later, there is no committed agreement.

Lessee

How does the lessee account for leases?

The two methods of accounting for a lease by the lessee are the operating method and the capital method.

What is an operating lease?

An operating lease is a regular rental of property.

How is recognition given to an operating lease?

- As rental payments become payable, rent expense is debited and cash and/or payables are credited.
- The lessee does not show anything on his balance sheet.
- Rent expense is reflected on a straight-line basis unless another method is more appropriate.
- Accrual-basis accounting is followed.

What is a capital lease?

The lessee uses the capital lease method if any *one* of these four criteria is met:

1. The lessee obtains ownership to the property at the end of the lease term.
2. There is a bargain purchase option where the lessee can either acquire the property at a nominal amount or renew the lease at nominal rental payments.

3. The life of the lease is 75 percent or more of the life of the property.
4. The present value of minimum lease payments at the inception of the lease equals or is greater than 90 percent of the fair market value of the property. Minimum lease payments exclude executory costs to be paid by the lessor such as maintenance, insurance, and property taxes.

Notes

If the first or second criterion is met, the depreciation period is the life of the property. If the third or fourth criterion is satisfied, the depreciation period is the life of the lease.

The third and fourth criteria do not apply where the beginning of the lease term falls within the last 25 percent of the total economic life of the property, including earlier years of use.

What is the accounting and reporting for a capital lease?

The asset and liability are recorded at the present value of the minimum lease payments plus the present value of the bargain purchase option. The expectation is that the lessee will take advantage of the nominal purchase price.

If the sum of present value of the minimum lease payments plus the bargain purchase option is greater than the fair value of the leased property at the time of lease inception, the asset should be capitalized at the fair market value of the property.

The discount rate used by the lessee is the lower of the lessee's incremental borrowing rate (the rate at which the lessee would have to borrow to be able to buy the asset) or the lessor's implicit interest rate (the rate implicit in the recovery of the fair value of the property at lease inception through the present value of minimum lease payments, including the lessee's guarantee of salvage value).

The liability is broken down between current and noncurrent.

What is the minimum lease payment (MLP)?

The lessee's minimum lease payment (MLP) usually includes:

- MLP over the lease term plus any residual value guaranteed by the lessee. The guarantee is the determinable amount for which the lessor has the right to require the lessee to buy the property at the lease termination. It is the stated amount when the lessee agrees to satisfy any dollar deficiency below a stated amount in the lessor's realization of the residual value.
- Any payment that the lessee must pay due to failure to extend or renew the lease at expiration.

Note

MLP includes only MLP over the lease term and exercise option payment, if a bargain purchase option exists.

MLP does not include:

- Contingent rentals
- Lessee's guarantee of lessor's debt
- Lessee's obligation for executory costs

Each minimum lease payment is allocated as a reduction of principal (debiting the liability) and as interest (debiting interest expense). The interest method is used to result in a constant periodic rate of interest. Interest expense equals the interest rate times the carrying value of the liability at the beginning of the year.

How is a capital lease shown on the balance sheet and income statement?

- *Balance sheet.* Show the asset under lease less accumulated depreciation.
- *Income statement.* Show interest expense and depreciation expense. In the first year, the expenses under a capital lease (interest expense and depreciation) are greater than the expenses under an operating lease (rent expense).

What if the lessee buys a leased asset that has been capitalized?

Per ASC 840-30-35, *Leases—Capital Leases—Subsequent Measurement* (FASB Interpretation 26, *Accounting for Purchase of a Leased Asset by the Lessee during the Term of the Lease*), when a lessee buys a leased asset during the lease term that has been originally capitalized, the transaction is considered an *extension* of a capital lease, not a termination. The difference between the purchase price and the carrying amount of the lease obligation recorded is an *adjustment* of the carrying amount of the asset.

Note

No loss recognition is required on an extension of a capital lease.

Example 5.9

On 1/1/2X11, the lessee enters into a capital lease for property. The minimum rental payment is $20,000 a year for six years to be made at year-end. The

(continued)

(Continued)

interest rate is 5 percent. The present value of an ordinary annuity factor for $n = 6$, $i = 5$ percent is 5.0757. The journal entries for the first two years are:

1/1/2X11 Asset	$101,514	
Liability		$101,514
12/31/2X11		
Interest Expense	5,076	
Liability	14,924	
Cash		20,000
5% × $101,514 = $5,076		
Depreciation	16,919	
Accumulated Depreciation		16,919
$\dfrac{\$101,514}{6} = \$16,919$		

The liability as of 12/31/2X11 is:

Liability

12/31/2X11	$14,924	1/1/12X11	$101,514
		12/31/2X11	86,590

12/31/2X12		
Interest Expense	4,330	
Liability	15,670	
Cash		20,000
5% × $86,590 = $4,330		
Depreciation	16,919	
Accumulated Depreciation		16,919

What footnote disclosures are necessary for leases?

Footnote disclosures under a capital lease include:

- Assets under lease by class
- Future minimum lease payments in total and for each of the next five years
- Contingent rentals (rentals based on terms other than time; e.g., sales)
- Total future sublease rentals
- Description of leasing arrangement including renewal terms, purchase options, escalation options, and restrictions in the lease agreement

Lessor

How does the lessor account for leases?

The three methods of accounting for leases by the lessor are:

1. Operating method
2. Direct-financing method
3. Sales-type method

What is the operating method?

The operating method is a regular rental by the lessor. *Example:* Avis rents automobiles.

How do I account for the operating method?

Under the operating method, the lessor records rental revenue less related expenses, including depreciation and maintenance expense.

- *Income statement.* Show rental revenue less expenses to obtain profit.
- *Balance sheet.* Present the asset under lease less accumulated depreciation to derive book value.

How is rental income recognized in the operating method?

Rental income is recognized as earned using the straight-line basis over the lease term, except if there is another preferable method.

Initial direct costs are deferred and amortized over the lease term on a pro rata basis based on rental income recognized. However, the initial direct costs can be expensed if immaterial relative to the allocation amount.

Example 5.10

Hall Corporation produced machinery costing $5,000,000, which it held for resale from January 1, 2X12, to June 30, 2X12, at a price to Travis Company under an operating lease. The lease is for four years, with equal monthly payments of $85,000 due on the first of the month. The initial payment was made on July 1, 2X12. The depreciation period is 10 years with no salvage value.

Lessee's Rental Expense for 2X12: $85,000 × 6	$510,000
Lessor's Income before Taxes for 2X12:	
Rental Income	510,000
Less: Depreciation	
$\dfrac{\$5,000,000}{10} \times \dfrac{6}{12}$	250,000
Income before Taxes	$260,000

What is the direct financing method?

The direct financing method satisfies one of the four criteria for a capital lease by the lessee *plus* both of the next two criteria for the lessor:

1. Collectibility of lease payments is assured.
2. No important uncertainties exist regarding future costs to be incurred.

The lessor is *not* a manufacturer or dealer. The lessor acquires the property for the sole purpose of leasing it out. *Example:* A bank leasing computers.

How do I account for the direct financing method?

The carrying value and the fair value of the leased property are the same at the inception of the lease.

The lessor uses as the discount rate the interest rate implicit in the lease.

Interest revenue equals the interest rate times the carrying value of the receivable at the beginning of the year. Interest income is recognized only in the financial statements over the life of the lease using the interest method. Unearned interest income is amortized as income over the lease term, resulting in a constant rate of interest.

Contingent rentals are recognized in earnings as earned.

The lessor's MLP includes:

- The MLP made by the lessee (net of any executory costs together with any profit thereon)
- Any guarantee of the salvage value of the leased property, or of rental payments after the lease term, made by a third party unrelated to either party in the lease, provided the third party is financially able to satisfy the commitment

Note

A guarantee by a third party related to the lessor makes the residual value unguaranteed. A guarantee by a third party related to the lessee implies a guaranteed residual value by the lessee.

What if there is a change in lease provisions?

A change in lease provisions that would have resulted in a different classification had it taken place at the beginning of the lease mandates that the lease be considered a new agreement and be classified under the new terms.

Exceptions

- Exercise of existing renewal options is not deemed lease changes.
- A change in estimate does not result in a new lease.

Note

A provision for escalation of the MLP during a construction or preacquisition period may exist. The resulting increase in MLP is considered in determining the fair value of the leased property at the lease inception. A salvage value increase resulting from an escalation clause may also exist.

What do initial direct costs include?

Initial direct costs are those costs incurred by the lessor directly applicable to negotiating and consummating *completed* leasing transactions, such as:

- Legal fees
- Commissions
- Document preparation and processing for new leases
- Credit investigation
- Relevant portion of salespersons' and other employees' compensation

Not included in initial direct costs are:

- Costs for *unconsummated* leases
- Supervisory, administrative, or other indirect expenses

Initial direct costs of the lease are expensed as incurred. A portion of the unearned income equal to the initial direct costs is recognized as income in the same accounting period.

What if the lease is terminated?

If the lease agreement contains a penalty for failure to renew and the penalty becomes inoperative due to lease renewal or other extension of time, the unearned interest income account must be adjusted for the difference between the present values of the old agreement and the revised agreement. The present value of the future MLP under the new agreement should be computed using the original rate for the initial lease.

Lease termination is accounted for by the lessor through eliminating the net investment and recording the leased property at the lower of cost or fair value. The net adjustment is then charged against earnings.

Balance Sheet

The lessor shows the total minimum lease payments plus salvage value of the property accruing to the lessor as the gross investment in the lease. This represents lease payments receivable. Deducted from lease payments receivable is unearned interest revenue. The balance sheet presentation follows:

> Lease Payments Receivable (Principal + Interest)
> Less: Unearned Interest Revenue (Interest)
> Net Receivable Balance (Principal)

(*continued*)

(Continued)

The income statement shows:

Interest Revenue
Less: Initial Direct Costs
Less: Executory Costs
Net Income

What footnote disclosure is necessary for the direct financing method?

Footnote disclosure should include:

- Assets leased out by category
- Future lease payments in total and for each of the next five years
- Contingent rentals
- The terms of the lease

What is the sales-type method?

The sales-type method must satisfy the same criteria as the direct financing method. The only difference is that the sales-type method involves a lessor who is a manufacturer or dealer in the leased item. Thus, a manufacturer or dealer profit results. Although legally there is no sale of the item, theoretical substance governs over legal form, and a sale is assumed to have taken place.

Note

The distinction between a sales-type lease and a direct financing lease affects only the lessor; for the lessee, either type would be a capital lease.

If there is a renewal or extension of an existing sales-type or financing lease, it shall not be classified as a sales-type lease.

Exception

A lease may sometimes be so classified (i.e., as a sales-type lease) when the renewal occurs toward the end of the lease term.

How do I account for a sales-type lease?

- In a sales-type lease, profit on the assumed sale of the item is recognized in the year of lease as well as interest income over the life of the lease. The cost and fair value of the leased property are different at the inception of the lease.
- An annual appraisal should be made of the salvage value. Where necessary, reduce the net investment and recognize a loss. Do not adjust the salvage value.
- The cost of the leased property is matched against the selling price in determining the assumed profit in the year of lease. Initial direct costs of the lease are expensed.
- Except for the initial entry to record the lease, the entries are the same for the direct financing and sales-type methods.

Example 5.11

Assume the same facts as in the capital lease illustration of Example 5.9. The accounting by the lessor assuming a direct financing lease and a sales-type lease follows:

Direct Financing			Sales Type		
1/1/2X12					
Receivable	$120,000		Receivable	$120,000	
Asset		$101,514	Cost of Sales	85,000	
Unearned			Inventory		$ 85,000
Interest			Sales		101,514
Revenue		18,486			
			Unearned		
			Interest		
			Revenue		18,846
12/31/2X12					
Cash	20,000				
Receivable		20,000			
Unearned					
Interest				Same entries	
Revenue	5,076				
Interest					
Revenue		5,076			
12/31/2X12					
Cash	20,000				
Receivable		20,000			
Unearned					
Interest				Same entries	
Revenue	4,330				
Interest					
Revenue		4,330			

(*continued*)

(*Continued*)

The income statement for 2X12 presents:

Interest		Sales	$101,514
Revenue	$5,076	Less: Cost of Sales	85,000
		Gross Profit	$ 16,514
		Interest Revenue	$ 5,076

Example 5.12

Jones leased equipment to Tape Company on October 1, 2X12. It is a capital lease to the lessee and a sales-type lease to the lessor. The lease is for eight years, with equal annual payments of $500,000 due on October 1 each period. The first payment was made on October 1, 2X12. The cost of the equipment to Tape Company is $2,500,000. The equipment has a life of 10 years with no salvage value. The appropriate interest rate is 10 percent.

Tape Company reports the following information in its income statement for 2X12:

Asset Cost ($500,000 × 5.868 = 2,934,000)		
Depreciation		
$\left(\dfrac{\$2,934,000}{10} \times \dfrac{3}{12}\right)$		$ 73,350
Interest Expense:		
Present Value of Lease Payments	$2,934,000	
Less: Initial Payment	500,000	
Balance	$2,434,000	
Interest Expense		60,850
$2,434,000 × 10% × 3/12		
Total Expenses		$134,200

Jones's income before tax is:

Interest Revenue		$ 60,850
Gross Profit on Assumed Sale of Property:		
Selling price	$2,934,000	
Less: Cost	2,500,000	
Gross Profit		434,000
Income before Tax		$494,850

Sales-Leaseback Arrangement

What is a sales-leaseback situation?

A sales-leaseback occurs when the lessor sells the property and then leases it back. The lessor may do this when in need of funds.

What is the accounting for a sales-leaseback arrangement?

The profit or loss on the sale is deferred and amortized as an adjustment in proportion to depreciation expense in the case of a capital lease, or in proportion to rental expense in the case of an operating lease. However, if the fair value of the property at the time of the sales-leaseback is below its book value, a loss is immediately recognized for the difference between book value and fair value.

Example 5.13

The deferred profit on a sales-leaseback is $50,000. An operating lease is involved, where rental expense in the current year is $10,000 and total rental expense is $150,000. Rental expense is adjusted as:

Rental Expense	$10,000
Less: Amortization of Deferred Gross Profit	
($50,000 × ($10,000/$150,000))	3,333
	$ 6,667

Subleases and Similar Transactions

What is a sublease?

There are three types of *subleases*:

1. The original lessee leases the property to a third party. The lease agreement of the original parties remains intact.
2. A new lessee is substituted under the original agreement. The original lessee may still be secondarily liable.
3. The new lessee is substituted in a new agreement. There is a cancellation of the original lease.

What accounting is necessary by the lessor?

The original lessor continues the present accounting method if the original lessee subleases or sells to a third party. If the original lease is replaced by a new agreement with a new lessee, the lessor terminates the initial lease and accounts for the new lease in a separate transaction.

What accounting does the original lessee have to do?

In accounting by the original lessee, if the original lessee is relieved of primary obligation by a transaction other than a sublease, terminate the original lease.

- If the original lease was a capital lease, remove the asset and liability, recognize a gain or loss for the difference, including any additional consideration paid or received, and accrue a loss contingency where secondary liability exists.
- If the original lease was an operating lease and the initial lessee is secondarily liable, recognize a loss contingency accrual.

If the original lessee is not relieved of *primary* obligation under a sublease, the original lessee (now sublessor) accounts in this manner:

- If the original lease met lessee criterion 1 or 2 (see "What is a capital lease?" in the earlier "Lessee" section), classify the new lease per normal classification criteria by lessor. If the sublease is a sales-type or direct financing lease, the unamortized asset balance becomes the cost of the leased property. Otherwise, it is an operating lease. Continue to account for the original lease obligation as before.
- If the original lease met only lessee criterion 3 or 4, classify the new lease using lessee criterion 3 and lessor criteria 1 and 2. Classify as a direct financing lease. The unamortized balance of the asset becomes the cost of the leased property. Otherwise, it is an operating lease. Continue to account for original lease obligation as before.

Note

If the original lease was an operating lease, account for old and new leases as operating leases.

Leveraged Leases

What is a leveraged lease?

A leveraged lease occurs when the lessor (equity participant) finances a small part of the acquisition, retaining total equity ownership. A third party (debt participant) finances the balance. The lessor maximizes the leveraged return by recognizing lease revenue and income tax shelter (e.g., interest deduction, rapid depreciation).

A leveraged lease must meet *all* of these criteria:

- It satisfies the tests for a direct financing lease. Sales-type leases are not leveraged leases.
- It involves at least three parties: lessee, long-term creditor (debt participant), and lessor (equity participant).

- The long-term creditor provides nonrecourse financing as to the general credit of the lessor. The financing is adequate to give the lessor significant leverage.
- The lessor's net investment (see "How does the lessor account for leveraged leases?") decreases during the initial lease years, then increases in subsequent years just before its liquidation by sale. These increases and decreases in the net investment balance may take place more than once during the lease life.

How does the lessee account for leveraged leases?

The lessee classifies and accounts for leveraged leases in the same way as for nonleveraged leases.

How does the lessor account for leveraged leases?

The lessor records investment in the leveraged lease net of the nonrecourse debt. The net of these balances represents the initial and continuing investment:

- Rentals receivable (net of the amount applicable to principal and interest on the nonrecourse debt)
- Estimated residual value
- Unearned and deferred income

The initial entry to record the leveraged lease is:

Lease Receivable
Residual Value of Asset
Cash Investment in Asset
Unearned Income

- The lessor's *net investment* in the leveraged lease for computing net income is the investment in the leveraged lease less deferred income taxes.

Periodic net income is determined in this manner employing the *net investment in the leveraged lease*:

- Determine annual cash flow equal to:

Gross Lease Rental (plus residual value of asset in last year of lease term)
Less: Loan Interest Payments
Less: Income Tax Charges (or add income tax credits)
Less: Loan Principal Payments
Annual Cash Flow

- Determine the return rate on the net investment in the leveraged lease. The rate of return is the one that when applied to the net investment in the years when it is positive, will distribute the net income (cash flow) to those positive years.

The *net investment* will be:

- Positive in the early years (but declining rapidly due to accelerated depreciation and interest expense)
- Negative during the middle years
- Again positive in the later years (because of the declining tax shelter)

How do I handle a change in income tax cash flows?

According to FASB Staff Position 13-2 (*Accounting for a Change in the Timing of Cash Flows Relating to Income Taxes Generated by a Leveraged Transaction*), a company has to recalculate its leverage lease when there is a change in the timing of income tax cash flows generated by the lease. If the projected timing of income tax cash flows is revised, the rate of return and the allocation of income to positive investment years should be recomputed from the beginning of the lease.

Pension Plans

How is a pension plan defined?

The pension plan relationship among the employer, trustee, and employee is depicted in Exhibit 5.3.

The two types of pension plans are:

1. *Defined contribution.* In a defined contribution plan, the employer's annual contribution amount is specified, not the benefits to be paid.
2. *Defined benefit.* In a defined benefit plan, the determinable pension benefit to be received by participants upon retirement is specified. The employer has to provide plan contributions so that sufficient assets are accumulated to pay for the benefits when due. Typically, an annuity of payments is made.

Notes

Pension expense applicable to administrative staff is expensed. Pension expense related to factory personnel can be inventoried.

Pension Plan Assets on Books of Trustee

EXHIBIT 5.3 Pension Plan Relationship

What terminology is important for understanding pension plans?

- *Actuarial assumptions.* Actuaries make assumptions as to variables in determining pension expense and related funding. *Examples:* Mortality rate, employee turnover, compensation levels, and rate of return.
- *Actuarial cost (funding) method.* This method is used by actuaries in determining the employer contribution to ensure that sufficient funds will be available at employee retirement. The method used determines the pension expense and related liability.
- *Actuarial present value of accumulated plan benefits.* This is the discounted amount of money that would be required to satisfy retirement obligations for active and retired employees.
- *Benefit information date.* This is the date the actuarial present value of accumulated benefits is presented.
- *Vested benefits.* An employee vests when he or she has accumulated pension rights to receive benefits upon retirement. The employee no longer has to remain in the company to receive pension benefits.
- *Projected benefit obligation.* This is the year-end pension obligation based on future salaries. It is the actuarial present value of vested and nonvested benefits for services performed before a particular actuarial valuation date based on expected future salaries. It measures the deferred compensation amount.
- *Accumulated benefit obligation.* This is the year-end obligation based on current salaries. It is the actuarial present value of benefits (vested and nonvested) attributable to the pension plan based on services performed before a specified date, based on current salary levels.
- *Net assets available for pension benefits.* This represents plan assets less plan liabilities. The plan's liabilities exclude participants' accumulated benefits.

In general, what are the accounting requirements for pension plans?

A company does not have to have a pension plan. If it does, the firm must conform to FASB and governmental rules regarding the accounting and reporting for the pension plan. ASC 715-20, *Compensation—Retirement Benefits—Defined Benefit Plans—General* and ASC 715-30, *Compensation—Retirement Benefits—Defined Benefit Plans—Pension* (FAS-158, *Employers' Accounting for Defined Benefit Pension and Other Postretirement Plans*) requires accounting for pension costs on the accrual basis.

Pension expense is reflected in the service periods using a method that considers the benefit formula of the plan. On the income statement, pension expense is presented as a single amount.

Defined Contribution Pension Plan

How do I account for a defined contribution plan?

- Pension expense equals the employer's cash contribution for the year. There is no deferred charge or deferred credit arising.

- If the defined contribution plan stipulates that contributions are to be made for years subsequent to an employee's rendering of services (e.g., after retirement), there should be an accrual of costs during the employee's service period.

Footnote disclosure includes:

- Description of plan including employee groups covered
- Basis of determining contributions
- Nature and effect of items affecting interperiod comparability
- Cost recognized for the period

Accounting Standards Update

Accounting Standards Update (ASU) No. 2010-25 (September 2010), Plan Accounting—Defined Contribution Pension Plans (Topic 962), Reporting Loans to Participants

Participant loans should be presented as notes receivable and are to be segregated from plan investments and valued at their unpaid principal amount plus any accrued but unpaid interest.

Defined Benefit Pension Plan

What is the accounting for a defined benefit plan?

ASC 715-20 and 715-30 amends ASC 962-10-05, *Plan Accounting—Defined Contribution Pension Plans: Overall* (FAS-87, *Employer's Accounting for Pensions*), FAS-88, FAS-106, and ASC 715-20-05, *Compensation—Retirement Benefits: Defined Benefit Plans—General* (FAS-132 [revised 2003], *Employers' Disclosures about Pension and Other Postretirement Benefits*). Pension accounting is segregated between the employer's accounting and the accounting for the pension fund. The employer incurs the cost and makes contributions to the pension fund. The fund (plan) is the entity that receives the contributions, administers plan assets, and makes benefit payments to retirees. The assets and liabilities of a pension plan are *not* included in the employer's financial statements. The pension fund is a distinct legal and accounting entity.

ASC 715-20 and 715-30 applies only to single-employer plans, *not* multiple-employer ones. Upon adoption of this statement, most companies will show a very substantial increase in liabilities as well as a reduction in stockholders' equity because most companies are underfunded.

What are the elements of pension expense?

The components of pension expense in a defined benefit pension plan are:

- Service cost
- Amortization of prior service cost

- Return on plan assets (reduces pension expense)
- Interest on projected benefit obligation
- Amortization of actuarial gain or loss (gain reduces pension expense but loss increases pension expense)

Service cost is based on the present value of future payments under the benefit formula for employee services of the current period. It is recognized in full in the current year. The calculation involves actuarial assumptions.

The company must incorporate future salary levels in measuring pension expense and the present obligation if the plan benefit includes them. ASC 715-20 and 715-30 adopts the benefits/years-of-service actuarial method, which computes pension expense based on future compensation levels. The employer must fund at a minimum the annual service cost.

Prior service cost is the pension expense applicable to services rendered before the adoption or amendment date of a pension plan. The cost of the retroactive benefits is the increase in the projected benefit obligation at the date of amendment. It involves the allocation of amounts of cost to future service years. Prior service cost determination involves actuarial considerations.

Amortization is accomplished by assigning an equal amount to each service year of active employees as of the amendment date who are expected to receive plan benefits. The amortization of prior service takes into account:

- Future service years
- Change in the projected benefit obligation
- Period in which employees will receive benefits
- Decrement in employees receiving benefits each year

"Other comprehensive income" is adjusted when amortizing prior service cost. Amortization of prior service cost typically increases pension expense.

The employer recognizes prior service cost as a component of pension expense over the remaining service lives of employees. FAS-158 prefers a three-step years-of-service amortization method:

1. The total number of service years to be worked by eligible participants is calculated.
2. Prior service cost is divided by the total number of service years to compute a cost per service year (unit cost).
3. The number of service years, each year, is multiplied by the cost per service year, to compute the annual amortization charge.

Companies can also use the straight-line method of amortization in which prior service cost is amortized over the average remaining service life of employees.

Prior service cost is reported as a component of accumulated other comprehensive income in the stockholders' equity section of the balance sheet.

IFRS Connection

For defined benefit plans, both IFRS and U.S. generally accepted accounting principles (GAAP) recognize the net of the pension assets and liabilities on the balance sheet. Some differences exist.

- Unlike U.S. GAAP, which recognizes prior service cost on the balance sheet (as an element of accumulated other comprehensive income), IFRS does not recognize prior service cost on the balance sheet. Both U.S. GAAP and IFRS amortize prior service cost into income over the expected service lives of employees.
- Another difference is that under IFRS, companies have the choice of recognizing actuarial gains and losses in income immediately or amortizing them over the expected remaining working lives of employees. U.S. GAAP does not permit choice; actuarial gains and losses (and prior service costs) are recognized in accumulated other comprehensive income and amortized to income over remaining service lives.

Example 5.14

X Company changes its pension formula from 2 percent to 5 percent of the past three years of pay multiplied by the service years on January 1, 2X12. This results in the projected benefit obligation being increased by $500,000. Employees are anticipated to receive benefits over the next 10 years.

Total future service years equals:

$$\frac{n(n+1)}{2} \times P$$

where

n is the number of years services are to be made
P is the population decrement each year

$$\frac{10(10+1)}{2} \times 9 = 495$$

Amortization of prior service cost in 2X12 equals:

$$\$500,000 \times \frac{10 \times 9}{495} = \underline{\$90,909}$$

Example 5.15

On 1/1/2X12, a company modifies its pension plan and grants $200,000 of prior service cost to employees. The workers are expected to provide 5,000 service years in the future with 250 service years in 2X12. The amortization of prior service cost for the year 2X12 is:

$$\text{Cost per service year} = \$200,000/5,000 = \$40$$

$$\text{2X12 amortization} = 250 \times \$40 = \$10,000$$

The return on plan assets (e.g., stocks, bonds) reduces pension expense. Plan assets are valued at the moving average of asset values for the accounting period.

The annual pension expense is adjusted for dividends and interest earned by the pension fund in addition to the appreciation or decline in the market value of plan assets.

Pension assets are increased from employer contributions and actual returns, but pension assets are decreased from benefit payments to retirees. Actual return on plan assets increases the fund balance and reduces the net cost to provide workers' pension benefits. Using assumed numbers, actual return on plan assets is calculated as:

Fair Market Value of Plan Assets—beginning of year	$600,000
Add: Contributions	80,000
Less: Benefit Payments	(30,000)
Add: Actual Return	?
Fair Market Value of Plan Assets—end of year	$725,000

Actual return must be $75,000 (the missing number).

Interest is on the projected benefit obligation at the beginning of the year. The settlement rate, representing the rate that pension benefits could be settled for, is employed.

$$\text{Interest} = \text{Interest rate} \times \text{Projected benefit obligation at beginning of year}$$

In determining the settlement rate, consideration is given to the return rate on high-quality fixed income investments whose cash flows match the amount and timing of the expected benefit obligations.

Actuarial gain or loss represents the difference between estimates and actual experience. *Example:* If the assumed interest rate is 10 percent and the actual interest rate is 12 percent, an actuarial gain results.

There may also be a change in actuarial assumptions regarding the future. Actuarial gains and losses are deferred and amortized as an adjustment to pension expense over future years. Actuarial gains and losses related to a single event not related to the pension plan and not in the ordinary course of business are immediately recognized in the current year's income statement. *Examples:* Plant closing and segment disposal.

Gains and losses are changes in the amount of either the projected benefit obligation (PBO) or pension plan assets because of experience different changes in assumptions. Gains and losses that are *not* recognized immediately as a component of pension expense shall be recognized as increases or decreases in other comprehensive income as they arise.

When is there an asset or liability gain or loss?

An asset gain or loss occurs on plan assets when the expected return is different from the actual return.

$$\text{Asset gain} = \text{Actual return} > \text{Expected return}$$
$$\text{Asset loss} = \text{Actual return} < \text{Expected return}$$

A liability gain or loss occurs when actuarial assumptions differ from actual experiences related to the computation of the projected benefit obligation.

$$\text{Liability gain} = \text{Unexpected decrease in the PBO}$$
$$\text{Liability loss} = \text{Unexpected increase in the PBO}$$

Asset gains and losses are combined with liability gains and losses to derive a *net* gain or loss. Net gain or loss is the change in the fair market value of plan assets and the amount of change in the projected benefit obligation.

What is the corridor method?

Asset gains and losses and liability gains and losses offset each other. The *corridor method* is used to amortize the "accumulated other comprehensive income" account balance when it becomes excessive. The FASB set a limit of 10 percent of the *greater* of the beginning balances of the market-related value of plan assets or the projected benefit obligation. Above the 10 percent limit, the "accumulated other comprehensive income" account related to gain and loss is too large and must be amortized. For example, if the projected benefit obligation and market-related asset value are $800,000 and $650,000, respectively, the corridor equals $80,000 (10% × $800,000). Any amount exceeding $80,000 would be amortized; if the "accumulated other comprehensive income" account balance was $120,000, the amount to be amortized would be $40,000 ($120,000 − $80,000). However, if the "accumulated other comprehensive income" account had a balance of $80,000 or less, *no* amortization is required.

If amortization is required, the *minimum* amortization is the excess ($40,000) divided by the average remaining service years of active employees to receive benefits. Assuming a 40-year service life, the amortization for the year would be $1,000 ($40,000/40 years).

The amortization of a loss increases pension expense whereas the amortization of a gain reduces it.

Note

A company can use any amortization method for gain and loss provided it is more than the minimum amount.

Note

Pension expense will not usually equal the employer's funding amount. Pension expense typically is based on the benefits/years-of-service method.

What if pension expense differs from the amount funded?

Pension expense > Cash paid = Pension liability

Pension expense < Cash paid = Pension asset

What is the financial statement presentation?

The change in the fair market value of pension plan assets equals:

Fair Market Value of Plan Assets—beginning of year
Plus: Actual Return on Plan Assets
Plus: Contributions
Minus: Benefit Payments
Fair Market Value of Plan Assets—end of year

The change in the projected benefit obligation equals:

Projected Benefit Obligation—beginning of year
Plus: Service Cost
Plus: Interest Cost
Plus: Amendments (prior service cost)
Plus: Actuarial Loss
Minus: Benefit Payments
Projected Benefit Obligation—end of year

Per ASC 715-20 and 715-30, the employer must measure the funded status (assets and liabilities) of a plan at its fiscal year-end date used for financial reporting.

The net funded status must be recognized on the balance sheet. If the projected benefit obligation exceeds the fair market value of plan assets, the plan is under-funded and there will be a pension liability. If the fair market value of plan assets exceeds the projected benefit obligation, the plan is overfunded and there will be a pension asset.

There should be an aggregation of the statuses of all overfunded plans, and the amount should be presented as a noncurrent asset. (*Note:* No part of a pension asset is reported as a current asset, because the pension plan assets are *restricted*.) There should be an aggregation of the statuses of all underfunded plans, and the amount should be presented as a liability. The liability for an underfunded plan can be classified as a current liability, noncurrent liability, or a combination of both. The current portion is the amount by which the actuarial present value of benefits

EXHIBIT 5.4   Pension Plan Accounting

Items	Journal Entry Account	Memo Account
Prior service cost (PSC) arising from amendment of plan	Other comprehensive income (OCI) (prior service cost) Dr.	Projected benefit obligation (PBO) Cr.
Service cost	Pension expense (PE) Dr.	PBO Cr.
Interest cost on PBO	Pension expense (PE) Dr.	PBO Cr.
Actual return	Pension expense (PE) Cr.	Plan assets (PA) Dr.
Amortization of PSC	PE Dr. and OCI (PSC) Cr.	
Contributions	Cash Cr.	Plan assets (PA) Dr.
Benefit payments		PBO Dr. and PA Cr.
Unexpected loss (expected return on PA exceeds actual return)	OCI (G/L) Dr. and PE Cr.	
Unexpected gain (actual return on PA exceeds expected return)	PE Dr. and OCI (G/L) Cr.	
Liability (PBO) increase	OCI (G/L) Dr.	PBO Cr.
Liability (PBO) decrease	OCI (G/L) Cr.	PBO Dr.
Amortization of excess loss over the corridor	PE Dr. and OCI (G/L) Cr.	
Amortization of excess gain over the corridor	OCI (G/L) Dr. and PE Cr.	

included in the benefit obligation payable within the year exceeds the fair market value of plan assets.

All overfunded plans should be combined and presented as a pension plan asset. Similarly, all underfunded plans should be combined and presented as a pension plan liability. It is *not* allowed to combine all plans and show a net amount as a single net asset or net liability.

Exhibit 5.4 presents a summary of the accounting for pension plans as required by ASC No. 715.

Example 5.16

Mr. A is hired six years before retirement. His estimated salary at retirement will be $50,000. The pension benefit is 3 percent of final salary for each service year payable at retirement. The retirement benefit is computed next.

Final Annual Salary	$50,000
Formula Rate	× 3%
	$ 1,500
Years of Service	× 6
Retirement Benefit	$ 9,000

Example 5.17

On 1/1/2X11, a company adopts a defined benefit pension plan. Return rate and interest rate are both 10 percent. Service costs for 2X11 and 2X12 are $100,000 and $120,000, respectively. The funding amounts for 2X11 and 2X12 are $80,000 and $110,000, respectively.

The entry for 2X11 is:

Pension Expense	$100,000	
Cash		$80,000
Pension Liability		20,000

The entry in 2X12 is:

Pension Expense	$122,000*	
Cash		$110,000
Pension Liability		12,000

*Computation:	
Service Cost	$120,000
Interest on Projected Benefit Obligation	
(10% × $100,000)	10,000
Return on Plan Assets	
(10% × $80,000)	(8,000)
	$122,000

At 12/31/2X12:

Projected Benefit Obligation = $230,000 ($100,000 + $120,000 + $10,000)

Pension Plan Assets = $198,000 ($80,000 + $110,000 + 8,000)

Example 5.18

Company X has a defined benefit pension plan for its 100 employees. On 1/1/2X12, pension plan assets have a fair value of $230,000, accumulated benefit obligation is $285,000, and the projected benefit obligation is $420,000. Ten employees are expected to resign each year for the next 10 years. They will be eligible to receive benefits. Service cost for 2X12 is $40,000. On 12/31/2X12, the projected benefit obligation is $490,000, the fair value of plan assets is $265,000, and the accumulated benefit obligation is $340,000. The return on plan assets

(continued)

(Continued)

and the interest rate are both 8 percent. No actuarial gains or losses occurred during the year. Cash funded for the year is $75,000.

Pension expense equals:

Service Cost	$40,000
Interest on Projected Benefit Obligation (8% × $420,000)	33,600
Return on Plan Assets (8% × $230,000)	(18,400)
Amortization of Actuarial Gains and Losses	—
Amortization of Prior Service Cost	34,545*
Pension Expense	$ 89,745
Obligation	$420,000
Fair Value of Pension Plan Assets	230,000
Initial Net Obligation	$190,000
Amortization $\dfrac{\$190,000}{5.5 \text{ years}^\dagger} = \underline{\$34,545}$	

*Projected Benefit

$^\dagger \dfrac{n(n+1)}{2} \times P = \dfrac{10(10+1)}{2} \times 10 = 550$

$\dfrac{550}{100} = 5.5$ years (average remaining service period)

The journal entry at 12/31/2X12 is:

Pension Expense	$89,745	
Cash		$75,000
Pension Liability		14,745

What information should be disclosed in the footnotes?

Footnote disclosure for a pension plan as required by ASC 715-20-05, *Compensation —Retirement Benefits: Defined Benefit Plans—General* (FAS-132 (revised 2003), *Employers' Disclosures about Pension and Other Postretirement Benefits*) and ASC 715-20 and 715-30 includes:

- Description of plan, including benefit formula, funding policy, employee groups covered, and retirement age
- Components of pension expense
- Pension assumptions (e.g., interest rate, mortality rate, employee turnover)
- Present value of vested and nonvested benefits
- Weighted-average assumed discount rate involved in measuring the projected benefit obligation
- Weighted-average return rate on pension plan assets
- Amounts and types of securities included in pension plan assets

- Amount of approximate annuity benefits to employees
- Investment policy, strategies, and objectives
- Measurement dates
- Risk management practices
- Unallowable investments in the pension plan, such as certain derivatives
- Benefits expected to be paid
- Expected contributions
- Rates of compensation increase
- Nature and amount of changes in pension plan assets and benefit obligations recognized in net income and in other comprehensive income
- Amortization method used for the excess of the "accumulated other comprehensive income" balance over the corridor amount
- Reconciliation of how the fair market value of plan assets and the projected benefit obligation changed from the beginning to end of year

When is there settlement in a pension plan?

According to FAS-88 and FAS-158, a settlement is discharging some or all of the employer's pension benefit obligation. A settlement must satisfy all of the following criteria:

- It is irrevocable.
- It relieves pension benefit responsibility.
- It materially curtails risk related to the pension obligation.

Excess plan assets may revert back to the employer.

How is settlement in a pension plan handled?

The amount of gain or loss recognized in the income statement when a pension obligation is settled is limited to the unrecognized net gain or loss from realized or unrealized changes in either the pension benefit obligation or plan assets. Changes arise when actual experiences deviate from the original assumptions. All or a pro rata share of the unrecognized gain or loss is recognized when a plan is settled.

- If full settlement occurs, all unrecognized gains or losses are recognized.
- If only a part of the plan is settled, a pro rata share of the unrecognized net gain or loss is recognized.

Example: When the employer furnishes employees with a lump-sum amount to give up pension rights, the gain or loss resulting is included in the current year's income statement.

When does curtailment occur in a pension plan?

Per ASC 715-20 and 715-30, a curtailment occurs when an event significantly reduces the future service years of present employees or eliminates for most employees the accumulation of defined benefits for future services. *Example:* A plant closing ends employee services prior to pension plan expectations.

How do I handle curtailment in a pension plan?

The gain or loss is recognized in the current year's income statement and contains these elements:

- Prior service cost attributable to employee services no longer needed
- Change in pension benefit obligation due to the curtailment

The projected benefit obligation may be decreased (a gain) or increased (a loss) by a curtailment. To the extent that such a gain (or loss) exceeds any net loss (or gain) included in accumulated other comprehensive income, it is a curtailment gain (or loss).

The amount of net periodic benefit cost should include the gain or loss recognized because of settlements or curtailments.

What is involved in a termination in a pension plan?

When termination benefits are offered by the employer and accepted by employees, and the amount can reasonably be determined:

- An expense and liability are recognized.
- The amount of the accrual equals the down payment plus the present value of future payments to be made by the employer.
- The entry is to debit loss and credit cash (down payment) and liability (future payments).
- Footnote disclosure of the arrangement should be made.

Trustee Reporting for a Defined Benefit Pension Plan

What recognition is made by the trustee?

This section discusses the reporting and disclosures by the trustee of a defined benefit pension plan. Generally accepted accounting principles (GAAP) must be followed. Financial statements are not required to be issued by the plan. If they are issued, reporting guidelines have to be followed. The prime objective is to assess the plan's capability to meet retirement benefits.

BALANCE SHEET   Present *pension assets and liabilities* as an offset. Operating assets are at book value. In determining net assets available, accrual accounting is followed. *Example:* Accruing for interest earned but not received. *Investments* are shown at fair market value. An asset shown is "contributions receivable due from employer."

In computing pension plan liability, the participants' accumulated benefits are *excluded*. In effect, plan participants are equity holders rather than creditors of the plan.

Disclosure is required of:

- Net assets available for benefits
- Changes in net assets available for benefits, including net appreciation in fair value of each major class of investments

- Actuarial present value of accumulated plan benefits (i.e., benefits anticipated to be paid to retired employees, beneficiaries, and present employees)
- Changes in actuarial present value of accumulated plan benefits
- Description of the plan, including amendments
- Accounting and funding policies

Note

An annuity contract may exist whereby an insurance company agrees to give specified pension benefits in return for receiving a premium.

IFRS Connection

Unlike U.S. GAAP, IFRS allows companies to have the option to report the funded status of their pension plans on the balance sheet.

Other Postretirement Benefits

What are the major differences between pensions and postretirement benefits?

The major differences between pension benefits and postretirement benefits are:

- Pension benefits are typically funded, whereas postretirement benefits are not.
- Pension benefits are well defined within a level dollar amount, whereas postretirement benefits are usually uncapped and show significant fluctuation.

How do I handle postretirement benefits other than pensions?

ASC 715-20 and 715-30 and ASC 750-10 (FAS-106, *Employers' Accounting for Postretirement Benefits Other Than Pensions*) apply to the employer's accounting and reporting for postretirement benefits other than pensions: (1) health care and welfare and (2) life insurance. These benefits are accrued as employee services are rendered. Under the defined contribution plan, the amount contributed yearly is presented as postretirement benefits expense. However, under the defined benefit plan, the amount contributed for the year will probably differ from the expense.

The postretirement benefit cost is based on actuarial determinations, and the benefits are allocated over the service periods of employees who will obtain them. Such benefits must be fully accrued by the date that the employee attains full eligibility, even if the employee is expected to continue working beyond that date.

Postretirement benefits for current and future retirees constitute deferred compensation. The time period during which the postretirement benefits accrue is called the *attribution period*.

The *accumulated postretirement benefit obligation* (*APBO*) is the actuarial present value of future benefits assigned to employees' services performed to a particular date. The *expected postretirement benefit obligation* (*EPBO*) is the actuarial present value as of a specified date of all benefits the employer expects to pay after retirement to workers, their beneficiaries, or covered dependents. The APBO equals the EPBO for retirees and active employees fully eligible for benefits at the end of the attribution period. Before full eligibility is reached, the APBO is a part of the EPBO. Therefore, the difference between the APBO and the EPBO is the future service costs of active employees who are not yet fully eligible.

Footnote disclosures include a description of the plan, types of benefits provided, components of postretirement expense, cost trend factors in health care, trend in compensation, fair market value of plan assets, accumulated postretirement benefit obligations, funding policy, return on plan assets, and the impact of a one-percentage-point increase in trend rates.

Income Tax Accounting

How do I account for taxes?

ASC 740-10-05-1 through 05-10, *Income Taxes: Overall* (FAS-109, *Accounting for Income Taxes*), applies to income tax allocation. Temporary differences occur between book income and taxable income. The deferred tax liability or asset is measured at the tax rate under current law that will exist when the temporary difference reverses. Furthermore, the deferred tax liability or asset must be adjusted for changes in tax law or in tax rate. Consequently, the liability method must be used to account for deferred income taxes. Comprehensive deferred tax accounting is practiced. Tax expense equals taxes payable plus the tax effects of all temporary differences. Interperiod tax allocation is used to account for temporary differences impacting the current year's results. The tax effects of future events should be reflected in the year they occur. It is improper to anticipate them and recognize a deferred tax liability or asset in the current year.

Temporary Differences

How do I handle temporary differences?

Temporary differences arise from four kinds of transactions:

1. Revenue included on the tax return after being reported on the financial records (e.g., installment sales)
2. Expenses deductible on the tax return after being deducted on the financial records (e.g., bad debts provision)
3. Revenue included on the tax return before being recognized in the financial records (e.g., unearned revenue)
4. Expenses deductible on the tax return before being deducted on the financial records (e.g., accelerated depreciation)

Footnote reference is made to the types of temporary differences. If tax rates are graduated based on taxable income, aggregate calculations can be made using an estimated average rate.

Permanent Differences

What about permanent differences?

Permanent differences do not reverse and thus do not require tax allocation. Examples are penalties and fines, which are not tax deductible, and interest on municipal bonds, which is not taxable.

Financial Statement Presentation

How do I present financial statement information?

Deferred charges and deferred credits must be offset and presented (1) net current and (2) net noncurrent. Deferred tax assets or liabilities are classified according to the related asset or liability to which they apply. For instance, a deferred liability arising from depreciation on a fixed asset would be noncurrent. Deferred taxes not applicable to specific assets or liabilities are classified as current or noncurrent depending on the expected reversal dates of the temporary differences.

Temporary differences reversing within one year are current, but those reversing after one year are noncurrent.

Intraperiod Tax Allocation

How is intraperiod tax allocation handled?

Intraperiod tax allocation takes place when tax expense is shown in different parts of the financial statements for the current year. The income statement presents the tax effect of income from continuing operations, income from discontinued operations, extraordinary items, and the cumulative effect of a change in accounting principle. In the statement of retained earnings, prior-period adjustments are presented net of tax.

Loss Carrybacks and Carryforwards

What about loss carrybacks and carryforwards?

The tax effects of net operating loss carrybacks are allocated to the loss period. A business can carry back a net operating loss two years and receive a tax refund for taxes paid in those years. The loss is first applied to the earliest year; any remaining loss is carried forward up to 20 years.

A loss carryforward can be recognized to the degree that there exist net taxable amounts in the carryforward period (deferred tax liabilities) to absorb them. A loss carryforward benefit can also be recognized if there is more than a 50 percent probability of future realization. Footnote disclosure should be provided of the amounts and expiration dates of operating loss carryforwards.

Deferred Tax Liability versus Deferred Tax Asset

What about the recognition of a deferred tax liability versus a deferred tax asset?

If book income is more than taxable income, then tax expense exceeds tax payable, causing a deferred tax credit. If book income is below taxable income, then tax expense is less than tax payable, resulting in a deferred tax charge.

Example 5.19

Assume that book income and taxable income are both $10,000. Depreciation for book purposes is $1,000 using the straight-line method, whereas depreciation for tax purposes is $2,000 based on the modified accelerated cost recovery system (MACRS) method. If we assume a 40 percent tax rate, the entry is:

Income Tax Expenses ($9,000 × 0.40)	$3,600	
Income Tax Payable ($8,000 × 0.40)		$3,200
Deferred Tax Liability ($1,000 × 0.40)		400

At the end of the asset's life, the deferred tax liability of $400 will be fully reversed.

A deferred tax asset can be recognized when it is more likely than not that the tax benefit will be realized in the future. The phrase *more likely than not* means at least slightly more than a 50 percent probability of occurring. The deferred tax asset must be reduced by a valuation allowance if it is more likely than not that some or all of the deferred tax asset will not be realized. The net amount is the amount likely to be realized. The deferred tax asset would be shown in the balance sheet as presented next, assuming a temporary difference of $200,000, the tax rate of 30 percent, and $140,000 of the tax benefit having a probability in excess of 50 percent of being realized.

Deferred Tax Asset (gross)	
($200,000 × 0.30)	$60,000
Less: Valuation Allowance	
($60,000 × 0.30)	$18,000
Deferred Tax Asset (net)	
($140,000 × 0.30)	$42,000

Example 5.20

In 2X12, a business sold a fixed asset at a gain of $35,000 for book purposes, which was deferred for tax purposes (installment method) until 2X13.

Furthermore, in 2X12, $20,000 of unearned revenue was received. The income was recognized for tax purposes in 2X12 but was deferred for book purposes until 2X13. The deferred tax asset may be recognized because the deductible amount in the future ($20,000) partially offsets the taxable amount ($35,000). Using a 40 percent tax rate and income taxes payable of $50,000, we find the entry in 2X12 is:

Income Tax Expense (balancing figure)	$56,000	
Deferred Tax Asset ($20,000 × 0.40)	8,000	
Deferred Tax Liability ($35,000 × 0.40)		$14,000
Income Tax Payable		50,000

A deferred tax asset can also be recognized for the tax benefit of deductible amounts realizable by carrying back a loss from future years to reduce taxes paid in the current or in a previous year.

IFRS Connection

The classification of deferred taxes under IFRS is always noncurrent. U.S. GAAP classifies deferred taxes based on the classification of the asset or liability to which it relates.

Tax Rates

How do I account for different tax rates in future years?

Deferred taxes are presented at the amounts of settlement when the temporary differences reverse.

Example 5.21

Assume in 2X09 a total temporary difference of $100,000 that will reverse in the future, generating these taxable amounts and tax rates:

	2X10	2X11	2X12	Total
Reversal	$30,000	$50,000	$20,000	$100,000
Tax rate	× 0.40	× 0.35	× 0.33	
Deferred tax liability	$12,000	$17,500	$ 6,600	$ 36,100

On December 31, 2X12, the deferred tax liability is recorded at $36,100.

How do I account for a change in tax rate because of a new tax law?

A change in tax rate must be accounted for immediately by adjusting tax expense and deferred tax.

Example 5.22

Assume that at the end of 2X08, a law is passed lowering the tax rate from 34 to 32 percent beginning in 2X10. In 2X08, the company had a deferred profit of $200,000 and presented a deferred tax liability of $68,000. The gross profit is to be reflected equally in 2X09, 2X10, 2X11, and 2X12. Therefore, the deferred tax liability at the end of 2X08 is $65,000, computed next.

	2X09	2X10	2X11	2X12	Total
Reversal	$50,000	$50,000	$50,000	$50,000	$200,000
Tax rate	× 0.34	× 0.32	× 0.32	× 0.32	
Deferred tax liability	$17,000	$16,000	$16,000	$16,000	$ 65,000

The required journal entry in 2X08 is:

Deferred Tax Liability	$3,000	
Income Tax Expense		$3,000

Footnote disclosures for income taxes include:

- Current and deferred portions of income taxes
- Reconciliation between tax expense per books and tax payable per the tax return
- Reconciliation between the actual and expected tax rates
- Adjustments to tax expense
- Government grants that reduce tax expense
- Tax-related balances due to or from affiliates

Indefinite Reversal

How are indefinite reversals handled?

As per ASC 740-30-05, *Income Taxes—Other Considerations or Special Areas* (APB Opinion 23, *Accounting for Income Taxes—Special Areas*, and APB Opinion 24, *Accounting for Income Taxes*), no interperiod tax allocation is needed for indefinite reversal situations. Indefinite reversal is when undistributed earnings of a foreign subsidiary will indefinitely be postponed as to remission back to the United States or when profit will be remitted in a tax-free liquidation. If a change in circumstances takes place and the assumption of indefinite reversal is no longer applicable, tax expense should be adjusted. Disclosure should be made not only of the declaration to reinvest indefinitely or to remit tax-free, but also of the cumulative amount of undistributed earnings.

Foreign Currency Translation and Transactions

ASC 830-10-15, *Foreign Currency Matters: Overall* (FAS-52, *Foreign Currency Translation*), applies to:

- Foreign currency transactions, such as exports and imports denominated in a currency other than a company's functional currency
- Foreign currency financial statements of branches, divisions, and other investees incorporated in the financial statements of a U.S. company by combination, consolidation, or the equity method

What are the purposes of a translation?

The purposes of translation are to:

- Furnish data of expected impacts of rate changes on cash flow and equity
- Provide data in consolidated financial statements relative to the financial results of each individual foreign consolidated entity

ASC 830-20 covers the translation of foreign currency statements and gains and losses on foreign currency transactions. Translation of foreign currency statements typically is needed when the statements of a foreign subsidiary or equity-method investee having a functional currency other than the U.S. dollar are to be included in the financial statements of a domestic enterprise (e.g., through consolidation or using the equity method).

Notes

Generally, foreign currency statements should be translated using the exchange rate at the end of the reporting year. Resulting translation gains and losses are shown as a separate item in the stockholders' equity section.

Also important is the accounting treatment of gains and losses emanating from transactions denominated in a foreign currency. These are presented in the current year's income statement.

What are important terms in foreign currency?

- *Conversion.* An exchange of one currency for another.
- *Currency swap.* An exchange between two companies of the currencies of two different countries per an agreement to reexchange the two currencies at the same rate of exchange at a specified future date.

- *Denominate.* To pay or receive in that same foreign currency. The payment or receipt can be denominated in only one currency (e.g., pounds). There is a real account (asset or liability) fixed in terms of a foreign currency regardless of exchange rate.
- *Exchange rate.* Ratio between a unit of one currency and that of another at a particular time. If there is a *temporary lack of exchangeability* between two currencies at the transaction date or balance sheet date, the *first rate available* thereafter at which exchanges could be made is used.
- *Foreign currency.* A currency other than the functional currency of a business (e.g., the dollar could be a foreign currency for a foreign entity).
- *Foreign currency statements.* Financial statements using as the unit of measure a functional currency that is not the reporting currency of the business.
- *Foreign currency transactions.* Transactions whose terms are denominated in a currency other than the entity's functional currency. Foreign currency transactions take place when a business:
  - Buys or sells on credit goods or services the prices of which are denominated in foreign currency
  - Borrows or lends funds, and the amounts payable or receivable are denominated in foreign currency
  - Is a party to an unperformed forward exchange contract
  - Acquires or disposes of assets, or incurs or settles liabilities denominated in foreign currency
- *Foreign currency translation.* Expressing in the reporting currency of the company those amounts that are denominated or measured in a different currency.
- *Foreign entity.* An operation (e.g., subsidiary, division, branch, joint venture) whose financial statements are prepared in a currency other than the reporting currency of the reporting entity.
- *Functional currency.* The currency of the primary economic environment in which the business operates. It is typically the currency of the environment in which the business primarily obtains and uses cash. The functional currency of a foreign operation may be the same as that of a related affiliate in the case where the foreign activity is an essential component or extension of the related affiliate.
- *Local currency.* The currency of a particular foreign country.
- *Measure.* To translate into a currency other than the original reporting currency. Foreign financial statements are measured in U.S. dollars by using the applicable exchange rate.
- *Reporting currency.* The currency in which the business prepares its financial statements, usually U.S. dollars.
- *Spot rate.* Exchange rate for immediate delivery of currencies exchanged.
- *Transaction gain or loss.* Transaction gains or losses occur due to a change in exchange rates between the functional currency and the currency in which a foreign currency transaction is denominated. They represent an increase or a decrease in (1) the actual functional currency cash flows realized upon settlement of foreign currency transactions and (2) the expected functional currency cash flows on unsettled foreign currency transactions.
- *Translation adjustments.* Adjustments arising from translating financial statements from the entity's functional currency into the reporting one.

What are the steps in a translation?

Four steps in translating the foreign country's financial statements into U.S. reporting requirements are:

Step 1. Conform the foreign country's financial statements to U.S. GAAP.

Step 2. Determine the functional currency of the foreign entity.

Step 3. Remeasure the financial statements in the functional currency, if necessary. Gains or losses from remeasurement are includable in remeasured current net income.

Step 4. Convert from the foreign currency into U.S. dollars (reporting currency).

What accounting recognition is given to foreign currency?

Prior to translation, the foreign country figures are remeasured in the functional currency. *Example:* If a company in Italy is an independent entity and received cash and incurred expenses in Italy, the euro currency is the functional currency. However, if the Italian company is an extension of a Canadian parent, the functional currency is the Canadian currency.

The functional currency should be consistently used except if material economic changes necessitate a change.

Exception

Previously issued financial statements are not restated for a change in the functional currency.

Consistent use of the functional currency of the foreign entity must exist over the years except if changes in circumstances occur warranting a change. If a change in the functional currency takes place, it is accounted for as a change in estimate.

If a company's books are *not* kept in its functional currency, remeasurement into the functional currency is mandated. The remeasurement process occurs before translation into the reporting currency takes place. When a foreign entity's functional currency is the reporting currency, remeasurement into the reporting currency obviates translation. The remeasurement process is intended to generate the same result as if the entity's books had been kept in the functional currency.

How do I determine the functional currency?

The following guidelines are referred to in determining the functional currency of a foreign operation.

- *Selling price.* The functional currency is the foreign currency when the foreign operation's selling prices of products or services are due primarily to local factors (e.g., government law and competition) and *not* due to changes in exchange rate. The functional currency is the parent's currency when the foreign operation's sales prices mostly apply in the short run to fluctuations in the exchange rate resulting from international factors (e.g., worldwide competition).

- *Market.* The functional currency is the foreign currency when the foreign activity has a strong local sales market for products or services, even though a significant amount of exports may exist. The functional currency is the parent's currency when the foreign operation's sales market is mostly in the parent's country.

- *Cash flow.* The functional currency is the foreign currency when the foreign operation's cash flows are primarily in foreign currency not directly affecting the parent's cash flows. The functional currency is the parent's currency when the foreign operation's cash flows directly impact the parent's cash flows. They are usually available for remittance via intercompany accounting settlement.

- *Financing.* The functional currency is the foreign currency if financing of the foreign activity is in foreign currency and funds obtained by the foreign activity are sufficient to meet debt obligations. The functional currency is the parent's currency when financing of foreign activity is provided by the parent or occurs in U.S. dollars (if a U.S. parent). Funds obtained by the foreign activity are insufficient to satisfy debt requirements.

- *Expenses.* The functional currency is the foreign currency when the foreign operation's production costs or services are usually incurred locally. However, some foreign imports may exist. The functional currency is the parent's currency when the foreign operation's production and service costs are primarily component costs obtained from the parent's country.

- *Intercompany transactions.* If there is a restricted number of intercompany transactions, the functional currency is the foreign currency—that is, when minor interrelationship occurs between the activities of the foreign entity and parent except for competitive advantages (e.g., patents). If many intercompany transactions exist, the functional currency is the parent's currency—that is, when a material interrelationship exists between the foreign entity and the parent.

Translation Process

What currency is used in a translation of inflationary foreign currency statements when the U.S. dollar is the functional currency?

The foreign entity's financial statement in a highly inflationary economy is not stable enough and should be remeasured as if the functional currency were the reporting currency. In effect, the reporting currency is used directly.

A *highly inflationary environment* is one that has cumulative inflation of about *100 percent or more over a three-year period.* In other words, the inflation rate must be increasing at a rate of about 35 percent a year for three consecutive years.

Note

The International Monetary Fund in Washington, D.C., publishes monthly figures on international inflation rates.

What currency is used in a translation of foreign currency statements when the foreign currency is the functional currency?

BALANCE SHEET Items are translated via the *current exchange rate*. For assets and liabilities, use the rate at the balance sheet date. If a current exchange rate is not available at the balance sheet date, use the first exchange rate available after that date. The current exchange rate is also used to translate the statement of cash flows, except for those items found in the income statement that are translated using the weighted-average rate.

INCOME STATEMENT For revenues, expenses, gains, and losses, use the exchange rates at the dates those items are recognized.

Recommendation

Since translation at the exchange rates at the dates when the many revenues, expenses, gains, and losses are recognized is almost always impractical, use a weighted-average exchange rate for the period in translating income statement items.

Disclosure should consist of:

- A material change occurring between the date of the financial statements and the audit report date (this should be disclosed as a subsequent event)
- The effects on unsettled balances pertaining to foreign currency transactions

Translation Adjustments

What are translation adjustments?

If a company's functional currency is a foreign currency, *translation adjustments* arise from translating that company's financial statements into the reporting currency. Translation adjustments are unrealized, and the current year's foreign translation gain or loss should be presented in the income statement under other comprehensive income. However, the total foreign translation gain or loss for all the years should be presented in the stockholders' equity section of the balance sheet under accumulated other comprehensive income.

How do I handle the sale or liquidation of an investment in a foreign entity?

Upon sale or liquidation of an investment in a foreign entity, the amount attributable to that entity and accumulated in the translation adjustment component of equity is removed from the stockholders' equity section. It is considered a part of the gain or loss on sale or liquidation of the investment in the income statement for the period during which the sale or liquidation occurs.

According to ASC 830-30-40-2, *Foreign Currency Matters: Translation of Financial Statements* (FASB Interpretation [FIN] No. 37, *Accounting for Translation Adjustment upon Sale of Part of an Investment in a Foreign Entity*), sale of an investment in a foreign entity may include a partial sale of an ownership interest. In that case, a pro rata amount of the cumulative translation adjustment reflected as a stockholders' equity component can be included in arriving at the gain or loss on sale. *Example:* If a business sells a 40 percent ownership interest in a foreign investment, 40 percent of the translation adjustment applicable to it is included in calculating gain or loss on sale of that ownership interest.

Foreign Currency Transactions

What are foreign currency transactions?

Foreign currency transactions may result in receivables or payables fixed in terms of the amount of foreign currency to be received or paid.

A foreign currency transaction requires settlement in a currency other than the functional currency. A change in exchange rates between the functional currency and the currency in which a transaction is denominated increases or decreases the expected amount of functional currency cash flows upon settlement of the transaction.

How are foreign currency transactions accounted for?

The change in expected functional currency cash flows is a *foreign currency transaction gain or loss* that is typically included in arriving at earnings in the income statement for the period in which the exchange rate is altered. *Example:* A transaction may result in a gain or loss when a British subsidiary has a receivable denominated in pounds from a French customer.

Similarly, a transaction gain or loss (measured from the *transaction date* or the most recent intervening balance sheet date, whichever is later) realized upon settlement of a foreign currency transaction usually should be included in determining net income for the period in which the transaction is settled.

Example 5.23

An exchange gain or loss occurs when the exchange rate changes between the purchase date and the sale date.

Merchandise is bought for 100,000 euros. The exchange rate is 0.77 euros to 1 U.S. dollar. The journal entry is:

Purchases	$129,870	
Accounts Payable		$129,870
(100,000/0.77 = $129,870)		

When the merchandise is paid for, the exchange rate is 0.8 to 1. The journal entry is:

Accounts Payable	$129,870	
Cash		$125,000
(100,000/0.8 = $125,000)		
Foreign exchange gain		4,870

The $125,000, using an exchange rate of 0.8 to 1, can buy 100,000 euros. The transaction gain is the difference between the cash required of $125,000 and the initial liability of $129,870.

Note

A foreign transaction gain or loss has to be determined at each balance sheet date on all recorded foreign transactions that have not been settled.

Example 5.24

A U.S. company sells goods to a customer in Italy; right on 11/15/2X11 for 10,000 euros. The exchange rate is 1 euro to $0.75. Thus, the transaction is worth $7,500 (10,000 euros × 0.75). Payment is due two months later. The entry on 11/15/2X11 is:

Accounts Receivable—Italy	$7,500	
Sales		$7,500

Accounts receivable and sales are measured in U.S. dollars at the transaction date employing the spot rate. Even though the accounts receivable are measured and reported in U.S. dollars, the receivable is fixed in euros. Thus, a transaction gain or loss can occur if the exchange rate changes between the transaction date (11/15/2X11) and the settlement date (1/15/2X12).

Since the financial statements are prepared between the transaction date and settlement date, receivables denominated in a currency other than the functional currency (U.S. dollar) must be restated to reflect the spot rate on the balance sheet date. On December 31, 2X11, the exchange rate is 1 euro equals $0.80. Hence, the 10,000 euros are now valued at $8,000 (10,000 × $0.80). Therefore, the accounts receivable denominated in euros should be upwardly adjusted by $500. The required journal entry on 12/31/2X11 is:

Accounts Receivable—Italy	$500	
Foreign Exchange Gain		$500

(continued)

(Continued)

The income statement for the year ended 12/31/2X11 shows an exchange gain of $500. Note that the sales account is not affected by the exchange gain since sales relate to operational activity.

On 1/15/2X12, the spot rate is 1 euro = $0.78. The journal entry is:

Cash	$7,800	
Foreign Exchange Loss	200	
Accounts Receivable—Italy		$8,000

The 2X12 income statement shows an exchange loss of $200.

Accounting Standards Update

Accounting Standards Update (ASU) No. 2010-19 (May 2010), *Foreign Currency* (Topic 830), *Foreign Currency Issues*

In the case of a foreign company's financial statements in a highly inflationary environment, there should be a remeasurement (assuming the functional currency is the reporting currency). If there is a difference existing before using the mandates of a highly inflationary accounting between the financial reporting balances and the U.S. dollar–denominated balances, it should be reflected in the profit and loss statement. Disclosure should be made of translation and remeasurement rates, why U.S. dollar–denominated balances are different from financial reporting balances, and the reasons why different rates were employed for translation and remeasurment.

What transaction gains and losses can be excluded from determination of net income?

Gains and losses on the following foreign currency transactions are not included in earnings but rather reported as translation adjustments:

- Foreign currency transactions designated as *economic hedges* of a net investment in a foreign entity, beginning as of the designation date
- Intercompany foreign currency transactions of a *long-term investment* nature (settlement is not planned or expected in the foreseeable future), when the entities to the transaction are consolidated, combined, or accounted for by the equity method in the reporting company's financial statements

A gain or loss on a forward contract or other foreign currency transaction that is intended to *hedge* an identifiable foreign currency commitment (e.g., an agreement to buy or sell machinery) should be deferred and included in the measurement of the related foreign currency transaction.

> **Note**
>
> Losses should not be deferred if it is anticipated that deferral would cause losses to be recognized in subsequent periods.

A foreign currency transaction is considered a hedge of an identifiable foreign currency commitment provided both of these criteria are satisfied:

- The foreign currency transaction is designated as a hedge of a foreign currency commitment.
- The foreign currency commitment is firm.

Forward Exchange Contracts

What is a forward exchange contract?

A forward exchange contract is an agreement to exchange different currencies at a given future date and at a specified rate (forward rate). A forward contract is a foreign currency transaction.

How do I handle forward contracts?

A gain or loss on a forward contract that does not meet the conditions described next is included in net income.

> **Note**
>
> Currency swaps are accounted for in a similar fashion.

- A *gain or loss on a forward contract*, except a speculative forward contract, should be computed by multiplying the foreign currency amount of the forward contract by the difference between the *spot rate* at the balance sheet date and the spot rate at the date of inception of the forward contract.
- The *discount or premium on a forward contract* (the foreign currency amount of the contract multiplied by the difference between the contracted forward rate and the spot rate at the date of inception of the contract) should be accounted for separately from the gain or loss on the contract. It should be included in computing net income over the life of the forward contract.
- A *gain or loss on a speculative forward contract* (a contract that does not hedge an exposure) should be computed by multiplying the foreign currency amount of the forward contract by the difference between the forward rate available from the remaining maturity of the contract and the contracted forward rate (or the forward rate last used to measure a gain or loss on that contract for an earlier period).

Note

No separate accounting recognition is given to the discount or premium on a speculative forward contract.

Hedging

How can foreign currency transactions be hedged?

Foreign currency transactions' gains and losses on assets and liabilities, denominated in a currency other than the functional currency, can be hedged if the U.S. company enters into a forward exchange contract.

A hedge can occur even if a forward exchange contract does not exist. *Example:* A foreign currency transaction can serve as an economic hedge offsetting a parent's net investment in a foreign entity when the transaction is entered into for hedging purposes and is effective.

Example 5.25

A U.S. parent completely owns a French subsidiary having net assets of $3 million in euros. The U.S. parent can borrow $3 million euros to hedge its net investment in the French subsidiary. Also assume that the euro is the functional currency and that the $3 million obligation is denominated in euros. Variability in the exchange rate for euros does not have a net impact on the parent's consolidated balance sheet, since increases in the translation adjustments balance arising from translation of the net investment will be netted against decreases in this balance emanating from the adjustment of the liability denominated in euros.

Derivative Products

What are derivatives?

A derivative is defined as a contract whose value is tied to the return in stocks, bonds, currencies, or commodities. Derivatives can also be contracts derived from an indicator such as interest rates or from a stock market or other index. For example, swaps usually are designed to track the interest rates or currencies.

ASC 815-10-05, *Derivatives and Hedging: Overall* (FAS-133, *Accounting for Derivative Instruments and Hedging Activities*), and ASC 815-20-25, *Derivatives and Hedging: Hedging—General* (FAS-138, *Accounting for Certain Derivative Instruments and Certain Hedging Activities—An Amendment of FASB Statement No. 133*), permit hedge accounting for foreign currency derivatives only if the following three conditions are satisfied:

1. The derivative is used to hedge either a fair value exposure or a cash flow exposure.

2. The derivative is highly effective in offsetting changes in the fair value or cash flows.
3. The derivative is documented as a hedge.

A fair value exposure exists if changes in exchange rates can affect the fair value of assets or liabilities. If the exposure is not hedged, it must have the potential to affect net income. A fair value hedge also may exist for foreign currency firm commitments.

A cash flow exposure exists if changes in exchange rates can affect the amount of cash flow that will be realized from a transaction, where changes in cash flow are reflected in net income.

To use hedge accounting, derivatives must be designated as either a fair value hedge or a cash flow hedge. An entity may use either a fair value hedge or a cash flow hedge for:

- Recognized foreign currency assets and liabilities
- Foreign currency firm commitments

Hedges of forecasted foreign currency transactions can qualify for only a cash flow hedge. Gains or losses on fair value hedges are recognized immediately in net income, whereas gains or losses on cash flow hedges are included in other comprehensive income.

To use hedge accounting, the hedge must be expected to be highly effective in offsetting gains and losses on the items being hedged. Critical terms of the hedging instrument, such as currency type, amount, and settlement date, should match those of the hedged item. The hedging entity should document the:

- Hedged item
- Hedging instrument
- Nature of risk
- Means of assessing the hedging instrument's effectiveness
- Management's objectives and strategies for undertaking the hedge

FAS-161, *Disclosures about Derivative Instruments and Hedging Activities—An Amendment of FASB Statement No. 133* (ASC 815-10-15-2, ASC 815-10-65-1), requires enhanced disclosures about the company's derivative and hedging activities thereby improving the transparency of financial reporting. This applies to all entities and all derivatives and hedged items.

What are specific enhanced disclosure requirements about derivative instruments and hedging activities?

Under ASC 815, a company must provide enhanced disclosures about (1) how and why a company uses derivative instruments, (2) how derivative instruments and related hedged items are accounted for, and (3) how derivative instruments and related hedged items impact a company's financial position, financial performance, and cash flows. Disclosure is required of the objective for using derivative instruments with respect to underlying risk and accounting designation. Further, disclosure is made of fair value of derivative instruments and their gains or losses in tabular format.

Finally, there should be disclosure of credit-risk-related contingent features to assess the company's liquidity from using derivatives. Disclosures for every reporting period for which a statement of financial position is issued are made for derivatives (and hedging nonderivatives) with contingent features that are related to credit risk:

- Nature of the features, how they may be activated in derivatives that are in a net liability position, and the aggregate fair values of such instruments
- An aggregate fair value of posted collateral, potentially required collateral, and immediate settlement amounts

Insurance Contracts

How do you account for insurance contracts?

FAS-163, *Accounting for Financial Guarantee Insurance Contracts—An Interpretation of FASB Statement No. 60* (ASC 944-20-15-66), requires that an insurance company record a claim liability before a default (insured event) when evidence exists of credit deterioration occurring in an insured financial obligation. ASC 944 is limited to financial guarantee insurance and reinsurance contracts, and is effective for financial statements issued for fiscal years beginning after December 15, 2008.

ASC 944FAS-163 relates to recognizing and measuring premium revenue and claim liabilities and to disclosures. The premium revenue recognition approach for a financial guarantee insurance contract links premium revenue recognition to the amount of insurance protection and the period it applies to. The amount of insurance protection provided is a function of the insured principal amount outstanding.

The recognition approach for a claim liability applying to a financial guarantee insurance contract mandates that an insurance company record a claim liability when the insurance company anticipates that a claim loss will be more than unearned premium revenue. The claim loss is based on the present value of anticipated net cash outflows to be paid, discounted using a risk-free rate.

U.S. GAAP versus IFRS

For several years, major accounting and reporting differences have existed between U.S. GAAP and international reporting standards. However, in a 2002 Memorandum of Understanding between the FASB and the IASB, commonly known as the Norwalk Agreement (http://72.3.243.42/news/memorandum.pdf), the two accounting standard-setting bodies made a firm commitment to develop high-quality accounting standards that converge. In effect, this effort has been a movement toward a globalization of accounting standards. Since the Norwalk Agreement, the FASB and IASB have issued new standards that closely converged and have revised many existing ones in order to attain a near-uniform set of accounting standards. While the challenge for practitioners is to learn and eventually implement this new set of global accounting standards, the benefits of a single set of worldwide standards are expected to produce financial reporting that is more comparable and transparent and achieves greater understandability. The American Institute of Certified Public Accountants (AICPA) amended Rules 202 and 203 of the AICPA Code of Professional Conduct by inserting the IASB into the allowable rules.

As of this writing, the U.S. Securities and Exchange Commission (SEC) has temporarily halted early adoption of IFRS. In the United States, registered companies were scheduled to issue financial statements using IFRS in 2014 as part of a proposed road map. The original time line for IFRS convergence with U.S. GAAP is as follows: U.S. companies registered with the SEC are currently required to file financial statements in accordance with U.S. GAAP. Foreign private issuers have been allowed to issue financial statements in accordance with IFRS without footnote reconciliation to U.S. GAAP. On August 27, 2008, the SEC voted unanimously to adopt a road map for convergence of accounting standards, thus adopting IFRS in the United States by as early as 2010 and requiring all companies to file financial statements under IFRS by 2014. In January 2009, the SEC announced that registered companies would be required to file with a two-year dual-reporting period beginning in 2012; by 2014, all large U.S. companies would be required to file financial statements using IFRS, with smaller U.S. companies delaying IFRS filing until 2016. However, on February 24, 2010, the SEC withdrew proposed rules that would have allowed early adoption of IFRS and announced it would table the decision until 2011. In addition, the SEC indicated that it was not ruling out the possibility that registered companies could be permitted to select to issue financial statements using either U.S. GAAP or IFRS. SEC Chairman Mary Schapiro formally indicated that the Commission is expected to issue its recommendation sometime in 2011. As of this writing, however, no action has been taken by the SEC.

In an effort to better understand how convergence will affect financial reporting in the United States, depending on the IFRS adoption action taken by the SEC in 2011, this chapter examines some of the material differences that currently exist between U.S. GAAP and IFRS.

What are the major differences between the proposed presentation of IFRS financial statements and the current presentation under U.S. GAAP?

Financial statements required under U.S. GAAP and IFRS are largely similar. IFRS requires a statement of financial position similar to U.S. GAAP, an income statement, a statement of changes in equity or a statement of recognized income and expense (reported as a separate financial statement), statement of cash flows, and disclosure notes, including a summary of significant accounting policies. Under U.S. GAAP, comprehensive income and changes in equity are reported as a separate financial statement (allowable under IFRS, and reported as a statement of changes in equity) or reported in the notes to the financial statements (not allowed under IFRS). However, U.S. GAAP allows for a combined statement of income and comprehensive income, which is not allowed under IFRS.

Unlike U.S. GAAP, IFRS requires comparative information on each financial statement for the preceding period only, with the option of providing additional years of comparable reporting. SEC registrants are required to present information on the current year and the prior year on the balance sheet, while other financial statements are required to report three years of comparable results.

In addition, in regard to consolidated financial reporting, under U.S. GAAP, the parent firm must present consolidated financial statements. However, IFRS allows for exemptions if the parent is a wholly owned or partially owned subsidiary, the parent does not trade bond or equity instruments in the public market, or it did not file (or will not file) financial statements with a regulatory agency.

How do you compare and contrast the approaches to income measurement and fair value use under IFRS and U.S. GAAP?

Both U.S. GAAP and IFRS recognize accrual accounting as the key concept underlying income measurement. However, IFRS and U.S. GAAP differ in their income measurement in that IFRS emphasizes measurement of assets and liabilities on the balance sheet at fair value and U.S. GAAP emphasizes the matching rule and measurement of items on the income statement. Whereas U.S. GAAP has various notions of value, including fair value, IFRS permits the use of a single concept of fair value as an exit value—that is, the amount an asset may be exchanged for or a liability settled between knowledgeable parties in an arm's-length transaction.

What are U.S. GAAP–IFRS differences affecting the statement of financial position?

Cash and Cash Equivalents

Cash and cash equivalents are defined similarly under IFRS and U.S. GAAP. However, U.S. GAAP does not allow bank overdraft offsets to the cash account and reports them as a liability. The only exception where offsetting is allowable is in the case of two accounts held by the same bank; an overdrawn account may be offset against another account in the same institution. IFRS allows offsetting of overdrafts to cash as long as it is integral to the entity's cash management.

Receivables

Under U.S. GAAP, receivables are not reported at fair value. However, under IFRS they are initially reported at fair value, with subsequent adjustments accounted for using amortized cost (effective interest method). In addition, under U.S. GAAP, an estimate of bad debts impacts earnings on the income statement. When a receivable is deemed uncollectible using the allowance method for accounting for bad debts, the write-off of the specific account does not impact earnings; any recovery of a previously written-off account also does not impact earnings. Under IFRS, impairment losses previously recognized on the income statement may be reversed in subsequent years, adjusting earnings. U.S. GAAP prohibits reversals of impairment losses on bad debts.

Inventories

U.S. GAAP generally measures inventory at lower of cost or market; under IFRS, inventory is measured at lower of cost or net realizable value (estimated selling price less estimated costs of completion and sale). IFRS includes distribution and marketing costs in its cost of sales, whereas U.S. GAAP excludes marketing costs in determining cost of sale.

Inventory write-downs under GAAP are normally determined on either an item-by-item, group, or categorical basis. IFRS writes inventory down to net realizable value (floor) on an item-by-item basis, but allows write-downs to occur by groups of similar products in special circumstances. In addition, any inventory write-downs under U.S. GAAP cannot subsequently be reversed, whereas IFRS allows previous inventory write-down reversals to be recognized in the same period as the write-down.

U.S. GAAP allows for the cost of inventory to be calculated using first in, first out (FIFO); last in, first out (LIFO); or a weighted-average calculation. IFRS allows FIFO and weighted-average calculation, but prohibits use of LIFO.

Investments

Accounting for trading, available-for-sale, and held-to-maturity instruments is similar between U.S. GAAP and IFRS. One clarifying difference is that under IFRS, securities are called *assets*, which is a much broader category. As with securities (asset) classification, under IFRS, any nontrading financial asset is classified as available for sale; under U.S. GAAP, only debt securities and marketable equity securities are classified as available-for-sale investments. Another major difference exists with unrealized gains and losses of available-for-sale securities, which are reported in comprehensive income under U.S. GAAP, whereas under IFRS, such gains and losses are reported in the equity section of the balance sheet. In addition, IFRS allows for impairment reversals for only available-for-sale debt (not equity) securities and held-to-maturity securities, while U.S. GAAP does not permit impairment reversals of any investments.

Another key difference is with debt security impairment. Under U.S. GAAP, a debt security is classified as other than temporarily impaired (OTTI) if the entity has the positive intent to sell an impaired debt security, or if the entity does not expect to recover the full amortized cost basis of the security and more likely than not will be required to sell the security prior to its recovery, or if the debt security has a credit loss. Under IFRS, a debt security is deemed to be impaired if there is objective evidence of impairment and the estimated future cash flows of the security are adversely affected. IFRS requires that impairment losses on debt securities are recognized in current earnings, whereas U.S. GAAP records other than temporarily impaired debt securities in other comprehensive income. Last, under U.S. GAAP, an equity security is other than temporarily impaired if the decline is considered significant *and* prolonged, whereas under IFRS, impairment is recorded if the decline is *either* significant *or* prolonged.

EQUITY-METHOD INVESTMENTS Both U.S. GAAP and IFRS account for investments where the investor possesses significant influence over the investee, holding at least 20 percent and up to 50 percent of an investee's outstanding stock but lacking control over the entity. IFRS refers to an equity investment as an investment in associates. Additionally, IFRS requires that the investee and investor firms follow the same accounting policies, whereas U.S. GAAP does not require such a practice.

Property, Plant, and Equipment

In general, U.S. GAAP and IFRS treat the accounting for property, plant, and equipment similarly, including the initial accounting for all costs necessary to bring the asset to its intended use. Under IFRS, International Accounting Standard (IAS) 16.16(b) describes costs of property, plant, and equipment as "any costs directly attributable to bring an asset to the location and condition necessary for it to be capable of operating in a manner intended by management." Additionally, there are no differences in depreciation methods used. Differences exist primarily in the treatment of capitalized interest, the components approach for depreciation, and the subsequent revaluation of the asset's fair value.

Interest incurred is capitalized under U.S. GAAP only during construction of a qualifying asset. Under IFRS, interest costs of borrowing may either be capitalized for the acquisition, construction, or production of a qualifying asset or be expensed in the period incurred. Whichever method selected must be consistently applied.

IAS 16, *Property, Plant and Equipment* requires that upon initial recognition of a depreciable asset, costs are allocated to significant components of the assets (including nonphysical components). Each component is then separately depreciated. For example, a roof would be one component and the remainder of the structure would be a separate component—each having different useful lives and depreciated separately. In addition, subsequent expenditures must be capitalized to the asset as long as probable future economic benefits will flow to the entity and the costs can be reliably measured. U.S. GAAP does not follow the components approach to depreciation.

Another difference between U.S. GAAP and IFRS is in the revaluation of property, plant, and equipment. U.S. GAAP requires that property, plant, and equipment be accounted for using the cost method. Under IFRS, the value of property, plant, and equipment is reported on a company's books at fair value less accumulated depreciation and impairment losses (if any). The accumulated depreciation account is used to revalue plant and equipment with the permission of two treatments, which use a revaluation surplus account. When a depreciable asset is revalued, depreciation is also revalued over the remaining useful life of the asset.

IAS 16 allows for two revaluation alternatives: revaluation of specific assets regularly or revaluation of assets of the same class. When revaluation occurs under IFRS and the revaluation requires a write-up (increase) to the asset (assuming no previous downward revaluation), the asset is debited and the incremental increase is credited to a surplus account (revaluation surplus account), which is an equity account. If there is a write-down (decrease) to the asset (assuming no previous upward revaluation), such downward revaluation is debited to an expense and the asset's book value is credited. If there had been a previous upward revaluation (causing surplus recognition) and a current downward revaluation occurs, the write-down cannot exceed the amount in the revaluation surplus account. Examples 5.26 through 5.28 deal with a land revaluation.

Example 5.26

Assume in year 1 QRS Corp. owns land costing $500,000 with a current fair value of $550,000. The journal entry to adjust the book value of the land to reflect its fair value is:

Land	$50,000	
Revaluation Surplus—Land		$50,000

Any subsequent decreases in the fair value of the land would be offset against the revaluation surplus account, with any excess charged to an expense.

Example 5.27

Assume in the following year (year 2), the fair value of QRS Corp.'s land has decreased to $480,000. The journal entry to adjust the book value of the land to reflect its fair value (with previous upward revaluation) is:

Revaluation Surplus—Land	$50,000	
Loss on Revaluation—Land*	20,000	
Land		$70,000

*The loss on revaluation is treated as an expense of the period.

For previous revaluation that had resulted in the recognition of an expense, followed by any subsequent revaluations resulting in an increase to the fair value of the asset, such incremental increases should be recognized as income to the extent of the previously recognized expense; any excess revaluation increase would be credited to the revaluation surplus account.

Example 5.28

Assume in year 3, the fair value of QRS Corp.'s land is $510,000. Given that there was a recent downward revaluation in year 2, the journal entry to adjust the book value of the land to reflect its fair value is:

Land	$30,000	
Revaluation Surplus—Land		$10,000
Gain on Revaluation—Land*		20,000

*The gain on revaluation is recognized as income in year 3 to the extent of expense recognition in the previous year(s).

Revaluations Involving Depreciable Assets

When depreciable assets are revalued annually, IAS 16 allows for two permissible treatments. The first is offsetting accumulated depreciation against the gross book value of the depreciable asset, with the difference restated to reflect the revalued amount of the asset.

Example 5.29

Assume KRF Corp. owns a building that cost $2,000,000 and has accumulated depreciation of $400,000, with a book value of $1,600,000. Assume KRF Corp.

(continued)

(Continued)

revalues the building to reflect its fair value of $1,800,000. Under this treatment, KRF Corp. would first remove its accumulated depreciation of $400,000, reducing the building by that amount of expired cost. Then, in the second entry, the building would be debited for $200,000 and the revaluation surplus credited, reflecting the net amount that is being restated. The entries are:

Accumulated Depreciation—Building	$400,000	
Building		$400,000
Building	200,000	
Revaluation Surplus—Building		200,000

The second permissible treatment is that accumulated depreciation is proportionately restated with the change in the revalued asset; the result is the book value of the asset, after revaluation, equaling the revalued amount of the asset.

Example 5.30

Assume KRF Corp. owns a building that cost $2,000,000 and has accumulated depreciation of $400,000, with a book value of $1,600,000. Assume KRF Corp. revalues the building to reflect its fair value of $1,800,000. KRF Corp. would restate the building account and accumulated depreciation based on the ratio of net book value to the revalued assets, which is 80 percent ($1,600,000/$2,000,000), and the entry is:

Building	$250,000*	
Accumulated Depreciation—Building		$ 50,000
Revaluation Surplus—Building		200,000

*$200,000 ÷ 80% = $250,000

The result of this entry will provide a book value that equals the revalued amount of the building.

Intangible Assets and Goodwill

U.S. GAAP and IFRS are similar in their definition of an intangible asset, which lacks physical substance and is not viewed as a financial asset. In addition, U.S. GAAP and IFRS consider intangibles as identifiable assets if they are separable or as a result of contractual or legal rights. Goodwill, in particular, is viewed similarly by both as a residual that arises from a business combination and is not amortized but is tested annually for impairment. Some significant differences do exist, however.

While U.S. GAAP bases amortization of intangibles based on historical cost less any impairment, IFRS allows revaluation of the value of the intangible by crediting any upward revision to the asset to a revaluation surplus account and adjusted against equity; downward revisions to fair value reduce the revaluation surplus account (until the account declines to zero). In addition, impairment for intangibles is treated differently under U.S. GAAP and IFRS (see the "Impairment" section later in this chapter).

Regarding research and development costs, such costs are segregated into two types: research phase costs and developmental phase costs. Under both U.S. GAAP and IFRS, research phase costs are expensed in the period incurred. Developmental phase costs are expensed in the period incurred under U.S. GAAP. Under IFRS, such costs are similarly expensed unless technological feasibility is achieved. If technical feasibility results, such development costs are capitalized only if there is an intention to complete the developed asset, if there exists an ability to either use or sell the asset, if future economic benefits are reasonably expected to result, and if the entity provides adequate resources to finish development of the asset. With regard to in-process research and development costs that are acquired as part of a business combination, U.S. GAAP and IFRS standards have converged, where acquired in-process research and development costs are capitalized and amortized, with annual testing for impairment.

Contingent Liabilities

U.S. GAAP and IFRS measure contingent liabilities similarly in that such a liability can be recognized only if the outcome is probable and can be reasonably estimated. However, IFRS contains a slight difference in estimating the contingent liability. Whereas U.S. GAAP uses a more conservative (low-end) estimate in recording the liability, IFRS recognizes a contingent liability at the midpoint of the estimate range.

Defined Benefit Plans

Under U.S. GAAP, prior service costs are retroactive benefits from a plan amendment based on the expected future service life of such participants. These prior service costs are often amortized proportionately (or using a straight-line basis) over the expected future period of service. IFRS uses the terminology *past service costs* and recognizes such costs using a straight-line basis over the average remaining service period until the amended benefits are vested. Therefore, under IFRS, entities are amortizing past service costs over a shorter period of time. Under IAS 19.96, should any past service costs be vested at the time the plan is amended, the entity must recognize them in the period of the amendment. U.S. GAAP makes no distinction as to whether the employees are vested or not vested.

Another area yet to be converged in regard to defined benefit plans is the issue of actuarial valuations and the measurement date. Under U.S. GAAP, actuarial valuations are required to be performed annually and are mandated by Employee Retirement Income Security Act (ERISA) regulations. In addition, the measurement date for valuation of the plan assets and the projected benefit obligation is the balance sheet date, unless a specific event causes a need for remeasurement. Under IFRS, there is no mandate as to the frequency of actuarial valuations; however, IAS

19.77 requires valuation results to be updated as of the balance sheet date for any significant changes since the previous valuation.

In addition to prior (past) service cost treatment, there are differences in procedures on handling actuarial gains and losses. Actuarial gains and losses are the differences between the actual result and the expected result in the valuation of the projected benefit obligation and plan assets. U.S. GAAP and IFRS allow a choice for recognition of actuarial gains and losses. Under U.S. GAAP, any actuarial gains and losses measured can be reflected as part of other comprehensive income (OCI) to the extent they are not recognized in earnings on the income statement. Alternatively, such gains and losses are permitted to be recognized in earnings in a systematic and rational method resulting in more rapid recognition than if the corridor method is used. Actuarial gains and losses that are recognized in accumulated other comprehensive income (AOCI) are reclassified to current earnings using a corridor approach (or using an alternative approach if it results in faster recognition). IFRS allows actuarial gains and losses to be recognized completely in either OCI or earnings of the period, or recognized in earnings using a corridor method (or using an alternative approach if it results in faster recognition).

U.S. GAAP also requires recognition of the funded status of the pension, either as a net pension asset or as a net pension liability. IFRS does not require funded status recognition on the balance sheet. As for asset ceilings, U.S. GAAP does not limit the amount of net pension assets, whereas under IFRS the prepaid pension amount is limited by an asset ceiling.

Income Tax Deferrals

In accounting for deferred income tax differences, U.S. GAAP and IFRS use the asset and liability approach in recognizing future tax differences arising from present transactions. There are a few differences in approaches. First, U.S. GAAP's recognition of a deferred tax asset (or liability) is based on the assumption that the underlying asset (or liability) will eventually be reversed (or recovered or settled) in a manner consistent with its use in the business. IFRS recognizes deferred taxes based on the expected manner of settlement or recovery.

Second, U.S. GAAP employs an asset valuation account to the extent that it is *more likely than not* that the deferred tax asset will eventually be realized (or reversed) at a future date. Under IFRS, a deferred tax asset is recognized if it is *probable* that it will eventually be realized (or reversed) in the future. Therefore, IFRS has a higher recognition threshold.

Third, U.S. GAAP allows for a deferred tax asset or liability classification to be either current or noncurrent, based on the classification of the related asset or liability. IFRS instead classifies all deferred tax differences as noncurrent.

Fourth, IFRS measures the deferred tax based on tax rates that are enacted or substantively enacted at the reporting date, whereas U.S. GAAP uses only the enacted tax rates at the reporting date (and ignores estimated future tax rate adjustments).

Fifth, one of the more relatively pervasive concerns is the temporary book-tax differences with regard to revaluations of property, plant, and equipment. IFRS requires that such temporary differences be recognized directly into equity; U.S. GAAP currently does not allow for such revaluations, so no deferred tax differences would exist.

Sixth, under U.S. GAAP, intercompany profits are derived using the seller's tax rate, whereas under IFRS, such intercompany profits are calculated using the buyer's tax rate. In addition, under U.S. GAAP, deferred tax liabilities are recognized on domestic subsidiaries if greater than 80 percent owned; IFRS does not recognize deferred taxes for joint ventures or investments in subsidiaries if the parent controls the timing of the deferred tax reversal and it is probable that the temporary difference is not expected to immediately reverse.

Finally, the last substantive difference exists with foreign nonmonetary assets. Under IFRS, deferred taxes are recognized for any differences related to foreign nonmonetary assets remeasured from the local to functional currency, whereas under U.S. GAAP deferred taxes are not recognized for such functional currency remeasurements.

Lease Accounting

U.S. GAAP and IFRS recognize the economic substance of recording leases of both the lessor and the lessee. However, there are some relatively significant differences in the accounting treatments. While U.S. GAAP refers to *capital lease* treatment, IFRS terminology refers to such leases as *finance leases*. Under U.S. GAAP, leased assets consist of only property, plant, and equipment, whereas under IFRS, the leased asset can consist of other types of assets, including leases to explore mineral or natural resources and other licensing agreements (e.g., motion pictures, plays, and manuscripts). U.S. GAAP is more rules-based; for example, four criteria are used by the lessee and lessor (plus two required additional criteria for the lessor) in determining if a lease should be capitalized. Many of these criteria are quantitative thresholds. IFRS similarly focuses on recording a lease where it transfers substantially all of the risks and rewards of ownership from the lessor to the lessee. Unlike the specific quantitative criteria under U.S. GAAP, IFRS provides a series of indicators that are used to determine whether a lease is classified as a finance lease. This criteria determination is much more general than U.S. GAAP and is not rules-based.

Another difference involves the accounting for executory costs. U.S. GAAP expenses and excludes specific costs from the calculation of minimum lease payments, including insurance, maintenance, and taxes, whereas IFRS excludes costs for services and taxes from minimum lease payments. Last, the present value of the minimum lease payment by the lessee is computed under U.S. GAAP as the *lower of* the lessor's implicit rate (if known by the lessee) or the lessee's incremental borrowing rate. IFRS uses the interest rate implicit in the lease if known by the lessee. If the lessee lacks knowledge of such rate, then the lessee uses its incremental borrowing rate.

Equity

There are several differences in the classification of items in the equity section of the statement of financial position under U.S. GAAP and IFRS. First, "common stock" is referred to as "share capital" under IFRS, "additional paid-in capital" is reported as "share premium" under IFRS, and "retained earnings" are often referred to as "accumulated profit and loss" or "retained profits." Similar to U.S. GAAP, treasury stock under IFRS is reported as a reduction to shareholders' equity; however,

IFRS allows treasury stock amounts to be offset against specific equity accounts. Furthermore, IFRS does not recognize gains or losses on the disposition of treasury shares and, instead, makes an adjustment to equity. Under U.S. GAAP, using the cost method, proceeds in excess of the purchase price are generally credited to a specific paid-in capital account from treasury stock, while subsequent losses are reduced from the paid-in capital account (to the extent of its balance) and then any residual is deducted from retained earnings.

In addition to the standard items classified in the equity section of the statement of financial position, two other common classification issues exist: the treatment of convertible bonds and the reporting of noncontrolling (minority) interest in a subsidiary. For corporate bonds that are convertible into common shares, U.S. GAAP reports such financial instruments as debt. However, under IFRS, proceeds of a debt instrument that are convertible into common shares are allocated between debt (reported at fair value) and equity (reported at residual value). As for reporting on noncontrolling interest in a subsidiary, U.S. GAAP formerly reported minority interest in the "mezzanine section" of the balance sheet. However, U.S. GAAP and IFRS methods recently converged and now report noncontrolling interest in a subsidiary in the equity section.

What are U.S. GAAP–IFRS differences affecting the income statement?

Revenue Recognition

One of the more complex differences between U.S. GAAP and IFRS is in the area of revenue recognition. IAS 18, *Revenue* deals with revenue recognition issues, specifically when to recognize revenues from the sale of goods or services, interest, dividend income, and royalties. Other revenue recognition issues are reflected in other IFRS pronouncements. For the most part, under IFRS income is the framework, with revenue being a subset of income. Conversely, under U.S. GAAP, revenue is considered an element of the income statement, whereas income is not considered an element, but a calculated result. Under U.S. GAAP, revenue is generally recognized when a product has been delivered or a service performed, the sales price is fixed and determinable, and collectability is reasonably assured. Following are some specific U.S. GAAP–IFRS differences involving revenue recognition.

SALE OF GOODS   Revenue recognition principles appear in several areas of authority within the literature, particularly with the application of the concepts of *realized*, *recognized*, and *earned* revenue. In addition, the SEC offers specific guidance on revenue recognition for listed companies. The IASB does not receive guidance from a regulatory body such as the SEC. Further, U.S. GAAP has several areas of specific industry guidance with regard to revenue recognition; IFRS has no industry guidance.

IFRS uses a risks and reward model when applying revenue recognition under IAS 18. In applying IFRS, revenue is generally recognized when probable economic benefits exist, the item(s) of revenue *and* costs can be reliably measured, the significant risks and rewards of ownership are conveyed from the seller to the buyer, and the seller does not retain managerial involvement to the degree of ownership or retain effective control over the buyer. According to ASC 605-10-S99, *Revenue Recognition—Overall—SEC Materials* (Staff Accounting Bulletin [SAB] No. 104), if there is to be revenue recognition from the sale of goods, there needs to be persuasive evidence of an arrangement, collectibility of the revenue is reasonably assured, the sales price is fixed and determinable, and the delivery occurred or services were rendered. Under IFRS, collectibility is not mentioned in IAS 18, but is considered inherent in the standard by the mention of the receipt of probable future economic benefits.

BILL-AND-HOLD TRANSACTIONS Under U.S. GAAP, revenue is recognized under bill-and-hold transactions after:

- The risks of ownership have passed to the buyer.
- The customer has a fixed commitment to purchase the goods.
- The buyer requests that the transaction be processed on a bill-and-hold basis.
- The buyer has a substantial business purpose for placing the order on a buy-and-hold basis.
- The seller cannot retain any performance obligations that would taint the completion of the earnings process.
- The acquired goods have to be held separate from the seller's inventory and not be used to fill orders.
- The product is ready for delivery.
- There is a fixed schedule for delivery to the buyer that includes the date of delivery consistent with the buyer's business purpose.

Under IFRS, revenue recognition for bill-and-hold arrangements occurs when the buyer takes title, provided it is probable that delivery will occur; goods are on hand, identified, and ready for delivery to the buyer; the buyer acknowledges deferred delivery arrangements; and usual payment terms exist. However, one noteworthy aspect of both U.S. GAAP and IFRS is that any time a buyer requests a delay in the delivery of goods, but takes title and acknowledges receipt of the invoice, revenue is not yet recognized. The seller still has to pay for storage, delivery, and insurance costs on the goods, so the significant risks and rewards have not yet passed to the buyer. Under IFRS, written orders are not required; however, U.S. GAAP requires that if written orders are customary business practices, then that format would be needed as evidence of the transaction.

MULTIPLE-ELEMENT ARRANGEMENTS A multiple-element contract involves goods sold with subsequent maintenance or support offered for no additional cost (such as a warranty). Under IFRS, revenue is recognized under IAS 18 based on separability of identifiable components of a transaction, and revenue is allocated to each component usually based on relative fair market value. IAS 18, paragraph 19, requires full revenue recognition and an accrual of costs. This approach ignores the matching principle.

Under U.S. GAAP, ASC 605-25-25, *Revenue Recognition—Multiple-Element Arrangements* (Emerging Issues Task Force [EITF] 08-01) provides criteria for separating the contract components in such arrangements. In general, the total consideration received should be allocated to each element of the contract based on relative fair values.

LONG-TERM CONSTRUCTION CONTRACTS   Under U.S. GAAP, ASC 605-35-25, *Revenue Recognition 35 Construction-Type and Production-Type Contracts* (Statement of Position [SOP] 81-1) permits, with specific guidance, the use of either the percentage of completion method, completed contract method (on a limited basis), or zero-profit method for recognition of gross profits for long-term construction contracts. Corresponding revenues and expenses related to the construction project are recognized on the income statement either by computing a ratio of stages of completion (using a cost-to-cost approach or other reasonable method) or basing recognition on the actual costs incurred of the project and deferring revenue recognition until project completion.

Under IFRS, IAS 11, *Construction Contracts* permits use of either the percentage of completion method or zero-profit method to account for long-term construction contracts. IAS 11 does not permit the completed contract method; therefore, revenues are recognized only by computing a ratio of stages of completion, and costs are expensed in the period incurred. In addition, IAS 11 includes the fair value of receivables in recognizing revenues. U.S. GAAP uses fair value only if the receivable is at fair value; otherwise, the amount of revenue is based on the negotiated amount (undiscounted). In addition, SOP 81-1 does not permit the application of construction accounting standards to service contracts; it must instead be accounted for based on the type of service provided. To contrast, IFRS allows either the percentage of completion method or zero-profit method for service contracts.

In the preceding discussion, in the case of real estate sales, according to International Financial Reporting Interpretations Committee (IFRIC) 15 *Agreements for the Construction of Real Estate*, if the agreement is a construction contract, IAS 11 applies and revenue is accounted for using the rules described. However, if the real estate agreement is not a construction contract, then IAS 18 would apply and revenue recognition would occur based on sale of goods or services criteria. The criteria in IFRIC 15 as to whether an agreement is a real estate contract centers on one criterion: if the agreement specifies major structural elements of design before or during construction, it is accounted for using IAS 11. If it does not specify major structural elements of design, but the contract specifies control and risks and rewards being transferred as the contract work progresses, then IAS 18 is used, but revenue is recognized in stages; otherwise, the contract is accounted for as a sale of goods under IAS 18.

CUSTOMER LOYALTY PROGRAMS   There are variations on how companies account for rewards programs granted to their customers. U.S. GAAP has mixed practices. ASC 605-25-25 may apply to such arrangements, where entities account for these programs similarly to a product warranty approach, accruing the incremental estimated cost of providing the goods or services that are to be redeemed. IFRIC 13, *Customer Loyalty Programmes* requires companies to estimate the value of points to the customer and defer the revenue as a liability until the concern has fulfilled its obligation to supply rewards. IFRIC 13 requires rewards to be recognized as a separate component of the sale if any consideration received is allocated to the loyalty program based on relative fair value or using a residual method.

In addition, IFRS includes gains in the definition of revenue rather than reporting them separately on the income statement, whereas U.S. GAAP records gains separately from revenue and defines gains as a specific element on the income statement.

Discontinued Operations

Currently, the definition of *discontinued operations* in ASC 360, *Property, Plant, and Equipment* (FAS-144) does not converge with IFRS 5, *Non-Current Assets Held For Sale And Discontinued Operations*. Under U.S. GAAP, discontinued operations apply to asset groups, whereas under IFRS, discontinued operations apply to major lines of business or geographical areas of operation. In addition, U.S. GAAP provides specific guidance on continuing involvement, whereas there is minimal guidance under IFRS. In presentation of discontinued operations under U.S. GAAP, disclosure of revenues, pretax profit (or loss), gain (or loss) on disposal of the unit, and the tax effect of discontinued operations are presented below income from continuing operations. Under IFRS, the same items are presented as under U.S. GAAP with the exception of also disclosing the expenses associated with the revenue segregated as part of the discontinued operation. Further, IFRS 5 requires that cash flows related to discontinued operations be separately presented by categories (i.e., operating, investing, and financing activities). U.S. GAAP has no cash flows disclosure requirement.

Share-Based Payment

U.S. GAAP and IFRS standards have closely converged in the accounting of share-based payment, where the fair value of shares and options that are awarded to employees are recognized over their period of service (period of benefit). One significant difference that remains regarding share-based payment is that under U.S. GAAP, ASC 718, *Compensation—Stock Compensation* (FAS-123R) applies to employee *and* nonemployee share-based payments, whereas IFRS 2, *Share-based Payment* generally applies only to employees of the concern. Share-based payments are classified as a liability under ASC 718 (FAS-123R) if the grantor can be compelled to deliver cash or other assets and no equity holder relationship is established. IFRS 2 classifies share-based payment awards as separated into components: cash-settled (the extent the liability will be settled in cash or other assets) and equity-settled (which is the award's fair value over the liability incurred).

In addition, there are differences in the treatment of the grant date under U.S. GAAP and IFRS. Under ASC 718 (FAS-123R), the grant date is the date when the employer and employee have a mutual understanding of the terms and conditions of the stock-based award and the employee begins to benefit from or be negatively impacted by the changes in the employer's share price. Under IFRS 2, the grant date is the date when the entity and the employee agree to a share-based payment arrangement and possess a mutual understanding of the terms and conditions of the arrangement.

Impairment

Discussed below are issues surrounding impairments for intangibles and property, plant, and equipment.

INTANGIBLE IMPAIRMENT   U.S. GAAP measures impairment as the excess of the intangible's carrying value over its fair value (expected future cash flows, undiscounted); IFRS recognizes impairment if the intangible's carrying value exceeds its recoverable amount (which is the higher of the intangible's fair value less costs to dispose of the asset and its value in use). Under U.S. GAAP, recorded impairment losses are not reversed in subsequent periods, as the intangible's revised basis for amortization reflects the written-down asset after impairment loss recognition. Under IFRS, IAS 36 allows for recovery of impairment losses (other than goodwill) in subsequent periods if there has been a change in economic conditions or a change in the expected use of the asset. Such allowable impairment recoveries (or asset write-ups) are limited to the intangible's preimpairment carrying value.

For goodwill, U.S. GAAP tests for impairment annually (or more often if evidence of impairment exists) and is based on a two-step recoverability test and impairment assessment. IFRS uses a one-step process in testing for goodwill impairment, where an impairment loss is recognized if the asset's carrying value is greater than its discounted fair value, less cost to sell and its discounted value in use.

PROPERTY, PLANT, AND EQUIPMENT IMPAIRMENT   According to U.S. GAAP and IFRS, a company must record an asset impairment when the book value of an asset is not recoverable. U.S. GAAP relies on a recoverability test to determine whether impairment has occurred. If the sum of expected future cash flows (undiscounted) is less than the carrying amount of the asset, the asset is considered impaired. Such an impairment loss is measured as the difference between the carrying amount of the asset and its fair value. U.S. GAAP prohibits subsequent impairment reversals.

Under IAS 36, an asset is impaired when its recoverable amount is less than its carrying amount. The recoverable amount is the greater of net selling price and its value in use. The net selling price is the market value of the asset less any disposal costs. Value in use is the present value of expected future net cash flows over the remaining useful life of the asset. The impairment loss is the difference between the asset's book value and its recoverable amount, which is recognized in income. IFRS permits asset write-ups for subsequent recoveries of impairments.

Earnings per Share

The calculations of basic and diluted EPS are similar under U.S. GAAP and IFRS, with some minor differences. First, both require EPS to be reported on the face of the income statement if the shares are traded publicly. U.S. GAAP and IFRS each report EPS for income from continuing operations and for net income or loss; however, U.S. GAAP requires EPS for discontinued operations and extraordinary items. In addition, under U.S. GAAP, if the treasury stock method of calculating incremental shares is used, a quarterly calculation of the average stock price is used. IFRS calculates the incremental shares based on a weighted average at the end of the accounting period, not at the end of each quarter. This topic is one that the two boards are jointly working on in order to converge accounting treatments.

Subsequent Events

Under U.S. GAAP, ASC 855, *Subsequent Events* (FAS-165) deals with accounting and disclosure requirements for subsequent events. Specifically, subsequent events are considered through the date when the financial statements are issued or are available to be issued. In addition, SEC registrants are not required to disclose the date through which the subsequent events have been evaluated. Under IFRS, IAS 10, *Events After the Reporting Period* defines subsequent events through the date of financial statement authorization; the date of authorization of financial statement issue is disclosed.

PART II

Analyzing Financial Statements

CHAPTER 6

Financial Statement Analysis

Financial statement analysis is an appraisal of a company's previous financial performance and its future potential. The CPA is often involved in analyzing the financial statements of an existing client, prospective client, or targeted company for a potential acquisition. Financial statement analysis aids the CPA in determining what areas to audit and in appraising the overall health of the business. A going-concern problem may be identified. After the CPA completes the financial statement analysis, he or she should consult with management to discuss their plans and prospects, identify problem areas, and offer possible solutions.

This chapter covers:

- Analytical techniques to be followed in appraising the balance sheet and income statement
- Indicators of prospective business failure

Introduction

Why analyze the financial statement?

The CPA analyzes the financial statement of a client for a number of important reasons:

- The financial statement indicates areas requiring audit attention. The CPA can look at the percentage change in an account over the years or relative to some base year to identify inconsistencies. *Example:* If the ratio of promotion and entertainment expense to sales was 2 percent last year and shot up to 16 percent this year, the auditor would want to uncover the reasons. This increase would be especially disturbing if other companies in the industry still had a percentage relationship of 2 percent. The auditor might suspect that the promotion and entertainment expense account contained some personal rather than business charges. Supporting documentation for the charges would be requested and carefully reviewed by the CPA.
- The financial statement indicates the financial health of the client, which is of interest to the CPA for these reasons:
  - A determination has to be made as to whether the client is financially sound enough to pay the accounting fees.

- The CPA must ascertain whether poor financial conditions exist that may cause a going-concern problem.
- The CPA wants to know his or her potential legal exposure. If the client has a poor financial condition, corporate failure may occur, resulting in lawsuits by creditors and others. If financial problems exist, the auditor would have to take proper audit and reporting steps, including suitable references in the audit report.
- The statement provides vital information to be included in the management letter.
- The statement assists in identifying areas of financial problems and means of corrective action for the client.
- The financial statement aids the client in determining the appropriateness of mergers and acquisitions.

A company's financial health has a bearing on its price-earnings ratio, bond rating, cost of financing, and availability of financing. CPAs should especially watch out for high-accounting-risk companies:

- Glamour companies known for earnings growth
- Companies in the public eye
- Companies having difficulty obtaining financing
- Companies whose management previously committed dishonest acts

How does the CPA draw conclusions from financial analysis?

To obtain worthwhile conclusions from financial ratios, the CPA has to make two comparisons: industry comparison and trend analysis.

Industry Comparison

The CPA should compare the company's ratios to those of competing companies in the industry or with industry standards. Industry norms can be obtained from such services as:

- *Risk Management Association (RMA).* RMA, formerly known as Robert Morris Associates, has been compiling statistical data on financial statements for more than 75 years. The RMA *Annual Statement Studies* provide statistical data from more than 150,000 actual companies on many key financial ratios, such as gross margin, operating margins, and return on equity and assets. The Statement Studies are organized by SIC codes, and you can obtain the financial statement studies for your industry in report form or over the Internet (www.rmahq.org).
- *Dun & Bradstreet.* Dun & Bradstreet publishes *Industry Norms & Key Business Ratios,* which covers over 1 million firms in over 800 lines of business.
- *Value Line. Value Line Investment Surveys* provide financial data and rate stocks of over 1,700 firms.
- *U.S. Department of Commerce.* The Department of Commerce Financial Report provides financial statement data and includes a variety of ratios and industry-wide common-size vertical financial statements.

- *Others.* Standard & Poor's, Moody's Investors Service, and various brokerages compile industry studies. Further, numerous online services such as Yahoo! Finance and MSN Money also provide these data.

In analyzing a company, the CPA should appraise the trends in its particular industry. What is the pattern of expansion or contraction in the industry? The profit dollar is worth more if earned in a healthy, expanding industry than in a declining one.

Trend Analysis

A company's ratio can be compared over several years to identify direction of financial health or operational performance.

The optimum value for any given ratio usually varies across industry lines, through time, and within different companies in the same industry. In other words, a ratio deemed optimum for one company may be inadequate for another. A particular ratio typically is deemed optimum within a given range of values. An increase or decrease beyond this range points to weakness or inefficiency. *Example:* Whereas a low current ratio may indicate poor liquidity, a very high current ratio may indicate inefficient utilization of assets (e.g., excessive inventory) or inability to use short-term credit to the firm's advantage.

Note

In appraising a seasonal business, the CPA may find that year-end financial data are not representative. Thus, averages based on quarterly or monthly information may be used to level out seasonality effects.

Horizontal and Vertical Analysis

How do horizontal and vertical analysis work?

Horizontal analysis looks at the trend in accounts over the years and aids in identifying areas of wide divergence mandating further attention. Horizontal analysis can also be presented by showing trends relative to a base year.

In *vertical analysis*, a significant item on a financial statement is used as a base value, and all other items on the financial statement are compared to it. In performing vertical analysis for the balance sheet, the total of assets is assigned 100 percent. Each asset is expressed as a percentage of total assets. The total of liabilities and stockholders' equity is also assigned 100 percent. Each liability and stockholders' equity account is then expressed as a percentage of total liabilities and stockholders' equity. In the income statement, net sales is given the value of 100 percent, and all other accounts are appraised in comparison to net sales. The resulting figures are then given in a common size statement.

Vertical analysis is helpful in disclosing the internal structure of the business. It shows the relationship between each income statement account and revenue. It indicates the mix of assets that produces the income and the mix of the sources of capital, whether by current or long-term liabilities or by equity funding. Besides making internal evaluation possible, the results of vertical analysis are also employed to appraise the company's relative position in the industry. Horizontal and vertical analysis point to possible problem areas to be evaluated by the CPA.

Balance Sheet Analysis

In analyzing the balance sheet, the CPA is concerned primarily with the realizability of the assets, turnover, and earning potential. The evaluation of liabilities considers arbitrary adjustments and understatements.

Assets

How do I appraise the quality of assets?

If assets are overstated, net income will be overstated, since the earnings do not include necessary charges to reduce earnings to their proper valuations. Asset quality depends on the amount and timing of the realization of assets. Therefore, assets should be categorized by risk category.

- Useful ratios are the percentage of high-risk assets to total assets and high-risk assets to sales. High asset realization risk points to poor quality of earnings due to possible future write-offs. *Example:* The future realization of accounts receivable is better than that of goodwill.
- Multipurpose assets are of better quality than single-purpose ones, as they have readier salability.
- Assets lacking separable value cannot be sold easily and as such have low realizability. *Examples:* Work-in-process and intangibles.

Notes

In appraising realization risk in assets, the effect of changing government policies on the entity has to be taken into account.

Risk may exist with chemicals and other products deemed hazardous to health. Huge inventory losses may have to be taken.

Example 6.1

Company A presents total assets of $6 million and sales of $10 million. Included in total assets are these high-risk assets, as perceived by the CPA:

Deferred plant rearrangement costs	$400,000
Receivables for claims under a government contract	200,000
Goodwill	150,000

Applicable ratios are:

$$\frac{\text{High-risk assets}}{\text{Total assets}} = \frac{\$750,000}{\$6,000,000} = \underline{12.5\%}$$

$$\frac{\text{High-risk assets}}{\text{Sales}} = \frac{\$750,000}{\$10,000,000} = \underline{7.5\%}$$

CASH

Is cash proper and unrestricted?

A high ratio of sales to cash may indicate inadequate cash. This may lead to financial problems if additional financing is not available at reasonable interest rates. A low turnover ratio indicates excessive cash being held.

The CPA should determine whether part of the cash is restricted and unavailable for use. *Examples:* A compensating balance that does not constitute free cash; cash in a politically unstable foreign country that may have remission restrictions.

ACCOUNTS RECEIVABLE

Are accounts receivable realizable?

Realization risk in receivables can be appraised by studying the nature of the receivable balance. *Examples:* High-risk receivables include:

- Amounts from economically unstable foreign countries
- Receivables subject to offset provisions
- Receivables due from a company experiencing severe financial problems

Companies dependent on a few customers have greater risk than those with a large number of important accounts. Receivables due from industry are usually safer than those arising from consumers. Fair trade laws are more protective of consumers.

What do increases in accounts receivable mean?

A significant increase in accounts receivable compared to the prior year may indicate increased realization risk. The firm may be selling to riskier customers. The trends in the ratios of accounts receivable to total assets and accounts receivable to sales should be evaluated.

The CPA should appraise the trends in the ratios of bad debts to accounts receivable and bad debts to sales. An unwarranted decrease in bad debts lowers the quality of earnings. This may happen when there is a decline in bad debts even though the company is selling to less creditworthy customers and/or actual bad debt losses are increasing.

A company may purposely overstate bad debts to provide accounting cushions for reporting understated profits. Also, companies may have substantial bad debt provisions in the current period because improper provisions were made in prior years, distorting the earnings trend. A sudden write-off of accounts receivable may arise from prior understated bad debt provisions. Earnings may be managed by initially increasing and then lowering the bad debt provision.

Receivables are of low quality if they arose from loading customers with unneeded merchandise by giving generous credit terms. Be alert for these red-flagged items:

- A significant increase in sales in the final quarter of the year
- A substantial amount of sales returns in the first quarter of the next year
- A material decrease in sales for the first quarter of the next year

In a *seasonal* business, the accounts receivable turnover (credit sales/average accounts receivable) may be based on monthly or quarterly sales figures so that a proper averaging takes place.

How significant are sales returns and allowances?

The trend in sales returns and allowances is often a good reflection of the quality of merchandise sold to customers. A significant decrease in a firm's sales allowance account as a percentage of sales is not in conformity with reality when a greater liability for dealer returns exists. This will result in lower earnings quality.

Example 6.2

Company X's sales and sales returns for the period 2X10 to 2X12 follow.

	2X12	2X11	2X10
Balance in Sales Returns Account at Year-End	$ 2,000	$ 3,800	$ 1,550
Sales	$240,000	$215,000	$100,000
Percentage of Sales Returns to Sales	0.0083	0.0177	0.0155

The reduction in the ratio of sales returns to sales from 2X11 to 2X12 indicates that the company is making less of a provision for returns. This is unrealistic if there is a greater liability for dealer returns and credits on an expanded sales base.

INVENTORY

What does an inventory buildup mean?

An inventory buildup may point to:

- *Greater realization risk.* The buildup may be at the plant, wholesaler, or retailer. A sign of buildup is when the inventory increases at a faster rate than sales.

- *A production slowdown*, when there is a reduction in raw materials coupled with an increase in work-in-process and finished goods. Furthermore, greater obsolescence risk exists with work-in-process and finished goods due to major buildups. Raw materials have the best realizability because of greater universality and their multipurpose nature.

What should I do in the event of inventory buildup?

Computation of the turnover rate should be made by each major inventory category and by department.

- A *low turnover rate* may indicate overstocking, obsolescence, or problems with the product line or marketing effectiveness. However, there are cases where a low inventory rate is appropriate. *Example:* A higher inventory level may arise because of expected future increases in price.
- A *high turnover rate* may point to inadequate inventory, possibly leading to a loss in business. At the natural year-end, the turnover rate may be unusually high because at that time the inventory balance may be very low.

The number of days inventory is held should be computed. The age of inventory should be compared to industry averages and to prior years of the company.

- *High realization risk* applies with specialized, technological, fad, luxurious, perishable, and price-sensitive merchandise. The CPA must be sure that the company has not assigned values to unsalable and obsolete merchandise. If there is a sudden inventory write-off, the CPA may be suspicious of the firm's deferral policy.
- *Low realization risk* applies to standard, staple, and necessity goods, owing to their better salability.
- *Collateralized inventory* has a greater risk, because creditors can retain it in the event of nonpayment of an obligation.
- *Political risk* may be associated with inventory.

Example: Increased gas prices due to a shortage situation making it infeasible to purchase large cars.

Look for inventory that is overstated due to mistakes in:

- Quantities
- Costing
- Pricing
- Valuation of work-in-process

The more technical the product and the more dependence there is on internally developed cost records, the greater the susceptibility of the cost estimates to misstatement.

Notes

If adequate insurance cannot be obtained at reasonable rates due to unfavorable geographic location of the merchandise (e.g., high-crime area, flood suscepti- bility), a problem exists.

The CPA should note the appropriateness of a change in inventory. Is it required by a new FASB pronouncement, SEC release, or IRS tax ruling?

INVESTMENTS

Are securities properly stated?

An indication of the fair value of investments may be the revenue (dividend income, interest income) obtained from them. Have decreases in portfolio market values been recognized in the accounts? Higher realization risk exists where there is a declining trend in the ratio of percentage of earnings derived from investments to their carrying value. Also check subsequent event disclosures for unrealized losses in the portfolio occurring after year-end.

Example 6.3

Company X presents this information:

	2X11	2X12
Investments	$50,000	$60,000
Investment Income	$ 7,000	$ 5,000

The ratio of percentage of investment income to total investments decreased from 14 percent in 2X11 to 8.3 percent in 2X12, pointing to higher realization risk in the portfolio.

If a company is buying securities in other companies for diversification purposes, this will reduce overall risk. Risk in an investment portfolio can be ascertained by computing the standard deviation of its rate of return.

An investment portfolio of securities fluctuating widely in price is of higher realization risk than a portfolio that is diversified by industry and economic sector. But the former portfolio will show greater profitability in a bull market.

Recommendations

Appraise the extent of diversification and stability of the investment portfolio. There is less risk when securities are negatively correlated (price goes in opposite directions) or not correlated compared to a portfolio of positively correlated securities (price goes in same direction).

Note cases where held-to-maturity securities have a cost in excess of market value.

FIXED ASSETS

Are property, plant, and equipment properly maintained?

Inadequate provision for the maintenance of property, plant, and equipment detracts from the long-term earning power of the firm. If obsolete assets are not replaced and repairs not made properly, breakdowns and declining operational efficiency will result. Failure to write down obsolete fixed assets results in overstated earnings.

Recommendations

- Determine the age and condition of each major asset along with its replacement cost.
- Review the trend in fixed asset acquisitions to total gross assets. This trend is particularly revealing for a technological company that has to keep up-to-date. A decrease in the trend points to the failure to replace older assets on a timely basis. Inactive and unproductive assets are a drain on the firm.
- Review asset efficiency by evaluating production levels, downtime, and discontinuances. Assets that have not been used for a long period of time may have to be written down.

Note

Pollution-causing equipment may necessitate replacement or modification to meet governmental ecology requirements.

Example 6.4

Company T presents this information regarding its fixed assets:

	2X11	2X12
Fixed Assets	$120,000	$105,000
Repairs and Maintenance	6,000	4,500
Replacement Cost	205,000	250,000

The company has inadequately maintained its assets, as indicated by:

- The reduction in the ratio of repairs and maintenance to fixed assets from 5 percent in 2X11 to 4.3 percent in 2X12
- The material variation between replacement cost and historical cost
- The reduction in fixed assets over the year

What does the fixed asset turnover ratio mean?

The fixed asset turnover ratio (net sales to average fixed assets) aids in appraising a company's ability to use its asset base efficiently to obtain revenue. A low ratio may mean that investment in fixed assets is excessive relative to the output generated.

When a company's rate of return on assets (e.g., ratio of net income to fixed assets) is poor, the firm may be justified in not maintaining fixed assets. If the industry is declining, fixed asset replacement and repairs may have been restricted.

A company having specialized or risky fixed assets has greater vulnerability to asset obsolescence. *Example:* Machinery used to manufacture specialized products and fad items.

Recommendations

A depreciation method should be used that most realistically measures the expiration in asset usefulness.

Example: The units-of-production method may result in a realistic charge for machinery. Unrealistic book depreciation may be indicated when depreciation for stockholder reporting is materially less than depreciation for tax return purposes.

Examine the trend in depreciation expense as a percentage of both fixed assets and net sales. A reduction in the trend may point to inadequate depreciation charges for the potential obsolescence of fixed assets. Another indication of inadequate depreciation charges is a concurrent moderate rise in depreciation coupled with a material increase in capital spending.

Example 6.5

This information applies to X Company:

	2X11	2X12
Depreciation Expense to Fixed Assets	5.3%	4.4%
Depreciation Expense to Sales	4.0%	3.3%

These declining ratios indicate improper provision for the deterioration of assets.

Notes

A change in classification of newly acquired fixed assets to depreciation categories different from those of the older assets (e.g., a change from accelerated depreciation to straight-line depreciation) will result in lower earnings quality.

A vacillating depreciation policy will distort continuity in earnings.

If there is a reduction in depreciation expense caused by an unrealistic change in the lives and salvage values of property, plant, and equipment, there will be overstated earnings.

An inconsistency exists when there is a material decline in revenue coupled with a major increase in capital expenditures. It may be indicative of overexpansion and later write-offs of fixed assets.

INTANGIBLES

When is there a high realization risk for intangible assets?

High realization risk is indicated when there are high ratios of:

- Intangible assets to total assets
- Intangible assets to net worth

Intangibles can be overstated compared to their market value or future earning potential. *Example:* A firm's goodwill can be overstated or worthless in a recessionary environment.

An unwarranted lengthening in the amortization period for intangibles overstates earnings. *Example:* An unjustified change is when the company's reputation has been worsened due to political bribes or environmental violations.

The ratio of the change in intangible assets to the change in net income should also be examined. A rising trend may mean this net income has been relieved of appropriate charges.

How do leasehold improvements affect intangibles?

Leasehold improvements are improvements made to rented property (e.g., paneling and fixtures). Leasehold improvements are amortized over the life of the rented property or the life of the improvement, whichever is shorter. Leasehold improvements have no cash realizability.

What about the goodwill value of an acquired company?

A company's goodwill account should be appraised to determine whether the acquired firm has superior earning potential to justify the excess of cost over fair market value of net assets paid for it. If the acquired company does not have superior profit potential, the goodwill has no value because excess earnings do not exist relative to other companies in the industry. However, internally developed goodwill is expensed and not capitalized. It represents an undervalued asset (e.g., the good reputation of McDonald's).

Are patents properly valued?

Patents may be undervalued. They are recorded at the registration cost plus legal fees to defend them. These costs may be far below the present value of future cash flows derived from the patents.

Patents are less valuable when they can easily be infringed on by minor alteration or when they apply to high-technology items. The company's financial condition must also be considered, since it may incur significant legal costs in defending patents. What are the expiration dates of the patents and the degree to which new patents are coming onstream?

DEFERRED CHARGES

Are deferred charges of poor quality?

Deferred expenses depend to a greater extent on estimates of future probabilities than do other assets. The estimates may be overly optimistic. Is the company deferring an item having no future benefit only for the purpose of deferring costs in order not to burden net income? Deferred charges are not cash-realizable assets and cannot be used to meet creditor claims. *Examples:* Questionable deferred charges are:

- Deferred exploration costs under the full cost method
- Deferred interest on borrowed funds for self-constructed assets

Recommendations

A company may try to hide declining profitability by deferring costs that were expensed in prior years. Be on the lookout for such a situation.

Examine the trends in ratios of deferred charges to sales, deferred charges to net income, and deferred charges (e.g., deferred promotion costs) to total expenditures. Increasing trends may be indicative of a more liberal accounting policy.

Example 6.6

Company G presents this information:

	2X11	2X12
Deferred Charges	$ 70,000	$150,000
Total Assets	500,000	590,000
Sales	800,000	845,000
Net Income	200,000	215,000
Computed ratios are:		
Deferred Costs to Total Assets	14%	25.4%
Deferred Costs to Sales	8.8%	17.8%
Deferred Costs to Net Income	35%	69.8%

The higher ratios of deferred charges to total assets, to sales, and to net income indicate more realization risk in assets in 2X12. Furthermore, 2X12's earnings quality may be lower because deferred costs may include items that should have been expensed.

Note

A high ratio of intangible assets and deferred charges to total assets points to an asset structure of greater realization risk. Overstated assets in terms of realizability may necessitate later write-off.

UNRECORDED ASSETS

Do off-balance-sheet assets exist?

Unrecorded assets are positive aspects of financial position even though they are not shown on the balance sheet. *Example:* Unrecorded assets include tax loss carryforward benefit and a purchase commitment in which the company has a contract to buy an item at a price materially less than the going rate.

Recommendation

Note the existence of unrecorded assets representing resources of the business or items expected to have future economic benefit.

Liabilities

What is the quality of liabilities?

If liabilities are understated, net income is overstated because it does not include necessary charges to reflect the proper valuation of liabilities.

Recommendations

Examine trends in ratios of current liabilities to total liabilities, to stockholders' equity, and to sales. Rising trends may point to liquidity problems.

Determine whether liabilities are "patient" or "pressing." A patient supplier with a long relationship may postpone or modify the debt payable for a financially troubled company. Pressing debt includes taxes and loans payable. These have to be paid without excuse. A high ratio of pressing liabilities to patient liabilities points to greater liquidity risk.

Example 6.7

Company A reports this information:

Current Liabilities	2X11	2X12
Accounts Payable	$ 30,000	$ 26,000
Short-Term Loans Payable	50,000	80,000
Commercial Paper	40,000	60,000
Total Current Liabilities	$ 120,000	$ 166,000
Total Noncurrent Liabilities	300,000	308,000
Total Liabilities	$ 420,000	$ 468,000
Sales	$1,000,000	$1,030,000

Relevant ratios follow		
Current Liabilities to Total Liabilities	28.6%	35.5%
Current Liabilities to Sales	12.0%	16.1%
Pressing Current Liabilities to Patient Current Liabilities (short-term loans payable plus commercial paper/accounts payable)	3.01	5.4

The company has greater liquidity risk in 2X12, as reflected by the higher ratios of current liabilities to total liabilities, current liabilities to sales, and pressing current liabilities to patient current liabilities.

How do adjustments of estimated liabilities affect earnings?

Arbitrary adjustments of estimated liabilities should be eliminated in deriving corporate earning power. Estimated liability provisions should be realistic given the nature of the circumstances. *Example:* Profits derived from a recoupment of prior-year reserves may necessitate elimination.

Recommendation

If reserves are used to manage earnings, add back the amounts charged to earnings and deduct the amounts credited to earnings.

A firm having an unrealistically low provision for future costs has understated earnings. *Example:* It is inconsistent for a company to have a lower warranty provision when prior experience points to a deficiency in product quality.

An overprovision in estimated liabilities sometimes is made. In effect, the company is providing a reserve for a rainy day. *Example:* Profits are too high, and management wants to bring them down.

Note

Poor earnings quality is indicated when more operating expenses and losses are being charged to reserve accounts compared to prior years.

Are some liabilities off the balance sheet?

- Unrecorded liabilities are not reported on the financial statements but do require future payment or services. *Examples*: Lawsuits and noncapitalized leases.
- Useful disclosures of long-term obligations are mandated by ASC 440-10-50-2, *Exit or Disposal Cost Obligations: Overall* (FAS-47, *Disclosure of Long-Term Obligations*).

Recommendation

Review commitments applicable to unconditional purchase obligations and future payments on long-term debt and redeemable stock.

- FASB Interpretation 34, *Disclosure of Indirect Guarantees of Indebtedness of Others*, requires disclosure of indirect guarantees of indebtedness. Included are contracts in which one company promises to advance funds to another if financial problems occur, as when sales drop below a stipulated level.
- Preferred stock with a maturity date or subject to sinking fund requirements is more like debt than equity. However, convertible bonds with an attractive conversion feature are more like equity than debt since there is an expectation of conversion.

Evaluation of Liquidity

How do I analyze a firm's liquidity?

In appraising a company's liquidity, sufficient funds flow is necessary so that current assets are sufficient to meet short-term debt. Measures of funds flow include:

- *Current ratio* equals current assets divided by current liabilities.
- *Quick ratio* equals cash plus marketable securities plus receivables divided by current liabilities. It is a stringent test of liquidity.
- *Working capital* equals current assets less current liabilities. A high working capital is needed when the company may have difficulty borrowing on short notice. Working capital should be compared to other financial statement items such as sales and total assets. *Example:* The ratio of working capital to sales indicates whether the company is optimally employing its liquid balance. To identify changes in the composition of working capital, ascertain the trend in the percentage of each current asset to total current assets. A movement from cash to inventory, for instance, points to less liquidity.
- *Sales to current assets.* A high turnover rate indicates inadequate working capital. Current liabilities may be due prior to inventories and receivables turning into cash.
- *Working capital provided from operations to net income* (net income plus nonworking capital expenses minus nonworking capital revenue). Liquidity is enhanced when net income is backed up by liquid funds.
- *Working capital provided from operations to total liabilities.* This ratio indicates the extent to which internally generated working capital is available to meet debt.
- *Cash plus marketable securities to current liabilities.* This ratio indicates the immediate amount of cash available to satisfy short-term obligations.
- *Cost of sales, operating expenses, and taxes to average total current assets.* The trend in this ratio indicates the adequacy of current assets in meeting ongoing business-related expenses.

- *Quick assets to year's cash expenses.* This ratio indicates the days of expenses that the highly liquid assets could support.
- *Sales to short-term trade liabilities.* This ratio indicates whether the firm can partly be financed by cost-free funds. A decline in trade credit means creditors have less faith in the financial strength of the business.
- *Net income to sales.* A decline in the profit margin of the business indicates financial deterioration.
- *Fixed assets to short-term debt.* A company financing long-term assets with short-term obligations has a problem satisfying debt when due, because the return and proceeds from the fixed asset will not be realized prior to the maturity date of the current liabilities.
- *Short-term debt to long-term debt.* A higher ratio points to greater liquidity risk because debt is of a current nature.
- *Accounts payable to average daily purchases.* This ratio indicates the number of days required for the company to pay creditors.
- *Liquidity index.* This indicates the days in which current assets are removed from cash.

Example 6.8

	Amount		Days Removed from Cash		Total
Cash	$ 10,000	×	—	=	—
Accounts Receivable	40,000	×	25	=	$1,000,000
Inventory	60,000	×	40	=	2,400,000
	$110,000				$3,400,000

$$\text{Index} = \frac{\$3,400,000}{\$110,000} = 30.9 \text{ days}$$

Example 6.9

Company B provides this financial information:

Current Assets	$ 400,000
Fixed Assets	800,000
Current Liabilities	500,000
Noncurrent Liabilities	600,000
Sales	5,000,000
Working Capital Provided from Operations	100,000

(continued)

(Continued)

Industry norms are:

Fixed Assets to Current Liabilities	4.0 times
Current Liabilities to Noncurrent Liabilities	45.0%
Sales to Current Assets	8.3 times
Working Capital Provided from Operations to Total Liabilities	30.5%

Company B's ratios are:

Fixed Assets to Current Liabilities	1.6 times
Current Liabilities to Noncurrent Liabilities	83.3%
Sales to Current Assets	12.5 times
Working Capital Provided from Operations to Total Liabilities	9.1%

Company B's liquidity ratios are all unfavorable compared to industry standards. There is a high level of short-term debt as well as deficiency in current assets. Also, working capital provided from operations to satisfy total debt is inadequate.

How does taking cash discounts affect a company financially?

A company's failure to take cash discounts raises a question as to management's financial astuteness because a high opportunity cost is involved.

Example 6.10

Company C bought goods for $300,000 on terms of 2/10, net/60. It failed to take advantage of the discount. The opportunity cost is:

$$\frac{\text{Discount foregone}}{\text{Proceeds use of}} \times \frac{360}{\text{Days delayed}}$$

$$\frac{\$6,000}{\$294,000} \times \frac{360}{50} = \underline{14.7\%}$$

The firm would have been better off financially paying within the discount period by taking out a loan, since the prime interest rate is below 14.7 percent.

Appraising Corporate Solvency

How do I evaluate a firm's solvency?

Corporate solvency depends on:

- The long-term debt-paying ability of the entity to ascertain whether the firm can meet long-term principal and interest payments
- Whether long-term funds are forthcoming to meet noncurrent debt
- The long-term financial and operating structure of the business
- The magnitude of noncurrent liabilities and the realization risk in noncurrent assets
- Earning power (a company will not be able to satisfy its obligations unless it is profitable)

Recommendation

When practical to do so, use the market value of assets instead of book value in ratio computations; it is more representative of true worth.

Measures of long-term debt-paying ability are:

- *Long-term debt to stockholders' equity.* High leverage indicates risk because it may be difficult for the company to meet interest and principal payments as well as obtain further reasonable financing. The problem is particularly acute when a company has cash problems. Excessive debt means less financial flexibility because the entity will have more problems obtaining funds during a tight money market.
- *Cash flow to long-term debt.* This ratio evaluates the adequacy of available funds to satisfy noncurrent obligations.
- *Net income before taxes and interest to interest (interest coverage ratio).* This ratio indicates the number of times interest expense is covered. It is a safety margin indicator that shows the degree of decline in income that a company can tolerate.
- *Cash flow generated from operations plus interest to interest.* This ratio indicates available cash to meet interest charges. Cash, not profit, pays interest.
- *Net income before taxes plus fixed charges to fixed charges.* This ratio helps in appraising a firm's ability to meet fixed costs. A low ratio points to risk—when corporate activity falls, the company is unable to meet its fixed charges.
- *Cash flow from operations plus fixed charges to fixed charges.* A high ratio indicates the ability of the company to meet its fixed charges. Furthermore, a company with stable operations is better able to meet fixed costs.
- *Noncurrent assets to noncurrent liabilities.* Long-term debt is ultimately paid from long-term assets. A high ratio affords more protection for long-term creditors.
- *Retained earnings to total assets.* The trend in this ratio reflects the firm's profitability over the years.

Example 6.11

The following partial balance sheet and income statement data are provided for Company D:

Long-Term Assets	$700,000
Long-Term Liabilities	500,000
Stockholders' Equity	300,000
Net Income before Tax	80,000
Cash Flow Provided from Operations	100,000
Interest Expense	20,000

Average norms taken from competitors:

Long-Term Assets to Long-Term Liabilities	2.0
Long-Term Debt to Stockholders' Equity	0.8
Cash Flow to Long-Term Liabilities	0.3
Net Income before Tax plus Interest to Interest	7.0

Company D's ratios are:

Long-Term Assets to Long-Term Liabilities	1.4
Long-Term Debt to Stockholders' Equity	1.67
Cash Flow to Long-Term Liabilities	0.2
Net Income before Tax plus Interest to Interest	5.0

After comparing the company's ratios with the industry norms, it is evident that the firm's solvency is worse than its competitors' due to the greater degree of long-term liabilities in the capital structure and the lower interest coverage.

What can financial management do to avoid solvency problems?

Ways for management to avoid solvency difficulties include:

- Avoid heavy debt.
- Lengthen the maturity date of debt.
- Ensure that there is a buffer between actual status and compliance requirements (e.g., working capital) in connection with loan agreements.
- Divest unprofitable segments and assets.
- Have adequate insurance.
- Avoid operations in risky foreign areas.

- Finance assets with liabilities of similar maturity.
- Adjust to changes in technology.
- Diversify horizontally and vertically.
- Avoid long-term fixed-fee commitments.

Income Statement Analysis

The analysis of the income statement indicates a company's earning power, quality of earnings, and operating performance.

Notes

Net income backed up by cash is important for corporate liquidity.

The accounting policies employed should be realistic in reflecting the substance of the transactions.

Accounting changes should be made only for proper reasons.

A high degree of estimation in the income measurement process results in uncertainty in reported figures.

Earnings stability enhances the predictability of future results based on currently reported profits.

Cash Flow from Operations

How does proximity to cash realization affect the quality of earnings?

The closer a transaction is to cash, the more objective is the evidence supporting revenue and expense recognition. As the proximity to cash becomes less, the transaction becomes less objective and the interpretations become more subjective. Higher earnings quality relates to recording transactions close to cash realization.

How is cash flow from operations treated?

Cash flow from operations equals net income plus noncash expenses less noncash revenue. Net income is of higher quality if it is backed up by cash. The trend in the ratio of cash flow from operations to net income should be evaluated.

In appraising the cash adequacy of a company, compute:

- Cash flow generated from operations before interest expense
- Cash flow generated from operations less cash payments to meet debt principal, dividends, and capital expenditures

Example 6.12

A condensed income statement for Company A follows.

Sales		$1,000,000
Less: Cost of Sales		300,000
Gross Margin		$ 700,000
Less: Operating Expenses		
Salary	$100,000	
Rent	200,000	
Telephone	50,000	
Depreciation	80,000	
Amortization Expense	60,000	
Total Operating Expenses		490,000
Income before Other Items		$ 210,000
Other Revenue and Expense		
Interest Expense	$ 70,000	
Amortization of Deferred Credit	40,000	
Total Other Revenue and Expense		30,000
Net Income		$ 180,000

The ratio of cash flow from operations to net income is 1.55, calculated as follows:

Cash Flow from Operations		$180,000
Add: Noncash Expenses		
Depreciation	$80,000	
Amortization Expense	60,000	140,000
Less: Noncash Revenue		
Amortization of Deferred Credit		(40,000)
Cash Flow from Operations		$ 280,000

$$\frac{\text{Cash Flow from Operations}}{\text{Net Income}} = \frac{\$280,000}{\$180,000} = 1.55$$

Discretionary Costs

What are discretionary costs?

Discretionary costs include:

- Advertising
- Repairs and maintenance
- Research and development

Discretionary costs can be changed by management easily. They may be decreased when a company is having problems or wants to show a stable earnings trend.

What are the effects of a change in discretionary costs?

A pullback in discretionary costs results in overstated earnings. It has a long-term negative effect because management is starving the company of needed expenses. Cost reduction programs may lower earnings quality when material cutbacks are made in discretionary costs.

Note

The CPA cannot always conclude that any reduction in discretionary costs is improper. The reduction may be necessary when the prior corporate strategy is deficient or ill-conceived.

Recommendations

Determine whether the present level of discretionary costs is in conformity with the company's prior trends and with current and future requirements. Index numbers can be used in comparing current discretionary expenditures with base-year expenditures. A vacillating trend in the ratio of discretionary costs to revenue may indicate the company is smoothing earnings by altering its discretionary costs. A substantial increase in discretionary costs may have a positive impact on corporate earning power and future growth.

A declining trend in the ratio of discretionary costs to net sales may indicate lower earnings quality. Review the relationship of discretionary costs to the assets they apply to.

Example 6.13

This relationship exists between advertising and sales:

	2X09	2X10	2X11
Sales	$120,000	$150,000	$100,000
Advertising	11,000	16,000	8,000

2X09 is the most typical year.
Increasing competition is expected in 2X12.
Ratio of advertising to sales equals:

2X09	2X10	2X11
9.2%	10.7%	8%

(continued)

(*Continued*)

In terms of base dollars, 2X09 is assigned 100. In 2X10, the index number is 145.5 ($16,000/$11,000); in 2X11, it is 72.7 ($8,000/$11,000).

The figures shown are negative indicators regarding 2X11. Advertising is at a lower level than in previous years. In fact, advertising should have risen due to expected increased competition.

Accounting Policies

What is the nature of the company's accounting principles and estimates?

Conservatively determined net income is of higher quality than liberally determined net income. Conservatism applies to the accounting methods and estimates used.

Recommendations

Compare the company's accounting policies with the prevailing accounting policies in the industry. If the firm's policies are more liberal, earnings quality may be lower. Take into account the company's timing of revenue recognition and the deferral of costs relative to prevailing industry practices.

The accounting policies employed should be realistic in reflecting the economic substance of the firm's transactions. The underlying business and financial realities of the company and industry have to be taken into account. *Example:* The depreciation method should most approximately measure the decline in usefulness of the asset.

The CPA may question the reasonableness of a company's accounting estimates when prior estimates have been materially different from what actually occurred. Examples of realistic accounting policies are cited in AICPA Industry Audit Guides and in accounting policy guides published by various CPA firms. If the use of realistic policies results in substantially lower earnings than the policies used, earnings quality is lower.

The artificial shifting of earnings from one year to another results in poor earnings quality. Income shifting encompasses:

- Bringing future revenue into the current year (or its converse)
- Shifting earnings from good years to bad years
- Shifting expenses and losses among the years

It is a questionable practice when a company immediately recognizes revenue even though services still have to be performed. *Example:* A magazine publisher recognizes subscription income immediately when payment is received, even though the subscription period may be three years.

The unrealistic deferral of revenue recognition results in poor earnings quality because profits are unjustifiably understated. When there is a reversal of previously recorded profits, the company's revenue recognition policies should be questioned.

If expenses are underaccrued or overaccrued, lower earnings quality results. *Examples:* An underaccrued expense is the failure of a computer manufacturer to provide for normal maintenance service for rented computers because they are being used by lessees.

An *overadorned expense* is a company with high earnings deciding to accrue for possible sales returns that are highly unlikely to materialize. Try to ascertain what these normal charges are and adjust reported earnings accordingly.

Accounting changes made to conform with new FASB Statements, AICPA Industry Audit Guides, and IRS Regulations are justifiable. However, an unjustified accounting change causes an earnings increment of low quality. Unwarranted changes made in accounting principles, estimates, and assumptions should be challenged.

Recommendation

Question whether accounting changes are being made in order to create artificial earnings growth. If there are numerous accounting changes, it will be more difficult to use current profits as a predictor for future earnings.

Degree of Certainty in Accounting Estimates

How are the estimates?

The more subjective accounting estimates and judgments are in arriving at earnings, the more uncertain is the net income figure. *Example:* A firm engaged in long-term activity (e.g., a shipbuilder using the percentage of completion contract method) has more uncertainty regarding earnings due to the material estimates involved. A higher percentage of assets subject to accounting estimates (intangibles) to total assets means uncertain earnings.

Recommendations

Determine the difference between estimated reserves and actual losses for previous years. A significant difference between the two may point to lower earnings quality. Further, substantial gains and losses on the sale of assets may point to inaccurate depreciation estimates being originally used.

Segregate cash expenses versus estimated expenses. Trends should be determined in:

- Cash expenses to net sales
- Estimated expenses to net sales

- Estimated expenses to total expenses
- Estimated expenses to net income

Example 6.14

The CPA assembles this information for Company B for the periods 2X11 and 2X12:

	2X11	2X12
Cash and Near-Cash (conversion period to cash is short) Revenue Items	$100,000	$110,000
Noncash Revenue Items (long-term receivables arising from credit sales to the government, revenue recognized under the percentage of completion method)	150,000	200,000
Total Revenue	$250,000	$310,000

	2X11	**2X12**
Cash and Near-Cash Expenses (salaries, rent, telephone)	$ 40,000	$ 60,000
Noncash Expenses (depreciation, depletion, amortization, bad debts)	70,000	120,000
Total Expenses	$110,000	$180,000
Net Income	$140,000	$130,000

Estimated revenue items to total revenue was 60 percent ($150,000/$250,000) in 2X11 and 65 percent ($200,000/$310,000) in 2X12. Estimated revenue to net income was 107 percent ($150,000/$140,000) in 2X11 and 154 percent ($200,000/$130,000) in 2X12.

Estimated expense items to total expenses was 64 percent ($70,000/$110,000) in 2X11 and 67 percent ($120,000/$180,000) in 2X12. Estimated expenses to total revenue was 28 percent ($70,000/$250,000) in 2X11 and 39 percent ($120,000/$310,000) in 2X12. Estimated expenses to net income was 50 percent ($70,000/$140,000) in 2X11 and 92 percent ($120,000/$130,000) in 2X12.

Due to the high percentages of estimated income statement items, uncertainty exists with respect to the earnings of 2X11 and 2X12. Also, a greater degree of estimation exists with regard to 2X12's income measurement process.

Residual Income

What are the implications of residual income?

An increasing trend in the ratio of residual income to net income points to a strong degree of corporate profitability because the company is earning enough to meet its imputed cost of capital. (Residual income is discussed in more detail in Chapter 7.)

Taxable Income

What about the discrepancy between taxable income and book income?

A company that has a significant deferred income tax credit account will have book profits in excess of taxable earnings. An increase in the deferred tax credit account may indicate the company is moving toward more liberal accounting policies. This is because a widening gap in the deferred tax credit account indicates a greater disparity between book earnings and taxable earnings.

A decline in the effective tax rate because of a nonrecurring source (e.g., a loss carryforward that will shortly expire) results in an earnings increment of low quality. The tax benefits will not continue in the future. However, the effective tax rate may be stable when it results from a recurring source (e.g., foreign tax credit, interest on municipal bonds).

Lower earnings quality exists if there is a high percentage of foreign earnings that will not be repatriated to the United States for a long time.

Recommendation

If a company reports significant stockholder earnings and a substantial tax loss, evaluate the quality of reported results.

Foreign Operations

How about foreign activities?

An erratic foreign exchange rate results in instability.

- To measure the degree of vacillation of the foreign exchange rate, determine its percentage change over time and/or its standard deviation.
- To evaluate the degree of stability, look at the trend in the ratio of foreign translation gains and losses to net income.

In evaluating the effect of foreign operations on the company's financial health, consider:

- Degree of intercountry transactions
- Different year-ends of foreign subsidiaries
- Foreign restrictions on the transfer of funds
- Tax structure of the foreign country
- Economic and political stability of the foreign country

Discontinued Operations

What is the analytical implication of discontinuing an operation?

Income from discontinued operations is usually of a one-time nature and should be ignored when forecasting future earnings. Furthermore, a discontinued operation implies that a company is in a state of decline or that a poor management decision was the cause for the firm's having entered the discontinued line of business in the first place.

Stability of Earnings

Are profits of a recurring nature?

A company with an unstable earnings trend has more risk associated with it. Measures of earnings stability are:

- *Average net income* (e.g., five years).
- *Average pessimistic earnings.* This measure represents the average earnings based on the worst possible scenario for the company's operational activities. The average minimum earnings is useful in appraising a risky company.
- *Standard deviation.*

$$SD = \sqrt{\frac{\sum (y - \bar{y})^2}{n}}$$

where:

y = reported earnings for period t
$\bar{y}$ = average earnings
n = number of years

A high standard deviation means instability in profits.
- *Coefficient of variation.*

$$CV = \frac{SD}{\bar{y}}$$

The coefficient of variation is useful in appraising relative instability in earnings among companies. A high coefficient indicates greater risk in the earnings stream.
- *Instability index of earnings.*

$$I = \sqrt{\frac{\sum (y - y^T)^2}{n}}$$

where:

y^T = trend earnings for period t and is computed by:

$$y^T = a + bt$$

where:

a = dollar intercept
b = slope of trend line
t = time period

A simple trend equation solved by computer is used to determine trend income. The index reflects the deviation between actual profit and trend income. A high index is indicative of instability.

- *Beta.* Beta is computed via a computer run with the use of this equation:

$$r_{jt} = a_j + B_j r_{Mt} + E_{jt}$$

where:
  r_{jt} = return on security j for period t
  a_j = constant
  B_j = beta for security j
  r_{Mt} = return on a market index, such as the New York Stock Exchange Composite index
  E_{jt} = error term

Beta is a measure of systematic or undiversifiable risk of a stock. A high beta means that the firm's stock price has vacillated more than a market index, indicating that it is a risky security.

Example 6.15

A beta of 1.7 means that the company's stock price tends to rise or fall 70 percent faster than the market. Beta values for particular stocks can be obtained from various financial services, such as Standard & Poor's.

Operating Leverage

What is operating leverage?

Operating leverage applies to the degree to which fixed costs exist in a company's cost structure. Operating leverage equals fixed costs divided by total costs.

How do I gauge operating leverage?

The three measures of operating leverage are:

1. Fixed costs to total costs ratio
2. Percentage change in operating income to the percentage change in sales volume ratio
3. Net income to fixed costs ratio

Notes

An increase in the first two operating leverage measures or a decrease in the third may point to lower earnings quality because higher fixed charges may result in greater earnings instability.

(continued)

> *(Continued)*
>
> A high percentage of variable costs to total costs indicates greater earnings stability. Variable costs can be adjusted more easily than fixed costs to meet a decline in product demand.
>
> A high-breakeven company is very susceptible to economic declines.

Profitability Measures

What about profitability?

Absolute dollar profit by itself has little meaning unless it is related to its source. A company's profit margin (net income to sales) indicates how well it is being managed and provides clues to a company's pricing, cost structure, and production efficiency.

A high gross profit percent (ratio of gross profit to sales) is favorable since it indicates that the company is able to control its manufacturing costs.

The return on common equity equals earnings available to common stockholders divided by average stockholders' equity. This ratio indicates the rate of return earned on common stockholders' investments.

Growth Rate

How do I compute growth rate?

Determine a company's growth rate in this way:

$$\frac{\text{EPS (end of year)} - \text{EPS (beginning of year)}}{\text{EPS (beginning of year)}}$$

Growth in dividends per share can be similarly computed:

$$\frac{\text{Change in retained earnings}}{\text{Stockholders' equity (beginning of year)}}$$

Other measures of growth are the changes in sales and total assets.

Market Value Measures

What indicators of market value exist?

Market value ratios apply to a comparison of the company's stock price to its earnings (or book value) per share. Also involved are dividend-related ratios. Included are:

- *Earnings per share.* This amount equals net income less preferred dividends divided by common stock outstanding.

- *Price-earnings ratio.* This ratio equals market price per share divided by earnings per share.
- *Book value per share.* This amount equals:

$$\frac{\text{Total stockholders' equity} - \left(\begin{array}{c}\text{Liquidation value of preferred stock} \\ + \text{Preferred dividends in arrears}\end{array}\right)}{\text{Common stock outstanding}}$$

  By comparing book value per share to market price per share, the CPA can see how investors feel about the business.
- *Dividend yield.* This amount equals dividends per share divided by market price per share.
- *Dividend payout.* This amount equals dividends per share divided by earnings per share. The investing public looks unfavorably on lower dividends since dividend payout is a sign of the financial health of the entity.

Bankruptcy Prediction

Will the company fail?

The following ratios are some of the key indicators to be examined by the CPA in predicting corporate bankruptcy:

- Cash flow from operations to total liabilities
- Net income to total assets
- Total liabilities to total assets
- Quick ratio
- Current ratio
- Operating income to total assets
- Interest coverage (income before interest and taxes to interest)
- Retained earnings to total assets
- Common equity to total liabilities
- Working capital to total assets
- Debt to equity
- Fixed assets to stockholders' equity

What is the "Z-score"?

Edward Altman's Z-score can be used to predict the likelihood of bankruptcy within the short run (one or two years).

The Z-score equals:

$$\frac{\text{Working capital}}{\text{Total assets}} \times 1.2 + \frac{\text{Retained earnings}}{\text{Total assets}} \times 1.4 + \frac{\text{Operating income}}{\text{Total assets}} \times 3.3$$

$$+ \frac{\text{Market value of common stock and preferred stock}}{\text{Total debt}} \times 0.6 + \frac{\text{Sales}}{\text{Total assets}} \times 0.999$$

Altman's scoring chart follows.

Score	Probability of Short-Term Illiquidity
1.80 or less	Very high
1.81 to 2.7	High
2.8 to 2.9	Possible
3.0 or higher	Not likely

Example 6.16

Company D provides this relevant information:

Working Capital	$ 250,000
Total Assets	900,000
Total Liabilities	300,000
Retained Earnings	200,000
Sales	1,000,000
Operating Income	150,000
Common Stock:	
Book Value	210,000
Market Value	300,000
Preferred Stock:	
Book Value	100,000
Market Value	160,000

The Z-score is:

$$\frac{\$250,000}{\$900,000} \times 1.2 + \frac{\$200,000}{\$900,000} \times 1.4 + \frac{\$150,000}{\$900,000} \times 3.3$$

$$+ \frac{\$460,000}{\$300,000} \times 0.6 + \frac{\$1,000,000}{\$900,000} \times 0.999 = 3.224$$

The score indicates that it is unlikely for business failure to occur.

Does company size bear a relationship to the probability of failure?

Many studies suggest that small companies have had higher failure rates than large companies. Size can be measured by total assets, sales, and age. According to the Small Business Administration (http://web.sba.gov/faqs/faqIndexAll.cfm?areaid=24), seven out of 10 new employer firms survive at least two years, half at least five years, a third at least 10 years, and a quarter stay in business 15 years or more. Census data report that 69 percent of new employer establishments born to new firms in the year 2000 survived at least two years, and 51 percent survived five or more years. Survival rates were similar across states and major industries. Bureau of Labor

Statistics data on establishment age show that 49 percent of establishments survive five years or more; 34 percent survive 10 years or more; and 26 percent survive 15 years or more. (*Source:* U.S. Department of Commerce, Census Bureau, Business Dynamics Statistics; U.S. Department of Labor, Bureau of Labor Statistics.)

What are indicators of financial distress?

Financial and operating deficiencies pointing to financial distress include:

- Significant decline in stock price
- Reduction in dividend payments
- Sharp increase in the cost of capital
- Inability to obtain further financing
- Inability to meet past-due obligations
- Poor financial reporting system
- Movement into business areas unrelated to the company's basic business
- Failure to keep up-to-date
- Failure to control costs
- High degree of competition

Liquidation Value

What is the expected liquidation value for a company?

J. Wilcox's "gambler's ruin" prediction formula can be used to determine a company's expected liquidation value:

- $+$ Cash and trading securities at market value
- $+$ (Inventory, accounts receivable, and prepaid expenses) $\times$ 70%
- $+$ (Other assets) $\times$ 50%
- $-$ Total liabilities

Example 6.17

Based on the following information, calculate A Company's liquidation value:

Cash	$200,000
Trading Securities	80,000
Accounts Receivable	70,000
Inventory	90,000
Prepaid Expenses	20,000
All Other Assets	300,000
Current Liabilities	100,000
Noncurrent Liabilities	250,000

(continued)

(*Continued*)

Liquidation value equals:

+ ($200,000 + $80,000)	=	$280,000
+ ($90,000 + $70,000 + $20,000) × 70%	=	+126,000
+ ($300,000) × 50%	=	+150,000
− ($100,000 + $250,000)	=	−350,000
Liquidation Value		$206,000

PART III

Managerial Accounting Applications

CHAPTER 7

Appraising Segmental Performance

Accountants typically look at budgeting and profit planning as tools for control of responsibility center operations and as facilitating factors in judging managerial performance. Accountants should be familiar with fundamental managerial accounting tools such as standard costing, flexible budgeting, and the contribution approach. They should have a thorough understanding of two important issues that arise frequently with decentralized operations: divisional performance and transfer pricing.

This chapter covers measures and guidelines for internally evaluating a company's performance, including:

- Responsibility accounting and responsibility centers
- Cost center performance and standard costs
- Flexible budgets and performance reports
- Profit centers and segmented reporting
- Evaluation of divisional performance
- Transfer pricing
- Budgeting and financial planning

The What and Why of Responsibility Accounting

What is responsibility accounting?

Responsibility accounting is the system for collecting and reporting revenue and cost information by areas of responsibility. It operates on the premise that managers should be held responsible for their performance, the performance of their subordinates, and all activities within their responsibility center.

What are the benefits of responsibility accounting?

Responsibility accounting, also called *profitability accounting* and *activity accounting*, has these advantages:

- It facilitates delegation of decision making.
- It helps management promote the concept of management by objective, in which managers agree on a set of goals. The manager's performance is then evaluated based on his or her attainment of these goals.
- It provides a guide to the evaluation of performance and helps establish standards of performance that are then used for comparison purposes.

- It permits effective use of the concept of *management by exception*, which means that the manager's attention is concentrated on the important deviations from standards and budgets.

What are responsibility centers?

A well-designed responsibility accounting system establishes *responsibility centers* within the organization. A responsibility center is a unit in the organization that has control over costs, revenues, and/or investment funds. A responsibility center can be a cost center, a profit center, or an investment center.

Cost Center

A cost center is the unit within the organization that is responsible only for costs. *Examples:* The production and maintenance departments of a manufacturing company, the admissions department of a university.

Recommendation

Variance analysis based on standard costs and flexible budgets would be a typical performance measure of a cost center.

Profit Center

A profit center is the unit that is held responsible for the revenues earned and costs incurred in that center. *Examples:* A sales office of a publishing company, an appliance department in a retail store, an auto repair center in a car dealership.

Recommendation

The contribution approach to cost allocation is widely used to measure the performance of a profit center.

Investment Center

An investment center is the unit within the organization that is held responsible for the costs, revenues, and related investments made in that center. *Examples:* The corporate headquarters, a division in a large decentralized organization.

Recommendation

Return on investment and residual income are two key performance measures of an investment center.

Exhibit 7.1 illustrates how responsibility accounting can be used within an organization and highlights profit and cost centers.

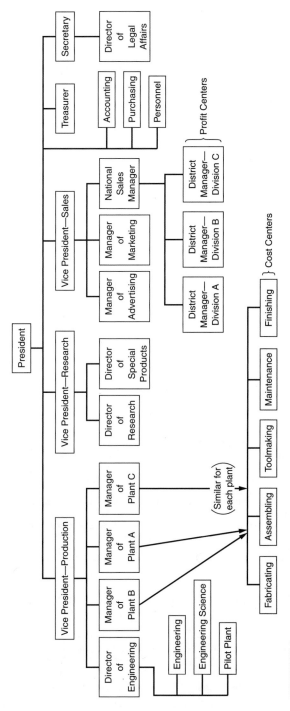

EXHIBIT 7.1 Organization Chart of Company XYZ

Cost Center Performance and Standard Costs

How do I measure the performance of a cost center?

One of the most important phases of responsibility accounting is establishing standard costs in order to evaluate performance by comparing actual costs with standard costs. The difference between the actual costs and the standard costs, called the *variance*, is calculated for individual cost centers. The variance analysis is a key tool for measuring the performance of a cost center.

The standard cost is based on physical and dollar measures. It is determined by multiplying the standard quantity of an input by its standard price. Two general types of variances (price and quantity) can be calculated for most cost items. The price variance is calculated as:

$$\text{Price variance} = \text{Actual quantity} \times (\text{Actual price} - \text{Standard price})$$

$$= AQ \times (AP - SP)$$

$$= \underset{(1)}{(AQ \times AP)} - \underset{(2)}{(AQ \times SP)}$$

The quantity variance is calculated as:

$$\text{Quantity variance} = (\text{Actual quantity} - \text{Standard quantity}) \times \text{Standard price}$$

$$= (AQ \times SQ) \times SP$$

$$= \underset{(2)}{(AQ \times SP)} - \underset{(3)}{(SQ \times SP)}$$

Exhibit 7.2 shows a general (three-column) model for variance analysis that incorporates the items (1), (2), and (3) from the preceding equations.

Actual Quantity of Inputs, at Actual Price (AQ × AP) (1)	Actual Quantity of Inputs, at Standard Price (AQ × SP) (2)	Standard Quantity Allowed for Output, at Standard Price (SQ × SP) (3)
Price Variance (1) − (2)		Quantity Variance (2) − (3)
Total Variance		
• Materials purchase price variance • Labor rate variance • Variable overhead spending variance	• Materials quantity (usage) variance • Labor efficiency variance • Variable overhead efficiency variance	

EXHIBIT 7.2   A General Model for Variance Analysis: Variable Manufacturing Costs

How is standard costing useful?

Standard costing has many advantages. It:

- Aids in cost control and performance evaluation
- Red-flags current and future problems through the "management by exception" principle
- Improves performance by recommending paths for corrective action in cost reduction
- Fixes responsibility
- Constitutes a vehicle of communication between top management and supervisors
- Establishes selling prices and transfer prices
- Determines bid prices on contracts
- Sets business goals
- Aids in the planning and decision-making processes
- Simplifies bookkeeping procedures and saves clerical costs

Standard costing is not without some drawbacks. *Examples:* The possible biases involved in deriving standards and the dysfunctional effects of setting improper norms and standards.

Materials Variances

How are materials variances computed?

A *materials price variance* is isolated at the time of purchase of the material. Therefore, it is normally computed based on the actual quantity purchased. The purchasing department is responsible for any materials price variance that might occur. The *materials quantity (usage) variance* is computed based on the actual quantity used.

Note

The production department is responsible for any materials quantity variance that might occur.

What causes materials variances?

The possible causes of *unfavorable* materials variances are:

Materials Price Variance
- Inaccurate standard prices
- Failure to take a discount on quantity purchases
- Failure to shop for bargains
- Inflationary cost increases
- Scarcity in raw material supplies resulting in higher prices
- Purchasing department inefficiencies

Materials Quantity (Usage) Variance
- Poorly trained workers
- Improperly adjusted machines
- Use of improper production method
- Outright waste on the production line
- Use of a lower-grade material purchased in order to economize on price

Example 7.1

ABC Corporation uses a standard cost system. The standard variable costs for Product J are:

Materials: 2 pounds at $3.00 per pound
Labor: 1 hour at $5.00 per hour
Variable overhead: 1 hour at $3.00 per hour

During March, 25,000 pounds of material were purchased for $74,750, and 20,750 pounds of material were used in producing 10,000 units of finished product. Direct labor costs incurred were $49,896 (10,080 direct labor hours), and variable overhead costs incurred were $34,776. Using the general (three-column) model, we find that the materials variances are:

Material Variances

Actual Quantity of Inputs, at Actual Price	Actual Quantity of Inputs, at Standard Price	Standard Quantity Allowed for Output, at Standard Price
(AQ × AP)	(AQ × SP)	(SQ × SP)
25,000 lb × $2.99 = $74,740	25,000 lb × $3.00 = $75,000	20,000 lb* × $3.00 = $60,000

Price Variance, $250 F†

20,750 lb × $3.00 = $62,250

Quantity Variance $2,250 U†

---

*10,000 units actually produced × 2 lb allowed per unit = 20,000 lb. *Note:* The amount of materials purchased (25,000 lb) differs from the amount of materials used in production (20,750 lb). The materials purchase price variance was computed using 25,000 lb purchased, whereas the material quantity (usage) variance was computed using the 20,750 lb used in production. A total variance cannot be computed because of the difference.
†A variance represents the deviation of actual cost from the standard or budgeted cost. U and F stand for "unfavorable" and "favorable," respectively.

Alternatively, we can compute the materials variances in this way:

Materials (purchase) price variance
$$= AQ \times (AP - SP) = (AQ \times AP) - (AQ \times SP)$$
$$= 25{,}000 \text{ lb } (\$2.99 - \$3.00) = \$74{,}750 - \$75{,}000$$
$$= \$250 \text{ F}$$

Materials quantity (usage) variance
$$= (AQ - SQ) \times SP$$
$$= (20{,}750 \text{ lb} - 20{,}000 \text{ lb}) \times \$3.00 = \$62{,}250 - \$60{,}000$$
$$= \$2{,}250 \text{ U}$$

Labor Variances

How are labor variances computed?

Labor variances are isolated when labor is used for production. They are computed in a manner similar to materials variances, except that in the three-column model the terms *hours* and *rate* are used in place of the terms *quantity* and *price*. The production department is responsible for both the prices paid for labor services and the quantity of labor services used. Therefore, the production department must explain the cause of any labor variances.

What causes labor variances?

Possible causes of unfavorable labor variances are:

- Labor price (rate) variance
  - Increase in wages
  - Poor scheduling of production, resulting in overtime work
  - Use of workers commanding higher hourly rates than contemplated in the standards
- Labor efficiency variance
  - Poor supervision
  - Use of unskilled workers paid lower rates
  - Wrong mixture of labor for a given job
  - Use of poor-quality machinery
  - Improperly trained workers
  - Poor quality of materials, requiring more labor time in processing
  - Machine breakdowns
  - Employee unrest
  - Production delays due to power failure

Variable Overhead Variances

How are variable overhead variances determined?

Variable overhead variances are computed in a way similar to labor variances. The production department usually is responsible for any variable overhead variance that might occur. Variances for fixed overhead are of questionable usefulness for control purposes, since they usually are beyond the control of the production department.

Example 7.2

Using the same data given in Example 7.1, the labor variances can be calculated as:

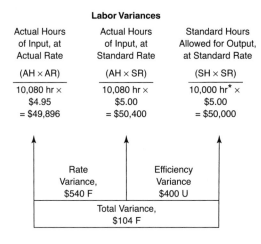

Labor Variances

Actual Hours of Input, at Actual Rate	Actual Hours of Input, at Standard Rate	Standard Hours Allowed for Output, at Standard Rate
(AH × AR)	(AH × SR)	(SH × SR)
10,080 hr × $4.95 = $49,896	10,080 hr × $5.00 = $50,400	10,000 hr* × $5.00 = $50,000

Rate Variance, $540 F

Efficiency Variance $400 U

Total Variance, $104 F

---

*10,000 units actually produced × 1 hour allowed per unit = 10,000 hrs.

Note

The symbols AQ, SQ, AP, and SP have been changed to AH, SH, AR, and SR to reflect the terms *hour* and *rate*.

Alternatively, we can calculate the labor variances in this way:

Labor Rate Variance $= AH \times (AR - SR)$
$= (AH \times AR) - (AH \times SR)$
$= 10,080 \text{ hrs } (\$4.95 - \$5.00) = \$49,896 - \$50,400$
$= \$504 \text{ F}$

Labor Efficiency Variance $= (AH - SH) \times SR$
$= (10,080 \text{ hrs} - 10,000 \text{ hrs}) \times \$5.00 = \$50,400 - \$50,000$
$= \$400 \text{ U}$

What causes unfavorable variable overhead variances?

Possible causes of unfavorable variable overhead variances are:

- Variable overhead spending variance
  - Increase in supplier prices
  - Increase in labor rates

- Inaccurate standards
- Waste
- Theft of supplies
- Variable overhead efficiency variance
  - Poorly trained workers
  - Use of poor-quality materials
  - Use of faulty equipment
  - Poor supervision
  - Employee unrest
  - Work interruptions
  - Poor production scheduling
  - Lack of automation and computerization in processing

Example 7.3

Using the same data given in Example 7.1, the variable overhead variances can be computed as:

Variable Overhead Variances

Actual Hours of Input, at Actual Rate	Actual Hours of Input, at Standard Rate	Standard Hours Allowed for Output at Standard Rate
(AH × AR)	(AH × SR)	(SH × SR)
10,080 hr × $3.45	10,080 hr × $3.00	10,000 hr* × $3.00
= $34,776	= $30,240	= $30,000

Spending Variance, $4,536 U   Efficiency Variance, $240 U

Total Variance, $4,776

---

*10,000 units actually produced × 1 hour allowed per unit = 10,000 hrs.

Alternatively, we can compute the variable overhead variances in this way:

Variable Overhead Spending Variance
$$= AH \times (AR - SR) = (AH \times AR) - (AH \times SR)$$
$$= 10{,}080 \text{ hrs } (\$3.45 - \$3.00) = \$34{,}776 - \$30{,}240$$
$$= \$4{,}536 \text{ U}$$

Variable Overhead Efficiency Variance
$$= (AH - SH) \times SR$$
$$= (10{,}080 \text{ hrs} - 10{,}000 \text{ hrs}) \times \$3.00 = \$30{,}240 - \$30{,}000$$
$$= \$240 \text{ U}$$

Fixed Overhead Variances

How are fixed overhead variances determined?

By definition, fixed overhead does not change over a relevant range of activity; the amount of fixed overhead per unit varies inversely with the level of production. In order to calculate variances for fixed overhead, it is necessary to determine a standard fixed overhead rate, which requires the selection of a predetermined level of activity (denominator activity). This activity should be measured on the basis of standard inputs allowed. The formula is:

$$\text{Standard fixed overhead rate} = \frac{\text{Budgeted fixed overhead}}{\text{Budgeted level of activity}}$$

Total fixed overhead variance is simply under- or overapplied overhead. It is the difference between actual fixed overhead incurred and fixed overhead applied to production (generally, on the basis of standard direct labor hours allowed for actual production). Total fixed overhead variance combines fixed overhead spending (flexible-budget) variance and fixed overhead volume (capacity) variance.

- *Fixed overhead spending (flexible-budget) variance.* This is the difference between actual fixed overhead incurred and budgeted fixed overhead. This variance is not affected by the level of production. Fixed overhead, by definition, does not change with the level of activity. The spending (flexible-budget) variance is caused solely by events such as unexpected changes in prices and unforeseen repairs.
- *Fixed overhead volume (capacity) variance.* This variance results when the actual level of activity differs from the denominator activity used in determining the standard fixed overhead rate. Note that the denominator used in the formula is the expected annual activity level. Fixed overhead volume variance is a measure of the cost of failure to operate at the denominator (budgeted) activity level and may be caused by such factors as failure to meet sales targets, idleness due to poor scheduling, and machine breakdowns. The volume variance is calculated as:

> Fixed overhead volume variance
>
>   = (Budgeted fixed overhead) − (Fixed overhead applied)
>
> or
>
>   = (Denominator activity − Standard hours allowed)
>   × Standard fixed overhead rate

When denominator activity exceeds standard hours allowed, the volume variance is unfavorable (U) because it is an index of less-than-denominator utilization of capacity.

There are no efficiency variances for fixed overhead. Fixed overhead does not change regardless of whether productive resources are used efficiently. For example, property taxes, insurance, and factory rents are not affected by whether production is being carried on efficiently.

	Incurred: Actual Hours x Actual Rate (1)	Flexible Budget Based on Actual Hours (2)	Flexible Budget Based on Standard Hours Allowed (3)	Applied (4)
3-Way Analysis	Spending Variance (1) – (2)	Efficiency Variance (Not Applicable)	Volume Variance (3) – (4)	
2-Way Analysis	Flexible Budget Variance (1) – (3)		Volume Variance (3) – (4)	
	(1) – (4) Under- or Overapplied			

EXHIBIT 7.3 Fixed Overhead Variances

Exhibit 7.3 illustrates the relationship between the various elements of fixed overhead and the possible variances.

Alternatively, fixed overhead volume variance can be calculated as:

$$\text{Fixed overhead volume variance overhead} = (\text{Denominator activity} - \text{Standard hours allowed}) \times \text{Standard fixed overhead rate}$$
$$= (1{,}300 \text{ hours} - 1{,}250 \text{ hours}) \times \$5.00 = 50 \text{ hours} \times \$5.00$$
$$= \$250 \text{ U}$$

Example 7.4

The Doubtfire Manufacturing Company has standard cost of factory overhead at a normal monthly production (denominator) volume of 1,300 direct labor hours:

Variable overhead: 1 hour at $2.00 per hour
Fixed overhead: 1 hour at $5.00 per hour

Fixed overhead budgeted is $6,500 per month. During the month of March, these two events occurred:

1. Actual overhead costs incurred (for 1,350 hours) were:

Variable	$2,853
Fixed	$6,725

(continued)

(*Continued*)

2. Standard hours allowed were 1,250 hours (1 hour × 1,250 units of output)

Note that:

- Flexible budget formula:

Variable overhead rate	$2.00 per direct labor hour
Fixed overhead budgeted	$6,500

- Standard overhead applied rates:

Variable	$2.00 per direct labor hour
Fixed	$5.00 per direct labor hour

Exhibit 7.4 shows all the variances for variable overhead as well as fixed overhead.

Incurred: Actual Hours x Actual Rate (1,350 hr) (1)	Flexible Budget Based on Actual Hours (1,250 hr) (2)	Flexible Budget Based on Standard Hours Allowed (1,250 hr) (3)	Applied (1,350 hr) (4)
V $2,853	$2,700 (1,350 × $2)	$2,500 (1,250 × $2)	$2,500
F 6,725	6,500	6,500	6,250
$9,578	$9,200	$9,000	$8,750

3-way	Spending Variance (1) − (2) V $153 U F 225 U $378 U	Efficiency Variance (Not Applicable) $200 U Not Applicable $200 U	Volume Variance (3) − (4) Not Applicable $250 U $250 U
2-way	Flexible Budget Variance (1) − (3) V $353 U F 225 U $578 U		Volume Variance (3) − (4) Not Applicable $250 U $250 U
	Under- or Overapplied (1) − (4) V $353 U F 475 U $828 U		

EXHIBIT 7.4   Variance Analysis for Variable Overhead and Fixed Overhead

What are the methods of variance analysis for factory overhead?

Variance analysis for factory overhead consists of a two-, three-, or four-way method of computation, depending on the significance of the variance amounts compared to the cost of analysis. These methods are indicated in the two previous figures.

The two-way analysis computes two variances: budget variance (sometimes called the flexible-budget or controllable variance) and volume variances, which means:

1. Budget variance = Variable spending variance + Fixed spending (budget) variance + Variable efficiency variance
2. Volume variance = Fixed volume variance

The three-way analysis computes three variances: spending, efficiency, and volume variances. Therefore:

1. Spending variance = Variable spending variance + Fixed spending (budget) variance
2. Efficiency variance = Variable efficiency variance
3. Volume variance = Fixed volume variance

The four-way analysis includes:

1. Variable spending variance
2. Fixed spending (budget) variance
3. Variable efficiency variance
4. Fixed volume variance

Mix and Yield Variances

What about the computation of mix and yield variances?

The *material mix variance* measures the impact of the deviation from the standard mix on material costs. The *material yield variance* measures the impact on material costs of the deviation from the standard input material allowed for actual production. The *material quantity variance* is divided into a material mix variance and a material yield variance.

- Compute the material mix variance by holding the total input units constant at their actual amount.
- Compute the material yield variance by holding the mix constant at the standard amount.

The computations for labor mix and yield variances are the same as those for materials. If there is no mix, the yield variance is the same as the quantity (or usage) variance.

What causes mix and yield variances?

Possible causes of unfavorable mix variances are:

- When capacity restraints force substitution
- Poor production scheduling
- Lack of certain types of labor
- Short supply of certain materials

Possible causes of unfavorable yield variances are:

- Low-quality materials and/or labor
- Faulty equipment
- Improper production methods
- Improper or costly mix of materials and/or labor

Example 7.5

J Company produces a compound composed of materials Alpha and Beta that is marketed in 20-lb bags. Material Alpha can be substituted for material Beta. Standard cost and mix data have been determined as:

	Unit Price	Standard Unit	Standard Mix Proportions
Material Alpha	$3.00	5 lb	25%
Material Beta	4.00	15	75
		20 lb	100%

Processing each 20-lb bag of material requires 10 hours of labor. The company employs two types of labor—skilled and unskilled—working on two processes, assembly and finishing. This standard labor cost has been set for a 20-lb bag:

	Standard Hours	Standard Wage Rate	Total	Standard Mix Proportions
Unskilled	4	$2.00	$ 8.00	40%
Skilled	6	3.00	18.00	60
	10	$2.60	$26.00	100%

At standard cost, labor averages $2.60 per unit. During the month of December, 100 20-lb bags were completed with the following labor costs:

	Actual Hours	Actual Rate	Actual Wages
Unskilled	380	$2.50	$ 950
Skilled	600	3.25	1,950
	980	$2.96	$2,900

We now want to determine these six variances from standard costs:

1. Material purchase price
2. Material mix
3. Material quantity
4. Labor rate
5. Labor mix
6. Labor efficiency

Material records show:

	Beginning Inventory	Purchase	Ending Inventory
Material Alpha	100 lb	800 @ $3.10	200 lb
Material Beta	225	1,350 @ $3.90	175

We also prepare appropriate journal entries. We show how to compute these variances in a tabular form.

Materials Variances

1. MATERIAL PURCHASE PRICE VARIANCE

	Material Price per Unit			Actual Quantity Purchased	Variance ($)
	Standard	Actual	Difference		
Material Alpha	$3.00	$3.10	$0.10 U	800 lb	$ 80 U
Material Beta	4.00	3.90	0.10 F	1,350	135 F
					$ 55 F

2. MATERIAL MIX VARIANCE

	Unit That Should Have Been Used at Standard Mix*	Actual Unit at Actual Mix[†]	Difference	Standard Unit Price	Variance ($)
Alpha	525 lb	700 lb	175 U	$3.00	$525 U
Beta	1,575	1,400	175 F	4.00	700 F
	2,100 lb	2,100 lb			$175 F

*This is the standard mix proportion of 25 percent and 75 percent applied to the actual material units used of 2,100 lb.

[†]Actual units used = Beginning inventory + Purchases – Ending inventory. Therefore,
   Material Alpha: 700 lb = 100 + 800 – 200
   Material Beta: 1,400 lb = 225 + 1,350 – 175

The material mix variance measures the impact of the deviation from the standard mix on material costs.

(continued)

(*Continued*)

Therefore, it is computed holding the total quantity used constant at its actual amount and allowing the material mix to vary between actual and standard. As shown, because of a favorable change in mix, we end up with a favorable material mix variance of $175.

3. MATERIAL QUANTITY VARIANCE

	Unit That Should Have Been Used at Standard Mix*	Standard Unit at Standard Mix	Difference	Standard Unit Price	Variance ($)
Alpha	525 lb	500 lb	25 U	$3.00	$ 75 U
Beta	1,575	1,500	75 U	4.00	300 U
	2,100 lb	2,000 lb	100 U		$375 U

*This is the standard mix proportion of 25 percent and 75 percent applied to the actual material units used of 2,100 lb.

The total material variance is the sum of the three variances:

Purchase price variance	$ 55 F
Mix variance	175 F
Quantity variance	375 U
	$145 U

The increase of $145 in material costs was due solely to an unfavorable quantity variance of 100 lb of materials Alpha and Beta. The unfavorable quantity variance, however, was compensated largely by favorable mix and price variances. J Company must look for ways to cut down waste and spoilage.

The labor cost increase of $300 ($2,900 − $2,600) is attributable to these causes:

- An increase of $0.50 per hour in the rate paid to skilled labor and $0.25 per hour in the rate paid to unskilled labor
- An unfavorable mix of skilled and unskilled labor
- A favorable labor efficiency variance of 20 hours

The labor variances are computed next.

Labor Variances

4. LABOR RATE VARIANCE

	Labor Rate per Hour			Actual Hour Used	Variance ($)
	Standard	Actual	Difference		
Unskilled	$2.00	$2.50	$0.50 U	380 U	$190 U
Skilled	3.00	3.25	0.25 U	600 U	150 U
					$340 U

5. LABOR MIX VARIANCE

	Actual Hours at Standard Mix*	Actual Hours at Actual Mix	Difference	Standard Rate	Variance ($)
Unskilled	392 hr	380 hr	12 F	$2.00	$24 F
Skilled	588	600	12 U	3.00	36 U
	980 hr	980 hr			$12 U

*This is the standard proportions of 40 percent and 60 percent applied to the actual total labor hours used of 980.

6. LABOR EFFICIENCY VARIANCE

	Actual Hours at Standard Mix	Standard Hours at Standard Mix	Difference	Standard Rate	Variance ($)
Unskilled	392 hr	400 hr	8 F	$2.00	$16 F
Skilled	588	600	12 F	3.00	36 F
	980 hr	1,000 hr			$52 F

The total labor variance is the sum of these three variances:

Rate variance	$340 U
Mix variance	12 U
Efficiency variance	52 F
	$300 U

which is proved to be:
Total Labor Variance

	Actual Hours Used	Actual Rate	Total Actual Cost	Standard Hours Allowed	Standard Hours Rate	Total Cost	Variance ($)
Unskilled	380 hr	$2.50	$ 950	400	$2.00	$ 800	$150 U
Skilled	600	3.25	1,950	600	3.00	1,800	150 U
			$2,900			$2,600	$300 U

The unfavorable labor variance, as evidenced by the cost increase of $300, may be due to:

- Overtime necessary because of poor production scheduling, resulting in a higher average labor cost per hour
- Unnecessary use of more expensive skilled labor (J Company should put more effort into better production scheduling)

Example 7.6

The Giffen Manufacturing Company uses a standard cost system for its production of a chemical product. This chemical is produced by mixing three major raw materials, A, B, and C. The company has these standards:

36 lb of Material A	@ 1.00	=	$ 36.00
48 lb of Material B	@ 2.00	=	$ 96.00
36 lb of Material C	@ 1.75	=	$ 63.00
120 lb of standard mix	@ 1.625	=	$195.00

The company should produce 100 lb of finished product at a standard cost of $1.625 per lb ($195/120 lb). Converting 120 lb of materials into 100 lb of finished chemical requires 400 direct labor hours at $3.50 per hour, or $14 per lb. During the month of December, the company completed 4,250 lb of output with this labor: direct labor 15,250 hours at $3.50 per hour. Material records show:

	Materials Purchased in Month		Materials Used in Month
Material A	1,200 lb @	$1.00	1,160 lb
Material B	1,800 @	1.95	1,820
Material C	1,500 @	1.80	1,480

The material *price variance is isolated at the time of purchase*. We want to compute the material purchase price, quantity, mix, and yield variances. We also want to prepare appropriate journal entries.

Next we show the computations of variances in tabular form.

Materials Variances

MATERIAL PURCHASE PRICE VARIANCE

	Material Price per Unit			Actual Quantity Purchased	Variance ($)
	Standard	Actual	Difference		
Material A	$1.00	$1.10	$0.10 U	1,200 lb	$120 U
Material B	2.00	1.95	0.05 F	1,800	90 F
Material C	1.75	1.80	0.05 U	1,500	75 U
					$105 U

The material quantity variance computed next results from the change in the mix of materials as well as from changes in the total quantity of materials. The standard input allowed for actual production consists of 1,275 lb of material A, 1,700 lb of material B, and 1,275 lb of material C, a total of 4,250 lb. The actual input consisted of 1,160 lb of material A, 1,820 lb of material B, and 1,480 lb of material C. The total of variance is subdivided into a material mix variance and a material yield variance, as shown.

MATERIAL QUANTITY VARIANCE

	Actual Units Used at Actual Mix	Should Have Been Inputs Based on Actual Output	Difference	Standard Unit Price	Variance ($)
Material A	1,160 lb	1,275 lb	115 F	$1.00	$115.00 F
Material B	1,820	1,700	120 U	2.00	240.00 U
Material C	1,480	1,275			358.75 U
	4,460 lb	4,250 lb			$483.75 U

The computations of the material mix variance and the material yield variance for the Giffen Manufacturing Company are given next.

MATERIAL MIX VARIANCE

	Actual Units Used at Actual Output*	Should Have Been Individual Input Based on Total Actual Throughput*	Difference	Standard Unit Price	Variance ($)
Material A	1,338 lb	1,160 lb	178 F	$1.00	$178.00 F
Material B	1,784	1,820	36 U	2.00	72.00 U
Material C	1,338	1,480	142 U	1.79	248.50 U
	4,460 lb	4,460 lb			$142.50 U

*This is the standard mix proportions of 30 percent, 40 percent, and 30 percent applied to the actual material units used of 4,460 lb.

MATERIAL YIELD VARIANCE

	Expected Input Units at Standard Mix	Should Have Been Inputs Based on Actual Output*	Difference	Standard Unit Price	Variance ($)
Material A	1,338 lb	1,275 lb	63 U	$1.00	$ 63.00 U
Material B	1,784	1,700	84 U	2.00	168.00 U
Material C	1,338	1,275	63 U	1.75	110.25 U
	4,460 lb	4,420 lb			$341.25 U

*This is the standard mix proportions of 30 percent, 40 percent, and 30 percent applied to the actual throughput of 4,460 lb or output of 4,250 lb.

The material mix and material yield variances are unfavorable, indicating that a shift was made to a more expensive (at standard) input mix and that an excessive quantity of material was used. Poor production scheduling requiring an unnecessarily excessive use of input material and an undesirable mix of materials A, B, and C was responsible for this result. To remedy the situation, the company must ensure that:

- The material mix is adhered to in terms of the least-cost combination without affecting product quality.

(continued)

(Continued)

- The proper production methods are being implemented so that inefficiencies, waste, and spoilage are within the standard allowance.
- Quality materials, consistent with established standards, are being used.

Journal Entries

TO RECORD MATERIAL PURCHASES:

Material and Supplies	7,425*	
Material Purchase Price Variance	105 U	
Cash (or Accounts Payable)		7,530†

*Actual quantities purchased at standard prices:

Material A (1,200 lb	@	$1.00)	$1,200	
Material B (1,800	@	2.00)	3,600	
Material C (1,500	@	1.75)	2,625	7,425

†Actual quantities purchased at actual prices:

Material A (1,200 lb	@	$1.10)	$1,320	
Material B (1,800	@	1.95)	3,510	
Material C (1,500	@	1.80)	2,700	7,530

TO CHARGE MATERIALS INTO PRODUCTION

Work-in-Process	$7,247.50*	
Material Mix Variance	42.50 U	
Material and Supplies		7,390†

*Actual quantities used at standard mix at standard prices:

Material A (1,338 lb	@	$1.00)	$1,338.00	
Material B (1,784	@	2.00)	3,568.00	
Material C (1,480	@	1.75)	2,341.50	7,247.50

†Actual quantities used at standard prices:

Material A (1,160 lb	@	$1.00)	$1,160	
Material B (1,820	@	2.00)	3,640	
Material C (1,480	@	1.75)	2,590	7,390.00

TO TRANSFER MATERIAL COSTS TO FINISHED GOODS

Finished Goods	$6,906.25*	
Material Yield Variance	341.25 U	
Work-in-Process		7,247.50*

*See the preceding for the numerical computations.

Employees seldom complete their operations according to standard times. Two factors should be considered in computing labor variances if the analysis and computation are to be used to fix responsibility:

1. The change in labor cost resulting from the efficiency of the workers, measured by a labor efficiency variance (in finding the change, allowed hours are determined through the material input)
2. The change in labor cost due to a difference in the yield, measured by a labor yield variance (in computing the change, actual output is converted to allowed input hours)

For the Giffen Manufacturing Company, more efficient workers resulted in a savings of 383.33 hours (15,250 hr − 14,866.67 hr). Priced at the standard rate per hour, this produced an unfavorable labor efficiency variance of $1,341.66, as shown next.

Labor Efficiency Variance

Actual hours at standard rate	$53,375.00
Actual hours at expected output	52,033.30
(4,460 hr × 400/120) = 14,866.67 hr @ $3.50	$ 1,341.60

With a standard yield of $83\frac{1}{3}$% (= 100/120), 4,250 lb of finished material should have required 17,000 hr of direct labor (4,250 lb × 400 direct labor hours (DLH)/100). Comparing the hours allowed for the actual input, 14,866.67 hr, with the hours allowed for actual output, 17,000 hr, we find a favorable labor yield variance of $7,466.66, as shown next.

Labor Yield Variance

Actual hours at expected output	$52,033.30
Actual output (4,250 lb × 400/100	59,500.00
= 17,000 hrs. @ $3.50 or 4,250 lb @ $14.00)	$ 7,466.60

The labor efficiency variance can be combined with the yield variance to give us the *traditional* labor efficiency variance, which turns out to be favorable, as shown.

Labor Efficiency Variance	$1,341.66 U
Labor Yield Variance	7,466.66 F
	$6,125.00 F

(*continued*)

(Continued)

This division is necessary when there is a difference between the actual yield and the standard yield, if responsibility is to be fixed. The producing department cannot be rightfully credited with a favorable efficiency variance of $6,125. Note, however, that a favorable yield variance, which is a factor most likely outside the control of the producing department, more than offsets the unfavorable labor efficiency variance of $1,341.66, for which the producing department rightfully should have been responsible.

Journal Entries

TO TRANSFER LABOR COSTS TO WORK-IN-PROCESS

Work-in-Process	$52,033.34	
Labor Efficiency Variance	1,341.66 U	
Payroll		$53,375.00

TO TRANSFER LABOR COSTS TO FINISHED GOODS

Finished Goods	$59,500	
Labor Yield Variance		7,466.66 F
Work-in-Process		$52,033.34

Flexible Budgets and Performance Reports

What are the implications of a flexible budget?

A flexible budget is an extremely useful tool in cost control. In contrast to a *static budget*, the flexible budget is:

- Geared toward a range of activity rather than a single level of activity
- Dynamic in nature rather than static

The static (fixed) budget is geared to only one level of activity and has problems in cost control. Flexible budgeting distinguishes between fixed and variable costs, thus allowing for a budget that can be automatically adjusted (via changes in variable cost totals) to the particular level of activity *actually* attained. By using the *cost-volume formula* (or *flexible budget formula*), a series of budgets can be easily developed for various levels of activity. Thus, variances between actual costs and budgeted costs are adjusted for volume ups and downs, before differences due to price and quantity factors are computed.

Note

The primary use of the flexible budget is for accurate measurement of performance by comparing actual costs for a given output with the budgeted costs for the same level of output.

Example 7.7

To illustrate the difference between the static budget and the flexible budget, assume that the fabricating department of Company X is budgeted to produce 6,000 units during June. Assume further that the company was able to produce only 5,800 units. The budget for direct labor and variable overhead costs is:

Company X
Direct Labor and Variable Overhead Budget Fabricating
Department for the Month of June

Budgeted Production	6,000 units
Actual Production	5,800 units
Direct Labor	$39,000
Variable Overhead Costs:	
Indirect Labor	6,000
Supplies	900
Repairs	300
	$46,200

If a static budget approach is used, the performance report will appear as:

Company X
Direct Labor and Variable Overhead Budget Fabricating
Department for the Month of June

	Budget	Actual*	Variance (U or F)
Production in Units	6,000	5,800	200 U
Direct Labor	$39,000	$38,500	$500 F
Variable Overhead Costs:			
Indirect Labor	6,000	5,950	50 F
Supplies	900	870	30 F
Repairs	300	295	5 F
	$46,200	$45,615	$585 F

*Provided by accounting record.

(*continued*)

(*Continued*)

These given cost variances are useless; they compare oranges with apples. The problem is that the budget costs are based on an activity level of 6,000 units, whereas the actual costs were incurred at an activity level below this (5,800 units). From a control standpoint, it makes no sense to try to compare costs at one activity level with costs at a different activity level. Such comparisons would make a production manager look good as long as the actual production is less than the budgeted production. Using the cost-volume formula while generating the budget based on the 5,800 actual units gives this performance report:

Company X Performance Report
Fabricating Department
for the Month of June

Budgeted Production	6,000 units
Actual Production	5,800 units

	Cost-Volume Formula	Budget 6,000 Units	Actual 5,800 Units	Variance (U or F)
Direct Labor	$6.50 per unit	$37,700	$38,500	$800 U
Variable Overhead:				
Indirect Labor	1.00	5,800	5,950	150 U
Supplies	0.15	870	870	0
Repairs	0.05	290	295	5 U
	$7.70	$44,660	$45,615	$955 U

Note

All cost variances are unfavorable (U), as compared to the favorable (F) cost variance on the performance report based on the static budget approach.

Profit Centers and Segmented Reporting

How do I evaluate business segments?

Segmented reporting is the process of reporting activities of profit centers of an organization such as divisions, product lines, or sales territories. The *contribution approach* is valuable for segmented reporting. It emphasizes the cost behavior patterns and the controllability of costs that are generally useful for profitability analysis of various segments of an organization. The contribution approach is based on the theses that:

- Fixed costs are much less controllable than variable costs are.
- *Direct fixed costs* and *common fixed costs* must be clearly distinguished. Direct fixed costs are those fixed costs that can be identified directly with a particular segment of an organization. Common fixed costs are those costs that cannot be identified directly with the segment.
- Common fixed costs should be clearly identified as unallocated in the contribution income statement by segments. Any attempt to allocate these types of costs arbitrarily to the segments of the organization can destroy the value of responsibility accounting. It would lead to unfair evaluation of performance and misleading managerial decisions.

The next concepts are highlighted in the contribution approach:

- *Contribution margin (CM).* Sales minus variable costs.
- *Contribution controllable by segment managers.* Contribution margin minus direct fixed costs controllable by segment managers. Direct fixed costs include discretionary fixed costs (e.g., certain advertising, research and development, sales promotion, and engineering).
- *Segment margin.* Contribution controllable by segment managers minus fixed costs controllable by others. Fixed costs controllable by others include traceable and committed fixed costs (e.g., depreciation, property taxes, insurance, and the segment managers' salaries).
- *Net income.* Segment margin minus unallocated common fixed costs.

Example 7.8

Exhibit 7.5 illustrates two levels of segmental reporting:

1. By segments defined as divisions
2. By segments defined as product lines of a division

The segment margin is the best measure of the profitability of a segment. Unallocated fixed costs are common to the segments being evaluated and should be left unallocated in order not to distort the performance results of segments.

(continued)

(Continued)

SEGMENTS DEFINED AS DIVISIONS

	Total Company	Segments Division 1	Division 2
Sales	$150,000	$90,000	$60,000
Variable costs:			
Manufacturing	40,000	30,000	10,000
Selling and admin.	20,000	14,000	6,000
Total variable costs	60,000	44,000	16,000
Contribution margin	$90,000	$46,000	$44,000
Less: Direct fixed costs controllable by division managers	55,000	33,000	22,000
Contribution controllable by division managers	$35,000	$13,000	$22,000
Less: Direct fixed costs controllable by others	15,000	10,000	5,000
Divisional segment margin	$20,000	$3,000	$17,000
Less: Unallocated common fixed costs	$10,000		
Net income	$10,000		

SEGMENTS DEFINED AS PRODUCT LINES OF DIVISION 2

	Division 2	Segments Deluxe Model	Regular Model
Sales	$60,000	$20,000	$40,000
Variable costs:			
Manufacturing	10,000	5,000	5,000
Selling and admin.	6,000	2,000	4,000
Total variable costs	16,000	7,000	9,000
Contribution margin	$44,000	$13,000	$31,000
Less: Direct fixed costs controllable by product line managers	22,000	8,000	14,000
Contribution controllable by product line managers	$22,000	$5,000	$17,000
Less: Direct fixed costs controllable by others	4,500	1,500	3,000
Product line margin	$17,500	$3,500	$14,000
Less: Unallocated common fixed costs	$ 500		
Divisional segment margin	$17,000		

EXHIBIT 7.5   Segmental Income Statement

Profit Variance Analysis

What is profit variance analysis?

Profit variance analysis, often called *gross profit analysis*, deals with how to analyze the profit variance that constitutes the departure between actual profit and the previous year's income or the budgeted figure. The primary goal of profit variance analysis is to improve performance and profitability in the future.

Profit, whether it is gross profit in absorption costing or contribution margin in direct costing, is affected by at least three basic items: sales price, sales volume, and costs. In addition, in a multiproduct firm, if not all products are equally profitable, profit is affected by the mix of products sold.

The differences between budgeted and actual profits are due to one or more of the following:

- Changes in unit sales price and cost, called *sales price variances* and *cost price variances*, respectively. The difference between sales price variance and cost price variance is often called a contribution margin per unit variance or a gross profit per unit variance, depending on what type of costing system is being referred to (i.e., absorption costing or direct costing). Contribution margin, however, is considered a better measure of product profitability because it deducts from sales revenue only the variable costs that are controllable in terms of fixing responsibility. Gross profit does not reflect cost–volume–profit relationships. Nor does it consider directly traceable marketing costs.
- Changes in the volume of products sold summarized as the sales volume variance and the cost volume variance. The difference between the two is called the *total volume variance*.
- Changes in the volume of the more profitable or less profitable items, referred to as the *sales mix variance*.

Detailed analysis is critical to management when multiple products exist. The volume variances can be used to measure a change in volume (while holding the mix constant), and the mix can be employed to evaluate the effect of a change in sales mix (while holding the quantity constant). This type of variance analysis is useful when the products are substituted for each other or when products that are not necessarily substitutes for each other are marketed through the same channel.

Types of Standards in Profit Variance Analysis

To determine the various causes for a favorable variance (an increase) or an unfavorable variance (a decrease) in profit, we need some kind of yardsticks to compare against the actual results. The yardsticks may be based on the prices and costs of the previous year, or any year selected as the base period. Some companies summarize profit variance analysis data in their annual reports by showing departures from the previous year's reported income. However, a more effective control and budgetary method can be established than the previous year's data. Standard or budgeted mix can be determined using such sophisticated techniques as linear and goal programming.

Single-Product Firms

Profit variance analysis is simplest in a single-product firm, for there is only one sales price, one set of costs (or cost price), and a unitary sales volume. An unfavorable profit variance can be broken down into four components: (1) sales price variance, (2) cost price variance, (3) sales volume variance, and (4) cost volume variance.

The sales price variance measures the impact on the firm's contribution margin (or gross profit) of changes in the unit selling price. It is computed as:

$$\text{Sales price variance} = (\text{Actual price} - \text{Budget price}) \times \text{Actual sales}$$

If the actual price is lower than the budgeted price, for example, this variance is unfavorable; it tends to reduce profit. The cost price variance, however, is simply the summary of price variances for materials, labor, and overhead. (This is the sum of material price, labor rate, and factory overhead spending variances.) It is computed as:

$$\text{Cost price variance} = (\text{Actual cost} - \text{Budget cost}) \times \text{Actual sales}$$

If the actual unit cost is lower than budgeted cost, for example, this variance is favorable; it tends to increase profit. We simplify the computation of price variances by taking the sales price variance less the cost price variance, and call it the gross profit per unit variance or contribution margin per unit variance.

The sales volume variance indicates the impact on the firm's profit of changes in the unit sales volume. This is the amount by which sales would have varied from the budget if nothing but sales volume had changed. It is computed as:

$$\text{Sales volume variance} = (\text{Actual sales} - \text{Budget sales}) \times \text{Budget price}$$

If actual sales volume is greater than budgeted sales volume, this is favorable; it tends to increase profit. The cost volume variance has the same interpretation. It is:

$$(\text{Actual sales} - \text{Budget sales}) \times \text{Budget cost per unit}$$

The difference between the sales volume variance and the cost volume variance is called the *total volume variance*.

Multiproduct Firms

When a firm produces more than one product, there is a fourth component of the profit variance. This is the *sales mix variance*, the effect on profit of selling a different proportionate mix of products than what has been budgeted. This variance arises when different products have different contribution margins (CMs). In a multiproduct firm, actual sales volume can differ from that budgeted in two ways.

1. The total number of units sold could differ from the target aggregate sales.
2. The mix of the products actually sold may not be proportionate to the target mix.

Each of these changes in volume is reflected in a separate variance.

The total volume variance is divided into the two variances: sales mix variance and sales quantity variance. These two variances should be used to evaluate the marketing department of the firm. The sales mix variance shows how well the department has done in terms of selling the more profitable products, whereas the sales quantity variance measures how well the firm has done in terms of its overall sales volume. They are computed as:

$$\text{Sales mix variance} = (\text{Actual sales at budget mix} - \text{Actual sales at actual mix})$$
$$\times \text{Budget CM (or Gross profit per unit)}$$

$$\text{Sales quantity variance} = (\text{Actual sales at budget mix} - \text{Budget sales at budget mix})$$
$$\times \text{Budget CM (or Gross profit per unit)}$$

$$\text{Sales volume variance} = (\text{Actual sales at actual mix} - \text{Budget sales at budget mix})$$
$$\times \text{Budget CM (or Gross profit per unit)}$$

Example 7.9   Profit Variance Analysis

The Lake Tahoe Ski Store sells two ski models: Model X and Model Y. For the years 2X11 and 2X12, the store realized a gross profit of $246,640 and $211,650, respectively. The owner of the store was astounded by the decrease since the total sales volume in dollars and in units was higher for 2X12 than for 2X11, yet the gross profit achieved actually declined. The following are the store's unaudited operating results for 2X11 and 2X12. No fixed costs were included in the cost of goods sold per unit.

		Model X				Model Y		
Year	Selling Price	Cost of Goods Sold per Unit	Sales in Units	Sales Revenue	Selling Price	Cost of Goods Sold per Unit	Sales in Units	Sales Revenue
1	$150	$110	2,800	$420,000	$172	$121	2,640	$454,080
2	160	125	2,650	424,000	176	135	2,900	510,400

To explain why the gross profit declined by $34,990, we include a detailed variance analysis of price changes and changes in volume for both sales and cost, and also subdivide the total volume variance into change in price and changes in quantity.

Sales price and sales volume variances measure the impact on the firm's CM or gross margin (GM) of changes in the unit selling price and sales volume. In computing these variances, all costs are held constant in order to stress changes in price and volume. Cost price and cost volume variances are computed in the same manner, holding price and volume constant. All these variances for the Lake Tahoe Ski Store are computed next.

(continued)

(Continued)

Sales Price Variance

Actual sales for 2X12:	$896,300
Model X: 2,650 × $160 = $424,000	
Model Y: 2,900 × $179 = $510,400	$934,400
Actual 2X12 sales at 2X11 prices:	
Model X: 2,650 × $150 = $397,500	
Model Y: 2,900 × $172 = $498,800	896,300
	$ 38,100 F

Sales Volume Variance

Actual 2X12 sales at 2X11 prices	$896,300
Actual 2X11 sales at 2X11 prices:	
Model X: 2,800 × $150 = $420,000	
Model Y: 2,640 × $172 = $454,080	874,080
	$ 22,220 F

Cost Price Variance

Actual cost of goods sold for 2X12:	$896,300
Model X: 2,650 × $125 = $331,250	
Model Y: 2,900 × $135 = $391,500	722,750
Actual 2X12 sales at 2X11 costs:	
Model X: 2,650 × $110 = $291,500	
Model Y: 2,900 × $121 = $350,900	$642,400
	$ 80,350 U

Cost Volume Variance

Actual 2X12 sales at 2X11 costs	$642,400
Actual 2X11 sales at 2X11 costs:	
Model X: 2,800 × $110 = $308,000	
Model Y: 2,640 × $121 = $319,440	627,440
	$ 14,960 U

Total volume variance = Sales volume variance − Cost volume variance

= $22,220 F − $14,960 U   = $7,260 F

The total volume variance is computed as the sum of a sales mix variance and a sales quantity variance:

Sales Mix Variance

	2X12 Actual Sales at 2X11 Mix*	2X12 Actual Sales at 2X12 Mix	Diff.	2X11 Gross Profit per Unit	Variance ($)
Model X	2,857	2,650	207 U	$40	$ 8,280 U
Model Y	2,693	2,900	207 F	51	10,557 F
	5,550	5,550			$ 2,277 F

*This is the 2X11 mix (used as standard or budget) proportions of 51.47 percent (or 2,800/5,440 = 51.47%) and 48.53 percent (or 2,640/5,440 = 48.53%) applied to the actual 2X12 sales figure of 5,550 units.

Sales Quantity Variance

	2X12 Actual Sales at 2X11 Mix*	2X12 Actual Sales at 2X12 Mix	Diff.	2X11 Gross Profit per Unit	Variance ($)
Model X	2,857	2,800	57 F	$40	$2,280 F
Model Y	2,693	2,640	52 F	51	2,703 F
	5,550	5,440			$4,983 F

A favorable total volume variance is due to a favorable shift in the sales mix (i.e., from Model X to Model Y) and also to a favorable increase in sales volume (by 110 units), which is shown next.

Sales mix variance	$2,277 F
Sales quantity	4,983 F
	$7,260

However, there remains the decrease in gross profit. The decrease in gross profit of $34,990 can be explained as:

	Gains	Losses
Gain due to increased sales price	$38,100 F	
Loss due to increased cost		80,350
Gain due to increase in units sold	4,983 F	
Gain due to shift in sales mix	2,277 F	
	$45,360 F	$80,350
	$80,350	$45,360
Hence, net decrease in gross profit =		
	$80,350 − $45,360	= $34,990 U

(continued)

(Continued)

Despite the increase in sales price and volume and the favorable shift in sales mix, the Lake Tahoe Ski Store ended up losing $34,990 compared to 2X11. The major reason for this comparative loss was the tremendous increase in cost of goods sold, as costs for both Model X and Model Y went up quite significantly over 2X11. The store has to take a close look at the cost picture, even though only variable and fixed costs should be analyzed in an effort to cut down on controllable costs. In doing that, it is essential that responsibility be clearly fixed to given individuals. In a retail business like the Lake Tahoe Ski Store, operating expenses, such as advertising and payroll of store employees, must also be closely scrutinized.

Example 7.10   Sales Mix Analysis

Shim and Siegel, Inc., sells two products, C and D. Product C has a budgeted unit contribution margin (CM) of $3.00, and Product D has a budgeted unit CM of $6.00. The budget for a recent month called for sales of 3,000 units of C and 9,000 units of D, for a total of 12,000 units. Actual sales totaled 12,200 units: 4,700 of C and 7,500 of D. We compute the sales volume variance and break this variance down into the sales quantity variance and sales mix variance.

Shim and Siegel's sales volume variance is computed next. As can be seen, while total unit sales increased by 200 units, the shift in sales mix resulted in a $3,900 unfavorable sales volume variance.

Sales Volume Variance

	Actual Sales at Actual Mix	Standard Sales at Budgeted Mix	Difference	Budgeted CM per Unit	Variance ($)
Product C	4,700	3,000	1,700 F	$3.00	$5,100 F
Product D	7,500	9,000	1,500 U	6.00	9,000 U
	12,200	12,000			$3,900 U

In multiproduct firms, the sales volume variance is further divided into a sales quantity variance and a sales mix variance. The computations of these variances are shown next.

Sales Quantity Variance

Product C	3,050	3,000	50 F	$3.00	$ 150 F
Product D	9,150	9,000	150 F	6.00	900 F
	12,200	12,000			$1,050 F

Sales Mix Variance

	Actual Sales at Actual Mix	Standard Sales at Budgeted Mix	Difference	Budgeted CM per Unit	Variance ($)
Product C	3,050	4,700	1,650 F	$3.00	$4,950 F
Product D	9,150	7,500	1,650 U	6.00	9,900 U
	12,200	12,200			$4,950 U

The sales quantity variance reflects the impact of deviations from the standard sales volume on the CM or GM, whereas the sales mix variance measures the impact on the CM of deviations from the budgeted mix. In the case of Shim and Siegel, Inc., the sales quantity variance came out to be favorable (i.e., $1,050 F), and the sales mix variance came out to be unfavorable (i.e., $4,950 U). These variances indicate that while there was a favorable increase in sales volume by 200 units, it was obtained by an unfavorable shift in the sales mix, that is, a shift from Product D, with a high margin, to Product C, with a low margin.

Note that the sales volume variance of $3,900 U is the algebraic sum of these two variances.

Sales quantity variance	$1,050 F
Sales mix variance	4,950 U
	$3,900 U

In conclusion, the product emphasis on high-margin sales is often a key to success for multiproduct firms. Increasing sales volume is one side of the story; selling the more profitable products is another.

Managerial Planning and Decision Making

In view of the fact that Shim and Siegel, Inc., in Example 7.10 experienced an unfavorable sales volume variance of $3,900 due to an unfavorable (or less profitable) mix in the sales volume, the company is advised to put more emphasis on increasing the sales of Product D.

In doing that, the company might wish to:

- Increase the advertising budget for succeeding periods to boost Product D sales.
- Set up a bonus plan in such a way that the commission is based on quantities sold rather than higher prices for higher-margin items such as Product D or revise the bonus plan to consider the sale of product D.
- Offer more lenient credit terms for Product D to encourage its sale.

- Reduce the price of Product D enough to maintain the present profitable mix while increasing the sale of the product. This strategy must take into account the price elasticity of demand for Product D.

SALES MIX ANALYSIS Many product lines include a lower-margin price leader model and often a high-margin deluxe model. For example, the automobile industry includes in its product line low-margin, energy-efficient small cars and higher-margin, deluxe models. In an attempt to increase overall profitability, management would want to emphasize the higher-margin, expensive items, but salespeople might find it easier to sell lower-margin, cheaper models. Thus, a salesperson might meet the unit sales quota with each item at its budgeted price, but because of mix shifts, the salesperson could be far short of contributing his or her share of budgeted profit.

Management should realize that:

- Greater proportions of more profitable products mean higher profits.
- Higher proportions of lower-margin sales reduce overall profit despite the increase in overall sales volume. That is to say, an unfavorable mix may easily offset a favorable increase in volume, and vice versa.

PERFORMANCE REPORTS Profit variance analysis aids in fixing responsibility by separating the causes of the change in profit into price, volume, and mix factors. With responsibility resting in different places, the segregation of the total profit variance is essential. Performance reports based on the analysis of profit variances must be prepared for each responsibility center, indicating:

- Is the profit variance controllable?
- Is it favorable or unfavorable?
- If it is unfavorable, is it significant enough for further investigation?
- Who is responsible for what portion of the total profit variance?
- What are the causes of an unfavorable variance?
- What remedial action can be taken?

The performance report must address such questions. The report is useful in two ways: (1) in focusing attention on situations in need of management action and (2) in increasing the precision of planning and control of sales and costs. The report should be produced as part of the overall standard costing and responsibility accounting system.

How to Measure the Performance of Investment Centers

Is the investment center healthy?

Two measurements of performance are widely used for the investment center division of a decentralized firm: rate of *return on investment* (ROI) and *residual income* (RI) (see Example 7.11).

Rate of Return on Investment

How do I calculate ROI?

Return on investment (ROI) relates operating income to operating assets. Specifically,

$$\text{ROI} = \frac{\text{Operating income}}{\text{Operating assets}}$$

Alternatively, ROI can be expressed as a product of these two important factors:

$$\text{ROI} = \text{Margin} \times \text{Turnover}$$
$$= \frac{\text{Operating income}}{\text{Sales}} \times \frac{\text{Sales}}{\text{Operating assets}} = \frac{\text{Operating income}}{\text{Operating assets}}$$

Margin is a measure of profitability or operating efficiency, whereas turnover measures how well a division manages its assets.

Example 7.11

Consider these financial data for a division:

Operating Assets	$100,000
Operating Income	$ 18,000
Sales	$200,000

$$\text{ROI} = \frac{\text{Operating income}}{\text{Operating assets}} = \frac{\$18,000}{\$100,000} = \underline{18\%}$$

Alternatively,

$$\text{Margin} = \frac{\text{Operating income}}{\text{Sales}} = \frac{\$18,000}{\$200,000} = \underline{9\%}$$

$$\text{Turnover} = \frac{\text{Sales}}{\text{Operating assets}} = \frac{\$200,000}{\$100,000} = \underline{2 \text{ times}}$$

Therefore,

$$\text{ROI} = \text{Margin} \times \text{Turnover} = 9\% \times 2 \text{ times} = \underline{18\%}$$

What are the benefits of breaking down ROI (the DuPont formula)?

The breakdown of ROI into margin and turnover (often called the DuPont formula) has several advantages over the original formula (operating income divided by operating assets) in terms of profit planning:

- The importance of turnover as a key to overall return on investment is emphasized in the breakdown. In fact, turnover is just as important as profit margin.

■ The importance of sales is explicitly recognized. The role of sales is not reflected in the regular formula.

The breakdown stresses the possibility of trading one off the other in an attempt to improve the overall performance of a division.

What effect does ROI have on the bottom line?

The breakdown of ROI into turnover and margin gives the manager of a division insight into planning for profit improvement. Generally speaking, a division manager can improve margin, turnover, or both.

■ *Improving margin* is a popular way of improving performance. Margins can be increased by reducing expenses, raising selling prices, or increasing sales faster than expenses.
■ *Improving turnover* can be achieved by increasing sales while holding the investment in assets relatively constant, or by reducing assets.
■ *Improving both margin and turnover* can be achieved by increasing sales revenue or by any combination of the first two.

Example 7.12

Assume that management sets a 20 percent ROI as a profit target. It is currently making an 18 percent return on its investment.

$$\text{ROI} = \frac{\text{Operating income}}{\text{Sales}} \times \frac{\text{Sales}}{\text{Operating assets}}$$

$$\text{Present: } 18\% = \frac{18,000}{200,000} \times \frac{200,000}{100,000}$$

Increase margin by reducing expenses:

$$20\% = \frac{20,000}{200,000} \times \frac{200,000}{100,000}$$

Increase turnover by reducing investment in assets:

$$20\% = \frac{18,000}{200,000} \times \frac{200,000}{90,000}$$

Increase both margin and turnover by disposing of obsolete and redundant inventories:

$$20\% = \frac{19,000}{200,000} \times \frac{200,000}{95,000}$$

Excessive investment in assets is just as much of a drag on profitability as excessive expenses are. In this case, cutting unnecessary inventories also helps cut down the expenses of carrying those inventories, so that both margin and turnover are improved at the same time. In practice, improving both margin and turnover is much more common than improving only one or the other.

Residual Income

What is residual income?

Residual income (RI) is the operating income that an investment center is able to earn above some minimum rate of return on its operating assets. RI, unlike ROI, is an absolute amount of income rather than a specific rate of return.

RI = Operating income − (Minimum required rate of return × Operating assets)

What are the benefits of RI?

When RI is used to evaluate divisional performance, the objective is to maximize the total amount of residual income, not to maximize the overall ROI figure.

Residual income is regarded as a better measure of performance than ROI because it encourages investment in projects that would be rejected under ROI. Other advantages of RI are:

- The incorporation of risk by varying the minimum rate of return based on the division's risk
- Varying the minimum return depending on the riskiness of a specific asset

A major disadvantage of RI is that it cannot be used to compare divisions of different sizes.

Note

Residual income (RI) tends to favor larger divisions due to the larger amount of dollars involved.

Example 7.13

Using the numbers in Example 7.11, assume the minimum required rate of return is 13 percent. Then the residual income of the division is:

$$\$18,000 - (13\% \times \$100,000) = \$18,000 - \$13,000 = \underline{\underline{\$5,000}}$$

Residual Income and Economic Value Added

Residual income is better known as *economic value added* (EVA$^{®}$). Many firms are addressing the issue of aligning division managers' incentives with those of the firm by using EVA as a measure of performance. EVA encourages managers to focus on increasing the value of the company to shareholders, because EVA is the value created by a company in excess of the cost of capital for the investment base. Improving EVA can be achieved in three ways:

1. Invest capital in high-performing projects.
2. Use less capital.
3. Increase profit without using more capital.

Investment Decisions under ROI and RI

How can I use ROI and RI?

The decision of whether to use ROI or RI as a measure of divisional performance affects the manager's investment decisions.

- Under the ROI method, division managers tend to accept only the investments whose returns exceed the division's ROI. Otherwise, the division's overall ROI would decrease if the investment were accepted.
- Under the RI method, division managers would accept an investment as long as it earns a rate in excess of the minimum required rate of return. The addition of such an investment would increase the division's overall RI.

Example 7.14

Consider the same data given in Examples 7.11 and 7.13.

Operating Assets	$100,000
Operating Income	$ 18,000
Minimum Required Rate of Return	13%
ROI = 18% and RI = $5,000.	

Assume that the division is presented with a project that would yield 15 percent on a $10,000 investment. The division manager would not accept this project under the ROI approach since the division is already earning 18 percent. Acquiring this project will bring down the present ROI to 17.73 percent, as shown next.

	Present	New Project	Overall
Operating Assets (a)	$100,000	$10,000*	$110,000
Operating Income (b)	18,000	1,500*	19,500
ROI (b) + (a)	18%	15%	17.73%

*$10,000 × 15% = $1,500.

Under the RI approach, the manager would accept the new project since it provides a higher rate than the minimum required rate of return (15 percent versus 13 percent). Accepting the new project will increase the overall residual income to $5,200, as shown next.

	Present	New Project	Overall
Operating Assets (a)	$100,000	$10,000*	$110,000
Operating Income (b)	18,000	1,500	19,500
Minimum Required Income at 13% (c)	13,000	1,300*	14,300
RI (b) − (c)	$ 5,000	$ 200	$ 5,200

*$10,000 × 13% = $1,300.

More on Economic Value Added

How does EVA differ from residual income?

$EVA^{®}$ is a concept similar to residual income, but often it is applied at the overall firm level as well as at the departmental level. It is a registered trademark of Stern Stewart & Co. (www.sternstewart.com), which developed the concept.

EVA is a measure of economic profit, but not the accounting profit we are accustomed to seeing in a corporate profit and loss statement. It is a measure of an operation's true profitability. The cost of debt capital (interest expense) is deducted when calculating net income, but no cost is deducted to account for the cost of common equity. Hence, in an economic sense, net income overstates true income. EVA overcomes this flaw in conventional accounting.

EVA is found by taking the net operating profit after taxes (NOPAT) for a particular period (such as a year) and subtracting the annual cost of *all* the capital a firm uses. EVA recognizes all capital costs, including the opportunity cost of the shareholder funds. It is a business's true economic profit. Such economic profits are the basis of shareholder value creation.

Note

The calculation of EVA can be complex because it makes various adjustments regarding costs of capital and accounting principles.

The formula is:

$$EVA = NOPAT - \text{After-tax cost of total capital}$$
$$= \text{Earnings before interest and taxes (EBIT)} \times (1 - \text{Tax rate})$$
$$- (\text{Total capital})(\text{After-tax cost of capital})$$

Total capital used here is total assets *minus* current liabilities. Hence, it is long-term liabilities *plus* equity (preferred stock and common equity). Thus, EVA is an estimate of a business's true economic profit for the year, and it differs sharply from accounting profit. EVA represents the residual income that remains after the cost of *all* capital, including equity capital, has been deducted, whereas accounting profit is determined without imposing a charge for equity capital. Equity capital has a cost, because funds provided by shareholders could have been invested elsewhere where they would have earned a return. In other words, shareholders give up the opportunity to invest funds elsewhere when they provide capital to the firm. The return they could earn elsewhere in investments of equal risk represents the cost of equity capital. This cost is an *opportunity cost* rather than an *accounting cost*, but it is quite real nevertheless.

Example 7.15 illustrates how an operation's economic profit differs from its accounting profit.

Example 7.15

A company with $100,000 in equity capital (stated at fair value) and $100,000 in 8 percent debt (also at fair value) had $60,000 in earnings before interest and taxes (EBIT). Assume also that $200,000 equals capital employed. The corporate tax rate is 40 percent. If that company's weighted-average after-tax cost of capital is 14 percent, the EVA is $8,000, calculated as:

EBIT	$60,000
Minus Taxes (40% × $60,000)	(24,000)
NOPAT	$36,000
Capital Charge (14% × $200,000)	(28,000)
EVA	$ 8,000

The company's traditional income statement reports income of $31,200, calculated as:

EBIT	$60,000
Minus Interest (8% × $100,000)	(8,000)
Income before Taxes	$52,000
Income Taxes (40% × $52,000)	(20,800)
Net Income after Taxes	$31,200

Initially, a 31.2 percent return on equity ($31,200 of net income/$100,000 of equity capital) seems favorable, but what is the cost of that equity capital? Given equal amounts of debt and equity, the cost of the equity capital must be 23.2 percent, because the after-tax weighted-average cost of capital was

14 percent, and the after-tax cost of debt capital was $4.8\% = 8\%(1 - 40\%)$. *Note:* Since $14\% = (4.8\%)(1/2) + X(1/2)$, $X = 23.2\%$.

Thus, $23,200 of the $31,200 of net income is nothing more than the opportunity cost of equity capital. The $8,000 of EVA is the only portion of earnings that has created value for the shareholders. Accordingly, if income after taxes had been only $20,000 (a 20 percent return on equity), shareholder value would have been reduced because the cost of equity capital would have exceeded the return.

EVA and Value Creation

In Example 7.15, the $8,000 of EVA is the only portion of earnings that has created value for the shareholders. EVA provides a good measure of whether the firm has added to shareholder value. Therefore, focusing on EVA will help to ensure that managers operate in a manner that is consistent with maximizing shareholder value. Note again that EVA can be determined for divisions—it is more often called *residual income*—as well as for the company as a whole, so it provides a useful basis for determining managerial compensation at all levels.

Although most companies adopt EVA for purposes of internal reporting and for calculating bonuses, some are publishing the results in the corporate annual reports. For example, Eli Lilly reports EVA in the Financial Highlights section of the annual report. SPX made it clear in its annual report: "EVA is the foundation of everything we do. ... It is a common language, a mind-set, and the way we do business."

Corporate Balanced Scorecard

What is the corporate Balanced Scorecard?

A problem with just assessing performance with financial measures like profit, ROI, and EVA is that the financial measures are backward-looking. In other words, today's financial measures tell about the accomplishments and failures of the past. An approach to performance measurement that also focuses on what managers are doing today to create future shareholder value is the Balanced Scorecard.

Essentially, a Balanced Scorecard is a set of performance measures constructed for four dimensions of performance. As indicated in Exhibit 7.6, the dimensions are financial, customer, internal processes, and learning and growth. Having financial measures is critical even if they are backward-looking. After all, they have a great effect on the evaluation of the company by shareholders and creditors. Customer measures examine the company's success in meeting customer expectations. Internal process measures examine the company's success in improving critical business processes. And learning and growth measures examine the company's success in improving its ability to adapt, innovate, and grow. The customer, internal processes, and learning and growth measures are generally thought to be predictive of future success (i.e., they are not backward-looking).

EXHIBIT 7.6   Balanced Scorecard

		Measures
Financial	Is the company achieving its financial goals?	Operating income Return on assets Sales growth Cash flow from operations Reduction of administrative expense
Customer	Is the company meeting customer expectations?	Customer satisfaction Customer retention New customer acquisition Market share On-time delivery Time to fill orders
Internal Processes	Is the company improving critical internal processes?	Defect rate Lead time Number of suppliers Material turnover Percent of practical capacity
Learning and Growth	Is the company improving its ability to innovate?	Amount spent on employee training Employee satisfaction Employee retention Number of new products New product sales as a percentage of total sales Number of patents

A variety of potential measures for each dimension of a Balanced Scorecard are indicated in Exhibit 7.6. After reviewing these measures, note how balance is achieved.

- Performance is assessed across a *balanced set of dimensions* (financial, customer, internal processes, and innovation).
- *Quantitative measures* (e.g., number of defects) are balanced with *qualitative measures* (e.g., ratings of customer satisfaction).
- There is a balance of *backward-looking measures* (e.g., financial measures like growth in sales) and *forward-looking measures* (e.g., number of new patents as an innovation measure).

How to Price Goods and Services Transferred

How are transfer prices determined?

Goods and services often are exchanged between various divisions of a decentralized organization. The question then is: What monetary values should be assigned to these exchanges or transfers—market price, some kind of cost, or some version of either? A single transfer price will please everyone involved in the transfer—that is, top management, the selling division, and the buying division.

The choice of a transfer pricing policy (i.e., which type of transfer price to use) normally is decided by top management. The decision typically will include consideration of:

- *Goal congruence.* Will the transfer price promote the goals of the company as a whole? Will it harmonize the divisional goals with organizational goals?
- *Performance evaluation.* Will the selling division receive enough credit for its transfer of goods and services to the buying division? Will the transfer price hurt the performance of the selling division?
- *Autonomy.* Will the transfer price preserve autonomy—the freedom of the selling and buying division managers to operate their divisions as decentralized entities?
- *Other factors*, such as minimization of tariffs and income taxes and observance of legal restrictions, must be taken into account.

Alternative Transfer Pricing Schemes

What other factors can determine transfer prices?

Transfer prices can also be based on:

- Market price
- Cost-based price—variable or full cost
- Negotiated price
- General formula that is usually the sum of variable costs per unit and opportunity cost for the company as a whole (lost revenue per unit on outside sales)

How suitable is market price for transfers?

Market price is the best transfer price in the sense that it will maximize the profits of the company as a whole, if it meets these two conditions:

1. A competitive market price exists.
2. Divisions are independent of each other.

If either of these conditions is violated, market price will not lead to an optimal economic decision for the company.

What are the pros and cons of cost-based prices?

Cost-based transfer price, another alternative transfer pricing scheme, is easy to understand and convenient to use. But there are some disadvantages:

- Inefficiencies of the selling divisions are passed on to the buying divisions with little incentive to control costs. The use of standard costs is recommended in such a case.

- The cost-based method treats the divisions as cost centers rather than profit or investment centers. Therefore, measures such as ROI and RI cannot be used for evaluation purposes.

The variable cost-based transfer price has an advantage over the full cost method because it can ensure the best use of the company's overall resources. The reason is that, in the short run, fixed costs do not change. Any use of facilities without incurrence of additional fixed costs will increase the company's overall profits.

When is a negotiated transfer price used?

A negotiated price generally is used when there is no clear outside market. A negotiated price is one agreed on between the buying and selling divisions that reflects unusual or mitigating circumstances.

Note

A negotiated transfer price is widely used when no intermediate market price exists for the product transferred and the selling division is assured of a normal profit.

Example 7.16   Negotiated Transfer Price

Company X just purchased a small company that specializes in the manufacture of Part 323. Company X is a decentralized organization. It will treat the newly acquired company as an autonomous division called Division B with full profit responsibility. Division B's fixed costs total $30,000 per month, and variable costs per unit are $18. Division B's operating capacity is 5,000 units. The selling price per unit is $30. Division A of Company X is currently purchasing 2,500 units of Part 323 per month from an outside supplier at $29 per unit, which represents the normal $30 price less a quantity discount. Top management of the company wants to decide what transfer price should be used.

Top management may consider these alternative prices:

- $30 market price
- $29, the price that Division A is currently paying to the outside supplier
- $23.50 negotiated price, which is $18 variable costs plus half of the benefits of an internal transfer (($29 – $18) × 1/2)
- $24 full cost, which is $18 variable costs plus $6 ($30,000/5,000 units) fixed cost per unit
- $18 variable costs

We next discuss each of these prices.

- $30 would not be an appropriate transfer price. Division B cannot charge a price more than the price Division A is paying now ($29).
- $29 would be an appropriate transfer price if top management wants to treat the divisions as autonomous investment centers. This price would cause all of the benefits of internal transfers to accrue to the selling division, with the buying division's position remaining unchanged.
- $23.50 would be an appropriate transfer price if top management wants to treat both divisions as investment centers, but wants to share the benefits of an internal transfer *equally* between them, in this way:

Variable costs of Division B	$18.00
1/2 of the difference between the variable costs of Division B and the price Division A is paying, ($29 − $18) × 1/2	5.50
Transfer price	$23.50

Note

The $23.50 amount is just one example of a negotiated transfer price. The exact price depends on how the divisions divide the benefits.

- $24 [$18 + ($30,000/5,000 units) = $24] would be an appropriate transfer price if top management treats the divisions like cost centers with no profit responsibility. All benefits from both divisions will accrue to the buying division. This will maximize the profits of the company as a whole but adversely affect the performance of the selling division. Another disadvantage of this cost-based approach is that inefficiencies (if any) of the selling division are being passed on to the buying division.
- $18 would be an appropriate transfer price for guiding top management in deciding whether transfers between the two divisions should take place. Since $18 is less than the outside purchase price of the buying division and the selling division has excess capacity, the transfer should take place, because it will maximize the profits of the company as a whole. However, if $18 is used as a transfer price, then all of the benefits of the internal transfer accrue to the buying division, and the performance of the selling division will be hurt.

Budgeting and Financial Planning

What is a budget?

A budget is:

- A formal statement of management's expectation regarding sales, expenses, volume, and other financial transactions of an organization for the coming period

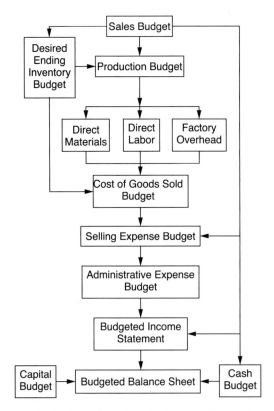

EXHIBIT 7.7   Comprehensive Budget: What Are the Types of Budgets?

- A set of pro forma (projected or planned) financial statements—income statement, balance sheet, and cash budget
- A tool for both planning and control
- At the beginning of the period, a plan or standard
- At the end of the period, a control device to help management measure its performance against the plan so that future performance can be improved

Exhibit 7.7 shows a simplified diagram of the various parts of the comprehensive budget, the master plan of the company.

Budgets are classified into two broad categories:

1. *Operating budget*, reflecting the results of operating decisions
2. *Financial budget*, reflecting the financial decisions of the firm

What is an operating budget?

The operating budget consists of:

- Sales budget
- Production budget
- Direct materials budget

- Direct labor budget
- Factory overhead budget
- Selling and administrative expense budgets
- Pro forma income statement

What does a financial budget contain?

The financial budget consists of:

- Cash budget
- Pro forma balance sheet
- Capital budget

How do I prepare a budget?

The five major steps in preparing the budget are:

Step 1. Prepare a sales forecast.
Step 2. Determine expected production volume.
Step 3. Estimate manufacturing costs and operating expenses.
Step 4. Determine cash flow and other financial effects.
Step 5. Formulate projected financial statements.

How can I prepare a budget quickly?

In actual practice, a shortcut approach is widely used in formulating a budget. The approach can be summarized in this way:

- A pro forma income statement is developed using past percentage relationships between certain expense and cost items and the firm's sales. These percentages are then applied to the firm's projected sales. The income statement can be set up in a traditional or contribution format.
- A pro forma balance sheet is estimated, using the percentage of sales method. This involves the following steps:

Step 1. Express balance sheet items that *vary directly with sales* as a percentage of sales. Any item that does not vary with sales (such as long-term debt) is designated *not applicable* (*n.a.*). Multiply these percentages by the sales projected to obtain the amounts for the future period.

Step 2. Where no percentage applies (such as long-term debt, common stock, and paid-in capital), simply insert the figures from the present balance sheet or their desired level in the column for the future period.

Step 3. Compute the projected retained earnings in this way:

Projected retained earnings
= Present retained earnings
+ Projected net income
− Cash dividend to be paid

Step 4. Sum the asset accounts and the liability and equity accounts to see if there is any difference. If there is any difference that is a *shortfall* for assets, this is the amount of financing the firm has to raise externally.

Computer-Based Budgeting

Should I use a computer to prepare budgets and do financial planning?

More and more companies are developing computer-based models for financial planning and budgeting, using powerful yet easy-to-use financial modeling languages such as Budget Maestro and Up Your Cash Flow. The models help not only build a budget for profit planning but also answer a variety of what-if scenarios. The resultant calculations provide a basis for choice among alternatives under conditions of uncertainty. Budget modeling also can be accomplished using spreadsheet programs, such as Microsoft's Excel.

In this section we illustrate the use of Excel to develop a financial model. For illustrative purposes, we present two examples of projecting an income statement.

CASE 1

Sales for first month = $60,000
Cost of sales = 42 percent of sales, all variable
Operating expenses = $10,000 fixed plus 5 percent of sales
Taxes = 30 percent of net income
Sales increase by 5 percent each month.

Based on this information, Exhibit 7.8 presents a spreadsheet for the contribution income statement for the next 12 months and in total.

Exhibit 7.9 shows the same, assuming that sales increase by 10 percent and operating expenses equal $10,000 plus 10 percent of sales. This is an example of what-if scenarios.

CASE 2   Delta Gamma Company wants to prepare a three-year projection of net income using this information:

1. 2X12 base-year amounts are:

Sales Revenues	$4,500,000
Cost of Sales	2,900,000
Selling and Administrative Expenses	800,000
Net Income before Taxes	800,000

2. Use these assumptions:
   - Sales revenues increase by 6 percent in 2X13, 7 percent in 2X14, and 8 percent in 2X15.
   - Cost of sales increase by 5 percent each year.
   - Selling and administrative expenses increase only 1 percent in 2X12 and will remain at the 2X12 level thereafter.
   - Income tax rate = 46 percent.

Exhibit 7.10 presents a spreadsheet for the income statement for the next three years.

EXHIBIT 7.8 Projected Income Statement

	1	2	3	4	5	6	7	8	9	10	11	12	TOTAL	PERCENT
Sales	$60,000	$63,000	$66,150	$69,458	$72,930	$76,577	$80,406	$84,426	$88,647	$93,080	$97,734	$102,620	$955,028	100%
Less: Variable Costs														
Cost of Sales	$25,200	$26,460	$27,783	$29,172	$30,631	$32,162	$33,770	$35,459	$37,232	$39,093	$41,048	$43,101	$401,112	42%
Operating Ex.	$ 3,000	$ 3,150	$ 3,308	$ 3,473	$ 3,647	$ 3,829	$ 4,020	$ 4,221	$ 4,432	$ 4,654	$ 4,887	$ 5,131	$ 47,751	5%
CM	$31,800	$33,390	$35,060	$36,812	$38,653	$40,586	$42,615	$44,746	$46,983	$49,332	$51,799	$54,389	$506,165	53%
Less: Fixed Costs														
Operating Ex.	$10,000	$10,000	$10,000	$10,000	$10,000	$10,000	$10,000	$10,000	$10,000	$10,000	$10,000	$10,000	$120,000	13%
Net Income	$21,800	$23,390	$25,060	$26,812	$28,653	$30,586	$32,615	$34,746	$36,983	$39,332	$41,799	$44,389	$386,165	40%
Less: Tax	$ 6,540	$ 7,017	$ 7,518	$ 8,044	$ 8,596	$ 9,176	$ 9,785	$10,424	$11,095	$11,800	$12,540	$13,317	$115,849	12%
NI after Tax	$15,260	$16,373	$17,542	$18,769	$20,057	$21,410	$22,831	$24,322	$25,888	$27,533	$29,259	$31,072	$270,315	28%

EXHIBIT 7.9 Projected Income Statement

	1	2	3	4	5	6	7	8	9	10	11	12	TOTAL	PERCENT
Sales	$60,000	$66,000	$72,600	$79,860	$87,846	$96,631	$106,294	$116,923	$128,615	$141,477	$155,625	$171,187	$1,283,057	134%
Less: VC														
Cost of Sales	$25,200	$27,720	$30,492	$33,541	$36,895	$40,585	$44,643	$49,108	$54,018	$59,420	$65,362	$71,899	$538,884	56%
Operating Ex.	$6,000	$6,600	$7,260	$7,986	$8,785	$9,663	$10,629	$11,692	$12,862	$14,148	$15,562	$17,119	$64,153	7%
CM	$28,800	$31,680	$34,848	$38,333	$42,166	$46,383	$51,021	$56,123	$61,735	$67,909	$74,700	$82,170	$615,867	64%
Less: FC														
Operating Ex.	$10,000	$10,000	$10,000	$10,000	$10,000	$10,000	$10,000	$10,000	$10,000	$10,000	$10,000	$10,000	$120,000	$13%
Net Income	$18,800	$21,680	$24,848	$28,333	$32,166	$36,383	$41,021	$46,123	$51,735	$57,909	$64,700	$72,170	$495,867	52%
Less: Tax	$5,640	$6,504	$7,454	$8,500	$9,650	$10,915	$12,306	$13,837	$15,521	$17,373	$19,410	$21,651	$148,760	$16%
NI after Tax	$13,160	$15,176	$17,394	$19,833	$22,516	$25,468	$28,715	$32,286	$36,215	$40,536	$45,290	$50,519	$347,107	$36%

EXHIBIT 7.10   Three-Year Income Projections

Delta Gamma Company
Three-Year Income Projections (2X12–2X15)

	2X12	2X13	2X14	2X15
Sales	$4,500,000	$4,770,000	$5,103,900	$5,512,212
Cost of Sales	2,900,000	3,045,000	3,197,250	3,357,113
Gross Margin	1,600,000	1,725,000	1,906,650	2,155,100
Selling & Adm. Exp.	800,000	808,000	808,000	808,000
Net Income before Tax	800,000	917,000	1,098,650	1,347,100
Tax	368,000	421,820	505,379	619,666
Net Income after Tax	$ 432,000	$ 495,180	$ 593,271	$ 727,434

Budgeting Software

There are many user-oriented software packages specifically designed for corporate planners, treasurers, budget preparers, managerial accountants, CFOs, and business analysts. In recent years, the focus has been on moving away from spreadsheets to enterprise budgeting applications in order to make the planning and budgeting process more efficient and the data more reliable. However, the underlying process remains fundamentally unchanged; it is still about capturing and consolidating line item expenses. Next, several popular software packages are described briefly.

BUDGET MAESTRO   Centage's Budget Maestro (www.centage.com) guides the financial executive through budgeting, planning, modeling, forecasting, resource management, consolidation, analysis, and reporting. With Budget Maestro, CFOs and budget managers can plan, analyze, and manage in new ways at a user's screen, and make changes directly without ever being there; can deliver budget models and deploy reconfigured software updates to many users at once; and can manage budgetary information, even enterprise-wide information systems, with a single consistent interface. As an alternative to spreadsheets, Budget Maestro automates many of the complex and repetitive tasks in the budgeting process while eliminating the need for creating complicated formulas and manual consolidation of multiple worksheets.

MICROSOFT BUSINESS SOLUTIONS FOR ANALYTICS—FORECASTER   Forecaster is a web-based budgeting and planning (B&P) solution from FRx Software (www.microsoft.com/en-us/dynamics/products/frx.aspx). Many organizations find it difficult to perform the ongoing budgeting and planning processes necessary to keep business performance on target. Financial surprises are met with panic, and, more often than not, companies are forced to make sacrifices in places they cannot afford. The result is a direct negative impact on their strategic objectives. But it is not for lack of trying. Finance departments simply do not have the time to combine multiple spreadsheets submitted from across the company (let alone the resources to make sure all line managers understand the importance of the budgeting and planning process, and of submitting well-planned information on time). Forecaster puts the systems and processes in place to help users immediately realize the

EXHIBIT 7.11   Budgeting and Planning Software

Companies	Websites	Software
ActiveStrategy	www.activestrategy.com	ActiveStrategy Enterprise
Actuate	www.actuate.com	e.Reporting Suite
Microsoft	www.microsoft.com/en-us/dynamics/ financial-planning-budgeting.aspx	FRx for Dynamics
IBM Cognos	www.cognos.com	Cognos Finance, Cognos Visualizer, Cognos Enterprise, Business Intelligence
Rocket CorVu	www.rocketsoftware.com	CorPlanning, CorStrategy, CorBusiness, CorPortfolio
Epicor	www.epicor.com	Epicor e.Intelligence Suite
Infor	www.geac.com	Infor Smartstream Financials, Enterprise Solutions Expert Series, FRx
Lawson Software	www.lawson.com	Enterprise Budgeting SEA Applications—including E-Scorecard; Analytic Extensions
Oracle	www.oracle.com	Oracle Strategic Enterprise Management (SEM), Hyperion Planning
SAP	www.sap.com	SAP Strategic Enterprise Management (SEM), SAP Financial Analyzer Business Intelligence with mySAP.com
SAS Institute	www.sas.com	SAS Total Financial Management, Strategic Vision, SAS/Warehouse Administrator, SAS Enabling Technology (OLAP), SAS BusinessObjects Portfolio, Oros Products
Silvon	www.silvon.com	Stratum

benefits of an effective budgeting and planning process, and make it an ongoing part of the business strategy.

HOST BUDGET   Host Budget (www.hostanalytics.com) is an integrated budgeting and planning software that provides streamlined budgeting, forecasting, reporting, and analysis. Modules are used to automatically manage, consolidate, and change information for planning and replanning. The modules included with Host Budget's performance measurement scorecard are sales, general, and administrative (SG&A) budgeting, human resources budgeting, sales and operation planning, capital expenditure budgeting, and sales forecasting. Host Budget is designed for the web so that users can either work online, directly with the database, for queries and updates or work off-line and easily upload the Excel file later or submit it via e-mail.

Because of the streamlined effects of Host Budget on an organization's budgeting process, budgets and forecasts can be refined on an ongoing basis. Managers can consider what has happened so far and can regularly look into the future aided by actual versus budgeted information, along with current forecast projections, in their effort to meet financial goals. Executive managers can create top-down budgets and "push down" the budget to lower levels of the organization. Line managers and department heads can create budgets from the bottom up and submit budgets for approval.

SAP BUSINESSOBJECTS BUDGETING AND CONSOLIDATION BusinessObjects Budgeting (www.sap.com) leverages the power of Microsoft Excel embedded in an enterprise application to create detailed, flexible plans and budgets. It improves accountability, reduces cycle time, and facilitates top-down adjustments.

Latest Generation of Budgeting and Planning Software

The new budgeting and planning (B&P) software represents a giant step forward for financial managers. Finance managers can use these robust, web-enabled programs to scan a wide range of data, radically speed up the planning process, and identify managers who have failed to submit budgets. More often known as active financial planning software, these packages include applications and the new level of functionality that combine budgeting, forecasting analytics, business intelligence, and collaboration. Exhibit 7.11 lists popular B&P software.

CHAPTER 8

Analysis of Projects, Proposals, and Special Situations

Accountants need to be equipped with various tools and techniques in order to cope with short-term and long-term decisions. Cost–volume–profit (CVP) analysis is an extremely useful tool for accountants. When used in conjunction with any spreadsheet program, it can help accountants choose a wise decision by simulating a variety of what-if scenarios. Analysis of short-term, special decisions typically requires such simple concepts as *contribution margin* and *relevant costs*. Long-term investment decisions, commonly called *capital budgeting*, however, require not only a good understanding of the time value concept and its application but also a working knowledge of how to analyze and evaluate investment proposals.

This chapter covers the tools and guidelines that facilitate various short-term, nonroutine decisions as well as long-term investment decisions. Specifically:

- Breakeven and cost–volume–profit analysis
- Short-term decisions (e.g., pricing decisions on special orders and make-or-buy decisions)
- Time value fundamentals
- Long-term investment decisions, commonly known as capital budgeting

Cost–Volume–Profit and Breakeven Analysis

What are variable and fixed costs?

Not all costs behave in the same way. Certain costs, called *variable costs*, vary in proportion to change in activity. Other costs that do not change, regardless of the volume, are called *fixed costs*.

Why analyze cost behavior?

An understanding of costs by behavior is very useful:

- For breakeven and CVP analysis
- For analysis of short-term, nonroutine decisions (e.g., make-or-buy decisions and sales mix decisions)
- For appraisal of profit center performance by means of the contribution approach and for flexible budgeting (see Chapter 7)

What is cost–volume–profit and breakeven analysis?

Cost–volume–profit analysis, together with cost behavior information, helps accountants perform many useful analyses. CVP analysis deals with how profit and costs change with a change in volume. It specifically looks at the effects on profits of changes in such factors as variable costs, fixed costs, selling prices, volume, and mix of products sold. By studying the relationships of costs, sales, and net income, accountants are better able to cope with planning decisions.

Breakeven analysis, a branch of CVP analysis, determines the breakeven sales, which is the level of sales at which total costs equal total revenue.

How can I use CVP analysis in solving business problems?

CVP analysis tries to answer these questions:

- What sales volume is required to break even?
- What sales volume is necessary in order to earn a desired profit?
- What profit can be expected on a given sales volume?
- How would changes in selling price, variable costs, fixed costs, and output affect profit?
- How would a change in the mix of products sold affect the breakeven and target income volume and profit potential?

Contribution Margin

What does contribution margin (CM) involve?

For accurate CVP analysis, a distinction must be made between variable and fixed costs. Semivariable costs (or mixed costs) must be separated into their variable and fixed components.

To compute the breakeven point and perform various CVP analyses, note these important concepts:

- *Contribution margin (CM).* The contribution margin is the excess of sales (S) over the variable costs (VC) of the product. It is the amount of money available to cover fixed costs (FC) and to generate profits. Symbolically, CM = S − VC.
- *Unit CM.* The unit CM is the excess of the unit selling price (p) over the unit variable cost (v). Symbolically, unit CM = $p - v$.
- *CM ratio.* The CM ratio is the contribution margin as a percentage of sales; that is,

$$\text{CM ratio} = \frac{\text{CM}}{\text{S}} = \frac{\text{S} - \text{VC}}{\text{S}} = 1 - \frac{\text{VC}}{\text{S}}$$

The CM ratio can also be computed using per-unit data:

$$\text{CM ratio} = \frac{\text{Unit CM}}{p} = \frac{p - v}{p} = 1 - \frac{v}{p}$$

Note

The CM ratio is 1 minus the variable cost ratio.

Example: If variable costs account for 70 percent of the price, the CM ratio is 30 percent.

Example 8.1

To illustrate the various concepts of CM, consider these data for Company Z:

	Per Unit	Total	Percentage
Sales (1,500 units)	$25	$37,500	100%
Less: Variable Costs	10	15,000	40
Contribution Margin	$15	$22,500	60%
Less: Fixed Costs		15,000	
Net Income		$ 7,500	

From the data listed, CM, unit CM, and the CM ratio are computed as:

$$CM = S - VC = \$37,500 - \$15,000 = \$22,500$$
$$\text{Unit CM} = p - v = \$25 - \$10 = \$15$$
$$CM \text{ ratio} = \frac{CM}{S} = \frac{\$22,500}{\$37,500}$$
$$= 60\% \text{ or } 1 - \frac{VC}{S}$$
$$= 1 - 0.4 = 0.6 = 60\%$$

How can the breakeven point be calculated?

The breakeven point—the point of no profit and no loss—provides accountants with insights into profit planning. It can be computed in three different ways: the equation approach, the contribution margin approach, and the graphical approach.

The *equation approach* is based on the cost-volume equation, which shows the relationships among sales, variable and fixed costs, and net income.

$$S = VC + FC + \text{Net income}$$

At the breakeven volume, $S = VC + FC + 0$. Defining x = volume in units, we can rewrite the relationship in terms of x:

$$px = vx + FC$$

To find the breakeven point in units, simply solve the equation for x.

Example 8.2

In Example 8.1, $p = \$25$, $v = \$10$, and FC $= \$15,000$. Thus, the equation is:

$$\$25X = \$10X + \$15,000$$
$$\$25X - \$10X = \$15,000$$
$$(\$25 - \$10)X = \$15,000$$
$$\$15X = \$15,000$$
$$X = \$15,000/\$15 = 1,000\,\text{units}$$

Therefore, Company Z breaks even at a sales volume of 1,000 units.

The *contribution margin approach*, another technique for computing the breakeven point, is based on solving the cost-volume equation. Solving the equation $px = vx + $ FC for x yields:

$$x_{BE} = FC/(p - v)$$

where $(p - v)$ is the unit CM by definition, and x_{BE} is the breakeven unit sales volume.

In words,

Breakeven point in *units* = Fixed costs/Unit CM

If the breakeven point is desired in terms of dollars, then:

Breakeven point in dollars = Breakeven point in units × Unit sales price

Alternatively,

Breakeven point in dollars = Fixed costs/CM ratio

Example 8.3

Using the same data given in Example 8.1, where the unit CM $= \$25 - \$10 = \$15$ and the CM ratio $= 60\%$, we get:

Breakeven point in units $= \$15,000/\$15 = 1,000\,\text{units}$
Breakeven point in dollars $= 1,000\,\text{units} \times \$25 = \$25,000$

Alternatively,

$$\$15,000/0.6 = \$25,000$$

The *graphical approach* is based on the so-called breakeven chart shown in Exhibit 8.1. Sales revenue, variable costs, and fixed costs are plotted on the vertical axis. Volume (x) (units of output) is plotted on the horizontal axis. The breakeven

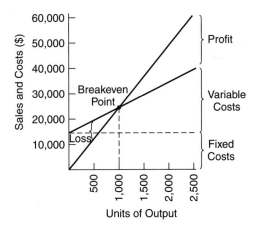

EXHIBIT 8.1 Breakeven Chart

point is the point where the total sales revenue line intersects the total cost line. This chart can also effectively report profit potential for a wide range of activity.

The *profit-volume (P/V) chart* shown in Exhibit 8.2 focuses more directly on how profits vary with changes in volume. Profits are plotted on the vertical axis, while units of output are shown on the horizontal axis.

Note

The slope of the chart is the unit CM.

Target Income Volume and Margin of Safety

How do I determine target income (TI) volume?

Besides being able to determine the breakeven point, CVP analysis determines the sales required to attain a particular income level or target net income. There are two ways target net income can be expressed.

EXHIBIT 8.2 Profit-Volume (P/V) Chart

As a *specific dollar amount*, the cost-volume equation specifying target net income is:

$$px = vx + FC + \text{Target income}$$

Solving the equation for x yields:

$$x_{TI} = \frac{FC + TI}{p - v}$$

where x_{TI} is the sales volume required to achieve a given target income.

In words,

$$\text{TI Sales Volume} = \frac{FC + TI}{\text{Unit CM}}$$

Specifying target income as a *percentage of sales*, the cost-volume equation is:

$$px = vx + FC + \%(px)$$

Solving this for x yields:

$$x_{TI} = \frac{FC}{p - v - \%(p)}$$

In words,

Target income sales volume = Fixed costs/(Unit CM − % of unit sales price)

Example 8.4

Using the same data given in Example 8.1, assume that Company Z wants to attain:

As a specific dollar amount: A target income of $15,000 before tax.
Target income sales volume (in units) required would be:

$$x_{TI} = \frac{FC + \text{Target income}}{p - v} = \frac{\$15,000 + \$15,000}{\$25 - \$10} = 2,000 \text{ units}$$

As a percentage of sales: A target income of 20 percent of sales.
The target income volume required would be:

$$x_{TI} = \frac{FC}{p - v - \%(p)} = \frac{\$15,000}{\$15 - 20\%(\$25)}$$

$$= \frac{\$15,000}{\$15 - \$5} = 1,500 \text{ units}$$

What is the impact of income taxes on target income volume?

If target income is given on an after-tax basis, the target income volume formula becomes:

$$\text{Target income volume} = \frac{\text{Fixed costs} + \dfrac{\text{Target after-tax income}}{1 - \text{Tax rate}}}{\text{Unit CM}}$$

Example 8.5

Assume in Example 8.1 that Company Z wants to achieve an after-tax income of $6,000. Income tax is levied at 40 percent. Then

$$\text{Target income volume} = \frac{\$15,000 + \dfrac{\$6,000}{1 - 0.04}}{\$15}$$

$$= \frac{\$15,000 + \$10,000}{\$15}$$

$$= 1,667 \text{ units}$$

What is the margin of safety?

The margin of safety is a measure of difference between the actual level of sales and the breakeven sales. It is the amount by which sales revenue may drop before losses begin and is expressed as a percentage of budgeted sales, as shown:

$$\text{Margin of safety} = \frac{\text{Budgeted sales} - \text{Breakeven sales}}{\text{Budgeted sales}}$$

What is the use of the margin of safety?

The margin of safety is often used as a measure of risk. The larger the margin of safety ratio, the safer the situation, since there is less risk of reaching the breakeven point.

Example 8.6

Assume Company Z projects sales of $30,000 with a breakeven sales level of $25,000. The expected margin of safety is:

$$\frac{\$30,000 - \$25,000}{\$30,000} = 16.7\%$$

How is CVP analysis used in practice?

The concepts of contribution margin have many applications in profit planning and short-term decision making. Applications are illustrated in Examples 8.7 through 8.11, using the data from Example 8.1.

Example 8.7

Recall from Example 8.1 that Z has a CM of 60 percent and fixed costs of $15,000 per period. Assume that the company expects sales to go up by $10,000 for the next period. How much will income increase?

Using the CM concepts, we can quickly compute the impact of a change in sales on profits. The formula for computing the impact is:

$$\text{Change in net income} = \text{Dollar change in sales} \times \text{CM ratio}$$

Thus, the increase in net income = $10,000 × 60% = $6,000. Therefore, the income will go up by $6,000, assuming there is no change. If we are given a change in sales in *units* instead of dollars, then the formula becomes:

$$\text{Change in net income} = \text{Change in unit sales} \times \text{unit CM}$$

Example 8.8

We now compute before-tax income expected on sales of $47,500.

CM: $47,500 × 60%	$28,500
Less: Fixed Costs	15,000
Net Income	$13,500

Example 8.9

Company Z is considering increasing the advertising budget by $5,000, which would increase sales revenue by $8,000. Should the advertising budget be increased? The answer is no, since the increase in the CM is less than the increased cost.

Increase in CM: $8,000 × 60%	$4,800
Increase in Advertising	5,000
Decrease in Net Income	($200)

Example 8.10

Company Z's accountant is considering a $3,000 increase in sales salaries. What additional sales are required to cover the higher cost?

The increase in fixed cost must be matched by an equal increase in CM:

$$\text{Increase in CM} = \text{Increase in cost}$$
$$0.60\,\text{sales} = \$3,000$$
$$\text{Sales} = \$5,000$$

Example 8.11

Consider the original data. Assume again that Company Z is currently selling 1,500 units per period. In an effort to increase sales, the accountant is considering cutting its unit price by $5 and increasing the advertising budget by $1,000. If these two steps are taken, the accountant feels that unit sales will go up by 60 percent. Should the two steps be taken?

A $5 reduction in the selling price would cause the unit CM to decrease from $15 to $10. Thus,

Proposed CM 2,400 units × $10	$24,000
Present CM 1,500 units × $15	22,500
Increase in CM	1,500
Increase in advertising outlay	1,000
Increase in net income	$ 500

The answer is yes. Alternatively, the same answer can be obtained by developing comparative income statements in contribution margin format:

	Present (1,500 units)	Proposed (2,400 units)	Difference
Sales	$37,500	$48,000	
	(@ 25)	(@ 20)	$10,500
Less: Variable Cost	15,000	24,000	9,000
CM	22,500	24,000	1,500
Less: Fixed Costs	15,000	16,000	1,000
Net Income	$ 7,500	$ 8,000	$ 500

Sales Mix Analysis

What effect does the sales mix have?

Breakeven and cost–volume–profit analyses require some additional computations and assumptions when a company produces and sells more than one product. Different selling prices and different variable costs result in different unit CM and different CM ratios. As a result, breakeven points vary with the relative proportions of the products sold, called the *sales mix*. In breakeven and CVP analysis, it is necessary to:

- Predetermine the sales mix and then compute a weighted-average CM.
- Assume that the sales mix does not change for a specified period.

The breakeven formula for the company as a whole is:

$$\text{Companywide breakeven in units (or in dollars)} = \frac{\text{Fixed costs}}{\textit{Average}\ \text{unit CM (or average CM ratio)}}$$

Example 8.12

Assume that Company X has two products with these CM data:

	A	B
Selling Price	$ 15	$10
Variable Costs	12	5
Unit CM	$ 3	$ 5
Sales Mix	60%	40%
Fixed Costs	$76,000	

The weighted average unit CM = $3(0.6) + $5(0.4) = $3.80.

Then the company's breakeven point in units is $76,000/$3.80 = 20,000 units.

This is divided as:

$$\text{A: } 20{,}000 \text{ units} \times 60\% = 12{,}000\ \text{units}$$
$$\text{B: } 20{,}000 \text{ units} \times 40\% = \underline{\ 8{,}000\ }$$
$$\underline{\underline{20{,}000}}\ \text{units}$$

Note

An alternative is to build a package containing three A models and two B models (3:2 ratio). By defining the product as a package, the multiple-product problem is converted into a single-product one. Then use these two steps:

Step 1. Compute the package CM:

	A	B
Selling Price	$15	$10
Variable Cost per Unit	12	5
Unit CM	$ 3	$ 5
Sales Mix	× 3	× 2
Package CM	$ 9	$10

$19 package total

$76,000/$19 per package = 4,000 packages

Step 2. Multiply this number by their respective mix units:

A: 4,000 packages × 3 units = 12,000 units

B: 4,000 packages × 2 units = _8,000_

20,000 units

Example 8.13

Assume that Company Y produces and sells three products with the following data:

	A	B	C	Total
Sales	$30,000	$60,000	$10,000	$100,000
Sales Mix	30%	60%	10%	100%
Less: VC	24,000	40,000	5,000	69,000
CM	$ 6,000	$20,000	$ 5,000	$ 31,000
CM Ratio	20%	$33\frac{1}{3}$%	50%	31%

Total fixed costs are $18,600.

The CM ratio for Company Y is $31,000/$100,000 = 31%. Therefore, the breakeven point in dollars is $18,600/0.31 = $60,000.

This will be split in the mix ratio of 3:6:1 to give us these breakeven points for the individual products A, B, and C:

A: $60,000 × 30% = $18,000

B: $60,000 × 60% = 36,000

C: $60,000 × 10% = _6,000_

$60,000

Example 8.14

Assume in Example 8.13 that total sales remain unchanged at $100,000, but a shift in mix from Product B to Product C is expected:

	A	B	C	Total
Sales	$30,000	$30,000	$40,000	$100,000
Sales Mix	30%	30%	40%	100%
Less: VC	24,000	20,000*	20,000	64,000
CM	$ 6,000	$10,000	$20,000	$ 36,000
CM Ratio	20%	$33^{1}/_{3}$%	50%	36%

*$20,000 = $30,000 × $66^{2}/_{3}$%.

Note

The shift in sales mix toward the more profitable line C has caused the CM ratio for the company as a whole to go from 31 percent to 36 percent. The new breakeven point will be $18,600/0.36 = $51,667. The breakeven dollar volume has decreased from $60,000 to $51,667.

What does breakeven and CVP analysis assume?

The basic breakeven and CVP models are subject to a number of limiting assumptions:

- The behavior of both sales revenue and expenses is *linear* throughout the entire *relevant* range of activity.
- All costs are classified as fixed or variable.
- There is only one product. In a multiproduct firm, the sales mix will not change during the planning period. If the sales mix changes, the breakeven point will also change.
- Inventories do not change significantly from period to period.
- Volume is the only factor affecting variable costs.

Short-Term, Nonroutine Decisions

What nonrecurring situations do I have to consider?

When analyzing the manufacturing and selling functions, accountants are constantly faced with the problem of choosing alternative courses of action. Typical questions include:

- What to make?
- How to make it?
- Where to sell the product or service?
- What price to charge?

In the short run, the accountant typically is confronted with these nonroutine, nonrecurring types of decisions:

- Acceptance or rejection of a special order
- Make or buy
- Add or drop a certain product line
- Utilization of scarce resources
- Sell or process further

What are relevant costs?

In each of the preceding situations, the ultimate decision rests on cost data analysis. Cost data are important in many decisions, since they are the basis for profit calculations. However, not all costs are of equal importance in decision making, and accountants must identify the costs that are relevant to a decision. Such costs are called *relevant costs*.

Which costs are relevant in a nonroutine decision?

The relevant costs are the expected future costs that differ between the decision alternatives. Therefore:

- *Sunk costs* are *not* relevant to the decision at hand, because they are past, historical costs.
- *Incremental costs* or *differential costs* are relevant, since they are the ones that differ between the alternatives.

  Example: In a decision on whether to sell an existing business for a new one, the cost to be paid for the new venture is relevant. However, the initial cost of the old business is not relevant to the decision because it is a sunk cost.

What is incremental analysis?

The method that uses the concept of *relevant costs* is called the *incremental approach*, also known as the *differential cost approach* or the *relevant cost approach*. Under this method, the decision involves these four steps:

Step 1. Gather all costs associated with each alternative.
Step 2. Drop the sunk costs.
Step 3. Drop those costs that do not differ between alternatives.
Step 4. Select the best alternative based on the remaining cost data.

Example 8.15

Assume that ABC Company is planning to expand its productive capacity. The plans consist of purchasing a new machine for $50,000 and disposing of the old machine without receiving anything. The new machine has a five-year life. The old machine has a five-year remaining life and a book value of $12,500. The new

(continued)

(Continued)

machine will reduce variable operating costs from $35,000 per year to $20,000 per year. Annual sales and other operating costs are shown next.

	Present Machine	New Machine
Sales	$60,000	$60,000
Variable Costs	35,000	20,000
Fixed Costs:		
Depreciation (straight-line)	2,500	10,000
Insurance, Taxes, etc.	4,000	4,000
Net Income	$18,500	$26,000

At first glance, it appears that the new machine provides an increase in net income of $7,500 per year. The book value of the present machine, however, is a sunk cost and is irrelevant in this decision. Furthermore, sales and fixed costs, such as insurance and taxes, are also irrelevant since they do not differ between the two alternatives being considered. Eliminating all the irrelevant costs leaves us with only these incremental costs:

Savings in variable costs	$15,000
Increase in fixed costs	10,000 (a $2,500 sunk cost is irrelevant)
Net annual cash savings arising from the new machine	$ 5,000

When should a company accept special orders at lower prices?

A company often receives a short-term, special order for its products at lower prices than usual. In normal times, the company may refuse such an order, since it will not yield a satisfactory profit.

Recommendation

If times are bad or when there is idle capacity, an order should be accepted if the incremental revenue exceeds the incremental costs involved.

A price lower than the regular price is called a *contribution price*. This approach to pricing is called the *contribution approach to pricing*, also called the *variable pricing model*. This approach is most appropriate when the company:

- Has idle capacity
- Is faced with sharp competition or is in a competitive bidding situation
- Is operating in a distress situation

Example 8.16

Assume that a company with 100,000-unit capacity is currently producing and selling only 90,000 units of product each year with a regular price of $2.00. If the variable cost per unit is $1.00 and the annual fixed cost is $45,000, the income statement shows:

		Per Unit
Sales (90,000 units)	$180,000	$2.00
Less: Variable Cost	90,000	1.00
Contribution Margin	$ 90,000	$1.00
Less: Fixed Cost	45,000	0.50
Net Income	$ 45,000	$0.50

The company has just received an order that calls for 10,000 units @ $1.20, for a total of $12,000. The acceptance of this special order will not affect regular sales. Management is reluctant to accept this order because the $1.20 price is below the $1.50 factory unit cost ($1.50 − $1.00 = $0.50).

Is filling the order advisable? The answer to this question is yes. The company can add to total profits by accepting this special order even though the price offered is below the factory unit cost. At a price of $1.20, the order will contribute $0.20 (CM per unit = $1.20 − $1.00 = $0.20) toward fixed cost, and profit will increase by $2,000 (10,000 units × $0.20). Using the contribution approach to pricing, the variable cost of $1.00 will be a better guide than the factory unit cost of $1.50.

Note

The fixed costs will not increase because of the presence of idle capacity.

What is a make-or-buy decision?

Often companies purchase subcomponents used to make their products instead of making them in their in-house manufacturing facilities. Buying services, products, or components of products from outside vendors instead of producing them is called *outsourcing*. The decision whether to produce a subcomponent in-house or to buy it externally from an outside vendor is called a *make-or-buy (outsource) decision*. Examples include:

- Processing payroll in-house or outsourcing it to an outside service bureau
- Developing a training program in-house or sending employees outside for training
- Providing data processing and network services internally or buying them (benefits: access to technology and cost savings)

Other strong candidates for outsourcing include managing fleets of vehicles, sales and marketing, and custodial services.

The make-or-buy decision involves both qualitative and quantitative factors.

- Qualitative considerations include ensuring product quality and the necessity for long-run business relationships with subcontractors.
- Quantitative factors, dealing with cost, are best seen through incremental analysis.

Example 8.17

Assume a firm has prepared these cost estimates for the manufacture of a sub-assembly component based on an annual production of 8,000 units:

	Per Unit	Total
Direct Materials	$ 5.00	$ 40,000
Direct Labor	4.00	32,000
Variable Overhead Applied	4.00	32,000
Fixed Overhead Applied (150% of direct labor cost)	6.00	48,000
Total Cost	$19.00	$152,000

The supplier has offered to provide the subassembly at a price of $16 each. Two-thirds of fixed factory overhead, which represents executive salaries, rent, depreciation, and taxes, continue regardless of the decision.

Should the company buy or make the product? The key to the decision lies in the investigation of those relevant costs that change between the make-or-buy alternatives. Assuming that the productive capacity will be idle if not used to produce the subassembly, the analysis takes this form:

	Per Unit		Total of 8,000 Units	
	Make	Buy	Make	Buy
Purchase Price		$16.00	$ 40,000	$128,000
Direct Materials	$ 5.00		32,000	
Direct Labor	4.00		32,000	
Variable Overhead	4.00			
Fixed Overhead Avoided by Not Making	2.00	—	16,000	
Total Relevant Costs	$15.00	$16.00	$120,000	$128,000
Difference in Favor of Making	$ 1.00		$ 8,000	

Note

The make-or-buy decision must be investigated in the broader perspective of available facilities. The alternatives are:

- Leaving facilities idle
- Buying the parts and renting out idle facilities
- Buying the parts and using unused facilities for other products

How do I decide whether to add or drop a product line?

The decision of whether to drop an old product line or add a new one must take into account both qualitative and quantitative factors. Ultimately, any final decision should be based on the impact the decision will have on contribution margin or net income.

Example 8.18

The ABC grocery store has three major product lines: produce, meats, and canned goods. The store is considering dropping the meat line because the income statement shows meats are being sold at a loss. Note the income statement for these product lines:

	Produce	Meats	Canned Food	Total
Sales	$10,000	$15,000	$25,000	$50,000
Less: Variable Costs	6,000	8,000	12,000	26,000
CM	$ 4,000	$ 7,000	$13,000	$24,000
Less: Fixed Costs				
Direct	2,000	6,500	4,000	12,500
Allocated	1,000	1,500	2,500	5,000
Total	$ 3,000	$ 8,000	$ 6,500	$17,500
Net Income	$ 1,000	($ 1,000)	$ 6,500	$ 6,500

In this example, *direct fixed costs* are those costs that are identified directly with each of the product lines. *Allocated fixed costs* are the amount of common fixed costs allocated to the product lines using some base such as space occupied. The amount of common fixed costs typically continues regardless of the decision and thus cannot be saved by dropping the product line to which it is distributed.

These calculations show the effects on the company as a whole with and without the meat line:

	Keep Meats	Drop Meats	Difference
Sales	$50,000	$35,000	($15,000)
Less: Variable Costs	26,000	18,000	(8,000)
CM	$24,000	$17,000	($ 7,000)
Less: Fixed Costs			
Direct	12,500	6,000	(6,500)
Allocated	5,000	5,000	—
Total	$13,500	$11,000	($ 6,500)
Net Income	$ 6,500	$ 6,000	($ 500)

From either of the two methods, we see that by dropping meats the store will lose an additional $500. Therefore, the meat product line should be kept.

Caution

One of the great dangers in allocating common fixed costs is that such alloca-tions can make a product line look less profitable than it really is.

Because of such an allocation, the meat line in Example 8.18 showed a loss of $1,000. In effect, however, it contributes $500 ($7,000 − $6,500) to the recovery of the store's common fixed costs.

How do I make the best use of scarce resources?

In general, the emphasis on products with higher contribution margin maximizes a firm's total net income, even though total sales may decrease. This is not true, however, where there are constraining factors and scarce resources. The constraining factor is the factor that restricts or limits the production or sale of a given product. *Examples:* Machine hours, labor hours, or cubic feet of warehouse space.

Note

In the presence of these constraining factors, maximizing total profits depends on getting the highest contribution margin per unit of the factor (rather than the highest contribution margin per unit of product output).

Example 8.19

Assume that a company produces products A and B with these contribution margins per unit:

	A		B
Sales	$8.00		$24.00
Variable Costs	6.00		20.00
CM	$2.00		$ 4.00
Annual Fixed Costs		$42,000	

As is indicated by CM per unit, B is more profitable than A since it contributes more to the company's total profits than A does ($4.00 versus $2.00). But assume that the firm has limited capacity of 10,000 labor hours. Further, assume that A requires two labor hours to produce and B requires five labor hours. One way to express this limited capacity is to determine the contribution margin per labor hour.

	A	B
CM per Unit	$2.00	$4.00
Labor Hours Required per Unit	2	5
CM per Labor Hour	$1.00	$0.80

Since A returns the higher CM per labor hour, it should be produced and B should be dropped.

Note

The presence of only one limited resource is unrealistic. Virtually all firms encounter multiple constraints: restrictions on materials, labor inputs, demand for each product, warehouse space, display space, and so on. The solution of the product mix problem with multiple constraints is considerably more complex and requires a technique known as *linear programming*.

Theory of Constraints

What is the theory of constraints?

A binding constraint can limit a company's profitability. For example, a manufacturing company may have a *bottleneck operation*, through which every unit of a product must pass before moving on to other operations. The *theory of constraints* (TOC) calls for identifying such limiting constraints and seeking ways to relax them. Also referred to as *managing constraints*, this management approach can significantly improve an organization's level of goal attainment. Among the ways that management can relax a constraint by expanding the capacity of a bottleneck operation are the following:

- Outsourcing (subcontracting) all or part of the bottleneck operation
- Investing in additional production equipment and employing parallel processing, in which multiple product units undergo the same production operation simultaneously
- Working overtime at the bottleneck operation
- Retaining employees and shifting them to the bottleneck
- Eliminating any non-value-added activities at the bottleneck operation

Life-Cycle Costs and Target Costing

What is life-cycle costing?

Life-cycle costing tracks and accumulates all product costs in the value chain from research and development and design of products and processes through production, marketing, distribution, and customer service. The value chain is the set of activities required to design, develop, produce, market, and service a product (or service). The terms *cradle-to-grave costing* and *womb-to-tomb costing* convey the sense of fully capturing all costs associated with the product.

Life-cycle costing focuses on minimizing locked-in costs by, for example, reducing the number of parts, promoting standardization of parts, and using equipment that can make more than one kind of product. The product life cycle is simply the time a product exists—from conception to abandonment. Life-cycle costs are all costs associated with the product for its entire life cycle. These costs include development (planning, design, and testing); manufacturing (conversion activities); and logistics support (advertising, distribution, warranty, and so on).

Can you achieve cost reduction through life-cycle costing?

Because total customer satisfaction has become a vital issue in the new business setting, whole-life cost has emerged as the central focus of life-cycle cost management. *Whole-life cost* is the life-cycle cost of a product plus after-purchase (postpurchase) costs that consumers incur, including operation, support, maintenance, and disposal. Since the costs a purchaser incurs after buying a product can be a significant percentage of whole-life costs and, thus, an important consideration in the purchase decision, managing activities so that whole-life costs are reduced can provide an important competitive advantage.

Note

Cost reduction, not cost control, is the emphasis. Moreover, cost reduction is achieved by judicious analysis and management of activities.

Studies show that 90 percent or more of a product's costs are committed during the development stage. Thus, it makes sense to emphasize management of activities during this phase of a product's existence. Every dollar spent on premanufacturing activities is known to save $8.00 to $10.00 on manufacturing and postmanufacturing activities. The real opportunities for cost reduction occur before manufacturing begins. Managers need to invest more in premanufacturing assets and dedicate more resources to activities in the early phases of the product life-cycle so that overall whole-life costs can be reduced.

What is the role of target costing? How does it differ from cost-plus pricing?

Life-cycle and whole-life cost concepts are associated with target costing and target pricing. A firm may determine that market conditions require that a product sell at a given target price. Hence, the target cost can be determined by subtracting the desired unit profit margin from the target price. The cost-reduction objectives of life-cycle and whole-life cost management can therefore be determined using target costing.

EXHIBIT 8.3   Cost-Plus Pricing versus Target Costing

	Formula	Implications
Cost-plus pricing	Cost base + Markup = Selling price	■ Cost is the base (given). ■ Markup is added (given). ■ The firm puts the product on the market and hopes the selling price is accepted.
Pricing based on target costing	Target selling price − Desired profit = Target cost	■ Markets determine prices (given). ■ Desired profit must be sustained for survival (given). ■ Target cost is the residual, the variable to be managed.

Thus, *target costing* becomes a particularly useful tool for establishing cost reduction goals. Toyota, for example, calculates the lifetime target profit for a new car model by multiplying a target profit ratio times the target sales. It then calculates the estimated profit by subtracting the estimated costs from target sales. Usually (at this point), target profit is greater than estimated profit. The cost-reduction goal is defined by the difference between the target profit and the estimated profit. Toyota then searches for cost-reduction opportunities through better design of the new model. Toyota's management recognizes that more opportunities exist for cost reduction during product planning than in actual development and production.

The Japanese developed target costing to enhance their ability to compete in the global marketplace. This approach to product pricing differs significantly from the cost-based methods just described. Instead of first determining the cost of a product or service and then adding a profit factor to arrive at its price, target costing reverses the procedure. Target costing is a pricing method that involves (1) identifying the price at which a product will be competitive in the marketplace, (2) defining the desired profit to be made on the product, and (3) computing the target cost for the product by subtracting the desired profit from the competitive market price. The formula is:

$$\text{Target price} - \text{Desired profit} = \text{Target cost}$$

Target cost is then given to the engineers and product designers, who use it as the maximum cost to be incurred for the materials and other resources needed to design and manufacture the product. It is their responsibility to create the product at or below its target cost.

Exhibit 8.3 compares the cost-plus philosophy with the target costing philosophy.

Example 8.20

A salesperson at Sunghi Products Company has reported that a customer is seeking price quotations for two electronic components: a special-purpose battery charger (Product X101) and a small transistorized machine computer (Product

(continued)

(Continued)

Y101). Competing for the customer's order are one French company and two Japanese companies. The current market price ranges for the two products are:

Product X101	$310–$370 per unit
Product Y101	$720–$820 per unit

The salesperson feels that if Sunghi could quote prices of $325 for Product X101 and $700 for Product Y101, the company would get the order and gain a significant share of the global market for those goods. Sunghi's usual profit markup is 25 percent of total unit cost. The company's design engineers and cost accountants put together these specifications and costs for the new products:

Activity-based cost rates:
Materials-handling activity cost $1.30 per dollar of raw materials
                                        and purchased parts
Production activity $3.50 per machine hour
Product delivery activity $24.00 per unit of X101
                                          $30.00 per unit of Y101

	Product X101	Product Y101
Projected unit demand	26,000	18,000
Per unit data:		
Raw materials cost	$30.00	$65.00
Purchased parts cost	$15.00	$45.00
Manufacturing labor		
Hours	2.6	4.8
Hourly labor rate	$12.00	$15.00
Assembly labor		
Hours	3.4	8.2
Hourly labor rate	$14.00	$16.00
Machine hours	12.8	28.4

The company wants to address three questions:

1. What is the target cost for each product?
2. What is the projected total unit cost of production and delivery?
3. Using the target costing approach, should the company produce the products?
    1. Target cost for each product:

$$\text{Product X101} = \$325.00 \div 1.25 = \$260.00^*$$
$$\text{Product Y101} = \$700.00 \div 1.25 = \$560.00$$

---

*Target price – Desired profit = Target cost

$$\$325.00 - 0.25X = X$$
$$\$325.00 = 1.25X$$
$$x = \frac{\$325.00}{1.25} = \$260.00$$

2. Projected total unit cost of production and delivery:

	Product X101	Product Y101
Raw materials cost	$ 30.00	$ 65.00
Purchased parts cost	15.00	45.00
Total cost of raw materials and parts	$ 45.00	$110.00
Manufacturing labor		
X101 (2.6 hours × $12.00)	31.20	
Y101 (4.8 hours × $15.00)		72.00
Assembly labor		
X101 (3.4 hours × $14.00)	47.60	
Y101 (8.2 hours × $16.00)		131.20
Activity-based costs		
Materials handling activity		
X101 ($45.00 × $1.30)	58.50	
Y101 ($110.00 × $1.30)		143.00
Production activity		
X101 (12.8 machine hours × $3.50)	44.80	
Y101 (28.4 machine hours × $3.50)		99.40
Product delivery activity		
X101	24.00	
Y101		30.00
Projected total unit cost	$251.10	$585.60

3. Production decision:

	Product X101	Product Y101
Target unit cost	$260.00	$560.00
Less: Projected unit cost	251.10	585.60
Difference	$ 8.90	($ 25.60)

Product X101 can be produced below its target cost, so it should be produced. As currently designed, Product Y101 cannot be produced at or below its target cost; either it needs to be redesigned or the company should drop plans to make it.

Activity-Based Costing

What is activity-based costing?

Many companies use a traditional cost system, such as job-order costing or process costing, or some hybrid of the two. However, these traditional systems may provide distorted product cost information. In fact, companies selling multiple products are making critical decisions about product pricing, making bids, or product mix based on inaccurate cost data. In all likelihood, the problem is not with assigning the costs of direct labor or direct materials. These prime costs are traceable to individual products, and most conventional cost systems are designed to ensure that this tracing takes place.

However, the assignment of overhead costs to individual products is another matter. The traditional methods of assigning overhead costs to products, using a single predetermined overhead rate based on any single activity measure, can produce distorted product costs. Activity-based costing (ABC) attempts to get around this problem. An ABC system assigns costs to products based on the product's use of activities, not on product volume. This approach has proved to produce more accurate product costing results in an environment where there is diversity in product line and services coming out of the same shop. A recent survey by the Institute of Management Accounting shows that over 30 percent of the companies that responded are using ABC systems to replace their existing traditional cost systems.

How is overhead costing handled in a single-product situation?

The accuracy of overhead cost assignment becomes an issue only when multiple products are manufactured in a single facility. If only a single product is produced, all overhead costs are traceable to it. The overhead cost per unit is simply the total overhead for the year divided by the number of hours or units produced, which was discussed in detail in previous chapters.

The cost calculation for a single-product setting is illustrated in Exhibit 8.4. There is no question that the cost of manufacturing the product illustrated in the exhibit is $28 per unit. All manufacturing costs were incurred specifically to make this product. Thus, one way to ensure product-costing accuracy is to focus on producing one product. For this reason, some multiple-product firms choose to dedicate entire plants to the manufacture of a single product.

By focusing on only one or two products, small manufacturers are able to calculate the cost of manufacturing the high-volume products more accurately and price them more effectively.

How is overhead costing handled in a multiple-product or job situation?

In a multiple-product or job situation, manufacturing overhead costs are caused jointly by all products or jobs. The problem becomes one of identifying the amount of overhead caused or consumed by each. This is accomplished by searching for *cost drivers*, or activity measures that cause costs to be incurred.

EXHIBIT 8.4   Unit Cost Computation: Single Product

	Manufacturing Costs	Units Produced	Cost per Unit
Direct Materials	$ 800,000	50,000	$16.00
Direct Labor	200,000	50,000	4.00
Factory Overhead	400,000	50,000	8.00
Total	$1,400,000	50,000	$28.00

In a traditional setting, it is normally assumed that overhead consumption is highly correlated with the volume of production activity, measured in terms of direct labor hours, machine hours, or direct labor dollars. These volume-related cost drivers are used to assign overhead to products to develop plantwide or departmental rates.

Example 8.21

Job No. 107 consists of 2,000 special-purpose machine tools with the following requirements:

Machine setups	2 setups
Waste materials required	2,000 pounds
Inspections	10 inspections
Machine hours	500 machine hours

The overhead assigned to Job No. 107 is computed next.

Overhead Cost Pool	Predetermined Overhead Rate	Level of Cost Driver	Assigned Overhead Cost
Machine setups	$1,000 per setup	2 setups	$ 2,000
Material handling	$2 per pound	10,000 pounds	20,000
Waste control	$5 per pound	2,000 pounds	10,000
Inspection	$75 per inspection	10 inspections	750
Other overhead costs	$10 per machine hour	500 machine hours	5,000
Total			$37,750

The total overhead cost assigned to Job No. 107 is $37,750, or $18.88 per tool ($37,750/2,000).

Compare this with the overhead cost that is assigned to the job if the firm uses a single predetermined overhead rate based on machine hours:

$$\frac{\text{Total budgeted overhead cost}}{\text{Total predicted machine hours}} = \frac{\$525,000}{20,000}$$

$$= \$26.25 \text{ per machine hour}$$

Under this approach, the total overhead cost assigned to Job No. 107 is $13,125 ($26.25 per machine hour × 500 machine hours). This is only $6.56 per tool ($13,125/2,000), which is about one-third of the overhead cost per tool computed when multiple-cost drivers are used.

The reason for this wide discrepancy is that these special-purpose tools require a relatively large number of machine setups, a sizable amount of waste materials, and several inspections. Thus, they are relatively costly in terms of driving overhead costs. Use of a single predetermined overhead rate obscures that fact.

(continued)

(*Continued*)

Inaccurately calculating the overhead cost per unit to the extent illustrated here can have serious adverse consequences for the firm. For example, it can lead to poor decisions about pricing, product mix, or contract bidding.

Note

In designing a product-costing system, the cost accountant needs to weigh such considerations carefully. A costing system using multiple-cost drivers is more costly to implement and use, but it may save millions through improved decisions.

How do I choose which cost drivers to use?

At least two major factors should be considered in selecting cost drivers: (1) the cost of measurement and (2) the degree of correlation between the cost driver and the actual consumption of overhead.

Cost of Measurement

In an ABC system, a large number of cost drivers can be selected and used. It is preferable, however, to select cost drivers that use information that is readily available. Information that is not available in the existing system must be produced, which will increase the cost of the firm's information system. A homogeneous cost pool could offer a number of possible cost drivers. For this situation, any cost driver that can be used with existing information should be chosen. This choice minimizes the costs of measurement.

Indirect Measures and the Degree of Correlation

The existing information structure can be exploited in another way to minimize the costs of obtaining cost-driver quantities. It is sometimes possible to replace a cost driver that directly measures the consumption of an activity with a cost driver that indirectly measures that consumption. For example, inspection hours could be replaced by the actual number of inspections associated with each product; this number is more likely to be known. This replacement works, of course, only if hours used per inspection are reasonably stable for each product. The least-squares method (regression analysis), which will be covered in Chapter 9, can be utilized to determine the degree of correlation.

A list of potential cost drivers is given in Exhibit 8.5.

The fundamental differences in the traditional and ABC cost systems are summarized in Exhibit 8.6.

Just-in-Time and Total Quality Management

Inventory control problems occur in almost every type of organization. They exist whenever products are held to meet some expected future demand. In most

EXHIBIT 8.5   Cost Drivers

Manufacturing

Number of setups	Square footage
Weight of material	Number of vendors
Number of units reworked	Asset value
Number of orders placed	Number of labor transactions
Number of orders received	Number of units scrapped
Number of inspections	Number of parts
Number of material-handling operations	Replacement cost
Number of orders shipped	Machine hours
Design time	Direct labor hours

Nonmanufacturing
Number of hospital beds occupied
Number of takeoffs and landings for an airline
Number of rooms occupied in a hotel

industries, cost of inventory represents the largest liquid asset under the control of management. Therefore, it is very important to develop a production- and inventory-planning system that will minimize both purchasing and carrying costs.

In recent years, the Japanese have demonstrated the ability to manage their production systems effectively. Much of their success has been attributed to what is known as the *just-in-time* (JIT) approach to production and inventory control, which has generated a great deal of interest among practitioners. The *kanban* system—as the Japanese call it—has been a focal point of interest, with its dramatic impact on the inventory performance and productivity of the Japanese auto industry.

What is just-in-time?

JIT is a demand-pull system. Demand for customer output (not plans for using input resources) triggers production. Production activities are pulled, not pushed, into action. JIT production, in its purest sense, is buying and producing in very small quantities just in time for use. As a philosophy, JIT believes that inventory is an evil presence that obscures problems that should be solved, and maintains that by contributing significantly to costs, large inventories keep a company from being as competitive or profitable as it otherwise might be. Practically speaking, JIT has as its principal goal the elimination of waste, and the principal measure of success is

EXHIBIT 8.6   Cost System Comparison

	Traditional	ABC
Cost pools	One or a limited number	Many—to reflect different activities
Applied rate	Volume-based, financial	Activity-based, nonfinancial
Suited for	Labor-intensive, low-overhead companies	Capital-intensive, product-diverse, high-overhead companies
Benefits	Simple, inexpensive	Accurate product costing, possible elimination of non-value-added activities

how much or how little inventory there is. Virtually anything that achieves this end can be considered a JIT innovation.

Furthermore, the little inventory that exists in a JIT system must be of good quality. This requirement has led to JIT purchasing practices uniquely able to deliver high-quality materials. This ties in very closely with the principle of *total quality management* (TQM).

JIT systems integrate five functions of the production process—sourcing, storage, transportation, operations, and quality control—into one controlled manufacturing process. In manufacturing, JIT means that a company produces only the quantity needed for delivery to dealers or customers. In purchasing, it means suppliers deliver subassemblies just in time to be assembled into finished goods. In delivery, it requires selecting a transportation mode that will deliver purchased components and materials in small-lot sizes at the loading dock of the manufacturing facilities just in time to support the manufacturing process.

How does JIT compare with traditional manufacturing?

JIT manufacturing is a demand-pull approach, rather than the traditional push approach. The philosophy underlying JIT manufacturing is to produce a product when it is needed and only in the quantities demanded by customers. Demand pulls products through the manufacturing process. Each operation produces only what is necessary to satisfy the demand of the succeeding operation. No production takes place until a signal from a succeeding process indicates a need to produce. Parts and materials arrive just in time to be used in production.

What is the main objective of JIT?

The primary goal of JIT is to reduce inventories to insignificant or zero levels. In traditional manufacturing, inventories result whenever production exceeds demand. Inventories are needed as a buffer when production does not meet expected demand.

What are manufacturing cells?

In traditional manufacturing, products are moved from one group of identical machines to another. Typically, machines with identical functions are located together in an area referred to as a department or process. Workers who specialize in the operation of a specific machine are located in each department. JIT replaces this traditional pattern with a pattern of manufacturing cells or work centers. Robots supplement people to do many routine operations.

Manufacturing cells contain machines that are grouped in families, usually in a semicircle. The machines are arranged so that they can be used to perform a variety of operations in sequence. Each cell is set up to produce a particular product or product family. Products move from one machine to another from start to finish. Workers are assigned to cells and are trained to operate all machines within the cell. Thus, labor in a JIT environment is multifunction labor, not specialized labor. Each manufacturing cell is basically a minifactory or a factory within a factory.

How does JIT result in better cost management?

Cost management differs from cost accounting in that it refers to the management of cost, whether or not the cost has direct impact on inventory or the financial statements. The JIT philosophy simplifies the cost accounting procedure and helps managers manage and control their costs.

JIT recognizes that with simplification come better management, better quality, better service, and better cost control. Traditional cost accounting systems have a tendency to be very complex, with many transactions and much reporting of data. Simplification of this process will transform a cost *accounting* system into a cost *management* system that can be used to support management's needs for better decisions about product design, pricing, marketing, and mix, and to encourage continual operating improvements.

What is total quality management?

JIT goes hand in hand with a stronger emphasis on quality control. A defective part brings production to a grinding halt. Poor quality simply cannot be tolerated in a stockless manufacturing environment. In other words, JIT cannot be implemented without a commitment to total quality management. TQM is essentially an endless quest for perfect quality. It is a *zero-defects* approach, which views the optimal level of quality costs as the level where zero defects are produced. This approach to quality is opposed to the traditional belief, called *acceptable quality level* (AQL), which allows a predetermined level of defective units to be produced and sold. AQL is the level where the number of defects minimizes total quality costs.

Quality costs are classified into three broad categories: prevention, appraisal, and failure costs. *Prevention costs* are those incurred to prevent defects. Amounts spent on quality training programs, researching customer needs, quality circles, and improved production equipment are considered prevention costs. Expenditures made for prevention will minimize the costs that will be incurred for appraisal and failure. *Appraisal costs* are costs incurred for monitoring or inspection; these costs compensate for mistakes not eliminated through prevention. *Failure costs* may be internal (such as scrap and rework costs and reinspection) or external (such as product returns due to quality problems, warranty costs, lost sales due to poor product performance, and complaint department costs).

Quality cost reports can be used to point out the strengths and weaknesses of a quality system. Improvement teams can use them to describe the monetary benefits and ramifications of proposed changes. Return on investment (ROI) models and other financial analyses can be constructed directly from quality cost data to justify proposals to management. In practice, quality costs can define activities of quality programs and quality improvement efforts in a language that management can understand and act on: dollars.

The negative effect on profits resulting from product or service of less than acceptable quality or from ineffective quality management is almost always dynamic. Once started, it continues to mushroom until ultimately the company finds itself in serious financial difficulties due to the two-pronged impact of an unheeded increase in quality costs coupled with a declining performance image. Management that clearly understands this fact understands the economics of quality.

Taguchi Method of Quality Control

The Taguchi method of quality control is a method of controlling quality, developed by Genichi Taguchi, a past winner of the Deming Award, that emphasizes robust quality design and the *quality loss function* (QLF). Taguchi claims that quality is largely determined at the design level. In addition to quality control in production, he emphasizes quality control in four other functions: (1) product planning, (2) product design, (3) process design, and (4) production service after purchase. Taguchi's QLF also quantitatively measures the success or failure of quality control. The traditional view is that any product that measures within the upper and lower specification limits is good and a product outside the limits is bad. In contrast, the QLF presumes that *any* deviation from the target specification is important since it means economic losses for the customer. Furthermore, the economic losses increase quadratically as the actual value deviates from the target value. The QLF can be described by this equation:

$$L(y) = k(y - T)^2$$

where:

    L = quality loss
    y = actual value of quality characteristic
    k = a proportionality constant dependent on the firm's external failure cost structure
    T = target value of quality characteristic

Example 8.22

Davidson Company has decided to estimate its quality loss using the Taguchi loss function. After some study, it was determined that $k = \$400$ and $T = 10$ inches in diameter. Exhibit 8.7 illustrates the computations of the quality loss for a sample of four units.

Note that the average loss per unit is $10. The total expected loss for, say, 1,000 units would be $10,000 ($10 × 1,000 units).

EXHIBIT 8.7   Quality-Loss Computation

Unit	Actual Diameter (y)	$y - T$	$(y - T)^2$	$k(y - T)^2$
1	9.9	−0.10	0.010	$ 4.00
2	10.1	0.10	0.010	4.00
3	10.2	0.20	0.040	16.00
4	9.8	−0.20	0.040	16.00
Total			0.100	$40.00
Average			0.025	$10.00

Is cost accounting simpler under JIT?

The cost accounting system of a company adopting JIT will be quite simple compared to job-order or processing costing. Under JIT, raw materials and work in process (WIP) accounts typically are combined into one account called *resources in process* or *raw and in-process* (RIP). Under JIT, the materials arrive at the receiving area and are whisked immediately to the factory area. The journal entries that accompany JIT costing are remarkably simple:

Raw and In-Process (RIP) Inventory	$45,000	
Accounts Payable or Cash		$45,000
To record purchases		
Finished Goods	$40,000	
RIP Inventory		$40,000
To record raw materials in completed units		

As can be seen, there are no stores control and WIP accounts under JIT. In summary, JIT costing can be characterized in this way:

- There are fewer inventory accounts.
- There are no work orders. Thus, there is no need for detailed tracking of actual raw materials.
- With JIT, activities can be eliminated on the premise that they do not add value. Prime targets for elimination are storage areas for WIP inventory and material-handling facilities.
- Direct labor costs and factory overhead costs are not tracked to specific orders. Direct labor is now regarded as just another part of factory overhead. Virtually all of the factory overhead incurred each month, now including direct labor, flows through to cost of goods sold in the same month. Tracking overhead through WIP and finished goods inventory provides no useful information. Therefore, it makes sense to treat manufacturing overhead as an expense charged directly to cost of goods sold.

The major differences between JIT manufacturing and traditional manufacturing are summarized in Exhibit 8.8.

Backflush Costing

Accounting in a JIT system focuses on the plant's output to the customer. *Note:* A company may wish to measure the output of each manufacturing cell or work center rather than total output. Although this practice may reveal problems in a given area, it does not correlate with the JIT philosophy, which emphasizes a team approach, plantwide attitude, and total cost picture. Because each area depends on the previous area, any problems will quickly stop the production process.

EXHIBIT 8.8   Comparison of JIT and Traditional Manufacturing

JIT	Traditional
Pull system	Push system
Insignificant or zero inventories	Significant inventories
Manufacturing cells	Process structure
Multifunction labor	Specialized labor
Total quality management (TQM)	Acceptable quality level (AQL)
Decentralized services	Centralized services
Simple cost accounting	Complex cost accounting

Daily accounting for the individual costs of production is no longer necessary; all costs should be standard, since variations are observed and corrected almost immediately.

Further, since costs are more easily traced to their related output in a JIT system, fewer costs are arbitrarily allocated to products. Costs are incurred in specified cells on a per-hour or per-unit basis. Energy costs are direct to production in a comprehensive JIT system because there should be a minimum of downtime by machines or unplanned idle time for workers. Virtually the only costs still being allocated are costs associated with the structure (building depreciation, rent, taxes, and insurance) and machinery depreciation. By comparison, activity-based costing attempts to allocate manufacturing overhead costs to products more accurately than under traditional cost accounting systems by using multiple cost drivers rather than by using departmental overhead application rates.

What is backflush costing?

Backflush costing is a streamlined cost accounting method that speeds up, simplifies, and reduces accounting effort in an environment that minimizes inventory balances, requires few allocations, uses standard costs, and has minimal variances from standard. During the accounting period, this costing method records purchases of raw material and accumulates actual conversion costs. Then, either at completion of production or upon the sale of goods, an entry is made to allocate the total costs incurred to cost of goods sold and to finished goods inventory, using standard production costs.

Implementation of a just-in-time system can result in significant cost reductions and productivity improvements. But even within a single company, not all inventories need to be managed according to a JIT philosophy. The costs and benefits of any inventory control system must be evaluated before management installs the system.

Example 8.23 provides information on a product of the Ivy Company. This information is used to illustrate the journal entries for backflush costing. The company has a long-term contract with its supplier for raw material at $75 per unit, so there is no material price variance. Ivy's JIT inventory system has minimum inventories that remain constant from period to period. Beginning inventories for June are assumed to be zero.

Example 8.23

Ivy Company's standard production cost per unit:

Raw Material	$ 75
Conversion	184
Total cost	$259

No beginning inventories exist.

1. Purchased $1,530,000 of raw material in June:

Raw and In-Process Inventory	$1,530,000	
Accounts Payable		$1,530,000
Purchased material at standard cost under		
a long-term agreement with supplier.		

2. Incurred $3,687,000 of conversion costs in June:

Conversion Costs	$3,687,000	
Various Accounts		$3,687,000
Record conversion costs. Various accounts include		
wages payable for direct and indirect labor,		
accumulated depreciation, supplies, etc.		

3. Completed 20,000 units of production in June:

Finished Goods (20,000 × $259)	$5,180,000	
Raw and In-Process Inventory (20,000 × $75)		$1,500,000
Conversion Costs (20,000 × $184)		3,680,000

4. Sold 19,800 units on account in June for $420 per unit:

(a) Cost of Goods Sold (19,800 × $259)	$5,128,200	
Finished Goods		$5,128,200
(b) Accounts Receivable (19,800 × $420)	8,316,000	
Sales		8,316,000
Ending Inventories:		
Raw and In-Process ($1,530,000 − $1,500,000)	30,000	
Finished Goods ($5,180,000 − $5,128,200)	51,800	

In addition, there are underapplied conversion costs of $7,000 ($3,687,000 − $3,680,000).

Three alternatives are possible to the entries in Example 8.23. First, if Ivy's production time were extremely short, the company might not journalize raw material purchases until completion of production. In that case, entries (1) and (3) from Example 8.23 could be combined as follows:

Raw and In-Process Inventory	$30,000	
Finished Goods	5,180,000	
Accounts Payable		$1,530,000
Conversion Costs		3,680,000

If goods were immediately shipped to customers on completion, Ivy could use a second alternative, in which entries (3) and (4)(a) from Example 8.23 could be combined in this manner to complete and sell the goods:

Finished Goods	$51,800	
Cost of Goods Sold	5,128,200	
Raw and In-Process Inventory		$1,500,000
Conversion Costs		3,680,000

The third alternative reflects the ultimate JIT system, in which only one entry is made to replace entries (1), (3), and (4)(a) in Example 8.23. For Ivy, this entry would be:

Raw and In-Process Inventory (minimal		
overpurchases)	$30,000	
Finished Goods (minimal overproduction)	51,800	
Cost of Goods Sold	5,128,200	
Accounts Payable		$1,530,000
Conversion Costs		3,680,000

Note that in all cases, entry (2) is not affected. All conversion costs must be recorded as incurred, or accrued at the end of a period, because of their effect on a variety of accounts.

Environmental Costs and Ecoefficiency

Why is there an increased interest in environmental costs?

Measuring environmental costs has become an important issue for many companies. Two reasons stand out relating to the increased interest in this issue:

1. Many countries have increased their regulations. Enormous fines or penalties have become part of these new regulations.
2. Successful treatment of environmental concerns is becoming a significant competitive issue.

What is ecoefficency?

Ecoefficiency is an important concept in dealing with the second reason listed. *Ecoefficiency* essentially maintains that organizations can produce more useful goods and services while simultaneously reducing negative environmental impacts, resource consumption, and costs. This means producing more goods and services using less materials, energy, water, and land, while minimizing polluting air emissions, water discharges, waste disposal, and the dispersion of toxic substances. Ecoefficiency implies a positive relationship between environmental and economic performance.

Ecoefficiency is not the only environmental cost paradigm. A competing paradigm is that of *compliance management*. Compliance management is the practice of achieving the minimal environmental performance required by regulations at the least cost. A second competing paradigm is that of *guided ecoefficiency*. Guided ecoefficiency maintains that pollution is a form of economic inefficiency and that properly designed environmental regulations will stimulate innovation such that environmental performance and economic efficiency will simultaneously improve.

There are at least five core objectives for the environmental perspective, including minimizing the use of raw or virgin materials; minimizing the use of hazardous materials; minimizing energy requirements for production and use of the product; minimizing the release of solid, liquid, and gaseous residues; and maximizing opportunities to recycle. Exhibit 8.9 summarizes the objectives and measures for the environmental perspective.

How can environmental costs be classified?

Environmental costs are costs that are incurred because poor environmental quality exists or may exist. Environmental costs can be classified into four categories: prevention costs, detection costs, internal failure costs, and external failure costs.

EXHIBIT 8.9 Objectives and Measures for the Environmental Perspective

Objective	Measures
Minimize hazardous materials	Types and quantities (total and per-unit)
	Percentage of total materials cost
	Productivity measures (output/input)
Minimize raw or virgin materials	Types and quantities (total and per-unit)
	Productivity measures (output/input)
Minimize energy requirements	Types and quantities (total and per-unit)
	Productivity measures (output/input)
Minimize release of residues	Pounds of toxic waste produced
	Cubic meters of effluents
	Tons of greenhouse gases produced
	Percentage reduction of packaging materials
Maximize opportunities to recycle	Pounds of materials recycled
	Number of different components recycled
	Percentage of units remanufactured
	Energy produced from incineration

Environmental prevention costs are the costs of activities carried out to prevent the production of contaminants and/or waste that could cause damage to the environment. Pollution prevention activities, often called "P2" activities, include:

- Evaluating and selecting suppliers
- Evaluating and selecting pollution-control equipment
- Designing processes
- Designing products
- Carrying out environmental studies
- Auditing environmental risks
- Developing environmental management systems
- Recycling products
- Obtaining ISO 14001 certification

Environmental detection costs are the costs of activities executed to determine if products, processes, and other activities within the firm are in compliance with appropriate environmental standards. Environmental detection costs include:

- Auditing environmental activities
- Inspecting products and processes
- Developing environmental performance measures
- Testing for contamination
- Verifying supplier environmental performance
- Measuring contamination levels

Environmental internal failure costs are costs of activities performed because contaminants and waste have been produced but not discharged into the environment. They are incurred to eliminate and manage contaminants or waste once produced.

Examples of environmental internal failure costs include:

- Operating pollution control equipment
- Treating and disposing of toxic waste
- Maintaining pollution equipment
- Licensing facilities for producing contaminants
- Recycling scrap

Environmental external failure costs are the costs of activities performed after discharging contaminants and waste into the environment. These costs are realized if incurred and paid for by the firm. They are unrealized or societal if they are caused by the firm but incurred and paid for by parties outside the firm. Examples of environmental external failure costs include:

- Cleaning up a polluted lake
- Cleaning up oil spills
- Cleaning up contaminated soil
- Settling personal injury claims (environmentally related)
- Restoring land to its natural state
- Losing sales due to poor environmental reputation

EXHIBIT 8.10 XYZ Chemicals Environmental Cost Report for the Year Ended December 31, 2X12

		Environmental Costs		Percentage*
Prevention costs				
	Evaluating suppliers	$ 120,000		
	Recycling products	$ 75,000	$ 195,000	0.33%
Detection costs				
	Inspecting products/ processes	$ 600,000		
	Developing performance measures	$ 60,000	$ 660,000	1.10%
Internal failure costs				
	Treating toxic waste	$4,800,000		
	Operating equipment	$ 840,000		
	Licensing facilities	$ 360,000	$6,000,000	10.00%
External failure costs				
	Settling claims	$1,200,000		
	Cleanup of soil	$1,800,000	$3,000,000	5.00%
Totals		$9,855,000		16.43%

*Of operating costs: $60,000,000.

- Using materials and energy inefficiently
- Receiving medical care due to polluted air
- Losing employment because of contamination
- Losing a lake for recreational use
- Damaging ecosystems from solid waste disposal

An *environmental cost report* may be prepared to report the details of environmental costs. It is a good idea to report the costs by category. Examples of environmental cost reports are presented in Exhibit 8.10 and Exhibit 8.11.

The relative distribution shown in the pie chart in Exhibit 8.11 reveals that the company is paying little attention to preventing and detecting environmental costs. To improve environmental performance, much more needs to be invested in the prevention and detection categories.

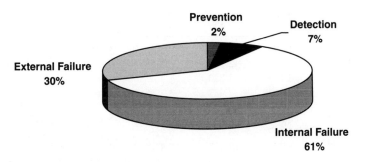

EXHIBIT 8.11 Sample Environmental Cost Report Pie Chart

Time Value Fundamentals

The time value of money is a critical consideration in investment decisions. *Examples:* Compound interest calculations are needed to appraise future sums of money resulting from an investment. Discounting, or the calculation of present values, which is inversely related to compounding, is used to evaluate future cash flow streams associated with the investment in fixed assets, such as machinery and equipment.

What is money worth in the future?

A dollar in hand today is worth more than a dollar to be received tomorrow because of the interest it could earn from putting it into a bank account or an investment. Compounding interest means that interest earns interest. For the discussion of this and the subsequent time value concepts, let us define:

F_n = future value; the amount of money at the end of year
P = principal
i = annual interest rate
n = number of years

To generalize, the future value of an investment if compounded annually at a rate of i for n years is:

$$F_n = P(1+i)^n = P \times T_1(i,n)$$

where $T_1(i,n)$ is the future value interest factor for $1.00 (found in Exhibit 8.12).

EXHIBIT 8.12   Future Value of $1.00

Period	4%	6%	8%	10%	12%	14%	20%
1	1.040	1.060	1.080	1.100	1.120	1.140	1.200
2	1.082	1.124	1.166	1.210	1.254	1.300	1.440
3	1.125	1.191	1.260	1.331	1.405	1.482	1.728
4	1.170	1.263	1.361	1.464	1.574	1.689	2.074
5	1.217	1.338	1.469	1.611	1.762	1.925	2.488
6	1.265	1.419	1.587	1.772	1.974	2.195	2.986
7	1.316	1.504	1.714	1.949	2.211	2.502	3.583
8	1.369	1.594	1.851	2.144	2.476	2.853	4.300
9	1.423	1.690	1.999	2.359	2.773	3.252	5.160
10	1.480	1.791	2.159	2.594	3.106	3.707	6.192
11	1.540	1.898	2.332	2.853	3.479	4.226	7.430
12	1.601	2.012	2.518	3.139	3.896	4.818	8.916
13	1.665	2.133	2.720	3.452	4.364	5.492	10.699
14	1.732	2.261	2.937	3.798	4.887	6.261	12.839
15	1.801	2.397	3.172	4.177	5.474	7.138	15.407
20	2.191	3.207	4.661	6.728	9.646	13.743	38.338
30	3.243	5.744	10.063	17.450	29.960	50.950	237.380
40	4.801	10.286	21.725	45.260	93.051	188.880	1,469.800

Example 8.24

Your client placed $1,000 in a savings account earning 8 percent interest compounded annually.

How much money will the client have in the account at the end of four years?

Substituting P = $1,000, $i = 0.08$, and $n = 4$ into the formula, and referring to Exhibit 8.12, gives:

$$F_4 = \$1,000(1 + 0.08)^4 = \$1,000(\text{Exhibit 8.12 value}) = \$1.000(1.361) = \$1,361$$

What is the future value of an annuity?

An *annuity* is defined as a series of equal payments (or receipts) for a specified number of periods. The future value of an annuity is a compound annuity that involves depositing or investing an equal sum of money at the end of each year for a certain number of years and allowing it to grow.

It is computed as:

$$F = AT_2(i,n)$$

where:

A = the amount of an annuity

$T_2(i,n)$ = the future value interest factor for an n-year annuity compounded at i percent (this can be found in Exhibit 8.13).

EXHIBIT 8.13 Future Value of an Annuity of $1.00

Period	4%	6%	8%	10%	12%	14%	20%
1	1.000	1.000	1.000	1.000	1.000	1.000	1.000
2	2.040	2.060	2.080	2.100	2.120	2.140	2.220
3	3.122	3.184	3.246	3.310	3.374	3.440	3.640
4	4.247	4.375	4.506	4.641	4.779	4.921	5.368
5	5.416	5.637	5.867	6.105	6.353	6.610	7.442
6	6.633	6.975	7.336	7.716	8.115	8.536	9.930
7	7.898	8.394	8.923	9.487	10.089	10.730	12.916
8	9.214	9.898	10.637	11.436	12.300	13.233	16.499
9	10.583	11.491	12.488	13.580	14.776	16.085	20.799
10	12.006	13.181	14.487	15.938	17.549	19.337	25.959
11	13.486	14.972	16.646	18.531	20.655	23.045	32.150
12	15.026	16.870	18.977	21.395	24.133	27.271	39.580
13	16.627	18.882	21.495	24.523	28.029	32.089	48.497
14	18.292	21.015	24.215	27.976	32.393	37.581	59.196
15	20.024	23.276	27.152	31.773	37.280	43.842	72.035
20	29.778	36.778	45.762	57.276	75.052	91.025	186.690
30	56.085	79.058	113.283	164.496	241.330	356.790	1,181.900
40	95.026	154.762	259.057	442.597	767.090	1,342.000	7,343.900

Example 8.25

Your client wants to determine the sum of money she will have in a savings account at the end of six years by depositing $1,000 at the end of each year for the next six years. The annual interest rate is 8 percent. The amount is:

$$\$1,000(\text{Exhibit } 8.13 \text{ value}) = \$1,000(7.336)$$
$$= \$7,336$$

What is present value?

Present value is the present worth of future sums of money. The process of calculating present values, or discounting, is the opposite of finding the compounded future value.

Recall from the future value formula:

$$F_n = P(1 + i)^n$$

Therefore,

$$P = F_n/(1 + i)^n = F_n T_3(i,n)$$

where $T_3(i,n)$ represents the present value interest factor for $1.00 (given in Exhibit 8.14).

Example 8.26

A client has been given an opportunity to receive $20,000 six years from now. If the client can earn 10 percent on the investment, what is the most he should pay for this opportunity?

We compute the present worth of $20,000 to be received six years from now at a 10 percent rate of discount. Use Exhibit 8.14 values:

$$\$20,000(\text{Exhibit } 8.14 \text{ value}) = \$20,000(0.564) = \$11,280$$

This means that the client should be indifferent to the choice between receiving $11,280 now and receiving $20,000 six years from now since the amounts are time equivalent. In other words, the client could invest $11,280 today at 10 percent and have $20,000 in six years.

What is the present value of an annuity?

Interest received from bonds, pension funds, and insurance obligations all involve annuities. To compare these financial instruments, we would like to know the

EXHIBIT 8.14 Present Value of $1.00

Period	4%	5%	6%	8%	10%	12%	14%	16%	18%	20%	22%	24%	26%	28%	30%	40%
1	0.962	0.952	0.943	0.926	0.909	0.893	0.877	0.862	0.847	0.833	0.820	0.806	0.794	0.781	0.769	0.714
2	0.925	0.907	0.890	0.857	0.826	0.797	0.769	0.743	0.718	0.694	0.672	0.650	0.630	0.610	0.592	0.510
3	0.889	0.864	0.840	0.794	0.751	0.712	0.675	0.641	0.609	0.579	0.551	0.524	0.500	0.477	0.455	0.364
4	0.855	0.823	0.792	0.735	0.683	0.636	0.592	0.552	0.516	0.482	0.451	0.423	0.397	0.373	0.350	0.260
5	0.822	0.784	0.747	0.681	0.621	0.567	0.519	0.476	0.437	0.402	0.370	0.341	0.315	0.291	0.269	0.186
6	0.790	0.746	0.705	0.630	0.564	0.507	0.456	0.410	0.370	0.335	0.303	0.275	0.250	0.227	0.207	0.133
7	0.760	0.711	0.665	0.583	0.513	0.452	0.400	0.354	0.314	0.279	0.249	0.222	0.198	0.178	0.159	0.095
8	0.731	0.677	0.627	0.540	0.467	0.404	0.351	0.305	0.266	0.233	0.204	0.179	0.157	0.139	0.123	0.068
9	0.703	0.645	0.592	0.500	0.424	0.361	0.308	0.263	0.225	0.194	0.167	0.144	0.125	0.108	0.094	0.048
10	0.676	0.614	0.558	0.463	0.386	0.322	0.270	0.227	0.191	0.162	0.137	0.116	0.099	0.085	0.073	0.035
11	0.650	0.585	0.527	0.429	0.350	0.287	0.237	0.195	0.162	0.135	0.112	0.094	0.079	0.066	0.056	0.025
12	0.625	0.557	0.497	0.397	0.319	0.257	0.208	0.168	0.137	0.112	0.092	0.076	0.062	0.052	0.043	0.018
13	0.601	0.530	0.469	0.368	0.290	0.229	0.182	0.145	0.116	0.093	0.075	0.061	0.050	0.040	0.033	0.013
14	0.577	0.505	0.442	0.340	0.263	0.205	0.160	0.125	0.099	0.078	0.062	0.049	0.039	0.032	0.025	0.009
15	0.555	0.481	0.417	0.315	0.239	0.183	0.140	0.108	0.084	0.065	0.051	0.040	0.031	0.025	0.020	0.006
16	0.534	0.458	0.394	0.292	0.218	0.163	0.123	0.093	0.071	0.054	0.042	0.032	0.025	0.019	0.015	0.005
17	0.513	0.436	0.371	0.270	0.198	0.146	0.108	0.080	0.060	0.045	0.034	0.026	0.020	0.015	0.012	0.003
18	0.494	0.416	0.350	0.250	0.180	0.130	0.095	0.069	0.051	0.038	0.028	0.021	0.016	0.012	0.009	0.002
19	0.475	0.396	0.331	0.232	0.164	0.116	0.083	0.060	0.043	0.031	0.023	0.017	0.012	0.009	0.007	0.002
20	0.456	0.377	0.312	0.215	0.149	0.104	0.073	0.051	0.037	0.026	0.019	0.014	0.010	0.007	0.005	0.001
21	0.439	0.359	0.294	0.199	0.135	0.093	0.064	0.044	0.031	0.022	0.015	0.011	0.008	0.006	0.004	0.001
22	0.422	0.342	0.278	0.184	0.123	0.083	0.056	0.038	0.026	0.018	0.013	0.009	0.006	0.004	0.003	0.001
23	0.406	0.326	0.262	0.170	0.112	0.074	0.049	0.033	0.022	0.015	0.010	0.007	0.005	0.003	0.002	
24	0.390	0.310	0.247	0.158	0.102	0.066	0.043	0.028	0.019	0.013	0.008	0.006	0.004	0.003	0.002	
25	0.375	0.295	0.233	0.146	0.092	0.059	0.038	0.024	0.016	0.010	0.007	0.005	0.003	0.002	0.001	
26	0.361	0.281	0.220	0.135	0.084	0.053	0.033	0.021	0.014	0.009	0.006	0.004	0.002	0.002	0.001	
27	0.347	0.268	0.207	0.125	0.076	0.047	0.029	0.018	0.011	0.007	0.005	0.003	0.002	0.001	0.001	
28	0.333	0.255	0.196	0.116	0.069	0.042	0.026	0.016	0.010	0.006	0.004	0.002	0.002	0.001	0.001	
29	0.321	0.243	0.185	0.107	0.063	0.037	0.022	0.014	0.008	0.005	0.003	0.002	0.001	0.001	0.001	
30	0.308	0.231	0.174	0.099	0.057	0.033	0.020	0.012	0.007	0.004	0.003	0.002	0.001	0.001	0.001	
40	0.208	0.142	0.097	0.046	0.022	0.011	0.005	0.003	0.001	0.001						

present value of each of these annuities. The way to find the present value of an annuity is:

$$P = AT_4(i,n)$$

where:

A = the amount of an annuity

$T_4(i,n)$ = the value for the present value interest factor for a \$1.00 annuity at i percent for n years (found in Exhibit 8.15).

Example 8.27

A client is to receive an annuity of \$1,000 each year for the next three years. You are asked to compute the present value of the annuity at 6 percent. Use Exhibit 8.15 for this purpose:

$$\$1,000(\text{Exhibit 8.15 value}) = \$1,000(2.673) = \$2,673$$

Capital Budgeting

What is capital budgeting?

Capital budgeting is the process of making long-term planning decisions for investments. There are typically two types of investment decisions:

1. *Selection decisions* in terms of obtaining new facilities or expanding existing facilities

    Examples:
    - Investments in long-term assets, such as property, plant, and equipment
    - Resource commitments in the form of new product development, market research, refunding of long-term debt, introduction of an information technology (IT) system, and so on

2. *Replacement decisions* in terms of replacing existing facilities with new facilities

    Examples:
    - Replacing a dial-up system with a broadband system
    - Replacing an inefficient lathe with one that is numerically controlled

What are the popular selection techniques?

There are several methods of evaluating investment projects:

- Payback period
- Accounting rate of return (ARR) (also called *simple rate of return*)
- Net present value (NPV)
- Internal rate of return (IRR) (also called *time-adjusted rate of return*)
- Profitability index (also called the *excess present value index*)

EXHIBIT 8.15 Present Value of an Annuity of $1.00

Period	4%	5%	6%	8%	10%	12%	14%	16%	18%	20%	22%	24%	26%	28%	30%	40%
1	0.962	0.952	0.943	0.926	0.909	0.893	0.877	0.862	0.847	0.833	0.820	0.806	0.794	0.781	0.769	0.714
2	1.886	1.859	1.833	1.783	1.736	1.690	1.647	1.605	1.566	1.528	1.492	1.457	1.424	1.392	1.361	1.224
3	2.775	2.723	2.673	2.577	2.487	2.402	2.322	2.246	2.174	2.106	2.042	1.981	1.868	1.816	1.816	1.589
4	3.630	3.546	3.465	3.312	3.170	3.037	2.914	2.798	2.690	2.589	2.494	2.404	2.320	2.241	2.166	1.879
5	4.452	4.330	4.212	3.993	3.791	3.605	3.433	3.274	3.127	2.991	2.864	2.745	2.635	2.532	2.436	2.035
6	5.242	5.076	4.917	4.623	4.355	4.111	3.889	3.685	3.498	3.326	3.167	3.020	2.885	2.759	2.643	2.168
7	6.002	5.786	5.582	5.206	4.868	4.564	4.288	4.039	3.812	3.605	3.416	3.242	3.083	2.937	2.802	2.263
8	6.733	6.463	6.210	5.747	5.335	4.968	4.639	4.344	4.078	3.837	3.619	3.421	3.241	3.076	2.925	2.331
9	7.435	7.108	6.802	6.247	5.759	5.328	4.946	4.607	4.303	4.031	3.786	3.566	3.366	3.184	3.019	2.379
10	8.111	7.722	7.360	6.710	6.145	5.650	5.216	4.833	4.494	4.192	3.923	3.682	3.465	3.269	3.092	2.414
11	8.760	8.306	7.887	7.139	6.495	5.988	5.453	5.029	4.656	4.327	4.035	3.776	3.544	3.335	3.147	2.438
12	9.385	8.863	8.384	7.536	6.814	6.194	5.660	5.197	4.793	4.439	4.127	3.851	3.606	3.387	3.190	2.456
13	9.986	9.394	8.853	7.904	7.103	6.424	5.842	5.342	4.910	4.533	4.203	3.912	3.656	3.427	3.223	2.468
14	10.563	9.899	9.295	8.244	7.367	6.628	6.002	5.468	5.008	4.611	4.265	3.962	3.695	3.459	3.249	2.477
15	11.118	10.380	9.712	8.559	7.606	6.811	6.142	5.575	5.092	4.675	4.315	4.001	3.726	3.483	3.268	2.484
16	11.652	10.838	10.106	8.851	7.824	6.974	6.265	5.669	5.162	4.730	4.357	4.033	3.751	3.503	3.283	2.489
17	12.166	11.274	10.477	9.122	8.022	7.120	6.373	5.749	5.222	4.775	4.391	4.059	3.771	3.518	3.295	2.492
18	12.659	11.690	10.828	9.372	8.201	7.250	6.467	5.818	5.273	4.812	4.419	4.080	3.786	3.529	3.304	2.494
19	13.134	12.085	11.158	9.604	8.365	7.366	6.550	5.877	5.316	4.844	4.442	4.097	3.799	3.539	3.311	2.496
20	13.590	12.462	11.470	9.818	8.514	7.469	6.623	5.929	5.353	4.870	4.460	4.110	3.808	3.546	3.316	2.497
21	14.029	12.821	11.764	10.017	8.649	7.562	6.687	5.973	5.384	4.891	4.476	4.121	3.816	3.551	3.320	2.498
22	14.451	13.163	12.042	10.201	8.772	7.645	6.743	6.011	5.410	4.909	4.488	4.130	3.822	3.556	3.323	2.498
23	14.857	13.489	12.303	10.371	8.883	7.718	6.792	6.044	5.432	4.925	4.499	4.137	3.827	3.559	3.325	2.499
24	15.247	13.799	12.550	10.529	8.985	7.784	6.835	6.073	5.451	4.937	4.507	4.143	3.831	3.562	3.327	2.499
25	15.622	14.094	12.783	10.675	9.077	7.843	6.873	6.097	5.467	4.948	4.514	4.147	3.834	3.564	3.329	2.499
26	15.983	14.375	13.003	10.810	9.161	7.896	6.906	6.118	5.480	4.956	4.520	4.151	3.837	3.566	3.330	2.500
27	16.330	14.643	13.211	10.935	9.237	7.943	6.935	6.936	5.492	4.964	4.525	4.154	3.839	3.567	3.331	2.500
28	16.663	14.898	13.406	11.051	9.307	7.984	6.961	6.152	5.502	4.970	4.528	4.157	3.840	3.568	3.331	2.500
29	16.984	15.141	13.591	11.158	9.370	8.022	6.983	6.166	5.510	4.975	4.531	4.159	3.841	3.569	3.332	2.500
30	17.292	15.373	13.765	11.258	9.427	8.055	7.003	6.177	5.517	4.979	4.534	4.160	3.842	3.569	3.332	2.500
40	19.793	17.159	15.046	11.925	9.779	8.244	7.105	6.234	5.548	4.997	4.544	4.166	3.846	3.571	3.333	2.500

> **Note**
>
> The NPV method and the IRR method are called *discounted cash flow* (DCF) methods since they both recognize the time value of money and thus discount future cash flows. Each of these methods is discussed in this chapter.

Payback Period

How do I determine the payback period?

The payback period measures the length of time required to recover the amount of the initial investment. The payback period is determined by dividing the amount of the initial investment by the cash inflow through increased revenues or cost savings.

Example 8.28

Assume:

Cost of investment	$18,000
Annual cash savings	$3,000

Then the payback period is:

$$\frac{\$18,000}{\$3,000} = 6 \text{ years}$$

When cash inflows are not even, the payback period is determined by trial and error. When two or more projects are considered, the rule for making a selection decision is:

Choose the project with the shorter payback period. The rationale is that the shorter the payback period, the less risky the project and the greater the liquidity.

Example 8.29

Consider two projects whose cash inflows are not even. Assume each project costs $1,000.

Year	A	B
1	$100	$500
2	200	400
3	300	300
4	400	$100
5	500	—
6	$600	—

Based on trial and error, the payback period of project A is four years ($100 + 200 + 300 + 400 = $1,000 in four years). The payback period of project B is

$$2 \text{ years } + \frac{\$100}{\$300} = 2\tfrac{1}{3} \text{ years}$$

Therefore, according to this method, choose project B over project A.

What are the pros and cons of the payback period method?

The advantages are:

- It is simple to compute and easy to understand.
- It handles investment risk effectively.

    The disadvantages are:

- It does not recognize the time value of money.
- It ignores the impact of cash inflows after the payback period. Essentially, cash flows after the payback period determine the profitability of an investment.

How do I not account for the time value of money?

To correct for the deficiency of not taking into account the time value of money, the discounted payback method can be used. In this case:

- Each year's cash inflows are expressed in present value terms.
- Each year's present value is added to determine how long it takes to recoup the initial investment.

Accounting (Simple) Rate of Return

What is the accounting rate of return?

Accounting rate of return (ARR) measures profitability from the conventional accounting standpoint by relating the required investment to the future annual net income. Sometimes the former is the average investment.

Example 8.30

Consider the investment:

Initial investment	$6,500
Estimated life	20 years
Cash inflows per year	$1,000
Depreciation (straight-line)	$ 325

(continued)

(Continued)

$$\text{Then, ARR} = \frac{\$1,000 - \$325}{\$6,500} = 10.4\%$$

Using the average investment, which is usually assumed to be one-half of the original investment, the resulting rate of return will be doubled, as shown.

$$\text{ARR} = \frac{\$1,000 - \$325}{1/2(\$6,500)} = \frac{\$675}{\$3,250} = 20.8\%$$

The justification for using the average investment is that each year the investment amount is decreased by $325 through depreciation. Therefore, the average is computed as one-half of the original cost.

Recommendation

Under the ARR method, choose the project with the higher rate of return.

What are benefits and drawbacks of the ARR method?

An advantage is that the method is easily understandable, simple to compute, and recognizes the profitability factor.

Disadvantages are:

- It fails to recognize the time value of money.
- It uses accounting data instead of cash flow data.

Net Present Value

What is net present value?

Net present value (NPV) is the excess of the present value (PV) of cash inflows generated by the project over the amount of the initial investment (I). Simply, NPV = PV − I. The present value of future cash flows is computed using the so-called cost of capital (or minimum required rate of return) as the discount rate.

Recommendation

If NPV is positive, accept the project; otherwise, reject it.

Example 8.31

Assume:

Initial investment	$12,950
Estimated life	10 years
Annual cash inflows	$ 3,000
Cost of capital (minimum required rate of return)	12%

Present value of cash inflows (PV):
$3,000 × PV of annuity of $1 for 10 years and 12%

$3,000(Exhibit 8.14 value) = $3,000(5.65) =	$16,950
Initial investment (I)	−$12,950
Net present value (NPV = PV − I)	$ 4,000

Since the investment's NPV is positive, the investment should be accepted.

What are the pros and cons of the NPV method?

Advantages are:

- It recognizes the time value of money.
- It is easy to compute regardless of whether the cash flows form an annuity or vary from period to period.

A disadvantage is that it requires detailed long-term forecasts of incremental cash flow data.

Internal Rate of Return (or Time-Adjusted Rate of Return)

What is internal rate of return?

Internal rate of return (IRR) is defined as the rate of interest that equates I with the PV of future cash inflows. In other words, at IRR, I = PV, or NPV = 0.

Recommendation

Accept if IRR exceeds the cost of capital; otherwise, reject.

Example 8.32

Assume the same data given in Example 8.31. We set up the following equality (I = PV):

$$\$12,950 = \$3,000 \times PV$$
$$PV = \$12,950/\$3,000 = 4.317$$

(continued)

(Continued)

which stands somewhere between 18 percent and 20 percent in the 10-year line of Exhibit 8.15. Using interpolation, we derive the exact rate.

PV Factor (Exhibit 8.15 Value)		
18%	4.494	4.494
IRR		4.317
20%	4.192	
Difference	0.302	0.177

$$\text{Therefore, IRR} = 18\% + \frac{0.177}{0.302}(20\% - 18\%)$$

$$= 18\% + 0.586\,(2\%)$$

$$= 18\% + 1.17\% = 19.17\%$$

Since the investment's IRR is greater than the cost of capital (12 percent), the investment should be accepted.

What are the benefits and drawbacks of the IRR method?

An advantage is that it considers the time value of money and is therefore more exact and realistic than ARR is.

Disadvantages are:

- It is difficult to compute, especially when the cash inflows are not even.
- It fails to recognize the varying sizes of investments in competing projects and their respective dollar profitabilities.

How is IRR computed by trial and error?

The trial-and-error method for computing IRR when cash inflows are different each year is summarized step-by-step next.

Step 1. Compute NPV at cost of capital, denoted here as r_1.

Step 2. See if NPV is positive or negative.

Step 3. If NPV is positive, then pick another rate (r_2) much higher than r_1. If NPV is negative, then pick another rate (r_2) much smaller than r_1. The true IRR at which NPV = 0 must be somewhere between these two rates.

Step 4. Compute NPV using r_2.

Step 5. Use interpolation for the exact rate.

Example 8.33

Consider the following investment whose cash flows are different from year to year:

Year	Cash Inflows
1	$1,000
2	$2,500
3	$1,500

Assume that the amount of initial investment is $3,000 and the cost of capital is 14 percent.

Step 1. NPV at 14 percent:

Year	Cash Inflows	PV Factor at 14%	Total PV
1	$1,000	0.877	$ 877
2	$2,500	0.769	1,923
3	$1,500	0.675	1,013
			$3,813

Thus, NPV = $3,813 − $3,000 = $813.

Step 2. We see that NPV = $813 is positive at $r_1 = 14$ percent.

Step 3. Pick, say, 30 percent to play safe as r_2.

Step 4. Computing NPV at $r_2 = 30\%$:

Year	Cash Inflows	PV Factor at 30%	Total PV
1	$1,000	0.769	$ 769
2	$2,500	0.592	1,480
3	$1,500	0.455	683
			$2,932

Thus, NPV = $2,932 − $3,000 = −$68.

Step 5. Interpolate:

	NPV	
14%	$813	$813
IRR		0
30%	−68	
Difference	$881	$813

(continued)

(*Continued*)

$$\text{Therefore, IRR} = 14\% + \frac{\$813}{\$881}(30\% - 14\%)$$
$$= 14\% + 0.923(16\%)$$
$$= 14\% + 14.76\%$$
$$= 28.76\%$$

Can a computer help?

Spreadsheet programs can be used in making IRR calculations. For example, Excel has a function IRR (*values, guess*). Excel considers negative numbers, such as the initial investment, as cash outflows and positive numbers as cash inflows. Many financial calculators have similar features. As in Example 8.31, suppose you want to calculate the IRR of a $12,950 investment (the value "–12950" entered in year 0 that is followed by 10 monthly cash inflows of 3000). Using a guess of 12 percent (the value of 0.12), which is in effect the cost of capital, the formula would be @IRR(values, 0.12) and Excel would return 19.15 percent, as shown next.

Year:	0	1	2	3	4	5	6	7	8	9	10
	$(12,950)	3,000	3,000	3,000	3,000	3,000	3,000	3,000	3,000	3,000	3,000
	IRR = 19.15%										
	NPV = $4,000.67										

Note: The Excel formula for NPV is NPV (discount rate, cash inflow values) + I, where I is given as a negative number.

What are the differences between NPV and IRR?

Net Present Value (NPV)
- Calculate the NPV, using the cost of capital as the discount rate.
- If the NPV is positive, accept the project; otherwise, reject it.

Internal Rate of Return (IRR)
- Using present value tables, compute the IRR by trial-and-error interpolation.
- If this rate of return exceeds the cost of capital, accept the project; if not, reject it.

Profitability Index (or Excess Present Value Index)

What is the profitability index?

The profitability index is the ratio of the total PV of future cash inflows to the initial investment, that is, PV/I. This index is used as a means of ranking projects in descending order of attractiveness.

Recommendation

If PV/I is greater than 1, then accept the project.

Example 8.34

Using the data in Example 8.31, the profitability index = PV/I = $16,950/$12,950 = $1.31. Since this project generates $1.31 for each dollar invested (its profitability index is greater than 1), you should accept the project.

How do I choose between mutually exclusive investments?

A project is said to be *mutually exclusive* if the acceptance of one project automatically excludes the acceptance of one or more other projects. The conditions under which contradictory rankings can occur are:

- Projects have different expected lives.
- Projects have different sizes of investment.
- The times of the projects' cash flows differ (e.g., the cash flows of one project increase over time, while those of the other decrease).

When you must choose between mutually exclusive investments, the NPV and IRR methods may give decision results contradictory to each other. The contradiction results from different assumptions with respect to the reinvestment rate on cash flows released from the projects.

- The NPV method discounts all cash flows at the cost of capital, thus implicitly assuming that these cash flows can be reinvested at this rate.
- The IRR method implies a reinvestment rate at IRR. Thus, the implied reinvestment rate will differ from project to project.

The NPV method generally gives correct ranking, since the cost of capital is a more realistic reinvestment rate.

Example 8.35

Assume:

		Cash Flows				
	0	1	2	3	4	5
A	(100)	120	—	—	—	—
B	(100)	—	—	—	—	201.14

(continued)

(Continued)

Computing IRR and NPV at 10 percent gives these different rankings:

	IRR	NPV at 10%
A	20%	9.08
B	15%	24.91

Note

The general rule is to go by NPV ranking, thus choosing project B over project A.

Limited Funds for Capital Spending

How do I deal with limited funds for capital spending?

Many firms specify a limit on the overall budget for capital spending. *Capital rationing* is concerned with the problem of selecting the mix of acceptable projects that provides the *highest overall NPV* in such a case. The profitability index is used widely in ranking projects competing for limited funds.

Example 8.36

Projects	I	PV	Profitability Index	Ranking
A	$ 70,000	$112,000	1.6	1
B	100,000	145,000	1.45	2
C	110,000	126,500	1.15	5
D	60,000	79,000	1.32	3
E	40,000	38,000	0.95	6
F	80,000	95,000	1.19	4

Assume that the company's fixed budget is $250,000. Using the profitability index, we select projects A, B, and D:

	I	PV
A	$ 70,000	$112,000
B	100,000	145,000
D	60,000	79,000
	$230,000	$336,000

Therefore, NPV = $336,000 − $230,000 = $106,000.

Effects of Income Tax Factors on Capital Budgeting Decisions

How do income tax factors affect capital budgeting decisions?

Income taxes make a difference in many capital budgeting decisions. The project that is attractive on a pretax basis may have to be rejected on an after-tax basis. Income taxes typically affect both the amount and the timing of cash flows. Since net income, not cash inflows, is subject to tax, after-tax cash inflows are not usually the same as after-tax net income.

Let us define:

S = sales
E = cash operating expenses
d = depreciation
t = tax rate

Before-tax cash inflows = $(S - E)$
Net income = $(S - E - d)$

By definition,

After-tax cash inflows = Before-tax cash inflows − Taxes
After-tax cash inflows = $(S - E) - (S - E - d) \times t$

Rearranging gives the shortcut formula:

After-tax cash inflows = $(S - E)(1 - t) + d \times t$

As can be seen, the deductibility of depreciation from sales in arriving at net income subject to taxes, reduces income tax payments and thus serves as a *tax shield*.

Tax shield = Tax savings on depreciation
$= d \times t$

Example 8.37

S = \$12,000
E = \$10,000
d = \$500 per year by straight-line depreciation
t = 40%

Then:
After-tax cash inflows

$$= (\$12,000 - \$10,000)(1 - 0.4) + \$500(0.4)$$
$$= \$1,200 + \$200 = \$1,400$$

Note

Tax shield = Tax savings on depreciation = $d \times t$ = \$500(0.4) = \$200.

How are after-tax outflows determined?

After-tax cash *outflows* are computed by simply dropping S in the previous formula. Therefore:

$$\text{After-tax cash outflows} = (-E)(1 - t) + d \times t$$

Example 8.38

Assume:

$E = \$6,000$
$d = \$800$ per year by straight-line depreciation
$t = 4\%$

Then:
After-tax cash *outflows*

$$= (-\$6,000)(1 - 0.4) + \$800(0.4) = -\$3,600 + \$320$$
$$= -\$3,280$$

What is the effect of accelerated depreciation on tax savings?

Since the tax shield is $d \times t$, the higher the depreciation deduction, the higher the tax savings on depreciation. Therefore, the accelerated depreciated methods, such as the double-declining-balance method and the sum-of-the-years'-digits method, produce higher tax savings than the straight-line method. They will produce higher present values for the tax savings, which greatly affect the investment decision. Let us look at the present values of tax shield effects of alternative depreciation methods.

Example 8.39

Assume:

Initial investment	$100,000
Estimated life	4 years
Salvage value	0
Cost of capital after taxes	15%
Tax rate	40%

Method of depreciation			15% PV Factor	PV of Tax Savings
Straight-Line Depreciation				
Annual depreciation				
($100,000 ÷ 4 = $25,000):				
Depreciation deduction		$25,000		
Multiply by 40%		× 40%		
Income tax savings, years 1–4		$10,000	2.855	$28,550

Sum-of-the-Years'-Digits Depreciation

Year	Multiplier*	Depreciation Deduction	Tax Shield: Income Tax Savings at 40%	15% PV Factor	PV of Tax Savings
1	4/10	$40,000	$16,000	0.870	$13,920
2	3/10	30,000	12,000	0.756	9,072
3	2/10	20,000	8,000	0.658	5,264
4	1/10	10,000	4,000	0.572	2,288
					$30,544

*The denominator for the sum-of-the-years'-digits method is: $1 + 2 + 3 + 4 = 10$ or
$$S = \frac{n(n+1)}{2} \quad S = \frac{4(4+1)}{2} = 10$$
where
S = sum of the years
n = life of the asset

Double-Declining Balance Depreciation

Year	Book Value	Rate* (%)	Depreciation Deduction	Tax Shield: Income Tax Savings at 40%		
1	$100,000	50	$50,000	$20,000	0.870	$17,400
2	50,000	50	25,000	10,000	0.756	7,560
3	25,000	50	12,500	5,000	0.658	3,290
4	12,500	50	12,500†	5,000	0.572	2,860
						$31,110

*The percentage rate for the double-declining method is: $2 \times$ Straight-line rate $= 2 \times 25\% = 50\%$.
†The asset is depreciated to zero salvage value in the fourth year.

MACRS Rule

How does the MACRS rule affect investment decisions?

Although the traditional methods still can be used for computing depreciation for book purposes, there is a new way of computing depreciation deductions for tax purposes, called the modified accelerated cost recovery system (MACRS) rule. Under this rule:

■ The concept of useful life is abandoned and depreciation deductions are accelerated by placing all depreciable assets into one of eight age property classes.

EXHIBIT 8.16   Modified Accelerated Cost Recovery System: Classification of Assets

	Property Class					
Year	3-Year	5-Year	7-Year	10-Year	15-Year	20-Year
1	33.3%	20.0%	14.3%	10.0%	5.0%	3.8%
2	44.5	32.0	24.5	18.0	9.5	7.2
3	14.8*	19.2	17.5	14.4	8.6	6.7
4	7.4	11.5*	12.5	11.5	7.7	6.2
5		11.5	8.9*	9.2	6.9	5.7
6		5.8	8.9	7.4	6.2	5.3
7			8.9	6.6*	5.9*	4.9
8			4.5	6.6	5.9	4.5*
9				6.5	5.9	4.5
10				6.5	5.9	4.5
11				3.3	5.9	4.5
12					5.9	4.5
13					5.9	4.5
14					5.9	4.5
15					5.9	4.5
16					3.0	4.4
17						4.4
18						4.4
19						4.4
20						4.4
21						2.2
Total	100%	100%	100%	100%	100%	100%

* Denotes the year of changeover to straight-line depreciation.

MACRS calculates deductions based on an allowable percentage of the asset's original cost. (See Exhibits 8.16 and 8.17.)

- Using a shorter time frame than useful life, the company can deduct depreciation more quickly and save more in income taxes in the earlier years, thereby making an investment more attractive. The rationale behind the system is that the company is encouraged to invest in facilities and increase its productive capacity and efficiency. Remember that the higher the d, the larger the tax shield ($d \times t$).
- There is no need to consider the salvage value of an asset in computing depreciation, since the allowable percentages in Exhibit 8.16 add up to 100 percent.
- The company may elect the straight-line method, which must follow what is called the *half-year convention*. This means that the company can deduct only half of the regular straight-line depreciation amount in the first year.
- If an asset is disposed of before the end of its class life, the half-year convention allows half the depreciation for that year (early disposal rule).

Why elect the straight-line method?

The reason for electing to use the MACRS optional straight-line method is that some firms may prefer to stretch out depreciation deductions rather than to accelerate

EXHIBIT 8.17   MACRS Tables by Property Class

MACRS Property Class and Depreciation Method	Useful Life (ADR Midpoint Life)*	Examples of Assets
3-year property 200% declining balance	4 years or less	Most small tools are included; the law specifically excludes autos and light trucks from this property class.
5-year property 200% declining balance	More than 4 years to less than 10 years	Autos and light trucks, computers, typewriters, copiers, duplicating equipment, heavy general-purpose trucks, and research and experimentation equipment are included.
7-year property 200% declining balance	10 years or more to less than 16 years	Office furniture and fixtures and most items of machinery and equipment used in production are included.
10-year property 200% declining balance	16 years or more to less than 20 years	Various machinery and equipment, such as used in petroleum distilling and refining and in the milling of grain, are included.
15-year property 150% declining balance	20 years or more to less than 25 years	Sewage treatment plants, telephone and electrical distribution facilities, and land improvements are included.
20-year property 150% declining balance	25 years or more	Service stations and other real property with an ADR midpoint life of less than 27.5 years are included.
27.5-year property straight-line	Not applicable	All residential rental property is included.
31.5-year property straight-line	Not applicable	All nonresidential real property is included.

* The term *asset depreciation range (ADR) midpoint life* means the useful life of an asset in a business sense; the appropriate ADR midpoint lives for assets are designated in the Tax Regulations.

them. Those firms may be just starting out and/or have little or no income and want to show more income on their income statements.

Example 8.40

Assume that a machine falls under a three-year property class and costs $3,000 initially. The straight-line option under MACRS differs from the traditional straight-line method in that under this method the company would deduct only $500 depreciation in the first year and in the fourth year ($3,000/3 years = $1,000; $1,000/2 = $500). The table shown compares the straight-line with half-year convention, with the standard MACRS rule.

(continued)

(Continued)

Year	Straight-Line (half-year) Depreciation	Cost × MACRS%	MACRS Deduction
1	$ 500	$3,000 × 33.3%	$ 999
2	1,000	3,000 × 44.5	1,335
3	1,000	3,000 × 14.8	444
4	500	3,000 × 7.4	222
	$3,000		$3,000

Example 8.41

A machine costs $10,000. Annual cash inflows are expected to be $5,000. The machine will be depreciated using the MACRS rule and will fall under the three-year property class. The cost of capital after taxes is 10 percent. The estimated life of the machine is five years. The salvage value of the machine at the end of the fifth year is expected to be $1,200. The tax rate is 30 percent. Should you buy the machine? Use the NPV method.

The formula for computation of after-tax cash inflows $(S - E)(1 - t) + (d)(t)$ needs to be computed separately. The NPV analysis can be performed as follows:

				Present Value Factor @ 10%	Present Value
$(S - E)$ $(1 - t)$:					
	$5,000	$5,000(1 − 0.3) = $3,500			
	for 5 years	for 5 years	$3.500	3.791*	$13,268.50

$(d)(t)$:

Year	Cost	MACRS %	d	(d)(t)		
1	$10,000 ×	33.3%	$3,330	$ 999	0.909† (b)	$ 908.09
2	$10,000 ×	44.5	4,450	1,335	0.826† (b)	1,102.71
3	$10,000 ×	14.8	1,480	444	0.751† (b)	333.44
4	$10,000 ×	7.4	740	222	0.683† (b)	151.63

Salvage
value:

$1,200 in $1,200(1 − 0.3) = $840** $ 840 0.621† (b) $ 521.64
year 5: in year 5
Present value (PV) $16,286.01

---

* T4 (10%, 4 years) = 3.170 (from Exhibit 8.15).
† T3 values (years 1, 2, 3, 4, 5) obtained from Exhibit 8.14.
** Any salvage value received under the MACRS rules is a *taxable gain* (the excess of the selling price over book value, $1,200 in this example), since the book value will be zero at the end of the life of the machine.

Since NPV = PV − I = $16,286.01 − $10,000 = $6,286.01 is positive, the machine should be bought.

What are the tax effects of disposal?

In general, gains and losses on disposal of equipment are taxed in the same way as ordinary gains and losses. Immediate disposal of the old equipment results in a loss that is fully tax deductible from current income. The loss (the excess of the book value over the disposal value) must be computed to isolate its effect on current income tax, but the total cash inflow is the selling price plus the current income tax benefit.

Example 8.42

Assume that the equipment has a salvage value of $1,200, while its book (undepreciated) value is $2,000. Two cash inflows are connected with this sale. The tax rate is 30 percent.

1. $1,200 cash inflow in the form of the sale price
2. $240 cash inflow in the form of a reduction in income taxes, resulting from the tax shield provided by the loss sustained on the sale, just like the tax shield provided by depreciation deduction, as computed in this way:

Book value	$2,000	
Selling price	1,200	
Loss	800	
Tax shield	× 0.3	$240

Thus, the total cash inflow from the disposal is $1,440 ($1,200 + $240).

CHAPTER 9

Quantitative Applications and Modeling in Accounting

Quantitative applications and modeling in accounting have been on the rise, coupled with the advent of microcomputers and the wide availability of software for various quantitative decision-making tools. The accountant should make use of quantitative techniques and modeling to analyze and solve the various accounting and financial problems faced by the client or the business entity he or she is employed by. These quantitative tools allow for the consideration of a multitude of data.

Statistical Analysis and Evaluation

How do I handle large volumes of data?

In many situations, accountants have a large volume of data that needs to be analyzed. These data could be earnings, cash flows, accounts receivable balances, weights of an incoming shipment, and so on. The statistics most commonly used to describe the characteristics of the data are the *mean* and the *standard deviation*. These statistics are also used to measure the return and risk in investment and financial decision making, in which the CPA may be asked to participate by the business entity.

Mean

What is a mean?

The mean gives us the average or central value of our data. Typically, there are three measures of central tendency:

1. Arithmetic mean
2. Weighted mean
3. Geometric mean

What is the arithmetic mean (x̄)?

The arithmetic mean is a simple average. To find it, we sum the values in our data and divide by the number of observations. Symbolically,

$$\bar{x} = \frac{\Sigma x}{n}$$

where:

n = number of observations

Example 9.1

John Jay Lamp Company has a revolving credit agreement with a local bank. The loan showed these ending monthly balances last year:

January	$18,500
February	21,000
March	17,600
April	23,200
May	18,600
June	24,500
July	60,000
August	40,000
September	25,850
October	33,100
November	41,000
December	28,400

Then the mean monthly balance for the loan last year is computed as shown.

Arithmetic mean balance:

$$= \frac{\$18,500 + \$21,000 + \$17,600 + \$23,200 + \$18,600 + \$24,500 + \$60,000 + \$40,000 + \$25,850 + \$33,100 + \$41,000 + \$28,400}{12}$$

$$= \frac{\$351,750}{12} = \$29,312.50$$

How do I determine a weighted mean?

The arithmetic mean is an unweighted average. It assumes equal likelihood of each value in one set of data. When observations have different degrees of importance or frequency, use the weighted mean. The weighted average enables us to take into account the importance of each value in the overall total. Symbolically, the formula for calculating the weighted average is:

$$\text{Weighted mean} = \Sigma w \cdot x$$

where:

w = weight (in percentage or in relative frequency) assigned to each observation

---

Example 9.2

Consider the company that uses three grades of labor to produce a finished product. The company wants to know the average cost of labor per hour for this product.

Grade of Labor	Labor Hours per Unit of Output	Hourly Wages (x)
Skilled	6	$10.00
Semiskilled	3	8.00
Unskilled	1	6.00

Using the arithmetic mean of the labor wage rates results in:

$$\text{Arithmetic mean} = \frac{\$10.00 + \$8.00 + \$6.00}{3}$$

$$= \frac{\$24.00}{3}$$

$$= \$8.00/\text{hr}$$

This implicitly assumes that the same amounts of each grade of labor were used to produce the output. More specifically,

$$\frac{\$10.00 + \$8.00 + \$6.00}{3} = \$10.00(1/3) + \$8.00(1/3) + \$6.00(1/3)$$

$$= \$8.00/\text{hr}$$

This is simply not true. We have to consider different amounts of each grade of labor in calculating the average cost of labor per hour. The correct way is to take a weighted average:

$$\text{Weighted mean} = \$10.00(6/10) + \$8.00(3/10) + \$6.00(1/10)$$

$$= \$9.00/\text{hr}$$

Note

Weight the hourly wage for each grade by its proportion of the total labor required to produce the product.

When should the geometric mean be used?

Sometimes we are dealing with quantities that change over a period of time. In such a case, we need to know an average rate of change, such as an average rate of return on investment or an average rate of growth in earnings over a period of several years. The formula for finding the geometric mean over n periods is:

$$\text{Geometric mean} = \sqrt[n]{(1 + x_1)(1 + x_2)\ldots(1 + x_n)} - 1$$

where:

x = percentage rate of change or percentage return on investment

Since it is cumbersome to calculate the nth root (although most scientific calculators have a key to compute this), we will illustrate only the two-period return calculation ($n = 2$).

The next example shows the inadequacy of the arithmetic mean return when the price of a stock doubles in one period and then depreciates back to the original price.

Example 9.3

	Time Periods		
	$t = 0$	$t = 1$	$t = 2$
Price (end of period)	$80	$160	$80
Rate of return	—	100%	−50%

The rates of return for periods 1 and 2 are computed as:

$$\text{Period 1 } (t = 1)\frac{(\$160 - \$80)}{\$80} = \frac{\$80}{\$80} = \underline{\underline{100\%}}$$

$$\text{Period 2 } (t = 2)\frac{(\$80 - \$160)}{\$160} = \frac{-\$80}{\$160} = \underline{\underline{-50\%}}$$

Therefore, the arithmetic mean return over the two periods is the average of 100 percent and −50 percent, which is 25 percent, as shown next.

$$\frac{100\% + (-50\%)}{2} = \underline{\underline{25\%}}$$

As can be easily seen, the stock purchased for $80 and sold for the same price two periods later did not earn a 25 percent return. It clearly earned a *zero* return. This can be shown by computing the geometric *mean* return.

Note that $n = 2$, $x_1 = 100\% = 1$, and $x_2 = -50\% = -0.5$.

Geometric mean return

$$= \sqrt[2]{(1 + 1)(1 - 0.5)} - 1$$
$$= \sqrt[2]{(2)(0.5)} - 1$$
$$= \sqrt{1} - 1 = 1 - 1 = \underline{\underline{0\%}}$$

Standard Deviation

What is the standard deviation?

The standard deviation measures the tendency of data to be spread out. Accountants can make important inferences from past data with this measure. The standard deviation, denoted with and read as sigma, is defined as:

$$\sigma = \sqrt{\frac{\Sigma(x - \bar{x})^2}{n - 1}}$$

where:

$\bar{x}$ = the mean

The standard deviation can be used to measure the variation of such items as the expected contribution margin (CM) or expected variable manufacturing costs. It can also be used to assess the risk associated with investment decisions.

How do I calculate standard deviation?

The standard deviation is calculated, step-by-step, in this way:

1. Subtract from the mean each value of the data.
2. Square each of the differences obtained in step 1.
3. Add together all the squared differences.
4. Divide the sum of all the squared differences by the number of values minus one.
5. Take the square root of the quotient obtained in step 4.

Example 9.4

The table shows one and a half years of quarterly returns for United Motors stock.

Time Period	x	$(x - \bar{x})$	$(x - \bar{x})^2$
1	10%	0	0
2	15	5	25
3	20	10	100
4	5	−5	25
5	−10	−20	400
6	20	10	100
	60%		650

From the table, note that $x = 60/6 = 10\%$.

$$\sigma = \sqrt{\Sigma(x - \bar{x})^2/(n - 1)} = \sqrt{650/(6 - 1)}$$
$$= \sqrt{130} = 11.40\%$$

The United Motors stock has returned on average 10 percent over the past six quarters. The variability about its average return was 11.40 percent. The high standard deviation (11.40 percent) relative to the average return of 10 percent indicates that the stock is very risky.

Regression Analysis

What is regression analysis?

Regression analysis is a very popular statistical method used to project sales and earnings.

It is also used to estimate the *cost–volume formula* (also called the *flexible budget formula*), which takes this functional form:

$$y = a + bx$$

where:

    y = semivariable (mixed) costs to be broken up
    a = fixed cost component
    b = variable rate per unit of x
    x = any given measure of activity, such as production volume, machine hours, or direct labor hours

The regression method is a statistical procedure for estimating mathematically the average relationship between the dependent variable y and the independent variable x.

- *Simple regression* involves one independent variable (e.g., direct labor hours [DLH] or machine hours alone).
- *Multiple regression* involves two or more activity variables.

(We assume simple linear regression throughout this chapter, which means that we maintain the $y = a + bx$ relationship.)

Method of Least Squares

How do I use least squares in making a decision?

In estimating the values of a and b, the regression method attempts to find a line of *best fit*. To find the line of best fit, a technique called the *method of least squares* is used.

To explain the least-squares method, we define the error as the difference between the observed value and the estimated value of some semivariable cost and denote it with u. Symbolically,

$$u = y - y'$$

where:

    y = observed value of a semivariable expense
    y' = estimated value based on $y' = a + bx$

The least-squares criterion requires that the line of best fit be such that the sum of the squares of the errors (or the vertical distance from the observed data points to the line shown in Exhibit 9.1) is a minimum; that is,

$$\min \Sigma U^2 = \Sigma(y - y)^2$$

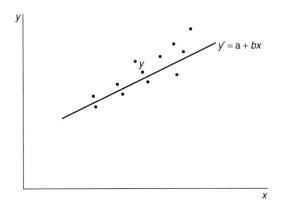

EXHIBIT 9.1 Actual (y) versus Estimated (y')

Using differential calculus we obtain these equations, called *normal equations*:

$$\Sigma y = n \cdot a + b \cdot \Sigma x$$
$$\Sigma xy = a \cdot \Sigma x + b \cdot \Sigma x^2$$

Solving the equations for b and a yields:

$$b = \frac{n\Sigma xy - (\Sigma x)(\Sigma y)}{n\Sigma x^2 - (\Sigma x)^2}$$

$$a = \bar{y} - b\bar{x} \text{ where } \bar{y} = \Sigma y/n \text{ and } \bar{x} = \Sigma x/n$$

Example 9.5

Use the data shown to illustrate the computations of b and a. All the sums required are computed and shown:

DLH (x)	Factory Overhead (y)	xy	x^2	y^2
9 hours	$ 15	$ 135	$ 81	$ 225
19	20	380	361	400
11	14	154	121	196
14	16	224	196	256
23	25	575	529	625
12	20	240	144	400
12	20	240	144	400
22	23	506	484	529
7	14	98	49	196
13	22	286	169	484
15	18	270	225	324
17	18	306	289	324
174 hours	$225	$3,414	$2,792	$4,359

(*continued*)

(Continued)

From the table:

$$\Sigma x = 174$$
$$\Sigma y = 225$$
$$\Sigma xy = 3,414$$
$$\Sigma x^2 = 2,792$$
$$\bar{x} = \Sigma x/n = 174/12 = 14.5$$
$$\bar{y} = \Sigma y/n = 225/12 = 18.75$$

Substituting these values into the formula first for b, then for a:

$$b = \frac{n\Sigma xy - (\Sigma x)(\Sigma y)}{n\Sigma x^2 - (\Sigma x)^2}$$

$$= \frac{(12)(3,414) - (174)(225)}{(12)(2,792) - (174)^2}$$

$$= \frac{1,818}{3,228} = \underline{0.5632}$$

$$a = \bar{y} - b\bar{x}$$

$$= (18.75) - (0.5632)(14.5) = 18.75 - 8.1664$$

$$= \underline{10.5836}$$

Note

Σy^2 is not used here but is computed for future use.
Our final regression equation is:

$$y' = \$10.5836 + \$0.5632x$$

where:
y' = estimated factory overhead (FO)
x = DLH

Use of a Spreadsheet Program for Regression

How do I use an electronic spreadsheet?

To utilize Excel for regression analysis, this procedure needs to be followed:

1. Click the *Tools* menu.
2. Click *Add-Ins.*
3. Click *Analysis ToolPak.*

After ensuring that the Analysis ToolPak is available, you can access the regression tool by completing these three steps:

Step 1. Click the *Tools* menu.
Step 2. Click *Data Analysis*.
Step 3. Click *Regression*.

Note

To obtain a scattergraph, use Excel's Chart Wizard.

Exhibit 9.2 captures the regression input dialogue screen. Exhibit 9.3 shows the Excel regression output.

The result shows:

$$y' = 10.58364 + 0.563197x \text{ (in the form of } y' = a + bx) \text{ with}$$
$$R\text{-squared } (r^2) = 0.608373 = 60.84\%$$

All of the values (a, b, and r^2) are the same as the ones obtained manually.

Exhibit 9.4 shows the regression output from the popular statistical software Minitab.

EXHIBIT 9.2   Regression Input Dialogue Screen

EXHIBIT 9.3   Excel Regression Output

Summary Output

Regression Statistics		
Multiple R		0.7800
R Square		0.6084
Adjusted R Square		0.5692
Standard Error		2.3436
Observations		12

ANOVA

	DF	SS	MS	F	Significance F
Regression	1	85.3243	85.3243	15.5345	0.0028
Residual	10	54.9257	5.4926		
Total	11	140.25			

	Coefficients	Standard Error	t-Stat	p-Value*	Lower 95%	Upper 95%
Intercept	10.583643	2.1796	4.8558	0.0007	5.7272	15.4401
DLH	0.563197	0.1429	3.9414	0.0028	0.2448	0.8816

*The p-value for x variable $= 0.0028$ indicates that we have a 0.28 percent chance that the true value of the variable coefficient is equal to 0, implying a high level of accuracy about the estimated value of 0.563197.

Trend Analysis

What is trend analysis?

Another common method for forecasting sales or earnings is the use of trend analysis, a special case of regression analysis. This method involves a regression whereby a trend line is fitted to a time series of data.

EXHIBIT 9.4   Minitab Regression Output

Regression Analysis

The regression equation is:

FO $= 10.6 + 0.563$ DLH

Predictor	Coef	Stdev	t-Ratio	p
Constant	10.584	2.180	4.86	0.000
DLH	0.5632	0.1429	3.94	0.003
$s = 2.344$		R-sq $= 60.8\%$	R-sq(adj) $= 56.9\%$	

Analysis of Variance

Source	DF	SS	MS	F	p
Regression	1	85.324	85.324	15.53	0.003
Error	10	54.926	5.493		
Total	11				

How do I apply trend analysis?

The trend line equation can be shown as:

$$y = a + bx$$

The formulas for the coefficients a and b are essentially the same as the formulas for simple regression. However, for regression purposes, a time period can be given a number so that $\Sigma x = 0$. When there is an odd number of periods, the period in the middle is assigned a zero value. If there is an even number, then -1 and $+1$ are assigned the two periods in the middle, so that again $\Sigma x = 0$.

With $\Sigma x = 0$, the formula for b and a reduces to:

$$b = \frac{n\Sigma xy}{n\Sigma x^2}$$

$$a = \Sigma y/n$$

Example 9.6

Case 1 (odd number)

2X08	2X09	2X10	2X11	2X12
$x = -2$	-1	0	$+1$	$+2$

Case 2 (even number)

2X07	2X08	2X09	2X10	2X11	2X12
$x = -3$	-2	-1	$+1$	$+2$	$+3$

In each case, $\Sigma x = 0$.

Example 9.7

Consider ABC Company's historical earnings per share (EPS) follow:

Year	EPS
2X08	$1.00
2X09	1.20
2X10	1.30
2X11	1.60
2X12	1.70

Since the company has five years' data, which is an odd number, the year in the middle is assigned a zero value.

(continued)

(Continued)

Year	x	EPS(y)	xy	x²
2X08	−2	$1.00	−2.00	4
2X09	−2	1.20	−1.20	1
2X10	0	1.30	0	0
2X11	+1	1.60	1.60	1
2X12	+2	1.70	3.40	4
	0	$6.80	1.80	10

$$b = \frac{(5)(1.80)}{(5)(10)} = \frac{9}{50} = \$0.18$$

$$a = \frac{\$6.80}{5} = \$1.36$$

Therefore, the estimated trend equation is:

$$\hat{y} = \$1.36 + \$0.18x$$

where:

$\hat{y}$ = estimated EPS

x = year index value

To project 2X13 sales, we assign +3 to the x value for the year 2X13. Thus,

$$\hat{y} = \$1.36 + \$0.18(+3) = \$1.36 + 54$$

$$= \$1.90$$

Regression Statistics

Regression analysis uses a variety of statistics that tell us about the accuracy and reliability of the regression results. They include:

- Correlation coefficient (r) and coefficient of determination (r^2)
- Standard error of the estimate (s_e)
- Standard error of the regression coefficient (s_b) and t-statistic

What is the correlation between variables y and x?

The correlation coefficient, r, measures the degree of correlation between y and x. The range of values it takes on is between −1 and +1. More widely used, however, is the coefficient of determination, designated r^2 (R-squared). Simply put, r^2 tells us how good the estimated regression equation is. In other words, it is a measure of *goodness of fit* in the regression. Therefore, the higher the r^2, the more confidence we have in the estimated cost formula.

More specifically, the coefficient of determination represents the proportion of the total variation in y that is explained by the regression equation. It has the range of values between 0 and 1.

Example 9.8

The statement "Factory overhead is a function of machine hours with $r^2 = 70\%$" can be interpreted as "Seventy percent of the total variation of factory overhead is explained by the regression equation or the change in machine hours, and the remaining 30 percent is accounted for by something other than machine hours."

The coefficient of determination is computed as shown:

$$r^2 = 1 - \frac{\Sigma(y - y')^2}{\Sigma(y - \bar{y})^2}$$

In a simple regression situation, however, there is the shortcut method available:

$$r^2 = \frac{[n \cdot \Sigma xy - (\Sigma x)(\Sigma y)]^2}{[n\Sigma x^2 - (\Sigma x)^2] \cdot [n\Sigma y^2 - (\Sigma y)^2]}$$

Comparing this formula with the one for b in Example 9.5, we see the only additional information we need to compute r^2 is Σy^2.

Example 9.9

From the table prepared in Example 9.5, $\Sigma y^2 = 4{,}359$. Using the shortcut method for r^2,

$$r^2 = \frac{(1{,}818)^2}{(3{,}228) \cdot [(12)(4{,}359) - (225)^2]}$$

$$= \frac{3{,}305{,}124}{(3{,}228)(52{,}308 - 50{,}625)}$$

$$= \frac{3{,}305{,}124}{(3{,}228)(1{,}683)} = \frac{3{,}305{,}124}{5{,}432{,}724}$$

$$= 0.6084 = 60.84\%$$

This means that about 60.84 percent of the total variation in total factory overhead is explained by direct labor hours (DLH) and the remaining 39.16 percent is still unexplained. A relatively low r indicates that there exists a lot of room for improvement in the estimated cost–volume formula ($y' = \$10.5836 + \$0.5632x$). Machine hours or a combination of DLH and machine hours might improve r^2.

Recommendations

- r^2 is a measure of goodness of fit. Even though the line obtained by the use of the least-squared error rule is supposed to be the line of best fit, it may still be inaccurate. The least-squares line may have been the best among the *linear* lines. The observed data, however, may exhibit a *curvilinear* pattern, which cannot be visualized, especially in multiple regressions. In other words, since it is impossible to draw the scatter diagram in a multivariable situation, we must rely on a statistic such as r^2 to determine the degree of the goodness of fit. Note that low values of r^2 indicate that the cost driver does not fully explain cost behavior.
- A low r^2 is an indication that the model is inadequate for explaining the y variable. The general causes for this problem are:
  - Use of a wrong functional form
  - Poor choice of an x variable as the predictor
  - The omission of some important variable or variables from the model

How can I compute the standard error of the estimate?

The standard error of the estimate, s_e, is defined as the standard deviation of the regression. It is computed:

$$s_e = \sqrt{\frac{\Sigma(y - y')^2}{n - 2}} = \sqrt{\frac{\Sigma y^2 - a\Sigma y - b\Sigma xy}{n - 2}}$$

The statistics can be used to gain some idea of the accuracy of our predictions.

Example 9.10

Going back to our example data, s_e is calculated as:

$$s_e = \sqrt{\frac{(4,359) - (10.5836)(225) - (0.5632)(3,414)}{12 - 2}}$$

$$= \sqrt{\frac{54.9252}{10}} = 2.3436$$

If a manager wants the prediction to be 95 percent confident, the confidence interval would be the estimated cost × 2(2.3436).

More specifically, the confidence interval for the prediction given as 10 hours of direct labor time would be:

$$\$16.2156^* \pm 2(2.3436) = \$16.2156 \pm 4.6872$$

which means from $11.5284 to $20.9028.

$$^*y' = \$10.5836 + \$0.5632x = \$10.5836 + \$0.5632(10)$$
$$= \$10.5836 + \$5.632 = \$16.2156$$

What is the relationship between the standard error of the coefficient and the t-statistic?

The standard error of the coefficient, s_b, and the t-statistic are closely related; s_b is calculated as:

$$s_b = \frac{s_e}{\sqrt{\Sigma(x - \bar{x})^2}}$$

or in shortcut form

$$s_b = \frac{s_e}{\sqrt{\Sigma x^2 - \bar{x}\Sigma x}}$$

The standard error of the coefficient, s_b, gives an estimate of the true coefficient's actual range. The t-statistic shows the statistical significance of x in explaining y. It is developed by dividing the estimated coefficient, b, by its standard error, s_b. That is, t-statistic $= b/s_b$. Thus, the t-statistic really measures how many standard errors the coefficient is away from zero.

Recommendation

Generally, any t-value greater than $+2$ or less than -2 is acceptable. The higher the t-value, the more significant the b is and, therefore, the greater the confidence in the coefficient as a predictor.

Example 9.11

The s_b for our example is:

$$s_b = \frac{2.3436}{\sqrt{2.792 - (14.5)(174)}}$$
$$= \frac{2.3436}{\sqrt{2,792 - 2,523}} = \frac{2.3436}{\sqrt{269}}$$
$$= \frac{2.3436}{16.40} = 0.143$$

(continued)

(Continued)

> *Note:*
>
> $$s_e = 2.3436, \; \Sigma x^2 = 2{,}792, \; \bar{x} = 14.5, \; \Sigma x = 174.$$
>
> Thus, t-statistic $= b/s_b = 0.5632/0.143 = 3.94$
> Since $t = 3.94 > 2$, we conclude that the b coefficient is statistically significant.

How can I estimate cash collection rates using regression?

Credit sales affect cash collections with time lags. In other words, there is a time lag between point of credit sale and realization of cash. More specifically, the lagged effect of credit sales and cash inflows is distributed over a number of periods, as shown:

$$C_t = b_1 S_{t-1} + b_2 S_{t-2} + \cdots + b_i S_{t-i}$$

where:

$$C_t = \text{cash collections}$$
$$S_t = \text{credit sales made in period } t$$
$$b_1, b_2, \ldots, b_i = \text{collection percentages}$$
$$i = \text{number of periods lagged}$$

By using the regression method discussed previously, we will be able to estimate these collection rates (or payment proportions). We can use Data Regression of Lotus 1-2-3 or special packages such as SPSS or SAS.

Note

The cash collection percentages ($b_1, b_2, \ldots, b_i$) may not add up to 100 percent because of the possibility of bad debts. Once we estimate these percentages, we should be able to compute the bad debt percentage with no difficulty.

Example 9.12

Exhibit 9.5 shows the regression results using actual monthly data on credit sales and cash inflows for a real company. Equation I can be written as shown:

$$C_t = 60.6\%(S_{t-1}) + 24.3\%(S_{t-2}) + 8.8\%(S_{t-3})$$

This result indicates that the receivables generated by the credit sales are collected at these rates:

- First month after sale, 60.6 percent
- Second month after sale, 24.3 percent
- Third month after sale, 8.8 percent

The bad debt percentage is computed as 6.3 percent (100% − 93.7%).

EXHIBIT 9.5   Regression Result for Cash Collection (C_1)

Independent Variables	Equation I
S_{t-1}	0.606*
	(0.062)†
S_{t-2}	0.243*
	(0.085)
S_{t-3}	0.088
	(0.157)
S_{t-4}	
r^2	0.754
Durbin-Watson	2.52‡
Standard error of the estimate (s_e)	11.63‡
Number of monthly observations	21
Bad debt percentages	0.063

*Statistically significant at the 5 percent significance level.
†This figure in the parentheses is the standard error of the estimate for the coefficient.
‡No autocorrelation present at the 5 percent significance level.

Caution

These collection and bad debt percentages are probabilistic variables—that is, variables whose values cannot be known with precision. However, the standard error of the regression coefficient and the t-value permit us to assess a probability that the true percentage is between specified limits. The confidence interval takes this form:

$$b \pm t' s_b$$

Example 9.13

To illustrate, assuming $t = 2$ as a rule of thumb at the 95 percent confidence level, we find the true collection percentage from the prior month's sales will be:

$$60.6\% \times 2(6.2\%) = 60.6\% \times 12.4\%$$

(continued)

(Continued)

Turning to the estimation of cash collections and allowance for doubtful accounts, we will use these values for illustrative purposes:

$$S_{t-1} = \$77.6$$
$$S_{t-2} = \$58.5$$
$$S_{t-3} = \$76.4$$

and forecast average monthly net credit sales = $75.20.

The forecast cash collection for period t would be:

$$C_t = 60.6\% \ (77.6) + 19.3\% \ (58.5) + 8.8\% \ (76.4) = \$65.04$$

If the accountant wants to be 95 percent confident about this forecast value, then he or she would set the interval in this way:

$$C_t \pm t s_e$$

To illustrate, using $t = 2$ as a rule of thumb at the 95 percent confidence level, the true value for cash collections in period t will be:

$$\$65.04 \pm 2(11.63) = 65.04 \pm 23.26$$

The estimated allowance for uncollectible accounts for period t will be:

$$6.3\% \ (\$75.2) = \$4.73$$

Note

By using the limits discussed so far, accountants can:

- Develop flexible (or probabilistic) cash budgets, where the lower and upper limits can be interpreted as pessimistic and optimistic outcomes, respectively.
- Simulate the cash budget in an attempt to determine both the expected change in cash collections each period and the variation about this value.

Quantitative Methods for Accounting

What are quantitative models?

Quantitative models, also known as *operations research (OR)* or *management science*, are sophisticated mathematical and statistical techniques for the solution of planning and decision-making problems.

What types of quantitative methods are available?

In recent years, much attention has been given to the use of a variety of quantitative models in accounting. Especially with the rapid development of microcomputers and software applications, accountants find them increasingly easy to use. It is becoming necessary to acquire knowledge about the use of those quantitative (mathematical and statistical) methods. The so-called Decision Support System (DSS) is in effect the embodiment of this trend. Numerous tools are available under the following subject headings. We explore six of the most important techniques that have broad applications in accounting:

1. Decision making under certainty or uncertainty
2. Linear programming and shadow prices
3. Goal programming and multiple goals
4. Learning curve
5. Inventory planning and control
6. Program Evaluation and Review Technique (PERT)

Decision Making

What is the difference between certainty and uncertainty in decision making?

Decisions are made under *certainty* or under *uncertainty*. Decision making under certainty means that for each decision, there is only one event and therefore only one outcome for each action. Decision making under uncertainty, which is more common in reality, involves several events for each action, each with its probability of occurrence.

Decision Making under Certainty

What is an example of decision making under certainty?

An accountant is often faced with a decision situation in which for each decision alternative, there is only one event and therefore only one outcome for each action.

Example 9.14

Assume there is only one possible event for each of the two possible actions:

1. Do nothing at a future cost of $3.00 per unit for 10,000 units.
2. Rearrange a facility at a future cost of $2.80 for the same number of units.

We can set up this table:

Actions	Possible Outcome with Certainty
Do nothing	$30,000 (10,000 units × $3.00)
Rearrange	$28,000 (10,000 units × $2.80)

(continued)

(Continued)

Since there is only one possible outcome for each action (with certainty), the decision is obviously to choose the action that will result in the more desirable outcome (least cost)—that is, to rearrange.

Decision Making under Uncertainty

What measures do I take when making a decision under uncertainty?

When decisions are made in a world of uncertainty, it is often helpful to make these computations:

- Expected value
- Standard deviation
- Coefficient of variation

How do I compute expected value?

For decisions involving uncertainty, the concept of *expected value* (Ā) provides a rational means for selecting the best course of action. The expected value of an alternative is an arithmetic mean, a weighted average using the probabilities as weights. More specifically, it is found by multiplying the probability of each outcome by its payoff.

$$\bar{A} = \Sigma A_x P_x$$

where:

A_x = outcome for the xth possible event
P_x = probability of occurrence of that outcome

Example 9.15

Consider two investment proposals, A and B, with the following probability distribution of cash flows in each of the next five years:

	Cash Inflows			
Probability	(0.2)	(0.3)	(0.4)	(0.1)
A	$ 50	200	300	400
B	$100	150	250	850

The expected value of the cash inflow in proposal A is:

$$\$50(0.2) + \$200(0.3) + \$300(0.4) + \$400(0.1) = \$230$$

The expected value of the cash inflow in proposal B is:

$$\$100(0.2) + \$150(0.3) + \$250(0.4) + \$850(0.1) = \$250$$

How is standard deviation determined?

The standard deviation (σ) measures the dispersion of a probability distribution. It is the square root of the mean of the squared deviations from the expected value.

$$\sigma = \sqrt{\sum_{x=1}^{n} (A_x - \bar{A})^2 P_x}$$

Note

The standard deviation is commonly used as an absolute measure of risk. The higher the standard deviation, the higher the risk.

Example 9.16

Using the data from Example 9.15, we can compute the standard deviations of proposals A and B.

For A:

$$\sigma = \sqrt{\begin{array}{l} [(\$50 - 230)^2 \, (0.2) + (200 - 230)^2 \, (0.3) \\ +(300 - 230)^2 \, (0.4) + (400 - 230)^2 \, (0.1)] \end{array}}$$

$$= \underline{\underline{\$107.70}}$$

For B:

$$\sigma = \sqrt{\begin{array}{l} [(\$100 - 250)^2 \, (0.2) + (150 - 250)^2 \, (0.3) \\ +(250 - 250)^2 \, (0.4) + (850 - 250)^2 \, (0.1)] \end{array}}$$

$$= \underline{\underline{\$208.57}}$$

Proposal B is riskier than proposal A, because its standard deviation is greater.

How is the coefficient of variation computed?

Coefficient of variation is a measure of relative dispersion, or relative risk. It is computed by dividing the standard deviation by the expected value:

$$CV = \frac{\sigma}{\bar{A}}$$

Example 9.17

Using the data from Examples 9.15 and 9.16, we calculate the coefficient of variation for each proposal as:

$$\text{For A: } \$107.70/\$230 = \underline{\underline{0.47}}$$

$$\text{For B: } \$208.57/\$250 = \underline{\underline{0.83}}$$

Therefore, because the coefficient is a relative measure of risk, B is said to have a greater degree of risk.

DECISION MATRIX

What is a decision matrix?

Although statistics such as expected value and standard deviation are essential for choosing the best course of action under uncertainty, the decision problem can best be approached using *decision theory*. Decision theory is a systematic approach to making decisions, especially under uncertainty. Decision theory uses an organized approach, such as a *payoff table* (or *decision matrix*), which is characterized by:

- The *row* representing a set of alternative courses of action available to the decision maker
- The *column* representing the state of nature or conditions that are likely to occur and that the decision maker has no control over
- The *entries* in the body of the table representing the outcome of the decision (payoffs in the form of costs, revenues, profits, or cash flows)

By computing expected value of each action, we will be able to pick the best one.

Example 9.18

Assume this probability distribution of daily demand for strawberries:

Daily demand	0	1	2	3
Probability	0.2	0.3	0.3	0.2

Also assume that unit cost = $3, selling price = $5 (i.e., profit on sold unit = $2), and salvage value on unsold units = $2 (i.e., loss on unsold unit = $1). We can stock 0, 1, 2, or 3 units.

How many units should be stocked each day? Assume that units from one day cannot be sold the next day. Then the payoff table can be constructed as shown.

		State of Nature			
Demand Stock	0	1	2	3	Expected Value
(Probability)	(0.2)	(0.3)	(0.3)	(0.2)	
0	$0	$0	$0	$0	$0.00
Actions 1	−1	2	2	2	1.40
2	−2	1*	4	4	1.90†
3	−3	0	3	6	1.50

*Profit for "stock 2, demand 1" equals (no. of units sold)(profit per unit) − (no. of units unsold)(loss per unit) = (1)($5 − $3) − (1)($3 − $2) = $1.
†Expected value for "stock 2" is: −$2(0.2) + $1(0.3) + $4(0.3) + $4(0.2) = $1.90.

The optimal stock action is the one with the highest *expected monetary value*, that is, stock 2 units.

EXPECTED VALUE OF PERFECT INFORMATION

How is expected value computed?

Suppose the decision maker can obtain a perfect prediction of which event (state of nature) will occur. The *expected value of perfect information* (EVPI) would be the total expected value of actions selected on the assumption of a perfect forecast. The EVPI can then be computed as:

$$\text{EVPI} = \text{Expected value with perfect information} - \text{Expected value with existing information}$$

Example 9.19

From the payoff table in Example 9.18, this analysis yields the expected value with perfect information:

		State of Nature			
Demand Stock	0	1	2	3	Expected Value
(Probability)	(0.2)	(0.3)	(0.3)	(0.2)	
0	$0				$0.00
Actions 1		$2			0.60
2			$4		1.20
3				$6	1.20
					$3.00

(continued)

(*Continued*)

Alternatively,

$$\$0(0.2) + \$2(0.3) + \$4(0.3) + \$6(0.2) = \$3.00$$

With existing information the best that the decision maker could obtain was $1.90 by selecting "stock 2." With perfect information (forecast), the decision maker could make as much as $3.00. Therefore, the expected value of perfect information is $3.00 − $1.90 = $1.10. This is the maximum price the decision maker is willing to pay for additional information.

DECISION TREE

How does decision tree analysis work?

Decision tree is another approach used in discussions of decision making under uncertainty. It is a pictorial representation of a decision situation. As in the case of the decision matrix approach discussed earlier, it shows decision alternatives, states of nature, probabilities attached to the states of nature, and conditional benefits and losses. The decision tree approach is most useful in a sequential decision situation.

Example 9.20

Assume XYZ Corporation wants to introduce one of two products to the market this year. The probabilities and present values (PVs) of projected cash inflows are given here.

Product	Initial Investment	PV of Cash Inflows	Probability
A	$225,000		1.00
		$450,000	0.40
		200,000	0.50
		−100,000	0.10
B	80,000		1.00
		320,000	0.20
		100,000	0.60
		−150,000	0.20

A decision tree analyzing the two products is given in Exhibit 9.6.

	Initial Investment (1)	Probability (2)	PV of Cash Inflow (3)	PV of Cash Inflow (2 × 3) = (4)
Product A	$225,000	0.40	$450,000	$180,000
		0.50	$200,000	100,000
		0.10	$100,000	10,000
		Expected PV of Cash Inflows		$270,000
Product B	$80,000	0.20	$320,000	$64,000
		0.60	$100,000	60,000
		0.20	-$150,000	30,000
		Expected PV of Cash Inflows		$94,000

Choice A or B

For Product A:

Expected NPV = Expected PV - 1 = $270,000 - $225,000 = $45,000

For Product B:

Expected NPV = $94,000 - $80,000 = $14,000

Based on the expected net present value, the company should choose product A over product B.

EXHIBIT 9.6 Decision Tree

Linear Programming and Shadow Prices

What is linear programming?

Linear programming (*LP*) addresses the problem of allocating limited resources among competing activities in an optimal manner. Specifically, it is a technique used to:

- *Maximize* a revenue, contribution margin, or profit function subject to constraints.
- *Minimize* a cost function subject to constraints.

Linear programming consists of two important ingredients:

1. Objective function
2. Constraints (including nonnegativity constraints), which are typically inequalities

What are the applications of linear programming?

A firm may want to:

- Find an optimal product mix so as to maximize its total contribution without violating restrictions imposed on the availability of resources.
- Determine a least-cost combination of input materials while satisfying production requirements, maintaining required inventory levels, staying within production capacities, and using available employees.

Other managerial applications include:

- Selecting an investment mix
- Blending chemical products
- Scheduling flight crews
- Assigning jobs to machines
- Determining transportation routes
- Determining distribution or allocation patterns

How do I formulate a linear programming problem?

To formulate the LP problem:

Step 1. Define the *decision variables* you are trying to solve for.
Step 2. Express the objective function and constraints in terms of these decision variables.

Note

As the name *linear* programming implies, all the expressions must be in *linear* form.

Example 9.21

A firm produces two products, A and B. Both products require time in two processing departments, the assembly department and finishing department. Data on the two products are:

	Products		Available Hours
Processing	A	B	
Assembly	2	4	100
Finishing	3	2	90
Contribution Margin per Unit	$25	$40	

The firm wants to find the most profitable mix of these two products.

Step 1. Define the decision variables:

A = Number of units of product A to be produced

B = Number of units of product B to be produced

Step 2. Express the objective function to maximize total contribution margin (CM) as:

Total CM = $25A + $40B

Step 3. Then formulate the constraints as inequalities:

$2A + 4B \leq 100$ (Assembly constraint)

$3A + 2B \leq 90$ (Finishing constraint)

Do not forget to add the nonnegativity constraints:

$A, B \geq 0$

Our LP model is:

Maximize total CM = $25A + 40B$

subject to $2A + 4B \leq 100$

$3A + 2B \leq 90$

$A, B \geq 0$

How are LP problems solved?

The solution methods available to solve LP problems include:

- The simplex method
- The graphical method

What is the simplex method?

The *simplex method* is the technique most commonly used to solve LP problems. It is an algorithm, which is an iteration method of computation, moving from one solution to another until it reaches the best solution. Virtually all computer software for LP uses this method of computation.

What is the graphical method?

The *graphical solution* is easier to use but limited to the LP problems involving two (or at most three) decision variables. The graphical method uses five steps:

Step 1. Change inequalities to equalities.
Step 2. Graph the equalities.
Step 3. Identify the correct side for the original inequalities.
Step 4. Identify the feasible region—the area of feasible solutions. *Feasible solutions* are values of decision variables that satisfy all the restrictions simultaneously.
Step 5. Determine the contribution margin at all of the corners in the feasible region.

Example 9.22

Using the data from Example 9.21, follow steps 1 through 4. We obtain the feasible region (shaded area in Exhibit 9.7) shown.

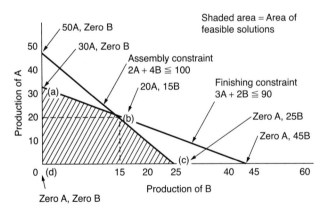

EXHIBIT 9.7   LP Graph

   Then we evaluate all of the corner points in the feasible region in terms of their CM.

Corner Points			Contribution Margin				
	A	B			$25A + $40B		
(a)	30	0	$25(30)	+	$40(0)	=	$ 750
(b)	20	15	25(20)	+	40(15)	=	1,100
(c)	0	25	25(0)	+	40(25)	=	1,000
(d)	0	0	25(0)	+	40(0)	=	0

The corner 20A, 15B produces the most profitable solution.

Shadow Prices (Opportunity Costs)

What are shadow prices?

An accountant who has solved an LP problem might want to know whether it pays to add capacity in hours in a particular department. He or she might be interested in the monetary value to the firm of adding an hour of assembly time per week. This monetary value is the additional contribution margin that could be earned and is called the *shadow price* of the given resource. A shadow price is in a way an opportunity cost, the contribution margin that would be lost by not adding an additional hour of capacity. To justify a decision in favor of a short-term capacity expansion, the accountant must be sure that the shadow price (or opportunity cost) exceeds the actual price of that expansion.

How are shadow prices determined?

Shadow prices are computed in three steps:

Step 1. Add one hour (preferably more than an hour to make it easier to show graphically) to the constraint under consideration.
Step 2. Resolve the problem and find the maximum CM.
Step 3. Compute the difference between CM of the original LP problem and the CM determined in step 2, which is the shadow price.

Other methods (e.g., using the dual problem) are available to compute shadow prices.

Example 9.23

Using the data in Example 9.21, compute the shadow price of the assembly capacity. To make it easier to show graphically, add eight hours of capacity to the assembly department rather than one hour. The new assembly constraint is shown in Exhibit 9.8.

(continued)

(Continued)

EXHIBIT 9.8   LP Graph

Corner Points			Contribution Margin			
	A	B		$25A + $40B		
(a)	30	0	$25(30)	+	$40(0)	=	$ 750
(b)	18	18	25(18)	+	40(18)	=	1,170
(c)	0	27	25(0)	+	40(27)	=	1,080
(d)	0	0	25(0)	+	40(0)	=	0

The new optimal solution of 18A, 18B has total CM of $1,170 per week. Therefore, the shadow price of the assembly capacity is $70: $1,170 − $1,100 = $70. The firm would be willing to pay up to $70 to obtain an additional eight hours per week, or $8.75 *per hour* per week.

Can the computer be used for LP problem solving?

We can use a computer LP software package—for example, LINDO (Linear Interactive and Discrete Optimization)—to quickly solve an LP problem. Exhibit 9.9 shows a computer output by an LP program for our LP model set up in Example 9.22.

Goal Programming and Multiple Goals

What is goal programming?

In the previous section, we saw how to develop an optimal program (or product mix) using LP. However, LP has one important drawback; it is limited primarily to solving problems where the objectives of management can be stated in a single goal (e.g., profit maximization or cost minimization). But management must now deal with multiple goals, which are often incompatible and in conflict with each other. Goal programming (GP) gets around this difficulty. In GP, unlike LP, the objective

EXHIBIT 9.9   Computer Printout for LP

** ** INFORMATION ENTERED ** **

NUMBER OF CONSTRAINTS	2
NUMBER OF VARIABLES	2
NUMBER OF < = CONSTRAINTS	2
NUMBER OF = CONSTRAINTS	0
NUMBER OF > = CONSTRAINTS	0

MAXIMIZATION PROBLEM

25×1 $+ 40 \times 2$

SUBJECT TO

2×1 $+ 4 \times 2$ $< = 100$
3×1 $+ 2 \times 2$ $> = 90$

NOTE:

$x_1 = A$
$x_2 = B$

RESULTS

VARIABLE	VARIABLE VALUE	ORIGINAL COEFF.	COEFF. SENS.
x 1	20	25	0
x 2	15	40	0

Solution:

$x_1 = A = 20$
$x_2 = B = 15$

CONSTRAINT NUMBER	ORIGINAL RHS	SLACK OR SURPLUS	SHADOW PRICE
1	100	0	8.75
2	90	0	2.5

OBJECTIVE FUNCTION VALUE: <u>1100</u> = CM
SENSITIVITY ANALYSIS
OBJECTIVE FUNCTION COEFFICIENTS

VARIABLE	LOWER LIMIT	ORIGINAL COEFFICIENT	UPPER LIMIT
x 1	20	25	60
x 2	16.67	40	50

RIGHT-HAND SIDE

CONSTRAINT NUMBER	LOWER LIMIT	ORIGINAL VALUE	UPPER LIMIT
1	60	100	180
2	50	90	150

Note: The printout shows the following optimal solution:

A = 20
B = 15
CM = $1,100

function may consist of multiple, incommensurable, and conflicting goals. Rather than maximizing or minimizing each objective criterion, the deviations from these set goals are minimized, often based on the priority factors assigned to each goal. The fact that management has multiple goals that are in conflict with each other means that management will look for a satisfactory solution rather than an optimal solution.

What are some examples of multiple conflicting goals?

Consider an investor who desires investments that will have a maximum return and minimum risk. These goals are generally incompatible and therefore unachievable. Other examples of multiple conflicting goals can be found in businesses that want to:

- Maximize profits and increase wages paid to employees.
- Upgrade product quality and reduce product costs.
- Pay larger dividends to shareholders and retain earnings for growth.
- Increase control of channels of distribution and reduce working-capital requirements.
- Reduce credit losses and increase sales.

How is a goal programming problem solved?

Example 9.24

In Example 9.23, the company during this planning period is facing a major organizational change and feels that maximizing contribution margin is not a realistic objective. However, it would like to achieve some satisfactory level of profit during this difficult period. Management feels that a CM of $750 would be satisfactory.

The GP problem is to determine, given the production time and material constraints, the product mix that would yield this rate of profit contribution.

To incorporate the $750 profit contribution into the GP model, we first define these *deviational* variables:

$$d- = \text{Underachievement of the target profit}$$

$$d+ = \text{Overachievement of the target profit}$$

This profit goal is now written into the model as a goal constraint:

$$25A + 40B + d- - d+ = \$750 \text{ (profit goal constraint)}$$

Then our GP model is:

$$
\begin{aligned}
\text{Min D} = \quad & d- + d+ \\
\text{subject to} \quad & 2A + 4B & < 100 \\
& 3A + 2B & < 90 \\
& 25A + 40B + d- - d+ & = 750 \\
& A, B, d-, d+ & > 0
\end{aligned}
$$

The solution is shown in Exhibit 9.10.

The GP solution is:

$$A = 0, \ B = 18.75, \ d- = 0, \ d+ = 0$$

This means that the company should make 18.75 units of product B (drop product A) in order to fully achieve the target profit of $750.

EXHIBIT 9.10   Computer Printout for GP

MINIMIZATION PROBLEM			
0×1	$+ 0 \times 2$	$+ 1 \times 3$	$+ 1 \times 4$
SUBJECT TO			
2×1	$+ 4 \times 2$	$+ 0 \times 3 < = 100$	$+ 0 \times 4$
3×1	$+ 2 \times 2$	$+ 0 \times 3 < = 90$	$+ 0 \times 4$
25×1	$+ 40 \times 2$	$+ 1 \times 3 = 750$	$- 1 \times 4$

Note:
$x_1 = A$
$x_2 = B$
$x_3 = d-$
$x_4 = d+$

** RESULTS **

VARIABLE	VARIABLE VALUE	ORIGINAL COEFF.	COEFF. SENS.
$\times 1$	0	0	0
$\times 2$	18.75	0	0
$\times 3$	0	1	1
$\times 4$	0	1	1

Solution:
$x_1 = A = 0$
$x_2 = B = 18.75$
$x_3 = d- = 0$
$x_4 = d+ = 0$

CONSTRAINT NUMBER	ORIGINAL RHS	SLACK OR SURPLUS	SHADOW PRICE
1	100	25	0
2	90	52.5	0
3	750	0	0

OBJECTIVE FUNCTION VALUE: 0

SENSITIVITY ANALYSIS
OBJECTIVE FUNCTION COEFFICIENTS

VARIABLE	LOWER LIMIT	ORIGINAL COEFFICIENT	UPPER LIMIT
$\times 1$	0	0	No Limit
$\times 2$	-40	0	40
$\times 3$	0	1	No Limit
$\times 4$	0	1	No Limit

(continued)

(Continued)

EXHIBIT 9.10

	RIGHT HAND SIDE		
CONSTRAINT NUMBER	LOWER LIMIT	ORIGINAL VALUE	UPPER LIMIT
1	75	100	No Limit
2	37.5	90	No Limit
3	0	750	1000

Note

One further step might be considered when formulating the GP model. The goal can be ranked according to *preemptive* priority factors. The deviational variables at the same priority level may be given different weights in the objective function, so that the deviational variables within the same priority have the different cardinal weights. (This topic is not treated here; refer to an advanced text for specifics.)

Learning Curve

What is the learning curve?

The *learning curve* is based on the proposition that labor hours per unit decrease in a definite pattern as labor operations are repeated. (See Exhibit 9.11.) More specifically, it is based on the statistical findings that as the cumulative output doubles,

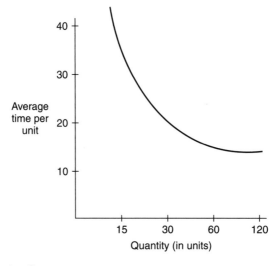

EXHIBIT 9.11   Learning Curve

the cumulative average labor input time required per unit will be reduced by some constraint percentage, ranging between 10 percent and 40 percent. The curve is usually designated by its complement. If the rate of reduction is 20 percent, the curve is referred to as an 80 percent learning curve.

Example 9.25

These data illustrate the 80 percent learning curve relationship:

Quantity (in units)		Time (in hours)	
Per Lot	Cumulative	Total (Cumulative)	Average Time per Unit
15	15	600	40.0
15	30	960	32.0 (40.0 × 0.8)
30	60	1,536	25.6 (32.0 × 0.8)
60	120	2,460	20.5 (25.6 × 0.8)
120	240	3,936	16.4 (20.5 × 0.8)

As can be seen, as production quantities double, the average time per unit decreases by 20 percent of its immediately preceding time.

What are some applications of the learning curve?

Applications of learning curve theory include:

- Scheduling labor requirements
- Capital budgeting decisions
- Setting incentive wage rates

Example 9.26

Stanley Electronics Products, Inc. finds that new-product production is affected by an 80 percent learning curve. The company has just produced 50 units of output at 100 hours per unit. Costs were:

Materials @ $20	$1,000
Labor and labor-related costs:	
Direct labor—100 hr @ $8.00	800
Variable overhead—100 hr @ $2.00	200
	$2,000

(continued)

(Continued)

The company has just received a contract calling for another 50 units of production. It wants to add a 50 percent markup to the cost of materials and labor and labor-related costs. Determine the price for this job.

Building up the table yields:

Quantity	Total Time	Average Time per Unit
50 units	100 hr	2 hr
100 units	160 hr	1.6 hr (80% × 2 hr)

Thus, the new 50-unit job takes 60 hours total.

Materials @ $20	$1,000
Labor and labor-related costs:	
Direct labor—60 hr @ $8.00	480
Variable overhead—60 hr @ $2.00	120
	$1,600
50% markup	800
Contract price	$2,400

Inventory Planning and Control

How do I plan and control inventory?

One of the most common problems that face managerial accountants is that of inventory planning and control. Inventory usually represents a sizable portion of a firm's total assets. Excess funds tied up in inventory are a drag on profitability. The purpose of inventory planning and control is to develop policies that will achieve an optimal investment in inventory. This objective is achieved by determining the optimal level of inventory necessary to minimize inventory-related costs.

What types of inventory costs are there?

Inventory costs fall into three categories:

1. *Order costs* include all costs associated with preparing a purchase order.
2. *Carrying costs* include storage costs for inventory items plus opportunity cost (i.e., the cost incurred by investing in inventory).
3. *Shortage (stockout) costs* include those costs incurred when an item is out of stock. These include the lost contribution margin on sales plus lost customer goodwill.

What are the basic types of inventory models?

There are many inventory planning and control models available that try to answer the basic questions of how much to order and when to order.

These models include:

- Basic economic order quantity (EOQ) model
- Reorder point
- Determination of safety stock

Economic Order Quantity

What is the optimal amount to order?

The EOQ model determines the order size that minimizes the sum of carrying and ordering costs.

- Demand is assumed to be a fixed amount and constant throughout the year.
- Order cost is assumed to be a fixed amount.
- Unit carrying costs are assumed to be constant.

Note

Since demand and lead time are assumed to be determinable, there are no shortage costs.

EOQ is computed as:

$$EOQ = \sqrt{\frac{2(\text{Annual demand})(\text{Ordering cost})}{\text{Carrying cost per unit}}}$$

Example: If the carrying cost is expressed as a percentage of average inventory value (e.g., 12 percent per year to hold inventory), then the denominator value in the EOQ formula would be 12 percent times the price of an item.

Example 9.27

ABC Store buys sets of steel at $40 per set from an outside vendor. ABC will sell 6,400 sets evenly throughout the year. ABC desires a 16 percent return on investment (cost of borrowed money) on its inventory investment. In addition, rent, taxes, and the like for each set in inventory total $1.60. The ordering cost is $100 per order.

The carrying cost per dozen is 16%($40) + $1.60 = $8.00. Therefore,

$$EOQ = \sqrt{\frac{2(6,400)(\$100)}{\$8.00}} = \sqrt{160,000} = 400 \text{ sets}$$

(continued)

(Continued)

$$\text{Total inventory costs} = \text{Carrying cost per unit} \times \frac{\text{EOQ}}{2}$$
$$+ \text{Ordering cost per order} \times \frac{\text{Annual demand}}{\text{EOQ}}$$
$$= (\$8.00)\,(400/2) + (\$100)(6{,}400/400) = \$1{,}600 + \$1{,}600 = \$3{,}200$$
$$\text{Total number of orders per year} = \text{Annual demand}/\text{EOQ}$$
$$= 6{,}400/400 = 16 \text{ orders}$$

How is the EOQ model applied?

The EOQ model described here is appropriate for a pure inventory system—that is, for single-item, single-stage inventory decisions for which joint costs and constraints can be ignored. EOQ assumes that both lead time and demand rates are constant and known with certainty. *Caution:* This may be unrealistic. Nevertheless, EOQ models have proven useful in inventory planning for many firms.

Many situations exist where such an assumption holds or nearly holds. *Examples:* Subcontractors who must supply parts on a regular basis to a primary contractor face a constant demand. Even where demand varies, the assumption of uniform usage is not unrealistic. For an auto dealer, demand for automobiles varies from week to week, but over a season the weekly fluctuations cancel each other out so that seasonal demand can be assumed constant.

How does EOQ handle quantity discounts?

The EOQ model does not take into account quantity discounts. This makes it unrealistic in many real-life cases. Usually the more you order, the lower the unit price you pay. Quantity discounts are price reductions for large orders offered to buyers to induce them to buy in large quantities. If quantity discounts are offered, the buyer must weigh the potential benefits of reduced purchase price and fewer orders that will result from buying in large quantities against the increase in carrying costs caused by higher average inventories. Hence, the buyer's goal is to select the order quantity that will minimize total cost, where total cost is the sum of carrying cost, ordering cost, and purchase cost:

$$\text{Total cost} = \text{Carrying cost} + \text{Ordering cost} + \text{Purchase cost}$$
$$= C \times (Q/2) + O(D/Q) + PD$$

where:
- C = carrying cost per unit
- Q = order quantity
- O = ordering cost per order
- D = annual demand
- P = unit price

How do I calculate EOQ with quantity discounts?

To find the EOQ with quantity discounts:

Step 1. Compute the EOQ ignoring price discounts, and compute the corresponding costs using the new cost formula given earlier.
Note: EOQ = $\sqrt{2OD/C}$
Step 2. Compute the costs for those quantities greater than the EOQ at which price reductions occur.
Step 3. Select the value of Q that will result in the lowest total cost.

Example 9.28

Using the data from Example 9.27, assume that ABC Store was offered this price discount schedule:

Order Quantity (Q)	Unit Price (P)
1 to 499	$40.00
500 to 999	39.90
1,000 or more	39.80

Step 1. The EOQ with no discounts is computed as:

$$EOQ = \sqrt{2(6,400)(100)/8.00} = \sqrt{160,000}$$
$$= 400 \text{ sets}$$
$$\text{Total cost} = \$8.00(400/2) + \$100(6,400/400) + \$40.00(6,400)$$
$$= \$1,600 + 1,600 + \$256,000 = \$259,200$$

Step 2. The value that minimized the sum of the carrying cost and the order cost but not the purchase cost was EOQ = 400 sets. As can be seen in Exhibit 9.12, the farther we move from the point 400, the greater the sum of the carrying and ordering costs is. Thus, 400 is obviously the only candidate for the minimum total cost value within the first price range. Q = 500 is the only candidate within the $39.90 price range, and Q = 1,000 is the only candidate within the $39.80 price bracket.
Step 3. These three quantities are evaluated in Exhibit 9.13 and illustrated in Exhibit 9.12, Inventory Cost and Quantity. The EOQ with price discounts is 500 sets. Hence, ABC is justified in going to the first price break, but the extra carrying cost of going to the second price break more than outweighs the savings in ordering and in the cost of the product itself.

(continued)

(Continued)

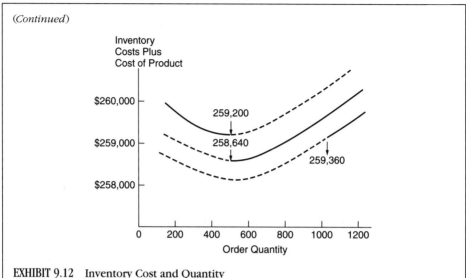

EXHIBIT 9.12　Inventory Cost and Quantity

EXHIBIT 9.13　Annual Costs with Varying Ordering Quantities

Order Quantity	400	500	1,000
Ordering cost $100 × (6,400/order quantity)	$ 1,600	$ 1,280	$ 640
Carrying cost $8 × (order quantity/2)	1,600	2,000	4,000
Purchase cost unit price × 6,400	256,000	255,360	254,720
Total cost	$259,200	$258,640	$259,360

What are the pros and cons of quantity discounts?

Buying in large quantities has some favorable and some unfavorable features for a firm. The advantages are:

- Lower unit costs
- Lower ordering costs
- Fewer stockouts
- Lower transportation costs

The disadvantages are:

- Higher inventory carrying costs
- Greater capital requirement
- Higher probability of obsolescence and deterioration

Reorder Point

When is the best time to place an order?

Reorder point (ROP), which answers *when* to place a new order, requires a knowl-edge of the *lead time*, the interval between placing an order and receiving delivery.

ROP is calculated in this way:

Reorder point = Average usage per unit of lead time × Lead time + Safety stock

Safety stock is extra units of inventory carried as protection against possible stockouts or shortages.

Step 1. Multiply average daily (or weekly) usage by the lead time in days (or weeks) yielding the lead time demand.

Step 2. Add safety stock to this to provide for the variation in lead time demand.

Note

If average usage and lead time are both certain, no safety stock is necessary and should be dropped from the reorder point formula.

Example 9.29

Using the data in Example 9.27, assume lead time is constant at one week, and there are 50 working weeks in a year.

Step 1. Reorder point is 128 sets = (6,400 sets/50 weeks) × 1 week. Therefore, when the inventory level drops to 128 sets, the new order should be placed.

Step 2. Suppose, however, that the store is faced with variable usage for its steel and requires a safety stock of 150 additional sets to carry. Then the reorder point will be 128 sets *plus* 150 sets, or 278 sets.

Exhibit 9.14 shows this inventory system when the order quantity is 400 sets and the reorder point is 128 sets.

EXHIBIT 9.14   Basic Inventory System with EOQ and Reorder Point

Safety Stock and Reorder Point

At what level should inventory be ordered?

When lead time and demand are not certain, the firm must carry extra units of inventory called *safety stock* as protection against possible stockouts. Stockouts can be quite expensive.

   Examples: Lost sales and disgruntled customers are external costs of stockouts. Idle machines and disrupted production scheduling are internal costs.

   The probability approach is used to show how the optimal stock size can be determined in the presence of stockout costs.

Example 9.30

Using the data from Examples 9.27 and 9.28, assume that the total usage over a one-week period is expected to be:

Total Usage	Probability
78	0.2
128	0.4
178	0.2
228	0.1
278	0.1
	1.0

   Further assume that a stockout cost is estimated at $12.00 per set. Recall that the carrying cost is $8.00 per set.

   The computation shows that the total costs are minimized at $1,200 when a safety stock of 150 sets is maintained. Therefore, the reorder point is: 128 sets + 150 sets = 278 sets.

Computation of Safety Stock

Safety Stock Levels in Units	Stockout and Probability	Average Stockout in Units	Average Stockout Costs	Number of Orders	Total Annual Stockout Costs	Carrying Costs	Total
0	50 with 0.2 100 with 0.1 150 with 0.1	35*	$420[†]	16	$6,720[‡]	$0	$7,140
50	50 with 0.1 100 with 0.1	15	180	16	2,880	400[§]	3,280
100	50 with 0.1	5	60	16	960	800	1,760
150	0	0	0	16	0	1,200	1,200

*50(0.2) + 100(0.1) + 150(0.1) = 10 + 10 + 15 = 35 units
[†]35 units × $12.00 = $420
[‡]$420 × 16 times = $6,720
[§]50 units × $8.00 = $400

Program Evaluation and Review Technique

What is PERT?

Program Evaluation and Review Technique (PERT) is a useful management tool for planning, scheduling, costing, coordinating, and controlling complex projects such as:

- Formulation of a master budget
- Construction of buildings
- Installation of computers
- Scheduling the closing of books
- Assembly of a machine
- Research and development activities

  Questions to be answered by PERT include:

- When will the project be finished?
- What is the probability that the project will be completed by any given time?

How do I schedule a project?

The PERT technique involves the diagrammatic representation of the sequence of activities comprising a project by means of a *network*. The network:

- Visualizes all of the individual tasks (activities) to complete a given job or program
- Points out interrelationships
- Consists of activities (represented by arrows) and events (represented by nodes [circles])

  In Exhibit 9.15, note two key features: arrows and nodes.

- *Arrows* represent tasks or activities that are distinct segments of the project requiring time and resources.
- *Nodes* (*circles*) symbolize events or milestone points in the project representing the completion of one or more activities and/or the initiation of one or more

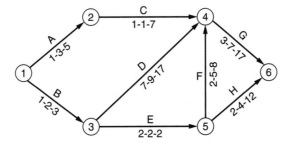

EXHIBIT 9.15   PERT Network Diagram

subsequent activities. An event is a point in time and, unlike an activity, does not consume any time in itself.

When will the project be finished?

In a real-world situation, estimates of activity completion times will seldom be certain.

Note

To cope with the uncertainty in activity time estimates, PERT proceeds by estimating three possible duration times for each activity. As shown in Exhibit 9.15, the numbers appearing on the arrows represent the three time estimates for activities needed to complete the various events. These three time estimates are:

1. The most optimistic time, a
2. The most likely time, m
3. The most pessimistic time, b

Example 9.31

For activity B in Exhibit 9.15:

- The optimistic time for completing activity B is one day.
- The most likely time is two days.
- The pessimistic time is three days.

The next step is to calculate an expected time (t_e), which is determined in this way:

$$t_e = (a + 4m + b)/6$$

For activity B, the expected time is:

$$t_e = [1 + 4(2) + 3]/6 = 12/6 = 2 \text{ days}$$

What quantitative calculations are involved in PERT?

As a measure of variation (uncertainty) about the expected time, the standard deviation is calculated as:

$$\sigma = (b - a)/6$$

The standard deviation of completion time for activity B is:

$$\sigma = (3 - 1)/6 = 2/6 = 0.33 \text{ day}$$

Expected activity times and their standard deviations are computed in this manner for all of the activities of the network and arranged in the following tabular format:

Activity	Predecessors	a	m	b	t_e	σ
A	None	1	3	5	3.0	0.67
B	None	1	2	3	2.0	0.33
C	A	1	1	7	2.0	1.00
D	B	7	9	17	10.0	1.67
E	B	2	2	2	2.0	0.00
F	E	2	5	8	5.0	0.67
G	C, D, F	3	7	17	8.0	2.33
H	E	2	4	12	5.0	1.67

What is a critical path?

To answer when the project will be finished, we need to determine the network's *critical path*. A path is a sequence of connected activities. In Exhibit 9.15, 1-2-4-6 is a path. The critical path for a project is the path that takes the longest time. The sum of the estimated activity times for all activities on the critical path is the total time required to complete the project. These activities are deemed critical because any delay in their completion causes a delay in the project.

The critical path is also the minimum amount of time needed for the completion of the project. Thus, the activities along this path must be shortened in order to speed up the project. Activities not on the critical path are not critical; they will be worked on simultaneously with critical path activities, and their completion could be delayed up to a point without delaying the project as a whole.

How do I find the critical path?

An easy way to find the critical path involves these two steps:

Step 1. Identify all possible paths of a project and calculate their completion times.
Step 2. Pick the one with the longest completion time; this is the critical path.

Note

When the network is large and complex, a more systematic and efficient approach is needed. Refer to an advanced management science text for specifics.

Example 9.32

Given the data in Example 9.31 and Exhibit 9.15, we have:

Path	Completion Time	
A-C-G	13 days	(3 + 2 + 8)
B-D-G	20 days	(2 + 10 + 8)
B-E-F-G	17 days	(2 + 2 + 5 + 8)
B-E-H	9 days	(2 + 2 + 5)

The critical path is B-D-G, which means it takes 20 days to complete the project.

What is the probability that the project will be completed on time?

The next important information to obtain is the probability of the project being completed within a contract time. To obtain this information, use the standard deviation of total project time around the expected time, as shown here:

$$\text{Standard deviation (project)} = \sqrt{\begin{array}{l}\text{The sum of the squares of the standard}\\ \text{deviations of all critical path activities}\end{array}}$$

Using the standard deviation and table of areas under the normal distribution curve (Exhibit 9.16), the probability of completing the project within any given time period can be determined.

EXHIBIT 9.16   Normal Distribution Table

Mean 1.81

Areas Under the Normal Curve

z	0	1	2	3	4	5	6	7	8	9
0.0	.5000	.5040	.5080	.5120	.5160	.5199	.5239	.5279	.5319	.5359
0.1	.5398	.5438	.5478	.5517	.5557	.5596	.5636	.5675	.5714	.5753
0.2	.5793	.5832	.5871	.5910	.5948	.5987	.6026	.6064	.6103	.6141
0.3	.6179	.6217	.6255	.6293	.6331	.6368	.6406	.6443	.6480	.6517
0.4	.6554	.6591	.6628	.6664	.6700	.6736	.6772	.6808	.6844	.6879

EXHIBIT 9.16 *(Continued)*

z	0	1	2	3	4	5	6	7	8	9
0.5	.6915	.6950	.6985	.7019	.7054	.7088	.7123	.7157	.7190	.7224
0.6	.7257	.7291	.7324	.7357	.7389	.7422	.7454	.7486	.7517	.7549
0.7	.7580	.7611	.7642	.7673	.7703	.7734	.7764	.7794	.7823	.7852
0.8	.7881	.7910	.7939	.7967	.7995	.8023	.8051	.8078	.8106	.8133
0.9	.8159	.8186	.8212	.8238	.8264	.8289	.8315	.8340	.8365	.8389
1.0	.8413	.8438	.8461	.8485	.8508	.8531	.8554	.8577	.8599	.8621
1.1	.8643	.8665	.8686	.8708	.8729	.8749	.8770	.8790	.8810	.8830
1.2	.8849	.8869	.8888	.8907	.8925	.8944	.8962	.8980	.8997	.9015
1.3	.9032	.9049	.9066	.9082	.9099	.9115	.9131	.9147	.9162	.9177
1.4	.9192	.9207	.9222	.9236	.9251	.9265	.9278	.9292	.9306	.9319
1.5	.9332	.9345	.9357	.9370	.9382	.9394	.9406	.9418	.9430	.9441
1.6	.9452	.9463	.9474	.9484	.9495	.9505	.9515	.9525	.9535	.9545
1.7	.9554	.9564	.9573	.9582	.9591	.9599	.9608	.9616	.9625	.9633
1.8	.9641	.9648	.9656	.9664	.9671	.9678	.9686	.9693	.9700	.9706
1.9	.9713	.9719	.9726	.9732	.9738	.9744	.9750	.9756	.9762	.9767
2.0	.9772	.9778	.9783	.9788	.9793	.9798	.9803	.9808	.9812	.9817
2.1	.9821	.9826	.9830	.9834	.9838	.9842	.9846	.9850	.9854	.9857
2.2	.9861	.9864	.9868	.9871	.9874	.9878	.9881	.9884	.9887	.9890
2.3	.9893	.9896	.9898	.9901	.9904	.9906	.9909	.9911	.9913	.9916
2.4	.9918	.9920	.9922	.9925	.9927	.9929	.9931	.9932	.9934	.9936
2.5	.9938	.9940	.9941	.9943	.9945	.9946	.9948	.9949	.9951	.9952
2.6	.9953	.9955	.9956	.9957	.9959	.9960	.9961	.9962	.9963	.9964
2.7	.9965	.9966	.9967	.9968	.9969	.9970	.9971	.9972	.9973	.9974
2.8	.9974	.9975	.9976	.9977	.9977	.9978	.9979	.9979	.9980	.9981
2.9	.9981	.9982	.9982	.9983	.9984	.9984	.9985	.9985	.9986	.9986
3.0	.9987	.9990	.9993	.9995	.9997	.9998	.9998	.9999	.9999	1.0000

Example 9.33

Using the last formula and the information in Exhibit 9.16, the standard deviation of completion time (the path B-D-G) for the project is:

$$\sqrt{(0.33)^2 + (1.67)^2 + (2.33)^2}$$
$$= \sqrt{0.1089 + 2.7889 + 5.4289}$$
$$= \sqrt{8.3267\%} = 2.885 \text{ days.}$$

Assume the expected delivery time is 21 days.

Step 1. Compute z, the number of standard deviations from the mean represented by our given time of 21 days. The formula for z is:

$$z = (\text{Delivery time} - \text{Expected time})/\text{Standard deviation}$$
$$\text{Therefore, } z = (21 \text{ days} - 20 \text{ days})/2.885 \text{ days} = 0.35$$

(continued)

(Continued)

Step 2. Find the probability associated with the calculated value of z by referring to a table of areas under a normal curve (Exhibit 9.16).

From Exhibit 9.16 we see that the probability is .6368, which means there is close to a 64 percent chance that the project will be completed in less than 21 days. To summarize:

- The expected completion time of the project is 20 days.
- There is a better than 60 percent chance of finishing before 21 days. The chances of meeting any other deadline can also be obtained, if desired.
- Activities B-D-G are on the critical path; they must be watched more closely than the others. If they fall behind, the whole project falls behind.

What other considerations are there with critical path?

If extra effort is needed to finish the project on time or before the deadline, it may be necessary to borrow resources (such as money and labor) from any activity not on the critical path.

It is possible to reduce the completion time of one or more activities. This will require an extra expenditure of cost. The benefit from reducing the total completion time of a project by accelerated efforts on certain activities must be balanced against this extra cost. A related problem is determining which activities must be accelerated in order to reduce the total project completion time. Critical Path Method (CPM), also known as PERT/COST, is widely used to deal with this subject.

Caution: PERT is a technique for project management and control. It is not an optimizing decision model, since the decision to undertake a project is initially assumed. It will not evaluate an investment project according to its attractiveness or the time specifications observed.

Project Budgeting and Control Using Earned Value Analysis

How do you prepare project budgeting?

There are several alternatives for assessing budgets over time. Fixed costs can be expensed at the start of the activity (e.g., equipment purchases) or at the end of the activity (e.g., paying a consultant). Variable costs can be expensed based on the project schedule or on the employees' calendar (e.g., payroll).

Example 9.34

The next project shows the budgeted costs associated with five activities. Assume that variable costs are incurred in proportion to the activity duration; thus, for instance, the cost for task B is spread out over the two weeks the task is scheduled. The resulting cost schedule is referred to as the budgeted cost of work scheduled (BCWS) and is calculated by adding all the costs on each week of the project, as shown in the last two lines of the table.

Task	Predecessor	Duration	Cost	By Week				
A	—	1	$ 1,500	$1,500				
B	A	2	3,510		$1,755	$ 1,755		
C	A	2	5,000		2,500	2,500		
D	B	2	2,000				$ 1,000	$ 1,000
E	B	2	3,000				1,500	1,500
Total project budget			$15,010	$1,500	$4,255	$ 4,255	$ 2,500	$ 2,500
Cumulative project budget = Budgeted cost of work scheduled (BCWS)				$1,500	$5,755	$10,010	$12,510	$15,010

Project Budgeting Example

Accurately tracking actual costs versus budgeted costs enables the project manager to obtain a better idea of the amount of managerial flexibility available. Thus, BCWS information is very useful for the project manager for controlling the project. For example, if by week 4 the project costs have exceeded BCWS in the amount of $12,510, then the project manager might wish to control future expenses more carefully, renegotiate the contract with the customer, and/or try to get more funds in order to complete the project. Similarly, if the project incurs less cost by week 4, this might indicate that the project is behind schedule and the pace of work needs to pick up. But how can a manager tell whether a cost overrun is due to greater expense than expected or to the work being completed faster than expected? Earned value analysis resolves this dilemma.

Why do you need the concept of earned value?

A separate analysis of schedule and cost does not provide an entirely accurate or comprehensive picture of overall project status. Evaluating how much work is getting done without considering how much has been paid to get that work done will give a distorted picture of your cost position. Likewise, using the rate of expenditure as a measure of project status will lead to a distorted picture of the schedule position. For example, say a company is under budget by about 10 percent. That is good news, right? What if the manager is told that the project is nearly completed? Good news becomes unbelievably great news: The project is nearly done and only about 75 percent of the money has been spent. Now imagine that the team has just barely gotten started; not much of anything has been done. This would be a disastrous situation.

The *earned value concept* integrates schedule and cost. A number of formulas are associated with earned value techniques. At the core of the earned value technique are three basic components of measurement:

1. Budgeted cost of work scheduled (BCWS)
2. Budgeted cost of work performed (BCWP)
3. Actual cost of work performed (ACWP)

Budgeted cost of work scheduled (BCWS) is a measure of *what is expected to be accomplished*. Specifically, it uses the original cost estimates for activities to chart the cost (or value) of the work that the manager plans to get done over time. It is equivalent to the conventional concept of the planned budget.

Budgeted cost of work performed (BCWP) is a measure of the value of *what has actually been accomplished*. It charts the cost (or value) of the work that has been done at any point in time. Again, the original activity-based cost estimates are used to perform these calculations. This is what earned value actually is.

Actual cost of work performed (ACWP) refers to *what has been paid for what has been accomplished*. This would be the actual cost expenditure at any point in time.

Conceptually, the schedule position is a comparison of BCWP and BCWS. In other words (using the preceding terminology), it compares *what is expected to be accomplished* and *what has actually been accomplished*, in terms of originally estimated dollar amounts.

The cost position can be evaluated by comparing BCWP and ACWP, in other words, *what the manager thought he or she would have to pay* and *what he or she actually paid—for a given amount of accomplishment*.

Earned value analysis is an approach for monitoring project costs and expenses. It involves specifying, on a periodic basis, how far each activity has progressed (percentage complete) and deriving the value of work completed from this information. Value is earned as activities are completed. The cumulative value of work completed on any week is then compared to actual costs incurred in completing that work and the amount of work budgeted for completion. Earned value is a uniform unit of measure and thus provides a consistent method for analyzing project progress and performance.

Establishing an earned value analysis system involves five steps:

Step 1. Establish the work breakdown structure (WBS) to divide the project into manageable portions.

Step 2. Identify the activities to be scheduled.

Step 3. Allocate the costs to be expended on each activity.

Step 4. Schedule the activities over time and assess percentage completion.

Step 5. Tabulate, plot, and analyze the data to confirm that the plan is acceptable.

Example 9.35

In Example 9.34, suppose that on week 4, a manager assesses the actual costs and percentage complete for each activity, as shown next.

						Earned Value = Budgeted Cost × %					
Task	Predecessor	Duration	Budgeted Cost	Actual Cost	% Complete	Complete			By-Week Allocated Cost		
A	—	1	$ 1,500	$ 1,600	100	$ 1,500	$1,500				
B	A	2	3,510	3,700	100	3,510		$1,755	$ 1,755		
C	A	2	5,000	4,600	80	4,000		2,500	2,500		
D	B	2	2,000	1,000	60	1,200				$ 1,000	$ 1,000
E	B	2	3,000	500	10	300				1,500	1,500
Total costs			$15,010	$11,400		$10,510	$1,500	$4,255	$ 4,255	$ 2,500	$ 2,500
Cumulative costs by period							$1,500	$5,755	$10,010	$12,510	$15,010

Earned Value Data

The earned value is calculated by multiplying the budgeted cost of the activity by the percentage complete and then adding the result over all activities. For instance, in week 4, the status of the project is:

- BCWS = $12,510
- ACWP = $11,400
- BCWP = $10,510 (earned value by week 4)

The distinction between the BCWS and the BCWP is that the former represents the budget of the activities that were planned to be completed and the latter represents the budget of the activities that actually were completed. BCWP is often referred to as *earned value*. In this case, the good news is that actual costs are less than planned costs (see Exhibit 9.17); however, the bad news is that work accomplished on the project is less than anticipated. For example, activity C should have been finished but is only 80 percent complete.

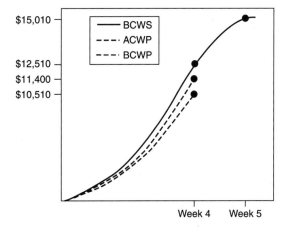

EXHIBIT 9.17 Cumulative Budgeted, Actual, and Earned Value: BCWS, ACWP, and BCWP

Forecasting Project Parameters Using Earned Value Methodology

Earned value methodology can be used for forecasting the estimated completion time and costs of a project given the current status of the project. To distinguish between cost slippage and schedule slippage on the project, we define:

SCHEDULE VARIANCE (SV)   Scheduled variance (SV) is the budgeted cost of work performed minus the budgeted cost of work scheduled = BCWP – BCWS. Schedule variance shows the difference between the scheduled completion of an activity and the actual completion of that activity. A negative schedule variance means it took longer than planned to perform the work, and a positive schedule variance means it took less time than planned to perform the work.

COST VARIANCE (CV)   Cost variance (CV) is the budgeted cost of work performed minus the actual cost of work performed = BCWP – ACWP. In other words, cost variance shows the difference between the estimated cost of an activity and the actual cost of that activity. If cost variance is a negative number, it means performing the work cost more than planned. If cost variance is a positive number, it means performing the work cost less than planned.

In our example project at week 4, we compute SV = $10,510 – $12,510 = ($2,000) and CV = $10,510 – $11,400 = ($890). The value of SV indicates that the project is severely behind schedule, and CV indicates that we are also overspending on the project because work with a value of $10,510 was done by actually spending $11,400.

We can forecast that, given the pace of work, the project is going to take longer than five weeks, and with the unfavorable cost variance, it is going to cost more than $15,010.

These forecasts can be made by calculating the following performance indexes.

SCHEDULE PERFORMANCE INDEX (SPI)   The schedule performance index (SPI) is the ratio of work performed to work scheduled (BCWP/BCWS) and can be used to estimate the projected time to complete the project. A schedule performance index of one or 100 percent means the project is on schedule. If the schedule performance index is greater than one or 100 percent, then the project is ahead of schedule. If the schedule performance index is less than one or 100 percent, the project is behind schedule.

COST PERFORMANCE INDEX (CPI)   The cost performance index (CPI) is the ratio of work performed to actual costs (BCWP/ACWP) and can be used to estimate the projected cost of completing the project. If the cost performance index is equal to one, or 100 percent, then the budged and actual costs are equal; the costs are exactly as planned. If the cost performance index is less than one or less than 100 percent, the project is over budget. If the cost performance index is greater than one or more than 100 percent, the project is under budget.

Note: In general, negative numbers for cost and schedule variances indicate problems in those areas. The project is costing more than planned or taking longer than planned. Likewise, CPI and SPI less than 100 percent also indicate problems. Earned value calculations for all project activities (or summary-level activities) are required to estimate the earned value for the entire project. Some activities may be over budget or behind schedule, but others may be under budget and ahead of schedule. By adding all of the earned values for all project activities, you can determine how the project as a whole is performing.

ESTIMATE AT COMPLETION (EAC) The estimate at completion (EAC) is an estimate of what it will cost to complete the project based on performance to date. It indicates where the project cost is heading. One simple way to calculate this is:

$$EAC = (BAC - BCWP)/CPI + ACWP$$

where BAC = budget at completion, the initial budget for the project.

This formula determines the unfinished or unearned work (BAC – BCWP) and divides it by the CPI. To that is added the sunk cost, or the cost of the completed work (ACWP). From this we can see that poor cost performance, a CPI less than 1, would result in an EAC that is greater than the BAC.

Example 9.36

For the example project:

$$SPI = \$10,510/\$12,510 = 0.84$$
$$CPI = \$10,510/\$11,400 = 0.92$$
$$EAC = (\$15,010 - \$10,510)/0.92 + \$11,400 = \$4,891.07 + \$11,400$$
$$= \$16,291.07$$

A similar forecast can be made for the project duration using the SPI; if work progresses at the current pace (84 percent schedule efficiency), then the time to complete the project would be:

Time to complete the project = Original project duration/SPI = 5/0.84
$$= 5.95 \text{ weeks}$$

PART IV

Auditing, Compiling, and Reviewing Financial Statements

CHAPTER 10

Auditing Procedures

The financial statement audit, commonly referred to as the attest function, involves (1) examination of financial statements through the gathering of sufficient appropriate evidence and (2) expression of an opinion on the fairness of the presentation of the financial statements in conformity with generally accepted accounting principles (GAAP) or other comprehensive basis of accounting.

In planning a financial statement audit, the practitioner needs to develop an overall strategy for performing:

- Risk assessment procedures
- Further audit procedures at the assertion level, including possible tests of controls and necessary substantive tests

This strategy must be documented in the audit work papers.

Risk Assessment Procedures

What are risk assessment procedures?

Risk assessment procedures are procedures performed by an auditor to obtain an understanding of the entity and its environment, including its internal control.

Must risk assessment procedures be performed separately from other audit procedures?

Risk assessment procedures can be performed concurrently with tests of controls and substantive procedures.

What are the types of risk assessment procedures?

Risk assessment procedures include:

- Inquiring of management and others within the entity, including those charged with governance, internal auditors, other employees, and in-house legal counsel
- Analytical procedures
- Inspection and observation

> ## Caution
>
> It should be noted that while all of the listed procedures need not be performed for each aspect of the requisite understanding, all of the procedures should be performed in the course of obtaining the understanding.

The Entity and Its Environment

What aspects of the entity and its environment should be of concern to an auditor?

An auditor should obtain an understanding of:

- Industry, regulatory, and other external factors: for example, competitive environment, supplier and customer relationships, technological developments, regulatory environment, environmental requirements, and general economic conditions
- The nature of the entity: for example, its operations, ownership, governance, types of investments, structure of the entity, and how it is financed
- Objectives (i.e., overall plans), strategies (i.e., operational approaches to achieving objectives), and related business risks (i.e., impediments to achieving objectives) that may result in material misstatement
- Measurement and review of financial performance, which are different from the monitoring of controls and create pressure on the entity that in turn may motivate management either to take action to improve performance or to misstate the financial statements—for example, key performance indicators, budgets, variance analysis, and reports of subsidiaries, divisions, and departments
- Internal control, which includes the selection and application of accounting policies

Internal Control

What are the components of internal control?

A client's internal control is a process—effected by those charged with governance, management, and other personnel—designed to provide reasonable, but not absolute, assurance that these entity objectives will be achieved:

- Reliable financial reporting
- Effective and efficient operations
- Compliance with laws and regulations

A client's internal control consists of five interrelated components:

1. Control environment
2. Risk assessment

3. Control activities
4. Information and communication systems
5. Monitoring

What is the control environment?

The control environment, which is the foundation for the other components of internal control, provides discipline and structure by setting the tone of an organization and influencing control consciousness. Factors to consider in assessing the client's control environment include:

- Communication and enforcement of integrity and ethical values, including (1) management's actions to eliminate or mitigate incentives and temptations on the part of personnel to commit dishonest, illegal, or unethical acts; (2) policy statements; and (3) codes of conduct
- Commitment to competence, including management's consideration of competence levels for specific tasks and how those levels translate into necessary skills and knowledge
- Participation of those charged with governance, including interaction with internal and external (independent) auditors
- Management's philosophy and operating style, such as management's attitude and actions regarding financial reporting, as well as management's approach to taking and monitoring risks
- The entity's organizational structure
- Assignment of authority and responsibility, including fulfilling job responsibilities
- Human resource policies and practices, including those relating to hiring, orientation, training, evaluating, counseling, promoting, and compensating employees

What is meant by risk assessment?

An entity's risk assessment for financial reporting purposes is its identification, analysis, and management of risks pertaining to financial statement preparation. Accordingly, risk assessment may consider the possibility of executed transactions that remain unrecorded.

These internal and external events and circumstances may be relevant to the risk of preparing financial statements that are not in conformity with generally accepted accounting principles (or another comprehensive basis of accounting):

- Changes in operating environment, including competitive pressures
- New personnel that have a different perspective on internal control
- Rapid growth that can result in a breakdown in controls
- New technology in information systems and production processes
- New business models, products, or activities
- Corporate restructuring that might result in changes in supervision and segregation of job functions

- Expanded foreign operations
- New accounting pronouncements requiring adoption of new accounting principles

What control activities are applicable to a financial statement audit?

Control activities are the policies and procedures management has implemented to ensure that directives are carried out. Control activities that may be relevant to a financial statement audit may be classified into these categories:

- *Performance reviews*, including comparisons of actual performance with budgets, forecasts, and prior-period results.
- *Information processing controls*, which generally are designed to verify accuracy, completeness, and authorization of transactions. Specifically, controls may be classified as *general controls* or *application controls*. General controls might include controls over data center operations, systems software acquisition and maintenance, and access security; application controls apply to the processing of individual applications and are designed to ensure that transactions that are recorded are valid, authorized, and complete.
- *Physical controls*, which involve adequate safeguards over the access to assets and records. These controls include authorization for access to computer programs and files, and periodic counting and comparison with amounts shown on control records.
- *Segregation of duties*, which is designed to reduce opportunities that allow any person to be in a position to both perpetrate and conceal errors or fraud in the normal course of his or her duties. This involves assigning different people the responsibilities of authorizing transactions, recording transactions, and maintaining custody of assets.

What knowledge about the information and communication systems component should an auditor obtain?

The auditor should obtain sufficient knowledge about the information system relevant to financial reporting. The information system generally consists of the methods and records established to record, process, summarize, and report entity transactions and to maintain accountability of related assets, liabilities, and equity.

Communication involves providing an understanding of individual roles and responsibilities pertaining to internal control over financial reporting.

What is meant by monitoring?

Monitoring is management's process of assessing the quality of internal control performance over time. Accordingly, management must assess the design and operation of controls on a timely basis and take necessary corrective actions. Monitoring may involve (1) separate evaluations, (2) the use of internal auditors, and (3) the use of communications from outside parties (e.g., complaints from customers and regulator comments).

Is there a relationship between objectives and components?

There is a direct relationship between objectives and components. This relationship results from the fact that objectives are what an entity strives to achieve, while components are what an entity needs to achieve the objectives. It is also important to remember that internal control is relevant not only to the entire entity, but also to an entity's operating units and business functions.

Caution

Not all of the objectives and related controls are relevant to a financial statement audit. Furthermore, an understanding of internal control relevant to each operating unit and business function may not be essential.

What objectives and controls are relevant to a financial statement audit?

In general, the auditor should consider the controls that pertain to the entity's objective of preparing financial statements for external use that are presented fairly in conformity with generally accepted accounting principles (GAAP) or some comprehensive basis of accounting other than GAAP.

The controls relating to operations and compliance objectives may be relevant to a financial statement audit if they pertain to data the auditor evaluates or uses. For example, the auditor may consider the controls relevant to nonfinancial data (such as production statistics) used in analytical procedures.

What is the auditor's primary consideration with respect to the components of internal control?

The auditor's primary consideration is whether a specific control affects the financial statement assertions rather than its classification into any particular component.

Although the five components are applicable to every audit, they should be considered in the context of:

- Entity size
- Organization and ownership characteristics
- Nature of the entity's business
- Diversity and complexity of operations
- Methods of transmitting, processing, maintaining, and accessing information
- Applicable legal and regulatory requirements

How does information technology affect internal control?

- An entity's use of information technology (IT) may affect any of the five interrelated components of internal control.
- Controls in systems that use IT consist of a combination of automated controls (e.g., controls embedded in computer programs) and manual controls.

What are the potential benefits of IT to internal control?

IT provides potential benefits of effectiveness and efficiency for internal control because it enables the entity to:

- Consistently apply predefined rules and perform complex calculations in processing large volumes of transactions or data.
- Enhance the timeliness, availability, and accuracy of information.
- Facilitate the additional analysis of information.
- Enhance the ability to monitor the performance of the entity's activities and its policies and procedures.
- Reduce the risk that controls will be circumvented.
- Enhance the ability to achieve effective segregation of duties by implementing security controls in applications, databases, and operating systems.

What risks does IT pose to internal control?

IT poses specific risks to internal control, including:

- Reliance on inaccurate systems or programs
- Unauthorized access to data that may result in destruction of data or improper alterations to data
- Unauthorized changes to master files
- Unauthorized changes to systems or programs
- Failure to make necessary changes to systems or programs
- Inappropriate manual intervention
- Potential loss of data

Note: The extent and nature of these risks to internal control depend on the nature and characteristics of the entity's information system.

To what extent must I consider the client's internal control?

The practitioner must obtain a sufficient understanding of internal control to enable (1) assessment of the risk of material misstatement and (2) design of the nature, extent, and timing of further audit procedures. The auditor should evaluate the design of the relevant controls and determine whether they have been implemented (i.e., they exist and are being used).

The understanding of the internal control should (1) provide a basis for identifying types of misstatements, (2) enable identification of factors affecting the risk of material misstatement, and (3) enable the auditor to design further audit procedures (i.e., tests of controls, when applicable, and substantive procedures).

What are the procedures used to obtain an understanding of internal control?

Ordinarily, a combination of these procedures is used to obtain a sufficient understanding of internal control:

- Previous experience with the client
- Inquiry of appropriate client personnel
- Observation of client activities
- Reference to prior-year working papers
- Inspection of client-prepared descriptions, such as organization charts and accounting manuals

How should I document my understanding of internal control?

The auditor must exercise professional judgment in determining the methods and extent of documentation. The most frequently used methods of documentation are:

- Flowcharts
- Questionnaires
- Narrative memos (written descriptions)

How are flowcharts helpful?

A flowchart is a pictorial representation of the flow of transactions. Flowcharts use standardized symbols and enable the auditor to visualize strengths and weaknesses in internal control. (See Exhibits 10.1A and B, Standardized Flowchart Symbols, and Exhibits 10.2A–D, Flowchart for a Typical Purchasing and Cash Disbursement System.)

How are questionnaires used?

A questionnaire is a series of questions designed to elicit a yes or no response as to whether a control exists. A *no* response, indicating a lack of the control, should prompt the auditor to pose another question in order to ascertain the existence of a compensating control. Questionnaires are useful because they can be tailored to fit a particular client. (See Exhibit 10.3.)

What is meant by assessing control risk?

The assessment of control risk is a process of evaluating the effectiveness of a client's internal controls in preventing or detecting material misstatements in the financial statements.

How do I assess control risk?

If the auditor concludes, based on his or her understanding of internal control, that controls are likely to be ineffective or that evaluation of their effectiveness would be inefficient, then the auditor may assess control risk at the maximum level for some or all financial statement assertions.

If specific controls are likely to prevent or detect material misstatements and the auditor performs tests of controls in order to evaluate the effectiveness of the

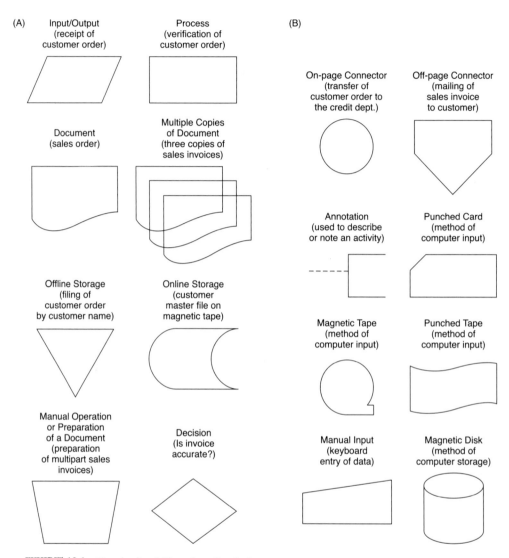

EXHIBIT 10.1   Standardized Flowchart Symbols

controls identified, then assessment of control risk below the maximum level is permissible.

What are tests of controls?

Tests of controls are tests directed toward the design or operation of an internal control to assess its effectiveness in preventing or detecting material misstatements in a financial statement assertion. Inquiry of company personnel, inspection of client documents and records, observation of client activities, and reperformance of controls represent some of the procedures used in performing tests of controls.

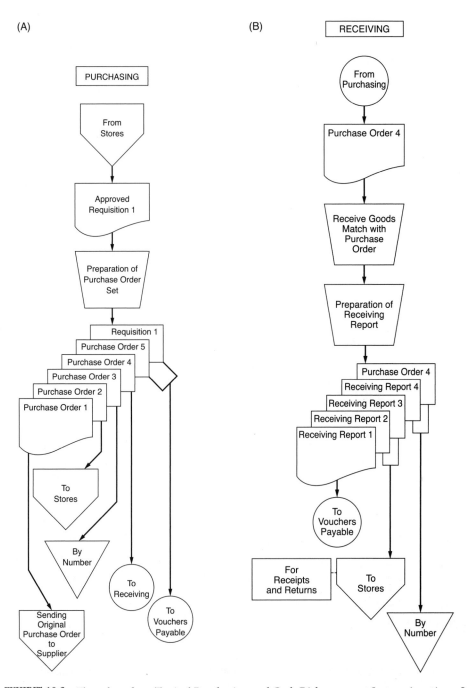

EXHIBIT 10.2   Flowchart for a Typical Purchasing and Cash Disbursement System (*continued*)

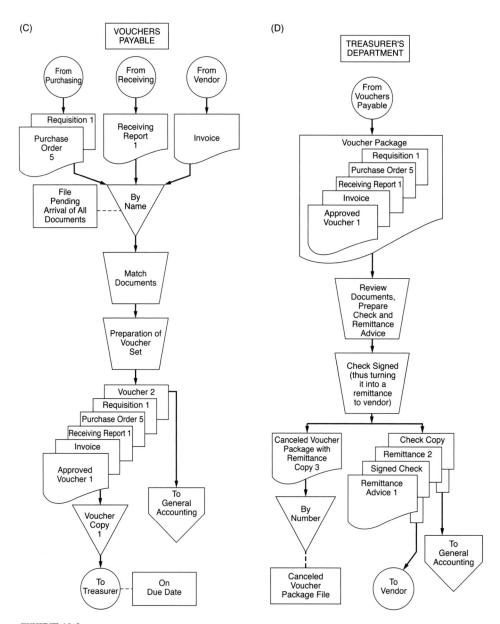

EXHIBIT 10.2   *(Continued)*

In performing tests of controls, the auditor seeks answers to these questions:

- Who performed the control?
- By what means was the control performed?
- How was the control performed?
- Was the control consistently applied?

EXHIBIT 10.3 Make-a-Million-Dollars Company Sample Internal Control Questionnaire for Investments

Authorized Execution of Transactions

		Yes	No	Basis for Answer	Comments
1.	Are investment transactions approved by the board of directors, the treasurer, or other responsible officer?				
2.	Is authorization required for access to vaults or safe-deposit boxes?				
3.	Is there proper documentation for initiation and approval of transactions?				

Limited Access to Assets

		Yes	No	Basis for Answer	Comments
1.	Are investment securities kept in safe-deposit boxes or vaults?				
2.	If not, is a bonded custodian utilized?				
3.	Are securities, other than bearer bonds, registered in the name of the company?				
4.	Does the company require two authorized signatures for access to the securities?				

Comparison of Recorded Amounts with Assets in Existence

		Yes	No	Basis for Answer	Comments
1.	Is there periodic inspection of investment securities?				
2.	Is there periodic comparison of recorded amounts with actual investment certificates?				
3.	Is there periodic review of worthless securities for possible realization?				

Recording of Transactions

		Yes	No	Basis for Answer	Comments
1.	Is an investment ledger maintained?				
2.	Are general ledger control totals compared to subsidiary investment ledgers?				
3.	Does management record investments using the lower-of-cost-or-market-value method?				
4.	Are investment transactions classified between current and long-term?				
5.	Is the cost or equity method being utilized?				

EXHIBIT 10.3   *(Continued)*

Technically Trained and Competent Personnel

	Yes	No	Basis for Answer	Comments
1. Are employees involved in the custody function bonded?				
2. Are employees involved in the custody function subjected to polygraph tests?				
3. Does the company maintain a prior work experience requirement for all employees involved in custody and recording of transactions?				

Segregation of Incompatible Functions

	Yes	No	Basis for Answer	Comments

1. Are the following functions segregated?
   a. Custody of investment securities
   b. Maintenance of subsidiary
   c. Journalizing transactions
   d. Posting to general ledger accounts
   e. Authorization for acquiring and disposing of investments
   f. Execution of authorized cash transactions				

Under what circumstances should tests of controls be performed?

The auditor should perform tests of controls when the auditor's risk assessment includes an expectation that internal controls are operating effectively or when the auditor is unable to reduce detection risk to an acceptably low level through substantive procedures alone.

Must an auditor test all internal controls?

An auditor need only test the operating effectiveness of controls that he or she concludes are suitably designed to prevent or enable detection of a material misstatement in a relevant assertion.

What must an auditor do if he or she plans to rely on controls that have not changed since they were last tested?

If, after obtaining an understanding of the entity and its environment, the auditor plans to rely on controls that have not changed since they were last tested, the auditor should test the effectiveness of such controls at least once in every third year in an annual audit.

It should be noted that the higher the risk of material misstatement or the greater the reliance on controls, the shorter should be the time elapsed between testing, if any. Further, when the auditor considers relying on a number of controls from prior audits, the auditor should test the operating effectiveness of some of the controls each year.

What should be the extent of tests of controls?

The extent, or amount, of tests of controls is a matter of professional judgment.

In general, however, the auditor should increase the extent of tests of controls the more he or she relies on the operating effectiveness of controls. If an entity uses information technology to process its transactions, the auditor may be able to limit tests of controls to one or a few instances because of the inherent consistent processing of transactions.

What is the relationship between the assessed level of control risk and substantive testing?

Since the auditor's determination of the nature, extent, and timing of substantive tests is dependent on detection risk, the assessed level of control risk must be considered in conjunction with inherent risk (see Statement on Auditing Standards [SAS] 107, Audit Risk and Materiality in Conducting on Audit). There is an inverse relationship between detection risk and the assurances to be provided from substantive tests. Accordingly, as detection risk decreases, the auditor should consider:

- Utilizing more effective substantive tests
- Performing substantive tests at year-end rather than at interim dates
- Increasing the amount of substantive testing

Do I have to document the assessed level of control risk?

The assessed level of control risk must be documented in the working papers in every audit engagement. Documentation should also include the basis for the auditor's conclusion.

How do cycles figure in assessing control risk?

Generally accepted auditing standards (GAAS) require that the auditor obtain a sufficient understanding of the entity and its environment, including its internal control, to assess the risk of material misstatement and to determine the nature, extent, and timing of further procedures to be performed.

Recommendation

The auditor should use the cycle approach, whereby broad areas of activity are selected and specific classes of transactions are identified. The five main cycles and their related classes of transactions are:

(*continued*)

(*Continued*)

1. *Revenue cycle:* Revenue and accounts receivable (order processing, credit approval, shipping, invoicing, and recording) and cash receipts
2. *Expenditure cycle:* Purchasing, receiving, accounts payable, payroll and cash disbursements
3. *Production or conversion cycle:* Inventories, cost of sales, and property, plant, and equipment
4. *Financing cycle:* Notes receivable and investments, notes payable, debt, leases, and other obligations and equity accounts
5. *External reporting:* Accounting principles and preparation of financial statements

Can I use statistical methods in performing tests of control?

To save time and money in performing tests of controls, auditors can use statistical sampling, in the form of attribute sampling. Seven steps should prove useful in this regard:

Step 1. *Determine the objective of the test*, namely, to obtain reasonable assurance that a particular control is in place (e.g., mathematical accuracy of invoices is verified by an individual other than the preparer of the invoice).

Step 2. *Define the deviation condition.* A deviation condition is a departure from a prescribed control (sometimes referred to as an attribute), such as the failure to initial an invoice that was mathematically verified. *Warning:* Deviation conditions increase the likelihood of, but do not necessarily result in, financial statement misstatements.

Step 3. *Define the population.*
- *Define the period covered.* If interim testing is performed, consider (1) inquiring about the period after testing and through the end of the year, and (2) the nature and amount of transactions and balances, and the length of the remaining period.
- *Define the sampling unit.* The sampling unit represents the item to be tested—for example, a document, a journal page, a transaction, or a line item.
- *Determine the completeness of the population.* The sample drawn must be representative of the population. *Example:* In testing purchase transactions, the population should include unpaid as well as paid invoices.

Step 4. *Determine the selection technique.*
- *Random number selection* provides assurance that each and every item in the population has a chance of being picked.
- *Systematic selection* involves picking every *n*th item from the population. The *n*th item, often referred to as the skip interval, is determined by dividing the population size by the sample size. *Example:* If the population size is 10,000 and the sample size is 50, the skip interval is 200. Thus, the auditor would pick every 200th item, beginning with a blind start.

EXHIBIT 10.4 Five Percent Risk of Assessing Control Risk Too Low

Statistical Sample Sizes for Tests of Controls (for large populations)

Expected Population Deviation Rate	Tolerable Rate								
	2%	3%	4%	5%	6%	7%	8%	9%	10%
0.00%	149	99	74	59	49	42	36	32	29
0.50	·	157	117	93	78	66	58	51	46
1.00	·	·	156	93	78	66	58	51	46
1.50	·	·	192	124	103	66	58	51	46
2.00	·	·	·	181	127	88	77	68	46
2.50	·	·	·	·	150	109	77	68	61
3.00	·	·	·	·	195	129	95	84	61
4.00	·	·	·	·	·	·	146	100	89
5.00	·	·	·	·	·	·	·	158	116
6.00	·	·	·	·	·	·	·	·	179

· Sample size is too large to be cost effective.

Step 5. *Determine the sample size by using the appropriate table.* (See Exhibits 10.4 and 10.5.)

Planned Degree of Reliance	Tolerable Rate
Substantial	2–7%
Moderate	6–12%
Little	11–20%

■ *Select an acceptable level of risk of assessing control risk too low.* Practically speaking, auditors select either a 5 percent or a 10 percent risk. These levels will provide the auditor 95 percent and 90 percent confidence,

EXHIBIT 10.5 Ten Percent Risk of Assessing Control Risk Too Low

Expected Population Deviation Rate	Tolerable Rate								
	2%	3%	4%	5%	6%	7%	8%	9%	10%
0.00%	114	76	57	45	38	32	28	25	22
0.50	194	129	96	77	64	55	48	42	38
1.00	·	176	96	77	64	55	48	42	38
1.50	·	·	132	105	64	55	48	42	38
2.00	·	·	198	132	88	75	48	42	38
2.50	·	·	·	158	110	75	65	58	38
3.00	·	·	·	·	132	94	65	58	52
4.00	·	·	·	·	·	149	98	73	65
5.00	·	·	·	·	·	·	160	115	78
6.00	·	·	·	·	·	·	·	182	116

· Sample size is too large to be cost effective.

respectively, that the sample is representative of the population. *Note:* The lower the risk the auditor selects, the bigger the sample size will be.

- *Select the tolerable rate.* This is the maximum rate of deviation the auditor is willing to tolerate while still being able to reduce assessed control risk. The tolerable rate is dependent on professional judgment and the planned degree of reliance on the control.
- *Assess the expected population deviation rate.* This may be based on (1) reference to actual deviation rates of the prior year, adjusted for current-year implementation of prior-year recommendations; (2) communication with prior-year accountants; or (3) a preliminary sample of 50 items.

Step 6. *Select the sample and perform tests of controls.*

Step 7. *Interpret the sample results.*

- *Calculate the sample deviation rate.* Divide the actual number of deviations by the sample size.
- *Determine the upper occurrence limit by using the appropriate table.* (See Exhibits 10.6 and 10.7.) Essentially the upper occurrence limit takes the sample deviation rate and adjusts it upward to reflect the fact that the population is likely to contain a greater rate of deviations.
- *Determine whether the deviations are a result of errors (unintentional) or fraud (intentional).*

EXHIBIT 10.6   Five Percent Risk of Assessing Control Risk Too Low

Statistical Sample Results Evaluation Table for Tests of Controls Upper Occurrence Limit (for large populations)

Sample Size	Actual Number of Occurrences Found								
	0	1	2	3	4	5	6	7	8
25	11.3	17.6	·	·	·	·	·	·	·
30	9.5	14.9	19.5	·	·	·	·	·	·
35	8.2	12.9	16.9	·	·	·	·	·	·
40	7.2	11.3	14.9	18.3	·	·	·	·	·
45	6.4	10.1	13.3	16.3	19.2	·	·	·	·
50	5.8	9.1	12.1	14.8	17.4	19.9	·	·	·
55	5.3	8.3	11.0	13.5	15.9	18.1	·	·	·
60	4.9	7.7	10.1	12.4	14.6	16.7	18.8	·	·
65	4.5	7.1	9.4	11.5	13.5	15.5	17.4	19.3	·
70	4.2	6.6	8.7	10.7	12.6	14.4	16.2	18.0	19.7
75	3.9	6.2	8.2	10.0	11.8	13.5	15.2	16.9	18.4
80	3.7	5.8	7.7	9.4	11.1	12.7	14.3	15.8	17.3
90	3.3	5.2	6.8	8.4	9.9	11.3	12.7	14.1	15.5
100	3.0	4.7	6.2	7.6	8.9	10.2	11.5	12.7	14.0
125	2.4	3.7	4.9	6.1	7.2	8.2	9.3	10.3	11.3
150	2.0	3.1	4.1	5.1	6.0	6.9	7.7	8.6	9.4
200	1.5	2.3	3.1	3.8	4.5	5.2	5.8	6.5	7.1

· Over 20 percent.

EXHIBIT 10.7   Ten Percent Risk of Assessing Control Risk Too Low

Sample Size	Actual Number of Occurrences Found								
	0	1	2	3	4	5	6	7	8
20	10.9	18.1	·	·	·	·	·	·	·
25	8.8	14.7	19.9	·	·	·	·	·	·
30	7.4	12.4	16.8	·	·	·	·	·	·
35	6.4	10.7	14.5	18.1	·	·	·	·	·
40	5.6	9.4	12.8	15.9	19.0	·	·	·	·
45	5.0	8.4	11.4	14.2	17.0	19.6	·	·	·
50	4.5	7.6	10.3	12.9	15.4	17.8	·	·	·
55	4.1	6.9	9.4	11.7	14.0	16.2	18.4	·	·
60	3.8	6.3	8.6	10.8	12.9	14.9	16.9	18.8	·
70	3.2	5.4	7.4	9.3	11.1	12.8	14.6	16.2	17.9
80	2.8	4.8	6.5	8.3	9.7	11.3	12.8	14.3	15.7
90	2.5	4.3	5.8	7.3	8.7	10.1	11.4	12.7	14.0
100	2.3	3.8	5.2	6.6	7.8	9.1	10.3	11.5	12.7
120	1.9	3.2	4.4	5.5	6.6	7.6	8.6	9.6	10.6
160	1.4	2.4	3.3	4.1	4.9	5.7	6.5	7.2	8.0
200	1.1	1.9	2.6	3.3	4.0	4.6	5.2	5.8	6.4

· Over 20 percent.

- *Accept or reject the sample as representative of the population.*
  - If the sample deviation is greater than the tolerable rate, no reliance may be placed on the control.
  - If the upper occurrence limit is less than the tolerable rate, reliance may be placed on the control.
  - If the upper occurrence limit is greater than the tolerable rate, no reliance should be placed on the control. In this case, the auditor might perform tests of controls on another control or proceed to substantive testing without modification.

Example 10.1

In determining whether the credit department is performing properly, Margie Scott, CPA, utilizes attribute sampling in testing controls over sales orders. Scott determines:

- The deviation condition is the absence of the credit manager's initials on a sales order.
- The population consists of the duplicate sales orders for the entire fiscal year.
- The sampling unit is the sales order itself.
- Random number selection will be utilized.

(continued)

(Continued)

- A 5 percent risk of assessing control risk too low will be utilized.
- The tolerable rate of deviation is 6 percent.
- The expected population deviation rate is 2 percent.

Using Exhibit 10.4, we find that the sample size will be 127. Scott uses a random number table (Exhibit 10.8) to select the sample. Since the population consists of sales orders numbered 1 to 500, Scott decides to use the first three digits of items selected from the random number table. Using a blind start at column 5, line 6, Scott selects these sales orders:

Number
277
188
174
496
482
312

After performing the sampling plan, Scott finds that four sales orders are missing the credit manager's signature (apparently an error on the credit manager's part). The sample deviation rate is therefore 4/127 or 3.1 percent. The upper occurrence limit, determined by using Exhibit 10.6, Five Percent Risk of Assessing Control Risk Too Low, is 7.2. (The sample size of 125 is used for conservative results.) Since the upper occurrence limit is greater than the tolerable rate of 6 percent, Scott rejects the control and attempts to identify a compensating control for additional testing.

Substantive Procedures

What is the purpose of substantive procedures?

To afford a reasonable basis for an opinion on the fairness of the financial statements, the third generally accepted fieldwork standard requires the gathering of sufficient appropriate audit evidence. Substantive procedures, which are performed to detect material misstatements at the relevant assertion level, provide the requisite audit evidence.

What are the types of substantive procedures?

In general, substantive procedures include:

- Tests of details of classes of transactions
- Tests of details of account balances
- Tests of details of disclosures
- Substantive analytical procedures

EXHIBIT 10.8   Random Number Table

Line	(1)	(2)	(3)	(4)	(5)	(6)	(7)	(8)	(9)	(10)	(11)	(12)	(13)	(14)
								Column						
1	50590	11592	10195	10244	81647	91646	69179	14194	62590	36207	20969	99570	91291	90700
2	22368	46573	25595	85393	30995	89198	27982	53402	93965	34095	52666	19174	39615	99505
3	24130	48360	22527	97265	76393	64809	15179	24830	49340	32081	30680	19655	63348	58629
4	42167	93093	06243	61680	07856	16376	39440	53537	71341	57004	00849	74917	97758	16379
5	37570	39975	81837	16656	06121	91782	60468	81305	49684	60672	14110	06927	01263	54613
6	77921	06907	11008	42751	27756	53498	18602	70659	90655	15053	21916	81825	44394	42880
7	99562	72905	56420	69994	98872	31016	71194	18738	44013	48840	63213	21069	10634	12952
8	96301	91977	05463	07972	18876	20922	94595	56869	69014	60045	18425	84903	42508	32307
9	89579	14342	63661	10281	17453	18103	57740	84378	25331	12566	58678	44947	05585	56941
10	85475	36857	53342	53988	53060	59533	38867	62300	08158	17983	16439	11458	18593	64952
11	28918	69578	88231	33276	70997	79936	56865	05859	90106	31595	01547	85590	91610	78188
12	63553	40961	48235	03427	49626	69445	18663	72695	52180	20847	12234	90511	33703	90322
13	09429	93969	52636	92737	88974	33488	36320	17617	30015	08272	84115	27156	30613	74952
14	10365	61129	87529	85689	48237	52267	67689	93394	01511	26358	85104	20285	29975	89868
15	07119	97336	71048	08178	77233	13916	47564	81056	97735	85977	29372	74461	28551	90707
16	51085	12765	51821	51259	77452	16308	60756	92144	49442	53900	70960	63990	75601	40719
17	02368	21382	52404	60268	89368	19885	55322	44819	01188	63255	64835	44919	05944	55157
18	01011	54092	33362	94904	31273	04146	18594	29852	71585	85030	51132	01915	92747	64951
19	52162	53916	46369	58586	23216	14513	83149	98736	23495	64350	94738	17752	35156	35749
20	07056	97628	33787	09998	42698	06691	76988	13602	51851	46104	88916	19509	25625	58104
21	48663	91245	85828	14346	09172	30168	90229	04734	59193	22178	30421	61666	99904	32812
22	54164	58492	22421	74103	47070	25306	76468	26384	58151	06646	21524	15227	96909	44592
23	32639	32363	05597	24200	13363	38005	94342	28728	35806	06912	17012	64161	18296	22851
24	29334	27001	87637	87308	58731	00256	45834	15398	46557	41135	10367	07684	36188	18510
25	02488	33062	28834	07351	19731	92420	60952	61280	50001	67658	32586	86679	50720	94953

(Continued)

EXHIBIT 10.8 *(Continued)*

Line							Column							
	(1)	(2)	(3)	(4)	(5)	(6)	(7)	(8)	(9)	(10)	(11)	(12)	(13)	(14)
26	81525	72295	04839	96423	24878	82651	66566	14778	76797	14780	13300	87074	79666	95725
27	29676	20591	68086	26432	46901	20849	89768	81536	86645	12659	92259	57102	80428	25280
28	00742	57392	39064	66432	84673	44027	32832	61362	98947	96067	64760	64584	96096	98253
29	05366	04213	25669	26422	44407	44048	37937	63904	45766	66134	75470	66520	34693	90449
30	91921	26418	64117	94305	26766	25940	39972	22209	71500	64568	91402	42416	07844	69618
31	00582	04711	87917	77341	42206	35126	74087	99547	81817	42607	43808	76655	62028	76630
32	00725	69884	62797	56170	86324	88072	76222	36086	84637	93161	76038	65855	77919	88006
33	69011	65795	95876	55293	18988	27354	26575	08625	40801	59920	29841	80150	12777	48501
34	25976	57948	29888	80604	67917	48708	18912	82271	65424	69774	33611	54262	85963	03547
35	09763	83473	73577	12908	30883	18317	28290	35797	05998	41688	34952	37888	38917	80050
36	91567	42595	29758	30134	04024	86385	29880	99730	55536	84855	29080	09250	79656	73211
37	17955	56349	90999	49127	20044	59931	06115	20542	18059	02008	73708	83517	36103	42791
38	46503	18584	18845	49618	02304	51038	20655	58727	28168	15475	56942	53389	20562	87338
39	92157	89634	94824	78171	84610	82834	09922	25417	44137	48413	25555	21246	35509	20468
40	14577	62765	35605	81263	39667	47358	56873	56307	61607	49518	89656	20103	77490	18062
41	98427	07523	33362	64270	01638	92477	66969	98420	04880	45585	46565	04102	46880	45709
42	34914	63976	88720	82765	34476	17032	87589	40836	32427	70002	70663	88863	77775	69348
43	70060	28277	39475	46473	23219	53416	94970	25832	69975	94884	19661	72828	00102	66794
44	53976	54914	06990	67245	68350	82948	11398	42878	80287	88267	47363	46634	06541	97809
45	76072	29515	40980	07391	58745	25774	22987	80059	39911	96189	41151	14222	60697	59583
46	90725	52210	83974	29992	65831	38857	50490	83765	55657	14361	31720	57375	56228	41546
47	64364	67412	33339	31926	14883	24413	59744	92351	97473	89286	38931	04110	23726	51900
48	08962	00358	31662	25388	61642	34072	81249	35648	56891	69352	48373	45578	78547	81788
49	95012	68379	93526	70765	10592	04542	76463	54328	02349	17247	28865	14777	62730	92277
50	15664	10493	20492	38391	91132	21999	59516	81652	27195	48223	46751	22923	32261	85653

444

Are substantive procedures required in every audit?

Regardless of the assessed risk of material misstatement, the auditor should design and perform substantive procedures for all relevant assertions related to each material class of transactions, account balance, and disclosure. Substantive procedures should include (1) agreeing the financial statements (including notes) with the underlying accounting records and (2) examining material journal entries and other adjustments.

Can an auditor perform substantive procedures before year-end?

In some circumstances, substantive procedures may be performed at an interim date.

Performing substantive procedures at an interim date increases the risk that material misstatements at year-end will not be detected by the auditor. The more time there is between the interim testing date and year-end, the more risk there is.

In considering whether to perform substantive procedures at an interim date, the auditor should consider such factors as:

- The control environment and other relevant controls
- The availability of information at a later date
- The objective of the substantive procedure
- The assessed risk of material misstatement
- The nature of the class of transactions or account balance and relevant assertions
- The ability to reduce the risk that misstatements existing at period-end will not be detected

What should an auditor do if misstatements are detected while performing interim testing?

If misstatements are detected in classes of transactions or account balances at an interim date, the auditor should consider modifying the related assessment of risk and the planned nature, timing, or extent of the substantive procedures covering the remainder of the period, or the auditor may extend or may repeat such audit procedures at period-end.

How should an auditor determine the extent of substantive procedures?

The extent or amount of substantive procedures is dependent on the risk of material misstatement. The greater the risk of material misstatement, the less detection risk that can be accepted; consequently, the greater the extent of substantive procedures.

In *testing transactions*, the auditor is concerned with tests of:

- Omitted transactions and account understatement (tracing source documents to the books of entry)
- Invalid or unsupported transactions and account overstatement (tracing recorded transactions to source documents)

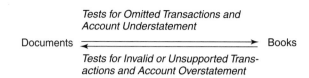

In analyzing *details of account balances*, auditors use professional judgment in determining which accounts to scrutinize. Some of the accounts commonly requiring scrutiny are:

- Repairs and maintenance
- Fixed assets
- Officers' salaries
- Contributions
- Travel and entertainment
- Income tax provisions

Substantive analytical procedures include the study and comparison of the relationships among data. This involves the comparison of current period financial information with:

- Prior-period information
- Expected results
- Predictable pattern information
- Intra-industry information
- Nonfinancial information

What is involved in developing an audit plan?

The auditor must develop an audit plan that documents the audit procedures to be performed.

To reduce audit risk to an acceptably low level, the audit plan should:

- Describe the nature, extent, and timing of planned risk assessment procedures.
- Describe the nature, extent, and timing of planned further audit procedures (i.e., substantive procedures and, if relevant, tests of controls) at the relevant assertion level.
- Describe other audit procedures needed in order to comply with generally accepted auditing procedures (i.e., procedures required in Statements on Auditing Standards).
- For initial engagements, include procedures regarding acceptance of both the client relationship and the specific audit engagement.
- For initial engagements, include procedures relating to communication with the predecessor auditor.

What should be included in an audit plan?

An audit plan should include audit programs for classes of transactions and events, account balances at period-end, and presentation and disclosure relevant to the financial statements. Specific procedures detailed in audit programs should be based on financial statement assertions.

What assertions should be considered for classes of transactions and events?

- *Occurrence.* Recorded transactions and events have occurred and pertain to the entity.
- *Completeness.* All transactions and events that should have been recorded have been recorded.
- *Accuracy.* Amounts and other data relating to recorded transactions and events have been recorded appropriately.
- *Cutoff.* Transactions and events have been recorded in the proper accounting periods.
- *Classification.* The proper accounts have been used to record transactions and events.

What assertions should be considered for account balances at period-end?

- *Existence.* Assets, liabilities, and equity interests exist.
- *Rights and obligations.* The entity holds or controls rights to assets, and liabilities represent obligations of the entity.
- *Completeness.* All assets, liabilities, and equity interests that should have been recorded have been recorded.
- *Valuation and allocation.* Assets, liabilities, and equity interests are recorded at appropriate amounts, and valuation or allocation adjustments are appropriately recorded.

What assertions should be considered regarding presentation and disclosure?

- *Occurrence and rights and obligations.* Disclosed transactions and events have occurred and pertain to the entity.
- *Completeness.* All disclosures that should have been included in the financial statements have been included.
- *Classification and understandability.* Financial information is appropriately presented and described and disclosures are clearly expressed.
- *Accuracy and valuation.* Financial and other information is disclosed fairly and at amounts that are appropriate.

Note

These assertions may be expressed differently as long as the substance of the information discussed has been taken into account.

What else is needed in preparing an audit plan?

The next steps in developing an audit plan are identifying the flow of transactions in the accounting process and developing an understanding of relevant generally accepted accounting principles.

Finally, the appropriate audit procedures must be selected from among these general procedures:

- Inspection of related documents or records
- Observation of procedures
- Confirmation of account balances and existence of assets, liabilities, and transactions
- Inquiry of company personnel
- Retracing of transactions from books to records
- Recalculation of extensions and footings
- Vouching of documents to verify propriety and validity
- Counting of tangible assets
- Scanning ("eyeballing") of documents, schedules, and accounts
- Scrutinizing of documents, schedules, and accounts
- Reading or reviewing of documents, minutes of board meetings, and financial statements
- Comparison of perpetual records with physical assets
- Analysis of account balances (see Exhibit 10.9)

EXHIBIT 10.9   Sample Audit Work Programs

I. Substantive Tests of Cash Balances
   A. Presentation and Disclosure
      1. Read or review the financial statements to verify proper classification.
      2. Read or review the financial statements to verify disclosures such as those relating to compensation balances.
      3. Determine the conformity with GAAP.
   B. Valuation and Allocation
      1. Simultaneously count cash on hand and negotiable securities.
      2. Confirm directly with the bank:
         a. Account balances
         b. Direct liabilities to bank
         c. Contingent liabilities to bank
         d. Letters of credit
         e. Security agreements under the Uniform Commercial Code
         f. Authorized signatures
      3. Count petty cash fund and reconcile with vouchers.
   C. Completeness
      1. Obtain bank cutoff statement and determine propriety of year-end outstanding checks and deposits-in-transit.
      2. Examine or prepare year-end bank reconciliation.
      3. Prepare a proof of cash.
      4. Perform analytical procedures.
   D. Existence (see Valuation and Allocation)
   E. Rights and Obligations
      1. Read minutes of the board of directors' meetings.
      2. Determine existence of compensating balances, levies, and so on.
      3. Verify names on accounts through confirmation requests.

EXHIBIT 10.9 *(Continued)*

II. Substantive Tests of Receivables Balances
  A. Presentation and Disclosure
    1. Determine appropriate classification of account balances.
    2. Read or review the financial statements in order to verify disclosure of:
      a. Restrictions—pledging, factoring, and discounting
      b. Related-party transactions
    3. Trace amounts on trial balance to general ledger control accounts and subsidiary ledger totals.
  B. Valuation and Allocation
    1. Confirm account balances where reasonable and practicable using positive and/or negative confirmation requests.
    2. Examine collections in the subsequent period cash receipts journal.
    3. Examine and verify amortization tables.
    4. Examine aging schedules.
    5. Review adequacy of allowance for doubtful accounts.
    6. Review collectibility by checking credit ratings (e.g., Dun & Bradstreet ratings).
    7. Verify clerical accuracy and pricing of sales invoices.
    8. Foot daily sales summaries and trace to journals.
    9. Perform tests for omitted and invalid (or unsupported) transactions with respect to subsidiary ledger account balances.
  C. Completeness
    1. Perform sales and sales return cutoff tests.
    2. Perform analytical procedures.
    3. Test for omitted transactions.
  D. Existence
    1. Inspect note agreements.
    2. Confirm accounts receivable and notes receivable balances.
    3. Review client documentation.
  E. Rights and Obligations
    1. Read minutes of board of directors' meetings.
    2. Read leases for pledging agreements.
    3. Determine pledging and contingent liabilities to bank by using a standard bank confirmation.
III. Substantive Tests of Inventory
  A. Presentation and Disclosure
    1. Read or review the financial statements to verify footnote disclosure of:
      a. Valuation method and inventory flow (e.g., lower of cost or market value; first in, first out)
      b. Pledged inventory
      c. Inventory in or out on consignment
      d. Existence of and terms of major purchase commitments
  B. Valuation and Allocation
    1. Verify the correct application of lower of cost or market value.
    2. Recalculate inventory valuation under the full absorption costing method.
    3. Verify the quality of inventory items.
    4. Vouch and test inventory pricing.
    5. Perform analytical procedures.
    6. Verify the propriety of inventory flow.
    7. Consider using the services of a specialist to corroborate the valuation of inventory (e.g., a gemologist to corroborate the valuation of precious stones).

(Continued)

EXHIBIT 10.9   *(Continued)*

    C. Completeness
       1. Perform cutoff tests for purchases, sales, purchase returns, and sales returns.
       2. With respect to tagged inventory, perform tests for omitted transactions and tests for invalid transactions.
       3. Verify the clerical and mathematical accuracy of inventory listings.
       4. Reconcile physical inventory amounts with perpetual records.
       5. Reconcile physical counts with general ledger control totals.
    D. Existence
       1. Observe client inventory counts.
       2. Confirm inventory held in public warehouses.
       3. Confirm existence of inventory held by others on consignment.
    E. Rights and Obligations
       1. Determine existence of collateral agreements.
       2. Read consignment agreements.
       3. Review major purchase commitment agreements.
       4. Examine invoices for evidence of ownership.
       5. Review minutes of the board of directors' meetings.
IV. Substantive Tests for Fixed Assets
    A. Presentation and Disclosure
       1. Read the financial statements in order to verify:
          a. Disclosure of historical cost
          b. Disclosure of depreciation methods under GAAP
          c. Financial statement classification
          d. Disclosure of restrictions
    B. Valuation and Allocation
       1. Examine invoices.
       2. Inspect lease agreements and ascertain the proper accounting treatment (e.g., capital versus operating lease).
       3. Analyze repairs and maintenance accounts.
       4. Analyze related accumulated depreciation accounts.
       5. Vouch entries in fixed asset accounts.
       6. Test extensions and footings on client-submitted schedules.
    C. Completeness
       1. Perform analytical procedures.
       2. Inspect fixed assets.
       3. Examine subsidiary schedules.
       4. Reconcile subsidiary schedules with general ledger control.
    D. Existence
       1. Inspect fixed assets.
       2. Examine supporting documentation.
    E. Rights and Obligations
       1. Inspect invoices.
       2. Inspect lease agreements.
       3. Inspect insurance policies.
       4. Inspect title documents.
       5. Inspect personal property tax returns.
       6. Read minutes of the board of directors' meetings.

Audit Reports

How does the auditor report?

After the auditor gathers sufficient appropriate audit evidence, pursuant to the fourth generally accepted reporting standard, he or she must form an opinion on the fairness of the presentation of the financial statements or disclaim an opinion.

The auditor's standard unqualified opinion can be modified when warranted.

How should the auditor's standard report be worded?

The wording of the auditor's report depends on whether it relates to the audit of (1) a private company or (2) a public company regulated by the Public Company Accounting Oversight Board (PCAOB).

An audit report on the financial statements of a private company should include a reference to either U.S. generally accepted auditing standards (GAAS) or auditing standards generally accepted in the United States of America.

Example 10.2   Standard Report—Private Company (Nonissuer)

Independent Auditor's Report

I (We) have audited the accompanying balance sheet of [*company name*] as of (at) [*date*] and the related statements of income, retained earnings, and cash flows for the year then ended. These financial statements are the responsibility of the Company's management. My (Our) responsibility is to express an opinion on these financial statements based on my (our) audit.

I (We) conducted my (our) audit in accordance with U.S. generally accepted auditing standards (or auditing standards generally accepted in the United States of America). Those standards require that I (we) plan and perform the audit to obtain reasonable assurance about whether the financial statements are free of material misstatement. An audit includes examining, on a test basis, evidence supporting the amounts and disclosures in the financial statements. An audit also includes assessing the accounting principles used and significant estimates made by management, as well as evaluating the overall financial statement presentation. I (We) believe that my (our) audit provides a reasonable basis for my (our) opinion.

In my (our) opinion, the financial statements referred to above present fairly, in all material respects, the financial position of [*company name*] as of (at) [*date*], and the results of its operations and its cash flows for the year then ended in conformity with U.S. generally accepted accounting principles (or accounting principles generally accepted in the United States of America).

[*Signature*]
[*Date*]

An audit report on the financial statements of a public company (issuer) regulated by the PCAOB should (1) be titled "Report of Independent Registered Public Accounting Firm," (2) refer to "the standards of the Public Company Accounting Oversight Board (United States)," (3) not include any reference to generally accepted auditing standards, and (4) include the city and state (or country, if a non-U.S. auditor) from which the audit report is issued.

Example 10.3   Standard Report—Public Company (Issuer)

Report of Independent Registered Public Accounting Firm

We have audited the accompanying balance sheet of [*company name*] as of (at) [*date*] and the related statements of income, retained earnings, and cash flows for the year then ended. These financial statements are the responsibility of the Company's management. Our responsibility is to express an opinion on these financial statements based on our audit.

We conducted our audit in accordance with the standards of the Public Company Accounting Oversight Board (United States). Those standards require that we plan and perform the audit to obtain reasonable assurance about whether the financial statements are free of material misstatement. An audit includes examining, on a test basis, evidence supporting the amounts and disclosures in the financial statements. An audit also includes assessing the accounting principles used and significant estimates made by management, as well as evaluating the overall financial statement presentation. We believe that our audit provides a reasonable basis for our opinion.

In our opinion, the financial statements referred to above present fairly, in all material respects, the financial position of [*company name*] as of (at) [*date*], and the results of its operations and its cash flows for the year then ended in conformity with accounting principles generally accepted in the United States of America.

[*Signature*]
[*City and state or country*]
[*Date*]

Note

The independent auditor's report should be (1) addressed to the company or its board of directors or stockholders and (2) dated no earlier than the date on which the auditor has obtained sufficient appropriate audit evidence.

How can the standard report be modified?

Using the auditor's standard report as a guideline, the practitioner can easily make modifications depending on the circumstances. These modifications can be classified by the type of report being issued. They are:

- Unqualified opinion
- Qualified opinion
- Disclaimer of opinion
- Adverse opinion

Note

All sample audit reports that follow contain wording applicable to financial statements of a private company. When reporting on financial statements of a public company, the practitioner is required to modify the audit report as indicated in Examples 10.2 and 10.3.

Unqualified Opinion

When does a division of responsibility apply?

A division of responsibility occurs, for instance, when the auditor of a consolidated group of companies is unable to audit one of the subsidiaries included in the group but another auditor is able to conduct that audit. The principal auditor has the choice of referring to the other auditor if he or she:

- Is satisfied as to the professional reputation of the other auditor.
- Has obtained a representation letter from the other auditor confirming his or her independence.
- Is satisfied that the other auditor is familiar with generally accepted auditing standards and generally accepted accounting principles.
- Coordinates the audit activities of the two auditors.

Requirement

If reference is to be made to another auditor, then all paragraphs of the report are modified to reflect the division of responsibility. The introductory paragraph should indicate the magnitude or the size of the portion of the financial statements audited by the other auditor. This may be accomplished through the use of dollars or percentages of total assets and revenues.

Example 10.4   Division of Responsibility

Independent Auditor's Report

I (We) have audited the consolidated balance sheets of KJB Company as of (at) December 31, 2X12, and the related consolidated statements of income, retained

(continued)

(Continued)

earnings, and cash flows for the year then ended. These financial statements are the responsibility of the Company's management. My (Our) responsibility is to express an opinion on these financial statements based on my (our) audit. I (We) did not audit the financial statements of KJB Company, a wholly owned subsidiary, which statements reflect total assets of $_____ as of December 31, 2X12, and total revenues of $_____ for the year then ended. Those statements were audited by other auditors whose report has been furnished to me (us), and my (our) opinion, insofar as it relates to the amounts included for KJB Company, is based solely on the report of the other auditors.

I (We) conducted my (our) audit in accordance with U.S. generally accepted auditing standards. Those standards require that I (we) plan and perform the audit to obtain reasonable assurance about whether the financial statements are free of material misstatement. An audit includes examining, on a test basis, evidence supporting the amounts and disclosures in the financial statements. An audit also includes assessing the accounting principles used and significant estimates made by management, as well as evaluating the overall financial statement presentation. I (We) believe that my (our) audit and the report of the other auditors provide a reasonable basis for my (our) opinion.

In my (our) opinion, based on my (our) audit and the report of other auditors, the consolidated financial statements referred to above present fairly, in all material respects, the financial position of KJB as of (at) December 31, 2X12, and the results of its operations and its cash flows for the year then ended in conformity with U.S. generally accepted accounting principles.

How can I emphasize a disclosure?

The practitioner, in his or her report, may emphasize a matter that is already disclosed and properly accounted for in the financial statements. Emphasis of a matter, such as a Type II subsequent event (discussed in Chapter 12), should be made in a separate paragraph between the scope and opinion paragraphs. No modification should be made to either the scope or the opinion paragraph.

How do I handle breaks in consistency?

When financial statements reflect a change in accounting principles, the auditor must modify the audit report by adding an explanatory paragraph following the opinion paragraph.

Example 10.5   Explanatory Paragraph

As discussed in Note X to the financial statements, the company changed its method of computing depreciation in 2X15.

> ## Caution
>
> In general, if the year of change is reported on in subsequent years, the additional paragraph must be presented.

When is the consistency modification required?

Changes in accounting principles requiring the consistency modification include:

- A change from one generally accepted accounting principle or method to another
- A change in reporting entity
- A change from a non-GAAP method to a method or principle that is generally accepted
- A change in principle that is inseparable from a change in accounting estimate

Changes in the following areas, however, do not require consistency modifications:

- Accounting estimates
- Correction of an error not involving a principle
- Financial statement classification, format, and terminology
- Reporting entity as a result of an accounting transaction

Qualified Opinion

When is the scope of the examination limited?

A scope limitation arises when the auditor is unable to do one or more of these:

- Gather enough evidential matter to afford the expression of an unqualified opinion.
- Apply a required auditing procedure.
- Apply one or more auditing procedures considered necessary under the circumstances.

What if the limitation is not a serious one?

When the scope limitation is not severe enough to warrant the expression of a disclaimer of an opinion, an "except for" qualified opinion should be issued. The necessary modifications to the report include:

- Adding the phrase "Except as discussed in the following paragraph" to the beginning or end of the second sentence of the scope paragraph
- Adding a paragraph before the opinion paragraph that explains the nature of the scope limitation

- Modifying the opinion paragraph for the possible effects of the scope limitation on the financial statements

---

Example 10.6   Report Modified to Indicate a Scope Limitation

Independent Auditor's Report

I (We) have audited the accompanying balance sheet of SMR Company as of (at) December 31, 2X12, and the related statements of income, retained earnings, and cash flows for the year then ended. These financial statements are the responsibility of the Company's management. My (Our) responsibility is to express an opinion on these financial statements based on my (our) audit.

Except as discussed in the following paragraph, I (we) conducted my (our) audit in accordance with U.S. generally accepted auditing standards. Those standards require that I (we) plan and perform the audit to obtain reasonable assurance about whether the financial statements are free of material misstatement. An audit includes examining, on a test basis, evidence supporting the amounts and disclosures in the financial statements. An audit also includes assessing the accounting principles used and significant estimates made by management, as well as evaluating the overall financial statement presentation. I (We) believe that my (our) audit provides a reasonable basis for my (our) opinion.

I was (We were) unable to obtain audited financial statements supporting the Company's investment in a foreign affiliate stated at $_____ at December 31, 2X12, or its equity in earnings of that affiliate of $_____, which is included in net income for the year then ended as described in Note X to the financial statements; nor was I (were we) able to satisfy myself (ourselves) as to the carrying value of the investment in the foreign affiliate or the equity in its earnings by other auditing procedures.

In my (our) opinion, except for the effects of such adjustments, if any, as might have been determined to be necessary had I (we) been able to examine evidence regarding the foreign affiliate investment and earnings, the financial statements referred to in the first paragraph above present fairly, in all material respects, the financial position of SMR Company as of (at) December 31, 2X12, and the results of its operations and its cash flows for the year then ended in conformity with U.S. generally accepted accounting principles.

How do I handle a departure from GAAP?

When financial statements contain a departure from GAAP and the client refuses to make the necessary modifications, the auditor will express a qualified opinion, unless the effects of the departure warrant the issuance of an adverse opinion. Departures from GAAP include the lack of adequate disclosure (e.g., the omission of the summary of significant accounting policies), the omission of the statement of cash flows (which results in incomplete presentation), as well as the use of an accounting method that does not reflect the substance of a particular transaction (e.g., the failure to capitalize lease obligations).

The necessary modifications to the report include:

- Adding an explanatory paragraph between the scope and opinion paragraphs describing the departure, the treatment required under GAAP, and the principal effects on the financial statements (or, if not practicable, a statement so indicating)
- Modifying the opinion paragraph by adding the phrase "except for" and including a reference to the explanatory paragraph

---

Example 10.7   Report Modified to Disclose a Departure from GAAP

Independent Auditor's Report

I (We) have audited the accompanying balance sheet of SR Company as of (at) December 31, 2X12, and the related statements of income, retained earnings, and cash flows for the year then ended. These financial statements are the responsibility of the Company's management. My (Our) responsibility is to express an opinion on these financial statements based on my (our) audit.

I (We) conducted my (our) audit in accordance with U.S. generally accepted auditing standards. Those standards require that I (we) plan and perform the audit to obtain reasonable assurance about whether the financial statements are free of material misstatement. An audit includes examining, on a test basis, evidence supporting the amounts and disclosures in the financial statements. An audit also includes assessing the accounting principles used and significant estimates made by management, as well as evaluating the overall financial statement presentation. I (We) believe that my (our) audit provides a reasonable basis for my (our) opinion.

The Company has excluded from property and debt in the accompanying balance sheet certain lease obligations, which in my (our) opinion should be capitalized in order to conform with generally accepted accounting principles. If these lease obligations were capitalized, property would be increased (decreased) by $_____, long-term debt by $_____, and retained earnings by $_____ as of December 31, 2X12, and net income and earnings per share would be increased (decreased) by $_____ and $_____, respectively, for the year then ended.

In my (our) opinion, except for the effects of not capitalizing certain lease obligations as discussed in the preceding paragraph, the financial statements referred to above present fairly, in all material respects, the financial position of SR Company as of (at) December 31, 2X12, and the results of its operations and its cash flows for the year then ended in conformity with U.S. generally accepted accounting principles.

> ## Note
>
> If the departure from GAAP is adequately disclosed in the notes to the financial statements, the explanatory paragraph may be shortened by referring to the applicable note (see Example 10.8, Explanatory Paragraph).

Example 10.8   Explanatory Paragraph

As more fully described in Note X to the financial statements, the Company has excluded certain lease obligations from property and debt in the accompanying balance sheet. In my (our) opinion, generally accepted accounting principles require that such obligations be included in the balance sheet.

What if an uncertainty exists?

Uncertainties involve matters that are expected to be resolved at a future date, at which time conclusive evidential matter concerning their outcome would be expected to become available. Uncertainties include, but are not limited to, situations pertaining to:

- Loss contingencies resulting from litigation, claims, and assessments
- Substantial doubt about the entity's ability to continue as a going concern for a reasonable period of time (i.e., going-concern uncertainties)

Do I have to modify the audit report for an uncertainty?

In general, management has the responsibility to estimate the effect of future events on financial statements (or determine that an estimate is not reasonably estimable) and to make the required disclosures under generally accepted accounting principles.

If the auditor concludes that sufficient evidential matter supports management's assertions about the nature of matters involving uncertainties (other than going-concern uncertainties) and their financial statement presentation and disclosure, then a standard unqualified opinion is normally warranted; accordingly, no modification is necessary.

If sufficient evidential matter concerning uncertainties exists but is not made available to the auditor, then a scope limitation exists. As is generally the case with a scope limitation, the auditor should modify the audit report by issuing a qualified opinion or a disclaimer of opinion.

If the auditor concludes that financial statements are materially misstated due to GAAP departures concerning uncertainties, then he or she should modify the audit report by issuing a qualified or adverse opinion.

Note

For a discussion of going-concern uncertainties, see the summary of SAS 59 in Chapter 12.

Disclaimer of Opinion

When is a disclaimer of opinion issued?

When a severe scope limitation exists and the auditor does not wish to express a qualified opinion, a disclaimer of opinion is warranted. A disclaimer of opinion indicates the practitioner's inability to form an opinion on the fairness of the financial statements.

These are the necessary modifications to the report:

- Modify the introductory paragraph.
- Omit the scope (second) paragraph of the standard report.
- Add an explanatory paragraph describing the reasons why the audit was not in conformity with generally accepted auditing standards.
- In lieu of an opinion paragraph, draft a disclaimer paragraph that includes wording to the effect that "I (We) do not express an opinion on these financial statements."

Example 10.9   Audit Report Containing a Disclaimer of Opinion

Independent Auditor's Report

I was (We were) engaged to audit the accompanying balance sheet of Harold Corporation as of (at) December 31, 2X12, and the related statements of income, retained earnings, and cash flows for the year then ended. These financial statements are the responsibility of the Company's management.

The Company did not make a count of its physical inventory in 2X12, stated in the accompanying financial statements at $_____ . Further, evidence supporting the cost of property and equipment acquired prior to December 31, 2X12, is no longer available. The Company's records do not permit the application of other auditing procedures to inventories or property and equipment.

Since the Company did not take physical inventories and I was (we were) not able to apply other auditing procedures to satisfy myself (ourselves) as to inventory quantities and the cost of property and equipment, the scope of my (our) work was not sufficient to enable me (us) to express, and I (we) do not express, an opinion on these financial statements.

Caution

In disclaiming an opinion, never identify the audit procedures that were actually performed.

Warning

A severe client-imposed scope limitation might warrant withdrawal from the audit engagement. Severe client-imposed scope limitations include the client's refusal to provide a representation letter required under SAS 85 and the client's refusal to send a letter of audit inquiry to the outside legal counsel as required under SAS 12.

Adverse Opinion

When is an adverse opinion warranted?

An adverse opinion should be expressed when financial statements do not present fairly in conformity with GAAP an entity's:

- Financial position
- Results of operations
- Retained earnings
- Cash flows

Issued when financial statements are misleading, the adverse opinion should include these modifications:

- Add a paragraph between the scope and opinion paragraphs disclosing all of the substantive reasons for the issuance of the adverse opinion as well as the principal effects on the financial statements. If the principal effects cannot be reasonably determined, the report should so state.
- Modify the opinion paragraph to indicate that the statements are not presented fairly in conformity with generally accepted accounting principles.

Example 10.10   Report Reflecting the Auditor's Adverse Opinion

Independent Auditor's Report

I (We) have audited the accompanying balance sheet of X Company as of (at) December 31, 2X12, and the related statements of income, retained earnings, and cash flows for the year then ended. These financial statements are the responsibility of the Company's management. My (Our) responsibility is to express an opinion on these financial statements based on my (our) audit.

I (We) conducted my (our) audit in accordance with U.S. generally accepted auditing standards. Those standards require that we plan and perform the audit to obtain reasonable assurance about whether the financial statements are free of material misstatement. An audit includes examining, on a test basis, evidence supporting the amounts and disclosures in the financial statements. An audit also includes assessing the accounting principles used and significant estimates made by management, as well as evaluating the overall financial statement presentation. I (We) believe that my (our) audit provides a reasonable basis for my (our) opinion.

In my (our) opinion, because of the effects of the matters discussed in the preceding paragraph, the financial statements referred to above do not present fairly, in conformity with U.S. generally accepted accounting principles, the financial position of X Company as of December 31, 2X12, or the results of its operations and its cash flows for the year then ended.

As discussed in Note X to the financial statements, the Company carries its property, plant, and equipment accounts at appraisal values, and provides depreciation on the basis of such values. Further, the Company does not provide for income taxes with respect to differences between financial income and taxable income arising because of the use, for income tax purposes, of the installment method of reporting gross profit from certain types of sales. Generally accepted accounting principles, in my (our) opinion, require that property, plant, and equipment be stated at an amount not in excess of cost, reduced by depreciation based on such amount, and that deferred income taxes be provided. Because of the departures from generally accepted accounting principles identified above, as of December 31, 2X12, inventories have been increased $_____ by inclusion in manufacturing overhead of depreciation in excess of that based on cost; property, plant, and equipment, less accumulated depreciation, is carried at $_____ in excess of an amount based on the cost to the Company; and allocated income tax of $_____ has not been recorded; the result is an increase of $_____ in retained earnings and in appraisal surplus of _____. For the year ended December 31, 2X12, cost of goods sold has been increased $_____ because of the effects of the depreciation accounting referred to above, and deferred income taxes of $_____ have not been provided, resulting in an increase in net income and earnings per share of $_____ and $_____, respectively.

CHAPTER 11

Compilation, Review, and Other Reporting Services

A practitioner whose client's stock is not publicly traded is often requested to compile or review financial statements. When an accountant is involved in the compilation or review of a client's financial statements, he or she is generally required to issue a report at the conclusion of the engagement.

Compilation and review services represent two types of engagements that practitioners face daily. This chapter explains these services and the reporting practices associated with them, in addition to special reports generally associated with audit engagements.

Engagements involving prospective financial statements and attestation services, which are also discussed, should be viewed by the practitioner as an important area for practice expansion.

Compilation of Financial Statements

What is a compilation of financial statements?

A compilation of financial statements is an engagement designed to assist management in presenting in the form of financial statements information that is the representation of management. A key characteristic of a compilation is that *no opinion* or any other form of assurance is expressed on the fairness of the presentation of the financial statements. Accordingly, the accountant is not required to make inquiries or perform procedures to verify or review management-furnished information. A compilation engagement is an attest engagement, because it requires independence. It is not, however, an assurance engagement, because it is not designed to enhance the degree of confidence users have in the financial statements.

How is a compilation conducted?

Inasmuch as a compilation engagement does not result in the expression of any assurance, the procedures to be performed are quite limited.

Recommendation: To facilitate the compilation engagement and to demonstrate that due care has been exercised, the practitioner should follow these 13 steps:

1. Establish an understanding with management. The understanding should be documented through a written communication with management (i.e., an engagement letter).

Note

The understanding should include, among other engagement-specific provisions, that:

- The objective of a compilation is to assist management in presenting financial information in the form of financial statements.
- The accountant uses management representations but does not obtain any assurance that no material modifications should be made in order for the financial statements to be in conformity with the applicable financial reporting framework.
- The preparation and fair presentation of the financial statements are management's responsibilities.
- Establishing and maintaining effective internal control over financial reporting are management's responsibilities.
- The prevention and detection of fraud are management's responsibilities.
- Compliance with laws and regulations is management's responsibility.
- All financial records will be made available to the accountant.
- Since a compilation is significantly less in scope than an audit or review, no opinion or any other form of assurance on the financial statements will be provided in a compilation.
- The engagement cannot be relied on to disclose error, fraud, or illegal acts.
- The accountant will communicate to the appropriate level of management evidence or information that comes to his or her attention indicating the possibility of fraud or illegal acts (unless clearly inconsequential).
- If independence is impaired, the compilation report will require modification.
- If applicable, management acknowledges that the financial statements are not expected to be used and not to be used by any third party.

2. Obtain an understanding of the industry in which the client operates. Specifically, research the accounting principles and practices applicable to the client's industry. Further, obtain knowledge of the client's business, including its organization, its unique operating characteristics, and the nature of its assets, liabilities, revenues, and expenses.
3. Obtain a general understanding of the flow and nature of the transactions underlying the client's financial records.
4. Obtain a general understanding of the client's accounting records.
5. Inquire about the stated qualifications of the client's accounting personnel.

6. Determine the applicable financial reporting framework—generally accepted accounting principles (GAAP) or another comprehensive basis of accounting (e.g., cash basis, modified cash basis, income tax basis, etc.).

7. Determine the necessity of performing these accounting services:
   - Adjustment of client books
   - Consultation with appropriate personnel regarding accounting-related matters
   - Bookkeeping services when the client's manual or automated bookkeeping does not produce financial statements as the end result

8. Although it is not required to verify or corroborate representations made by management and personnel, obtain satisfaction as to representations that appear incorrect, incomplete, or otherwise unsatisfactory. If the accountant has communicated to management evidence or information indicating the possibility of fraud or illegal acts, he or she should (1) request that management consider the possible effect(s) on the financial statements and (2) consider the effect, if any, on the compilation report to be issued.

9. When financial statements depart from the basis of accounting in use and the client refuses to make the necessary adjustments, modify the accountant's report to disclose this fact.

10. Read the financial statements to determine that the statements are free from obvious material errors. *Examples:* Mathematical mistakes, omission of relevant disclosures, and departures from relevant accounting principles.

11. If a higher level of service was performed (e.g., a review or an audit), issue the report that relates to the highest level of service performed.

12. If the accountant is not independent with respect to the client, indicate this fact and, if desired, the reasons for it in the compilation report.

13. Document the compilation engagement.

What reports can be issued at the conclusion of a compilation engagement?

At the conclusion of a compilation engagement in which the financial statements are reasonably expected to be used by a third party, the accountant should issue a report that includes:

- A title; for example, "Accountant's Compilation Report" or "Independent Accountant's Compilation Report"
- An addressee
- An *introductory paragraph* that:
  - Identifies the entity
  - States that the financial statements have been compiled
  - Identifies the financial statements
  - Specifies the date or period covered by the financial statements
  - Indicates that the accountant has not audited or reviewed the financial statements and, accordingly, no opinion or any other form of assurance is expressed as to whether the financial statements are in conformity with the applicable financial reporting framework
- A paragraph that states management's responsibility for the preparation and fair presentation of the financial statements in accordance with the applicable financial reporting framework

- A paragraph that states that:
  - The accountant is responsible for conducting the compilation in accordance with Statements on Standards for Accounting and Review Services issued by the American Institute of Certified Public Accountants.
  - The objective of a compilation is to assist management in presenting financial information in the form of financial statements without obtaining or providing any assurance that no material modifications should be made to the financial statements.
- The manual or printed signature of the accountant
- The date of the compilation report, which should coincide with the date on which the compilation was completed

---

Warning

The compilation report should not describe the actual compilation procedures performed.

Note

Each page of the financial statements should be labeled "See accountant's compilation report" or "See independent accountant's compilation report."

What if the financial statements are prepared in accordance with some other comprehensive basis of accounting?

Other comprehensive basis of accounting (OCBOA) financial statements are considered appropriate in form only if the financial statements include both a description of the OCBOA and informative disclosures that include a summary of significant accounting policies and description of the differences between GAAP and OCBOA.

Example 11.1   Standard Compilation Report

Accountant's Compilation Report

[*Appropriate salutation*]

I (We) have compiled the accompanying balance sheet of XYZ Company as of December 31, 2X12, and the related statements of income, retained earnings, and cash flows for the year then ended. I (We) have not audited or reviewed the accompanying financial statements and, accordingly, do not express an opinion or provide any assurance about whether the financial statements are in accordance with accounting principles generally accepted in the United States of America.

Management (Owners) is (are) responsible for the preparation and fair presentation of the financial statements in accordance with accounting principles generally accepted in the United States of America and for designing, implementing, and maintaining internal control relevant to the preparation and fair presentation of the financial statements.

My (Our) responsibility is to conduct the compilation in accordance with Statements on Standards for Accounting and Review Services issued by the American Institute of Certified Public Accountants. The objective of a compilation is to assist management in presenting financial information in the form of financial statements without undertaking to obtain or provide any assurance that there are no material modifications that should be made to the financial statements.

[*Signature of accounting firm or accountant, as appropriate*]
[*Date*]

Note

It is permissible to compile and report on only one of the financial statements normally included in the complete set.

When should the standard compilation report be modified?

Seven circumstances warrant modification of the standard compilation report:

1. *Omission of substantially all disclosures.* When financial statements that purport to be in conformity with an applicable financial reporting framework lack the necessary disclosures (e.g., notes to the financial statements, parenthetical comments on the face of the statements, etc.), the accountant should add this paragraph immediately after the standard three-paragraph report:

   Management has elected to omit substantially all of the disclosures required by accounting principles generally accepted in the United States of America. If the omitted disclosures were included in the financial statements, they might influence the user's conclusions about the company's financial position, results of operations, and cash flows. Accordingly, these financial statements are not designed for those who are not informed about such matters.

> **Note**
>
> If the financial statements are based on an OCBOA, the additional paragraph should be modified. For example, if an income tax basis of accounting was used, the wording should be as follows:
>
> *Management has elected to omit substantially all of the disclosures ordinarily included in financial statements prepared in accordance with the income tax basis of accounting. If the omitted disclosures were included in the financial statements, they might influence the user's conclusions about the company's assets, liabilities, equity, revenue, and expenses. Accordingly, these financial statements are not designed for those who are not informed about such matters.*

2. *Selected information presented.* When notes to the financial statements include only a few matters, the presentation of this information should be labeled "Selected Information—Substantially All of the Disclosures Required by [*identify the applicable financial reporting framework*] Are Not Included." The compilation report should include the additional paragraph just described.
3. *Omission of the statement of cash flows.* See the first departure. Modify the first sentence of the additional paragraph to reflect the omission of either the statement of cash flows alone or the statement of cash flows and substantially all of the required disclosures. Further, the introductory paragraph should omit any reference to the statement of cash flows.

> **Note**
>
> Financial statements that are prepared using a comprehensive basis of accounting other than GAAP do not *require* presentation of a statement of cash flows.

4. *Lack of independence.* While an accountant who is not independent with respect to a client's financial statements may issue a compilation report, he or she must state in the report that "I am (We are) not independent with respect to X Company." *Caution:* The accountant is permitted, but not required, to disclose the reason(s) for the lack of independence. If the accountant elects to do so, however, *all* reasons for the impairment of independence must be disclosed.
5. *Departure from the applicable financial reporting framework.* Although the accountant is under no obligation to search for departures from the applicable financial reporting framework, such departures, if uncovered and not corrected, must be disclosed in the compilation report. This is accomplished by adding a separate paragraph, after the third paragraph of the standard report, that discloses the departures and either the principal effects of the departures on the financial statements or a statement that such effects have not been determined.

6. *Emphasis of a matter.* The account is permitted to add one or more paragraphs to the standards compilation report in order to emphasize one or more matters that are already disclosed in the financial statements.

Note

Matters that are often emphasized include uncertainties, significant related-party transactions, and subsequent events.

---

7. *Supplementary information.* When both the basic financial statements and other data presented for supplementary analysis purposes are compiled, the compilation report should refer to the other data. Alternatively, the accountant may issue a separate report on the supplementary data that states that (1) the other data are presented for supplementary analysis purposes only, (2) the information has been compiled without audit or review from information that is the representation of management, and (3) no opinion of any other assurance on the data is expressed.

What communications are necessary when an accountant compiles financial statements that are not expected to be used by a third party?

If an accountant submits unaudited financial statements to a client that are not expected to be used by a third party, a decision must be made either to (1) issue a compilation report or (2) document an understanding with the client in an engagement letter, preferably signed by management, regarding the services to be performed and the limitations on the use of the financial statements.

What statements or descriptions should be included in the written understanding regarding an engagement in which a compilation report is not issued?

The written understanding should include these statements or descriptions:

- The nature and limitations of the engagement.
- The definition of a compilation.
- The financial statements will not be audited or reviewed.
- No opinion or any other form of assurance about the financial statements will be expressed.
- Management possesses knowledge of the nature of the procedures performed, and the basis of accounting and assumptions utilized in the preparation of the financial statements.
- Acknowledgment of management's representation and agreement that the financial statements are not to be used by any third party.
- The engagement cannot be relied on to disclose errors, illegal acts, or fraud.

- Material departures from the applicable financial reporting framework may exist, and their related financial statement effects may not be disclosed.
- If applicable, substantially all disclosures (and the statement of cash flows, if applicable) required by the applicable financial reporting framework may be omitted.
- The accountant's lack of independence, if applicable.
- Reference to supplementary information, if applicable.

What action is necessary if the accountant does not establish an understanding with the client?

An accountant should not accept or perform the engagement if he or she fails to establish an understanding with the client.

If the accountant decides not to issue a compilation report on financial statements not expected to be used by third parties, do the financial statements require any special marking?

Each page of the financial statements that are not accompanied by a compilation report and that are not expected to be used by third parties should be marked "Restricted for management's use only" or "Solely for the information and use by the management of [*name of entity*] and not intended to be and should not be used by any other party."

What should an accountant do if he or she becomes aware that the "restricted" financial statements have been distributed to third parties?

If the accountant becomes aware that the "restricted" financial statements have been distributed to third parties, then he or she should discuss the matter with the client and request the return of the financial statements. The client's failure to comply should cause the accountant to notify known third parties that the financial statements are not intended for their use.

Review of Financial Statements

What constitutes a review of financial statements?

A review is a step up in the level of service from a compilation engagement, since some form of assurance on the financial statements will be expressed.

Review procedures generally are limited to inquiries of company personnel and analytical procedures applied to financial data. These provide the accountant with a reasonable basis for expressing limited assurance that no material modifications need be made to the financial statements in order for them to be in conformity with the applicable financial reporting framework.

Since review procedures do not include consideration of the client's internal control or the gathering of audit evidence, an opinion may not be expressed. In a review, the practitioner may identify matters that significantly affect the financial statements. However, the review engagement may not be relied on to disclose all significant matters that would surface in an audit.

Accumulating review evidence is an integral part of a review engagement. It should be noted that a review engagement is both an attest engagement and an assurance engagement.

What are the steps in a review engagement?

The steps in a review engagement should be tailored to each engagement, but generally include these eight:

1. Establish an understanding with management. The understanding should be documented through a written communication with management (i.e., an engagement letter).

Note

The understanding should include, among other engagement-specific provisions, that:

- The objective of a review is to obtain limited assurance that there are no material modifications that should be made to the financial statements in order for them to be in conformity with the applicable financial reporting framework.
- The preparation and fair presentation of the financial statements are management's responsibilities.
- Establishing and maintaining effective internal control over financial reporting are management's responsibilities.
- The prevention and detection of fraud are management's responsibilities.
- Compliance with laws and regulations is management's responsibility.
- All financial records will be made available to the accountant.
- Management will provide a representation letter to the accountant at the conclusion of the engagement.
- The accountant will communicate to the appropriate level of management evidence or information that comes to his or her attention indicating the possibility of fraud or illegal acts (unless clearly inconsequential).
- The review is to be performed in accordance with Statements on Standards for Accounting and Review Services issued by the American Institute of Certified Public Accountants.
- A review is substantially less in scope than an audit, the objective of which is to express an opinion on the financial statement presentation. Accordingly, no opinion will be expressed.

---

2. Obtain an understanding of the industry in which the client operates. Specifically, research the accounting principles and practices applicable to the client's industry.

3. Obtain a general understanding of:
   - The client's organization
   - The client's operating characteristics
   - The nature of the client's assets, liabilities, equity, revenues, and expenses
   - The client's production, distribution, and compensation methods
   - The types of products and services offered
   - The client's operating locations
   - Any material related-party transactions
4. Perform analytical procedures. Analytical procedures should be performed in order to identify and provide a basis for inquiries about unusual relationships and individual items that may be indicative of material misstatement.

   An accountant should:
   - Develop expectations by identifying and using plausible relationships that are reasonably expected to exist based on the accountant's understanding of the entity and the industry in which the entity operates.
   - Compare recorded amounts, or ratios developed from recorded amounts, to accountant-developed expectations.

Recommendation

To identify unusual relationships and individual items, an accountant should consider performing these analytical procedures:

- Compare current-period financial information with that of prior periods.
- Compare current-period financial information with anticipated results. *Example:* Budgeted and forecasted amounts.
- Compare current financial information with pertinent nonfinancial information. *Example:* Number of units of inventory to square footage of a storage facility.
- Compare current-period financial ratios and other indicators with prior-period expectations. *Examples:* Current ratio, gross margin, accounts receivable turnover, and debt to equity.
- Compare current-period financial ratios and other indicators to industry norms.
- Compare relationships among current-period financial statement elements with corresponding prior-period relationships. *Example:* A specific expense item as a percentage of sales.

Analytical procedures may also encompass statistical techniques, including trend analysis and regression analysis.

5. Consider asking management personnel who have financial and accounting oversight about:
   - Whether the financial statements have been prepared in conformity with GAAP or an OCBOA on a consistent basis

- The accounting principles and practices and the methods followed in applying them and procedures for recording, classifying, and summarizing transactions, and accumulating information relevant to financial statement disclosure
- Unusual or complex situations that may affect the financial statements
- Significant transactions occurring or recognized near the end of the accounting period
- Uncorrected misstatements identified during the previous engagement
- Questions that have surfaced during the application of review procedures
- Subsequent events that could have a material effect on the financial statements
- Their knowledge of any fraud or suspected fraud affecting the entity involving management or others that could have a material effect on the financial statements—for example, communications received from employees, former employees, or others
- Significant journal entries and other adjustments
- Communications from regulatory agencies
- Actions taken at meetings of shareholders, the board of directors, committees of the board of directors, or comparable meetings that may affect the financial statements

6. Perform other review procedures, including:
    - Reading the financial statements to consider, on the basis of information coming to the accountant's attention, whether the financial statements appear to conform with the applicable financial reporting framework
    - Obtaining reports from other accountants, if any, who have been engaged to audit or review the financial statements of significant components of the reporting entity, its subsidiaries, and other investees
    - Communicating to the appropriate level of management any material errors as well as evidence or information indicating the possibility of fraud or illegal acts (unless clearly inconsequential)
    - Requesting that management consider the possible effect(s) on the financial statements of evidence or information indicating the possibility of fraud or illegal acts communicated by the accountant
    - Considering the effect, if any, on the review report to be issued of the evidence or information indicating the possibility of fraud or illegal acts communicated by the accountant
7. Obtain a representation letter from management.
8. Document the review engagement.

Are illustrative inquiries available?

The appendix to Statement on Standards for Accounting and Review Services (SSARS) No. 10 contains guidance on the inquiries applicable to review engagements.

The list of illustrative inquiries presented in Exhibit 11.1 (by permission of the American Institute of Certified Public Accountants) should not be construed as a mandatory work program or all-inclusive checklist. The practitioner must be guided by professional judgment in tailoring inquiries and procedures to the needs of the client given all facts and circumstances.

EXHIBIT 11.1   Illustrative Inquiries

1. General
    a. Have there been any changes in the entity's business activities?
    b. Are there any unusual or complex situations that may have an effect on the financial statements (for example, business combinations, restructuring plans, or litigation)?
    c. What procedures are in place related to recording, classifying, and summarizing transactions and accumulating information related to financial statement disclosures?
    d. Have the financial statements been prepared in conformity with generally accepted accounting principles or, if appropriate, a comprehensive basis of accounting other than generally accepted accounting principles? Have there been any changes in accounting principles and methods of applying those principles?
    e. Have there been any instances of fraud or illegal acts within the entity?
    f. Have there been any allegations or suspicions that fraud or illegal acts might have occurred or might be occurring within the entity? If so, where and how?
    g. Are any entities, other than the reporting entity, commonly controlled by the owners? If so, has an evaluation been performed to determine whether those other entities should be consolidated into the financial statements of the reporting entity?
    h. Are there any entities other than the reporting entity in which the owners have significant investments (for example, variable interest entities)? If so, has an evaluation been performed to determine whether the reporting entity is the primary beneficiary related to the activities of these other entities?
    i. Have any significant transactions occurred or been recognized near the end of the reporting period?
2. Cash and Cash Equivalents
    a. Is the entity's policy regarding the composition of cash and cash equivalents in accordance with Financial Accounting Standards Board Statement of Financial Accounting Standards No. 95, Statement of Cash Flows (paragraphs 7–10)? Has the policy been applied on a consistent basis?
    b. Are all cash and cash equivalents accounts reconciled on a timely basis?
    c. Have old or unusual reconciling items between bank balances and book balances been reviewed and adjustments made where necessary?
    d. Has there been a proper cutoff of cash receipts and disbursements?
    e. Has a reconciliation of intercompany transfers been prepared?
    f. Have checks written but not mailed as of the financial statement date been properly reclassified into the liability section of the balance sheet?
    g. Have material bank overdrafts been properly reclassified into the liability section of the balance sheet?
    h. Are there compensating balances or other restrictions on the availability of cash and cash equivalents balances? If so, has consideration been given to reclassifying these amounts as noncurrent assets?
    i. Have cash funds been counted and reconciled with control accounts?
3. Receivables
    a. Has an adequate allowance for doubtful accounts been properly reflected in the financial statements?
    b. Have uncollectible receivables been written off through a charge against the allowance account or earnings?
    c. Has interest earned on receivables been properly reflected in the financial statements?
    d. Has there been a proper cutoff of sales transactions?
    e. Are there receivables from employees or other related parties? Have receivables from owners been evaluated to determine if they should be reflected in the equity section (rather than the asset section) of the balance sheet?

EXHIBIT 11.1 *(Continued)*

    f. Are any receivables pledged, discounted, or factored? Are recourse provisions properly reflected in the financial statements?

    g. Have receivables been properly classified between current and noncurrent?

    h. Have there been significant numbers of sales returns or credit memoranda issued subsequent to the balance sheet date?

    i. Is the accounts receivable subsidiary ledger reconciled to the general ledger account balance on a regular basis?

4. Inventory

    a. Are physical inventory counts performed on a regular basis, including at the end of the reporting period? Are the count procedures adequate to ensure an appropriate count? If not, how have amounts related to inventories been determined for purposes of financial statement presentation? If so, what procedures were used to take the latest physical inventory and what date was that inventory taken?

    b. Have general ledger control accounts been adjusted to agree with the physical inventory count? If so, were the adjustments significant?

    c. If the physical inventory counts were taken at a date other than the balance sheet date, what procedures were used to determine changes in inventory between the date of the physical inventory counts and the balance sheet date?

    d. Were consignments in or out considered in taking physical inventories?

    e. What is the basis of valuing inventory for purposes of financial statement presentation?

    f. Does inventory cost include material, labor, and overhead where applicable?

    g. Has inventory been reviewed for obsolescence or cost in excess of net realizable value? If so, how are these costs reflected in the financial statements?

    h. Have proper cutoffs of purchases, goods in transit, and returned goods been made?

    i. Are there any inventory encumbrances?

    j. Is scrap inventoried and controlled?

5. Prepaid Expenses

    a. What is the nature of the amounts included in prepaid expenses?

    b. How are these amounts being amortized?

6. Investments

    a. What is the basis of accounting for investments reported in the financial statements (for example, securities, joint ventures, or closely held businesses)?

    b. Are derivative instruments properly measured and disclosed in the financial statements? If those derivatives are utilized in hedge transactions, have the documentation or assessment requirements related to hedge accounting been met?

    c. Are investments in marketable debt and equity securities properly classified as trading, available-for-sale, and held-to-maturity?

    d. How were fair values of the reported investments determined? Have unrealized gains and losses been properly reported in the financial statements?

    e. If the fair values of marketable debt and equity securities are less than cost, have the declines in value been evaluated to determine whether the declines are other than temporary?

    f. For any debt securities classified as held-to-maturity, does management have the positive ability and intent to hold the securities until they mature? If so, have those debt securities been properly measured?

    g. Have gains and losses related to disposal of investments been properly reflected in the financial statements?

    h. How was investment income determined? Is investment income properly reflected in the financial statements?

(Continued)

EXHIBIT 11.1 *(Continued)*

    i. Has appropriate consideration been given to the classification of investments between current and noncurrent?

    j. For investments made by the reporting entity, have consolidation, equity, or cost method accounting requirements been considered?

    k. Are any investments encumbered?

7. Property and Equipment

    a. Are property and equipment items properly stated at depreciated cost or other proper value?

    b. When was the last time a physical inventory of property and equipment was taken?

    c. Are all items reflected in property and equipment held for use? If not, have items that are held for sale been properly reclassified from property and equipment?

    d. Have gains or losses on disposal of property and equipment been properly reflected in the financial statements?

    e. What are the criteria for capitalization of property and equipment? Have the criteria been consistently and appropriately applied?

    f. Are repairs and maintenance costs properly reflected as an expense in the income statement?

    g. What depreciation methods and rates are utilized in the financial statements? Are these methods and rates appropriate and applied on a consistent basis?

    h. Are there any unrecorded additions, retirements, abandonments, sales, or trade-ins?

    i. Does the entity have any material lease agreements? If so, have those agreements been properly evaluated for financial statement presentation purposes?

    j. Are there any asset retirement obligations associated with tangible long-lived assets? If so, has the recorded amount of the related asset been increased because of the obligation and is the liability properly reflected in the liability section of the balance sheet?

    k. Has the entity constructed any of its property and equipment items? If so, have all components of cost been reflected in measuring these items for purposes of financial statement presentation, including, but not limited to, capitalized interest?

    l. Has there been any significant impairment in value of property and equipment items? If so, has any impairment loss been properly reflected in the financial statements?

    m. Are any property and equipment items mortgaged or otherwise encumbered? If so, are these mortgages and encumbrances properly reflected in the financial statements?

8. Intangibles and Other Assets

    a. What is the nature of the amounts included in other assets?

    b. Do these assets represent costs that will benefit future periods? What is the amortization policy related to these assets? Is this policy appropriate?

    c. Have other assets been properly classified between current and noncurrent?

    d. Are intangible assets with finite lives being appropriately amortized?

    e. Are the costs associated with computer software properly reflected as intangible assets (rather than property and equipment) in the financial statements?

    f. Are the costs associated with goodwill (and other intangible assets with indefinite lives) properly reflected as intangible assets in the financial statements? Has amortization ceased related to these assets?

    g. Has there been any significant impairment in value of these assets? If so, has any impairment loss been properly reflected in the financial statements?

    h. Are any of these assets mortgaged or otherwise encumbered?

9. Accounts and Short-Term Notes Payable and Accrued Liabilities

    a. Have all payables been reflected in the financial statements?

    b. Are loans from financial institutions and other short-term liabilities properly classified in the financial statements?

EXHIBIT 11.1   *(Continued)*

   c. Have all significant accruals (for example, payroll, interest, provisions for pension and profit-sharing plans, or other postretirement benefit obligations) been properly reflected in the financial statements?

   d. Has a liability for employees' compensation for future absences been properly accrued and disclosed in the financial statements?

   e. Are any liabilities collateralized or subordinated? If so, are those liabilities disclosed in the financial statements?

   f. Are there any payables to employees and related parties?

10. Long-Term Liabilities

   a. Are the terms and other provisions of long-term liability agreements properly disclosed in the financial statements?

   b. Have liabilities been properly classified between current and noncurrent?

   c. Has interest expense been properly accrued and reflected in the financial statements?

   d. Is the company in compliance with loan covenants and agreements? If not, is the noncompliance properly disclosed in the financial statements?

   e. If so, are these facts disclosed in the financial statements?

   f. Are there any obligations that, by their terms, are due on demand within one year from the balance sheet date? If so, have these obligations been properly reclassified into the current liability section of the balance sheet?

11. Income and Other Taxes

   a. Do the financial statements reflect an appropriate provision for current and prior-year federal income taxes payable?

   b. Have any assessments or reassessments been received? Are there tax authority examinations in process?

   c. Are there any temporary differences between book and tax amounts? If so, have deferred taxes on these differences been properly reflected in the financial statements?

   d. Do the financial statements reflect an appropriate provision for taxes other than income taxes (for example, franchise, sales)?

   e. Have all required tax payments been made on a timely basis?

12. Other Liabilities, Contingencies, and Commitments

   a. What is the nature of the amounts included in other liabilities?

   b. Have other liabilities been properly classified between current and noncurrent?

   c. Are there any guarantees, whether written or verbal, whereby the entity must stand ready to perform or is contingently liable related to the guarantee? If so, are these guarantees properly reflected in the financial statements?

   d. Are there any contingent liabilities (for example, discounted notes, drafts, endorsements, warranties, litigation, and unsettled asserted claims)? Are there any potential unasserted claims? Are these contingent liabilities, claims, and assessments properly measured and disclosed in the financial statements?

   e. Are there any material contractual obligations for construction or purchase of property and equipment and/or any commitments or options to purchase or sell company securities? If so, are these facts clearly disclosed in the financial statements?

   f. Is the entity responsible for any environmental remediation liability? If so, is this liability properly measured and disclosed in the financial statements?

   g. Does the entity have any agreement to repurchase items that previously were sold? If so, have the repurchase agreements been taken into account in determining the appropriate measurements and disclosures in the financial statements?

(Continued)

EXHIBIT 11.1   (*Continued*)

    h. Does the entity have any sales commitments at prices expected to result in a loss at the consummation of the sale? If so, are these commitments properly reflected in the financial statements?

    i. Are there any violations, or possible violations, of laws or regulations the effects of which should be considered for financial statement accrual or disclosure?

13. Equity

    a. What is the nature of any changes in equity accounts during each reporting period?

    b. What classes of stock (other ownership interests) have been authorized?

    c. What is the par or stated value of the various classes of stock (other ownership interests)?

    d. Do amounts of outstanding shares of stock (other ownership interests) agree with subsidiary records?

    e. Have pertinent rights and privileges of ownership interests been properly disclosed in the financial statements?

    f. Does the entity have any mandatorily redeemable ownership interests? If so, have these ownership interests been evaluated so that a proper determination has been made related to whether these ownership interests should be measured and reclassified to the liability section of the balance sheet? Are redemption features associated with ownership interests clearly disclosed in the financial statements?

    g. Have dividend (distribution) and liquidation preferences related to ownership interests been properly disclosed in the financial statements?

    h. Do disclosures related to ownership interests include any applicable call provisions (prices and dates), conversion provisions (prices and rates), unusual voting rights, significant terms of contracts to issue additional ownership interests, or any other unusual features associated with the ownership interests?

    i. Are syndication fees properly reflected in the financial statements as a reduction of equity (rather than an asset)?

    j. Have any stock options or other stock compensation awards been granted to employees or others? If so, are these options or awards properly measured and disclosed in the financial statements?

    k. Has the entity made any acquisitions of its own stock? If so, are the amounts associated with these reacquired shares properly reflected in the financial statements as a reduction in equity? Is the presentation in accordance with applicable state laws?

    l. Are there any restrictions or appropriations on retained earnings or other capital accounts? If so, are these restrictions or appropriations properly reflected in the financial statements?

14. Revenue and Expenses

    a. What is the entity's revenue recognition policy? Is the policy appropriate? Has the policy been consistently applied and appropriately disclosed?

    b. Are revenues from sales of products and rendering of services recognized in the appropriate reporting period (that is, when the products have been delivered and when the services have been performed)?

    c. Were any sales recorded under a "bill and hold" arrangement? If yes, have the criteria been met to record the transaction as a sale?

    d. Are purchases and expenses recognized in the appropriate reporting period (that is, matched against revenue) and properly classified in the financial statements?

    e. Do the financial statements include discontinued operations items that might be considered extraordinary? If so, are amounts associated with discontinued operations, extraordinary items, or both properly displayed in the income statement?

EXHIBIT 11.1 *(Continued)*

---

   f. Does the entity have any gains or losses that would necessitate the display of comprehensive income (for example, gains/losses on available-for-sale securities or cash flow hedge derivatives)? If so, have these items been properly displayed within comprehensive income (rather than included in the determination of net income)?

15. Other

   a. Have events occurred subsequent to the balance sheet date that would require adjustment to, or disclosure in, the financial statements?

   b. Have actions taken at stockholders, board of directors, committees of directors, or comparable meetings that affect the financial statements been reflected in the financial statements?

   c. Are significant estimates and material concentrations (for example, customers or suppliers) properly disclosed in the financial statements?

   d. Are there plans or intentions that may materially affect the carrying amounts or classification of assets and liabilities reflected in the financial statements?

   e. Have there been material transactions between or among related parties (for example, sales, purchases, loans, or leasing arrangements)? If so, are these transactions properly disclosed in the financial statements?

   f. Are there uncertainties that could have a material impact on the financial statements? Is there any change in the status of previously disclosed material uncertainties? Are all uncertainties, including going-concern matters, that could have a material impact on the financial statements properly disclosed in the financial statements?

   g. Are barter or other nonmonetary transactions properly recorded and disclosed?

Presented by permission of the American Institute of Certified Public Accountants.

What action should the accountant take if incorrect, incomplete, or otherwise unsatisfactory information comes to his or her attention?

If such instances arise, the accountant should:

- Request that management consider the effects of such matters on the financial statements.
- Consider the effect of management's response on the accountant's ability to express limited assurance.
- Consider the need to perform additional review procedures.

What should be included in the representation letter obtained from management?

It is important that the representation letter obtained from management cover all financial statements and periods that the accountant is reporting on. Although the specific items to be addressed in the representation letter will vary depending on the circumstances of the engagement and the applicable financial reporting framework, representations pertaining to GAAP financial statements should relate to:

- Management's acknowledgment of its responsibility for the fairness of the financial statement presentation

- Management's belief that the financial statements are fairly presented in conformity with GAAP
- Management's acknowledgment of its responsibility for the prevention and detection of fraud
- Knowledge of any fraud or suspected fraud involving members of management or others that could materially affect the financial statements, including communications received from current or former employees or others
- Management's full and truthful response to all accountant inquiries
- Completeness of information
- Subsequent events

In general, the representation letter should be (1) dated no earlier than the date of the accountant's review report and (2) signed by the chief executive officer and chief financial officer. In the event that the current management team is different from the management team of prior periods on which the accountant is reporting on a comparative basis, the current management team is responsible for all of the representations.

Accountant's Consideration of Obtaining an Updating Representation Letter from Management

When should I consider obtaining an updating representation letter from management?

The accountant should consider obtaining an updating representation letter from management when:

- The accountant obtains a representation letter after completion of the review procedures but does not issue the review report for a significant period of time thereafter.
- A material subsequent event occurs after the completion of the review procedures.
- A predecessor accountant is requested by a former client to reissue his or her report on the financial statements of a prior period that are to be presented on a comparative basis with reviewed financial statements of a subsequent period.

What additional information should be included in the updating representation letter?

The updating management representation letter should state whether:

- Information has come to management's attention that would cause management to believe that modifications should be made to previous representations.
- Events have occurred subsequent to the balance sheet date of the latest financial statements reported on that would require adjustment to or disclosure in those financial statements.

Documentation in a Review Engagement

What are the documentation requirements applicable to a review engagement?

The form and content of the documentation should be tailored to meet the circumstances of the engagement. A review report may also be supported by other means in addition to the documentation of the review. For example, documentation of a compilation engagement and documentation contained in quality control files may supplement the documentation of the review engagement.

Specifically, the documentation of the review should include:

- The engagement letter
- Significant findings or issues that could result in material misstatement of the financial statements, including actions to address such findings or issues, and the accountant's basis for his or her final conclusion
- The matters covered in the accountant's inquiry
- The analytical procedures performed
- The accountant-developed expectations where significant expectations are not otherwise readily determinable from the documentation of the work performed, and factors considered in the development of those expectations
- Results of the comparison of the expectations to the recorded amounts or ratios developed from recorded amounts
- Additional procedures performed in response to significant unexpected differences arising from analytical procedures and the results of such additional procedures
- Unusual matters identified by the accountant and their disposition
- Oral or written communications to the appropriate level of management concerning fraud or illegal acts that come to the accountant's attention
- The representation letter

Reports on Reviewed Financial Statements

What should the review report contain?

The accountant's review report should include:

- A title that includes the word *independent* (e.g., "Independent Accountant's Review Report")
- An addressee
- An *introductory paragraph* that:
  - Identifies the entity
  - States that the financial statements have been reviewed
  - Identifies the financial statements
  - Specifies the date or period covered by the financial statements
  - Indicates that a review includes primarily performance of analytical procedures and making inquiries of management
  - States that a review is substantially less in scope than an audit, the objective of which is the expression of an opinion, and that no opinion is being expressed

- A paragraph that states management's responsibility for (1) the preparation and fair presentation of the financial statements in accordance with the applicable financial reporting framework and (2) establishing and maintaining effective internal control over financial reporting
- A paragraph that states that
  - The accountant is responsible for conducting the review in accordance with Statements on Standards for Accounting and Review Services issued by the American Institute of Certified Public Accountants
  - That the accountant believes that the results of the review procedures provide a reasonable basis for the review report
- A paragraph that includes the expression of limited assurance
- The manual or printed signature of the accountant
- The date of the review report, which should be no earlier than the date on which the accountant has obtained review evidence sufficient to enable the expression of limited assurance

Warning

The review report should not describe the actual review procedures performed.

Note

Each page of the financial statements should be labeled "See independent accountant's review report."

What if the financial statements are prepared in accordance with an OCBOA?

OCBOA financial statements are considered appropriate in form only if the financial statements include both a description of the OCBOA and informative disclosures that include a summary of significant accounting policies and a description of the differences between GAAP and the OCBOA.

What does a standard review report look like?

Example 11.2   Independent Accountant's Review Report

[*Appropriate salutation*]

I (We) have reviewed the accompanying balance sheet of XYZ Company as of December 31, 2X12, and the related statements of income, retained earnings, and cash flows for the year then ended. A review includes primarily applying analytical procedures to management's (owners') financial data and making inquiries of company management (owners). A review is substantially less in scope than an audit, the objective of which is the expression of an opinion regarding the financial statements as a whole. Accordingly, I (we) do not express such an opinion.

Management (owners) is (are) responsible for the preparation and fair presentation of the financial statements in accordance with accounting principles generally accepted in the United States of America and for designing, implementing, and maintaining internal control relevant to the preparation and fair presentation of the financial statements.

My (Our) responsibility is to conduct the review in accordance with Statements on Standards for Accounting and Review Services issued by the American Institute of Certified Public Accountants. Those standards require me (us) to perform procedures to obtain limited assurance that there are no material modifications that should be made to the financial statements.

I (We) believe that the results of my (our) procedures provide a reasonable basis for our report.

Based on my (our) review, I am (we are) not aware of any material modifications that should be made to the accompanying financial statements in order for them to be in conformity with accounting principles generally accepted in the United States of America.

[*Signature of accounting firm or accountant, as appropriate*]
[*Date*]

What should I be cautious about in review engagements?

If the practitioner is precluded from performing review procedures that he or she considers necessary, then a review report should not be issued. In such circumstances, the accountant might consider issuing a compilation report.

Caution

Professional judgment must be exercised in considering the circumstances that precluded the review report.

Independence is a requirement for the issuance of a review report.

An accountant may undertake an engagement to review less than a complete set of financial statements. *Example:* The practitioner may accept an engagement to review only a client's balance sheet.

Under certain circumstances, a client may request that an accountant who was engaged to perform an audit under generally accepted accounting standards (GAAS) change the engagement to a lower level of service, namely a change to a compilation or a review. Before undertaking the step-down, the accountant should take into consideration:

- The client's reasons for the step-down, including any client-imposed scope limitations
- The extent of any additional procedures to complete the audit engagement
- The cost to the client of performing the additional auditing procedures

When justification exists for the step-down, as in the case of a client who no longer requires an audit report to secure a bank loan because alternative financing was arranged, the accountant's report should not refer to the step-down or to the application of any audit procedures performed. Accordingly, the standard compilation or review report is appropriate.

Caution

If the accountant is precluded from discussing litigation, claims, and assessments with the client's legal counsel because the client refuses to authorize the communication or refuses to furnish a representation letter, then the situation is tantamount to a scope limitation sufficient to preclude the issuance of an opinion. Such scope limitations similarly preclude the accountant from issuing a review or compilation report on the financial statements.

When must the standard report be modified?

DEPARTURES FROM THE APPLICABLE FINANCIAL REPORTING FRAMEWORK   When the accountant becomes aware of a material departure from the applicable financial reporting framework, it is necessary to modify the standard report by:

- Beginning the fourth paragraph with wording such as "Based on my (our) review, with the exception of the matter(s) described in the following paragraph(s), I am (we are) not aware of any material modifications. . . ."
- Presenting an additional paragraph in order to disclose the effects of the departure

In situations in which the principal effects of the departure cannot reasonably be determined, the practitioner should state this in the report.

SUPPLEMENTARY INFORMATION   When the basic financial statements are accompanied by additional information, such as a supporting schedule of selling, general, and administrative expenses, the accountant should indicate the responsibility he or she is taking with respect to this supplementary information. This may be accomplished by presenting either of the following:

1. One report that covers both the basic financial statements and the supplementary information
2. Separate reports on the basic financial statements and the supplementary information

Whichever approach is followed, the report should include a statement that the additional information is presented for the purpose of analysis only and was or was not subjected to the review procedures applicable to the review of the basic financial statements.

Note

If the additional information was reviewed, the report should contain the expression of limited assurance, that is, that the accountant is not aware of any material modifications that should be made to the additional information. If the practitioner did not review the supplementary information, the report should state this fact. In this circumstance, it would be appropriate to state that the additional information was compiled from information that is the representation of management, without audit or review, and that no opinion or any other form of assurance is being expressed.

EMPHASIS OF A MATTER The accountant is permitted to add one or more paragraphs to the standard review report in order to emphasize one or more matters that are already disclosed in the financial statements.

Note

Matters that are often emphasized include uncertainties, significant related-party transactions, and subsequent events.

Restricting the Use of an Accountant's Compilation or Review Report

What is the difference between general-use and restricted-use reports?

General-use reports are those reports issued by the accountant that are not restricted to specified parties. Financial statements prepared in conformity with an applicable financial reporting framework ordinarily are not restricted regarding use.

Restricted-use reports are those reports issued by the accountant that are intended to be used only by one or more specified third parties. A report should be restricted as to use when the subject matter of the report or the presentation being reported on is based on measurement or disclosure criteria contained in contractual agreements or regulatory provisions not in conformity with an applicable financial reporting framework.

What wording should be included in a restricted-use report?

A restricted-use report should include a separate paragraph at the end that includes:

- A statement indicating that the report is intended solely for the information and use of the specified parties.
- An identification of the specified parties to whom use is restricted.
- A statement that the report is not intended to be and should not be used by anyone other than the specified parties. For example:

> *This report is intended solely for the information and use of [the specified parties] and is not intended to be and should not be used by anyone other than these specified parties.*

Consideration of an Entity's Ability to Continue as a Going Concern

What is the accountant's responsibility in a compilation or review engagement concerning an entity's ability to continue as a going concern?

During a compilation or review engagement, the accountant is not required to evaluate whether there is uncertainty as to entity's ability to continue as a going concern. However, during either type of engagement, the accountant may come across evidence or other information indicative of such an uncertainty. If the accountant becomes aware of such an uncertainty, he or she should:

- Request that management consider the possible effects of the uncertainty on the financial statements.
- Consider the reasonableness of management's response.
- If management's response is deemed to be unreasonable or management's financial statement disclosure is considered to be inadequate, treat the situation as a departure from the applicable financial reporting framework and modify the accountant's report accordingly.

Note

The accountant may emphasize uncertainty as to an entity's ability to continue as a going concern in his or her report provided the uncertainty has been disclosed in the financial statements.

Subsequent Events

What is the accountant's responsibility in a compilation or review engagement concerning subsequent events?

During either type of engagement, the accountant is not required to perform procedures to identify subsequent events.

However, during either type of engagement, the accountant may come across evidence or other information indicative of subsequent events. If the accountant becomes aware of subsequent events, he or she should:

- Request that management consider the possible effects of the subsequent events on the financial statements.
- Consider the reasonableness of management's response.
- If management's accounting treatment or financial statement disclosure is considered to be inadequate, treat the situation as a departure from the applicable financial reporting framework and modify the accountant's report accordingly.

Note

The accountant may emphasize subsequent events in his or her report provided the subsequent events have been disclosed in the financial statements.

Subsequent Discovery of Facts Existing at the Date of the Report

What is the accountant's responsibility in a compilation or review engagement concerning subsequent discovery of facts existing at the date of the report?

During either type of engagement, after the date of the accountant's report, the accountant is not required to perform other procedures with respect to the financial statements unless new information comes to his or her attention.

However, subsequent to the date of the compilation or review report, if the accountant becomes aware of facts that may have existed at that date, he or she should take action similar to the action to be taken in an audit situation (see SAS 1 in Chapter 12).

Recommendation

The accountant should consider consulting with his or her legal counsel in such circumstances.

Change in Engagement from Audit or Review to Compilation

What should be done if a client requests a change in engagement from audit or review to compilation?

Before agreeing to a step-down in the level of service, the practitioner should consider:

■ The reason for the client's request

Caution

If the reason for the request is based on a scope restriction imposed by the client or other circumstances, the practitioner should consider withdrawal from the engagement.

■ The additional effort needed to complete the higher level of service
■ The additional cost to complete the additional procedures

Recommendation

If the procedures applicable to the higher level of service are substantially complete or the cost to complete the additional procedures is relatively immaterial, the practitioner should consider completing the higher level of service.

Note

It would be appropriate to agree to a reduced level of service if (1) circumstances change, such that the client no longer requires the higher level of service or (2) the client misunderstood the nature of original service requested.

Warning

If the accountant agrees to a lower level of service, the report that is issued should not refer to the original engagement or any procedures previously performed.

Reporting on Prescribed Forms

How do I report on compiled financial statements included in certain prescribed forms?

A prescribed form is a preprinted form designed and adopted by the body to which it is to be submitted (e.g., forms used by industry trade associations and banks).

Generally, the accountant has no responsibility to advise the designer of the prescribed form of departures from GAAP.

Example 11.3   Accountant's Compilation Report

[Appropriate salutation]

I (We) have compiled the *[identify financial statements, including period covered and the name of entity]* included in the accompanying prescribed form; I (we) have not audited or reviewed the financial statements included in the accompanying prescribed form and, accordingly, do not express an opinion or provide any assurance about whether the financial statements are in accordance with accounting principles generally accepted in the United States of America.

Management (Owners) is (are) responsible for the preparation and fair presentation of the financial statements included in the form prescribed by *[name of body]* in accordance with accounting principles generally accepted in the United States of America and for designing, implementing, and maintaining internal control relevant to the preparation and fair presentation of the financial statements.

My (Our) responsibility is to conduct the compilation in accordance with Statements on Standards for Accounting and Review Services issued by the American Institute of Certified Public Accountants. The objective of compilation is to assist management in presenting financial information in the form of financial statements without undertaking to obtain or provide any assurance that there are no material modifications that should be made to the financial statements.

The financial statements included in the accompanying prescribed form are presented in accordance with the requirements of *[name of body]*, and are not intended to be a presentation in accordance with accounting principles generally accepted in the United States of America.

This report is intended solely for the information and use of *[the specified parties]* and is not intended to be and should not be used by anyone other than these specified parties.

[Signature of accounting firm or accountant, as appropriate]
[Date]

Warning

Do not sign a preprinted report form that does not conform to the reporting standards contained in the Statements on Standards for Accounting and Review Services issued by the American Institute of Certified Public Accountants.

Communication between Successor and Predecessor Accountants

If I am a successor accountant, do I have a responsibility to communicate with the predecessor accountant in either a compilation or a review engagement?

The successor accountant must decide whether to communicate with the predecessor accountant regarding acceptance of a compilation or review engagement. If the successor decides to contact the predecessor, after permission is granted by the client to both the successor and the predecessor, inquiry may be made about:

- Facts that bear on the integrity of management
- Disagreements about accounting principles
- Disagreements about the performance of relevant procedures
- Cooperation of management in providing additional or revised information
- The predecessor's understanding of the reason for the change in accountants

It is generally expected that the predecessor will respond promptly and fully. However, unusual conditions, such as impending litigation, may preclude a full response. In such cases, the predecessor should indicate that his or her response is limited.

The successor may also request that the predecessor release copies of certain working papers. If the client grants permission for such release, the predecessor should provide access to working papers relating to (1) matters of continuing accounting significance and (2) contingencies. It should be noted, however, that valid business reasons may lead the predecessor to decide not to provide the requested access.

Finally, if the successor becomes aware of information that may require revision of the financial statements reported on by the predecessor, the successor has a responsibility to request that his or her client communicate this information to the predecessor. The client's refusal to communicate with the predecessor regarding such information should result in the successor contacting his or her attorney.

Compilation of Specified Elements, Accounts, or Items of a Financial Statement

Can an accountant compile specified elements, accounts, or items of a financial statement?

An accountant is permitted to accept an engagement to prepare or assist a client in preparing one or more specified elements, accounts, or items of a financial statement. This type of engagement may be undertaken as a separate engagement or as part of an engagement to compile financial statements.

Must a compilation report accompany a schedule of one or more specified elements, accounts, or items of a financial statement?

If an accountant has prepared or assisted a client in preparing a schedule of one or more specified elements, accounts, or items of a financial statement and the accountant believes that he or she will be associated with such a schedule, the accountant should consider issuing a compilation report.

Is the accountant required to establish an understanding with the entity regarding an engagement to compile specified elements, accounts, or items of a financial statement?

Before accepting such an engagement, the accountant should establish an understanding with the entity, preferably in writing, regarding the services to be performed.

What are the performance and communication requirements applicable to an engagement to compile specified elements, accounts, or items of a financial statement?

In general, the accountant should follow the performance and communication requirements applicable to engagements to compile financial statements.

What should be included in the compilation report prepared at the end of the engagement?

The basic elements of a compilation report on one or more specified elements, accounts, or items of a financial statement are:

- A title; for example, "Accountant's Compilation Report" or "Independent Accountant's Compilation Report"
- An addressee
- An *introductory paragraph* that:
    - Identifies the entity
    - States that the specified element(s), account(s), or item(s) has/have been compiled
    - Identifies the specified element(s), account(s), or item(s) that has/have been compiled
    - Specifies the date or period covered by the specified element(s), account(s), or item(s)
    - Indicates that the accountant has not audited or reviewed the specified element(s), account(s), or item(s) and, accordingly, no opinion or any other form of assurance is expressed as to whether the specified element(s), account(s), or item(s) are in conformity with the applicable financial reporting framework
    - If the financial statements were also compiled, states so and then indicates the date of the report issued thereon
- A paragraph that states management's responsibility for (1) the preparation and fair presentation of the specified element(s), account(s), or item(s) in accordance with the applicable financial reporting framework and (2) the establishment and maintenance of effective internal control over financial reporting relevant to the specified element(s), account(s), or item(s)

- A paragraph that states that:
  - The accountant is responsible for conducting the compilation in accordance with Statements on Standards for Accounting and Review Services issued by the American Institute of Certified Public Accountants
  - The objective of a compilation is to assist management in presenting financial information in the form of specified element(s), account(s), or item(s) of a financial statement without obtaining or providing any assurance that no material modifications should be made to the specified element(s), account(s), or item(s).
  - The manual or printed signature of the accountant
  - The date of the compilation report, which should coincide with the date on which the compilation was completed

Warning

The compilation report should not describe the actual compilation procedures performed.

Note

Each page of the specified element(s), account(s), or item(s) should be labeled "See accountant's compilation report" or "See independent accountant's compilation report."

- A statement that the specified element(s), account(s), or item(s) identified in the report was/were compiled. If the compilation was in conjunction with a compilation of the entity's financial statements, this should be stated along with the date of the report and any departure from the standard report.
- A statement that the compilation was performed in accordance with Statements on Standards for Accounting and Review Services issued by the American Institute of Certified Public Accountants.
- If other than GAAP, a description of the basis of accounting used in preparing the specified element(s), account(s), or item(s) of the financial statement, and a statement that the basis is a comprehensive basis of accounting other than GAAP.
- A statement that a compilation is limited to presenting financial information that is the representation of management (or owners).
- A statement that the accountant has not audited or reviewed the specified element(s), account(s), or item(s) of the financial statement, and, accordingly, no opinion or any other form of assurance on it/them is being expressed.
- A signature, which may be manual, stamped, electronic, or typed.
- The date of the report, which should be the date of the completion of the compilation.

Note

Each page of the compiled schedule should include a reference, such as "See accountant's compilation report."

Example 11.4   Accountant's Compilation Report

[*Appropriate salutation*]

I (We) have compiled the accompanying schedule of accounts receivable of XYZ Company as of December 31, 2X12. I (we) have not audited or reviewed the accompanying schedule of accounts receivable and, accordingly, do not express an opinion or provide any assurance about whether the schedule of accounts receivable is in accordance with accounting principles generally accepted in the United States of America.

Management (owners) is (are) responsible for the preparation and fair presentation of the schedule of accounts receivable in accordance with accounting principles generally accepted in the United States of America and for designing, implementing, and maintaining internal control relevant to the preparation and fair presentation of the schedule of accounts receivable.

My (Our) responsibility is to conduct the compilation in accordance with Statements on Standards for Accounting and Review Services issued by the American Institute of Certified Public Accountants. The objective of a compilation is to assist management in presenting financial information in the form of a schedule of accounts receivable without undertaking to obtain or provide any assurance that there are no material modifications that should be made to the schedule of accounts receivable.

[*Signature of accounting firm or accountant, as appropriate*]
[*Date*]

Example 11.5   Accountant's Compilation Report

[*Appropriate salutation*]

I (We) have compiled the accompanying schedule of depreciation of XYZ Company as of December 31, 2X12. I (We) have not audited or reviewed the accompanying schedule of depreciation and, accordingly, do not express an opinion or provide any assurance about whether the schedule of depreciation is in accordance with the basis of accounting the Company uses for federal income tax purposes.

(continued)

(Continued)

Management (Owners) is (are) responsible for the preparation and fair presentation of the schedule of depreciation in accordance with the basis of accounting the Company uses for federal income tax purposes and for designing, implementing, and maintaining internal control relevant to the preparation and fair presentation of the schedule of depreciation.

My (Our) responsibility is to conduct the compilation in accordance with Statements on Standards for Accounting and Review Services issued by the American Institute of Certified Public Accountants. The objective of a compilation is to assist management in presenting financial information in the form of a schedule of depreciation without undertaking to obtain or provide any assurance that there are no material modifications that should be made to the schedule of depreciation.

[Signature of accounting firm or accountant, as appropriate]
[Date]

If an accountant lacks independence with respect to an entity, can he or she accept an engagement to compile specified elements, accounts, or items of a financial statement?

The accountant is permitted to accept such an engagement provided he or she discloses the lack of independence in the compilation report.

Caution

The accountant is permitted, but not required, to disclose the reason(s) for the lack of independence. If the accountant elects to do so, however, *all* reasons for the impairment of independence must be disclosed.

Compilation of Pro Forma Financial Information

What is pro forma financial information?

Pro forma financial information is intended to show what the significant effects on historical financial statements might have been had a consummated or proposed transaction (or event) occurred at an earlier date.

Pro forma financial information is commonly used to show the effects of a transaction such as a business combination, change in capitalization, or disposition of a significant portion of the business.

How should pro forma financial information be presented?

Pro forma financial information should be labeled as such in order to distinguish it from historical financial information. A presentation of pro forma financial information should:

- Describe the transaction or event.
- Describe the source of the historical financial information on which it is based.
- Describe the significant assumptions used (including any significant uncertainties).
- Indicate that the pro forma financial information should be read in conjunction with the related historical financial information.
- Indicate that the pro forma financial information is not necessarily indicative of the results that would have been attained had the transaction (or event) occurred at an earlier date.

Can an accountant compile pro forma financial information?

An accountant is permitted to accept an engagement to prepare (compile) or assist a client in preparing pro forma financial information. This type of engagement may be undertaken as a separate engagement or as part of an engagement to compile financial statements.

Must a compilation report accompany pro forma financial information?

If an accountant has prepared or assisted a client in preparing pro forma financial information and the accountant believes that he or she will be associated with the presentation, the accountant should consider issuing a compilation report.

Is there anything unique about compiling pro forma financial information in connection with a business combination?

In the case of a business combination, the document containing the pro forma financial information should include (or incorporate by reference) the historical financial information of the combined entity's significant components. Further, the historical financial statements must have been compiled, reviewed, or audited and the related accountant's or auditor's report should be included (or incorporated by reference).

Is the accountant required to establish an understanding with the entity regarding an engagement to compile pro forma financial information?

Before accepting such an engagement, the accountant should establish an understanding with the entity, preferably in writing, regarding the services to be performed.

What are the performance and communication requirements applicable to an engagement to compile pro forma financial information?

In general, the accountant should follow the performance and communication requirements applicable to engagements to compile financial statements.

What should be included in the compilation report prepared at the end of the engagement?

The basic elements of a compilation report on pro forma financial information are:

- A title; for example, "Accountant's Compilation Report" or "Independent Accountant's Compilation Report"
- An addressee
- An *introductory paragraph* that:
  - Identifies the entity
  - States that the pro forma financial information has been compiled
  - Identifies the pro forma financial information that has been compiled
  - Specifies the date or period covered by the pro forma financial information
  - Indicates that the accountant has not audited or reviewed the pro forma financial information and, accordingly, no opinion or any other form of assurance is expressed as to whether the pro forma financial information is in conformity with the applicable financial reporting framework
  - If the financial statements were also compiled, states so and then indicates date of the report issued thereon
- A paragraph that states management's responsibility for (1) the preparation and fair presentation of the pro forma financial information in accordance with the applicable financial reporting framework and (2) the establishment and maintenance of effective internal control over financial reporting relevant to the pro forma financial information
- A paragraph that states that:
  - The accountant is responsible for conducting the compilation in accordance with Statements on Standards for Accounting and Review Services issued by the American Institute of Certified Public Accountants.
  - The objective of a compilation is to assist management in presenting financial information in the form of pro forma financial information without obtaining or providing any assurance that no material modifications should be made to the pro forma financial information.
- The manual or printed signature of the accountant
- The date of the compilation report, which should coincide with the date on which the compilation was completed

Warning

The compilation report should not describe the actual compilation procedures performed.

Note

Each page of the pro forma financial information should be labeled "See accountant's compilation report" or "See independent accountant's compilation report."

Example 11.6 Accountant's Compilation Report

[*Appropriate salutation*]

I (We) have compiled the accompanying pro forma financial information of XYZ Company as of December 31, 2X12, reflecting the business combination of the Company and ABC Company. The historical condensed financial statements are derived from the historical unaudited financial statements of XYZ Company, which were compiled by me (us), and of ABC Company, which were compiled by another (other) accountant(s). I (We) have not audited or reviewed the accompanying pro forma financial information and, accordingly, do not express an opinion or provide any assurance about whether the pro forma financial information is in accordance with accounting principles generally accepted in the United States of America.

Management (Owners) is (are) responsible for the preparation and fair presentation of the pro forma financial information in accordance with accounting principles generally accepted in the United States of America and for designing, implementing, and maintaining internal control relevant to the preparation and fair presentation of the pro forma financial information.

My (Our) responsibility is to conduct the compilation in accordance with Statements on Standards for Accounting and Review Services issued by the American Institute of Certified Public Accountants. The objective of a compilation is to assist management in presenting financial information in the form of pro forma financial information without undertaking to obtain or provide any assurance that there are no material modifications that should be made to the pro forma financial information.

The objective of this pro forma financial information is to show what the significant effects on the historical financial information might have been had the transaction (or event) occurred at an earlier date. However, the pro forma financial information is not necessarily indicative of the results of operations or related effects on financial position that would have been attained had the transaction (or event) actually occurred earlier.

Paragraph the accountant may add after the previous paragraph.

Management (Owners) has (have) elected to omit substantially all disclosures, but the pro forma financial information is otherwise in conformity with accounting principles generally accepted in the United States of America.

[*Signature of accounting firm or accountant, as appropriate*]
[*Date*]

If the accountant lacks independence with respect to an entity, can he or she accept an engagement to compile pro forma financial information?

The accountant is permitted to accept such an engagement provided he or she discloses the lack of independence in the compilation report.

Caution

The accountant is permitted, but not required, to disclose the reason(s) for the lack of independence. If the accountant elects to do so, however, *all* reasons for the impairment of independence must be disclosed.

Communicating to Management and Others in a Compilation or Review Engagement

What are an accountant's communication requirements in a compilation or review engagement?

When evidence or information comes to the accountant's attention during the performance of a compilation or review engagement that fraud or an illegal act may have occurred, the matter should be brought to the attention of the appropriate level of management. An illegal act that is clearly inconsequential need not be communicated.

If the fraud or illegal act involves senior management, it should be reported to an individual or group of individuals at a higher level within the entity, such as the manager (owner) or board of directors.

The communication of fraud or illegal acts may be oral or written. If the communication is oral, the accountant should document it in the work papers.

What should I do if the fraud or illegal act involves an owner of the business?

The accountant should consider withdrawing from an engagement if fraud or an illegal act involves an owner of the business.

When is it necessary to contact my attorney and my insurance carrier?

The accountant should consider consulting with an attorney and his or her insurance provider unless the fraud or illegal act is clearly inconsequential.

Are there circumstances where communication to outside parties is necessary?

Disclosure of fraud or illegal acts to parties other than senior management ordinarily is not part of the accountant's responsibility. In fact, disclosure of such information to parties other than management is ordinarily precluded by ethical or regulatory provisions pertaining to confidentiality.

However, disclosure to outside parties may be necessary in order to:

- Comply with legal or regulatory requirements.
- Communicate with a successor accountant.
- Respond to a subpoena or an ethics inquiry.
- Comply with a report review required by the American Institute of Certified Public Accountants (AICPA).

Reports on Prospective Financial Statements

What are prospective financial statements?

Prospective financial statements encompass financial forecasts and financial projections. Pro forma financial statements and partial presentations are specifically excluded from this category.

Financial forecasts are prospective financial statements that present, to the best of the responsible party's knowledge and belief, an entity's expected financial position, results of operations, and cash flows. They are based on assumptions about conditions *actually* expected to exist and the course of action expected to be taken.

Financial projections are prospective financial statements that present, to the best of the responsible party's knowledge and belief, an entity's expected financial position, results of operations, and cash flows. They are based on assumptions about conditions expected to exist and the course of action expected to be taken, given one or more hypothetical (i.e., what-if) assumptions.

Responsible parties are those who are responsible for the underlying assumptions. While the responsible party is usually management, it may be a third party. *Example:* If a client is negotiating with a bank for a large loan, the bank may stipulate the assumptions to be used. Accordingly, in this case, the bank would represent the responsible party.

What are my reporting responsibilities regarding prospective financial statements?

Statement on Standards for Attestation Engagements (SSAE) No. 10, "Attestation Standards: Revision and Codification," specifically precludes an accountant from compiling, examining, or applying agreed-upon procedures to prospective financial statements that fail to include a summary of significant assumptions. The practice standards in the Statement are *not* applicable to:

- Engagements involving prospective financial statements that are restricted to internal use
- Those used solely in litigation support services (e.g., in circumstances where the practitioner is serving as an expert witness)

How are prospective financial statements used?

The intended use of an entity's prospective financial statements governs the type of prospective financial statements to be presented.

- When an entity's prospective financial statements are for general use, only a financial forecast is to be presented. *General use* means that the statements will be used by persons not negotiating directly with the responsible party. *Example:* In a public offering of a tax shelter interest.
- When an entity's prospective financial statements are for limited use, either a financial forecast or a financial projection may be presented. *Limited use* refers to situations in which the statements are to be used by the responsible party alone or by the responsible party and those parties negotiating directly with the responsible party. *Example:* If a client is negotiating directly with a bank, either a forecast or a projection is appropriate.

How do I compile prospective statements?

Compilation procedures applicable to prospective financial statements are not designed to provide any form of assurance on the presentation of the statements or the underlying assumptions.

They are essentially the same as those applicable to historical financial statements. Additional procedures are:

- Inquire of the responsible party as to the underlying assumptions developed.
- Compile or obtain a list of the underlying assumptions and consider the possibility of obvious omissions or inconsistencies.
- Verify the mathematical accuracy of the assumptions.
- Read the prospective financial statements in order to identify departures from AICPA presentation guidelines.
- Obtain a client representation letter in order to confirm that the responsible party acknowledges its responsibility for the prospective statements (including the underlying assumptions).

Caution

An accountant is precluded from compiling forecasts and projections that do not present the summary of significant assumptions. Furthermore, the practitioner should not compile a projection that fails to identify the underlying hypothetical assumptions or describe the limitations on the utility of the projection.

What do I include in a compilation report on prospective statements?

The accountant's report on compiled prospective financial statements should include:

- An identification of the prospective financial statements presented
- A statement as to the level of service provided and the fact that the prospective financial statements were compiled in accordance with attestation standards established by the AICPA

- A statement describing the limited scope of a compilation and the fact that no opinion or any other form of assurance is being expressed
- A warning that the prospective results may not materialize
- A statement that the accountant is under no responsibility to update his or her report for conditions occurring after the compilation report is issued
- The date of the report, which should coincide with the completion of the compilation procedures
- The accountant's signature
- In the case of a projection, a separate middle paragraph describing the limitations on the utility of the statements
- A separate paragraph when the statements present the expected results in the form of a range of values
- If the accountant is not independent, a statement as to this fact; the accountant may disclose a description concerning the reason(s) for the impairment of independence; however, all reasons for impairment must then be disclosed
- A separate explanatory paragraph when the prospective statements contain a departure from AICPA presentation guidelines or omit disclosures unrelated to the significant assumptions

---

Example 11.7   Standard Report on Compiled Forecasts

I (We) have compiled the accompanying forecasted balance sheet, statement of income, retained earnings, and cash flows of Future Corporation as of (at) December 31, 2X12, and for the year then ending, in accordance with attestation standards established by the American Institute of Certified Public Accountants.

A compilation is limited to presenting, in the form of a forecast, information that is the representation of management (or other responsible party) and does not include evaluation of the support for the assumptions underlying the forecast. I (We) have not examined the forecast and, accordingly, do not express an opinion or any other form of assurance on the accompanying statements or assumptions. Furthermore, there will usually be differences between the forecasted and actual results, because events and circumstances frequently do not occur as expected, and those differences may be material. I (We) have no responsibility to update this report for events and circumstances occurring after the date of this report.

Example 11.8   Standard Report on Compiled Projections

I (We) have compiled the accompanying projected balance sheet, statements of income, retained earnings, and cash flows of Future Corporation as of December 31, 2X12, and for the year then ending, in accordance with attestation standards established by the American Institute of Certified Public Accountants.

(continued)

(Continued)

The accompanying projection and this report were prepared for [*state special purpose, e.g., "the Takeover Corporation for the purpose of negotiating a buyout of the Company"*] and should not be used for any other purpose.

A compilation is limited to presenting, in the form of a projection, information that is the representation of management (or other responsible party) and does not include evaluation of the support for the assumptions underlying the projection. I (We) have not examined the projection and, accordingly, do not express an opinion or any other form of assurance on the accompanying statements or assumptions. Furthermore, even if [*describe hypothetical assumption, e.g., "the buyout is consummated"*], there will usually be differences between the projected and actual results, because events and circumstances frequently do not occur as expected, and those differences may be material. I (We) have no responsibility to update this report for events and circumstances occurring after the date of this report.

Example 11.9   Paragraph Included When Statements Contain a Range of Values

As described in the summary of significant assumptions, management of Future Corporation (or another responsible party) has elected to portray forecasted (or projected) [*describe financial statement element(s) for which expected results of one or more assumptions fall within a range, and identify the assumptions expected to fall within a range, e.g., "revenue at the amounts of $XXX,XXX and $YYY,YYY, which is based on a buyout purchase price of X percent of 2X12 net income and Y percent of 2X12 net income"*], rather than as a single-point estimate. Accordingly, the accompanying forecast (projection) presents forecasted (projected) financial position, results of operations, and cash flows [*describe assumption(s) expected to fall within a range, e.g., "at such buyout rates"*]. However, there is no assurance that the actual results will fall within the range of [*describe assumption(s) expected to fall within a range, e.g., "buyout rates"*] presented.

Example 11.10   Sample Paragraph Included When Prospective Financial Statements Depart from AICPA Presentation

Management (or another responsible party) has elected to omit the summary of significant accounting policies required by the guidelines for presentation of a financial forecast (or projection) established by the American Institute of Certified Public Accountants. If the omitted disclosures were included in the forecast (projection), they might influence the user's conclusions about the Company's financial position, results of operations, and cash flows for the forecasted (projected) period. Accordingly, this forecast (projection) is not designed for those who are not informed about such matters.

What is involved in an examination of prospective financial statements?

An examination of prospective financial statements evaluates:

- The preparation of the statements
- The support of the related underlying assumptions
- The conformity of the statements with AICPA presentation guidelines

The practitioner's report should contain an opinion as to whether:

- The statements are presented in conformity with the AICPA guidelines
- The underlying assumptions provide a reasonable basis for the forecast
- The underlying assumptions provide a reasonable basis for the projection in light of the hypothetical assumptions

How do I conduct an examination of prospective financial statements?

In performing an examination of prospective financial statements, the practitioner should take these seven steps.

1. Assess inherent and control risk, as well as limit detection risk.
2. Consider the sufficiency of external sources (such as government and industry publications) and internal sources (such as management-prepared budgets) of information supporting the underlying assumptions.
3. Determine the consistency of the assumptions and the sources on which they are predicated.
4. Determine the consistency of the assumptions themselves.
5. Determine the reliability and consistency of the historical financial information used.
6. Evaluate the preparation and presentation of the prospective financial statements:
   - Does the presentation reflect the underlying assumptions?
   - Are the assumptions mathematically accurate?
   - Do the assumptions reflect an internally consistent pattern?
   - Do the accounting principles in use reflect those expected to be in effect in the prospective period?
   - Are the AICPA presentation guidelines followed?
   - Is there adequate disclosure of the assumptions?
7. Obtain a client representation letter to confirm that the responsible party acknowledges its responsibility for the presentation of the prospective financial statements and the underlying assumptions.

What is included in examination reports on prospective statements?

The accountant's report on examined prospective financial statements should include:

- A title that includes the word *independent*
- Identification of the prospective financial statements presented
- Identification of the responsible party and a statement that the prospective financial statements are the responsibility of the responsible party
- A statement that the practitioner's responsibility is to express an opinion on the prospective financial statements based on his or her examination
- A statement that the examination was performed in accordance with attestation standards established by the AICPA and, accordingly, included such procedures as the practitioner considered necessary in the circumstances
- A statement that the practitioner believes that the examination provides a reasonable basis for his or her opinion
- An opinion on the presentation of the prospective financial statements in terms of their conformity with AICPA presentation guidelines
- An opinion as to whether the underlying assumptions provide a reasonable basis for the prospective financial statements
- A warning that the prospective results may not materialize
- A statement that the accountant is under no responsibility to update his or her report for conditions occurring after the examination report is issued
- The accountant's signature, which may be manual or printed
- The date of the report, which should coincide with the completion of the examination procedures

---

Example 11.11   Standard Report on Examined Forecasts

Independent Accountant's Report

I (We) have examined the accompanying forecasted balance sheet, statements of income, retained earnings, and cash flows of Travis Company as of December 31, 2X12, and for the year then ending. Travis Company's management is responsible for the forecast. My (Our) responsibility is to express an opinion on the forecast based on my (our) examination.

My (Our) examination was conducted in accordance with attestation standards established by the American Institute of Certified Public Accountants and, accordingly, included such procedures as I (we) considered necessary to evaluate both the assumptions used by management and the preparation and presentation of the forecast. I (We) believe that my (our) examination provides a reasonable basis for my (our) opinion.

In my (our) opinion, the accompanying forecast is presented in conformity with guidelines for presentation of a forecast established by the American Institute of Certified Public Accountants, and the underlying assumptions provide a reasonable basis for management's forecast. However, there will usually be differences between the forecasted and actual results, because events and circumstances frequently do not occur as expected, and those differences may be material. I (We) have no responsibility to update this report for events and circumstances occurring after the date of this report.

[Signature]
[Date]

Example 11.12   Standard Report on Examined Projections

Independent Accountant's Report

I (We) have examined the accompanying projected balance sheet, statements of income, retained earnings, and cash flows of Jordan Company as of December 31, 2X12, and for the year then ending. Jordan Company's management is responsible for the projection, which was prepared for [*state special purpose, e.g., "the purpose of negotiating a loan to expand Jordan Company's plant"*]. My (Our) responsibility is to express an opinion on the projection based on my (our) examination.

My (Our) examination was conducted in accordance with attestation standards established by the American Institute of Certified Public Accountants and, accordingly, included such procedures as I (we) considered necessary to evaluate both the assumptions used by management and the preparation and presentation of the projection. I (We) believe that my (our) examination provides a reasonable basis for my (our) opinion.

In my (our) opinion, the accompanying projection is presented in conformity with guidelines for presentation of a projection established by the American Institute of Certified Public Accountants, and the underlying assumptions provide a reasonable basis for management's projection [*describe the hypothetical assumption, e.g., "assuming the granting of the requested loan for the purpose of expanding Jordan Company's plant as described in the summary of significant assumptions"*]. However, even if [*describe hypothetical assumption, e.g., "the loan is granted and the plant is expanded"*], there will usually be differences between the projected and actual results, because events and circumstances frequently do not occur as expected, and those differences may be material. I (We) have no responsibility to update this report for events and circumstances occurring after the date of this report.

The accompanying projection and this report are intended solely for the information and use of [*identify specified parties, e.g., "Jordan Company and DEF National Bank"*] and are not intended to be and should not be used by anyone other than these specified parties.

[Signature]
[Date]

Modification and Other Issues

When should the standard examination report be modified?

RANGE OF VALUES   When prospective financial statements contain a range of values, the report should contain an additional paragraph clearly indicating this. The explanatory paragraph should be similar to the one added to compilation reports on prospective financial statements containing a range of values.

DEPARTURE FROM AICPA PRESENTATION GUIDELINES   When the prospective financial statements contain a departure from the AICPA presentation guidelines, issue either an "except for" qualified opinion or an adverse opinion. An "except for" qualified opinion should contain an explanatory middle paragraph that describes the departure. The opinion paragraph should specifically refer to the explanatory middle paragraph.

> In my (our) opinion, except for [*describe the departure, e.g., "the omission of the disclosures of the reasons for significant variation in the relationship between income tax expense and pretax accounting income as discussed in the preceding paragraph"*], . . .

Note

The issuance of an adverse opinion is mandated if the prospective financial statements fail to disclose the significant underlying assumptions.

SIGNIFICANT ASSUMPTION DOES NOT PROVIDE REASONABLE BASIS   When the accountant believes that one or more significant assumptions (including hypothetical assumptions) do not provide a reasonable basis for the prospective financial statements, the issuance of an adverse opinion is justified.

Note

The examination report should include a middle paragraph that discloses all of the substantive reasons for the issuance of the adverse opinion. The opinion paragraph should specifically refer to the middle explanatory paragraph.

Example 11.13   Paragraph Used When Expressing an Adverse Opinion

In my (our) opinion, the accompanying forecast is not presented in conformity with guidelines for presentation of a financial forecast established by the

American Institute of Certified Public Accountants, because management's (or another responsible party's) assumptions, as discussed in the preceding paragraph, do not provide a reasonable basis for management's (or another responsible party's) forecast. I (We) have no responsibility to update this report for events or circumstances occurring after the date of this report.

SCOPE LIMITATION   When the accountant is unable to perform one or more examination procedures considered necessary for the particular engagement, a disclaimer of an opinion should be expressed. The disclaimer should clearly describe the scope limitation in a separate explanatory paragraph.

Note

The scope paragraph of the examination report should be modified to indicate the existence of a scope limitation and the explanatory middle paragraph.

Example: "Except as explained in the following paragraph,..." The disclaimer paragraph should also refer to the explanatory paragraph.

Example 11.14   Sample Disclaimer

Because, as described in the preceding paragraph, I am (we are) unable to evaluate management's (or another responsible party's) assumptions regarding income from an equity investee and other assumptions depend thereon, I (we) express no opinion with respect to the presentation of or the assumptions underlying the accompanying forecast. I (We) have no responsibility to update this report for events and circumstances occurring after the date of this report.

EMPHASIS OF A MATTER   The accountant may emphasize a matter in a separate paragraph while simultaneously expressing an unqualified opinion. This is accomplished in a manner similar to emphasizing a matter already disclosed in historical financial statements.

DIVISION OF RESPONSIBILITY   When another auditor is involved and the principal auditor wishes to divide the responsibility for the overall examination report, the principal auditor should modify the report in a manner similar to the modifications pertinent to historical financial statements.

Agreed-Upon Procedures

When can I undertake an engagement with agreed-upon procedures?

It is permissible to undertake an engagement involving the application of agreed-upon procedures to prospective financial statements provided that:

- The accountant is independent.
- The procedures performed or to be performed are agreed on by the accountant and the specified users.
- The specified users take responsibility for the sufficiency of the agreed-upon procedures.
- A summary of significant assumptions is included in the prospective financial statements.
- The prospective financial statements are subject to reasonably consistent estimation or measurement.
- The accountant and the specified users agree upon the criteria to be used in the determination of findings.
- The procedures to be applied are expected to result in reasonably consistent findings.
- Evidential matter is expected to exist to provide a reasonable basis for expressing the accountant's findings.
- A description of any agreed-upon materiality limits for reporting purposes is included in the accountant's report.
- The accountant's report is restricted to use by the specified users.

How do I report on the results of applying agreed-upon procedures?

The accountant's report on prospective financial statements subjected to agreed-upon procedures should include:

- A title including the word *independent*
- An identification of the specified parties
- A reference to the prospective financial statements and the character of the engagement
- A statement that the procedures performed were those agreed to by the specified parties
- An identification of the responsible party and a statement that the prospective financial statements are the responsibility of the responsible party
- A statement that the agreed-upon procedures engagement was conducted in accordance with attestation standards established by the American Institute of Certified Public Accountants
- A statement that the specified users are responsible for the sufficiency of the procedures and a disclaimer of responsibility for the sufficiency of those procedures
- A listing of the procedures performed (or a reference thereto) and the related findings
- A description of any agreed-upon materiality limits
- A statement that the accountant was not engaged to examine and did not examine the prospective financial statements; a disclaimer of opinion; and a statement that if the accountant had performed additional procedures, other matters might have been reported
- A restriction on the use of the report because it is generally intended to be used solely by the specified parties

- A description of any reservations or restrictions concerning procedures or findings
- A warning that the prospective results might not materialize
- A statement that the accountant is under no responsibility to update his or her report for conditions occurring after the report is issued
- A description of the nature of the assistance provided by any specialists
- The accountant's signature, which may be manual or printed
- The date of the report

Caution

Negative assurance should not be expressed; the results of an agreed-upon procedures engagement should be presented in the form of findings.

Example 11.15   Report After Applying Agreed-Upon Procedures

Independent Accountant's Report on Applying Agreed-Upon Procedures

Board of Directors—Katie Corporation
Board of Directors—Mike Company

At your request, we have performed certain agreed-upon procedures, as enumerated below, with respect to the forecasted balance sheet and the related forecasted statements of income, retained earnings, and cash flows of Karen Company, a subsidiary of Mike Company, as of December 31, 2X12, and for the year then ending. These procedures, which were agreed to by the Boards of Directors of Katie Corporation and Mike Company, were performed solely to assist you in evaluating the forecast in connection with the proposed sale of Karen Company to Katie Corporation. This agreed-upon procedures engagement was performed in accordance with attestation standards established by the American Institute of Certified Public Accountants. The sufficiency of these procedures is solely the responsibility of the specified users of the report. Consequently, we make no representation regarding the sufficiency of the procedures described below either for the purpose for which this report has been requested or for any other purpose.

[Include paragraphs to enumerate procedures and findings.]

We were not engaged to, and did not, perform an examination, the objective of which would be the expression of an opinion on the accompanying prospective financial statements. Accordingly, we do not express an opinion on whether the prospective financial statements are presented in conformity with AICPA

(continued)

(Continued)

presentation guidelines or on whether the underlying assumptions provide a reasonable basis for the presentation. Had we performed additional procedures, other matters might have come to our attention that would have been reported to you. Furthermore, there will usually be differences between the forecasted and actual results, because events and circumstances frequently do not occur as expected, and those differences may be material. We have no responsibility to update this report for events and circumstances occurring after the date of this report.

This report is intended solely for the use of the Boards of Directors of Mike Company and Katie Corporation and is not intended to be and should not be used by anyone other than these specified parties.

[*Signature*]
[*Date*]

What are the minimum items to be included in prospective financial statements?

Financial forecasts and financial projections may be in the form of either complete basic financial statements or financial statements containing at least the 12 items that follow:

1. Sales or gross revenues
2. Gross profit or cost of sales
3. Unusual or infrequently occurring items
4. Provision for income taxes
5. Discontinued operations or extraordinary items
6. Income from continuing operations
7. Net income
8. Basic and fully diluted earnings per share
9. Significant changes in financial position
10. Management's (or another responsible party's) intent as to what the prospective statements present, a statement indicating that management's (or another responsible party's) assumptions are predicated on facts and circumstances in existence when the statements were prepared, and a warning that the prospective results may not materialize
11. Summary of significant assumptions
12. Summary of significant accounting policies

Caution

A partial presentation (omitting one or more of the first nine items) is not appropriate for general use. Presentations omitting only the last three items are

> not considered partial presentations. Accordingly, in such circumstances, the practitioner must adhere to the requirements of the statement.

Attest Engagements

What is an attest engagement?

An *attest engagement* is when an accountant is engaged to issue or does issue an examination, a review, or an agreed-upon procedures, report on subject matter, or an assertion about the subject matter that is the responsibility of another party. *Examples:* Assertions that may require attest engagements include:

- A client write-up computer program is capable of generating a monthly, quarterly, and year-to-date payroll ledger without the need for a separate payroll module.
- The value of stocks and bonds in a particular mutual fund has grown at the rate of 48 percent over the past two years.

What is meant by an "unconditional requirement"?

An *unconditional requirement* included in a Statement on Standards for Attestation Engagements means that the practitioner is required to comply with the requirement in all cases. The word *must* and phrase *is required* are indicative of an unconditional requirement.

What is a "presumptively mandatory requirement"?

A *presumptively mandatory requirement* included in a Statement on Standards for Attestation Engagements means that, under normal conditions, the practitioner is required to comply with the requirement. However, in rare circumstances, the practitioner may depart from a presumptively mandatory requirement, provided he or she documents the justification for the departure and how alternative procedures performed were sufficient. The word *should* indicates a presumptively mandatory requirement.

What is explanatory material?

In general, *explanatory material* is text included in a Statement on Standards for Attestation Engagements that:

- Provides additional explanation and guidance on a professional requirement
- Identifies and describes other audit procedures or actions

The words *may*, *might*, and *could* are used in the context of explanatory material.

How do I conduct an attestation engagement?

In performing an attestation engagement, the practitioner must:

- Possess sufficient knowledge of the subject matter of the assertion.
- Perform engagements only if the assertion is capable of evaluation (or measurement) against reasonable criteria and the assertion can be consistently estimated or measured.
- Be independent in fact (i.e., possess independence in mental attitude).
- Exercise due professional care.
- Plan the engagement and supervise any assistants.
- Obtain sufficient competent evidence in order to express the written conclusion.

What constitutes "subject matter"?

Subject matter, which may be as of a point in time or for a period of time, may exist in many forms, including:

- Historical or prospective performance or condition, such as a mutual fund's performance
- Physical characteristics, such as the square footage of a warehouse
- Historical events, such as the price of goods at a particular date
- Analyses, such as breakeven analysis
- Systems or processes, such as internal control over financial reporting
- Behavior, such as compliance with terms of an agreement

Must the practitioner obtain a representation letter in an attest engagement?

If the attest engagement constitutes either an examination or a review, the practitioner should obtain a representation letter from the responsible party. The representation letter should cover both oral and written representations pertinent to the engagement.

Examination Engagements

What is the purpose of an examination engagement?

The purpose of an examination engagement is to express an opinion about whether (1) the subject matter is based on (or in conformity with) the criteria in all material respects, or (2) the written assertion is presented (or fairly stated), in all material respects, based on the criteria. If necessary, the practitioner may express a qualified opinion or a disclaimer of opinion. *Note:* The practitioner may modify the report in order to emphasize a matter.

What items should be included in the examination report?

- A title that includes the word *independent*
- An identification of the subject matter or an identification of the assertion (or a statement of the assertion, if the assertion does not accompany the examination report) and the responsible party

- A statement that the subject matter (or the assertion) is the responsibility of the responsible party
- A statement that the practitioner's responsibility is to express an opinion on the subject matter (or the assertion) based on his or her examination
- A statement that the examination was conducted in accordance with attestation standards established by the American Institute of Certified Public Accountants and, accordingly, included procedures that the practitioner considered necessary in the circumstances
- A statement that the practitioner believes the examination provides a reasonable basis for his or her opinion
- The practitioner's opinion on whether:
  - The subject matter is based on (or in conformity with) the criteria in all material respects, or
  - The assertion is presented (or fairly stated), in all material respects, based on the criteria
- A statement restricting the use of the report to specified parties when any of the following are the case:
  - The criteria used to evaluate the subject matter are determined by the practitioner to be appropriate for only a limited number of parties who either participated in their establishment or can be presumed to have an adequate understanding of the criteria.
  - The criteria used to evaluate the subject matter are available only to the specified parties.
  - A written assertion has not been provided by the responsible party. (A statement to that effect should also be included in the explanatory paragraph of the report.)
- The practitioner's signature, which may be manual or printed
- The date of the examination report

Example 11.16   Standard Report for an Examination Engagement on Subject Matter

Independent Accountant's Report

I (We) have examined [*identify the subject matter, e.g., "the accompanying Schedule of Investment Performance Statistics of Reap the Benefits Fund for the year ended December 31, 2X12"*]. Reap the Benefits Fund's management is responsible for the schedule of investment performance statistics. My (Our) responsibility is to express an opinion based on my (our) examination.

My (Our) examination was conducted in accordance with attestation standards established by the American Institute of Certified Public Accountants and, accordingly, included examining, on a test basis, evidence supporting [*identify the subject matter, e.g., "Reap the Benefits Fund's Schedule of Investment Performance Statistics"*] and performing such other procedures as (I) we considered necessary in the circumstances. I (We) believe that my (our) examination provides a reasonable basis for my (our) opinion.

(continued)

(Continued)

[*Additional paragraph(s) may be added to emphasize certain matters relating to the attest engagement or the subject matter.*]

In my (our) opinion, the schedule referred to above presents, in all material respects, [*identify the subject matter, e.g., "the investment performance statistics of Reap the Benefits Fund for the year ended December 31, 2X12"*] based on [*identify criteria, e.g., "the ABC criteria set forth in Note 1"*].

[*Signature*]
[*Date*]

Example 11.17   Standard Report for an Examination Engagement on an Assertion

Independent Accountant's Report

(I) We have examined management's assertion that [*identify the assertion, e.g., "the accompanying Schedule of Investment Performance Statistics of Reap the Benefits Fund for the year ended December 31, 2X12, is presented in accordance with ABC criteria set forth in Note 1"*]. Reap the Benefits Fund's management is responsible for the assertion. My (Our) responsibility is to express an opinion on the assertion based on my (our) examination.

My (Our) examination was conducted in accordance with attestation standards established by the American Institute of Certified Public Accountants and, accordingly, included examining, on a test basis, evidence supporting management's assertion and performing such other procedures as I (we) considered necessary in the circumstances. I (We) believe that my (our) examination provides a reasonable basis for my (our) opinion.

[*Additional paragraph(s) may be added to emphasize certain matters relating to the attest engagement or the assertion.*]

In my (our) opinion, management's assertion referred to above is fairly stated, in all material respects, based on [*identify established or stated criteria, e.g., "the ABC criteria set forth in Note 1"*].

[*Signature*]
[*Date*]

Review Engagements

What is the objective of a review engagement?

The purpose of a review engagement is to express negative assurance.

What items should be included in the review report?

- A title that includes the word *independent*
- An identification of the subject matter or an identification of the assertion (or a statement of the assertion, if the assertion does not accompany the examination report) and the responsible party
- A statement that the subject matter (or the assertion) is the responsibility of the responsible party
- A statement that the review was conducted in accordance with attestation standards established by the American Institute of Certified Public Accountants
- A statement that a review is substantially less in scope than an examination, the objective of which is the expression of opinion on the subject matter (or the assertion), and accordingly, no such opinion is expressed
- A statement about whether the practitioner is aware of any material modifications that should be made to:
  - The subject matter in order for it to be based on (or in conformity with), in all material respects, the criteria, other than those modifications, if any, indicated in the review report, or
  - The assertion in order for it to be presented (or fairly stated), in all material respects, based on (or in conformity with) the criteria, other than those modifications, if any, indicated in the review report
- A statement restricting the use of the report to specified parties when any of the following is the case:
  - The criteria used to evaluate the subject matter are determined by the practitioner to be appropriate for only a limited number of parties who either participated in their establishment or can be presumed to have an adequate understanding of the criteria.
  - The criteria used to evaluate the subject matter are available only to the specified parties.
  - A written assertion has not been provided by the responsible party. (A statement to that effect should also be included in the explanatory paragraph of the report.)
- The practitioner's signature, which may be manual or printed
- The date of the review report

Example 11.18   Standard Report for a Review Engagement on Subject Matter

Independent Accountant's Report

I (We) have reviewed the accompanying [*identify the subject matter, e.g., "the accompanying schedule of investment returns of Reap the Benefits Fund for the year ended December 31, 2X12"*]. Reap the Benefits Fund's management is responsible for the schedule of investment returns.

My (Our) review was conducted in accordance with attestation standards established by the American Institute of Certified Public Accountants. A review

(continued)

(Continued)

is substantially less in scope than an examination, the objective of which is the expression of an opinion on [*identify the subject matter, e.g., "Reap the Benefits Fund's schedule of investment returns"*]. Accordingly, I (we) do not express such an opinion.

[*If desired, the practitioner may present additional paragraphs to emphasize matters pertaining to the attest engagement or the subject matter.*]

Based on my (our) review, nothing came to my (our) attention that caused me (us) to believe that the [*identify the subject matter, e.g., "schedule of investment returns of Reap the Benefits Fund for the year ending December 31, 2X12"*] is not presented, in all material respects, in conformity with [*identify the criteria, e.g., "the ABC criteria set forth in Note X"*].

[*Signature*]
[*Date*]

Example 11.19   Standard Report for a Review Engagement on an Assertion

Independent Accountant's Report

I (We) have reviewed management's assertion that [*identify the assertion, e.g., "the accompanying schedule of investment returns of Reap the Benefits Fund for the year ended December 31, 2X12, is presented in accordance with the ABC criteria referred to in Note X"*]. Reap the Benefits Fund's management is responsible for the assertion.

My (Our) review was conducted in accordance with attestation standards established by the American Institute of Certified Public Accountants. A review is substantially less in scope than an examination, the objective of which is the expression of an opinion on management's assertion. Accordingly, I (we) do not express such an opinion.

[*If desired, the practitioner may present additional paragraphs to emphasize matters pertaining to the attest engagement or the assertion.*]

Based on my (our) review, nothing came to my (our) attention that caused me (us) to believe that management's assertion referred to above is not stated fairly, in all material respects, based on [*identify the criteria, e.g., "the ABC criteria referred to in the investment management agreement between Reap the Benefits Fund and Holdem Investment Managers, dated November 15, 2X12"*].

[*Signature*]
[*Date*]

Engagements to Apply Agreed-Upon Procedures

How do I report when applying agreed-upon procedures to subject matter?

The results of applying agreed-upon procedures should be in the form of findings. Accordingly, neither an opinion nor negative assurance should be provided.

All findings should be reported unless a definition of materiality is agreed on by the specified users and described in the practitioner's report.

The practitioner's report should include:

- A title including the word *independent*
- Identification of the specified parties
- Identification of the subject matter and the character of the engagement
- Identification of the responsible party
- A statement that the subject matter is the responsibility of the responsible party
- A statement that the procedures performed were those agreed to by the specified parties identified in the report
- A statement that the agreed-upon procedures engagement was conducted in accordance with attestation standards established by the AICPA
- A statement that the sufficiency of the procedures is solely the responsibility of the specified parties and a disclaimer of responsibility for the sufficiency of those procedures
- A list of the procedures performed (or reference thereto) and related findings (negative assurance should not be provided)
- If applicable, the agreed-upon materiality limits
- A statement that the practitioner was not engaged to and did not perform an examination of the subject matter; a disclaimer of opinion; and a statement that if the practitioner had performed additional procedures, other matters might have come to his or her attention that would have been reported
- A statement of restrictions on the use of the report because it is intended to be used solely by the specified parties
- Any reservations or restrictions concerning procedures or findings
- Where applicable, a description of the nature of the assistance provided by a specialist
- The practitioner's signature, which may be manual or printed
- The date of the agreed-upon procedures report

Example 11.20   Report on Applying Agreed-Upon Procedures

Independent Accountant's Report on Applying Agreed-Upon Procedures

To the Audit Committees and Managements of ME Inc. and YOU Fund:

We have performed the procedures enumerated below, which were agreed to by the audit committees and managements of ME Inc. and YOU Fund, solely to assist you in evaluating the accompanying Statement of Investment Performance Statistics of YOU Fund (prepared in accordance with the criteria specified

(continued)

(Continued)

therein) for the year ended December 31, 2X12. YOU Fund's management is responsible for the statement of investment performance statistics. This agreed-upon procedures engagement was conducted in accordance with attestation standards established by the American Institute of Certified Public Accountants. The sufficiency of these procedures is solely the responsibility of those parties specified in this report. Consequently, we make no representation regarding the sufficiency of the procedures described below either for the purpose for which this report has been requested or for any other purpose.

[Include paragraphs to enumerate procedures and findings.]

We were not engaged to and did not conduct an examination, the objective of which would be the expression of an opinion on the accompanying Statement of Investment Performance Statistics of YOU Fund. Accordingly, we do not express such an opinion. Had we performed additional procedures, other matters might have come to our attention that would have been reported to you.

This report is intended solely for the information and use of the audit committees and managements of ME Inc. and YOU Fund, and is not intended to be and should not be used by anyone other than these specified parties.

[Signature]
[Date]

Examination of an Entity's Internal Control over Financial Reporting That Is Integrated with an Audit of Its Financial Statements (SSAE 15)

When are the provisions of SSAE 15 applicable?

The provisions of SSAE 15 are applicable when a practitioner is engaged to perform an examination of the design and operating effectiveness of an entity's internal control over financial reporting (*examination of internal control*) that is integrated with a financial statement audit (*integrated audit*). While the examination of the "effectiveness of internal control over financial reporting (*internal control*)" generally is applicable to internal control at an entity's fiscal year-end, management is permitted to choose a different date. The examination may cover internal control for a period of time rather than at a point in time. The practitioner should follow the guidance in this section even if the examination (1) is applicable to internal control at a date other than fiscal year-end or (2) covers a period of time.

When are the provisions of SSAE 15 not applicable?

SSAE 15 does not provide guidance to the practitioner who is engaged to:

- Examine (1) the suitability of design of internal control and (2) internal controls over the effectiveness and efficiency of operations.
- Examine internal controls over compliance with laws and regulations.

- Report on internal controls at a service organization.
- Perform agreed-upon procedures on internal controls.

The examination of internal control includes engagements to report directly on internal control or on a written assertion made by management about the effectiveness of internal control.

Caution

Under no circumstances should a practitioner accept an engagement to review an entity's internal control or a written assertion about the entity's internal control.

Note

The *practitioner* performing an integrated audit may be referred to as the *auditor* because the examination of internal control results in the same level of assurance as is provided in an audit of financial statements.

What definitions should the practitioner be familiar with?

Control objectives, which relate to relevant financial statement assertions, represent the aims or purposes of specific internal controls, and accordingly address the risk that one or more controls will not provide reasonable assurance that a misstatement or an omission relevant to an assertion will not be prevented, or detected and corrected timely.

A *deficiency in internal control* exists when the design or operation of an internal control does not allow management or other employees performing their normal assigned functions, to prevent or detect financial statement misstatements on a timely basis.

A *deficiency in design* exists when either (1) a control needed to meet a control objective is not present or (2) an existing control, when operating as designed, would not enable a control objective to be met.

A *deficiency in operation* exists when (1) a control that is in fact properly designed does not operate as intended or (2) the person performing the control lacks the necessary authority or competency to effectively perform the control.

A *detective control* is a control that is designed to detect and correct existing errors or fraud that could result in financial statement misstatement.

Internal control over financial reporting is a process effected by those charged with governance, management, and other employees that is designed to provide reasonable, but not absolute, assurance that the financial statements are reliable. Internal control has inherent limitations such as lapse in judgment, breakdown due to human failure, possible management override, and circumvention by collusion.

Management's assertion represents management's conclusion concerning the effectiveness of internal control that they include in their report on internal control.

A *material weakness* is a deficiency in internal control or a combination of deficiencies in internal control, resulting in a reasonable possibility that a material financial statement misstatement will not be prevented or detected and corrected timely. (It is important to note that internal control cannot be considered effective if one or more material weaknesses exist.)

A *preventive control* is a control that is designed to prevent errors or fraud that could result in financial statement misstatement.

A *relevant assertion* is a financial statement assertion that has a reasonable possibility of containing one or more misstatements that could result in materially misstated financial statements.

A *significant account or disclosure* is an account balance or disclosure item that has a reasonable possibility of containing one or more misstatements that could result in materially misstated financial statements.

A *significant deficiency* is a deficiency in internal control or a combination of deficiencies in internal control that is less severe than a material weakness, but is important enough to warrant attention by those charged with governance.

What is the objective of an examination of internal control?

The expression of an opinion on the effectiveness of internal control is the objective of an examination. Accordingly, an examination of internal control should be planned and performed to obtain sufficient appropriate evidence in order to obtain reasonable assurance about whether material weaknesses exist.

Is the practitioner required to search for deficiencies in internal control other than material weaknesses?

There is no requirement to search for deficiencies that are less severe than a material weakness.

What conditions are necessary for engagement performance?

A practitioner may examine the effectiveness of an entity's internal control if the following four conditions are met:

1. Management accepts responsibility for the effectiveness of internal control over financial reporting.
2. Management evaluates the effectiveness of internal control using suitable and available criteria (i.e., control criteria) that need not necessarily be established by the American Institute of Certified Public Accountants.
3. Management has sufficient appropriate evidence to support its assertion about the effectiveness of the entity's internal control.
4. Management's assertion about the effectiveness of the entity's internal control is presented in a report accompanied by the auditor's report.

Warning

An auditor should withdraw from an engagement if management refuses to provide a written assertion; however, if the examination is required by law or regulation and the auditor is legally precluded from withdrawing, the auditor should issue a disclaimer of opinion.

What types of evidence are considered to support management's assertion?

Management must identify and document the entity's controls and their related objectives. The form of documentation is discretionary and may include, for example:

- Policy manuals
- Accounting manuals
- Narrative memoranda
- Flowcharts
- Decision tables
- Procedural write-ups
- Questionnaires

Are there additional considerations applicable to integrating the examination with the financial statement audit?

The auditor should integrate the examination of internal control with the audit of the financial statements. While the objectives of an examination of internal control and a financial statement audit differ, an auditor should plan and perform the integrated audit to achieve the objectives of both engagements. Accordingly,

- Tests of controls should be designed to obtain sufficient appropriate evidence to support both (1) an opinion on the effectiveness of internal control at period-end and (2) the auditor's assessment of control risk, which is an integral part of the financial statement audit.
- The "as-of" date specified in management's assertion should be the same as the date of the balance sheet being audited.

When assessing control risk, which is a component of the risk of material misstatement, as part of a financial statement audit, an auditor may choose not to perform tests of controls. However, tests of controls must be performed as part of an integrated audit. As such, tests of controls would be performed primarily to provide a basis for the opinion on whether internal control is effective at period-end.

What is necessary in planning the engagement?

The examination of internal control should be properly planned. Accordingly, the auditor should consider the following 12 items:

1. Knowledge of internal control obtained during other types of engagements or a review of a predecessor's working papers
2. Intra-industry matters such as pertinent laws and regulations, economic factors, and financial reporting practices
3. Matters specific to the entity's business such as operating characteristics and its organizational and capital structure
4. Any significant changes in the entity, its operations, or its internal control
5. Preliminary judgments concerning materiality, audit risk, and other factors pertaining to material weaknesses in internal control
6. Prior communications to those charged with governance about deficiencies in internal control
7. Pertinent legal or regulatory matters
8. The nature and extent of available evidence concerning internal control effectiveness
9. Publicly available information relevant to the possibility of financial statement misstatement and the effectiveness of internal control
10. Known risks considered in evaluating the acceptance of the engagement or the retention of the client
11. Preliminary judgments concerning the effectiveness of internal control
12. The complexity of the client's operations

The risk assessment process applicable to an audit of financial statements is also applicable to planning and performing the examination of internal control. Attention should be directed to areas that represent the highest risk. The greater the risk that a material weakness could exist, the more attention the area warrants.

What is meant by scaling the engagement?

The examination should be scaled based on the size and complexity of the entity, its business processes, and its business units. Accordingly, when scaling the examination, the auditor should consider these six factors:

1. The number of business lines
2. The complexity of business processes
3. The complexity of the financial reporting systems
4. The centralization or decentralization of the accounting functions
5. The extent of senior management's involvement in daily business activities
6. The number of management levels

When performing an integrated audit, should the practitioner address the risk of fraud?

An integral component of a financial statement audit is the assessment of the risk of fraud, which may result in the identification of deficiencies in controls. This assessment, including any control deficiencies identified, should be incorporated into the planning and performance of the examination of internal control. Conversely, deficiencies in internal control identified during an examination of internal control should be considered when assessing the risk of fraud as part of the financial statement audit.

Am I permitted to use the work of other practitioners?

The auditor may use the work performed by or receive direct assistance from:

- Entity personnel
- Third parties working under the direction of management or those charged with governance
- Internal auditors

Before using the work of others, the auditor should assess the competency and objectivity of the persons whose work the auditor plans to utilize.

The extent to which the auditor may use the work of others should also be based on the risk associated with a particular control. An auditor should increase the extent of his or her own work as the risk associated with a particular control increases.

How should materiality be determined in an integrated audit?

Materiality for planning and performing the examination of internal control should be the same as materiality for planning and performing the audit of the financial statements.

What is a top-down approach?

A *top-down* approach should be used when examining internal control. The top-down approach is intended to describe the appropriate thought process for identifying risks and controls to test rather than a required sequence of examination procedures.

A top-down approach, which begins at the financial statement level, involves six procedures:

1. Utilizing an understanding of the overall risks to internal control.
2. Focusing on entity-level internal controls.
3. Working down to significant accounts and disclosure items and their relevant assertions.
4. Directing attention to significant accounts, disclosure items, and assertions that indicate a reasonable possibility of material misstatement.

Note

As in an audit of financial statements, identification of significant accounts, disclosure items, and assertions should be based on evaluation of qualitative and quantitative risk factors, as well as the source of potential misstatements.

Walk-throughs assist the auditor in identifying significant accounts, disclosure items, and assertions, as they enable the auditor to determine the likely sources of potential financial statement misstatements. A walk-through involves following a transaction from its initiation to its recording in the journals and ledgers. A walk-through is usually performed through a combination of inquiry, observation, inspection of documentation, recalculation, and reperformance of relevant controls.

5. Verifying the understanding of the risks in the entity's processes.
6. Choosing internal controls to test that adequately address the assessed risk of material misstatement at the relevant assertion level.

What are examples of entity-level controls?

Entity-level controls, which vary in nature and precision, include these eight:

1. Controls relating to the control environment
2. Controls addressing possible management override
3. The entity's risk assessment process
4. Centralized processing and related controls
5. Controls used to monitor operating results
6. Controls used to monitor other controls (e.g., use of internal auditors)
7. Controls over the period-end reporting process
8. Controls concerning risk management

Should the practitioner consider the period-end financial reporting process?

The period-end financial reporting process, which should be evaluated during the integrated audit, involves procedures used to:

- Post transaction totals into general ledger accounts
- Select and apply accounting policies
- Initiate, authorize, record, and process journal entries in the general ledger
- Record recurring and nonrecurring financial statement adjustments
- Prepare the entity's financial statements and related disclosures

In order to evaluate the period-end financial reporting process, the auditor should assess these six items:

1. The inputs, procedures performed, and outputs of the financial statement preparation processes
2. The extent to which information technology impacts the financial reporting process
3. Who from management participates in the financial reporting process
4. The locations where the period-end financial reporting process occurs
5. The types of adjusting and consolidating journal entries
6. The nature and extent of the oversight by management and those charged with governance

How should the practitioner select controls to test?

The controls selected for testing should be those that would influence the auditor's conclusion about whether the controls sufficiently address the assessed risk of material misstatement at the assertion level.

The auditor should evaluate design effectiveness of controls in terms of their ability either to prevent or to detect and correct financial statement misstatements. Procedures used to perform this evaluation commonly include a combination of inquiry, observation, and inspection of documentation. Walk-throughs are usually sufficient for evaluation purposes because they generally include these procedures.

Tests of operating effectiveness should be performed to determine whether the control is operating as designed and whether the individual performing the control has the authority and competence to effectively perform the control.

Procedures used to test operating effectiveness include inquiry, observation, inspection of documentation, recalculation, and reperformance of controls.

What is the relationship of risk to the evidence to be obtained?

The need to obtain more evidence increases when there is an increase in the risk that a control might not be effective (and accordingly, a risk of material misstatement exists).

The auditor is not required to obtain evidence to support an opinion on specific controls. The auditor should obtain sufficient appropriate evidence to support an opinion on internal control taken as a whole.

What should be considered in determining the nature, extent, and timing of tests of controls?

Procedures used to test operating effectiveness, in order of the quality of evidence produced, are inquiry, observation, inspection of documentation, recalculation, and reperformance of controls. It should be noted that evidence obtained from inquiry alone would not provide a basis for an opinion concerning the effectiveness of internal control.

The auditor should realize that more evidence will be obtained when tests of controls are performed over a longer period of time rather than over a shorter period of time. Additionally, more evidence can be obtained when tests of controls are performed closer to the date of management's assertion as opposed to performing tests of controls at an earlier point in time.

Finally, there is a direct relationship between the amount of evidence obtained from a test and the amount of testing.

May roll-forward procedures be used?

Evidence obtained at an interim date may be used when reporting on the effectiveness of internal control at a later date. However, the auditor should consider the need to obtain additional evidence for the remaining period of time. Accordingly, the auditor should take into account (1) the length of the remaining period,

(2) possible subsequent significant changes in internal control, and (3) the nature of the control tested at the interim date.

What is important to consider when evaluating identified deficiencies?

The severity of each deficiency identified should be considered in order to determine whether deficiencies, individually or in combination, represent a material weakness. Severity is a measure of (1) the magnitude of potential misstatement resulting from the ineffectiveness of the control and (2) the possibility that, based on the control, a financial statement misstatement will not be prevented or will not be detected and corrected.

The existence of one or more compensating controls can mitigate the severity of a control deficiency such that it is not a material weakness. However, compensating controls do not eliminate control deficiencies. It should be readily apparent that the auditor should perform tests of controls to evaluate the effectiveness of compensating controls.

What should the practitioner do to conclude the engagement?

At the conclusion of the engagement, after evaluating the evidence obtained from all sources, the auditor should form an opinion regarding the effectiveness of internal control. The opinion should be based on the following four items:

1. The examination of internal control
2. Misstatements detected during the course of the financial statement audit
3. Identified deficiencies in internal control, if any
4. A review of pertinent sections of reports prepared by internal auditors

The auditor should then evaluate management's report on the effectiveness of internal control to ensure inclusion of the following six items:

1. A statement that management is responsible for internal control
2. A description of the subject matter examined (e.g., internal controls over the preparation of the entity's financial statements in accordance with GAAP)
3. Identification of the measurement criteria (e.g., criteria established in the Committee of Sponsoring Organizations of the Treadway Commission's Internal Control—Integrated Framework)
4. Management's assertion about the effectiveness of the entity's internal control
5. If applicable, a description of material weaknesses identified
6. The date as of which management's assertion is made

If the auditor considers management's report to be incomplete or inaccurate, the auditor should request that management revise its report. In the absence of appropriate revision, the auditor should modify his or her report. Failure of management to furnish a report generally should cause the auditor to withdraw from the engagement.

Must the practitioner obtain written representations from management in order to conclude the engagement?

An important procedure in an examination of internal control is to obtain written representations from management covering these eight areas:

1. Acknowledging its responsibility for establishing and maintaining effective internal control
2. Stating that management has evaluated the effectiveness of internal control using specified criteria (which must also be stated)
3. Stating that management did not consider the auditor's procedures in developing its written assertion
4. Stating management's assertion concerning the effectiveness of internal control based on control criteria as of (at) a specified date
5. Stating that all internal control deficiencies have been disclosed to the auditor, including separate disclosure of material weaknesses and significant deficiencies
6. Describing instances of fraud (1) resulting in material misstatement of the financial statements and (2) not resulting in material misstatement of the financial statements, but involving senior management or others having a significant role in internal control
7. Stating whether previously communicated significant deficiencies and material weaknesses have been remediated (those not remediated should be specifically identified)
8. Stating whether there were any subsequent-period changes in internal control or other factors (including remediation of significant deficiencies or material weaknesses) that could have a significant effect on internal control

What if management refuses to furnish the written representations requested by the practitioner?

Management's failure to furnish written representations is tantamount to a scope limitation. The auditor should then consider his or her ability to rely on other representations, including those obtained during the financial statement audit.

What are the communication requirements?

The auditor should communicate, in writing, to management and those charged with governance, significant deficiencies and material weaknesses identified during the integrated audit. Significant deficiencies and material weaknesses that were previously communicated but have not been remediated should also be communicated in writing. This may be accomplished by reference to the previous communication, including the date of the communication.

If the auditor concludes that the audit committee's oversight of the financial reporting process and internal control is ineffective, this conclusion should be communicated to the board of directors.

The written communications just discussed should generally be made by the report release date, which is the date that the auditor gives the entity permission to use the auditor's report.

Oral communication of significant matters may be made during the integrated audit. The auditor, however, is not relieved of his or her responsibility for the written communications just discussed.

All deficiencies not considered to be material weaknesses or significant deficiencies should be communicated to management, in writing, no later than 60 days from the report release date. Further, those charged with governance should be advised of this communication. However, any of these deficiencies previously communicated need not be communicated again.

Warning

The auditor should never state in a report that no material weaknesses were identified during the integrated audit.

Example 11.21   Written Communication of Significant Deficiencies and Material Weaknesses

In connection with my (our) audit of W Company's financial statements as of December 31, 2X12, and for the year then ended, and my (our) audit of the W Company's internal control over financial reporting as of December 31, 2X12 ("integrated audit"), the standards established by the American Institute of Certified Public Accountants require that I (we) advise you of the following internal control matters identified during my (our) integrated audit.

My (Our) responsibility is to plan and perform my (our) integrated audit to obtain reasonable assurance about whether the financial statements are free of material misstatement, whether caused by error or fraud, and whether effective internal control over financial reporting was maintained in all material respects (that is, whether material weaknesses exist as of the date specified in management's assertion). The integrated audit is not designed to detect deficiencies that, individually or in combination, are less severe than a material weakness. However, I am (we are) responsible for communicating to management and those charged with governance significant deficiencies and material weaknesses identified during the integrated audit. I am (We are) also responsible for communicating management deficiencies that are of a lesser magnitude than a significant deficiency, unless previously communicated, and inform those charged with governance when such a communication was made.

A deficiency in internal control over financial reporting exists when the design or operation of a control does not allow management or employees, in the normal course of performing their assigned functions, to prevent or detect and correct misstatements on a timely basis. [*A material weakness is a deficiency, or a combination of deficiencies, in internal control over financial reporting, such that there is a reasonable possibility that a material misstatement of the company's financial statement will not be prevented, or detected and corrected on a timely basis.*] I (We) believe the following deficiencies constitute material weaknesses:

[*Describe the material weaknesses that were identified during the integrated audit. The auditor may separately identify those material weaknesses that exist as of the date of management's assertion by referring to the auditor's report.*]

[*A significant deficiency is a deficiency or a combination of deficiencies in internal control over financial reporting that is less severe than a material weakness, yet important enough to merit attention by those charged with governance.*] I (We) consider the following deficiencies to be significant deficiencies:

[*Describe the significant deficiencies that were identified during the integrated audit.*]

This communication is intended solely for the information and use of management, [*identify the body or individuals charged with governance*], others within the organization, and [*identify any specified governmental authorities*], and is not intended to be and should not be used by anyone other than these specified parties.

What should be included in the auditor's examination report on internal control?

The auditor's examination report on internal control should include:

- A title that includes the word *independent*
- A statement that management is responsible for maintaining effective internal control and for evaluating the effectiveness of internal control
- Identification of management's assertion on internal control that accompanies the auditor's report, including a reference to management's report
- A statement that the auditor's responsibility is to express an opinion on the entity's internal control (or management's assertion) based on the examination
- A statement that the examination was conducted in accordance with attestation standards established by the American Institute of Certified Public Accountants
- A statement that those standards require the auditor to plan and perform the examination to obtain reasonable assurance about whether effective internal control was maintained in all material respects
- A statement that an examination includes obtaining an understanding of internal control over financial reporting, assessing the risk that a material weakness exists, testing and evaluating the design and operating effectiveness of internal control based on the assessed risk, and performing such other procedures as the auditor considered necessary in the circumstances
- A statement that the auditor believes the examination provides a reasonable basis for the opinion
- A definition of internal control, which should be the same as used by management in its report

- A paragraph stating that, because of inherent limitations, internal control may not prevent or not detect and correct misstatements and that projections of any evaluation of effectiveness to future periods are subject to the risk that controls may become inadequate because of changes in conditions, or that the degree of compliance with the policies or procedures may deteriorate
- An opinion on whether:
  - The entity maintained, in all material respects, effective internal control as of the specified date, or during a period of time, based on the control criteria; or
  - Management's assertion about the effectiveness of the entity's internal control as of the specified date is fairly stated, in all material respects, based on the control criteria
- A signature of the auditor's firm, which may be manual or printed
- The date of the examination report

Example 11.22

Standard form to be used when the practitioner is reporting directly on the effectiveness of an entity's internal control as of a specified date.

Independent Accountant's Report

[*Introductory paragraph*]

I (We) have examined the effectiveness of W Company's internal control over financial reporting as of December 31, 2X12, based on [*identify criteria*]. W Company's management is responsible for maintaining effective internal control over financial reporting. My (Our) responsibility is to express an opinion on the effectiveness of internal control based on my (our) examination.

[*Scope paragraph*]

My (Our) examination was conducted in accordance with attestation standards established by the American Institute of Certified Public Accountants and, accordingly, included obtaining an understanding of internal control over financial reporting, testing, and evaluating the design and operating effectiveness of internal control, and performing such other procedures as I (we) considered necessary in the circumstances. I (We) believe that my (our) examination provides a reasonable basis for my (our) opinion.

[*Inherent limitations paragraph*]

Because of inherent limitations in any internal control, misstatements due to error or fraud may occur and not be detected. Also, projections of any evaluation of internal control over financial reporting to future periods are subject to the risk that the internal control may become inadequate because of changes in conditions, or that the degree of compliance with the policies or procedures may deteriorate.

[*Opinion paragraph*]

In my (our) opinion, W Company maintained, in all material respects, effective internal control over financial reporting as of December 31, 2X12, based on [*identify criteria*].

[*Signature*]
[*Date*]

Example 11.23

Standard form to be used when the practitioner is reporting on management's assertion about the effectiveness of an entity's internal control.

Independent Accountant's Report

[*Introductory paragraph*]

I (We) have examined management's assertion, included in the accompanying [*title of management report*], that W Company maintained effective internal control over financial reporting as of December 31, 2X12, based on [*identify criteria*]. W Company's management is responsible for maintaining effective internal control over financial reporting. My (Our) responsibility is to express an opinion on management's assertion based on my (our) examination.

[*Standard scope and inherent limitations paragraphs*]
[*Opinion paragraph*]

In my (our) opinion, management's assertion that W Company maintained effective internal control over financial reporting as of December 31, 2X12, is fairly stated, in all material respects, based on [*identify criteria*].

[*Signature*]
[*Date*]

May the auditor choose to issue separate or combined reports?

The auditor may issue (1) a combined report that contains the auditor's opinion on the financial statements and his or her opinion on internal control or (2) separate reports on the financial statements and on internal control. If the auditor chooses the latter, the following paragraph should be added to the auditor's report on the financial statements:

> *I (We) have also examined* [or audited], *in accordance with attestation standards established by the American Institute of Certified Public Accountants,* [company name]'s *internal control over financial reporting as of December 31, 2X12, based*

on [identify control criteria]*, and our report dated* [date of report, which should be the same as the date of the report on the financial statements] *expressed* [include nature of opinion].

In addition, the following paragraph should be added to the report on internal control:

> *We have also audited, in accordance with auditing standards generally accepted in the United States of America, the* [identify financial statements] *of* [company name]*, and our report dated* [date of report, which should be the same as the date of the report on internal control] *expressed* [include nature of opinion].

How should the practitioner date the report on internal control?

The report on internal control should be dated no earlier than the date on which the auditor has obtained sufficient appropriate evidence to support his or her opinion. This should be the same date used in the audit report on the financial statements.

When should the auditor issue an adverse opinion?

An adverse opinion should be issued if the auditor identifies deficiencies that, individually or in combination, result in one or more material weaknesses.

The existence of one or more material weaknesses precludes the auditor from expressing an opinion on management's assertion. Rather, the auditor should report directly on the effectiveness of internal control. The auditor's report should also be modified to include (1) the definition of a material weakness and (2) a statement that one or more material weaknesses have been identified and an identification of the material weaknesses described in management's assertion. Reference to the material weaknesses included in management's report is permissible, and the auditor need not describe each material weakness, as long as management's report fully discloses each material weakness and is fairly presented. In the event that one or more material weaknesses have not been disclosed in management's report, the auditor's report should be modified to (1) indicate the omission and (2) include a description of each material weakness, including the actual and potential effect on the entity's financial statements. Those charged with governance should be notified in writing of the situation and the appropriate details.

The issuance of an adverse opinion on internal control may have an effect on the auditor's opinion on the financial statements. Finally, the auditor should disclose whether the opinion on the financial statements was influenced by the material weaknesses.

When is it appropriate to modify the report on internal control?

Modification of the auditor's report is warranted when:

- Elements of management's report are incomplete or improperly presented.
- The scope of the examination is restricted.
- The auditor's report contains a reference to the report of another auditor.
- Other information is included in management's report.

What should the auditor do if elements of management's report are incomplete or improperly presented?

Management is responsible for revising its report if any element is incomplete or improperly presented. Management's failure to make the appropriate revisions should cause the auditor to modify his or her report to include an explanatory paragraph that describes the situation.

What action is necessary if the auditor encounters scope restrictions?

The auditor is precluded from expressing an opinion on an entity's internal control if there are restrictions on the scope of the auditor's work. Accordingly, scope restrictions should cause the auditor to withdraw from the engagement or issue a disclaimer of opinion.

When issuing a disclaimer of opinion, the auditor should specifically state that he or she does not express an opinion on the effectiveness of internal control. Additionally, the auditor should add explanatory language to indicate the substantive reasons for the disclaimer but should omit any description of the engagement characteristics.

If material weaknesses were identified by the limited procedures performed, the auditor's report containing the disclaimer of opinion should include the definition of a material weakness and a description of the material weaknesses identified.

The inability to (1) complete the examination of internal control and (2) express an opinion should be communicated in writing to management and those charged with governance.

What is an auditor's responsibility with respect to other information included in management's report?

The auditor should disclaim an opinion on other information included in management's report accompanying the auditor's report by adding the following paragraph to his or her examination report:

> *We do not express an opinion or any other form of assurance on* [describe additional information, such as management's cost-benefit statement].

Do subsequent events have any impact on the integrated audit engagement?

It is important that the auditor inquire of management about changes in internal control and other related factors occurring subsequent to the date as of which internal control is being examined, but before the audit report date. The auditor should also obtain written representations from management concerning such matters. The provisions concerning subsequent events applicable to audits of financial statements may be useful in connection with subsequent events that could affect the auditor's report on internal control.

Identification in the subsequent events period of a material weakness that existed as of the date specified in management's assertion should prompt the auditor (1) to report directly on internal control and (2) to express an adverse opinion.

The auditor should add an explanatory paragraph to his or her report on internal control to describe any condition that (1) did not exist as of the date specified in management's assertion, (2) arose after that date and before the release of the examination report, and (3) could have a material effect on internal control.

While the auditor has no responsibility to keep informed of matters after the issuance of the examination report, if the auditor does become aware of matters that existed at the report date that might have had an effect on the report had he or she been aware of them, the auditor's actions should be guided by the financial statement auditing provisions applicable to subsequent discovery of facts existing at the date of the auditor's report.

Integration with the Financial Statement Audit

How do tests of controls in an examination of internal control differ from tests of controls in an audit of financial statements?

Tests of controls in an examination of internal control are performed in order to obtain sufficient appropriate evidence to support the auditor's opinion on the effectiveness of internal control as of a point in time. To express his or her opinion, the auditor needs to:

- Be satisfied that internal control operated effectively for a sufficient period of time, which need not be the entire period covered by entity's financial statements.
- Obtain evidence concerning the effectiveness of selected controls over all relevant assertions. (This involves testing controls not ordinarily tested in a financial statement audit.)

Note

The auditor's opinion on the effectiveness of internal control may be based in part on the results of tests of controls performed in the financial statement audit.

Tests of controls in an audit of financial statements are usually performed when the auditor (1) wants to base his or her assessment of the risk of material misstatement on effective internal control or (2) concludes that detection risk cannot be reduced to an acceptably low level based on substantive procedures alone.

Tests of controls in an audit of financial statements should be designed to obtain sufficient appropriate evidence concerning the effectiveness of controls throughout the period covered by the financial statements. However, there is no requirement to test controls for *all* relevant assertions.

Note

The results of tests of controls performed in the examination of internal control (including deficiencies identified) should be considered in the financial statement audit when determining (1) the need for further tests of controls and (2) the nature, extent, and timing of substantive procedures.

Caution

Procedures performed to opine on the effectiveness of internal control never eliminate the need to perform substantive procedures for all relevant assertions in a financial statement audit.

What effect do substantive procedures have on conclusions about the operating effectiveness of internal controls?

As part of the examination of internal control, the auditor should evaluate the results of substantive procedures performed in the financial statement audit to determine the effect, if any, on the effectiveness of internal control. At a minimum, the evaluation should take into account:

- Risk assessments, especially those related to fraud, pertinent to substantive procedures
- Findings in connection with illegal acts and related-party transactions
- Any management bias in formulating estimates and selecting accounting principles
- Financial statement misstatements identified

Warning

The auditor's conclusion that there are no material misstatements in the financial statements should not cause the auditor to conclude that an internal control is operating effectively. Effectiveness of an internal control must be based on direct testing of the control. However, failure of substantive procedures to detect material misstatements may impact the auditor's risk assessment for purposes of determining tests of controls needed to form a conclusion about the operating effectiveness of a control.

The following examples are of illustrative reports applicable to engagements to examine an entity's internal control over financial reporting. (Please note that the word *audit* may be substituted for the word *examination* throughout the illustrative reports.)

Example 11.24   Unqualified Opinion on Internal Control

The following represents a standard report expressing an unqualified opinion directly on internal control.

Independent Auditor's Report

[Introductory paragraph]

    I (We) have examined W Company's internal control over financial reporting as of December 31, 2X12, based on [*identify criteria*]. W Company's management is responsible for maintaining effective internal control over financial reporting, and for its assertions of the effectiveness of internal control over financial reporting, included in the accompanying [*title of management's report*]. My (Our) responsibility is to express an opinion on W Company's internal control over financial reporting based on my (our) examination.

    [Scope paragraph]

    I (We) conducted my (our) examination in accordance with attestation standards established by the American Institute of Certified Public Accountants. Those standards require that I (we) plan and perform the examination to obtain reasonable assurance about whether effective internal control over financial reporting was maintained in all material respects. My (Our) examination included obtaining an understanding of internal control over financial reporting, assessing the risk that a material weakness exists, and testing and evaluating the design and operating effectiveness of internal control based on the assessed risk. My (Our) examination also included performing such other procedures as I (we) considered necessary in the circumstances. I (We) believe that my (our) examination provides a reasonable basis for my (our) opinion.

    [Definition paragraph]

    An entity's internal control over financial reporting is a process effected by those charged with governance, management, and other personnel, designed to provide reasonable assurance regarding the preparation of reliable financial statements in accordance with [*applicable financial reporting framework, such as accounting principles generally accepted in the United States of America*]. An entity's internal control over financial reporting includes those policies and procedures that (1) pertain to the maintenance of records that, in reasonable detail, accurately and fairly reflect the transactions and dispositions of the assets of the entity; (2) provide reasonable assurance that transactions are recorded as necessary to permit preparation of financial statements in accordance with [*applicable financial reporting framework, such as accounting principles generally accepted in the United States of America*], and that receipts and expenditures of the entity are being made only in accordance with authorizations of management and those charged with governance; and (3) provide reasonable assurance regarding prevention or timely detection and correction of unauthorized acquisition, use, or disposition of the entity's assets that could have a material effect on the financial statements.

[*Inherent limitations paragraph*]

Because of its inherent limitations, internal control over financial reporting may not prevent or detect and correct misstatements. Also, projections of any evaluation of effectiveness to future periods are subject to the risk that controls may become inadequate because of changes in conditions, or that the degree of compliance with the policies or procedures may deteriorate.

[*Opinion paragraph*]

In my (our) opinion, W Company maintained, in all material respects, effective internal control over financial reporting as of December 31, 2X12, based on [*identify criteria*].

[*Audit of financial statements paragraph*]

I (We) also have audited, in accordance with auditing standards generally accepted in the United States of America, the [*identify financial statements*] of W Company, and my (our) report dated [*date of report, which should be the same as the date of the report on the examination of internal control*] expressed [*include nature of opinion*].

[*Signature*]
[*Date*]

Example 11.25   Unqualified Opinion on Management's Assertion

The following represents a standard report expressing an unqualified opinion on management's assertion.

Independent Auditor's Report

[*Introductory paragraph*]

We have examined management's assertion, included in the accompanying [*title of management report*], that W Company maintained effective internal control over financial reporting as of December 31, 2X12, based on [*identify criteria*]. W Company's management is responsible for maintaining effective internal control over financial reporting, and for its assertion of the effectiveness of internal

(continued)

(Continued)

control over financial reporting, included in the accompanying [*title of management's report*]. Our responsibility is to express an opinion on management's assertion based on our examination.

[*Scope paragraph*]

We conducted our examination in accordance with attestation standards established by the American Institute of Certified Public Accountants. Those standards require that we plan and perform the examination to obtain reasonable assurance about whether effective internal control over financial reporting was maintained in all material respects. Our examination included obtaining an understanding of internal control over financial reporting, assessing the risk that a material weakness exists, and testing and evaluating the design and operating effectiveness of internal control based on the assessed risk. Our examination also included performing such other procedures as we considered necessary in the circumstances. We believe that our examination provides a reasonable basis for our opinion.

[*Definition paragraph*]

An entity's internal control over financial reporting is a process effected by those charged with governance, management, and other personnel, designed to provide reasonable assurance regarding the preparation of reliable financial statements in accordance with [*applicable financial reporting framework, such as accounting principles generally accepted in the United States of America*]. An entity's internal control over financial reporting includes those policies and procedures that (1) pertain to the maintenance of records that, in reasonable detail, accurately and fairly reflect the transactions and dispositions of the assets of the entity; (2) provide reasonable assurance that transactions are recorded as necessary to permit preparation of financial statements in accordance with [*applicable financial reporting framework, such as accounting principles generally accepted in the United States of America*], and that receipts and expenditures of the entity are being made only in accordance with authorizations of management and those charged with governance; and (3) provide reasonable assurance regarding prevention, or timely detection and correction of unauthorized acquisition, use, or disposition of the entity's assets that could have a material effect on the financial statements.

[*Inherent limitations paragraph*]

Because of its inherent limitations, internal control over financial reporting may not prevent or detect and correct misstatements. Also, projections of any evaluation of effectiveness to future periods are subject to the risk that controls may become inadequate because of changes in conditions, or that the degree of compliance with the policies or procedures may deteriorate.

[*Opinion paragraph*]

In our opinion, management's assertion that W Company maintained effective internal control over financial reporting as of December 31, 2X12, is fairly stated, in all material respects, based on [*identify criteria*].

[*Audit of financial statements paragraph*]

We also have audited, in accordance with auditing standards generally accepted in the United States of America, the [*identify financial statements*] of W Company, and our report dated [*date of report, which should be the same as the date of the report on the examination of internal control*] expressed [*include nature of opinion*].

[*Signature*]
[*Date*]

Example 11.26   Adverse Opinion on Internal Control

The following is an illustrative report expressing an adverse opinion on internal control when the opinion on the financial statements is not affected by the adverse opinion on internal control.

Independent Auditor's Report

[*Introductory paragraph*]

I (We) have examined W Company's internal control over financial reporting as of December 31, 2X12, based on [*identify criteria*]. W Company's management is responsible for maintaining effective internal control over financial reporting, and for its assertion of the effectiveness of internal control over financial reporting, included in the accompanying [*title of management's report*]. My (Our) responsibility is to express an opinion on W Company's internal control over financial reporting based on my (our) examination.

[*Scope paragraph*]

I (We) conducted my (our) examination in accordance with attestation standards established by the American Institute of Certified Public Accountants. Those standards require that I (we) plan and perform the examination to obtain reasonable assurance about whether effective internal control over financial reporting was maintained in all material respects. My (Our) examination included obtaining an understanding of internal control over financial reporting, assessing the risk that a material weakness exists, and testing and evaluating the design and operating effectiveness of internal control based on the assessed risk. My (Our)

(continued)

(Continued)

examination also included performing such other procedures as I (we) considered necessary in the circumstances. I (We) believe that my (our) examination provides a reasonable basis for my (our) opinion.

[Definition paragraph]

An entity's internal control over financial reporting is a process effected by those charged with governance, management, and other personnel, designed to provide reasonable assurance regarding the preparation of reliable financial statements in accordance with *[applicable financial reporting framework, such as accounting principles generally accepted in the United States of America]*. An entity's internal control over financial reporting includes those policies and procedures that (1) pertain to the maintenance of records that, in reasonable detail, accurately and fairly reflect the transactions and dispositions of the assets of the entity; (2) provide reasonable assurance that transactions are recorded as necessary to permit preparation of financial statements in accordance with *[applicable financial reporting framework, such as accounting principles generally accepted in the United States of America]*, and that receipts and expenditures of the entity are being made only in accordance with authorizations of management and those charged with governance; and (3) provide reasonable assurance regarding prevention or timely detection and correction of unauthorized acquisition, use, or disposition of the entity's assets that could have a material effect on the financial statements.

[Inherent limitations paragraph]

Because of its inherent limitations, internal control over financial reporting may not prevent or detect and correct misstatements. Also, projections of any evaluation of effectiveness to future periods are subject to the risk that controls may become inadequate because of changes in conditions, or that the degree of compliance with the policies or procedures may deteriorate.

[Explanatory paragraph]

A material weakness is a deficiency or a combination of deficiencies in internal control over financial reporting such that there is a reasonable possibility that a material misstatement of the entity's financial statements will not be prevented, or detected and corrected on a timely basis.

The following material weakness has been identified and included in the accompanying *[title of management's report]*.

[Identify the material weakness described in management's report.]
[Opinion paragraph]

In my (our) opinion, because of the effect of the material weakness described above on the achievement of the objectives of the control criteria, W Company has not maintained effective internal control over financial reporting as of December 31, 2X12, based on *[identify criteria]*.

[Audit of financial statements paragraph]

I (We) also have audited, in accordance with auditing standards generally accepted in the United States of America, the *[identify financial statements]* of W Company. I (We) considered the material weakness identified above in determining the nature, timing, and extent of audit tests applied in my (our) audit of the 2X12 financial statements, and this report does not affect my (our) report dated *[date of report, which should be the same as the date of the report on the examination of internal control]*, which expressed *[include nature of opinion]*.

[Signature]
[Date]

Example 11.27   Disclaimer of Opinion on Internal Control

The following is an illustrative report expressing a disclaimer of opinion on internal control when a material weakness was identified during the limited procedures performed by the auditor.

Independent Auditor's Report

[Introductory paragraph]

I was (We were) engaged to examine W Company's internal control over financial reporting as of December 31, 2X12, based on *[identify criteria]*. W Company's management is responsible for maintaining effective internal control over financial reporting, and for its assertion of the effectiveness of internal control over financial reporting, included in the accompanying *[title of management's report]*.

[Paragraph that describes the substantive reasons for the scope limitation]

Accordingly, I was (we were) unable to perform auditing procedures necessary to form an opinion on W Company's internal control over financial reporting as of December 31, 2X12.

[Definition paragraph]

An entity's internal control over financial reporting is a process effected by those charged with governance, management, and other personnel, designed to provide reasonable assurance regarding the preparation of reliable financial statements in accordance with *[applicable financial reporting framework, such as accounting principles generally accepted in the United States of America]*. An entity's internal control over financial reporting includes those policies and

(continued)

(Continued)

procedures that (1) pertain to the maintenance of records that, in reasonable detail, accurately and fairly reflect the transactions and dispositions of the assets of the entity; (2) provide reasonable assurance that transactions are recorded as necessary to permit preparation of financial statements in accordance with [*applicable financial reporting framework, such as accounting principles generally accepted in the United States of America*], and that receipts and expenditures of the entity are being made only in accordance with authorizations of management and those charged with governance; and (3) provide reasonable assurance regarding prevention or timely detection and correction of unauthorized acquisition, use, or disposition of the entity's assets that could have a material effect on the financial statements.

[*Inherent limitations paragraph*]

Because of its inherent limitations, internal control over financial reporting may not prevent or detect and correct misstatements. Also, projections of any evaluation of effectiveness to future periods are subject to the risk that controls may become inadequate because of changes in conditions, or that the degree of compliance with the policies or procedures may deteriorate.

[*Explanatory paragraph*]

A material weakness is a deficiency or a combination of deficiencies in internal control over financial reporting, such that there is a reasonable possibility that a material misstatement of the entity's financial statements will not be prevented or detected and corrected on a timely basis.

The following material weakness has been identified and included in the accompanying [*title of management's report*].

[*Identify the material weakness described in management's report.*]
[*Opinion paragraph*]

In my (our) opinion, because of the effect of the material weakness described above on the achievement of the objectives of the control criteria, W Company has not maintained effective internal control over financial reporting as of December 31, 2X12, based on [*identify criteria*].

[*Audit of financial statements paragraph*]

I (We) also have audited, in accordance with auditing standards generally accepted in the United States of America, the [*identify financial statements*] of W Company. I (We) considered the material weakness identified above in determining the nature, timing, and extent of audit tests applied in my (our) audit of the 2X12 financial statements, and this report does not affect my (our) report dated [*date of report, which should be the same as the date of the report on the examination of internal control*], which expressed [*include nature of opinion*].

[*Signature*]
[*Date*]

Example 11.28 Unqualified Opinion on Internal Control Based in Part on the Report of Another Auditor

The following is an illustrative report expressing an unqualified opinion on internal control when the auditor decides to refer to the report of another auditor as the basis, in part, for the auditor's own report.

Independent Auditor's Report

[Introductory paragraph]

I (We) have examined W Company's internal control over financial reporting as of December 31, 2X12, based on *[identify criteria]*. W Company's management is responsible for maintaining effective internal control over financial reporting, and for its assertion of the effectiveness of internal control over financial reporting, included in the accompanying *[title of management's report]*. My (Our) responsibility is to express an opinion on W Company's internal control over financial reporting based on my (our) examination. I (We) did not examine the effectiveness of internal control over financial reporting of B Company, a wholly owned subsidiary, whose financial statements reflect total assets and revenues constituting 20 percent and 30 percent, respectively, of the related consolidated financial statement amounts as of December 31, 2X12, and for the year ended December 31, 2X12. The effectiveness of B Company's internal control over financial reporting was examined by another auditor whose report has been furnished to me (us), and my (our) opinion, insofar as it relates to the effectiveness of B Company's internal control over financial reporting, is based solely on the report of the other auditor.

[Scope paragraph]

I (We) conducted our examination in accordance with attestation standards established by the American Institute of Certified Public Accountants. Those standards require that I (we) plan and perform the examination to obtain reasonable assurance about whether effective internal control over financial reporting was maintained in all material respects. My (Our) examination included obtaining an understanding of internal control over financial reporting, assessing the risk that a material weakness exists, and testing and evaluating the design and operating effectiveness of internal control based on the assessed risk. My (Our) examination also included performing such other procedures as I (we) considered necessary in the circumstances. I (We) believe that my (our) examination and the report of the other auditor provide a reasonable basis for my (our) opinion.

[Definition paragraph]

An entity's internal control over financial reporting is a process effected by those charged with governance, management, and other personnel, designed to provide reasonable assurance regarding the preparation of reliable financial

(continued)

(Continued)

statements in accordance with [*applicable financial reporting framework, such as accounting principles generally accepted in the United States of America*]. An entity's internal control over financial reporting includes those policies and procedures that (1) pertain to the maintenance of records that, in reasonable detail, accurately and fairly reflect the transactions and dispositions of the assets of the entity; (2) provide reasonable assurance that transactions are recorded as necessary to permit preparation of financial statements in accordance with [*applicable financial reporting framework, such as accounting principles generally accepted in the United States of America*], and that receipts and expenditures of the entity are being made only in accordance with authorizations of management and those charged with governance; and (3) provide reasonable assurance regarding prevention or timely detection and correction of unauthorized acquisition, use, or disposition of the entity's assets that could have a material effect on the financial statements.

[*Inherent limitations paragraph*]

Because of its inherent limitations, internal control over financial reporting may not prevent or detect and correct misstatements. Also, projections of any evaluation of effectiveness to future periods are subject to the risk that controls may become inadequate because of changes in conditions, or that the degree of compliance with the policies or procedures may deteriorate.

[*Opinion paragraph*]

In my (our) opinion, based on my (our) examination and the report of the other auditor, W Company maintained, in all material respects, effective internal control over financial reporting as of December 31, 2X12, based on [*identify criteria*].

[*Audit of financial statements paragraph*]

I (We) also have audited, in accordance with auditing standards generally accepted in the United States of America, the [*identify financial statements*] of W Company, and our report dated [*date of report, which should be the same as the date of the report on the examination of internal control*] expressed [*include nature of opinion*].

[*Signature*]
[*Date*]

Example 11.29　Combined Report Expressing an Unqualified Opinion on Internal Control and on the Financial Statements

The following is an illustrative combined report expressing an unqualified opinion directly on internal control and on the financial statements. This report refers to the examination of internal control as an audit.

Independent Auditor's Report

[Introductory paragraph]

I (We) have audited the accompanying balance sheet of W Company as of December 31, 2X12, and the related statements of income, retained earnings, and cash flows for the year then ended. I (We) also have audited W Company's internal control over financial reporting as of December 31, 2X12, based on *[identify criteria]*. W Company's management is responsible for these financial statements, for maintaining effective internal control over financial reporting, and for its assertion of the effectiveness of internal control over financial reporting, included in the accompanying *[title of management's report]*. My (Our) responsibility is to express an opinion on these financial statements and an opinion on W Company's internal control over financial reporting based on my (our) audits.

[Scope paragraph]

I (We) conducted my (our) audit of the financial statements in accordance with auditing standards generally accepted in the United States of America and my (our) audit of internal control over financial reporting in accordance with attestation standards established by the American Institute of Certified Public Accountants. Those standards require that I (we) plan and perform the audits to obtain reasonable assurance about whether the financial statements are free of material misstatement and whether effective internal control over financial reporting was maintained in all material respects. My (Our) audit of the financial statements included examining, on a test basis, evidence supporting the amounts and disclosures in the financial statements, assessing the accounting principles used and significant estimates made by management, as well as evaluating the overall financial statement presentation. My (Our) audit of internal control over financial reporting included obtaining an understanding of internal control over financial reporting, assessing the risk that a material weakness exists, and testing and evaluating the design and operating effectiveness of internal control based on the assessed risk. My (Our) audits also included performing such other procedures as I (We) considered necessary in the circumstances. I (We) believe that our audits provide a reasonable basis for our opinion.

[Definition paragraph]

An entity's internal control over financial reporting is a process effected by those charged with governance, management, and other personnel, designed to provide reasonable assurance regarding the preparation of reliable financial statements in accordance with *[applicable financial reporting framework, such as accounting principles generally accepted in the United States of America]*. An entity's internal control over financial reporting includes those policies and procedures that (1) pertain to the maintenance of records that, in reasonable detail, accurately and fairly reflect the transactions and dispositions of the assets of the

(continued)

(Continued)

entity; (2) provide reasonable assurance that transactions are recorded as necessary to permit preparation of financial statements in accordance with [*applicable
financial reporting framework, such as accounting principles generally accepted
in the United States of America*], and that receipts and expenditures of the entity are being made only in accordance with authorizations of management and
those charged with governance; and (3) provide reasonable assurance regarding prevention, or timely detection and correction of unauthorized acquisition,
use, or disposition of the entity's assets that could have a material effect on the
financial statements.

[*Inherent limitations paragraph*]

Because of its inherent limitations, internal control over financial reporting
may not prevent or detect and correct misstatements. Also, projections of any
evaluation of effectiveness to future periods are subject to the risk that controls
may become inadequate because of changes in conditions, or that the degree of
compliance with the policies or procedures may deteriorate.

[*Opinion paragraph*]

In my (our) opinion, the financial statements referred to above present fairly,
in all material respects, the financial position of W Company as of December 31,
2X12, and the results of its operations and its cash flows for the year then ended
in conformity with accounting principles generally accepted in the United States
of America. Also in my (our) opinion, W Company maintained, in all material
respects, effective internal control over financial reporting as of December 31,
2X12, based on [*identify criteria*].

[*Signature*]
[*Date*]

Reporting on Controls at a Service Organization

What is a service organization?

A service organization is an entity that provides services to user entities that are likely
to be relevant to those user entities' internal control over financial reporting—for
example, a payroll processing company and a bank trust department that makes
investments for an entity's pension plan.

What type of attest engagements are permitted?

An engagement may lead to the issuance of either of these reports:

Type 1 report, which is a report on management's description of a service organization's system and the suitability of the design of controls.

Type 2 report, which is a report on management's description of a service organization's system and the suitability of the design and operating effectiveness of controls.

What is required in an engagement to report on controls at a service organization?

The auditor of the service organization should:

- Obtain a written assertion from management that will be included in or attached to management's description of the entity's system and will be issued to user entities.

Caution

Management's refusal to furnish a written assertion is tantamount to a scope limitation that should result in the service auditor's withdrawal from the engagement.

- Assess the suitability of the criteria (i.e., the standards used to measure and present the subject matter and against which the auditor evaluates the subject matter).
- Obtain an understanding of the service organization's system.
- Obtain evidence concerning management's description of the service organization's system.
- Obtain evidence regarding the design of relevant internal controls.
- In an engagement to issue a type 2 report,
  - Obtain evidence regarding the operating effectiveness of relevant internal controls by performing tests of controls.
  - Investigate the nature and cause of deviations identified.

Is the service auditor required to obtain any written representations from management?

The service auditor should obtain written representations from management that:

- Reaffirm the assertion provided by management.
- State that it has provided the auditor with all requested information.
- State, if applicable, that it has disclosed:
  - Instances of noncompliance with laws and regulations
  - Knowledge of actual, suspected, or alleged intentional management acts that could negatively affect its description of the entity's system
  - Deficiencies in the design of internal control
  - Situations in which internal controls have not operated as described
  - Subsequent events that could have a significant impact on management's assertion

Note

Management's written representations should be in the form of a representation letter addressed to the auditor and dated as of the date of the auditor's report.

Caution

Management's refusal to furnish the requested written representations should result in the issuance of a disclaimer of opinion or the auditor's withdrawal from the engagement.

How do type 1 and type 2 reports differ?

Since the two reports are based on engagements that have different objectives, type 1 and type 2 reports differ, as illustrated in Examples 11.30 to 11.35.

Example 11.30   Independent Service Auditor's Report on a Description of a Service Organization's System and the Suitability of the Design of Controls (Type I Service Auditor's Report)

To: XYZ Service Organization

Scope

I (We) have examined XYZ Service Organization's description of its [*type or name of*] system for processing user entities' transactions [*or identification of the function performed by the system*] as of [*date*], and the suitability of the design of controls to achieve the related control objectives stated in the description.

[*Service organization's responsibilities*]

On page XX of the description, XYZ Service Organization has provided an assertion about the fairness of the presentation of the description and suitability of the design of the controls to achieve the related controls objectives stated in the description. XYZ Service Organization is responsible for preparing the description and for its assertion, including the completeness, accuracy, and method of presentation of the description and the assertion; providing the services covered by the description; specifying the control objectives and stating them in the description; identifying the risks that threaten the achievement of the control objectives; selecting the criteria; and designing, implementing, and documenting controls to achieve the related control objectives stated in the description.

[*Service auditor's responsibilities*]

My (Our) responsibility is to express an opinion on the fairness of the presentation of the description and on the suitability of the design of the controls to achieve the related control objectives stated in the description, based on my (our) examination. I (We) conducted my (our) examination in accordance with attestation standards established by the American Institute of Certified Public Accountants. Those standards require that I (we) plan and perform my (our) examination to obtain reasonable assurance, in all material respects, about whether the description is fairly presented and the controls were suitably designed to achieve the related control objectives stated in the description as of [*date*].

An examination of a description of a service organization's system and the suitability of the design of the service organization's controls to achieve the related control objectives stated in the description involves performing procedures to obtain evidence about the fairness of the presentation of the description of the system and the suitability of the design of the controls to achieve the related control objectives stated in the description. My (Our) procedures included assessing the risks that the description is not fairly presented and that the controls were not suitably designed to achieve the related control objectives stated in the description. An examination engagement of this type also includes evaluating the overall presentation of the description and the suitability of the control objectives stated therein, and the suitability of the criteria specified by the service organization and described at page XX.

I (We) did not perform any procedures regarding the operating effectiveness of the controls stated in the description and, accordingly, do not express an opinion thereon.

I (We) believe that the evidence I (we) obtained is sufficient and appropriate to provide a reasonable basis for my (our) opinion.

[*Inherent limitations*]

Because of their nature, controls at a service organization may not prevent or detect and correct, all errors or omissions in processing or reporting transactions [*or identification of the function performed by the system*]. The projection to the future of any evaluation of the fairness of the presentation of the description, or any conclusions about the suitability of the design of the controls to achieve the related control objectives, is subject to the risk that controls at a service organization may become ineffective or fail.

[*Opinion*]

In my (our) opinion, in all material respects, based on the criteria described in XYZ Service Organization's assertion, a. the description fairly presents the [*type or name of*] system that was designed and implemented as of [*date*], and b. the controls related to the control objectives stated in the description were suitably designed to provide reasonable assurance that the control objectives would be achieved if the controls operated effectively as of [*date*].

(continued)

(Continued)

[Restricted use]

This report is intended solely for the information and use of XYZ Service Organization, user entities of XYZ Service Organization's *[type or name of]* system as of *[date]*, and the independent auditors of such user entities, who have a sufficient understanding to consider it, along with other information, including information about controls implemented by user entities themselves, when obtaining an understanding of user entities information and communication systems relevant to financial reporting. This report is not intended to be and should not be used by anyone other than these specified parties.

[Service auditor's signature]
[Date of the service auditor's report]
[Service auditor's city and state]

Example 11.31   Independent Service Auditor's Report on a Description of a Service Organization's System and the Suitability of the Design and Operating Effectiveness of Controls (Type 2 Service Auditor's Report)

To: XYZ Service Organization

[Scope]

I (We) have examined XYZ Service Organization's description of its *[type or name of]* system for processing user entities' transactions *[or identification of the function performed by the system]* throughout the period *[date]* to *[date]* (description) and the suitability of the design and operating effectiveness of controls to achieve the related control objectives stated in the description.

[Service organization's responsibilities]

On page XX of the description, XYZ Service Organization has provided an assertion about the fairness of the presentation of the description and suitability of the design and operating effectiveness of the controls to achieve the related control objectives stated in the description. XYZ Service Organization is responsible for preparing the description and for the assertion, including the completeness, accuracy, and method of presentation of the description and the assertion; providing the services covered by the description; specifying the control objectives and stating them in the description; identifying the risks that threaten the achievement of the control objectives; selecting the criteria; and designing, implementing, and documenting controls to achieve the related control objectives stated in the description.

[Service auditor's responsibilities]

My (Our) responsibility is to express an opinion on the fairness of the presentation of the description and on the suitability of the design and operating effectiveness of the controls to achieve the related control objectives stated in the description, based on our examination. I (We) conducted my (our) examination in accordance with attestation standards established by the American Institute of Certified Public Accountants. Those standards require that I (we) plan and perform my (our) examination to obtain reasonable assurance about whether, in all material respects, the description is fairly presented and the controls were suitably designed and operating effectively to achieve the related control objectives stated in the description throughout the period [*date*] to [*date*].

An examination of a description of a service organization's system and the suitability of the design and operating effectiveness of the service organization's controls to achieve the related control objectives stated in the description involves performing procedures to obtain evidence about the fairness of the presentation of the description and the suitability of the design and operating effectiveness of those controls to achieve the related control objectives stated in the description. My (Our) procedures included assessing the risks that the description is not fairly presented and that the controls were not suitably designed or operated effectively to achieve the related control objectives stated in the description. My (Our) procedures also included testing the operating effectiveness of those controls that I (we) consider necessary to provide reasonable assurance that the related control objectives stated in the description were achieved. An examination engagement of this type also includes evaluating the overall presentation of the description and the suitability of the control objectives stated therein, and the suitability of the criteria specified by the service organization and described at page XX. I (We) believe that the evidence I (we) obtained is sufficient and appropriate to provide a reasonable basis for my (our) opinion.

[*Inherent limitations*]

Because of their nature, controls at a service organization may not prevent or detect and correct, all errors or omissions in processing or reporting transactions [*or identification of the function performed by the system*]. Also, the projection to the future of any evaluation of the fairness of the presentation of the description, or conclusions about the suitability of the design or operating effectiveness of the controls to achieve the related control objectives is subject to the risk that controls at a service organization may become inadequate or fail.

[*Opinion*]

In my (our) opinion, in all material respects, based on the criteria described in XYZ Service Organization's assertion on page XX:

- The description fairly presents the [*type or name of*] system that was designed and implemented throughout the period [*date*] to [*date*].
- The controls related to the control objectives stated in the description were suitably designed to provide reasonable assurance that the control objectives

(continued)

(Continued)

would be achieved if the controls operated effectively throughout the period [*date*] to [*date*].
- The controls tested, which were those necessary to provide reasonable assurance that the control objectives stated in the description were achieved, operated effectively throughout the period [*date*] to [*date*].

[Description of tests of controls]

The specific controls tested and the nature, timing, and results of those tests are listed on pages YY–ZZ.

[Restricted use]

This report, including the description of tests of controls and results thereof on pages YY–ZZ, is intended solely for the information and use of XYZ Service Organization, user entities of XYZ Service Organization's [*type or name of*] system during some or all of the period [*date*] to [*date*], and the independent auditors of such user entities, who have a sufficient understanding to consider it, along with other information, including information about controls implemented by user entities themselves, when assessing the risks of material misstatements of user entities' financial statements. This report is not intended to be and should not be used by anyone other than these specified parties.

[Service auditor's signature]
[Date of the service auditor's report]
[Service auditor's city and state]

What situations might result in modified opinions?

The service auditor's opinion might require modification if:

- Management's description of the entity's system is not presented fairly, in all material respects. (See Example 11.32.)
- The internal controls are not suitably designed. (See Example 11.33.)
- In the case of a type 2 engagement, the auditor concludes that the internal controls did not operate effectively. (See Example 11.34.)
- The service auditor encounters a restriction on the scope of the engagement. (See Example 11.35.)

Example 11.32   Qualified Opinion for a Type 2 Report—The Description of the Service Organization's System Is Not Fairly Presented in All Material Respects

The following paragraph would be inserted before the modified opinion paragraph. (All other report paragraphs are unchanged from Example 11.31.)

[Basis for qualified opinion]

The accompanying description states on page XX that XYZ Service Organization uses operator identification numbers and passwords to prevent unauthorized access to the system. Based on inquiries of staff personnel and observation of activities, I (we) have determined that operator identification numbers and passwords are employed in applications A and B but are not required to access the system in applications C and D.

[Opinion]

In my (our) opinion, except for the matter described in the preceding paragraph, and based on the criteria described in XYZ Service Organization's assertion on page XX, in all material respects...

Example 11.33   Qualified Opinion—The Controls Are Not Suitably Designed to Provide Reasonable Assurance That the Control Objectives Stated in the Description of the Service Organization's System Would Be Achieved If the Controls Operated Effectively

The following paragraph would be inserted before the modified opinion paragraph. (All other report paragraphs are unchanged from Example 11.31.)

[Basis for qualified opinion]

As discussed on page XX of the accompanying description, from time to time, XYZ Service Organization makes changes in application programs to correct deficiencies or to enhance capabilities.

The procedures followed in determining whether to make changes, in designing the changes, and in implementing them do not include review and approval by authorized individuals who are independent from those involved in making the changes. There also are no specified requirements to test such changes or provide test results to an authorized reviewer prior to implementing the changes. As a result, the controls are not suitably designed to achieve the control objective "Controls provide reasonable assurance that changes to existing applications are authorized, tested, approved, properly implemented, and documented."

[Opinion]

In my (our) opinion, except for the matter described in the preceding paragraph, and based on the criteria described in XYZ Service Organization's assertion on page XX, in all material respects...

Example 11.34   Qualified Opinion for a Type 2 Report—The Controls Did Not Operate Effectively Throughout the Specified Period to Achieve the Control Objectives Stated in the Description of the Service Organization's System

The paragraph would be inserted before the modified opinion paragraph. (All other report paragraphs are unchanged from Example 11.31.)

[Basis for qualified opinion]

XYZ Service Organization states in its description that it has automated controls in place to reconcile loan payments received with the various output reports. However, as noted on page XX of the description of tests of controls and results thereof, this control was not operating effectively throughout the period [*date*] to [*date*] due to a programming error. This resulted in the nonachievement of the control objective "Controls provide reasonable assurance that loan payments received are properly recorded" throughout the period January 1, 2X12, to April 30, 2X12. XYZ Service Organization implemented a change to the program performing the calculation as of May 1, 2X12, and my (our) tests indicate that it was operating effectively throughout the period May 1, 2X12, to December 31, 2X12.

[Opinion]

In my (our) opinion, except for the matter described in the preceding paragraph, and based on the criteria described in XYZ Service Organization's assertion on page XX, in all material respects . . .

Example 11.35   Qualified Opinion—The Service Auditor Encounters a Restriction on the Scope of the Engagement

The paragraph would be inserted before the modified opinion paragraph. (All other report paragraphs are unchanged from Example 11.31.)

[Basis for qualified opinion]

XYZ Service Organization states in its description that it has automated controls in place to reconcile loan payments received with the output generated. However, electronic records of the performance of this reconciliation for the period from [*date*] to [*date*] were deleted as a result of a computer processing error and, therefore, I was (we were) unable to test the operation of this control for that period. Consequently, I was (we were) unable to determine whether the control objective "Controls provide reasonable assurance that loan payments received are properly recorded" was achieved throughout the period [*date*] to [*date*].

[*Opinion*]

In my (our) opinion, except for the matter described in the preceding paragraph, and based on the criteria described in XYZ Service Organization's assertion on page XX, in all material respects . . .

Compliance Attestation

SSAE 10 provides guidance for engagements related to (1) an entity's compliance with specified requirements (i.e., requirements of specified laws, regulations, rules, contracts, or grants) and (2) the effectiveness of an entity's internal control over compliance with specified requirements.

What levels of service are applicable to engagements pertaining to compliance attestation?

The practitioner may be engaged to examine (1) an entity's compliance with specified requirements (or a written assertion thereon) or (2) the effectiveness of the entity's internal control over compliance (or a written assertion thereon). Alternatively, the practitioner may be engaged to perform an agreed-upon procedures engagement.

Note

A review engagement cannot be performed in connection with compliance attestation.

What report should a practitioner use when expressing an opinion directly on an entity's compliance with specified requirements during a period of time?

Example 11.36   Expressing Opinion Directly on an Entity's Compliance with Specified Requirements During a Period of Time

Independent Accountant's Report

[*Introductory paragraph*]

I (We) have examined [*name of entity*]'s compliance with [*list specified compliance requirements*] during the [*period*] ended [*date*]. Management is

(*continued*)

(Continued)

responsible for [*name of entity*]'s compliance with those requirements. My (Our) responsibility is to express an opinion on [*name of entity*]'s compliance based on my (our) examination.

[*Scope paragraph*]

My (Our) examination was conducted in accordance with attestation standards established by the American Institute of Certified Public Accountants and, accordingly, included examining, on a test basis, evidence about [*name of entity*]'s compliance with those requirements and performing such other procedures as I (we) considered necessary in the circumstances. I (We) believe that my (our) examination provides a reasonable basis for my (our) opinion. My (Our) examination does not provide a legal determination on [*name of entity*]'s compliance with specified requirements.

[*Opinion paragraph*]

In my (our) opinion, [*name of entity*] complied, in all material respects, with the aforementioned requirements for the year ended December 31, 2X12.

[*Signature*]
[*Date*]

What report should a practitioner use when expressing an opinion on management's assertion about compliance with specified requirements during a period of time?

Example 11.37   Expressing an Opinion on Management's Assertion about Compliance with Specified Requirements during a Period of Time

Independent Accountant's Report

[*Introductory paragraph*]

I (We) have examined management's assertion, included in the accompanying [*title of management report*], that [*name of entity*] complied with [*list specified compliance requirements*] during the [*period*] ended [*date*]. Management is responsible for [*name of entity*]'s compliance with those requirements. My (Our) responsibility is to express an opinion on management's assertion about [*name of entity*]'s compliance based on my (our) examination.

[*Scope paragraph*]

My (Our) examination was conducted in accordance with attestation standards established by the American Institute of Certified Public Accountants and, accordingly, included examining, on a test basis, evidence about [*name of entity*]'s compliance with those requirements and performing such other procedures as I (we) considered necessary in the circumstances. I (We) believe that my (our) examination provides a reasonable basis for my (our) opinion. My (Our) examination does not provide a legal determination on [*name of entity*]'s compliance with specified requirements.

[*Opinion paragraph*]

In my (our) opinion, management's assertion that [*name of entity*] complied, in all material respects, with the aforementioned requirements during the [*period*] ended [*date*] is fairly stated in all material respects.

[*Signature*]
[*Date*]

Management's Discussion and Analysis

What is Management's Discussion and Analysis?

Management's Discussion and Analysis (MD&A) is a document that needs to be prepared in accordance with rules and regulations of the Securities and Exchange Commission. MD&A, which is usually presented in annual reports to shareholders, generally covers three years of audited financial statements as well as any available interim-period financial statements. MD&A is designed to provide users with a useful analysis of significant changes in a publicly traded company's financial condition and results of operations.

What types of attest services can a practitioner perform with respect to MD&A?

A practitioner may accept an engagement to examine, review, or apply agreed-upon procedures to MD&A. An attest engagement with respect to MD&A should be performed in accordance with the general attestation rules previously discussed in this chapter.

Personal Financial Statements Included in Written Personal Financial Plans

What are my responsibilities when personal financial statements are included in a financial plan?

When the accountant prepares personal financial statements that are included in a written personal financial plan, the accountant may:

- Follow the compilation standards applicable to compilation engagements involving historical basic financial statements.

- Issue the report specified in Statement on Standards for Accounting and Review Services (SSARS) No. 6, "Reporting on Personal Financial Statements Included in Written Personal Financial Plans."

In order to make use of the exemption from SSARS 19, "Compilation and Review Engagements," provided in SSARS 6, the accountant must reach an understanding with the client that the personal financial statements:

- Are prepared only to assist in the development of goals and objectives pertaining to the client's personal finances
- Will not be used in securing credit

Caution

If the accountant, during the engagement, discovers that the personal financial statements are to be used to obtain credit or for some purpose other than to develop a financial strategy, the accountant may not utilize the exemption from SSARS 19.

Example 11.38   Report Based on Exemption from SSARS 19

The standard report for personal financial statements in financial plans based on exemption from SSARS 19 follows.

[*Exemption paragraph*]

The accompanying Statement of Financial Condition of Karen B, as of December 31, 2X12, was prepared solely to help you develop your personal financial plan. Accordingly, it may be incomplete or contain other departures from accounting principles generally accepted in the United States of America and should not be used to obtain credit or for any other purposes other than developing your financial plan. I (We) have not audited, reviewed, or compiled the statement.

What must I do when examining personal financial statements?

Engagements to examine personal financial statements are subject to the standards applicable to audits of historical financial statements. Accordingly, the auditor must gather sufficient appropriate audit evidence to form the basis of his or her opinion. While the accountant normally expresses the opinion on a statement of financial condition, he or she may report on:

- A statement of changes in net worth
- Comparative financial statements

Note

If warranted, the practitioner may express a qualified opinion, an adverse opinion, or a disclaimer of opinion on personal financial statements.

Example 11.39   Report Based on Audit of Personal Financial Statements

Independent Auditor's Report

I (We) have audited the accompanying statement of financial condition of Marc and Susan Janes as of December 31, 2X12, and the related statement of changes in net worth for the year then ended. These financial statements are the responsibility of Marc and Susan Janes. My (Our) responsibility is to express an opinion on these financial statements based on my (our) audit.

I (We) conducted my (our) audit in accordance with auditing standards generally accepted in the United States of America. Those standards require that I (we) plan and perform the audit to obtain reasonable assurance about whether the financial statements are free of material misstatement. An audit includes examining, on a test basis, evidence supporting the amounts and disclosures in the financial statements. An audit also includes assessing the accounting principles used and significant estimates made by the individuals, as well as evaluating the overall financial statement presentation. I (We) believe that my (our) audit provides a reasonable basis for my (our) opinion.

In my (our) opinion, the financial statements referred to above present fairly, in all material respects, the financial condition of Marc and Susan Janes as of December 31, 2X12, and the changes in their net worth for the year then ended in conformity with accounting principles generally accepted in the United States of America.

[*Signature*]
[*Date*]

Reporting on Comparative Statements

What are the reporting requirements for comparative statements?

Guidance for reporting on audited comparative financial statements is provided in Statement on Auditing Standards (SAS) No. 58, "Reports on Audited Financial Statements."

The practitioner may report on financial statements of one or more prior periods that are presented with financial statements of the current period.

If the accountant is the continuing auditor, having performed the audit of the current period and immediately preceding period(s), he or she has the responsibility of updating the report on the financial statements of the prior period(s).

Note

In updating the audit report, the practitioner should either express a previous opinion again or express an opinion different from the one previously expressed. The latter circumstance may arise when, for example, prior-period financial statements are subsequently restated.

Example 11.40   Continuing Auditor's Standard Report on Comparative Financial Statements

Independent Auditor's Report

I (We) have audited the accompanying balance sheets of M Corporation as of (at) December 31, 2X14 and 2X13, and the related statements of income, retained earnings, and cash flows for the years then ended. These financial statements are the responsibility of the Company's management. My (Our) responsibility is to express an opinion on these financial statements based on my (our) audits.

I (We) conducted my (our) audits in accordance with auditing standards generally accepted in the United States of America. Those standards require that I (we) plan and perform the audit to obtain reasonable assurance about whether the financial statements are free of material misstatement. An audit includes examining, on a test basis, evidence supporting the amounts and disclosures in the financial statements. An audit also includes assessing the accounting principles used and significant estimates made by management, as well as evaluating the overall financial statement presentation. I (We) believe that my (our) audits provide a reasonable basis for my (our) opinion.

In my (our) opinion, the financial statements referred to above present fairly, in all material respects, the financial position of M Corporation as of (at) December 31, 2X14 and 2X13, and the results of its operations and its cash flows for the years then ended in conformity with accounting principles generally accepted in the United States of America.

How can the continuing auditor's standard report be modified?

The practitioner may issue a report that contains differing opinions. *Example:* A qualified opinion on the current year's financial statements and an unqualified opinion on the prior year's financial statements.

If the practitioner deems it necessary to modify the opinion expressed on prior-period financial statements, he or she should include an explanatory paragraph (preceding the opinion paragraph) in the updated report. The explanatory paragraph should disclose:

- Date of the original audit report
- Type of the original opinion (e.g., unqualified, qualified)
- Reasons for the change in opinion
- Statement that the updated opinion is different from the opinion previously expressed

---

Example 11.41 Explanatory Paragraph Added When the Standard Report Needs to Be Modified

In my (our) report dated April 3, 2X15, I (we) expressed an opinion that the 2X14 financial statements did not present fairly financial position, results of operations, and cash flows in conformity with generally accepted accounting principles because of two departures from such principles: (1) the Company carried its property, plant, and equipment at appraisal values and provided for depreciation on the basis of such values, and (2) the Company did not provide for deferred income taxes with respect to differences between income for financial reporting purposes and taxable income. As described in Note X, the Company has changed its method of accounting for these items and restated its 2X14 financial statements to conform with generally accepted accounting principles. Accordingly, my (our) present opinion on the 2X14 financial statements, as presented herein, is different from that expressed in my (our) previous report.

When can I reissue a report on prior-period statements?

If a client requests that a predecessor auditor reissue a report on prior-period financial statements, he or she must first:

- Read the current-period financial statements.
- Compare the original prior-period financial statements with the statements to be presented.
- Obtain a representation letter from the successor auditor.

Note

The representation letter should disclose events and circumstances that came to the successor's attention that might have a significant effect on the predecessor's report or on the prior-period financial statements.

- If events and circumstances arose after the original report was issued, perform inquiry and other necessary procedures.

Note

The date of a reissued report should coincide with the date of the original report. However, if the predecessor revises his or her report, or if the financial statements of the prior period need to be restated, the practitioner should utilize dual dating in the report.

What if the predecessor auditor's report is not with the successor's?

When the report of the predecessor auditor is not presented with the report of the successor auditor, add the following information to the introductory paragraph of the successor auditor's report:

- A statement that another auditor audited the financial statements of the prior period(s)
- The date of the predecessor's report
- A statement as to the type of opinion expressed by the predecessor
- If the predecessor's report was not standard, a statement of the substantive reasons for the type of opinion

Example 11.42   Additional Wording for Introductory Paragraph of the Successor's Report

The financial statements of KJB Company as of December 31, 2X14, were audited by other auditors whose report, dated April 1, 2X15, on those statements included an explanatory paragraph that described the litigation discussed in Note X to the financial statements.

How do I compile and review comparative statements?

If a client requests that the practitioner report on comparative financial statements of a non-publicly traded entity, the practitioner should be guided by the provisions of SSARS 2. Accordingly, the accountant must reissue or update the report issued in connection with the financial statements of the prior period.

Same Level of Service

When a continuing accountant performs the same level of service for each of the comparative periods (e.g., compilation for all periods or review for all periods), the accountant's report is modified by merely including the comparative dates.

Higher Level of Service

When the continuing accountant is requested to step up the level of service, the resulting report must be modified to reflect the levels of service provided and the responsibility the practitioner is taking.

GUIDELINE If the prior period involved a compilation and the current period involves a review, the report should contain the standard wording of a review report for the current period and the additional paragraph shown in Example 11.43.

Example 11.43   Wording Added to the Comparative Report for Step-Up to a Review

The accompanying 2X11 financial statements of SJD Corporation were compiled by me (us). A compilation is limited to presenting in the form of financial statements information that is the representation of management (owners). I (We) have not audited or reviewed the 2X11 financial statements and, accordingly, do not express an opinion or any other form of assurance on them.

Lower Level of Service

The accountant may be involved in a step-down in the level of service provided. Accordingly, the accountant may perform an audit with respect to the financial statements of one period and a review or compilation in a subsequent period.

In a step-down from an audit to a compilation or a review, the practitioner should issue the appropriate compilation or review report with respect to the statements of the current period. An additional paragraph should:

- Describe the responsibility assumed for the prior period.
- Indicate the date of the previous report.
- State the type of opinion expressed in the audit report.
- State that subsequent to the date of the audit report no additional auditing procedures have been performed.

Similarly, if an engagement involves a step-down from a review to a compilation, the comparative report should contain the standard compilation report and an additional paragraph that:

- Describes responsibility for the prior period
- Indicates the date of the review report
- Provides the limited assurance normally expressed in a standard review report

- States that no additional review procedures have been performed subsequent to the date of the review report

---

Example 11.44   Wording Added to the Comparative Report for Step-Down to a Compilation

The accompanying 2X14 financial statements of SJD Company were previously reviewed by me (us), and my (our) report dated April 1, 2X15, stated that I was (we were) not aware of any material modifications that should be made to those statements in order for them to be in conformity with generally accepted accounting principles. I (We) have not performed any procedures in connection with that review engagement after the date of my (our) report on the 2X14 financial statements.

Special Reports

What is a special report?

Statement on Auditing Standards (SAS) No. 62, "Special Reports," states that a special report is an auditor's report issued in connection with any of these items:

- Financial statements based on a comprehensive basis of accounting other than GAAP
- Specified elements, accounts, or items contained in a basic set of financial statements
- Compliance with contractual agreements or regulations related to financial statements subjected to an audit
- Special-purpose financial presentations to comply with contractual agreements or regulatory provisions
- Financial information included in prescribed forms

What constitutes a comprehensive basis of accounting other than GAAP?

A comprehensive basis of accounting other than GAAP includes:

- The cash basis of accounting, which recognizes income when collected and expenses when paid
- The modified cash basis of accounting, which recognizes income when collected and expenses when paid, except for the capitalization of fixed assets and the recognition of depreciation expense, which is a noncash item
- A basis of accounting that follows the requirements of a regulatory agency
- Any basis of accounting that uses a definite set of criteria having substantial support, such as the price-level basis of accounting

Note

With respect to financial statements based on a comprehensive basis of accounting other than GAAP, an auditor may perform an audit in conformity with generally accepted auditing standards.

What should a special report include?

The report issued at the conclusion of the audit engagement should include:

- A title that includes the word *independent*
- An identification of the financial statements audited and a statement as to whether the audit was performed in accordance with generally accepted auditing standards
- An opinion on the fairness of presentation of the financial statements, considered in light of the comprehensive basis of accounting used

An additional paragraph placed before the opinion paragraph should:

- Identify the basis of accounting utilized.
- Refer to the note to the financial statement that describes the basis of accounting used.
- State that the basis of accounting is a comprehensive basis of accounting other than GAAP.

Recommendation

Change the titles of financial statements based on a comprehensive basis of accounting other than GAAP.

    Example: In the cash basis of accounting, use "statement of assets and liabilities arising from cash transactions" instead of "balance sheet."

Example 11.45　Report for Income Tax Basis Financial Statements

Independent Auditor's Report

I (We) have audited the accompanying statements of assets, liabilities, and capital (income tax basis) of ABC Partnership as of December 31, 2X12 and 2X11, and the related statements of revenue and expenses (income tax basis) and

(continued)

(Continued)

of changes in partners' capital accounts (income tax basis) for the years then ended. These financial statements are the responsibility of the Partnership's management. My (Our) responsibility is to express an opinion on these financial statements based on my (our) audits.

I (We) conducted my (our) audits in accordance with auditing standards generally accepted in the United States of America. Those standards require that I (we) plan and perform the audit to obtain reasonable assurance about whether the financial statements are free of material misstatement. An audit includes examining, on a test basis, evidence supporting the amounts and disclosures in the financial statements. An audit also includes assessing the accounting principles used and significant estimates made by management, as well as evaluating the overall financial statement presentation. I (We) believe that my (our) audits provide a reasonable basis for my (our) opinion.

As described in Note X, these financial statements were prepared on the basis of accounting the Partnership uses for income tax purposes, which is a comprehensive basis of accounting other than generally accepted accounting principles.

In my (our) opinion, the financial statements referred to above present fairly, in all material respects, the assets, liabilities, and capital of ABC Partnership as of (at) December 31, 2X12 and 2X11, and its revenue and expenses and changes in partners' capital accounts for the years then ended, on the basis of accounting described in Note X.

Example 11.46   Sample Report for Cash Basis Financial Statements

Independent Auditor's Report

I (We) have audited the accompanying statements of assets and liabilities arising from cash transactions of XYZ Company as of December 31, 2X12 and 2X11, and the related statements of revenue collected and expenses paid for the years then ended. These financial statements are the responsibility of the Company's management. My (our) responsibility is to express an opinion on these financial statements based on my (our) audits.

I (We) conducted my (our) audits in accordance with auditing standards generally accepted in the United States of America. Those standards require that I (we) plan and perform the audit to obtain reasonable assurance about whether the financial statements are free of material misstatement. An audit includes examining, on a test basis, evidence supporting the amounts and disclosures in the financial statements. An audit also includes assessing the accounting principles used and significant estimates made by management, as well as evaluating the overall financial statement presentation. I (We) believe that my (our) audits provide a reasonable basis for my (our) opinion.

As described in Note X, these financial statements were prepared on the basis of cash receipts and disbursements, which is a comprehensive basis of accounting other than generally accepted accounting principles.

In my (our) opinion, the financial statements referred to above present fairly, in all material respects, the assets and liabilities arising from cash transactions of XYZ Company as of December 31, 2X12 and 2X11, and its revenue collected and expenses paid during the years then ended, on the basis of accounting described in Note X.

What about the statement of cash flows?

The presentation of a statement of cash flows is required under GAAP. Accordingly, when financial statements are intended to be in conformity with a comprehensive basis of accounting other than GAAP, a statement of cash flows need not be presented.

Specific Elements, Accounts, or Items in a Basic Set of Financial Statements

What should I do when asked to evaluate specific elements or items?

With respect to specific elements, accounts, or items (such as rentals, royalties, and the provision for income tax expense) contained in a basic set of financial statements, an accountant may undertake an engagement to:

- Express an opinion
- Apply agreed-upon procedures

What report should generally be issued in connection with an engagement to express an opinion on specified elements, accounts, or items of a financial statement?

Example 11.47   Report for Adequacy of Provision for Income Taxes in the Basic Financial Statements

Independent Auditor's Report

I (We) have audited, in accordance with auditing standards generally accepted in the United States of America, the financial statements of XYZ Company, Inc., for the year ended June 30, 2X12, and have issued my (our) report thereon dated August 15, 2X12. I (We) have also audited the current and deferred provision for the Company's federal and state income taxes for the year ended June 30, 2X12, included in those financial statements, and the related asset and liability tax

(continued)

(Continued)

accounts as of June 30, 2X12. This income tax information is the responsibility of the Company's management. My (Our) responsibility is to express an opinion on it based on my (our) audit.

I (We) conducted my (our) audit of the income tax information in accordance with auditing standards generally accepted in the United States of America. Those standards require that I (we) plan and perform the audit to obtain reasonable assurance about whether the federal and state income tax accounts are free of material misstatement. An audit includes examining, on a test basis, evidence supporting the amounts and disclosures related to the federal and state income tax accounts. An audit also includes assessing the accounting principles used and significant estimates made by management, as well as evaluating the overall presentation of the federal and state income tax accounts. I (We) believe that my (our) audit provides a reasonable basis for my (our) opinion.

In my (our) opinion, the Company has paid or, in all material respects, made adequate provision in the financial statements referred to above for the payment of all federal and state income taxes and for related deferred income taxes that could be reasonably estimated at the time of my (our) audit of the financial statements of XYZ Company, Inc., for the year ended June 30, 2X12.

Caution

In general, do not express an opinion on specified elements, accounts, or items included in financial statements if you expressed an adverse opinion or disclaimed an opinion on the basic financial statements.

Can agreed-upon procedures be used on specific items?

An engagement to apply agreed-upon procedures to specific elements, accounts, or items is more limited in scope than an audit that leads to the expression of an opinion. Accordingly, the practitioner should issue a disclaimer of opinion.

Caution

Engagements involving the application of agreed-upon procedures may be accepted provided that:

- An understanding between the accountant and client has been reached regarding the specific procedures to be performed.
- The accountant's report is to be distributed only to the named parties involved.

- The accountant follows the guidance in SSAE 10 relative to agreed-upon procedures.

Compliance with Contracts or Regulations Relating to Audited Financial Statements

What are my responsibilities regarding compliance with contracts?

Clients sometimes request an independent accountant to issue a report concerning compliance with contractual agreements or regulations. *Example:* A report on compliance with the terms, provisions, and covenants of bond indentures. Such a report should express the requisite negative assurance either in a separate report or as part of the audit report on the basic financial statements.

In either reporting situation, the report should specifically state that the negative assurance is being expressed in connection with the audit (of the financial statements).

Note

The practitioner should state that "The audit was not directed primarily toward obtaining knowledge of such noncompliance."

What format should generally be used if the report on contractual provisions related to audited financial statements is given in a separate report?

The separate report to be used in connection with contractual provisions should contain negative assurance.

Example 11.48   Separate Report Issued in Connection with Contractual Provisions

Independent Auditor's Report

I (We) have audited, in accordance with auditing standards generally accepted in the United States of America, the balance sheet of XYZ Company as of December 31, 2X12, and the related statement of income, retained earnings, and cash flows for the year then ended, and have issued my (our) report thereon dated February 16, 2X13.

In connection with my (our) audit, nothing came to my (our) attention that caused me (us) to believe that the Company failed to comply with the terms, covenants, provisions, or conditions of sections XX to YY, inclusive, of the indenture dated July 21, 2X10, with ABC Bank insofar as they relate to

(continued)

(Continued)

accounting matters. However, my (our) audit was not directed primarily toward obtaining knowledge of such noncompliance.

This report is intended solely for the information and use of the boards of directors and management of XYZ Company and ABC Bank and should not be used for any other purpose.

What is meant by special-purpose financial presentations to comply with contractual agreements or regulatory provisions?

Special-purpose financial presentations are intended to be used only by the parties to the agreement, regulatory agencies, or other specified parties. Accordingly, such presentations:

- May not represent a complete presentation of assets, liabilities, revenues, and expenses, but may nevertheless be in conformity with GAAP or OCBOA
- May represent a complete presentation of assets, liabilities, revenues, and expenses that is not in conformity with GAAP or OCBOA

What report should generally be issued in connection with special-purpose financial presentations?

Example 11.49   Report Issued in Connection with a Statement of Assets Sold and Liabilities Transferred to Comply with a Contractual Agreement

Independent Auditor's Report

I (We) have audited the accompanying statement of net assets sold of ABC Company as of June 8, 2X12. This statement of net assets sold is the responsibility of ABC Company's management. My (Our) responsibility is to express an opinion on the statement of net assets sold based on my (our) audit.

I (We) conducted my (our) audit in accordance with auditing standards generally accepted in the United States of America. Those standards require that I (we) plan and perform the audit to obtain reasonable assurance about whether the statement of net assets sold is free of material misstatement. An audit includes examining, on a test basis, evidence supporting the amounts and disclosures in the statement. An audit also includes assessing the accounting principles used and significant estimates made by management, as well as evaluating the overall presentation of the statement of net assets sold. I (We) believe that my (our) audit provides a reasonable basis for my (our) opinion.

The accompanying statement was prepared to present the net assets of ABC Company sold to XYZ Corporation pursuant to the purchase agreement described in Note X and is not intended to be a complete presentation of ABC Company's assets and liabilities.

In my (our) opinion, the accompanying statement of net assets sold presents fairly, in all material respects, the net assets of ABC Company as of June 8, 2X12, sold pursuant to the purchase agreement referred to in Note X, in conformity with accounting principles generally accepted in the United States of America.

This report is intended solely for the information and use of the boards of directors and managements of ABC Company and XYZ Corporation and should not be used for any other purpose.

Financial Information Included in Prescribed Forms

What are the requirements for financial information in prescribed forms?

Accountants often accept engagements to audit financial information included in prescribed forms.

Example 11.50

The accountant may be requested to certify the financial information presented in forms prescribed by the United States government for the reimbursement of expenses paid by health care facilities.

In such circumstances, the practitioner must be satisfied that the form prescribed for the auditor's report adheres to relevant reporting standards. When the prescribed audit report contains inappropriate or unacceptable wording, the practitioner should either modify the wording or attach a separate report that conforms to the relevant reporting standards.

CHAPTER 12

Auditing Standards

This chapter provides the practitioner with a handy reference guide to the major practical provisions of the Statements on Auditing Standards (SAS) and Auditing Standards (AS) of the Public Company Accounting Oversight Board (PCAOB) not previously covered.

Statements on Auditing Standards set forth authoritative guidance for properly conducting an audit of a nonpublic company. Audits of publicly traded companies should also be based on SAS unless provisions are superseded by Auditing Standards issued by the PCAOB. In applying the substantive material of these Statements, the practitioner must exercise professional judgment and due professional care.

SAS 1—Codification of Auditing Standards and Procedures

This statement covers the material contained in Statements on Auditing Procedures numbers 33 through 54. While much of SAS 1 has been superseded by subsequent pronouncements, the information presented here remains in effect.

What are "subsequent events"?

Subsequent events are events that occur after the balance sheet date but before the issuance of the financial statements and the auditor's report. They provide additional information about conditions or circumstances:

- Existing at or before the balance sheet date (Type I)
- Arising after the balance sheet date (Type II)

How should subsequent events be handled?

- Type I subsequent events require adjustment of the financial statements.
- Type II subsequent events may require disclosure in the financial statements in order to prevent readers from being misled.

Example 12.1 Type I Subsequent Event

A client has advised you that one of their accounts receivable is deemed to be uncollectible as of the balance sheet date. Accordingly, the client has made an adjusting entry to record the bad debt expense and to remove the account receivable from the subsidiary ledger. However, while examining the cash receipts of the period subsequent to the balance sheet date, you find a partial collection of the receivable. Accordingly, you should suggest to the client that an adjusting entry be made to properly reflect the receivable at its net realizable value.

Example 12.2 Type II Subsequent Event

Fifteen days after the end of the year, a client's building is completely destroyed in a fire. Since the building was in existence as of the balance sheet date, no adjusting entry is necessary. In order to prevent readers from being misled, the casualty should be disclosed in the notes to the financial statements.

How do I handle the subsequent discovery of facts existing at the date of the auditor's report?

Subsequent discovery of facts existing at the date of the auditor's report differs from subsequent events in that the audit report is already issued in the case of subsequent discovery of facts.

In such a case, the auditor should:

- Determine the reliability of the facts and verify their existence as of the date of the audit report.
- Ascertain whether the audit report would have been affected had the facts been known at the date of the report.
- Determine whether readers of the financial statements might be materially influenced.
- Advise the client that disclosure is necessary through revised financial statements.

The audit report may need to be modified, especially if the client refuses to make the necessary disclosures. In such circumstances, the practitioner should withdraw from the engagement and take steps to recall the financial statements.

SAS 2—Reports on Audited Financial Statements

Superseded by SAS 58.

SAS 3—The Effects of EDP on the Auditor's Study and Evaluation of Internal Control

Superseded by SAS 48.

SAS 4—Quality Control Considerations for a Firm of Independent Auditors

Superseded by SAS 25.

SAS 5—The Meaning of "Present Fairly in Conformity with Generally Accepted Accounting Principles" in the Independent Auditor's Report

Superseded by SAS 69.

SAS 6—Related Party Transactions

Superseded by SAS 45.

SAS 7—Communication between Predecessor and Successor Auditor

Superseded by SAS 84.

SAS 8—Other Information in Documents Containing Audited Financial Statements

Superseded by SAS 118.

SAS 9—The Effect of an Internal Audit Function on the Scope of the Independent Auditor's Examination

Superseded by SAS 65.

SAS 10—Limited Review of Interim Financial Information

Superseded by SAS 24 and later superseded by SAS 36. SAS 36 was subsequently superseded by SAS 71 and then by SAS 100.

SAS 11—Using the Work of a Specialist

Superseded by SAS 73.

SAS 12—Inquiry of a Client's Lawyer Concerning Litigation, Claims, and Assessments

The independent auditor must obtain sufficient competent evidential matter concerning the existence of a possible loss from litigation, claims, and assessments. In this connection, he or she should identify the period in which the underlying cause occurred, the probability of an unfavorable outcome, and an estimate of the potential loss.

The auditing procedures to be performed by the independent auditor include:

- Inquiry of management personnel
- Obtaining a client-prepared description of litigation, claims, and assessments
- Examination of documents in the possession of the client
- Obtaining written assurance from management as to the disclosure and proper accounting of all unasserted claims
- Reading the minutes of the board of directors' meetings
- Reading contracts, loan agreements, leases, and correspondence with governmental agencies and legal counsel

How do I corroborate information furnished by the client?

The auditor's primary means of corroborating information provided by the client concerning litigation, claims, and assessments is a letter of audit inquiry sent to the client's legal counsel. The client's legal counsel, after obtaining the permission of the client to respond, is expected to respond promptly and fully, but may, however, limit his or her response to the matters to which he or she has devoted substantial attention.

Example 12.3 Letter of Audit Inquiry

[Prepared on client's letterhead—See Note A]

Date [See Note B]

[Name of lawyer]
[Address of lawyer]
Dear _____:

    In connection with an audit of our financial statements at *[balance sheet date]* and for the *[period]* then ended, management of the Company has prepared and furnished to our auditors *[name and address of auditors]* a description and evaluation of certain contingencies, including those set forth below involving matters with respect to which you have been engaged and to which you have devoted substantive attention on behalf of the Company in the form of legal consultation or representation. These contingencies are regarded by management of the Company as material for this purpose *[management may indicate a materiality limit if an understanding has been reached with the auditor]*. Your response should include matters that existed at *[balance sheet date]* and during the period from that date to the date of your response.

Pending or Threatened Litigation

[Excluding unasserted claims]

[Ordinarily the information would include: (1) the nature of the litigation, (2) the progress of the case to date, (3) how management is responding or intends to respond to the litigation (e.g., to contest the case vigorously or to seek an out-of-court settlement), and (4) an evaluation of the likelihood of an unfavorable outcome and an estimate, if one can be made, of the amount or range of potential loss.]

Please furnish to our auditors such explanation, if any, that you consider necessary to supplement the foregoing information, including an explanation of those matters as to which your views may differ from those stated and an identification of the omission of any pending or threatened litigation, claims, and assessments or a statement that the list of such matters is complete.

Unasserted Claims and Assessments

[Considered by management to be probable of assertion, and that, if asserted, would have at least a reasonable possibility of an unfavorable outcome]

[Ordinarily management's information would include: (1) the nature of the matter, (2) how management intends to respond if the claim is asserted, and (3) an evaluation of the likelihood of an unfavorable outcome and an estimate, if one can be made, of the amount or range of potential loss.]

Please furnish to our auditors such explanation, if any, that you consider necessary to supplement the foregoing information, including an explanation of those matters as to which your views may differ from those stated.

We understand that whenever, in the course of performing legal services for us with respect to a matter recognized to involve an unasserted possible claim or assessment that may call for financial statement disclosure, you have formed a professional conclusion that we should disclose or consider disclosure concerning such possible claim or assessment, as a matter of professional responsibility to us, you will so advise us and will consult with us concerning the question of such disclosure and the applicable requirements of Statement of Financial Accounting Standards No. 5. Please specifically confirm to our auditors that our understanding is correct.

Please specifically identify the nature of and reasons for any limitation on your response.

[The auditor may request the client to inquire about additional matters, for example, unpaid or unbilled charges or specified information on certain contractually assumed obligations of the company, such as guarantees of indebtedness of others.]

Very truly yours,

[Authorized signature for client]

(continued)

(Continued)

Notes to User:

(A) Auditors should carefully consider the provisions of SAS 12 in drafting this letter.

(B) Sending of this letter should be timed so that the lawyer's response is dated as close to the auditor's opinion date as is practicable. However, the auditor and the client should consider early mailing of a draft inquiry as a convenience for the lawyer in preparing a timely response to the formal inquiry letter.

What if the lawyer does not respond to the inquiry?

The lawyer's refusal to respond to the letter of audit inquiry is tantamount to a scope limitation sufficient to preclude the issuance of an unqualified opinion.

SAS 13—Reports on a Limited Review of Interim Financial Information

Superseded by SAS 24 and subsequently superseded by SAS 36. SAS 36 was subsequently superseded by SAS 71 and then by SAS 100.

SAS 14—Special Reports

Superseded by SAS 62.

SAS 15—Reports on Comparative Financial Statements

Superseded by SAS 58.

SAS 16—The Independent Auditor's Responsibility for the Detection of Errors or Irregularities

Superseded by SAS 53.

SAS 17—Illegal Acts by Clients

Superseded by SAS 54.

SAS 18—Unaudited Replacement Cost Information

Withdrawn by the Auditing Standards Board.

SAS 19—Client Representations

Superseded by SAS 85.

SAS 20—Required Communication of Material Weaknesses in Internal Accounting Control

Superseded by SAS 60.

SAS 21—Segment Information

Rescinded by the Auditing Standards Board.

SAS 22—Planning and Supervision

Superseded by SAS 108.

SAS 23—Analytical Review Procedures

Superseded by SAS 56.

SAS 24—Review of Interim Financial Information

Superseded by SAS 36 and later superseded by SAS 71. SAS 71 was subsequently superseded by SAS 100.

SAS 25—The Relationship of Generally Accepted Auditing Standards to Quality Control Standards

Am I responsible for quality control?

When performing an audit, the independent auditor is responsible for complying with generally accepted auditing standards.

When conducting an audit practice, an independent auditor (or firm of independent auditors) is responsible for complying with quality control standards in order to provide assurance of compliance with generally accepted auditing standards.

> ### Note
>
> Refer to Chapter 16 for guidance in establishing an effective system of quality control.

SAS 26—Association with Financial Statements

When am I considered associated with financial statements?

An accountant is deemed to be associated with financial statements when:

- He or she has consented to the use of his or her name in a report, document, or any written communication containing the financial statements.
- The accountant has prepared or assisted in the preparation of the financial statements, even though his or her name is not on the financial statements.

Note: This statement applies to association with audited or unaudited financial statements of a public entity.

Recommendation

The practitioner engaged to compile or review unaudited financial statements of a nonpublic entity should comply with Statements on Standards for Accounting and Review Services.

Can I use a disclaimer?

When the practitioner is associated with unaudited financial statements of a public entity, it is appropriate to issue a disclaimer of opinion. Such a disclaimer may be in the form of a report on the financial statements, or the disclaimer may be placed directly on the statements. In addition to providing the disclaimer of opinion, the practitioner should clearly mark every page of the financial statements "Unaudited."

SAS 27—Supplementary Information Required by the Financial Accounting Standards Board

Superseded by SAS 52.

SAS 28—Supplementary Information on the Effects of Changing Prices

Withdrawn by the Auditing Standards Board.

SAS 29—Reporting on Information Accompanying the Basic Financial Statements in Auditor-Submitted Documents

Superseded by SAS 118 and SAS 119.

SAS 30—Reporting on Internal Accounting Control

Superseded by SSAE 2, which was later superseded by SSAE 10.

SAS 31—Evidential Matter

Superseded by SAS 106.

SAS 32—Adequacy of Disclosure in Financial Statements

How much disclosure is enough?

If the independent auditor concludes that the audited financial statements omit information required by generally accepted accounting principles (GAAP), the auditor should express either a qualified opinion or an adverse opinion.

Recommendation

If practicable, present the omitted information in an explanatory paragraph of the audit report. *Practicable* means that the information is obtainable from the client's records and the auditor is not put in the position of being the preparer of the information.

SAS 33—Supplementary Oil and Gas Reserve Information

Superseded by SAS 45.

SAS 34—The Auditor's Considerations When a Question Arises about an Entity's Continued Existence

Superseded by SAS 59.

SAS 35—Special Reports: Applying Agreed-Upon Procedures to Specified Elements, Accounts, or Items of a Financial Statement

Superseded by SAS 75.

SAS 36—Review of Interim Financial Information

Superseded by SAS 71.

SAS 37—Filings under Federal Securities Statutes

What are my responsibilities in filings under federal securities statutes?

The accountant involved in filings under the federal securities statutes is considered to be an expert. Therefore, the accountant's responsibility is based on the "reasonable man/person" standard.

The "subsequent events" period is extended from the date of the audit report to the effective date of the filing under the federal securities statutes. In addition, if the accountant finds that any unaudited information is not in conformity with GAAP, he or she should insist that an appropriate revision be made.

SAS 38—Letters for Underwriters

Superseded by SAS 49. SAS 49 was subsequently superseded by SAS 72.

SAS 39—Audit Sampling

What risks are involved in statistical sampling?

This statement provides guidance in situations in which the independent auditor decides to utilize statistical or nonstatistical sampling plans or approaches in performing tests of controls, substantive tests, or both.

While sampling plans create uncertainty, the uncertainty is justified due to the cost-benefit relationship since a well-designed sample is presumed to be representative of a population.

In performing sampling plans, the auditor should assess and control *sampling risk*, which is the risk that a sample may not be representative of a population and therefore might cause the auditor to draw an invalid conclusion.

- In *substantive testing*, sampling risk involves the risk of incorrect acceptance and the risk of incorrect rejection.
- In *tests of controls*, it includes the risk of assessing control risk too low and the risk of assessing control risk too high.

Nonsampling risk should also be controlled. Nonsampling risk includes the risk that the auditor will fail to detect material misstatements due to nonapplication of a required procedure or the application of a procedure inconsistent with a given audit objective.

Note

The audit objective is the detection of unrecorded liabilities, and the audit procedure is the confirmation of recorded account balances.

Audit risk is a combination of sampling and nonsampling risks.

SAS 40—Supplementary Mineral Reserve Information

Superseded by SAS 52.

SAS 41—Working Papers

Superseded by SAS 96 and later superseded by SAS 103.

SAS 42—Reporting on Condensed Financial Statements and Selected Financial Data

What about client-prepared documents?

This statement is applicable to reporting on a client-prepared document containing:

- Condensed financial statements that are derived from audited financial statements
- Selected financial data derived from audited financial statements

Condensed Financial Statements

What should be in the report on condensed financial statements?

The auditor's report on condensed financial statements should contain:

- A statement that the auditor has audited, in accordance with auditing standards generally accepted in the United States of America, the complete set of financial statements
- An indication that an opinion has been expressed on the complete set of financial statements
- The date of the auditor's report on the complete set of financial statements
- The type of opinion expressed on the complete set of financial statements
- An opinion as to whether the information contained in the condensed financial statements is presented fairly in all material respects in relation to the complete set of financial statements

Caution

To prevent readers from being misled, condensed financial statements should be so marked.

Example 12.4 Wording of a Report on Condensed Financial Statements

I (We) have audited, in accordance with auditing standards generally accepted in the United States of America, the consolidated balance sheet of Mat Corporation as of December 31, 2X13, and the related statements of income, retained earnings, and cash flows for the year then ended (not presented herein); and in my (our) report dated March 2, 2X14, I (we) expressed an unqualified opinion on those financial statements.

In my (our) opinion, the information set forth in the accompanying condensed financial statements is fairly stated in all material respects in relation to the consolidated financial statements from which it has been derived.

Selected Financial Data

Since selected financial data are not a required part of the basic financial statements, the auditor's report on such data should be limited to data that are derived from financial statements subjected to an audit.

What should be in the report on selected financial data?

The auditor's report on selected financial data should include:

- A statement that the auditor has audited, in accordance with auditing standards generally accepted in the United States of America, the complete set of financial statements
- An indication that an opinion has been expressed on the complete set of financial statements
- The type of opinion expressed on the complete set of financial statements
- An opinion as to whether the information contained in the selected financial data is presented fairly in all material respects in relation to the complete set of financial statements

Example 12.5 Wording of Additional Paragraph Added to the Auditor's Standard Report

I (We) have also previously audited, in accordance with generally accepted auditing standards, the balance sheets as of December 31, 2X13, 2X12, and 2X11, and the related statements of income, retained earnings, and cash flows for the years ended December 31, 2X13, 2X12, and 2X11 (none of which are presented herein); and I (we) expressed unqualified opinions on those consolidated financial statements. In my (our) opinion, the information set forth in the selected financial data for each of the five years in the period ended December 31, 2X15, appearing on page XX, is fairly stated, in all material respects, in relation to the consolidated financial statements from which it has been derived.

SAS 43—Omnibus Statement on Auditing Standards

This statement amends parts of selected Statements on Auditing Standards. These amendments have been incorporated into the summaries of the pertinent Statements.

SAS 44—Special-Purpose Reports on Internal Accounting Control at Service Organizations

Superseded by SAS 70.

SAS 45—Omnibus Statement on Auditing Standards—1983

This statement amends parts of selected Statements on Auditing Standards.

Related Parties

How do I handle related-party transactions?

With respect to related-party transactions, the auditor should be aware that the substance of a particular transaction could be significantly different from its legal form. Whenever a client transacts business with another entity at terms more favorable than would be afforded under usual circumstances, it is possible that a related-party relationship exists.

Recommendation

The auditor should design substantive tests in order to identify the existence and terms of related-party transactions. This is crucial, since Financial Accounting Standards Board (FASB) Statement No. 57 requires that related-party information be disclosed in financial statements.

How do I identify related-party transactions?

In order to identify transactions with related parties, the auditor should review:

- The minutes of meetings of the board of directors
- Transactions with major customers, suppliers, borrowers, and lenders
- Large, unusual, and nonrecurring transactions

Once identified, related-party transactions should be examined in order for the auditor to gain satisfaction as to the purpose, extent, and nature of the transactions. In addition, the practitioner must be satisfied with the related-party disclosures contained in the financial statements.

SAS 46—Consideration of Omitted Procedures after the Report Date

What if one or more procedures were omitted?

Under certain circumstances, such as peer review, the auditor may conclude, after the issuance of an audit report, that he or she omitted one or more auditing procedures. In these situations, the auditor has the responsibility of assessing the importance of the omitted procedures to his or her present ability to support the previously expressed opinion. In making this assessment, the auditor should consider any alternative auditing procedures performed.

If the auditor still feels that the omitted procedures impair the current ability to support the audit report, he or she should undertake to apply the omitted or alternative procedures. If the auditor is unable to apply the necessary procedures, he or she should contact legal counsel in order to discuss the appropriate course of action.

SAS 47—Audit Risk and Materiality in Conducting an Audit

Superseded by SAS 107.

SAS 48—The Effects of Computer Processing on the Audit of Financial Statements

What effect does computer processing have on an audit?

An auditor should consider these issues in planning an engagement to audit an entity that records its transactions by computer:

- The extent of electronic data processing
- The complexity of the electronic data processing operations
- The organizational structure of the electronic data processing department
- The availability of financial data
- The application of computer-assisted audit techniques
- The need for a specialist to explain the effects of electronic data processing

How do computer processing and manual systems differ?

When considering a client's internal control in an electronic data processing environment, the auditor should consider the characteristics that distinguish computer processing from manual recording:

- *Transaction trails*. Audit trails in a computerized environment are either nonexistent or short-lived.
- *Uniform processing of transactions*. If a computer handles a particular type of transaction correctly, then it will handle all subsequent transactions of the same type in the same manner. *Caution:* The converse is also true. If a transaction is handled incorrectly, all subsequent similar transactions processed will also be incorrectly handled.
- *Segregation of functions*. Since many functions are performed internally by the computer, there is an inherent lack of segregation of functions in a computerized environment. To compensate for this situation, job functions should be segregated within the electronic data processing activities.
- *Potential for errors and fraud*. The potential for errors and fraud in a computerized environment depends on the human involvement in the computerized applications and the extent of the segregation of functions.
- *Potential for increased management supervision*. Given that a computer can generate data more quickly than manual preparation, financial information is provided on a more timely basis. This enables management to use information before it outlives its utility.
- *Initiation or subsequent execution of transactions by computer*. Authorization for initiation or subsequent execution of transactions is built into the computer. Documentation for this authorization is therefore not always apparent.
- *Dependence of other controls on controls over computer processing*. The output derived from computer processing is often useful in performing manual control procedures.

SAS 49—Letters for Underwriters

Superseded by SAS 72.

SAS 50—Reports on the Application of Accounting Principles

When might I have to report on the application of accounting principles?

An accountant may be requested to prepare a written report on:

- The application of accounting principles to specified transactions
- The type of opinion that may be expressed on an entity's financial statements

Note

An accountant should not prepare a written report on a hypothetical transaction.

What should be in a report on the application of accounting principles?

The accountant's report on the application of accounting principles should include:

- The appropriate address (the report should be addressed to the principal to the transaction or to the intermediary)
- A statement describing the type of engagement
- An indication that the engagement was performed in accordance with the relevant standards of the American Institute of Certified Public Accountants
- A description of the transaction and its related facts, circumstances, and assumptions (including their source)
- An identification of the principals to the transaction
- A description of the relevant accounting principles
- A statement fixing the responsibility for the proper accounting treatment with the preparers of the financial statements, who should consult with their continuing accountants
- A warning that the report may change if differences of facts, circumstances, or assumptions arise
- A statement restricting the use of the report to the specified parties

---

Example 12.6 Wording for a Report on Accounting Applications

I (We) have been engaged to report on the appropriate application of accounting principles generally accepted in the United States of America to the specific transaction described below. This report is being issued to the Karen Company (DBA Intermediaries) for assistance in evaluating accounting principles for the described specific transaction. My (Our) engagement has been conducted in accordance with standards established by the American Institute of Certified Public Accountants.

The facts, circumstances, and assumptions relevant to the specific transaction as provided to me (us) by the management of the Karen Company (DBA Intermediaries) are as follows:

> [*Description of transaction*]
> [*Description of appropriate accounting principles*]

The ultimate responsibility for the decision on the appropriate application of accounting principles generally accepted in the United States of America for an actual transaction rests with the preparers of financial statements, who should consult with their continuing accountants. My (Our) judgment on the appropriate application of accounting principles generally accepted in the United States of America for the described specific transaction is based solely on facts provided to me (us) as described above; should these facts and circumstances differ, my (our) conclusion may change.

This report is intended solely for the information and use of the board of directors and management of the Karen Company (DBA Intermediaries) and is not intended to be and should not be used by anyone other than these specified parties.

SAS 51—Reporting on Financial Statements Prepared for Use in Other Countries

When reporting on financial statements for overseas use, what should I do?

Generally accepted auditing standards as developed in the United States should be adhered to when examining financial statements of a U.S. entity prepared in conformity with accounting principles accepted in another country. Under certain circumstances, the auditor may also have to adhere to the auditing standards of the foreign country.

If the financial statements are for use only in a foreign country, the auditor may issue:

- A U.S.-style report modified for reporting on the foreign country's accounting principles
- A report based on the foreign country's standards

Example 12.7 U.S.-Style Report Modified for Use in a Foreign Country

Independent Auditor's Report

I (We) have audited the accompanying balance sheet of Transcontinental Company as of December 31, 2X12, and the related statements of income, retained earnings, and cash flows for the year then ended, which, as described in Note X, have been prepared on the basis of accounting principles accepted in [*name of country*]. These financial statements are the responsibility of the Company's management. My (our) responsibility is to express an opinion on these financial statements based on my (our) audit.

I (We) conducted my (our) audit in accordance with auditing standards generally accepted in the United States of America (and in [*name of country*]). U.S. standards require that I (we) plan and perform the audit to obtain reasonable assurance about whether the financial statements are free of material misstatement. An audit includes examining, on a test basis, evidence supporting the amounts and disclosures in the financial statements. An audit also includes assessing the accounting principles used and significant estimates made by management, as

(continued)

(Continued)

well as evaluating the overall financial statement presentation. I (We) believe that my (our) audit provides a reasonable basis for my (our) opinion.

In my (our) opinion, the financial statements referred to above present fairly, in all material respects, the financial position of Transcontinental Company as of (at) December 31, 2X12, and the results of its cash flows for the year then ended in conformity with accounting principles generally accepted in [*name of country*].

SAS 52—Omnibus Statement on Auditing Standards—1987

Superseded by various SAS.

SAS 53—The Auditor's Responsibility to Detect and Report Errors and Irregularities

Superseded by SAS 82.

SAS 54—Illegal Acts by Clients

What is an illegal act?

An illegal act is a violation of law or government regulations.

Caution

The auditor should seek legal counsel when determining what is an illegal act.

What is my responsibility for the detection and reporting of illegal acts?

The auditor's responsibility is essentially the same as his or her responsibility to detect and report errors and fraud (as discussed in SAS 99).

Note

The auditor is concerned with the illegal act's effect on the financial statements rather than the illegality itself.

What if I detect an illegal act that does not have a material effect on the financial statements?

If the client refuses to take appropriate action with respect to any illegal act, material or otherwise, the auditor should consider withdrawing from the engagement.

SAS 55—Consideration of Internal Control in a Financial Statement Audit

Modified by SAS 78 and SAS 94. Subsequently superseded by SAS 109 and SAS 110; refer to Chapter 10.

SAS 56—Analytical Procedures

Analytical procedures must be performed in the planning and overall review stages of all audits. Because analytical procedures enable identification of unusual relationships and fluctuations, the auditor can better determine the nature and extent of substantive tests.

> **Note**
>
> Analytical procedures do not have to be used in substantive testing. This is a matter of professional judgment.

What are analytical procedures?

Analytical procedures include comparison of recorded amounts, or ratios based on recorded amounts, to expectations derived by the auditor. Accordingly, analytical procedures include comparison of current-period financial information with:

- Prior-period information
- Expected results
- Predictable pattern information
- Intra-industry information
- Nonfinancial information

SAS 57—Auditing Accounting Estimates

What is meant by an accounting estimate?

An accounting estimate is an approximation of a financial statement element, item, or account.

Examples include:
- Net realizable values of inventory
- Pension and warranty expenses
- Obsolete inventories
- Amount of a probable loss contingency

What is my responsibility with respect to accounting estimates?

Whereas management is responsible for developing accounting estimates, the auditor is responsible for evaluating the reasonableness of such estimates.

The auditor must evaluate accounting estimates in order to obtain reasonable assurance that (1) all material accounting estimates have been developed, (2) the accounting estimates are reasonable, (3) the accounting estimates are in conformity with GAAP, and (4) the accounting estimates are properly disclosed in the financial statements.

How do I evaluate the reasonableness of accounting estimates?

The auditor should review and test the process employed by management in developing a particular accounting estimate. Furthermore, the auditor should develop an independent expectation of the estimate to corroborate the reasonableness of the client's estimate. Finally, the auditor should review subsequent events.

SAS 58—Reports on Audited Financial Statements

Modified by SAS 79; refer to Chapter 10.

SAS 59—The Auditor's Consideration of an Entity's Ability to Continue as a Going Concern

The auditor is responsible for evaluating whether there is substantial doubt about the entity's ability to continue as a going concern for a reasonable time period, not to exceed one year beyond the date of the audited financial statements.

What conditions and events may indicate a going-concern problem?

These issues might be considered indicative of a going-concern problem:

- *Negative trends*, such as a poor current working capital ratio
- *Indicators of possible financial trouble*, such as defaults on note agreements
- *Internal matters*, such as a strike by employees
- *External matters*, such as pending or actual litigation or legislation

Caution

The auditor should consider mitigating circumstances by evaluating management's plans. For example, management may be planning to restructure its debt in a manner that will increase equity ownership.

Do going-concern problems affect financial statements?

Certain informative disclosures might be necessary if the client is experiencing a going-concern problem. These disclosures include:

- The conditions and events causing the going-concern problem
- The possible effects of such conditions
- Management's evaluation of the significance of those conditions and events, along with any mitigating factors
- The possible cessation of operations
- Management's plans for overcoming the going-concern problem
- Significant information regarding the recoverability or classification of assets and liabilities

What is my reporting responsibility?

If the auditor concludes that there is substantial doubt about the entity's ability to continue as a going concern for a reasonable time period, then the audit report should be modified to include an additional paragraph (to be inserted after the opinion paragraph) that reflects the auditor's conclusion.

Example 12.8 Sample Wording of an Additional Paragraph Regarding the Entity's Ability to Continue as a Going Concern

The accompanying financial statements have been prepared assuming that the Company will continue as a going concern. As discussed in Note X to the financial statements, the Company has suffered recurring losses from operations and has a net capital deficiency that raises substantial doubt about its ability to continue as a going concern. Management's plans in regard to these matters are also described in Note X. The financial statements do not include any adjustments that might result from the outcome of this uncertainty.

> ## Caution
>
> A going-concern problem should not result in a qualified opinion. It would still be appropriate to issue an unqualified opinion.

> ## Warning
>
> Do not use conditional language (e.g., "if the company . . . , then . . . ") in the additional paragraph.

SAS 60—Communication of Internal Control Related Matters Noted in an Audit

Superseded by SAS 112.

SAS 61—Communication with Audit Committees

Superseded by SAS 114.

SAS 62—Special Reports

See Chapter 11.

SAS 63—Compliance Auditing Applicable to Governmental Entities and Other Recipients of Governmental Financial Assistance

Superseded by SAS 68.

SAS 64—Omnibus Statement on Auditing Standards

This statement amends parts of selected Statements on Auditing Standards. These amendments have been incorporated into the summaries of the pertinent statements.

SAS 65—The Auditor's Consideration of the Internal Audit Function in an Audit of Financial Statements

What is required of me as an independent auditor?

The work performed by a client's *internal* auditors may affect the nature, extent, and timing of the *independent* auditor's procedures. Internal auditors may provide direct assistance to the independent auditor. Accordingly, the practitioner should review the competency and objectivity of the internal auditors as well as evaluate their work.

- *Competency* of the internal auditors may be evaluated in light of their:
  - Education
  - Experience
  - Professional certification
  - Audit programs, policies, and procedures
  - Supervision and review
  - Working-papers documentation, including recommendations
- In judging *objectivity*, the independent auditor should consider:
  - The organizational level to which the internal audit reports are sent
  - Whether the internal audit staff has direct access to (and reports to) the board of directors, the audit committee, or the equivalent

Caution

Given that the independent auditor is responsible for expressing an opinion on the financial statements, he or she is responsible for all judgments concerning risks associated with the audit, materiality levels, sufficiency of tests performed, and evaluations of audit evidence. Furthermore, the practitioner should not allow internal auditors to gather evidence that the independent auditor cannot corroborate.

Note

The practitioner should not allow internal auditors to prepare and mail the accounts receivable confirmations. Rather, the internal auditors may be requested to prepare the confirmations, but the practitioner should both verify the balances (by inspecting the subsidiary ledger) and mail the confirmations.

SAS 66—Communication of Matters about Interim Financial Information Filed or to Be Filed with Specified Regulatory Agencies

Superseded by SAS 71.

SAS 67—The Confirmation Process

What is the confirmation process?

Confirmation is the process of obtaining and evaluating a direct communication from a third party in response to a request for information about an item relating to financial statement assertions. Throughout the confirmation process, the auditor should exercise professional skepticism.

What forms of confirmation exist?

The two types of confirmations that may be used are:

1. Positive forms that request a response whether or not the recipient is in agreement with the information stated on the confirmation request (a positive form can be a blank form that requests the recipient to fill in requested information)
2. Negative forms that request a response only if the recipient disagrees with the information stated on the confirmation request

Is there risk involved in using the negative form?

The use of negative confirmation requests may increase audit risk. Accordingly, judgment should be exercised in considering their use. In general, negative confirmation requests may be used when:

- The combined assessed level of inherent and control risk is low.
- Many small balances are involved.
- The auditor believes that the recipients are likely to give the requests consideration.

What should be done if a response to a confirmation request is not received?

- If a negative confirmation request was used and no response is received, the auditor ordinarily concludes that the recipient is in agreement with the stated information; accordingly, no additional procedures are necessary.
- If a positive confirmation request was used and no response is received, the auditor should perform alternative procedures. For example, in auditing accounts receivable, alternative procedures might include examination of subsequent-period cash receipts and inspection of shipping documents.

Are there any special considerations in evaluating the results of confirmation procedures?

In evaluating the results of the confirmation process, the auditor should consider:

- The reliability of the confirmations and/or applicable alternative procedures
- The nature and cause of exceptions
- The evidence generated from the application of other procedures
- The need for additional information

What guidance does SAS 67 provide in connection with the confirmation of accounts receivable?

The definition of accounts receivable is rather narrow. Accounts receivable include an entity's claims against customers created from the sale of goods or services in the normal course of business operations. Also included are a financial institution's loans.

Confirmation of accounts receivable is generally required.

Note

Confirmation of accounts receivable may not be necessary when (1) accounts receivable are immaterial, (2) the use of the confirmations is not likely to be effective, and (3) the combined assessed level of inherent and control risk is low.

Caution

If the auditor does not confirm accounts receivable, he or she should document in the working papers the justification for the omission and any details of any relevant alternative procedures performed.

SAS 68—Compliance Auditing Applicable to Governmental Entities and Other Recipients of Governmental Financial Assistance

Superseded by SAS 74.

SAS 69—The Meaning of Present Fairly in Conformity with Generally Accepted Accounting Principles in the Independent Auditor's Report

Withdrawn by the Auditing Standards Board.

SAS 70—Service Organizations

What is a service organization?

A service organization is an entity that provides a service to a client of the practitioner (i.e., user organization). *Example:* A company that processes the payroll for a client of the CPA.

What is the responsibility of an auditor of a user organization?

If an auditor wants to assess control risk below the maximum level, he or she should obtain from the auditor of the service organization a report on controls placed in operation and tests of operating effectiveness.

Note

When reporting on internal controls at a service organization relevant to a user entity's internal control over financial reporting, the practitioner should follow the provisions in SSAE 16, *Reporting on Controls at a Service Organization.*

SAS 71—Interim Financial Information

Superseded by SAS 100.

SAS 72—Letters for Underwriters and Certain Other Requesting Parties

What is a comfort letter?

A CPA may issue a letter for an underwriter, called a *comfort letter*. A comfort letter may refer to one or more of these issues:

- The accountant's independence
- Compliance of the financial statements included in the registration statement with the Securities Act of 1933
- Unaudited financial statements, condensed financial statements, capsule information, pro forma financial information, and forecasts
- Changes in financial statement items after the date of the financial statements included in the registration statement
- Tables and statistics

Note

A typical comfort letter includes (1) an opinion as to whether the audited financial statements and related schedules included in a registration statement are in compliance with applicable accounting requirements of the Securities Act of 1933 and pertinent accounting requirements adopted by the Securities and Exchange Commission (SEC) and (2) negative assurance as to whether the unaudited condensed interim financial information included in a registration statement is in compliance with applicable accounting requirements of the Securities Act of 1933 and pertinent accounting requirements adopted by the SEC.

SAS 73—Using the Work of a Specialist

How is a specialist used?

During the course of an audit, the independent auditor may need to employ a specialist. A specialist has expertise in an area other than accounting or auditing. Matters that might require the use of a specialist include:

- Valuation of assets. *Example:* A gemologist may be consulted in valuing inventories consisting of diamonds or other precious stones.
- Determination of physical characteristics. *Example:* A specialist may be consulted in connection with mineral reserves.
- Determination or verification of amounts determined through the use of specialized methods and techniques. *Example:* An actuary may be consulted in order to corroborate a client's accrual for contributions to a defined benefit pension plan.
- Interpretation of technical requirements, regulations, or agreements. *Example:* An attorney may be consulted in connection with contracts or other legal documents.

What must be considered before using a specialist?

The auditor must:

- Consider the professional competency and reputation of the specialist.
- Consider the relationship, if any, of the specialist to the client to determine if objectivity is impaired. *Note:* Independence of the specialist from the client is not required, but a lack of independence may require additional auditing procedures.
- Understand the nature of the work of the specialist, including:
  - The objectives and scope of the work
  - The accounting assumptions and methods used
  - The appropriateness of using the work for the intended purpose
  - The form and content of the report to be issued by the specialist

Does using a specialist affect reporting requirements?

If the findings of the specialist support the representations or assertions made by management, then the auditor could appropriately express a standard unqualified opinion. In such circumstances, the auditor should not refer to the use of the specialist.

The auditor may make reference to and identify the specialist if he or she decides to:

- Add explanatory language to the standard audit report. *Example:* The findings of the specialist raise substantial doubt about the entity's ability to continue as a going concern for a reasonable period of time.

- Issue a qualified opinion or adverse opinion because the findings of the specialist do not corroborate the representations or assertions made by management.
- Disclaim an opinion because of the inability to obtain sufficient competent evidential matter regarding a material client representation or assertion. *Example:* When a difference of opinion exists among specialists and the auditor cannot perform alternative auditing procedures.

SAS 74—Compliance Auditing Considerations in Audits of Governmental Entities and Recipients of Governmental Financial Assistance

Superseded by SAS 117.

SAS 75—Engagements to Apply Agreed-Upon Procedures to Specified Elements, Accounts, or Items of a Financial Statement

Withdrawn by SAS 93.

SAS 76—Amendments to Statement on Auditing Standards No. 72, Letters for Underwriters and Certain Other Requesting Parties

Refer to the summary of SAS 72, which includes the appropriate amendments.

SAS 77—Amendments to Statements on Auditing Standards No. 22, Planning and Supervision; No. 59, The Auditor's Consideration of an Entity's Ability to Continue as a Going Concern; and No. 62, Special Reports

Amendments in this pronouncement have been incorporated into the summaries of SAS 22 and SAS 59 as well as Chapter 11.

SAS 78—Consideration of Internal Control in a Financial Statement Audit: An Amendment to SAS 55

Refer to Chapter 10, which includes the appropriate amendments.

SAS 79—Amendment to Statement on Auditing Standards No. 58, Reports on Audited Financial Statements

Refer to Chapter 10, which includes the appropriate amendments.

SAS 80—Amendment to Statement on Auditing Standards No. 31, Evidential Matter

Refer to the summary of SAS 31, which includes the appropriate amendments.

SAS 81—Auditing Investments

Superseded by SAS 92.

SAS 82—Consideration of Fraud in a Financial Statement Audit

Superseded by SAS 99.

SAS 83—Establishing an Understanding with the Client

What are the documentation requirements relative to the understanding established with the client?

The understanding should be documented in the working papers, preferably by means of a written communication with the client.

Note

Under SAS 83, an engagement letter is highly recommended, but it is not required. However, see SAS 108, which imposes a presumptively mandatory requirement to issue an engagement letter.

What are the matters that should be considered when establishing an understanding with a client?

The understanding should cover (1) the objective(s) of the engagement, (2) management's responsibilities, and (3) the limitations of the engagement.

What are management's responsibilities that should be addressed in the understanding?

Management's responsibilities include:
- The financial statements
- Establishing and maintaining effective internal control
- Compliance with laws and regulations
- Making all financial records and related information available to the auditor
- Providing the auditor with a representation letter at the conclusion of the audit

- Adjusting the financial statements for those items that are deemed to be individually or collectively material to the financial statements
- Affirming in the representation letter that the financial statements have not been adjusted for those items that are deemed to be individually or collectively immaterial to the financial statements

What other matters may be relevant to the understanding?

Other matters that may be part of the understanding include:

- Terms of the engagement, including the timing of the audit, assistance of client personnel, fees, and billing
- Any arrangements involving the use of specialists (see SAS 73) and internal auditors (see SAS 65)
- Any arrangements involving a predecessor auditor (see SAS 84)
- Any additional services to be performed
- Any limitations of or arrangements regarding liability of either the auditor or the client
- Conditions under which access to audit documentation may be granted to others

SAS 84—Communications between Predecessor and Successor Accountants

As a successor auditor, are there any required communications with the predecessor auditor?

Yes. An auditor should not accept an engagement until the required communications with the predecessor have been properly evaluated. *Note:* The communications addressed in this pronouncement are not required if the most recent audited financial statements are more than two years prior to the beginning of the earliest period the successor auditor is requested to audit.

The successor auditor should communicate with the predecessor primarily to determine whether there are any reasons the engagement should not be accepted. Accordingly, the successor is interested in:

- Reasons for the change in auditors, including any facts that bear on the integrity of management
- Any disagreements the predecessor may have had with the client regarding application of generally accepted auditing principles and/or generally accepted auditing standards
- Any phases of the predecessor's audit that required an unusually large amount of time, possibly indicative of problems with the client's financial records
- Any communications to audit committees (or their equivalent) regarding fraud (see SAS 99), illegal acts (see SAS 54), and reportable conditions (see SAS 60)

The successor should also request that the client authorize the predecessor to allow a review of the predecessor's working papers that may have continuing and auditing significance.

The predecessor's response should be prompt and full but may indicate that the response is limited due to, for example, impending, threatened, or potential litigation or disciplinary proceedings.

Do the required communications violate confidentiality?

There is no violation of confidentiality as long as the client authorizes (1) the successor to communicate with the predecessor and (2) the predecessor to respond to the successor's inquiries. The authorization may be oral or in writing.

What action is appropriate if a prospective client will not allow the predecessor to respond fully?

The refusal of a prospective client to allow the predecessor auditor to respond fully should cause the successor auditor to (1) question the reason(s) for the refusal and (2) consider declining the engagement.

What should the successor do if he or she becomes aware of information that may require the revision of the financial statements reported on by the predecessor?

If the successor becomes aware of information that leads him or her to conclude that the financial statements reported on by the predecessor may require revision, then the successor should request that the client inform the predecessor and arrange a meeting of the three parties in order to discuss the matter and arrive at an appropriate resolution.

Caution

A client's refusal to inform the predecessor of the need to revise prior financial statements should cause the successor to consider whether withdrawal from the engagement is appropriate. Furthermore, the successor should consider the need to consult with his or her legal counsel.

SAS 85—Management Representations

What type of representations do I need from the client?

At the conclusion of the audit, the auditor must obtain from the client a representation letter confirming oral and written representations or assertions made by the client during the course of the audit. The representation letter, to be addressed to the auditor, is usually signed by the chief executive officer and chief financial officer. The representation letter should cover all financial statements and periods covered by the audit report. It should be dated as of the audit report date.

What items should be included in the representation letter?

The items included in the client representation letter will vary depending on the engagement and the nature and basis of financial statement presentation. Some commonly included items are:

- Management's acknowledgment of its responsibility for the fair presentation in the financial statements of financial position, results of operations, and cash flows in conformity with GAAP
- Management's belief that the financial statements are fairly presented in conformity with GAAP
- Availability of all financial records and related data
- Completeness and availability of all minutes of meetings of stockholders, directors, and committees of directors
- Communication from regulatory agencies concerning noncompliance with or deficiencies in financial reporting practices
- Absence of unrecorded transactions
- Management's belief that the effects of any uncorrected financial statement misstatements aggregated by the auditor during the current engagement and pertaining to the latest period presented are immaterial, both individually and in the aggregate, to the financial statements taken as a whole (a summary of such items should be included in or attached to the letter)
- Management's acknowledgment of its responsibility for the design and implementation of programs and controls to prevent and detect fraud
- Knowledge of fraud or suspected fraud affecting the entity involving (1) management, (2) employees who have significant roles in internal control, or (3) others where the fraud could have a material effect on the financial statements
- Knowledge of any allegations of fraud or suspected fraud affecting the entity received in communications from employees, former employees, analysts, regulators, short sellers, or others
- Plans or intentions that may affect the carrying value or classification of assets or liabilities
- Information concerning related-party transactions and amounts receivable from or payable to related parties
- Guarantees, whether written or oral, under which the entity is contingently liable
- Significant estimates and material concentrations known to management that are required to be disclosed in accordance with the AICPA's Statement of Position 94-6, *Disclosure of Certain Significant Risks and Uncertainties*
- Violations or possible violations of laws or regulations whose effects should be considered for disclosure in the financial statements or as a basis for recording a loss contingency
- Unasserted claims or assessments that the entity's lawyer has advised are probable of assertion and must be disclosed in accordance with FASB Statement No. 5, *Accounting for Contingencies*

- Other liabilities and gain or loss contingencies that are required to be accrued or disclosed by FASB 5
- Satisfactory title to assets, liens, or encumbrances on assets, and assets pledged as collateral
- Compliance with aspects of contractual agreements that may affect the financial statements
- Information concerning subsequent events

Can a representation letter replace audit procedures?

Although the management representation letter is a form of evidential matter, it is not a substitute for the application of auditing procedures.

Caution

Management's refusal to furnish the representation letter to the auditor is tantamount to a scope limitation sufficient to preclude the issuance of an unqualified opinion. The refusal to issue a representation letter ordinarily will lead the auditor to doubt the integrity of management. As a result, the auditor should reconsider his or her ability to rely on other management assertions or representations. This situation usually will result in a disclaimer of opinion.

Example 12.9 Illustrative Representation Letter

[*Prepared on client's letterhead*]
[*Date*]
To [*name of independent auditor*]:

   I am (We are) providing this letter in connection with your audit(s) of the [*identify financial statements*] of [*name of entity*] as of [*dates*] and for the [*periods*] for the purpose of expressing an opinion as to whether the [*consolidated*] financial statements present fairly, in all material respects, the financial position, results of operations, and cash flows of [*name of entity*] in conformity with accounting principles generally accepted in the United States of America. I (We) confirm that I (we) are responsible for the fair presentation in the [*consolidated*] financial statements of financial position, results of operations, and cash flows in conformity with generally accepted accounting principles.

   Certain representations in this letter are described as being limited to matters that are material. Items are considered material, regardless of size, if they involve an omission or misstatement of accounting information that, in the light of surrounding circumstances, makes it probable that the judgment of a

(continued)

(*Continued*)

reasonable person relying on the information would be changed or influenced by the omission or misstatement.

I (We) confirm, to the best of my (our) knowledge and belief, as of [*date of auditor's report*], the following representations made to you during your audit(s).

1. The financial statements referred to above are fairly presented in conformity with accounting principles generally accepted in the United States of America.
2. I (We) have made available to you, all:
   (a) Financial records and related data.
   (b) Minutes of the meetings of stockholders, directors, and committees of directors, or summaries of actions of recent meetings for which minutes have not yet been prepared.
3. There have been no communications from regulatory agencies concerning noncompliance with or deficiencies in financial reporting practices.
4. There are no material transactions that have not been properly recorded in the accounting records underlying the financial statements.
5. I (We) believe that the effects of the uncorrected financial statement misstatements summarized in the accompanying schedule are immaterial, both individually and in the aggregate, to the financial statements taken as a whole.
6. I (We) acknowledge my (our) responsibility for the design and implementation of programs and controls to prevent and detect fraud.
7. I (We) have no knowledge of any fraud or suspected fraud affecting the entity involving:
   (a) Management,
   (b) Employees who have significant roles in internal control, or
   (c) Others where the fraud could have a material effect on the financial statements.
   The company has no plans or intentions that may materially affect the carrying value or classification of assets and liabilities.
8. I (We) have no knowledge of any allegations of fraud or suspected fraud affecting the entity received in communications from employees, analysts, regulators, short sellers, or others.
9. The company has no plans or intentions that may materially affect the carrying value or classification of assets and liabilities.
10. The following have been properly recorded or disclosed in the financial statements:
    (a) Related-party transactions, including sales, purchases, loans, transfers, leasing arrangements, and guarantees, and amounts receivable from or payable to related parties.
    (b) Guarantees, whether written or oral, under which the company is contingently liable.

(c) Significant estimates and material concentrations known to management that are required to be disclosed in accordance with the AICPA's Statement of Position 94-6, *Disclosure of Certain Significant Risks and Uncertainties*. [*Significant estimates are estimates at the balance sheet date that could change materially within the next year. Concentrations refer to volumes of business, revenues, available sources of supply, or markets or geographical areas for which events could occur that would significantly disrupt normal finances within the next year.*]

11. There are no:

   (a) Violations or possible violations of laws or regulations whose effects should be considered for disclosure in the financial statements or as a basis for recording a loss contingency.

   (b) Unasserted claims or assessments that my (our) lawyer has advised me (us) are probable of assertion and must be disclosed in accordance with Financial Accounting Standards Board (FASB) Statement No. 5, *Accounting for Contingencies*.

   (c) Other liabilities or gain or loss contingencies that are required to be accrued or disclosed by FASB Statement No. 5.

12. The company has satisfactory title to all owned assets, and there are no liens or encumbrances on such assets, nor has any asset been pledged as collateral.

13. The company has complied with all aspects of contractual agreements that would have a material effect on the financial statements in the event of noncompliance.

   [*Add additional representations that are unique to the entity's business or industry.*]

   To the best of my (our) knowledge and belief, no events have occurred subsequent to the balance sheet date and through the date of this letter that would require adjustment to or disclosure in the aforementioned financial statements.

   [*Name of chief executive officer and title*]

   [*Name of chief financial officer and title*]

SAS 86—Amendment to Statement on Auditing Standards No. 72, Letters for Underwriters and Certain Other Requesting Parties

Refer to the summary of SAS 72, which includes the appropriate amendments.

SAS 87—Restricting the Use of an Auditor's Report

What is the difference between general-use and restricted-use reports?

General-use reports are auditor's reports that are not restricted as to use by specified parties—for example, audit reports on historical financial statements.

Restricted-use reports are auditor's reports that are intended only for specified parties.

When can an auditor issue a restricted-use report?

An auditor can issue a restricted-use report in these circumstances:

- The subject matter of the report or the presentation being reported on is based on measurement or disclosure criteria included in contractual agreements or regulatory provisions not in conformity with generally accepted accounting principles or another comprehensive basis of accounting.
- The report is based on agreed-upon procedures.
- The report is a by-product of a financial statement audit—for example, communication of internal control–related matters noted in an audit (see SAS 60) and communications with audit committees (see SAS 61).

What is the appropriate language to include in restricted-use reports?

An example of appropriate language is: "This report is intended solely for the information and use of [*the specified parties*] and is not intended to be and should not be used by anyone other than these specified parties."

SAS 88—Service Organizations and Reporting on Consistency

Refer to the summary of SAS 70 and Chapter 10, which include the appropriate amendments.

SAS 89—Audit Adjustments

The amendments contained in this pronouncement have been integrated within other areas of this book.

SAS 90—Audit Committee Communications

The amendments contained in this pronouncement have been integrated within other areas of this book.

SAS 91—Federal GAAP Hierarchy

Refer to the summary of SAS 69, which includes the appropriate amendments.

SAS 92—Auditing Derivative Instruments, Hedging Activities, and Investments in Securities

What special skills or knowledge are required in order to audit derivative instruments, hedging activities, and other investments in securities?

The auditor should:

- Obtain an understanding of an entity's information system for derivative instruments and securities, including services provided by a service organization when significant information about them is transmitted, processed, maintained, or accessed electronically.
- Identify controls placed in operation by the entity's service organization that are part of the entity's information system for derivative instruments and securities.
- Obtain special knowledge to evaluate the measurement, disclosure, and other U.S. GAAP requirements for derivative instruments and securities.
- Obtain an understanding of the determination of the fair values, including the appropriateness of various types of valuation models and the reasonableness of key factors and assumptions used in such models.
- Obtain an understanding of the general risk management concepts and typical asset/liability management strategies to assess inherent risk and control risk for assertions about derivatives used in hedging activities.

How can inherent risk be affected in the audit of derivative instruments, hedging activities, and other investments in securities?

The assessment of inherent risk for assertions pertaining to derivative instruments, hedging activities, and other investments in securities can be affected by:

- Accounting requirements based on management's objectives.
- The complexity of the features of the derivative financial instruments or securities, which may impact the measurement disclosure requirements.
- Derivatives without an initial exchange of cash that may be inadvertently ignored for valuation and disclosure considerations.
- An entity's inexperience with derivative instruments or securities.
- Embedded derivatives, which are less likely to be identified by management.
- Risks related to external factors, including:
  - *Credit risk*—risk of loss as a result of the issuer of a debt security or the counterparty to a derivative failing to meet its obligation.
  - *Market risk*—risk of loss from adverse changes in market factors that affect the fair value of a derivative instrument or security (i.e., changes in interest rates, foreign exchange rates, market indexes for equity securities).
  - *Basis risk*—risk of loss from ineffective hedging activities. Basis risk is the difference between the fair value (or cash flows) of the hedged item and the fair value (or cash flows) of the hedging derivative. The risk is that fair values (or cash flows) will change so that the hedge will no longer be effective.
  - *Legal risk*—risk of loss from a legal or regulatory action that invalidates or otherwise precludes performance by one or both parties to the derivative instrument or security.

What control risk considerations should the auditor be aware of when auditing derivative instruments, hedging activities, and other investments in securities?

The auditor's understanding of internal controls over derivative instruments and securities will not only encompass controls of the entity but may also include those of service organizations; outside services may be part of the entity's information system.

It may not be practicable or possible to reduce audit risk to an acceptable level without identifying controls placed in operation by a service organization and gathering evidential matter about the operating effectiveness of those controls.

What substantive auditing procedures should the auditor consider with respect to financial statement assertions for derivative instruments and other investments?

Substantive procedures for the financial statement assertions for derivative instruments and other investments include:

- Existence or occurrence
- Completeness
- Rights and obligations
- Valuation
- Impairment losses

Existence or Occurrence

- Confirmation with the issuer of the derivative instrument or security
- Confirmation with the holder or with the counterparty to the derivative instrument or security
- Confirmation of settled transactions with the broker-dealer or counterparty
- Confirmation of unsettled transactions with the broker-dealer or counterparty
- Physical inspection of the derivative instrument or security contract
- Reading executed partnership or similar agreements
- Inspecting underlying agreements and other forms of supporting documentation, in paper or electronic form, to determine amounts reported, evidence that might preclude sales treatment of a transfer, or unrecorded repurchase agreements
- Inspecting supporting documentation for subsequent realization or settlement after the balance sheet date
- Performing analytical procedures

Completeness

- Requesting the counterparty to a derivative instrument or the holder of a security to provide information such as whether there are any side agreements or agreements to repurchase securities sold

- Requesting counterparties or holders who are frequently used, but with whom there is at present no record of derivative instruments or securities, to state whether they are counterparties to derivative instruments with the entity or holders of its securities
- Inspecting agreements to identify embedded derivatives
- Inspecting documentation in paper or electronic form for activity subsequent to the balance sheet date
- Performing analytical procedures
- Comparing previous and current account detail to determine whether assets removed from the accounts met the criteria for sales treatment
- Reading other information, such as minutes of meetings of the board of directors or finance, asset/liability, investment, or other committees

Rights and Obligations

- Confirming significant terms with the counterparty, including the absence of any side agreements
- Inspecting agreements and other forms of supporting documentation, in paper or electronic form
- Considering whether the findings of other auditing procedures, such as reviewing minutes of meetings of the board of directors and reading contracts and other agreements, provide evidence about rights and obligations, such as pledging of securities as collateral or selling securities with a commitment to repurchase them

Valuation

- Evidence about the cost of securities may include inspection of documentation of the purchase price, confirmation with issuer or holder, and testing discount or premium amortization, either by recomputation or by analytical procedures.
- For valuations based on an investee's financial results, including but not limited to the equity method of accounting, the auditor should read available financial statements of the investee and the accompanying audit report, if any. Financial statements of the investee that have been audited by an auditor whose report is satisfactory to the investor's auditor may constitute sufficient evidential matter. If additional evidential matter is needed, the auditor should review information in the investor's files that relates to the investee, such as investee minutes and budgets and cash flows information about the investee. The auditor should also inquire of investor management about the investee's financial results. If the investee's financial statements are not audited, or if the report of the investee's auditor is not satisfactory, the investor's auditor should apply, or should request to have another auditor apply, appropriate auditing procedures to such financial statements.
- For valuations based on fair value, the auditor should determine whether a specified valuation method is to be used to determine the fair value of the entity's derivative instruments and securities. The auditor should evaluate whether the determination of fair value is consistent with the specified method. Quoted market prices for derivative instruments and securities listed on national exchanges

or over-the-counter markets are generally considered to provide sufficient evidence of their fair value.

- If quoted market prices are not available for the derivative instruments or securities, estimates of fair value may be obtained from broker-dealer or other third-party sources based on proprietary valuation models or from the entity based on internally or externally developed valuation models. The auditor should understand the method used, and may determine that it is necessary to obtain estimates from more than one pricing source. This may be appropriate if:
  - The pricing source has a relationship with an entity that might impair its objectivity, such as an affiliate or a counterparty involved in selling or structuring the product.
  - The valuation is based on assumptions that are highly subjective or particularly sensitive to changes in the underlying circumstances.
- If the estimated value of the derivative instrument or security is from a valuation model, the auditor is not expected to substitute his or her judgment for that of management. The auditor should obtain evidence by performing procedures such as:
  - Assessing the reasonableness and appropriateness of the model
  - Calculating the value; for example, using a model developed by the auditor or by a specialist engaged by the auditor to develop an independent expectation to corroborate the reasonableness of the value calculated by the entity's model
  - Comparing the fair value with subsequent or recent transactions

Impairment Losses

Management is required to determine whether to recognize an impairment loss for a decline in fair value that is other than temporary. Accordingly, the auditor should determine whether factors indicating an impairment loss exist, such as:

- Fair value is significantly below cost.
  - The decline is attributable to adverse conditions specifically related to the security or to specific conditions in an industry or in a geographical area.
  - The decline has existed for an extended period of time.
  - Management does not possess either the intent or the ability to hold the security for a period of time sufficient to allow for any anticipated recovery in fair value.
- The security has been downgraded by a rating agency.
- The financial condition of the issuer has deteriorated.
- Dividends have been reduced or eliminated, or scheduled interest payments have not been made.
- The entity recorded losses from the security subsequent to the end of the reporting period.

What additional considerations should the auditor be aware of in connection with hedging activities?

The auditor should determine whether management complied with the hedge accounting requirements, including designation and documentation requirements, to support management's expectation at the inception of the hedge that the hedging relationship would be highly effective. The auditor should also review management's periodic assessment of the ongoing effectiveness of the hedging relationship.

When the entity designates a derivative as a fair value hedge, management is required to adjust the carrying amount of the hedged item for the change in the hedged item's fair value that is attributable to the hedged risk.

For a cash flow hedge of a forecasted transaction, management must determine that the forecasted transaction has probability of occurrence, and that the likelihood is not based solely on management's intent. The transaction's probability should be supported by facts and circumstances, such as:

- The frequency of similar past transactions
- The financial and operational ability of the entity to carry out the transaction
- The extent of loss that could result if the transaction does not occur
- The likelihood that transactions with substantially different characteristics might be used to achieve the same business purpose

The auditor should evaluate management's determination of whether a forecasted transaction is probable.

What additional considerations should the auditor be aware of in connection with assertions about securities based on management's intent and ability?

Management's intent and ability are a key factor in valuing certain securities, such as:

- Debt securities classified as held-to-maturity securities and reported at cost depending on management's intent and ability to hold them to their maturity
- Equity securities reported using the equity method depending on management's ability to significantly influence the investee
- Equity securities classified as trading or available-for-sale securities based on management's intent and objectives

In order to evaluate management's intent and ability, the auditor should:

- Obtain an understanding of the process used by management to classify securities as trading, available-for-sale, or held-to-maturity securities.
- For an investment accounted for using the equity method, inquire of management as to whether the entity has the ability to exercise significant influence over the operating and financial policies of the investee.
- If the entity accounts for the investment contrary to the presumption established by GAAP for use of the equity method, determine whether that presumption has been overcome and whether appropriate disclosure is made regarding the reasons for not accounting for the investment in keeping with that presumption.
- Consider whether management's activities corroborate or conflict with its stated intent.

- Determine whether management's activities, contractual agreements, or the entity's financial condition provide evidence of its ability. This can be done by auditor review of:
  - The entity's financial position, working capital needs, operating results, debt agreements, guarantees, alternative sources of liquidity, and other relevant contractual obligations, as well as laws and regulations
  - Management's cash flow projections
  - Management's ability to obtain information from an investee

SAS 93—Omnibus Statement on Auditing Standards—2000

This pronouncement includes amendments to existing pronouncements that have been integrated within other areas of this book.

SAS 94—The Effect of Information Technology on the Auditor's Consideration of Internal Control in a Financial Statement Audit

Refer to Chapter 10.

SAS 95—Generally Accepted Auditing Standards

This pronouncement indicates that interpretive publications (1) are not auditing standards, but rather recommendations on application of the SAS in specific circumstances and (2) consist of auditing interpretations of the SAS, auditing guidance in AICPA Audit and Accounting Guides and AICPA Statements of Position. Furthermore, although other auditing publications have no authoritative status, they may assist the auditor in understanding and applying the SAS. Other auditing publications include auditing articles in professional journals, continuing professional education programs, textbooks, and state CPA society publications.

SAS 96—Audit Documentation

Superseded by SAS 103.

SAS 97—Amendment to Statement on Auditing Standards No. 50, Reports on the Application of Accounting Principles

Refer to the summary of SAS 50, which includes the appropriate amendments.

SAS 98—Omnibus Statement on Auditing Standards—2002

The provisions in this pronouncement have been integrated within other areas of this book.

SAS 99—Consideration of Fraud in a Financial Statement Audit

What is the difference between error and fraud?

The distinction between error and fraud is dependent on whether the underlying action that results in financial statement misstatement is intentional or unintentional.

Error refers to unintentional misstatements or omissions of financial statement amounts or disclosures—for example, misinterpretation, mistakes, and use of incorrect accounting estimates. *Fraud*, however, refers to acts that are intentional.

What types of misstatements are relevant to an auditor's consideration of fraud?

- Misstatements arising from fraudulent financial reporting, including manipulation, falsification, or alteration of accounting records or supporting documents, and intentional misapplication of accounting principles, practices, and methods
- Misstatements arising from misappropriation of assets (i.e., defalcation), including outright theft, embezzlement schemes, and causing an entity to pay for goods or services that the entity does not actually receive

What conditions are usually present when fraud occurs?

- Pressure or incentive to commit fraud
- Opportunity to perpetrate fraud
- Ability to rationalize or justify committing fraud

Is an auditor responsible for detecting fraud in a financial statement audit?

An auditor is responsible for planning and performing a financial statement audit in order to obtain reasonable, but not absolute, assurance about whether the financial statements are free of material misstatement (whether caused by fraud or by error).

Note

An auditor is not trained as, or normally expected to be, an expert in authentication. Accordingly, an auditor might not discover material misstatements caused by fraud that is concealed through falsified (forged) documents. Collusion might also prevent an auditor's detection.

Because of the characteristics of fraud, the auditor is advised to exercise professional judgment. Accordingly, the auditor should have a questioning mind and critically assess evidence obtained throughout the conduct of the audit.

What is meant by brainstorming?

SAS 99 requires members of the audit team to discuss the potential for material misstatement due to fraud. *Brainstorming*, or exchanging of ideas, is therefore emphasized. Audit team members should brainstorm about:

- How and where the financial statements might be susceptible to material misstatement due to fraud
- How management could perpetrate and conceal fraudulent financial reporting
- How an entity's assets could be misappropriated
- The need to emphasize professional skepticism throughout the audit
- The risk of management override of internal controls
- How the audit team might respond to the susceptibility of the financial statements to material misstatement caused by fraud

In general, how can an auditor identify risks that may result in material misstatement caused by fraud?

An auditor should consider the attributes of the risk of material misstatement caused by fraud:

- *Type of risk*—that is, whether the risk involves fraudulent financial reporting or misappropriation of assets
- *Significance of risk*—that is, whether it is of a magnitude that could result in material misstatement
- *Likelihood of risk*
- *Pervasiveness of risk*—that is, whether the risk is isolated to a particular assertion, account, or class of transaction or has a potentially pervasive effect on the financial statements

How should an auditor respond to the results of the assessment of the risk of material misstatement caused by fraud?

An auditor generally responds to the risk of material misstatement caused by fraud by:

- Developing a response that has an overall effect on the conduct of the audit
- Modifying the nature, extent, and timing of specific auditing procedures
- Performing additional auditing procedures to address the risk of material misstatement due to fraud arising from management override of internal controls

How might the risk of material misstatement caused by fraud have an overall effect on the audit?

Judgments about the risk of material misstatement caused by fraud may have an overall effect on the audit in these ways:

- *Assignment of personnel.* The knowledge, skill, and ability of audit personnel should be commensurate with the assessed level of risk.
- *Accounting principles.* The auditor should be more skeptical about management's selection and application of accounting principles, practices, and methods.
- *Predictability of auditing procedures.* The auditor should incorporate an element of unpredictability in selecting auditing procedures performed from year to year.

What procedures should be performed to address the risk of management override of internal controls?

The auditor should examine journal entries and other adjustments. More specifically, the auditor should:

- Obtain an understanding of the financial reporting process and the relevant internal controls.
- Identify and select journal entries and other adjustments for substantive testing.
- Determine the timing of substantive tests, with special focus on journal entries and other adjustments made at the end of the reporting period.
- Make inquiries of individuals involved in the financial reporting process about inappropriate or unusual activity concerning the processing of journal entries and other adjustments.

What should an auditor be aware of when evaluating audit evidence?

It is important to keep in mind that the assessment of the risk of material misstatement caused by fraud is not a one-time assessment, but rather should be ongoing through the conduct of the audit.

Accordingly, on an ongoing basis, the auditor should watch out for:

- Discrepancies in the accounting records
- Conflicting or missing evidential matter
- Problematic or unusual relationships between management and the auditor

The auditor should also:

- Evaluate whether analytical procedures in the substantive testing and overall review stages of the audit indicate previously unrecognized risks of material misstatement caused by fraud.
- At or near the end of fieldwork, evaluate the accumulated results of audit tests to determine the effect on the auditor's earlier risk assessment.

What actions should an auditor take if he or she believes that financial statement misstatements are or may be caused by fraud?

If the auditor believes that the effect of the misstatement is immaterial, he or she should nevertheless evaluate the implications, especially those dealing with the organizational position of the individual(s) involved.

If the auditor believes that the effect of the misstatement is material or he or she is unable to determine the materiality of the misstatement, these actions are appropriate:

- Undertake to obtain additional evidential matter in order to ascertain whether material fraud has occurred or is likely to have occurred, and if so, its related effects on the financial statements as well as the auditor's report.
- Consider the possible effects on other aspects of the audit.
- Discuss the matter as well as the approach for further investigation with an appropriate level of management that is at least one level above those involved, as well as with senior management and the audit committee.
- Consider whether it is appropriate to advise the client to consult with its legal counsel.

What communications concerning fraud or its possibility are necessary?

An appropriate level of management should be notified if the auditor determines that there is evidence of fraud, even if the fraud is inconsequential.

The audit committee should be notified directly if the auditor determines that there is fraud:

- Involving senior management
- That results in material misstatement in the financial statements

If the auditor concludes that identified fraud risk factors have continuing internal control implications, he or she should determine whether such factors represent reportable conditions requiring communication to senior management or the audit committee.

Although an auditor is generally precluded from communicating with nonclient personnel about fraud, he or she is permitted to disclose such information when:

- Permitted by law or regulatory requirements
- A predecessor auditor communicates with a successor auditor pursuant to the provisions of SAS 84
- Responding to a subpoena
- Required to notify a funding agency or other specified agency pursuant to requirements for the audits of entities that receive governmental financial assistance

Does SAS 99 contain any specific documentation requirements?

Yes. The auditor is required to document:

- The details of the required brainstorming
- The procedures performed to identify and assess the risks of material misstatement caused by fraud

- Specific risks of material misstatement caused by fraud that the auditor identified as well as a description of the auditor's response
- The basis for the conclusion if the auditor has not identified in a particular circumstance improper revenue recognition as a risk of material misstatement caused by fraud
- The results of the procedures to further address the risk of management override of internal controls
- Other conditions and results of analytical procedures that led the auditor to believe that additional audit procedures were necessary, as well as any further responses the auditor considered necessary
- The nature of the communications concerning fraud made to management, the audit committee, and others

Does SAS 99 provide lists of risk factors relating to misstatements arising from fraudulent financial reporting and misappropriation of assets?

The list of risk factors shown in Example 12.10 is derived from the appendix to SAS 99.

Example 12.10 Examples of Fraud Risk Factors

Risk Factors Relating to Misstatements Arising from Fraudulent Financial Reporting

INCENTIVES/PRESSURES

A. Financial stability or profitability is threatened by economic, industry, or entity operating conditions, such as (or as indicated by):
   1. High degree of competition or market saturation, accompanied by declining margins
   2. High vulnerability to rapid changes, such as changes in technology, product obsolescence, or interest rates
   3. Significant declines in customer demand and increasing business failures in either the industry or the overall economy
   4. Operating losses making the threat of bankruptcy, foreclosure, or hostile takeover imminent
   5. Recurring negative cash flows from operations or an inability to generate cash flows from operations while reporting earnings and earnings growth
   6. Rapid growth or unusual profitability, especially compared to that of other companies in the same industry
   7. New accounting, statutory, or regulatory requirements

(continued)

(Continued)

B. Excessive pressure exists for management to meet the requirements or expectations of third parties due to the following:
1. Profitability or trend level expectations of investment analysts, institutional investors, significant creditors, or other external parties (particularly expectations that are unduly aggressive or unrealistic), including expectations created by management in, for example, overly optimistic press releases or annual report messages
2. Need to obtain additional debt or equity financing to stay competitive—including financing of major research and development or capital expenditures
3. Marginal ability to meet exchange listing requirements or debt repayment or other debt covenant requirements
4. Perceived or real adverse effects of reporting poor financial results on significant pending transactions, such as business combinations or contract awards

C. Information available indicates that management's or the board of directors' personal financial situation is threatened by the entity's financial performance arising from the following:
1. Significant financial interests in the entity
2. Significant portions of their compensation (for example, bonuses, stock options, and earn-out arrangements) being contingent on achieving aggressive targets for stock price, operating results, financial position, or cash flow
3. Personal guarantees of debts of the entity

D. There is excessive pressure on management or operating personnel to meet financial targets set up by the board of directors or management, including sales or profitability incentive goals.

OPPORTUNITIES

A. The nature of the industry or the entity's operations provides opportunities to engage in fraudulent financial reporting that can arise from the following:
1. Significant related-party transactions not in the ordinary course of business or with related entities not audited or audited by another firm
2. A strong financial presence or ability to dominate a certain industry sector that allows the entity to dictate terms or conditions to suppliers or customers that may result in inappropriate or non-arm's-length transactions
3. Assets, liabilities, revenues, or expenses based on significant estimates that involve subjective judgments or uncertainties that are difficult to corroborate
4. Significant, unusual, or highly complex transactions, especially those close to period-end that pose difficult substance-over-form questions
5. Significant operations located or conducted across international borders in jurisdictions in which differing business environments and cultures exist

6. Significant bank accounts or subsidiary or branch operations in tax-haven jurisdictions for which there appears to be no clear business justification

B. There is ineffective monitoring of management as a result of the following:

1. Domination of management by a single person or small group (in a non-owner-managed business) without compensating controls
2. Ineffective board of directors or audit committee oversight over the financial reporting process and internal control

C. There is a complex or unstable organizational structure, as evidenced by the following:

1. Difficulty in determining the organization or individuals that have controlling interest in the entity
2. Overly complex organizational structure involving unusual legal entities or managerial lines of authority
3. High turnover of senior management, counsel, or board members

D. Internal control components are deficient as a result of the following:

1. Inadequate monitoring of controls, including automated controls and controls over interim financial reporting (where external reporting is required)
2. High turnover rates or employment of ineffective accounting, internal audit, or information technology staff
3. Ineffective accounting and information systems, including situations involving reportable conditions

ATTITUDES/RATIONALIZATIONS

- Ineffective communication, implementation, support, or enforcement of the entity's values or ethical standards by management or the communication of inappropriate values or ethical standards
- Nonfinancial management's excessive participation in or preoccupation with the selection of accounting principles or the determination of significant estimates
- Known history of violations of securities laws or other laws and regulations, or claims against the entity, its senior management, or board members alleging fraud or violations of laws and regulations
- Excessive interest by management in maintaining or increasing the entity's stock price or earnings trend
- A practice by management of committing to analysts, creditors, and other third parties to achieve aggressive or unrealistic forecasts
- Management failing to correct known reportable conditions on a timely basis
- An interest by management in employing inappropriate means to minimize reported earnings for tax-motivated reasons
- Recurring attempts by management to justify marginal or inappropriate accounting on the basis of materiality
- Strained relationship between management and the current or predecessor auditor, as exhibited by the following:

(continued)

(Continued)

- Frequent disputes with the current or predecessor auditor on accounting, auditing, or reporting matters
- Unreasonable demands on the auditor, such as unreasonable time constraints regarding the completion of the audit or the issuance of the auditor's report
- Formal or informal restrictions on the auditor that inappropriately limit access to people or information or the ability to communicate effectively with the board of directors or audit committee
- Domineering management behavior in dealing with the auditor, especially involving attempts to influence the scope of the auditor's work or the selection or continuance of personnel assigned to or consulted on the audit engagement

Risk Factors Relating to Misstatements Arising from Misappropriation of Assets

INCENTIVES/PRESSURES

A. Personal financial obligations may create pressure on management or employees with access to cash or other assets susceptible to theft to misappropriate those assets.
B. Adverse relationships between the entity and employees with access to cash or other assets susceptible to theft may motivate those employees to misappropriate those assets. For example, adverse relationships may be created by:
- Known or anticipated future employee layoffs
- Recent or anticipated changes to employee compensation or benefit plans
- Promotions, compensation, or other rewards inconsistent with expectations

OPPORTUNITIES

A. Certain characteristics or circumstances may increase the susceptibility of assets to misappropriation. For example, opportunities to misappropriate assets increase when there are:
- Large amounts of cash on hand or processed
- Inventory items that are small in size, of high value, or in high demand
- Easily convertible assets, such as bearer bonds, diamonds, or computer chips
- Fixed assets that are small in size, marketable, or lacking observable identification of ownership
B. Inadequate internal control over assets may increase the susceptibility of misappropriation of those assets. For example, misappropriation of assets may occur because there is:
- Inadequate segregation of duties or independent checks
- Inadequate management oversight of employees responsible for assets—for example, inadequate supervision or monitoring of remote locations

- Inadequate job applicant screening of employees with access to assets
- Inadequate record keeping with respect to assets
- Inadequate system of authorization and approval of transactions—for example, in purchasing
- Inadequate physical safeguards over cash, investments, inventory, or fixed assets
- Lack of complete and timely reconciliations of assets
- Lack of timely and appropriate documentation of transactions—for example, credits for merchandise returns
- Lack of mandatory vacations for employees performing key control functions
- Inadequate management understanding of information technology, which enables information technology employees to perpetrate a misappropriation
- Inadequate access controls over automated records, including controls over and review of computer systems event logs

ATTITUDES/RATIONALIZATIONS

Risk factors reflective of employee attitudes/rationalizations that allow them to justify misappropriations of assets are generally not susceptible to observation by the auditor. Nevertheless, the auditor who becomes aware of the existence of such information should consider it in identifying the risks of material misstatement arising from misappropriation of assets. For example, auditors may become aware of the following attitudes or behavior of employees who have access to assets susceptible to misappropriation:

- Disregard for the need for monitoring or reducing risks related to misappropriations of assets
- Disregard for internal control over misappropriation of assets by overriding existing controls or by failing to correct known internal control deficiencies
- Behavior indicating displeasure or dissatisfaction with the company or its treatment of the employee
- Changes in behavior or lifestyle that may indicate assets have been misappropriated

SAS 100—Interim Financial Information

Superseded by SAS 116.

SAS 101—Auditing Fair Value Measurements and Disclosures

How is fair value defined?

The fair value of an asset (or liability) is the amount at which that asset (or liability) could be bought (or incurred) or sold (or settled) in a current transaction between willing parties—that is, other than in a forced sale or liquidation sale.

Notes

Observable market pricing is the preferable method for measuring an item's fair value.

Management is responsible for establishing an accounting and reporting process for determining fair value measurements.

Management is responsible for making the fair value measurements and disclosures in its financial statements.

What is an auditor's responsibility with respect to fair value measurements and disclosures included in financial statements?

An auditor must obtain sufficient competent audit evidence that fair value measurements and disclosures included in financial statements are in conformity with generally accepted accounting principles.

Accordingly, an auditor should:

- Obtain an understanding of the entity's process for determining fair value measurements and disclosures and the relevant controls.
- Evaluate management's intent and ability to carry out specific courses of action when intent is relevant to the use and disclosure of fair value measurements. Therefore, an auditor might:
  - Consider management's past history of carrying out its stated intentions.
  - Review written plans and other documentation (e.g., budgets and minutes).
  - Consider management's stated reasons for its choice of a particular course of action.
  - Consider the entity's economic circumstances.
- Evaluate whether (1) the entity's method for determining fair value measurements is applied consistently and (2) consistency is appropriate in light of changing circumstances.
- Consider the need to engage a specialist when auditing fair value measurements.
- Test the entity's fair value measurements and disclosures to evaluate whether:
  - Management's assumptions are reasonable and reflect, but are not inconsistent with, market information.
  - The fair value measurement was determined using an appropriate model, if applicable.
  - Management used relevant information that was reasonably available at the time.

> **Note**
>
> The auditor may make an independent estimate of fair value to corroborate the entity's fair value measurement.

SAS 102—Defining Professional Requirements in Statements on Auditing Standards

What is meant by an unconditional requirement?

An unconditional requirement included in a Statement on Auditing Standards means that the auditor is required to comply with the requirement in all cases. The word *must* and phrase *is required* are indicative of an unconditional requirement.

What is a presumptively mandatory requirement?

A presumptively mandatory requirement included in a Statement on Auditing Standards means that under normal conditions the auditor is required to comply with the requirement. However, in rare circumstances the auditor may depart from a presumptively mandatory requirement, provided he or she documents the justification for the departure and how alternative procedures performed were sufficient. The term *should* indicates a presumptively mandatory requirement.

What is explanatory material?

In general, explanatory material is text included in a Statement on Auditing Standards that:

- Provides additional explanation and guidance on a professional requirement
- Identifies and describes other audit procedures or actions

The words *may, might*, and *could* are used in the context of explanatory material.

SAS 103—Audit Documentation

Audit documentation, which may be referred to as working papers, is the main record of the audit procedures performed, the audit evidence gathered from those procedures, and the judgments and evaluations made throughout the audit.

What are the purposes of audit documentation?

Audit documentation:

- Provides support that the auditor performed the audit in accordance with generally accepted auditing standards

- Provides support for the auditor's opinion
- Assists the auditor in planning and performing the audit
- Assists the auditor in directing and supervising the audit
- Assists in demonstrating the accountability of the audit team for its work
- Assists quality control reviewers
- Enables an *experienced auditor* to conduct inspections or peer reviews
- Assists a successor auditor who reviews a predecessor's audit documentation

Note

An *experienced auditor* is an individual who possesses the competence and skills that would enable him or her to perform the audit. An experienced auditor understands the audit process, auditing pronouncements and legal and regulatory requirements, the entity's business environment, and pertinent industry audit and reporting issues.

In what form should audit documentation be maintained?

Audit documentation may be in paper form, electronic format, or other suitable media.

What should be the content of audit documentation?

The auditor should use professional judgment when determining the content of audit documentation. Factors in this determination include the risk of material misstatement, the nature of the auditing procedures, the significance of the evidence obtained, the nature and extent of exceptions identified, and the need to document a conclusion and basis for that conclusion.

In general, audit documentation should enable an experienced auditor to understand:

- The nature, timing, and extent of auditing procedures
- The results of the audit procedures and the audit evidence obtained
- Conclusions reached
- That the accounting records agree or reconcile with the audited financial statements

Note

Oral explanations alone are not sufficient support for the audit work, but can be used to clarify or explain information in the audit documentation.

Must matters that are not engagement specific (e.g., quality control considerations) be documented in the working papers for a particular engagement?

Matters that are not engagement specific (e.g., quality control considerations, such as independence and staff training) can be documented either centrally within the firm or in the documentation for a specific audit engagement.

What items are commonly included in audit documentation?

Audit documentation generally includes:

- Audit programs
- Analyses
- Issues memoranda
- Summaries of significant findings
- Letters of confirmation and representation
- Checklists
- Abstracts or copies of important documents
- Correspondence (including e-mail)
- Schedules of work performed

Note

The audit documentation applicable to a specific engagement should be assembled in an audit file. The audit file does not need to contain superseded audit documentation.

Does SAS 103 include specific audit documentation requirements?

According to SAS 103, audit documentation should include:

- *Significant findings or issues*
  The auditor should document significant findings or issues, discussions with management about them, the auditor's response, and the basis for the final conclusions reached. Significant audit findings or issues include (1) matters that are significant and involve the selection, application, and consistency of accounting principles; (2) results of auditing procedures that indicate possible financial statement misstatement or the need to significantly modify auditing procedures; (3) circumstances that result in significant difficulty in applying auditing procedures; and (4) matters that might suggest the need to modify the auditor's report.
- *Identification of preparer and reviewer*
  Documentation of the nature, extent, and timing of audit procedures should indicate (1) who performed the audit procedures and the date completed and (2) who reviewed specific audit documentation and the date of the review.

- *Specific items tested*

    Audit documentation should include the identifying characteristics of the specific items tested. This is applicable to tests of controls and substantive tests of details involving inspection of documents or confirmation.

- *Departures from Statements on Auditing Standards*

    The auditor must document the justification for a departure from a presumptively mandatory requirement and how alternative procedures performed were sufficient to achieve the objectives of the presumptively mandatory requirement.

What is meant by the documentation completion date?

The document completion date is the date on which the auditor has completed the assembly of the final audit file. The auditor should complete the assembly of the final audit file on a timely basis, but within 60 days following the report release date, unless a shorter period of time is specified by statute, regulation, or the firm's quality control policies.

The auditor is permitted to revise the audit documentation prior to the documentation completion date. After the documentation completion date, the auditor is not allowed to delete or discard audit documentation before the end of the specified retention period. The auditor, however, may make additions (including amendments).

Is an auditor permitted to make changes to audit documentation after the date of the audit report?

The audit report should be dated no earlier than the date on which the auditor has obtained sufficient appropriate evidence to support his or her opinion. *Sufficient appropriate audit evidence* includes evidence of audit documentation review and evidence that the financial statements have been prepared and that management has asserted its responsibility for them.

> **Note**
>
> In general, the report date will be close to the report release date, which is the date that the auditor grants the client permission to use his or her report.

In connection with documentation of new information, the auditor should comply with SAS 46, *Consideration of Omitted Procedures after the Report Date*, and the provisions in SAS 1 pertaining to subsequent discovery of facts existing at the date of the auditor's report.

To whom does audit documentation belong?

Since the auditor prepares audit documentation, he or she is the owner and is responsible for adopting reasonable procedures in order to retain and access audit documentation for a period of time. The retention period should not be shorter than five years from the report release date.

It is imperative that the auditor maintain confidentiality of client information, and he or she should establish reasonable procedures to do so.

> ### Note
>
> Audit documentation is not part of or a substitute for a client's records. However, audit documentation sometimes may serve as a reference source for a client.

What is the difference between a current file and a permanent file?

SAS 103 does not specifically address the distinction between a current file and a permanent file. However, many practitioners split their audit documentation into these two types of files. A current file consists of documentation that pertains only to the current engagement. A permanent file, sometimes referred to as a continuing file, includes documents that are pertinent to the current audit engagement as well as to future audit engagements.

SAS 104—Amendment to SAS 1, Codification of Auditing Standards and Procedures ("Due Professional Care in the Performance of Work")

This pronouncement clarifies that reasonable assurance is defined as a "high level of assurance." "Absolute assurance" is not attainable in the course of an audit.

SAS 105—Amendment to SAS 95—Generally Accepted Auditing Standards

What changes in terminology are included in SAS 105?

This pronouncement includes two changes in terminology applicable to Statements on Auditing Standards:

- The term *audit evidence* replaces the term *evidential matter*.
- The term *further audit procedures* replaces the term *tests to be performed*.

Which Generally Accepted Auditing Standards have been revised?

The Standards of Field Work are modified in three ways:

1. The auditor must adequately plan the work and must properly supervise any assistants.
2. The auditor must obtain a sufficient understanding of the entity and its environment, including its internal control, to assess the risk of material misstatement of

the financial statements whether due to error or fraud, and to design the nature, timing, and extent of further audit procedures.

Note

The key change is that the scope of the auditor's required understanding has been expanded to include the client entity and its environment.

---

3. The auditor must obtain sufficient appropriate audit evidence by performing audit procedures to afford a reasonable basis for an opinion regarding the financial statements under audit.

SAS 106—Audit Evidence

What is audit evidence?

Audit evidence consists of all information utilized by the auditor in forming conclusions on which his or her opinion on the financial statements is based.

What constitutes audit evidence?

Audit evidence consists of:

- Information in the accounting records underlying the financial statements
- Other information.

What are examples of accounting records?

Examples of accounting records include:

- Records of initial entries and supporting records, including but not limited to checks and records of electronic fund transfers
- General and subsidiary ledgers, journal entries, and other adjustments not in formalized journal entries
- Records such as worksheets, reconciliations, and spreadsheets

What other information should an auditor consider during the course of the audit?

Other information includes:

- Minutes of meetings
- Confirmations obtained from third parties
- Industry analysts' reports
- Comparable data about competitors (i.e., benchmarking)

- Controls manuals
- Information obtained through inquiry, observation, and inspection

How much audit evidence is enough?

The sufficiency of audit evidence is a measure of quantity. While the sufficiency of audit evidence is a matter of professional judgment, the greater the risk of material misstatement, the more evidence is likely to be required. Accordingly, there is a direct relationship between the risk of material misstatement and the quantity of audit evidence needed to afford a reasonable basis for the auditor's opinion.

What is meant by the appropriateness of audit evidence?

Appropriateness is a measure of quality of audit evidence. Audit evidence is deemed to be appropriate if it is relevant and reliable. The higher the quality of audit evidence, the less audit evidence may be required. Accordingly, there is an inverse relationship between the quality of audit evidence and the quantity of audit evidence needed.

What factors should be considered in determining the reliability of audit evidence?

Because reliability is influenced by the source and nature of audit evidence, the auditor should take into account the following facts:

- Audit evidence is more reliable if obtained from knowledgeable independent outside sources.
- Internally generated audit evidence is more reliable when internal control is effective.
- Audit evidence obtained directly by the auditor is more reliable than evidence indirectly obtained.
- Documentary audit evidence is more reliable than oral evidence.

Warning

Auditors do not authenticate documents. Further, all available audit evidence need not be examined. Accordingly, audit evidence may be persuasive and need not be conclusive.

Warning

While cost versus usefulness of audit evidence should be considered, difficulty and expense of obtaining audit evidence, by themselves, should not govern.

SAS 107—Audit Risk and Materiality in Conducting an Audit

What constitutes audit risk?

The risk that the independent auditor may unknowingly fail to modify his or her audit opinion on materially misstated financial statements is known as *audit risk*.

The components of audit risk (AR), which may be assessed quantitatively or nonquantitatively, are:

- *Inherent risk (IR)*. This is the built-in susceptibility of an assertion to material misstatement regardless of internal control. *Example:* The existence assertion over cash has a high inherent risk due to its liquidity.
- *Control risk (CR)*. This is the risk that a material misstatement that could occur in an assertion will not be prevented or detected on a timely basis by the entity's internal control.
- *Detection risk (DR)*. This is the risk that the auditor will fail to identify a material misstatement that exists in an assertion. Detection risk is a combination of tests of detail (TD) risk and substantive analytical procedures (AP) risk.

Recommendation

The auditor can control detection risk by applying the appropriate auditing procedures. It is management's responsibility to minimize control risk by establishing and maintaining effective internal control.

Recommendation

An auditor can never eliminate detection risk. Furthermore, inherent risk and control risk exist independently of the audit; only control risk can be controlled by the entity.

What is the "risk of material misstatement"?

The risk of material misstatement (RMM) is a combination of inherent risk (IR) and control risk (CR).

In every audit, the auditor needs to assess RMM at both the financial statement level and the relevant assertion level as a basis for determining further audit procedures.

Note

$$AR = RMM \times DR$$

This is the same as $AR = (IR \times CR) \times DR$.

What is materiality?

Materiality relates to the financial importance of an item or a group of items in the financial statements. The concept of materiality, which is a matter of professional judgment, is based on the fact that some matters, but not all, either individually or in the aggregate, affect the fairness of the financial statement presentation. The determination of materiality should take into account, among other items, prior-period results, period-to-date results, and current-period budgets and forecasts.

What must I do with respect to audit risk and materiality?

Both audit risk and materiality must be considered in planning an audit and expressing an opinion on the financial statements. The auditor should limit audit risk to a relatively low level.

In addition, audit risk and materiality are inversely related. Accordingly, the risk that an account may be materially misstated may be low, although the risk that an account may be misstated by a small amount may be very high.

Finally, the auditor should consider audit risk at the individual account balance, class of transactions, or disclosure level because the consideration directly assists in determining the nature, timing, and extent of further audit procedures for the related relevant assertions.

What misstatements must be communicated to management?

The auditor must accumulate all known and likely misstatements, other than those considered trivial, and communicate them on a timely basis to an appropriate level of management. The communication should distinguish between known misstatements and likely misstatements.

Known misstatements are the specific misstatements identified during the audit. *Likely misstatements* are misstatements that (1) arise from the difference between management's and the auditor's judgments concerning accounting estimates that the auditor considers unreasonable or inappropriate and (2) the auditor considers likely to exist based on extrapolation from audit evidence obtained (e.g., amount obtained by projecting known misstatements in an audit sample to the entire population).

What should an auditor do if management fails to correct misstatements?

The auditor should obtain an understanding of management's decision not to correct some or all of the misstatements communicated. Management's explanation should be taken into account when considering the qualitative aspects of the entity's accounting practices and implications for the audit report. Ultimately, if the auditor believes that the financial statements are materially misstated, he or she should consider the effects on the audit report.

What documentation requirements should the auditor be aware of?

The auditor should document:

- The levels of materiality and tolerable misstatement (i.e., the maximum error in the population that the auditor is willing to accept)

- A summary of uncorrected misstatements, other than those that are considered trivial
- The auditor's conclusion as to whether uncorrected misstatements do or do not cause the statements to be materially misstated, and the basis for that conclusion
- All known and likely misstatements, other than those that are trivial, that have been corrected by management

SAS 108—Planning and Supervision

This statement provides guidance in planning the audit (including supervision of assistants) as required by the first standard of fieldwork. Planning the audit involves developing an overall audit strategy (see Chapter 10) that varies with the size and complexity of the client organization, the auditor's previous experience with the entity, and an understanding of the entity and its environment, including its internal control.

Planning the audit includes establishing an understanding with the client regarding the services to be performed. Guidance for establishing the understanding may be found in SAS 83. The auditor should document the understanding through a written communication with the client.

What matters should be part of the understanding established with the client?

The understanding generally includes these matters:

- Objective of the audit.
- Management is responsible for:
  - The financial statements and accounting policies
  - Establishing and maintaining effective internal control
  - Preventing and detecting fraud
  - Complying with laws and regulations
  - Making all financial records and related information available to the auditor
  - Providing the auditor with a representation letter (see SAS 85)
  - Adjusting financial statements to correct material misstatements and affirming in the representation letter that immaterial misstatements are not adjusted
- The auditor is responsible for conducting the audit in accordance with generally accepted auditing standards. Accordingly, the auditor must obtain reasonable, but not absolute, assurance that the financial statements are free of material misstatement. Further, an audit is not designed to detect immaterial error or fraud.
- An audit includes obtaining an understanding of the entity and its environment, including internal control. An audit is not designed to provide assurance about internal control. Significant deficiencies in internal control that are identified during the audit, however, must be communicated to those charged with governance.

These items should be communicated in the form of an engagement letter.

> ## Note
>
> It is logical to conclude that effective with the issuance of SAS 108, there is a presumptively mandatory requirement to issue an engagement letter before commencing audit work.

Are there other items that may be part of the understanding established with the client?

Other items that may be communicated include:

- The overall audit strategy
- The possible use of specialists (SAS 73) or internal auditors (SAS 65)
- Possible communication with predecessor auditors (SAS 84)
- Fees and billing
- Limitations or other arrangements—for example, indemnification
- The possible need to grant access to audit documentation to others
- Additional services to be performed

What are some of the preliminary engagement activities that the auditor should consider?

The auditor should consider, among other relevant activities:

- Procedures pertaining to the appointment of the auditor
- Establishing an understanding of the terms of the engagement
- Procedures concerning continuance of the client relationship and the specific audit engagement
- Evaluation of the auditor's compliance with ethical requirements, including independence

> ## Note
>
> See Chapter 10 for an in-depth discussion about the development of an audit plan.

How are the auditor's assistants to be supervised?

Supervision involves directing assistants who are involved in accomplishing the audit objectives and determining whether the objectives were accomplished.

Elements of supervision include:

- Instructing assistants
- Keeping informed of significant issues

- Reviewing the work performed at every level of supervision
- Resolving differences of opinion among firm personnel

Caution

Differences of opinion concerning auditing and accounting matters, when resolved, should be documented in the audit work papers.

SAS 109—Understanding the Entity and Its Environment and Assessing the Risks of Material Misstatement

This pronouncement:

- Provides guidance relative to the procedures needed to obtain the required understanding of the entity and its environment, including its internal control (these procedures are referred to as *risk assessment procedures* and are discussed in detail in Chapter 10)
- Requires discussion among audit team members, including the individual with final responsibility, about the susceptibility of the financial statements to material misstatement (also see SAS 99)

What are some considerations that an auditor should take into account in assessing the risks of material misstatements?

An auditor should identify and assess the risks of material misstatement at the financial statement level and at the relevant assertion level related to classes of transactions, account balances, and disclosures. Accordingly, the auditor should:

- Identify risks throughout the process of obtaining an understanding of the entity and its environment, including relevant controls that relate to the risks.
- Relate the identified risks to what can go wrong at the assertion level.
- Consider whether the risks are so significant that they could result in material misstatement.
- Consider the likelihood that the risks could result in material misstatement.

What identified risks require special audit consideration?

Identified risks that require special audit consideration are referred to as *significant risks*. The determination of significant risks is a matter of the auditor's professional judgment. It should be noted that significant risks often relate to significant nonroutine transactions (i.e., those that are unusual due to size or nature and are therefore infrequent) and judgmental matters (e.g., development of estimates).

If the entity's management has not implemented appropriate controls over significant risks, and if the auditor concludes that there is a significant deficiency or material weakness in internal control, the auditor should communicate the matter to those charged with governance. (See SAS 112.)

What are the specific documentation requirements contained in this pronouncement?

Under this pronouncement, the auditor is generally required to document:

- The required discussion among the audit team members regarding the susceptibility of the financial statements to material misstatement, including how and when the discussion occurred, the subject matter discussed, the audit team participants, and the significant decisions reached
- Key elements of the understanding obtained regarding each aspect of the entity and its environment, including each component of internal control identified, the source of information obtained, and risk assessment procedures
- The assessment of the risks of material misstatement both at the financial statement level and at the relevant assertion level and the basis for the assessment
- The risks identified and the related controls evaluated

Note

The form of documentation is a matter of professional judgment. Generally, the more complex the entity and its environment and the more extensive the audit procedures performed, the more extensive the documentation will be.

SAS 110—Performing Audit Procedures in Response to Assessed Risks and Evaluating the Audit Evidence Obtained

What is the focus of this pronouncement?

This pronouncement requires the auditor to determine "overall responses" to address the assessed risks of material misstatement at the financial statement level. The auditor should also design and perform "further audit procedures" that are responsive to the assessed risks of material misstatement at the relevant assertion level.

What are possible overall responses to the risks of material misstatement at the financial statement level?

The auditor's overall response may include:

- Emphasizing to members of the audit team the need to exercise professional skepticism

- Assigning more experienced audit personnel or those with specialized skills
- Using specialists (see SAS 73)
- Providing more supervision
- Incorporating additional elements of unpredictability in the selection of further audit procedures
- Making general changes to the nature, timing, and extent of further audit procedures.

What should an auditor consider with respect to further audit procedures at the relevant assertion level?

In designing further audit procedures, the auditor should consider the:

- Significance of the risk
- Likelihood that a material misstatement will occur
- Characteristics of the class of transactions, account balances, and disclosures involved
- Nature of specific controls used by the entity—in particular, whether they are manual or automated

Can audit procedures be limited to substantive procedures?

The auditor needs to be satisfied that a substantive approach, which emphasizes substantive procedures, would be effective in reducing detection risk to an acceptably low level. A combined approach, which incorporates both tests of controls and substantive procedures, may be more effective.

Regardless of the audit approach, the auditor should design and perform substantive procedures for all relevant assertions related to each material class of transactions, account balance, and disclosure. The performance of tests of controls does not eliminate the need to perform substantive procedures.

What is meant by the "nature" of further audit procedures?

The *nature* of further audit procedures refers to their purpose (i.e., tests of controls or substantive procedures) and their type (e.g., inquiry, observation, and inspection).

How should an auditor select audit procedures?

The risk of material misstatement should guide the auditor's selection of audit procedures. The higher the assessment of risk, the more reliable and relevant is the audit evidence desired from substantive procedures. The auditor also needs to consider the reasons for the risk assessment at the relevant assertion level—that is, the inherent risks and control risks.

What is meant by "timing" of audit procedures?

Timing refers to when audit procedures are performed or the period or date to which the audit evidence applies.

What audit procedures can be performed at interim dates?

Both tests of controls and substantive procedures can be performed at interim dates instead of at period-end.

Caution

Higher risk of material misstatement may prompt the auditor to perform substantive procedures nearer to or at period-end rather than at an interim date.

What matters should an auditor consider in determining the timing of audit procedures?

In considering when to perform audit procedures, the auditor should consider such matters as:

- The entity's control environment
- When relevant information is available
- The nature of the assessed risk
- The period or date to which the evidence relates

Warning

Certain audit procedures should be performed only at or after period-end; these include agreeing the financial statements to the accounting records.

What is meant by the "extent" of audit procedures?

The *extent* of audit procedures refers to the quantity of a specific audit procedure, and is based on auditor's professional judgment after considering tolerable misstatement, the assessed risk of material misstatement, and the degree of assurance the auditor plans to obtain.

It should be readily apparent that there normally is a direct relationship between the extent of audit procedures and the risk of material misstatement; that is, increased risk should result in an increase in the amount of procedures.

What should an auditor consider in evaluating the sufficiency and appropriateness of audit evidence?

In order to express an opinion of the fairness of the financial statements, an auditor needs to conclude that sufficient appropriate audit evidence has been obtained so that the risk of material misstatement has been reduced to an appropriately low level.

While the sufficiency and appropriateness of audit evidence are matters of professional judgment, the auditor should consider these factors:

- Significance of the potential misstatement and its likelihood of having a material effect
- Effectiveness of management's responses and controls to address the risks
- Experience gained during previous audits with respect to similar misstatements
- Results of audit procedures, including detection of error or fraud
- Source(s) and reliability of available information
- Persuasiveness of the audit evidence
- Understanding of the entity and its environment, including internal control

What should an auditor do if he or she has not obtained sufficient appropriate audit evidence?

If the auditor has not obtained sufficient appropriate audit evidence as to a material financial statement assertion, he or she should attempt to obtain further audit evidence. Ultimately, if the auditor is unable to obtain sufficient appropriate audit evidence, he or she is precluded from expressing an unqualified opinion; the auditor should express a qualified opinion or a disclaimer of opinion.

Does SAS 110 contain any specific documentation requirements?

Pursuant to SAS 110, the auditor should document:

- The overall responses to address the assessed risks of misstatement at the financial statement level
- The nature, timing, and extent of the further audit procedures
- The linkage of those procedures with the assessed risks at the relevant assertion level
- The results of the audit procedures
- The conclusions reached with regard to the use in the current audit of audit evidence about the operating effectiveness of controls that was obtained in a prior audit

Note

Other provisions contained in SAS 110 applicable to tests of controls and substantive procedures have been incorporated into Chapter 10.

SAS 111—Amendment to Statement on Auditing Standards No. 39, Audit Sampling

Refer to the summary of SAS 39 and Chapter 10, which include the appropriate amendments.

SAS 112—Communication of Internal Control–Related Matters Identified in an Audit

Superseded by SAS 115.

SAS 113—Omnibus 2006

This pronouncement amends various other pronouncements by clarifying terminology. In particular, all references to "completion of the fieldwork" have been replaced with "the date of the auditor's report."

SAS 114—The Auditor's Communication with Those Charged with Governance

Certain matters pertaining to an audit must be communicated to those charged with governance.

What is meant by "those charged with governance"?

Those charged with governance are the individual(s) responsible for overseeing the strategic direction of the entity and obligations related to the accountability of the entity. This includes the individuals responsible for overseeing the financial reporting process. Those charged with governance commonly include the board of directors or audit committee. Management represents the individual(s) responsible for achieving the entity's objectives and possessing the authority to establish policies and make decisions relative to the entity's objectives. Management is responsible for (1) the fairness of the financial statement presentation and (2) establishing and maintaining effective internal control. Management may or may not be charged with a governance role.

What matters are to be included in a communication to those charged with governance?

In general, the matters to be communicated are those related to the financial statement audit that the auditor considers significant and relevant to those charged with governance in overseeing the financial reporting process.

Some of the matters to be communicated concern:

- The auditor's responsibilities under generally accepted auditing standards
- The planned scope and timing of the audit
- Significant findings from the audit
- Qualitative aspects of the entity's significant accounting policies, including accounting estimates and financial statement disclosures
- Significant difficulties encountered during the audit
- Uncorrected misstatements

- Disagreements with management
- Management's consultations with other accountants
- Significant issues discussed, or subject to correspondence, with management
- Situations that might impair the auditor's required independence

Note

Other Statements on Auditing Standards require additional matters to be communicated to those charged with governance.

When should the required communication be made?

The auditor should communicate with those charged with governance on a sufficiently timely basis to enable the recipients to take the appropriate action(s).

SAS 115—Communicating Internal Control Related Matters Identified in an Audit

What is a deficiency in internal control?

A deficiency in internal control exists when the design or operation of an internal control does not allow management or other employees performing their normal assigned functions, to prevent or detect financial statement misstatements on a timely basis.

What is a material weakness?

A material weakness is a deficiency in internal control or a combination of deficiencies in internal control, resulting in a reasonable possibility that a material financial statement misstatement will not be prevented or not be detected and corrected on a timely basis.

What is a significant deficiency?

A significant deficiency is a deficiency in internal control or a combination of deficiencies in internal control that is less severe that a material weakness, but is important enough to warrant attention by those charged with governance.

What is meant by the phrase "reasonable possibility"?

"Reasonable possibility," which is the threshold for evaluating the significance of a deficiency in internal control, exists when the likelihood of an event resulting in a material financial statement misstatement not being prevented or not being detected and corrected on a timely basis is either reasonably possible or probable.

What is an auditor's responsibility with respect to deficiencies in internal control?

While an auditor is not required to search specifically for deficiencies in internal control, he or she is required to evaluate identified internal control deficiencies and determine whether they are material weaknesses or significant deficiencies.

Can an auditor conclude that there are no material weaknesses or significant deficiencies because he or she concludes that the financial statements are not materially misstated?

The absence of identified material financial statement misstatements does not imply that there are no material weaknesses or significant deficiencies. Potential for material misstatement governs.

What is an auditor's responsibility if deficiencies in internal control are identified?

If an auditor concludes that identified deficiencies in internal control are material weaknesses or significant deficiencies, then he or she is required to communicate the deficiencies in writing to management and those charged with governance. (See SAS 114.) Deficiencies in internal control that the auditor does not consider to be material weaknesses or significant deficiencies need not be communicated.

Must I recommunicate material weaknesses and significant deficiencies that have not been corrected?

An auditor is required to recommunicate material weaknesses and significant deficiencies previously communicated if not yet remediated. The written communication may be made by referring to the written communication (and the date of that communication) previously issued.

When should an auditor communicate material weaknesses and significant deficiencies?

The issuance of the written communication should generally coincide with the audit report release date (i.e., the date that the auditor grants the entity permission to use the auditor's report on the financial statements), but in no event should the communication be made later than 60 days after the report release date. Earlier communication, during the audit, may be important and need not be in writing. Early communication, however, does not relieve the auditor of the ultimate responsibility to communicate material weaknesses and significant deficiencies in writing. This responsibility exists even if such material weaknesses and significant deficiencies are corrected during the audit.

The auditor's responsibility to communicate significant deficiencies and material weaknesses is not eliminated in instances where management (1) is already aware of such deficiencies and (2) decides not to remediate such deficiencies because of cost constraints or other considerations.

Is an auditor required to make suggestions to improve internal control?

The auditor is permitted, but not required, to communicate orally or in writing to management and those charged with governance recommendations for improving internal controls.

What should be included in the written communication?

The written communication of significant deficiencies and material weaknesses should:

- State that the purpose of the auditor's consideration of internal control was to express an opinion on the financial statements, but not to express an opinion on the effectiveness of the entity's internal control.
- State that the auditor is not expressing an opinion on the effectiveness of internal control.
- State that the auditor's consideration of internal control was not designed to identify all deficiencies in internal control that might be significant deficiencies or material weaknesses.
- Define material weakness and, where relevant, significant deficiency.
- Identify significant deficiencies and those deemed to be material weaknesses.
- State that the communication is intended solely for the information and use of management, those charged with governance, and others within the organization and is not intended to be and should not be used by anyone other than these specified parties (reference to a government authority is permissible).

The auditor may, but is not required to, include additional statements regarding (1) the general inherent limitations of internal control, including the possibility of management override, and (2) the specific nature and extent of the auditor's consideration of internal control during the audit.

Note

An auditor may issue a communication stating that no material weaknesses were identified during the audit for submission to governmental authorities.

Caution

The auditor should not issue a written communication stating that no significant deficiencies were identified.

Example 12.11   Sample Communication of Material Weaknesses and Significant Deficiencies

In planning and performing our audit of the financial statements of Kate Company as of and for the year ended December 31, 20XX, in accordance with auditing standards generally accepted in the United States of America, we considered the Company's internal control over financial reporting (internal control) as a basis for designing our auditing procedures for the purpose of expressing our opinion on the financial statements, but not for the purpose of expressing an opinion on the effectiveness of the Company's internal control. Accordingly, we do not express an opinion on the effectiveness of the Company's internal control.

Our consideration of internal control was for the limited purposes described in the preceding paragraph and was not designed to identify all deficiencies in internal control that might be significant deficiencies or material weaknesses and therefore, there can be no assurance that all deficiencies, significant deficiencies, or material weaknesses have been identified. However, as discussed below, we identified certain deficiencies in internal control that we considered to be material weaknesses [and other deficiencies that we considered to be significant deficiencies].

A deficiency in internal control exists when the design or operation of a control does not allow management or employees, in the normal course of performing their assigned functions, to prevent or detect and correct misstatements on a timely basis. A material weakness is a deficiency, or a combination of deficiencies, in internal control, such that there is a reasonable possibility that a material misstatement of the entity's financial statements will not be prevented, or detected and corrected on a timely basis. [We consider the following deficiencies in the Company's internal control to be material weaknesses:]

[Describe the material weaknesses that were identified.]

[A significant deficiency is a deficiency, or a combination of deficiencies, in internal control that is less severe than a material weakness, yet important enough to merit attention by those charged with governance. We consider the following deficiencies in the Company's internal control to be significant deficiencies:]

[Describe the significant deficiencies that were identified.]

This communication is intended solely for the information and use of management, [identify the body or individuals charged with governance], others within the organization, and [identify any specified governmental authorities] and is not intended to be and should not be used by anyone other than these specified parties.

Does SAS 115 provide examples of deficiencies in internal control?

The pronouncement lists the following examples of circumstances that may be deficiencies, significant deficiencies, or material weaknesses.

Deficiencies in the Design of Controls
- Inadequate design of internal control over the preparation of the financial statements being audited.
- Inadequate design of internal control over a significant account or process.
- Inadequate documentation of the components of internal control.
- Insufficient control consciousness within the organization—for example, the tone at the top and the control environment.
- Absent or inadequate segregation of duties within a significant account or process.
- Absent or inadequate controls over the safeguarding of assets (this applies to controls that the auditor determines would be necessary for effective internal control over financial reporting).
- Inadequate design of information technology (IT) general and application controls that prevent the information system from providing complete and accurate information consistent with financial reporting objectives and current needs.
- Employees or management who lack the qualifications and training to fulfill their assigned functions. For example, in an entity that prepares financial statements in accordance with generally accepted accounting principles, the person responsible for the accounting and reporting function may lack the skills and knowledge to apply generally accepted accounting principles in recording the entity's financial transactions or preparing its financial statements.
- Inadequate design of monitoring controls used to assess the design and operating effectiveness of the entity's internal control over time.
- The absence of an internal process to report deficiencies in internal control to management on a timely basis.

Failures in the Operation of Internal Control
- Failure in the operation of effectively designed controls over a significant account or process—for example, the failure of a control such as dual authorization for significant disbursements within the purchasing process.
- Failure of the information and communication component of internal control to provide complete and accurate output because of deficiencies in timeliness, completeness, or accuracy—for example, the failure to obtain timely and accurate consolidating information from remote locations that is needed to prepare the financial statements.
- Failure of controls designed to safeguard assets from loss, damage, or misappropriation. This circumstance may need careful consideration before it is evaluated as a significant deficiency or material weakness. For example, assume that a company uses security devices to safeguard its inventory (preventive controls) and also performs periodic physical inventory counts (detective controls) on a timely basis in relation to its financial reporting. Although the physical inventory count does not safeguard the inventory from theft or loss, it prevents a material misstatement of the financial statements if performed effectively and on a timely basis.

Therefore, given that the definitions of material weakness and significant deficiency relate to likelihood of misstatement of the financial statements, the failure of a preventive control such as inventory tags will not result in a significant deficiency or material weakness if the detective control (physical inventory) prevents a misstatement of the financial statements. Material weaknesses relating to controls over the safeguarding of assets would exist only if the company does not have effective controls (considering both safeguarding and other controls) to prevent or detect a material misstatement of the financial statements.

- Failure to perform reconciliations of significant accounts—for example, if accounts receivable subsidiary ledgers are not reconciled to the general ledger account in a timely or accurate manner.
- Undue bias or lack of objectivity by those responsible for accounting decisions—for example, consistent understatement of expenses or overstatement of allowances at the direction of management.
- Misrepresentation by client personnel to the auditor (an indicator of fraud).
- Management override of controls.
- Failure of an application control caused by a deficiency in the design or operation of an IT general control.
- An observed deviation rate that exceeds the number of deviations expected by the auditor in a test of the operating effectiveness of a control. For example, if the auditor designs a test in which he or she selects a sample and expects no deviations, the finding of one deviation is a nonnegligible deviation rate because, based on the results of the auditor's test of the sample, the desired level of confidence was not obtained.

SAS 116—Interim Financial Information

To which entities is this pronouncement applicable?

In general, this statement applies to reviews of a nonissuer's (i.e., a nonpublic entity's) interim financial statements if the latest annual financial statements have been or are expected to be audited.

Is there a difference between a review under Statements on Standards for Accounting and Review Services (SSARS) and a review under SAS 116?

The review procedures and reporting requirements applicable to reviews of financial statements under SSARS and SAS 116 are essentially the same. However, with respect to a review of interim financial information under SAS 116, the following two conditions should be noted:

1. The accountant must have sufficient knowledge of the client's internal controls as they relate to both annual and interim financial information. If the accountant has performed the audit for the most recent annual period, he or she may have the requisite knowledge pertinent to the latest annual information.

> ## Caution
>
> Even if the accountant has audited the financial statements of the most recent annual period, he or she should inquire about any significant changes in internal control.

2.   Each page of the interim financial statements should be labeled "Unaudited."

SAS 117—Compliance Audits

What is the objective of a compliance audit?

The objective of a compliance audit is to express an opinion as to whether an entity has complied in all material respects with applicable governmental compliance requirements.

What guidance is contained in SAS 117?

This statement provides guidance for testing and reporting on compliance with laws and regulations applicable to certain governmental audits. In general, when performing governmental auditing, the practitioner has a responsibility to follow generally accepted auditing standards and certain supplemental standards known as generally accepted government auditing standards.

> ## Suggestion
>
> Practitioners undertaking a governmental audit engagement would be well advised to refer to "Government Auditing Standards" (known as the Yellow Book) issued by the Comptroller General of the United States, the Single Audit Act of 1984, and Office of Management and Budget (OMB) Circular A-133, "Audits of States, Local Governments and Non-Profit Organizations."

SAS 118—Other Information in Documents Containing Audited Financial Statements

What are documents containing audited financial statements?

In general, "documents containing audited financial statements" refers to annual reports (or similar documents) issued to business owners (shareholders).

What is meant by "other information"?

Other information is financial and nonfinancial information, excluding an entity's financial statements and required supplementary information (see SAS 120).

Examples include a report by management or those charged with governance, financial summaries or highlights, employment data, planned capital expenditures, financial ratios, names of officers and directors, and selected quarterly data. Other information does not include, for example, a press release, a cover letter accompanying the financial statements (and auditor's report), and information found on an entity's website.

What is an auditor's responsibility with respect to other information?

An auditor should:

- Read the other information to identify any material inconsistencies with the audited financial statements.
- Arrange with management and those charged with governance to obtain the other information before the report release date, or if not possible, read the other information as soon as practicable.
- Communicate to those charged with governance (1) the auditor's responsibility with respect to the other information, (2) the procedures performed, and (3) the results of the procedures performed.

What is an inconsistency?

An inconsistency is other information conflicting with information in audited financial statements. Material inconsistencies may raise doubt about audit evidence obtained and the basis for the auditor's opinion on the financial statements.

What should an auditor do if a material inconsistency is found?

Identification of material inconsistencies should cause the auditor to determine whether the audited financial statements or other information needs to be revised.

If material inconsistencies are identified in other information obtained prior to the report release date, the auditor should consider whether the financial statements require revision. If management refuses to revise the financial statements, the auditor's opinion should be modified, and the auditor should communicate the matter to those charged with governance. The auditor should also add an explanatory paragraph to the auditor's report that describes the material inconsistency. Alternatively, the auditor may withhold the auditor's report or withdraw from the engagement when possible.

If material inconsistencies are identified in other information obtained subsequent to the report release date, the auditor should:
- Follow the rules applicable to subsequent discovery of facts existing at the date of the auditor's report when the financial statements require revision.
- Perform the procedures necessary under the circumstances, including reviewing the actions taken by management to ensure that applicable users are notified

of the need for revision, when the other information requires revision that management agrees to.
- Notify those charged with governance and take further appropriate action, which might include obtaining advice from the auditor's legal counsel, when the other information requires revision that management refuses to make.

What is an auditor's responsibility with respect to material misstatements of fact?

Material misstatements of fact identified in the other information should be discussed with management. Management might need to contact its legal counsel regarding the matter. Management's refusal to correct the material misstatements of fact should be communicated to those charged with governance. Additionally, the auditor might need to contact his or her own legal counsel, withhold the auditor's report, or withdraw from the engagement.

Are there any additional matters the auditor should consider with respect to "other information"?

SAS 120, *Required Supplementary Information*, addresses the auditor's responsibility for other information in a document containing audited financial statements required to be included by a designated accounting standard setter.

The other information to which SAS 118 applies is not required to be referenced in the auditor's report on the financial statements. An explanatory paragraph disclaiming an opinion on the other information is permissible. For example:

> *My (Our) audit was conducted for the purpose of forming an opinion on the basic financial statements as a whole. The* [identify the other information] *is presented for purposes of additional analysis and is not a required part of the basic financial statements. Such information has not been subjected to the auditing procedures applied in the audit of the basic financial statements, and accordingly, I (we) do not express an opinion or provide any assurance on it.*

SAS 119—Supplementary Information in Relation to the Financial Statements as a Whole

What is supplementary information?

Supplementary information is information presented outside the basic financial statements, excluding required supplementary information that is not considered necessary for the fair presentation of the financial statements. Supplementary information may be presented in a document containing audited financial statements or separate from the financial statements. Examples of supplementary information include additional details or explanations of financial statement items, consolidating information, historical summaries of items extracted from financial statements, and statistical data.

What is an auditor's objective in an engagement to report on supplementary information?

The objective of such an engagement is to evaluate the presentation of the supplementary information in relation to the financial statements as a whole and report on whether the supplementary information is fairly stated, in all material respects, in relation to the financial statements as a whole.

What procedures should an auditor perform to determine whether the supplementary information is fairly stated, in all material respects, in relation to the financial statements as a whole?

The auditor should determine that all five of the following conditions are satisfied:

1. The supplementary information was derived from, and relates directly to, the underlying accounting and other records.
2. The supplementary information relates to the same period covered by the financial statements.
3. The financial statements were audited, and the auditor served as the principal auditor.
4. Neither an adverse opinion nor a disclaimer of opinion was issued on the financial statements.
5. The supplementary information will accompany the audited financial statements, or such statements will be readily available (i.e., a third party can obtain the audited financial statements without further action by the entity).

The auditor should obtain management's agreement that it acknowledges and understands its responsibility:

- For the supplementary information
- To provide the auditor with certain written representations concerning the supplementary information
- To include the auditor's report on the supplementary information in any document containing the supplementary information that indicates that the auditor has reported on the supplementary information
- To either present the supplementary information with the audited financial statements or, if the supplementary information is not presented with them, to make the audited financial statements available no later than the date of issuance of the supplementary information

Using the same materiality level used in the financial statement audit, the auditor should also:

- Inquire of management about the purpose of the supplementary information and the criteria used to prepare the supplementary information.
- Determine that the form and content of the supplementary information comply with the applicable criteria.

- Obtain an understanding of the methods used in preparing the supplementary information and determine the consistency in the application of such methods.
- Compare and reconcile the supplementary information to the accounting and other records applicable to the financial statements.
- Inquire of management about underlying significant assumptions or interpretations.
- Evaluate appropriateness and completeness of the supplementary information, considering information derived from the financial statement audit.
- Obtain written representations from management:
  - That it acknowledges its responsibility for the presentation of the supplementary information
  - That it believes the supplementary information, including its form and content, is fairly presented
  - That the measurement or presentation methods have not changed from the prior period or, if they have, the reasons for the changes
  - Regarding significant assumptions or interpretations underlying the supplementary information
  - That management will make the audited financial statements readily available to users of the supplementary information no later than the issuance of the supplementary information and the audit report thereon when the supplementary information is not presented with the audited financial statements

The auditor does not have to consider subsequent events with respect to the supplementary information.

What are the reporting requirements applicable to supplementary information?

When supplementary information is presented with financial statements, the auditor should report on the supplementary information by either (1) adding an explanatory paragraph after the opinion paragraph or (2) issuing a separate report on the supplementary information. The following six elements should be included in either reporting situation:

1. A statement that the audit was conducted in order to form an opinion on the financial statements as a whole
2. A statement that the supplementary information is presented for additional analysis purposes and is not a required part of the financial statements
3. A statement that the supplementary information is the responsibility of management and was derived from, and relates directly to, the underlying accounting and other records used to prepare the financial statements
4. A statement that the supplementary information has been subjected to the auditing procedures applied in the audit of the financial statements and certain additional procedures, in accordance with generally accepted auditing standards
5. If an unqualified opinion is expressed on the financial statements and the auditor believes that the supplementary information is fairly stated in relation to the

audited financial statements, a statement that the supplementary information is fairly stated, in all material respects, in relation to the financial statements as a whole

6. If a qualified opinion on the financial statements has an effect on the supplementary information, a statement that, except for the effects on the supplementary information, such information is fairly stated, in all material respects, in relation to the financial statements as a whole

A separate report on supplementary information should be issued when the audited financial statements are presented separately from the supplementary information. The separate report should include a reference to the report on the financial statements, the date of the report, the type of opinion expressed, and any report modifications.

A separate report on supplementary information may be restricted to use by specified parties.

Caution

An auditor should not express an opinion on supplementary information when he or she expressed an adverse opinion or disclaimed an opinion on the financial statements.

Material misstatement of supplementary information should be discussed with management, and the auditor should propose appropriate revisions. Management's failure to make the appropriate revisions should cause the auditor to either modify the opinion expressed on the supplementary information or, if applicable, withhold the auditor's separate report on the supplementary information.

Example 12.12 Illustrative Explanatory Paragraph

My (Our) audit was conducted for the purpose of forming an opinion on the financial statements as a whole. The [*identify accompanying supplementary information*] is presented for purposes of additional analysis and is not a required part of the financial statements. Such information is the responsibility of management and was derived from and relates directly to the underlying accounting and other records used to prepare the financial statements. The information has been subjected to the auditing procedures applied in the audit of the financial statements and certain additional procedures, including comparing and reconciling such information directly to the underlying accounting and other records used to prepare the financial statements or to the financial statements themselves, and other additional procedures in accordance with auditing standards

(continued)

> *(Continued)*
>
> generally accepted in the United States of America. In my (our) opinion, the information is fairly stated in all material respects in relation to the financial statements as a whole.

SAS 120—Required Supplementary Information

What is required supplementary information?

Required supplementary information is information that a designated accounting standard setter requires to accompany basic financial statements. While required supplementary information is not part of the basic financial statements, it is considered an important part of the reporting process.

Are there specific examples of designated accounting standard setters?

Bodies designated to set accounting standards are the FASB, the Governmental Accounting Standards Board (GASB), the Federal Accounting Standards Advisory Board (FASAB), and the International Accounting Standards Board (IASB).

What are an auditor's responsibilities with respect to required supplementary information?

In connection with required supplementary information, an auditor should perform the following three procedures:

1. Make inquiries of management regarding the methods and any changes in the methods of preparing the required supplementary information.
2. Determine the consistency of the information with both the inquiries made and the basic financial statements.
3. Obtain written representations from management, including management's acknowledgement of its responsibility for the information, the conformity of the information with applicable prescribed guidelines, and changes in the measurement or presentation of the information.

What should an auditor do if the necessary procedures cannot be performed?

If management was responsible for the auditor's inability to perform the necessary procedures, the auditor should promptly inform those charged with governance.

What are the reporting requirements with respect to required supplementary information?

The auditor's report on the basic financial statements should include an explanatory paragraph, placed after the opinion paragraph, to refer to the required supplementary information.

Example 12.13   Explanatory Paragraph When the Required Supplementary Information Is Included, and the Auditor Has Applied the Necessary Procedures and Determined That There Are No Material Departures from Prescribed Guidelines

[Identify the applicable financial reporting framework (e.g., "Accounting principles generally accepted in the United States of America")] require that the *[identify the required supplementary information]* on page XX be presented to supplement the basic financial statements. Such information, although not a part of the basic financial statements, is required by *[identify designated accounting standard setter]*, which considers it to be an essential part of financial reporting for placing the basic financial statements in an appropriate operational, economic, or historical context. I (We) have applied certain limited procedures to the required supplementary information in accordance with auditing standards generally accepted in the United States of America, which consisted of inquiries of management about the methods of preparing the information and comparing the information for consistency with management's responses to my (our) inquiries, the basic financial statements, and other knowledge I (we) obtained during my (our) audit of the basic financial statements. I (We) do not express an opinion or provide any assurance on the information, because the limited procedures do not provide me (us) with sufficient evidence to express an opinion or provide any assurance.

Caution

The explanatory paragraph should be modified if (1) some or all required supplementary information is omitted, (2) the required supplementary information contains material departures from prescribed guidelines, or (3) the auditor is unable to perform certain specified procedures.

SAS 121—Revised Applicability of Statement on Auditing Standards No. 100, Interim Financial Information

This pronouncement indicates that SAS 100 is applicable when the accountant has audited an entity's latest annual financial statements, and the appointment of another accountant to audit the current year financial statements is not effective prior to the beginning of the period covered by the review.

Alert

About four years ago, the Auditing Standards Board of the American Institute of Certified Public Accountants began its "clarity project." The objective of the project is to simplify and clarify its auditing pronouncements and, where possible, align its standards with International Standards of Auditing. Accordingly, there will be consistency in the use of terminology, making it easier for auditors to determine practice requirements. Rather than replace each extant SAS with the clarified pronouncement, when the project is completed, the Auditing Standards Board will issue what amounts to a "supersized" pronouncement that codifies all of the redrafted standards. While this "clarified SAS" will not, in most instances, substantially change what is required of the auditor, the structure of the SAS will be modified and new terminology introduced. Two of the most significant anticipated changes are a revised auditor's report and the introduction of "group audit" requirements; the latter will replace current guidance for situations involving a division of responsibility as discussed in Chapter 10. The revised and clarified standards are expected to be effective with respect to 2012 calendar-year audits.

AS 1—References in Auditor's Reports to the Standards of the Public Company Accounting Oversight Board

Refer to Chapter 10.

AS 2—An Audit of Internal Control over Financial Reporting Performed in Conjunction with an Audit of Financial Statements

Superseded by AS 5.

AS 3—Audit Documentation

When are the documentation requirements in this pronouncement applicable?

The documentation requirements in this pronouncement are applicable to financial statement audits, audits of internal control over financial reporting (see AS 5), and reviews of interim financial information.

Under AS 3, an auditor must document "significant findings or issues." What does the PCAOB consider to be significant findings or issues?

The PCAOB defines *significant findings or issues* as substantive matters that are important to the procedures performed, evidence obtained, or conclusions reached. Examples of significant findings or issues include:

- Significant matters pertaining to the selection, application, and consistency of accounting principles, including related disclosures
- Results of auditing procedures that indicate a need for significant modification of the audit program
- Audit adjustments
- Disagreements among audit team members
- Difficulties encountered in applying auditing procedures
- Significant changes in the auditor's assessed level of audit risk
- Matters that might impact the auditor's report
- The existence of significant deficiencies in internal control, including material weaknesses

Note

All significant findings or issues must be identified in an engagement completion document.

What retention requirements should an auditor be aware of?

- In general, audit documentation must be retained for a period of seven years, which commences on the date that the auditor grants permission to use the audit report in connection with the issuance of the company's financial statements (report release date). A specific law, however, may require a longer retention period.
- A complete and final set of audit documentation is required to be assembled for retention not more than 45 days after the report release date (documentation completion date).
- No audit documentation is permitted to be deleted or discarded after the document completion date.
- Information may be added after the documentation completion date provided that the documentation includes the date of addition, the name of the preparer of the additional documentation, and the reason for the addition.
- The office of the firm issuing the auditor's report is responsible for the documentation and its retention.

AS 4—Reporting on Whether a Previously Reported Material Weakness Continues to Exist

Is an auditor required to report on whether a previously reported material weakness continues to exist?

An issuer may voluntarily engage an independent auditor to report on whether a previously reported material weakness continues to exist.

> ## Caution
>
> In this type of engagement, an auditor is not reporting on the overall effectiveness of internal control over financial reporting. The auditor's report in this type of engagement relates to a specific previously identified material weakness.

What are the conditions for this type of engagement?

This type of engagement may be accepted only if management:

- Accepts responsibility for the effectiveness of internal control
- Evaluates the effectiveness of the controls it believes address the material weakness
- Asserts that the controls are effective in correcting the material weakness
- Has sufficient evidence, including documentation, to support its assessment
- Presents a written report that will accompany the report of the auditor

How should an auditor conduct this type of engagement?

In performing this type of engagement, an auditor is required to comply with the standards of the PCAOB and accordingly must:

- Properly plan the engagement.
- Obtain a sufficient understanding of internal control over financial reporting.
- Test and evaluate whether a material weakness continues to exist.
- Evaluate whether to use the work of other auditors.
- Form an opinion as to whether a previously reported material weakness continues to exist.

> ## Note
>
> In order to evaluate whether a material weakness continues to exist, an auditor needs to obtain sufficient evidence concerning the effectiveness of the controls identified by management as addressing the material weakness.

Is a representation letter required in connection with this type of engagement?

An auditor should obtain certain written management representations. AS 4 indicates that the auditor should obtain written representations from management:

- Acknowledging management's responsibility for establishing and maintaining effective internal control over financial reporting

- Stating that management has evaluated the effectiveness of the specified controls using the specified criteria and management's stated control objective(s)
- Stating management's assertion that the specified controls are effective in achieving the stated control objective(s) as of a specified date
- Stating management's assertion that the identified material weakness no longer exists as of the same specified date
- Stating that management believes that its assertions are supported by sufficient evidence
- Describing any material fraud and any other fraud that, although not material, involves senior management or management or other employees who have a significant role in the company's internal control over financial reporting and that has occurred or come to management's attention since the date of management's most recent annual assessment of internal control over financial reporting
- Stating whether there were, subsequent to the date being reported on, any changes in internal control over financial reporting or other factors that might significantly affect the stated control objective(s) or indicate that the identified controls were not operating effectively as of or subsequent to the date specified in management's assertion

What must management include in its report that will accompany the report of the auditor?

Management's report should include:

- A statement of management's responsibility for establishing and maintaining effective internal control over financial reporting
- A statement identifying the control criteria used by management to conduct the required annual assessment of the effectiveness of internal control over financial reporting
- An identification of the material weakness that was identified as part of management's annual assessment
- An identification of the control objective(s) addressed by the specified controls and a statement that the specified controls achieve the stated control objective(s) as of a specified date
- A statement that the identified material weakness no longer exists as of the same specified date because the specified controls address the material weakness

What is involved in an auditor's evaluation of management's report?

An auditor should evaluate whether:

- Management's responsibility is stated properly.
- The control criteria used by management are suitable.
- The material weakness, stated control objectives, and specified controls have been described properly.
- Management's assertions, as of the specified date, are free of material misstatement.

Is an auditor required to issue a report at the conclusion of the engagement?

Given that this type of engagement is voluntary, an auditor is not required to issue a report.

If a continuing auditor decides to issue a report after concluding that a previously reported material weakness no longer exists, what would be appropriate wording?

Example 12.14 represents an illustrative standard report that includes an opinion that a material weakness no longer exists.

Example 12.14 Report of Independent Registered Public Accounting Firm

We have previously audited and reported on management's annual assessment of XYZ Company's internal control over financial reporting as of December 31, 2X12, based on [*identify control criteria, for example, "criteria established in Internal Control—Integrated Framework issued by the Committee of Sponsoring Organizations of the Treadway Commission (COSO)"*]. Our report, dated [*date of report*], identified the following material weakness in the Company's internal control over financial reporting:

[*Describe material weakness*]

We have audited management's assertion, included in the accompanying [*title of management's report*], that the material weakness in internal control over financial reporting identified above no longer exists as of [*date of management's assertion*] because the following control(s) address(es) the material weakness:

[*Describe control(s)*]

Management has asserted that the control(s) identified above achieve(s) the following stated control objective, which is consistent with the criteria established in [*identify control criteria used for management's annual assessment of internal control over financial reporting*]: [*state control objective addressed*]. Management also has asserted that it has tested the control(s) above and concluded that the control(s) was (were) designed and operated effectively as of [*date of management's assertion*]. XYZ Company's management is responsible for its assertion. Our responsibility is to express an opinion on whether the identified material weakness continues to exist as of [*date of management's assertion*] based on our auditing procedures.

Our engagement was conducted in accordance with the standards of the Public Company Accounting Oversight Board (United States). Those standards require that we plan and perform the engagement to obtain reasonable assurance about whether a previously reported material weakness continues to exist at the company. Our engagement included examining evidence supporting management's assertion and performing such other procedures as we considered necessary in the circumstances. We obtained an understanding of the company's internal control over financial reporting as part of our previous audit of management's annual assessment of XYZ Company's internal control over financial reporting as of December 31, 2X12, and updated that understanding as it specifically relates to changes in internal control over financial reporting associated with the material weakness described above. We believe that our auditing procedures provide a reasonable basis for our opinion.

In our opinion, the material weakness described above no longer exists as of [*date of management's assertion*].

We were not engaged to and did not conduct an audit of internal control over financial reporting as of [*date of management's assertion*], the objective of which would be the expression of an opinion on the effectiveness of internal control over financial reporting. Accordingly, we do not express such an opinion. This means that we have not applied auditing procedures sufficient to reach conclusions about the effectiveness of any controls of the company as of any date after December 31, 2X12, other than the control(s) specifically identified in this report. Accordingly, we do not express an opinion that any other controls operated effectively after December 31, 2X12.

Because of its inherent limitations, internal control over financial reporting may not prevent or detect misstatements. Also, projections of any evaluation of the effectiveness of specific controls or internal control over financial reporting overall to future periods are subject to the risk that controls may become inadequate because of changes in conditions or that the degree of compliance with the policies or procedures may deteriorate.

[*Signature*]
[*City and state or country*]
[*Date*]

Can the auditor's standard report be modified?

An auditor should modify the standard report if:

- Other material weaknesses that were previously reported are not addressed by the current opinion.
- A significant subsequent event has occurred since the date being reported on.
- Management's report includes additional information.

What is an auditor's reporting responsibility when a previously reported material weakness continues to exist?

In this situation, an auditor can either (1) issue a report expressing an opinion that the material weakness exists as of the date specified by management or (2) issue a written communication to the audit committee containing the conclusion that the material weakness continues to exist.

AS 5—An Audit of Internal Control over Financial Reporting That Is Integrated with an Audit of Financial Statements

What is an auditor's objective in auditing internal control over financial reporting?

The objective of an audit of internal control over financial reporting is to express an opinion on the effectiveness of a company's internal control over financial reporting.

Note

If an auditor determines that one or more material weaknesses in internal control exist, he or she may not conclude that internal control over financial reporting is effective.

What is meant by integrating the audit of financial statements with the audit of internal control over financial reporting?

In an integrated audit, an auditor needs to design tests of controls to accomplish the objectives of both types of audits simultaneously. Accordingly, tests of controls should enable an auditor to obtain sufficient evidence to support (1) an opinion on the effectiveness of internal control over financial reporting and (2) the assessments of control risk for the audit of financial statements.

What is meant by scaling the audit?

The PCAOB recognizes that the size and complexity of an entity, its business processes, and business units may affect (1) the achievement of an entity's control objectives and (2) the risks of material misstatement and the controls necessary to address the risks. Accordingly, the audit of internal control over financial reporting should be tailored to the size and complexity of the entity. AS 5 emphasizes the significance of fraud risk and antifraud controls and requires the auditor to assess risk at the assertion level rather than at the control level. Further, an auditor is not required to evaluate management's process of evaluating its internal control over financial reporting.

Is it permissible to use the work of others during the performance of an integrated audit?

During the performance of an integrated audit, it is permissible to use the work of others. As such, the work or use of internal auditors is allowed. (See SAS 65.)

Also permitted is the use of other company personnel and outside parties working under the direction of management or the audit committee.

Caution

As the risk associated with a control increases, the use of others and/or their work should decrease.

What approach should be used in an audit of internal control over financial reporting?

In selecting controls to be subjected to testing, an auditor should use a top-down approach. Accordingly, an auditor should start at the financial statement level and with his or her understanding of the overall risks to internal control. The auditor should then focus on entity-level controls and work down to accounts and disclosures along with the relevant assertions. As a result, the auditor's attention is directed toward accounts, disclosures, and assertions that may be materially misstated. Subsequent steps involve verification of the required understanding of the risks in the entity's processes and selection of controls to test. The controls to be tested should sufficiently address the assessed risk of misstatement to each relevant assertion. The auditor is not required to identify specifically major classes of transactions and significant processes before identifying relevant assertions.

What are examples of entity-level controls?

Entity-level controls include:

- Controls related to the control environment
- Controls over management override of controls
- The entity's risk assessment process
- Controls pertaining to monitoring results of operations
- Controls over the period-end financial reporting process (e.g., procedures relative to adjusting entries and their entry in the general ledger)
- Policies regarding significant business control and risk management practices

What is the focus of tests of controls?

The auditor should test both the design and the operating effectiveness of controls. This may be accomplished by a combination of inquiry, observation, inspection of relevant documentation, and reperformance of controls. The auditor should use judgment in determining the nature, extent, and timing of tests of controls.

How should the auditor evaluate identified control deficiencies?

The severity of each control deficiency should be evaluated to determine whether the deficiency alone, or in combination with one or more other control deficiencies, represents a material weakness as of the date of management's assessment of its internal control. The severity of a control deficiency is dependent on (1) whether there is a reasonable possibility that the entity's controls will not prevent or detect a financial statement misstatement and (2) the magnitude (materiality) of the potential misstatement.

Definitions

A *deficiency* in internal control over financial reporting (i.e., a control deficiency) exists when the design or operation of a control does not allow management or employees, while performing their normal assigned functions, to prevent or detect financial statement misstatements in a timely fashion.

A *significant deficiency* is a deficiency (i.e., control deficiency) or a combination of deficiencies that is less severe than a material weakness yet important enough to merit attention by those having financial reporting oversight responsibility.

A *material weakness* is a deficiency (i.e., control deficiency), or a combination of deficiencies, such that there is a reasonable possibility (i.e., reasonably possible or probable) that a material misstatement of the company's annual or interim financial statements will not be prevented or detected on a timely basis.

What are some indicators of material weaknesses in internal control over financial reporting?

Indicators of material weaknesses include:

- Identification of fraud committed by senior management
- Correction of a material misstatement through restatement of prior-period financial statements
- Ineffective audit committee oversight of the entity's external financial reporting and internal control
- Identification of a material misstatement in circumstances indicating that the entity's internal controls would not enable its detection

What is an auditor's reporting responsibility?

An opinion should be expressed on the effectiveness of internal control over financial reporting. The opinion should be based on evaluation of evidence obtained from all sources, including results of tests of controls, misstatements detected in the course of the financial statement audit, and identified control deficiencies.

Caution

If a scope limitation is encountered, the auditor is required to disclaim an opinion or withdraw from the engagement.

An auditor should then evaluate management's presentation concerning internal control included in the entity's annual report, as required by the Securities and Exchange Commission.

Must an auditor obtain written representations from management before expressing an opinion?

An auditor should obtain written representations from management, including:

- Acknowledgment of management's responsibility for establishing and maintaining effective internal control over financial reporting
- A statement that management has performed an evaluation and made an assessment of the effectiveness of the company's internal control over financial reporting and specification of the control criteria
- A statement that management did not use the auditor's procedures performed during the audits of internal control over financial reporting or the financial statements as part of the basis for management's assertion of the effectiveness of internal control over financial reporting
- A statement of management's conclusion, as set forth in its assessment, about the effectiveness of the company's internal control over financial reporting based on the control criteria as of a specified date
- A statement that management has disclosed to the auditor all deficiencies in the design or operation of internal control over financial reporting identified as part of management's evaluation, including separate disclosure to the auditor of all such deficiencies that it believes to be significant deficiencies or material weaknesses in internal control over financial reporting
- A description of any fraud resulting in a material misstatement and any fraud that does not result in a material misstatement but involves senior management or management, or other employees who have a significant role in the company's internal control over financial reporting
- A statement whether control deficiencies identified and communicated to the audit committee during previous engagements have been resolved, and specific identification of any that have not
- A statement whether there were, subsequent to the date being reported on, any changes in internal control over financial reporting or other factors that might significantly affect internal control over financial reporting, including any corrective actions taken by management with regard to significant deficiencies and material weaknesses.

Caution

The failure to obtain written representations from management is tantamount to a severe scope limitation that warrants either a disclaimer of opinion or withdrawal from the engagement.

What are an auditor's communication requirements?

Prior to issuing the audit report on internal control over financial reporting, the auditor is required to communicate, in writing, to management and the audit committee all identified material weaknesses.

If applicable, the auditor must communicate in writing to the board of directors the conclusion that the oversight of the company's external financial reporting and internal control over financial reporting by the audit committee is ineffective.

Further, significant deficiencies, even though not considered to be material weaknesses, must be communicated in writing to the audit committee.

Additionally, the auditor should communicate in writing to management all control deficiencies not considered to be material weaknesses and inform the audit committee of this communication. The auditor need not repeat information about such deficiencies included in previously issued written communications.

Note

The auditor does not need to perform procedures to identify all control deficiencies. Only those control deficiencies that he or she identifies are required to be communicated.

Caution

Under no circumstance should an auditor issue a report stating that no deficiencies less severe than a material weakness were noted during the audit.

What should be included in the auditor's report on the audit of internal control over financial reporting?

These elements must be included in the auditor's report:

- A title that includes the word *independent*
- A statement that management is responsible for maintaining effective internal control over financial reporting and for assessing the effectiveness of internal control over financial reporting
- An identification of management's report on internal control
- A statement that the auditor's responsibility is to express an opinion on the company's internal control over financial reporting based on his or her audit
- A definition of internal control over financial reporting as stated in AS 5
- A statement that the audit was conducted in accordance with the standards of the Public Company Accounting Oversight Board (United States)
- A statement that the standards of the PCAOB require that the auditor plan and perform the audit to obtain reasonable assurance about whether effective internal control over financial reporting was maintained in all material respects

- A statement that an audit includes obtaining an understanding of internal control over financial reporting, assessing the risk that a material weakness exists, testing and evaluating the design and operating effectiveness of internal control based on the assessed risk, and performing such other procedures as the auditor considers necessary in the circumstances
- A statement that the auditor believes the audit provides a reasonable basis for his or her opinion
- A paragraph stating that, because of inherent limitations, internal control over financial reporting may not prevent or detect material misstatements and that projections of any evaluation of effectiveness to future periods are subject to the risk that controls may become inadequate because of changes in conditions or that the degree of compliance with the policies or procedures may deteriorate
- The auditor's opinion on whether the company maintained, in all material respects, effective internal control over financial reporting as of the specified date, based on the control criteria
- The manual or printed signature of the auditor or the auditor's firm
- The city and state (or city and country, in the case of non-U.S. auditors) from which the auditor's report has been issued
- The date of the audit report, which should be no earlier than the date on which the auditor has obtained sufficient competent evidence to support the opinion

Notes

Instead of issuing separate audit reports on the company's financial statements and on internal control, the auditor may issue a combined report that contains both an opinion on the financial statements and an opinion on internal control over financial reporting.

A separate report on internal control over financial reporting necessitates the inclusion of this paragraph to the auditor's report on the company's financial statements:

I (We) have also audited, in accordance with the standards of the Public Company Accounting Oversight Board (United States), W Company's internal control over financial reporting as of December 31, 2X12, based on [identify control criteria], *and my (our) report dated* [date of report, which should be the same as the date of the report on the financial statements] *expressed* [include nature of opinion].

In addition, the auditor should include the following paragraph to the auditor's report on internal control over financial reporting:

I (We) have also audited, in accordance with the standards of the Public Company Accounting Oversight Board (United States), the [identify financial statements] *of W company, and our report dated* [date of report, which should be the same as the date of the report on the effectiveness of internal control over financial reporting] *expressed* [include nature of opinion].

Example 12.15 Combined Reports Expressing an Unqualified Opinion on Financial Statements and an Unqualified Opinion on Internal Control over Financial Reporting

Report of Independent Registered Public Accounting Firm

[*Introductory paragraph*]

We have audited the accompanying balance sheets of W Company as of December 31, 2X18 and 2X17, and the related statements of income, stockholders' equity and comprehensive income, and cash flows for each of the years in the three-year period ended December 31, 2X18. We also have audited W Company's internal control over financial reporting as of December 31, 2X18, based on [*identify control criteria, for example, "criteria established in Internal Control—Integrated Framework issued by the Committee of Sponsoring Organizations of the Treadway Commission (COSO)"*]. W Company's management is responsible for these financial statements, for maintaining effective internal control over financial reporting, and for its assessment of the effectiveness of internal control over financial reporting, included in the accompanying [*title of management's report*]. Our responsibility is to express an opinion on these financial statements and an opinion on the company's internal control over financial reporting based on our audits.

[*Scope paragraph*]

We conducted our audits in accordance with the standards of the Public Company Accounting Oversight Board (United States). Those standards require that we plan and perform the audits to obtain reasonable assurance about whether the financial statements are free of material misstatement and whether effective internal control over financial reporting was maintained in all material respects. Our audits of the financial statements included examining, on a test basis, evidence supporting the amounts and disclosures in the financial statements, assessing the accounting principles used and significant estimates made by management, and evaluating the overall financial statement presentation. Our audit of internal control over financial reporting included obtaining an understanding of internal control over financial reporting, assessing the risk that a material weakness exists, and testing and evaluating the design and operating effectiveness of internal control based on the assessed risk. Our audits also included performing such other procedures as we considered necessary in the circumstances. We believe that our audits provide a reasonable basis for our opinions.

[*Definition paragraph*]

A company's internal control over financial reporting is a process designed to provide reasonable assurance regarding the reliability of financial reporting and the preparation of financial statements for external purposes in accordance with generally accepted accounting principles. A company's internal control over financial reporting includes those policies and procedures that (1) pertain to the maintenance of records that, in reasonable detail, accurately and fairly reflect the transactions and dispositions of the assets of the company; (2) provide reasonable assurance that transactions are recorded as necessary to permit preparation of financial statements in accordance with generally accepted accounting principles and that receipts and expenditures of the company are being made only in accordance with authorizations of management and directors of the company; and (3) provide reasonable assurance regarding prevention or timely detection of unauthorized acquisition, use, or disposition of the company's assets that could have a material effect on the financial statements.

[Inherent limitations paragraph]

Because of its inherent limitations, internal control over financial reporting may not prevent or detect misstatements. Also, projections of any evaluation of effectiveness to future periods are subject to the risk that controls may become inadequate because of changes in conditions or that the degree of compliance with the policies or procedures may deteriorate.

[Opinion paragraph]

In our opinion, the financial statements referred to above present fairly, in all material respects, the financial position of W Company as of December 31, 2X18 and 2X17, and the results of its operations and its cash flows for each of the years in the three-year period ended December 31, 2X18, in conformity with accounting principles generally accepted in the United States of America. Also in our opinion, W Company maintained, in all material respects, effective internal control over financial reporting as of December 31, 2X18, based on *[identify control criteria, for example, "criteria established in Internal Control—Integrated Framework issued by the Committee of Sponsoring Organizations of the Treadway Commission (COSO)"]*.

[Signature]
[City and state or country]
[Date]

When is it appropriate to modify the standard report?

The standard report should be modified if:

- Elements of management's annual report on internal control are incomplete or inaccurate. (The auditor's report should be modified to include appropriate explanatory language describing the reasons for the auditor's determination.)
- There is a restriction on the scope of the engagement. (As discussed, a restriction generally warrants a disclaimer of opinion or withdrawal from the engagement.)

- The auditor decides to refer to the report of other auditors as the basis, in part, for his or her own report. (See Chapter 10 for guidance when dividing responsibility with other auditors.)
- Other information is included in management's annual report on internal control over financial reporting. (In this circumstance, the auditor should generally disclaim an opinion with respect to the other information. Material misstatement of the other information should be discussed with management, and, if necessary, both management and the audit committee should be notified in writing.)
- Management's annual certification pursuant to Section 302 of the Sarbanes-Oxley Act is misstated. (If the auditor believes that modifications to the disclosures about changes in internal control during the fourth quarter are necessary for accurate annual certification, he or she should comply with the communication requirements in SAS 116.)

How should I modify my audit report on internal control over financial reporting if I have identified one or more material weaknesses?

Since the identification of a material weakness necessitates the expression of an adverse opinion on internal control over financial reporting, the auditor's report must include:

- The definition of a material weakness
- A statement that a material weakness has been identified and an identification of the material weakness described in management's assessment

Is the auditor required to report on management's evaluation of its internal control?

Effective with the issuance of AS 5, an auditor is *not* required to express an opinion on either (1) management's own evaluation of the effectiveness of its internal control or (2) the adequacy of management's process.

AS 6—Evaluating Consistency of Financial Statements

What is the auditor's responsibility with respect to consistency of an entity's financial statements?

The auditor should evaluate whether the comparability of financial statements between periods has been materially affected by (1) changes in accounting principles or (2) material adjustments to the financial statements of prior periods to correct misstatements.

What is considered to be a change in accounting principle?

A change in accounting principle is a change from one generally accepted accounting principle (GAAP) to another. This includes a change in accounting principle when the previously applied principle is no longer acceptable.

> ## Notes
>
> A change from a principle not considered to be a GAAP to a principle that is a GAAP is deemed to be a correction of a misstatement.
>
> The use of retrospective application to account for a change in accounting principle generally is not considered to be an inconsistency in the application of an accounting principle.

What is the effect of a change in accounting principle on the auditor's report?

The effect of a change in accounting principle under AS 6, applicable to financial statements of an issuer, is essentially the same as the effect of a change in accounting principle in the financial statements of a nonissuer.

What is the effect of a correction of a material misstatement in previously issued financial statements?

If the financial statement disclosure pertaining to restatements to correct financial statements previously issued is considered inadequate, the auditor should be guided by AS 14, *Evaluating Audit Evidence*, and SAS 58 (as modified by SAS 79).

How should changes in financial statement classification be handled by the auditor?

Unless the change in classification is considered to be a correction of a material misstatement or a change in accounting principle, there is no effect on the auditor's report.

AS 7—Engagement Quality Review

This pronouncement requires an engagement quality review and concurring approval of issuance for each audit engagement and for each engagement to review an entity's interim financial information.

Who may perform an engagement quality review?

The reviewer must be associated with a public accounting firm registered with the PCAOB. Further, the reviewer must be (1) a partner of the accounting firm, (2) someone in an equivalent position, or (3) an outsider. The reviewer must be competent, independent, and objective, and must possess integrity.

In general terms, what is required in an engagement quality review?

Among other procedures, an engagement quality review should include:

- Evaluation of significant judgments concerning planning of the engagement
- Evaluation of the engagement team's assessment of significant risks, including fraud risks
- Evaluation of materiality and internal control deficiencies
- Consideration of the firm's independence
- Review of the engagement documentation, including the engagement completion document
- Review of the financial statements and management's internal control report
- Evaluation of the nature and extent of the engagement documentation

Under what circumstances may the engagement quality reviewer provide concurring approval of issuance?

Concurring approval of issuance may be provided only if the reviewer is not aware of a significant engagement deficiency.

What is considered to be a significant engagement deficiency?

A significant engagement deficiency is defined as any of the following:

- Failure of the engagement team to obtain sufficient appropriate audit evidence
- An inappropriate overall conclusion reached on the engagement's subject matter
- An engagement for which the firm lacks independence

AS 8—Audit Risk

This pronouncement reinforces the auditor's responsibility to consider audit risk and its components during an audit of financial statements as part of an integrated audit or an audit of financial statements only.

What guidance does the pronouncement offer in addition to the guidance in SAS 107, Audit Risk and Materiality in Conducting an Audit?

Two points of interest are:

1. To determine the accounting principles that the entity being audited should follow, the auditor should consider the requirements of the Securities and Exchange Commission
2. The auditor should follow AS 12, *Identifying and Assessing Risks of Material Misstatement*; accordingly, risks of material misstatement should be assessed at both the financial statement level and the assertion level. At the assertion level, the risk of material misstatement is a combination of inherent risk and control risk.

AS 9—Audit Planning

Who is responsible for properly planning the audit?

Since the engagement partner is responsible for the engagement and its performance, he or she ultimately is responsible for planning the audit.

What factors affect the planning of the engagement?

AS 9 states that the following factors affect the planning of the audit:

- The size and complexity of the entity
- The auditor's previous experience with the entity

> **Note**
>
> In an initial engagement, the auditor should plan to obtain sufficient appropriate audit evidence regarding the opening balances.

- Changes in circumstances occurring during the audit

What specific matters affect the audit procedures?

The auditor should consider whether the following matters are significant to the company's financial statements and internal control over financial reporting:

- Knowledge of the entity's internal control over financial reporting obtained during other engagements
- Matters affecting the industry in which the client operates, such as financial reporting practices, economic conditions, laws and regulations, and changes in technology.
- Matters pertaining to the entity's business, including its organization, operating characteristics, and capital structure
- The extent of any recent changes in the entity's operations or its internal control over financial reporting
- The auditor's preliminary judgment about materiality, risk, and, in integrated audits, other factors concerning the determination of material weaknesses
- Previously communicated internal control deficiencies
- Legal or regulatory matters that the entity is aware of
- The type and extent of available evidence concerning the effectiveness of internal control over financial reporting
- Preliminary judgments concerning the effectiveness of internal control over financial reporting
- Public information concerning the entity relevant to the evaluation of the likelihood of material misstatements and the effectiveness of internal control over financial reporting

- Knowledge about risks concerning the entity evaluated as part of the client acceptance and retention process
- The relative complexity of the entity's operations

What should the auditor do if the client has multiple locations or business units?

To determine whether consolidated financial statements in multilocation engagements are free of material misstatements, the auditor should determine the extent to which audit procedures should be performed at selected locations or business units (e.g., subsidiaries, branches, components, divisions, or investments).

What factors are relevant in both (1) the assessment of the risks of material misstatement associated with a particular location or business unit and (2) the determination of the specific audit procedures to be performed?

The following factors should be considered:

- The nature and amount of assets, liabilities, and transactions at the location or business unit
- The materiality of the location or business unit
- The specific risks associated with the location or business unit that could result in misstatement of the consolidated financial statements
- Whether specific risks associated with one location or unit could have an effect on another location or unit
- The extent of centralization of records and information processing
- The effectiveness of the entity's control environment
- The nature, extent, and timing of monitoring activities at the location or business unit

Note

In determining which locations or business units to consider, the auditor may:

- Take into account the work of internal auditors. Accordingly, the auditor should consider the relevant provisions in SAS 65 and AS 5.
- Use the work and reports of other auditors. Refer to Chapter 10 for guidance in this area.

AS 10—Supervision of the Audit Engagement

Who is responsible for supervising the work of the audit team members?

The engagement partner is responsible for supervising the work of the audit team members and complying with standards of the PCAOB. The engagement partner is, however, permitted to seek assistance from engagement team members in fulfilling his or her supervisory responsibilities.

What are the engagement partner's supervisory responsibilities?

The engagement partner is responsible for:

- Informing engagement team members of their responsibilities, including the nature, extent, and timing of audit procedures to be performed
- Directing engagement team members to inform him or her of significant accounting and auditing issues
- Reviewing the work of the audit team members

What factors should be considered in determining the extent of necessary supervision?

In determining the extent of supervision needed, the engagement partner should consider:

- The nature of the entity, including its size and complexity
- The nature of the work assigned to each engagement team member, including the procedures to be performed and the controls or accounts and disclosures to be tested
- The risk of material misstatement
- The knowledge, skill, and ability of the engagement team members

---

Note

There should be a direct relationship between the risks of material misstatements and the extent of supervision.

AS 11—Consideration of Materiality in Planning and Performing an Audit

What is materiality?

According to the U.S. Supreme Court, a fact is material if there is "a substantial likelihood that the . . . fact would have been viewed by the reasonable investor as having significantly altered the 'total mix' of information made available."

Caution

Both quantitative and qualitative factors should be considered in designing audit procedures to detect material misstatements.

What levels of materiality should be established?

In planning and performing the audit, the auditor needs to establish materiality levels for:

- The financial statements taken as a whole
- Particular accounts or disclosures

Note

The materiality level for the financial statements taken as a whole needs to be expressed as a specified amount.

There may be accounts or disclosures for which there is a substantial likelihood that misstatements of lesser amounts than the financial statement materiality level would affect an investor's judgment. In such cases, separate materiality levels for those accounts or disclosures should be established in order to test those accounts or disclosures.

What should an auditor consider concerning tolerable misstatement?

The auditor should determine the amount(s) of tolerable misstatement for both (1) assessing the risks of material misstatement and (2) planning and performing specific audit procedures at the account or disclosure level.

Tolerable misstatement should be less than the materiality level for the financial statements taken as a whole and, if applicable, the materiality level(s) established for particular accounts or disclosures.

If an auditor is performing an audit of consolidated financial statements involving multiple locations or business units, tolerable misstatement at an individual location should be less than the materiality level for the consolidated financial statements taken as a whole.

When is it necessary to reevaluate the established materiality level(s) and tolerable misstatement?

An auditor may need to reevaluate the established materiality level(s) and tolerable misstatement if (1) changes in circumstances arise or (2) additional information comes to the auditor's attention. For example:

- Materiality levels and tolerable misstatement were initially based on estimated or preliminary financial statement amounts that significantly differ from actual amounts.
- Events or changes (such as changes in laws, regulations, the applicable financial reporting framework, and contractual agreements) occurred subsequent to the establishment of initial materiality levels and tolerable misstatement that are likely to affect readers of the financial statements.

AS 12—Identifying and Assessing Risks of Material Misstatements

What risk assessment procedures should an auditor perform?

Risk assessment procedures that should be performed by the auditor encompass:

- Obtaining an understanding of the entity and its environment
- Obtaining an understanding of the entity's internal control over financial reporting (see Chapter 10 and AS 5)
- Evaluating information concerning client acceptance and retention, audit planning, audits of prior periods, and other engagements performed
- Performing analytical procedures
- Conducting brainstorming sessions with key engagement team members regarding the selection and application of accounting principles and risks of material misstatements
- Inquiry of the audit committee, management, and others in the client organization (e.g., internal auditors, accounting personnel, and in-house legal counsel) about risks of material misstatements caused by error or fraud (see SAS 99)

What should an auditor understand about the entity and its environment?

The auditor should perform risk assessment procedures sufficient to understand:

- Relevant industry, regulatory, and other external factors (e.g., the competitive environment and changes in technology, the applicable financial reporting framework, the legal and political environment, and general economic conditions)
- The nature of the entity, including the entity's organizational structure, the entity's source of funding, operating characteristics, and key supplier and customer relationships
- The selection and application of accounting principles, including related disclosures
- The entity's objectives and strategies, including related business risks
- The measurement and analysis of the entity's financial performance

What procedures should an auditor perform to obtain an understanding of the entity and its environment?

Procedures the auditor should consider performing include:

- Reading public information about the entity (e.g., entity-issued press releases and analyst reports)
- Obtaining information about trading activity in the entity's securities and holdings
- Considering compensation agreements with senior management, including incentive plans and special bonuses

What should an auditor consider relative to the entity's selection and application of accounting principles, including related disclosures?

The auditor should determine whether the entity's selection and application of accounting principles are (1) appropriate for its business and (2) consistent with the appropriate financial reporting framework. The auditor should also develop expectations concerning necessary financial statement disclosures.

Accordingly, the following matters should be considered:

- Significant changes in accounting principles, financial reporting policies, or disclosures
- The competency of accounting personnel
- The accounts or disclosures for which judgment is used
- Controversial or emerging areas affecting significant accounting principles
- The accounting for significant and unusual transactions
- New financial reporting standards, laws, and regulations

What situations affecting business risks might result in material misstatement?

Examples of situations in which business risks might result in material misstatement include:

- Industry developments
- New products and services
- Use of information technology
- New accounting requirements
- Business expansion
- Implementation of new business strategies
- Financing requirements
- Regulatory requirements

What company performance measures affect the risks of material misstatement?

Examples of performance measures that could affect the risks of material misstatement include those:

- That form the basis for contractual commitments or incentive compensation arrangements
- Used by external parties, including financial analysts and credit rating agencies, to review the entity's performance
- Used by the entity to monitor its operations

What should be the focus of analytical procedures performed as risk assessment procedures?

The auditor should perform analytical procedures pertaining to revenue to identify unusual or unexpected relationships that might be indicative of material misstatement, whether caused by error or by fraud. The results of analytical procedures performed during a review of interim financial information should also be considered.

What should an auditor do in order to identify and assess risks of material misstatement?

The auditor is responsible for identifying and assessing the risks of material misstatements at both the financial statement and the assertion levels. To fulfill this responsibility, the auditor should:

- Perform risk assessment procedures in order to identify risks of misstatement.
- Evaluate whether identified risks have a pervasive effect on the financial statements.
- Consider the identified risks and the accounts, disclosures, or assertions that could be affected, and evaluate the types of potential misstatements
- Assess the likelihood of misstatement(s) and the magnitude of potential misstatement(s)
- Consider inherent risk, and identify significant accounts and disclosures along with their relevant assertions

What factors should be considered in identifying significant accounts and disclosures along with their relevant assertions?

The auditor should evaluate the following qualitative and quantitative risk factors:

- Size and composition of the account
- Susceptibility to misstatement
- Volume of activity, complexity, and homogeneity of transactions processed
- Nature of the account or disclosure
- Accounting and reporting complexities of the account or disclosure
- The account's exposure to losses
- Possibility of significant contingent liability associated with the account or disclosure
- Existence of related-party transactions in the account
- Changes from the prior period in account and disclosure characteristics

Note

The auditor should also determine the sources of potential misstatements by simply considering what could go wrong within an account or a disclosure.

What factors are relevant to identifying fraud risks?

Guidance concerning factors relevant to identifying fraud risks can be found in SAS 99, *Consideration of Fraud in a Financial Statement Audit.*

What factors are relevant to identifying significant risks?

A significant risk exists when the risk requires special audit consideration because of the nature of the risk or the likelihood or potential magnitude of misstatement. Determination as to whether a risk is a significant risk is based on inherent, but not control, risk.

Factors to consider in determining the significance of risk include:

- The effect of both quantitative and qualitative risk factors
- Whether the risk is a fraud risk, which always should be considered a significant risk
- The relationship of the risk to recent significant economic, accounting, or other developments
- The complexity of transactions
- Whether the risk involves significant related-party transactions
- The complexity or judgment in recognition or measurement of financial information
- Whether the risk is based on significant transactions outside the normal course of business

When should the auditor assess the risks of material misstatement?

The auditor's assessment of the risks of material misstatement is not a one-time assessment. The assessment should continue throughout the conduct of the audit. Accordingly, it may be necessary to revise the risk assessment and therefore modify the nature, extent, and timing of audit procedures.

AS 13—The Auditor's Responses to the Risks of Material Misstatement

What are the types of audit responses that address the risks of material misstatement assessed and identified?

There are two types of audit responses:

- Overall responses
- Responses involving the nature, extent, and timing of audit procedures to be performed

Note

The auditor should refer to SAS 99 and SAS 110 for guidance regarding both types of responses. In general, the two types of responses are not dependent on whether the entity is an issuer or a nonissuer.

What about testing controls in an audit of the financial statements of an issuer?

Tests of controls must be performed when the auditor plans to assess control risk at less than the maximum and thereby rely on controls and modify the nature, extent, and timing of substantive procedures. In such instances, the auditor must obtain evidence that the selected controls are designed and operating effectively during the entire period of reliance.

Tests of design effectiveness generally include a combination if inquiry of entity personnel, observation of entity operations, and inspection of pertinent documentation. It should be noted that walk-throughs that include these procedures are sufficient to evaluate design effectiveness.

Tests of operating effectiveness include similar procedures as well as reperformance of the control. Inquiry alone does not provide sufficient evidence concerning the effectiveness of a control.

Further guidance concerning test of controls and assessing control risk may be found in Chapter 10 and AS 5.

Are substantive procedures required in all audits?

Yes. Substantive procedures should be performed for each relevant assertion of each significant account and disclosure, regardless of the assessed level of control risk.

Guidance regarding the performance of substantive procedures may be found in Chapter 10 and AS 15.

May an auditor perform dual-purpose tests?

Dual-purpose tests, in which a substantive test of a transaction is performed concurrently with a test of a control relevant to the same transaction, are acceptable.

AS 14—Evaluating Audit Results

How should an auditor evaluate the audit results?

The auditor's evaluation of audit results should include evaluation of the following:

- The results of analytical procedures performed in the overall review stage of the audit
- Financial statement misstatements accumulated during the audit, especially those that remain uncorrected
- Qualitative aspects of the entity's accounting practices
- Conditions identified during the course of the audit concerning fraud risk
- The financial statement presentation
- The sufficiency and appropriateness of audit evidence gathered

In connection with the preceding, the following should be noted:

- The auditor should perform analytical procedures pertaining to revenue through the end of the reporting period.

- Analytical procedures performed during the overall review stage of the audit may be similar to those analytical procedures performed as risk assessment procedures.

Which misstatements should be accumulated?

All misstatements, except those that are clearly trivial, should be accumulated. The phrase *clearly trivial* is not synonymous with the phrase *not material*. A matter that is clearly trivial is of a smaller order of magnitude than the materiality level established pursuant to AS 11. A matter is not considered trivial if there is uncertainty about whether it is clearly trivial.

Accumulated misstatements should include identified misstatements and likely misstatements.

What should be considered when evaluating the qualitative aspects of an entity's accounting practices?

An auditor should consider potential bias in management's judgment concerning amounts and disclosures.

Management bias might involve:

- Selective correction of misstatements brought to management's attention during the audit
- Identification by management of additional adjustments that offset misstatements accumulated by the auditor
- Bias in selecting and applying accounting principles
- Bias in accounting estimates

The auditor should consider whether management bias, along with the effect of uncorrected misstatements, results in material misstatement of the financial statements.

AS 15—Audit Evidence

What financial statement assertions are relevant to the meaningful presentation of financial statements?

Assertions that are relevant to the meaningful presentation of financial statements may be classified into the following categories:

- *Existence or occurrence.* Assets or liabilities of the entity exist at a given date, and recorded transactions have occurred during a given period.
- *Completeness.* All transactions and accounts that should be presented in the financial statements are so included.
- *Valuation or allocation.* Asset, liability, equity, revenue, and expense components have been included in the financial statements at appropriate amounts.

- *Rights and obligations.* The entity holds or controls rights to the assets, and liabilities are obligations of the entity at a given date.
- *Presentation and disclosure.* The components of the financial statements are properly classified, described, and disclosed.

Notes

Audit work may be based on different assertions if the assertions are sufficient for the auditor to identify material misstatements and to respond appropriately to the risks of material misstatement.

The assertions referred to in AS 15 are different from the assertions in SAS 106 (as discussed in Chapter 10).

Additional guidance concerning audit evidence may be found in Chapter 10 and SAS 106.

CHAPTER 13

Sarbanes-Oxley Act of 2002

The Sarbanes-Oxley Act of 2002 (SOX) was enacted, in part, in response to the accounting scandals of several publicly traded companies. SOX resulted in changes to corporate governance, increased corporate reporting (disclosure), and partial regulation of the accounting profession. This chapter focuses on the impact that SOX has on independent auditors of publicly traded entities.

In general, what are the major provisions of SOX that impact auditors of publicly traded entities?

Major provisions in SOX that impact auditors of publicly traded entities include:

- Stricter rules regarding independence of the auditor
- Partner rotation
- Creation of the Public Company Accounting Oversight Board
- A requirement to attest to, and report on, the effectiveness of internal control over financial reporting (discussed in Chapter 12)

Auditor Independence

What employment situations impair auditor independence?

Under SOX, an auditor will lose independence if an employee of the company being audited was part of the audit engagement team at any time during the *cooling-off period*. In order for the loss of independence to occur, the employee of the auditee must have had a financial accounting oversight role. Accordingly, prohibited employee positions include the chief executive officer, the chief financial officer, the controller, and the chief accounting officer, as well as any other position in which the individual can impact the preparation or contents of the entity's financial statements. The cooling-off period is generally the one-year period that precedes the commencement of audit procedures.

What are the services under SOX that impair auditor independence?

Under SOX, independence is impaired if an auditor performs these services for a client:

- Bookkeeping
- Design and implementation of financial information systems

- Appraisal or valuation
- Expression of fairness opinions
- Issuance of contribution-in-kind reports
- Actuarial advice concerning amounts included in financial statements
- Internal audit outsourcing
- Legal advice
- Providing expert opinions in litigation or in regulatory or administrative proceedings or investigations

Notes

Under SOX, an auditor may provide tax services, including providing tax advice and preparing tax returns. However, the services must be preapproved by the client's audit committee. Furthermore, the fees for tax services must be disclosed in the client's annual reports and proxy statements.

As under prior Securities and Exchange Commission (SEC) rules, auditor independence is lost if the auditor:

- Provides management functions, such as serving as a director or officer of the auditee
- Conducts human resources functions for the auditee
- Serves as a broker-dealer, promoter, or underwriter for the auditee

Partner Rotation

What are the new partner rotation rules under SOX?

SOX classifies partners into two categories:

1. Lead and concurring audit partners
2. All other audit partners

Lead and concurring partners must be rotated after five years and are subject to a time-out period of five years. All other audit partners must be rotated after seven years and are subject to a time-out period of two years.

Public Company Accounting Oversight Board

What is the PCAOB?

The Public Company Accounting Oversight Board (PCAOB) is a nongovernmental organization established under Title I of SOX. As an independent organization, the

PCAOB is charged with oversight of audits of public companies and their auditors. Specifically, the PCAOB is responsible for:

- Registering auditors of publicly traded entities
- Disciplining auditors of publicly traded entities
- Investigating financial irregularities of publicly traded entities
- Establishing auditing and accounting standards

How will the PCAOB discipline auditors?

Public accounting firms registered with the PCAOB will be subject to inspections to ensure compliance with SOX. National audit firms will be inspected annually; other firms will be inspected every three years. The PCAOB is empowered to impose disciplinary action (including sanctions on accepting new audit clients) on firms that have unsatisfactory inspections.

Will the PCAOB replace existing auditing and accounting standards?

Currently, the PCAOB has no plans to take away the power of the Financial Accounting Standards Board (FASB) to promulgate accounting standards. Accordingly, the PCAOB intends to adopt the current and future accounting standards of the FASB.

Although the PCAOB has stated that it will establish its own auditing standards, it has temporarily adopted the promulgations issued by the Auditing Standards Board of the AICPA, which no longer is empowered to set rules applicable to audits of public companies. It should be noted that promulgations of the PCAOB are not effective until approved by the SEC.

Has the PCAOB issued new auditing standards?

Yes. To date, the PCAOB has issued 15 new auditing standards (one of which has been superseded), which are applicable only to audits of publicly traded companies. The new standards are discussed in Chapter 12.

PART V

Taxation

CHAPTER 14

Tax Research

One of the greatest assets for an accountant is the ability to conduct tax research. Whether the accountant is attempting to solve an existing tax problem or is formulating suggestions for proposed tax transactions, the practitioner should be familiar with the many sources of tax information.

Sources of Tax Law

What is the Internal Revenue Code?

The Internal Revenue Code represents the U.S. tax law. Amendments to the Internal Revenue Code must be approved by both the House of Representatives and the Senate before the president signs them into law.

How are committee reports helpful?

The legislative intent of the law can be found in the committee reports of the House Ways and Means Committee, the Senate Finance Committee, and the Joint Conference Committee. Committee reports often provide examples that may closely approximate your client's transactions and proposals.

When defending positions in court, the use of congressional intent is quite forceful. Each section in the Code includes a reference to the legislative history of the law—that is, a reference to Revenue Acts and their years of enactment. Standard tax services, such as those published by the Research Institute of America and Commerce Clearing House, reprint congressional committee reports upon issuance. Another source for the committee reports is the *Cumulative Bulletin* issued twice a year by the Internal Revenue Service (IRS). The *Cumulative Bulletin* is the hardbound version containing 26 weekly *Internal Revenue Bulletins*.

What is the importance of Treasury Department regulations?

U.S. Treasury Department regulations represent the government's interpretation of the Internal Revenue Code. Regulations are issued in three forms:

1. *Proposed regulations* are not authoritative since their adoption has not been finalized.

2. *Temporary regulations*, although not in their final form, do represent an authoritative source for the practitioner.
3. *Final regulations* are completely authoritative and are published in the Federal Register.

What is a revenue ruling?

- *Revenue rulings*, which are interpretive in nature, are issued by the National Office of the Internal Revenue Service in Washington, D.C. They are published weekly in the *Internal Revenue Bulletin* and are reprinted in the semiannual *Cumulative Bulletin*.
- A *letter ruling* is issued in response to a taxpayer's request for a ruling on a particular transaction. If the IRS feels that the substance of the ruling could affect the public, it converts the letter ruling into a revenue ruling.

What should you know about revenue procedures?

Revenue procedures offer guidance on practices and procedures of the IRS. *Example:* A revenue procedure may instruct the practitioner on how to apply for a ruling on a particular type of tax transaction.

Revenue procedures are published in the same manner as revenue rulings.

What is the purpose of Treasury Decisions?

Published in the weekly *Internal Revenue Bulletin* and the semiannual *Cumulative Bulletin*, Treasury Decisions are issued to:

- Promulgate new regulations
- Amend current regulations
- Announce the Treasury's position relative to certain court decisions

How are Technical Information Releases useful?

This source of tax information is used to locate announcements of various publications.

How about technical advice memoranda?

Technical advice memoranda represent responses by the IRS to requests made by auditors. Technical advice memoranda are not published officially and cannot be cited or used as precedent since they are applicable to specific audit situations.

The Court System

What should I know about the Tax Court?

Taxpayers may wish to seek relief in the Tax Court since it hears only cases involving tax law and therefore specializes in tax matters.

Although most Tax Court cases are ruled on by one of 19 judges, all 19 judges will rule on a case (sit en banc) when novel issues are of concern. Furthermore, Tax Court judges travel around the country in order to hear cases.

Decisions issued by the Tax Court are either regular decisions or memorandum decisions.

- *Regular decisions* involve new issues never before resolved by the court. They are published in semiannual volumes of *Tax Court of the United States Reports*.
- *Memorandum decisions* involve only the application of existing doctrines of law.

An important distinction between regular and memorandum decisions is that for regular decisions, the IRS will publicly announce, in its *Internal Revenue Bulletin*, its decision as to whether it will acquiesce. Acquiescence means that the Internal Revenue Service has agreed to follow the Tax Court's decision in all subsequent cases involving the issue in question.

Note

Taxpayers do not have to pay tax assessments before they bring suit in the Tax Court. Suits of $50,000 or less are the jurisdiction of the Small Claims Division of the U.S. Tax Court.

How does the U.S. Claims Court differ from the Tax Court?

The U.S. Claims Court, like the U.S. Tax Court, is a court of original jurisdiction. The U.S. Claims Court can rule on any claim against the United States that involves constitutional law, congressional acts, or executive department regulations. Accordingly, the decisions of the U.S. Claims Court are not restricted to tax matters.

Note

To bring suit in the U.S. Claims Court, taxpayers must first pay the tax assessed.

What is the role of U.S. district courts?

District court cases are ruled on by only one judge. A minimum of one U.S. district court is found in every state. Like the U.S. Claims Court, the district courts rule on both tax and nontax matters.

A distinguishing characteristic of a district court is that a jury trial is available in cases that involve only questions of fact. Questions of law must be decided by a judge. District court decisions are valid only in the court's geographical jurisdiction.

> **Note**
>
> To bring suit in a U.S. district court, a taxpayer must first pay the deficiency assessed by the government.

How do I appeal a court decision?

When a taxpayer loses a case in either U.S. Tax Court or a U.S. district dourt, an appeal may be made to a regional circuit of the U.S. Court of Appeals. Losses in the U.S. Claims Court may be appealed by seeking relief in the court of appeals for the federal circuit.

Trial courts (district courts, the Tax Court, and the Claims Court) are bound by the decisions established by the court of appeals having jurisdiction. A court of appeals, however, does not have to follow the decisions handed down by a court of appeals in a different jurisdiction.

Can a tax case go to the Supreme Court?

The U.S. Supreme Court represents the highest appellate court. The U.S. Supreme Court decides which cases it will hear by granting a *writ of certiorari*. Although the U.S. Supreme Court usually will not hear cases involving tax matters, it will agree to resolve conflicts between courts of appeals.

> **Note**
>
> All courts must abide by the decisions of the U.S. Supreme Court.

Which court should be used in a particular case?

The decision to use a particular court for tax litigation depends on many factors, including:

- The expertise in tax matters possessed by the judges
- The ability to request a jury trial
- Whether there is a requirement that the assessed tax be paid before legal action can be taken

PART VI

Other Professional Standards

CHAPTER 15

Consulting Services

Certified public accountants (CPAs) have become more than specialists in accounting, auditing, attestation, and tax-related matters. Clients have come to rely on CPAs as business advisors in many diverse areas, such as mergers and acquisitions, information technology, and controllership activities. The American Institute of Certified Public Accountants has long recognized the involvement of CPAs in nontraditional services and previously issued Statements on Standards for Management Advisory Services. In 1992, those statements were superseded by a Statement on Standards for Consulting Services (SSCS) to (1) indicate a broader range of professional services and (2) provide standards for the practitioner to follow.

What are consulting services?

Consulting services are professional services involving the application of technical skills, education, observations, and experiences.

Consulting services include:

- *Consultations*, in which the CPA provides counsel based on existing knowledge of the client. This service usually spans a short time period—for example, providing guidance in connection with a client-prepared business plan.
- *Advisory services*, in which the CPA formulates findings, conclusions, and recommendations; an example is analysis of an information technology–based accounting system.
- *Implementation services*, in which the CPA, alone or with client assistance, puts an action plan into effect, such as actual installation of a computer system.
- *Transaction services*, which involve providing services applicable to a specific client transaction, typically with an outside party—for example, insolvency services.
- *Staff and other support services*, in which the CPA provides staff and other support to perform client-specified tasks, such as computer programming and controllership activities.
- *Product services*, in which the CPA sells a product to a client, along with related support; an example is the sale and training of computer programs.

> **Note**
>
> Consulting services exclude, among other services, (1) tax return preparation, (2) tax planning and tax advisory services, (3) financial planning, (4) bookkeeping services, and (5) financial statement services governed by SASs, SSAEs, and SSARSs.

What standards are applicable to consulting services?

The practitioner should comply with the general standards of the profession, which can be found in Rule 201 of the AICPA Code of Professional Conduct (see Chapter 17).

In addition, the practitioner should adhere to these general standards specifically applicable to consulting services:

- *Client interest.* While maintaining integrity and objectivity, the CPA should serve the client's best interest and accordingly attempt to achieve client objectives.
- *Understanding with client.* Before accepting an engagement, the CPA should establish a written or oral understanding with the applicable parties concerning the nature, scope, and limitations of the services to be performed.
- *Communication with client.* The CPA should notify the client of (1) conflicts of interest that arise, (2) significant reservations concerning the engagement, and (3) significant findings.

Can a CPA perform consulting services for attest clients?

A CPA should be cautious when considering the performance of a consulting service for an attest client. By itself, performance of a consulting service does not impair an accountant's independence. A CPA should take steps to comply with independence requirements of the AICPA, applicable regulatory agencies, state boards of accountancy, and state societies of CPAs.

> **Caution**
>
> The practitioner should be aware that the Public Company Accounting Oversight Board for the most part precludes an auditor of a publicly traded entity from performing any additional services other than preparation of the entity's tax returns.

CHAPTER 16

Quality Control

In 1979, the Auditing Standards Board of the American Institute of Certified Public Accountants (AICPA) issued SAS 25, *The Relationship of Generally Accepted Auditing Standards to Quality Control Standards*. As indicated in the pronouncement, generally accepted auditing standards (GAAS) relate to the conduct of an audit, whereas quality controls relate to the conduct of the accounting firm's practice.

Subsequent to the issuance of SAS 25, the Auditing Standards Board began issuing a series of pronouncements titled Statements on Quality Control Standards (SQCS). Firms enrolled in the AICPA practice-monitoring program are required to comply with the provisions in these statements.

Recommendation

Firms not enrolled in the AICPA practice-monitoring program are encouraged to comply with the provisions in the SQCS.

Caution

SQCS do not specify guidance for quality control considerations of the Public Company Accounting Oversight Board, which regulates the audits of publicly traded entities (i.e., issuers).

What is a system of quality control?

A system of quality control is a process, consisting of policies and procedures, designed to provide reasonable, but not absolute, assurance that CPA firm personnel comply with professional standards and applicable legal and regulatory requirements.

A system of quality control should be established for a CPA firm that performs any of these services:

- Auditing (governed by SASs)
- Attest engagements (governed by SSAEs)
- Accounting and review services (governed by SSARSs)

What factors should be considered in establishing a system of quality control?

In designing a system of quality control, the CPA firm should take into account:

- Size of the firm
- Number of offices the firm maintains
- Qualifications and experience of its personnel and the authority granted the personnel
- Nature and complexity of the practice, including the types of services performed
- Cost/benefit considerations

What are the relevant elements of a system of quality control?

A system of quality control should consist of these interrelated elements:

- Relevant ethical requirements
- Human resources
- Acceptance and continuance of client relationships and engagements
- Engagement performance
- Monitoring
- Leadership responsibilities for quality within the firm

What should be taken into account when considering the element of "relevant ethical requirements"?

A CPA firm should design and implement policies and procedures to maintain independence in fact and in appearance in circumstances requiring independence. A CPA firm should take steps necessary to ensure that firm personnel possess integrity (i.e., honesty) and are capable of making professional decisions objectively (i.e., with an unbiased mental attitude). For example, a CPA firm may periodically require personnel to complete a checklist indicating ownership interests in clients.

What factors should a CPA firm consider in connection with "human resources"?

Human resources should include policies and procedures relating to:

- Hiring staff, including resume and application submission followed by the interview process
- Assignment of staff to specific engagements, based on experience and other qualifications
- Professional development, including continuing professional education
- Advancement (i.e., promotion)
- Competency of supervisory personnel in such areas as the Code of Professional Conduct, the specific service to be performed, the industry in which the client is operating, and the client's information technology systems

What affects the decision to accept or continue a client relationship or a specific engagement?

Whether a firm accepts or continues a client relationship or a specific engagement is based on professional judgment that should take into account:

- The integrity of the client
- Whether the CPA firm reasonably expects to complete a specific engagement
- Risks associated with performing specific professional services

Recommendation

Before undertaking an engagement, the CPA firm should establish an understanding with the client regarding the needs and expectations of the client, the responsibilities of the client and the CPA firm, and any limitations relevant to the engagement.

An engagement letter documenting the understanding is generally a presumptively mandatory requirement.

What is meant by the element "engagement performance"?

A CPA firm needs to establish policies and procedures to provide reasonable assurance that each engagement is performed in accordance with professional and, where applicable, regulatory standards. Engagement performance must also meet the firm's standards of quality.

Policies and procedures regarding engagement performance should reasonably ensure that engagements are planned, performed properly, supervised, reviewed, and documented. Engagement results also need to be properly communicated to interested parties.

In view of these points, policies regarding engagement performance might include disseminating copies of new pronouncements and providing means for consulting with others inside and outside the CPA firm.

What is "monitoring"?

Monitoring, which should be an ongoing process, involves considering:

- Relevance and adequacy of the firm's policies and procedures relevant to the other elements of quality control
- Appropriateness of the firm's practice aids and other materials used by firm personnel
- Effectiveness of the firm's professional development activities
- Compliance with the firm's policies and procedures

Monitoring may be accomplished by a variety of means, including, but not limited to, inspection procedures applied to personnel records, engagement work papers and reports, and pre- and postissuance review of specific engagements. Peer review, by itself, is not sufficient for monitoring purposes, but may be a substitute for some or all inspection procedures.

A sole practitioner may monitor his or her own compliance with quality controls. However, for additional assurance regarding compliance, a sole practitioner may decide to engage another individual to perform an independent inspection.

What should be considered in connection with "leadership responsibilities for quality within the firm"?

Leadership responsibilities for quality within the firm, also referred to as the "tone at the top", should stress the need for a quality-oriented culture within the firm. Accordingly, quality control policies and procedures should recognize and reward the quality of work performed by firm members. To accomplish this, a firm may (1) conduct training seminars and staff brainstorming sessions and (2) distribute firm newsletters and briefing memos.

What should a CPA firm document in connection with quality control?

A CPA firm should document the quality control policies and procedures designed and implemented. Compliance with the policies and procedures should also be documented. The form and content of the documentation should be based on professional judgment.

Why is the relationship of quality control standards to professional standards applicable to specific engagements?

Deficiencies in or instances of noncompliance with a CPA firm's quality control policies and procedures do not, in and of themselves, indicate that a specific engagement was not performed in accordance with professional standards applicable to that engagement.

CHAPTER 17

Code of Professional Conduct

The AICPA Code of Professional Conduct is applicable to members of the American Institute of Certified Public Accountants. A practicing member must also comply with ethical provisions promulgated by applicable state societies and licensing jurisdictions. Most likely, the principles and rules contained in the various codes of conduct will be similar or identical. However, CPAs should ensure that the ethical provisions of their licensing jurisdiction take precedence.

The principles contained in the AICPA Code of Professional Conduct are aspirational in nature and provide basic guidance on general ethical and professional conduct.

What principles are contained in the AICPA Code of Professional Conduct?

These principles are designed to express a member's responsibilities to the public, the member's clients, and other members:

- Exercise sensitive professional and moral judgments.
- Serve the best interest of the profession.
- Perform all services with integrity.
- Maintain objectivity and, where applicable, independence in fact and appearance.
- Exercise due professional care; that is, perform services with diligence and competency.

How do the rules contained in the Code differ from the principles?

The rules contained in the Code specify the minimum level of conduct expected of members. Accordingly, they are rather specific, and members must be able to justify any departures from the rules.

Rule 101—Independence

What is the general requirement of Rule 101—Independence?

In essence, Rule 101 indicates that a practitioner shall maintain independence when performing professional services that require independence. The AICPA has issued many interpretations under Rule 101 that specify situations and relationships with clients that either are allowed or need to be avoided in order to prevent a breach of independence.

What are some situations that a member should avoid?

A practitioner should:

- Avoid any direct or material indirect financial interest in a client
- Generally not lend money to or borrow money from a client
- Not perform an attest service for a client for a period during which the member was an employee
- Not perform an attest service where an outstanding fee for a prior-period service is more than one year past due
- Not accept a more than insignificant gift from an attest client

Can a member perform nonattest services for an attest client?

Under Interpretation 101-3, a member may be permitted to perform nonattest services for a nonpublic attest client. In order to do so, these general requirements need to be satisfied:

- The member does not perform any managerial functions or make decisions for management.
- With respect to the nonattest services, the client must agree to:
  - Perform all managerial functions and make all management decisions.
  - Designate an individual within the client organization to oversee the nonattest service.
  - Evaluate the adequacy and results of the nonattest service.
  - Accept responsibility for the nonattest service results.
  - Set up and maintain internal controls, including monitoring ongoing activities.

The member should establish and document in writing the understanding reached with the client regarding the objectives of the engagement, the services to be performed, the client's acceptance of its responsibilities, the practitioner's responsibilities, and any limitations relevant to the engagement.

Note

The member's understanding need not be documented in an engagement letter. A memo to the client's file is an acceptable form of documentation.

What are examples of nonattest services?

These are some of the more common nonattest services:

- Bookkeeping
- Payroll preparation
- Administration of employee benefit plans
- Providing investment advice or management services
- Conducting executive or employee searches
- Design or installation of computer systems

Rule 102—Integrity and Objectivity

Rule 102 requires a member to maintain objectivity and integrity throughout the conduct of all professional engagements. Accordingly, the member shall be free of conflicts of interest and must not knowingly misrepresent facts or subordinate his or her professional judgment to anyone.

Rule 201—General Standards

Briefly, Rule 201 requires a member to:

- Possess professional competence before accepting an engagement.
- Exercise due professional care.
- Plan and supervise an engagement.
- Obtain sufficient relevant data in order to afford a reasonable basis for any conclusions or recommendations.

Rule 202—Compliance with Standards

Under this rule, when performing an engagement, a member must comply with promulgated standards applicable to a specific type of service.

What are specific types of services for which promulgated standards exist?

Promulgated standards and interpretations exist for these services:

- Auditing
- Compilation
- Review
- Attestation
- Consulting
- Tax

Rule 203—Accounting Principles

In general, a member should not express an unqualified opinion based on an audit, or limited assurance based on a review, of financial statements if the financial statements contain one or more departures from generally accepted accounting principles (GAAP).

Is there an exception to this general rule?

If a member can demonstrate that compliance with GAAP would result in misleading financial statement presentation, he or she can still issue an unqualified opinion based on an audit, or limited assurance based on a review, if the report is modified to reflect (1) a description of the departure(s), (2) the approximate effects of the departure(s) if practicable, and (3) the reasons why adherence to GAAP would render the financial statements misleading.

Rule 301—Confidential Client Information

A member in public practice is generally precluded from disclosing confidential client information without the express consent of the client.

Are there situations in which a member may or is required to disclose confidential client information without client consent?

Rule 301 would not be breached if the member disclosed confidential client information without client consent in order to:

- Respond to a subpoena or summons
- Comply with laws or government regulations
- Undergo peer review
- Initiate or respond to a complaint concerning professional ethics

Rule 302—Contingent Fees

Essentially, a member is precluded from accepting a contingent fee in connection with (1) an audit or a review of financial statements, (2) a compilation of financial statements that are reasonably expected to be used by a third party and the accountant's report fails to disclose the lack of independence, (3) an engagement to examine a financial forecast or projection, or (4) preparation of a tax return.

What is a contingent fee?

A contingent fee is a fee that is dependent on a specified finding or result. Contingent fees do not include fees that (1) are fixed by courts or other public authorities or (2) with respect to tax matters, are determined based on judicial proceedings or government agencies.

Rule 501—Acts Discreditable

Simply stated, a member shall not commit an act that would discredit the profession.

What member acts would be deemed to be discreditable to the profession?

A member would commit an act discreditable to the profession if he or she:

- Withholds client records
- Discriminates or harasses in employment practices
- Fails to follow standards in government audits
- Is negligent in the preparation of financial statements
- Fails to comply with laws and government regulations
- Fails to file tax returns or pay outstanding tax liabilities

Rule 502—Advertising and Other Forms of Solicitations

A member is permitted to advertise or otherwise solicit clients if the advertising or manner of solicitation is not false, deceptive, or misleading.

Rule 503—Commissions and Referral Fees

Can a member accept commissions?

In general, if a member performs an attest engagement with respect to historical financial statements or an examination with respect to prospective financial information, the member is prohibited from accepting a commission for recommending or referring:

- Any product or service to a client
- Any product to be furnished by a client

A member is also precluded from accepting commissions as described when he or she compiles financial statements that are reasonably expected to be used by a third party and the member's report fails to disclose his or her lack of independence.

If a commission is permissible, the member should disclose the receipt of the commission (or the expectation of receipt) to the party to whom he or she recommends or refers the product or service that generated the commission.

Can a member accept a referral fee?

A member may accept or pay a referral fee if the client is made aware of the referral fee.

Rule 505—Form of Organization and Name

A member is permitted to conduct an accounting practice in any form allowed by state law. Further, the name of the practice must not be misleading. If all of the firm's

CPA owners are members of the AICPA, the firm may designate itself "Members of the American Institute of Certified Public Accountants." Names of one or more past owners may be included in the firm name of a successor organization.

Note

Most states permit CPAs to conduct their practices as sole proprietors, general partnerships, limited liability companies (LLCs), limited liability parnerships (LLPs), or professional corporations (or associations).

Caution

While the AICPA permits an accounting practice to use a fictitious name, many states do not allow such use.

Index